STATISTICAL HANDBOOK ON WOMEN IN AMERICA

Second Edition

Compiled and Edited by Cynthia M. Taeuber

Forewords by
Gail Sheehy
Wilma Vaught
Sheila Wellington

Oryx Press
1996

The rare Arabian Oryx is believed to have inspired the myth of the unicorn. This desert antelope became virtually extinct in the early 1960s. At that time several groups of international conservationists arranged to have 9 animals sent to the Phoenix Zoo to be the nucleus of a captive breeding herd. Today the Oryx population is over 1000, and over 500 have been returned to the Middle East.

© 1996 by The Oryx Press
4041 North Central at Indian School Road
Phoenix, Arizona 85012-3397

Published simultaneously in Canada
Printed and Bound in the United States of America

∞ The paper used in this publication meets the minimum requirements of
American National Standard for Information Science—Permanence of Paper
for Printed Library Materials, ANSI Z39.48, 1984.

Library of Congress Cataloging-in-Publication Data
Statistical handbook on women in America / edited by Cynthia M.
Taeuber. —2nd ed.
    p. cm.
    Includes bibliographical references and index.
    ISBN 1-57356-005-7 (cloth: perm. paper)
    1. Women—United States—Statistics. I. Taeuber, Cynthia Murray.
HQ1420.T34 1996   96-1521
305.4'021—dc20   CIP

In memory of my courageous and funny best friend
Robin Wright
and
Mary Abigail McCarthy
who gave her knowledge, heart, and uncompromising
advocacy to the needs of women and children.

Contents

List of Tables and Charts

of Non-Hispanic Origin: 1990 (46 Reporting States, the District of Columbia, and New York City)

A3. Birth Expectations and Childlessness

A4. Births to Unmarried Women

A5. Death and Life Expectancy

A6. Causes of Death

B. EMPLOYMENT AND ECONOMIC STATUS

B1. Labor Force Participation

B2. Earnings and Pension Coverage

C. HEALTH CHARACTERISTICS

C1.   Health and Disability Status

C2. Personal Health Practices and Sports

Foreword

We are constantly bombarded by often contradictory "facts" regarding women. In an era of increasingly polarized politics, more and more of these assertions are self-serving—and a stretch of the truth. For example, a legislator has recently claimed that requiring unwed mothers to live with their parents will stem the flow of welfare. However, those who work with teens point out that for many teen mothers their home environment is often inappropriate or even dangerous for raising a child. As a teenage mother in Arizona told authorities, "I love my mother, but if I lived with her and my AFDC check came into her household, she would drink it away."

A senior policy analyst for a conservative think tank calls the rise in unwed mothers over 30 "a sign of the continuing breakdown of the family and culture." Yet a new Census Bureau study reveals that this group is in many ways better able to support and care for their children than other parent groups in America. "Murphy Brown Moms"—30-something college graduates with a professional or management career who have never married—are twice as likely today to choose to have a baby and support it on their own than they were a decade ago.

Each of these "facts" is true but also false, depending on the perspective of the person either reacting to or giving the argument. Some arguments fall into the gray area in between true and false, causing people to question the data that support these hypotheses. Responsible people, whether students, demographers, members of government or social agencies, or just people listening and reading, must try to determine for themselves the basis of the hypotheses presented and the skew of the person making the statement. They must look at the data and draw their own conclusions. Sometimes those conclusions will be the same; at other times they will be vastly different. Whatever the outcome, it is this dialogue and debate that will inform the next chapter in the story of women in America.

Statistical Handbook on Women in America is the essential source for a sound and accurate picture of women in America today, one based on cold, hard facts. It is tremendously helpful as a "reality check" of unbiased information with which to analyze the "facts" that bombard us from slanted and skewed sources. It should be within arm's reach of any inquisitive person who is trying, for whatever reason, to sort through the often disparate, sometimes startling, information from which our perceptions of today's women's experience is constructed.

As a group, women have changed more, and more quickly, than any other group in America. The facts confirm the many ways in which their lives are fundamentally different from those of their mothers and grandmothers. Women are living longer, working more, and more often raising families on their own. Women also are a larger sector of the American population than any other group. In fact, a portrait of the average American would depict a 35-year-old woman. At the same time, the facts clearly show that there is no universal "women's experience," that women all around the country lead very different lives. All these things make it ever more important that people use the data and statistics present in *Statistical Handbook on Women in America* to question the "facts" presented to them.

If you are writing a grant proposal or a policy paper, firing off an angry letter to the editor of a newspaper or magazine, researching a term paper, designing a demographic study, casting a vote, or, like me, looking for statistical backup to support the kind of theoretical leaps that make the most exciting books, you need the responsible analysis of unbiased, statistical information—the type of information found in this book.

I encourage you to use the tables and charts presented here. They will help you make responsible analyses and decisions that will better serve women now and in years to come.

GAIL SHEEHY
Best-selling Author

Foreword

When I went to the University of Illinois, I postponed taking algebra, a freshman level course, until my last semester in college, and then as a senior, barely got a C. Some years later, when the Air Force sent me to the University of Alabama for a master's degree in business administration, I found that one of the first courses I had to take was undergraduate statistics—and there was no way I could postpone or get out of taking it.

To say that I had no interest in the probability of a coin coming up heads or tails or the probability of anything else happening for that matter is an understatement. But take the course, I did, and found, through the rest of my military career, that what I learned about statistics, probability, and demographics in that course was of increasing value to me in my job. For example, it was essential for me to understand demographic trends and people's attitudes toward the military and a military career when I spent three years working with recruiters for each of the military services. The command I headed was responsible for aptitude testing in the high schools and for processing new recruits for entry into the service. It was critical to plan ahead in order to place our resources correctly and in order to detect demographic shifts in where recruits were enlisting.

Now, as a woman and as executive manager and fundraiser for The Women in Military Service Memorial Foundation, a major project honoring women, I need to understand more than ever what's happening throughout the country—and particularly with respect to women.

This book does a superb job of bringing needed information and data together in a reference book that can be used by all of us as we go about meeting our challenges. My only hope is that someday it will be twice as thick and filled with twice as many types of data. But that will come!

As those of us associated with The Women's Memorial continue collecting data about the women who have served in the military over time, it's our goal to be ready to add some pages of relevant information about these women in a later edition of this book, so that researchers and analysts can have that information at their fingertips. As it is, when we need such information, as Cynthia Taeuber knows, we must painstakingly build it bit by bit. And when we get phone calls asking for data, more often than not they just aren't available—here or anyplace else.

We need more sources of reliable data on women, and we need more people to record, tabulate, and analyze statistics so that they will be available. Cynthia Taeuber has done a masterful job of meeting this need. She has conscientiously collected the data and organized a stunningly comprehensive statistical record of women. Those of us interested, whether professionally or personally, in the past, present, and future of women in America, owe her a good deal for taking the initiative to do what has been needed for a long time.

WILMA VAUGHT
The Women in Military Service
Memorial Foundation

Foreword

In America, we measure what we value—and what gets measured gets done. This second edition of the *Statistical Handbook on Women in America* provides the tools needed to assess and derive policy about the status of women in our nation. The volume contains countless measurements of women's lives and, as such, brings into focus what the nation must value in order to thrive in the next century.

It is my hope that this handbook will serve as a catalyst for change for women. The unbiased data herein tell the real story of the status of women and their unique contributions to this country—as workers and students, as soldiers, immigrants, athletes, voters, wives, and mothers. These statistics hold up a mirror to the economic, health, and social lives of American women, and although not always pretty, the statistics enlighten. Indeed, they allow us to identify and quantify where the disparities and inequities lie, so that remedies can be found. The statistics also empower—motivating companies, institutions, and individual women to value women's contributions.

As Catalyst president, I can speak about one area of the enormous undertaking that this book represents: women at work. One of the most important demographic—and economic—phenomena occurring in the United States in the last three decades is the large-scale entry of women into the workforce. As you will see by the charts in the Employment and Economic Status section, more women are working than ever before. In 1994, the latest year for which figures are available, women represented 46 percent of all participants in the civilian labor force, up from 30 percent in 1950; 59 percent of women 16 and older were labor force participants in 1994, up from 34 percent in 1950 (*U.S. Bureau of Labor Statistics,* 1994). In addition to their improved position in the labor force, more women than ever before own their own businesses. According to the last economic census (1987), 4.1 million women are business owners, a 58 percent increase from 1982. And recent reports indicate that this is a long-term trend, extending into the next century. Women's integration into the workplace also has spilled over into society as a whole: as reflected in the statistics in this book, it is related to such basic factors of American life as household incomes, birth rates, child care, education, and marriage.

For over 30 years, Catalyst has both documented and facilitated women's progress in the workplace. We have relied on labor force statistics to demonstrate the incremental advances women have made, as well as the barriers that remain. Our workplace cultures have not kept pace with the swelling tide of working women— indeed, these cultures were created by and for another age and another gender—and have kept women out of fair and open competition for leadership. As a result, U.S. companies and the American economy are not fully benefiting from the brainpower, the education, and the training of women— who represent over half the nation's population. Catalyst's statistics illustrate this point: Today, women make up less than 5 percent of senior management and less than 10 percent of corporate board seats. No woman serves as CEO of a Fortune 500 company, and only two women CEOs run Fortune 1000 companies, the same number as in 1978.

The statistics in this book not only document the *value* women have added to the American economy, they also help debunk the myths about women and their potential, such as the following:

- **Married women don't really need to work.**

  Economic realities dictate that most families need two incomes to obtain and maintain a middle-class lifestyle, keep a decent roof over their heads, and educate their children. Only 3.1 percent of married-couple families have a wage-earning father, stay-at-home mother, and two children (*BLS,* 1993). The entire 8 percent growth in the average income of married-couple families with children from 1979–89 is attributed to the increased earnings of wives.

- **When women become mothers, they drop out of the workforce.**

  Over 68 percent of mothers with children under 18 work. Catalyst finds mothers working late into pregnancy and returning soon after childbirth. In 1993, 55 percent of mothers with children under the age of two were in the labor force, up from 32 percent in 1975 (*BLS*, 1993). Seventy-five percent of new mothers are back working by the time their children are two (*Rand Corporation*, 1989).

- **Women are not prepared for professional and managerial careers.**

  Women hold more than half the bachelor and masters degrees from United States academic institutions. In addition, they hold more than one-third of MBAs and PhDs and over 40 percent of law degrees.

These are just three of the misperceptions that the *Statistical Handbook on Women in America,* Second Edition, refutes; the data in this book substantiate that these are three major obstacles blocking women's advance-

ment. Catalyst finds that time alone does not eliminate the barriers faced by women. Women who entered the workforce in the 1960s have not advanced in lockstep with the men, who still hold 95 percent of top managerial positions. Such numbers speak loudly.

This handbook helps set the record straight. Documenting where women are in the business world—and in all other areas—allows us to see how far we have come and what work still needs to be done. This book, with its vast yet accessible array of statistical information, will, I hope, inspire women and men alike to chip away vigorously at the inequities which remain.

SHEILA WELLINGTON
President, Catalyst

Preface

This statistical handbook is, on the surface, mere numbers. But these seemingly cold facts are much more. They are a story, a story about the lives of real women, women we know, women we see as we pass down the streets, women we will never see but must always know are there. It tells us about their growing diversity, the changes in their family and work lives, their education and health, and their part in our social, economic, and political institutions. It also tells us that women are not all the same. How often have we heard, "women think this," and "women do that"? The numbers in this *Handbook* show how false, how simplistic such sweeping generalizations are. Women from different race and ethnic groups, age groups, and with different economic resources have different lifetime experiences.

Birth, education, family life, health, economic circumstances, and death have all changed dramatically for women across the decades. Young women today live fundamentally different lives from those their mothers, grandmothers, and great-grandmothers have experienced. Very long lives for women, and hence the four-generation family, are becoming common in American society. Most women will live well into their 80s, thus requiring a less well-charted need for women to plan for their future economic security with the long run in mind. Many of today's young women, who were held by their great-grandmothers when they were babies, will eventually provide care for both frail grandmothers and mothers. This change in the length of life for most women brings unprecedented changes in the traditional role of the nurturing woman. It portends a life of providing "serial care," first for children and, finally, for parents and other relatives, most of whom are women.

Many women, especially younger women, have broken from the traditions of past generations. They have obtained college degrees, broken into the ranks of traditional male occupations, stayed in the labor force continuously, even when they have very young children, and have improved their wages relative to men. Nearly 15 million women (29 percent of employed women) were in managerial and professional occupations (including nursing and teaching) in 1994. Nevertheless, most women still do work traditionally done by women at relatively low pay. The majority of women workers are secretaries and other clerical workers (28 percent of employed women in 1990); nurses and other health assessment and treating workers (4 percent); teachers, counselors, or librarians (8 percent); or service workers such as those in cleaning and food service (16 percent). It is still the case, however, that most of America's poor are women and their children.

This is the second edition of the *Statistical Handbook on Women in America*. In many ways, the second edition is more a companion than a replacement to the first edition. It updates some tables and charts from the first edition and includes many new tables within each section and new topics such as reproductive health and sports. There are over 260 tables and 80 charts. The statistical charts and tables in the *Handbook* are reproduced from federal government sources (including unpublished tables) and nongovernment publications as shown in the last paragraph of this Preface. The most recent survey data are used here, often up to 1994. At the end of the book there is a glossary that defines technical terms and a "Guide to Informative Sources" to help readers find additional material.

There is always a tradeoff in data between being up-to-date versus having geographic and subject-matter detail. In general, if you want demographic, social, or economic data for states and local areas, the census, which is done once every 10 years, is the only source. If you want very detailed information (such as a detailed list of 400+ occupations), the decennial census is again the only source. More current, but general demographic, social, economic (such as 10 general occupation categories), and health data come from surveys for the United States (and sometimes large states or regions). Vital statistics (fertility, mortality, cause of death) are provisional if you want current information; final and more detailed data are older (for example, the table included in this *Handbook* on deaths by single years of age for race groups is from 1989, the most recent data available in early 1995).

Most sections in the *Handbook* include substantial information on young women. The experiences of young women have lifelong implications and give us hints about the future. Highlights of the second edition of the *Handbook* include data from the 1990 census and a new section on women's reproductive health. Because a variety of sources were used, a variety of table formats are found here. In most cases, entire charts and tables are displayed, while some were edited to better represent women, the focus of this compilation.

The subject of "women," of course, is broad and includes every physical, mental, emotional, and spiritual aspect of life. We cannot include every possible topic on women in one book. I have used data availability and quality, space considerations, and personal areas of expertise as guides in choosing what topics to include or exclude from this book. Data quality considerations, for example, led to limited treatment of the choices women make of sexual partners. Some women are heterosexual, some are lesbians, and some are bisexual. Estimates of the numbers and proportions vary widely among surveys and advocates and there are no generally agreed-upon counts of the sexual preferences of women. Section D2 includes a table on same-sex households with two adults who were willing to indicate in the government-sponsored Current Population Survey that they were "partners." This table is no more than a minimum count of lesbians who live openly in a committed relationship. Also, religion is not included here because men and women do not differ significantly in the data available.

Finally, the *Statistical Handbook on Women in America* could not exist without the willingness of the American public to respond to surveys and the intellectual and physical labor of thousands of field interviewers and statisticians. These are the unnamed champions behind a book such as this who help us see where we as a people have been and where we are heading. There are champions who have contributed to this book, however, who can be named. As with the first edition, my husband Forrest McIlwain contributed his loving encouragement and his equally vital technical abilities to tame the computer monster. I am also grateful to particular statisticians who have given so much thought on how to present data, how to ensure high-quality data, and how to analyze key aspects of American life. I particularly note and thank statisticians from the Bureau of the Census who generously share their extensive knowledge and insight: Martin O'Connell, Carmen DeNavas, Arlene Saluter, Donald Hernandez, Jack McNeil, and Paula Coupe. Many questions about women in the labor force were answered for me by specialists from the Department of Labor including Harriet Harper (Women's Bureau) and Howard Hayghe (Bureau of Labor Statistics). From the Centers for Disease Control and Prevention, Susan Bradley was especially helpful in providing statistical data on sexually transmitted diseases. For permission to reprint statistical information from their work, I thank the following: Jacqueline Forrest and Stanley Henshaw of the Alan Guttmacher Institute, New York City, who provided information on unwanted pregnancies, contraceptive practices, abortions, and adoptions; Anthony Gamboa, Jr., of Vocational Econometrics, Louisville, KY (502-589-0995) for information on worklife expectancy; Roberta Spalter-Roth, Heidi Hartmann, Nancy Collins, and Lois Shaw of the Institute for Women's Policy Research for information on working women; Elaine Sorensen from the Urban Institute in Washington, D.C., for trends in earnings; April Brayfield on childcare costs; and Thomas Doyle of the National Sporting Goods Association (708-439-4000), who provided information on women in sports. In all cases, more detailed information (both data and analyses) is available from the original source. And finally, I thank my editor, Garth Weber, who devoted much creative energy and good counsel to the production of this statistical picture of women in America.

Symbols Used in This Book

The following is a complete list of symbols and their respective definitions, which are used in the tables of this statistical handbook.

–	Represents zero or rounds to zero
* or (**B**)	Figure does not meet standards of reliability or precision
— or (**NA**)	Not available
r	Revised from the previously published number
... or (**X**)	Not applicable

STATISTICAL HANDBOOK ON WOMEN IN AMERICA

Demographic Events and Characteristics

A1. POPULATION CHANGE AND IMMIGRATION

The Census Bureau estimates there were about 260 million Americans in 1994, and more than half (133 million) were women. That makes the "average" American a woman and she is about 35 years old. As recently as 1970, however, half of American women were under 29 years old. There were more women than men for the first time in the census of 1950. Women are expected to remain just slightly over half of the U.S. population for many decades to come.

Even though there are more women than men, the female population has grown slower than the male population since the early 1980s. The last time that happened was the 1900–1910 period. The major contributors to the faster growth of men (10.3 percent from 1980 to 1991 compared with 9.5 percent for women) were changes in birth and death trends. There was an increase in the number of births late in the decade, and slightly more boy babies than girl babies were born. At the same time, more men are living somewhat longer. There also has been an increased number of deaths among women (particularly because of heart disease and cancer, which many blame on the increased number of women who started smoking in the 1950s). The decade of the 1980s was the first time since early this century that male life expectancy rose more rapidly than female life expectancy. Illegal male immigrants also contributed to the increasing male population in the United States.

One in four American women live in California, New York, or Texas, and more than three in four women live in the metropolitan areas of our nation. It's not a surprise to hear that most women live in our central cities or suburbs (about 40 million in each in 1990). It may be more surprising to learn 31 million women live in rural areas (that is, where towns and villages have a population of less than 2,500 people or there is only open country).

Women come from different race and ethnic groups and have different lifetime experiences. Of 100 women in 1994, 83 were White, 13 were Black, 3 were Asian and Pacific Islanders (API), and 1 was American Indian, Eskimo, and Aleut (AIEA); 10 were of Hispanic origin (they may have been of any race). By the middle of the next century, much more racial and ethnic diversity is expected among women. If today's rates of birth, mortality, and net migration continue through the middle of the next century, of 100 women, 72 will be White; 16, Black; 10, API; 1, AIEA; and 22 of Hispanic origin.

On average, White women tended to be the oldest in 1990 with a median age of 36 years. By comparison, half of Hispanic women had not yet reached their 26th birthday, our youngest group of women. Among White women, 7 percent are 75 years or older compared to only 4 percent of Black women, and about 2 percent of AIEA, API, and Hispanic women.

In 1994, almost one in five women were aged 60 or older and another one in four were under 18 years. In 1970, when the Baby Boom was young, one in three women were under 18 and one in six were 60 or older. Women of the Baby-Boom generation (born 1946 to 1964) make up the largest age group, and so, as they age, the overall female population becomes older on average. By the middle of the next century, when the World War II Baby-Boom generation becomes our oldest old population, the "average" woman could be about 40 years old. In 2050, more than one in four women could be aged 60 or older and those under 18 would be one in five women, a reversal of the 1990 proportions for each age group.

The elderly population is itself becoming older on average also. The elderly population will grow steadily but undramatically until 2011. After 2011, when the first of the Baby Boom reaches age 65, growth of the elderly population will be rapid. After 2030, the Baby-Boom generation will begin to reach age 85. Care of our oldest old, those 85 years and older, most of whom are likely to be women, could become one of the most significant issues of that period. It is women in their late 50s and 60s who are likely to be asked to provide much of the care of frail, very old mothers, mothers-in-law, and other relatives. This will come just as they are trying to prepare for their own retirement. They will face difficult decisions about whether to continue in the labor force as they juggle caring for their elderly with work, just as they once did with child care.

In 1993, 904,000 persons legally immigrated, over half of whom were women; most of these women were married. In the Census Bureau's middle projection series shown here, it is assumed there are about 200,000 undocumented immigrants annually, most of whom are male.

Recent immigrant women tend to be young, married, and have 1 or 2 children. Foreign-born women (25 years old and over) are often poorly educated and tend to work in lower level jobs. They are more likely than American-born women to be poor. The 1990 Census counted more than 10 million foreign-born women living in the United States; nearly 6 in 10 were not American citizens. Of the 5.8 million women who were not citizens, 4 in 10 reported they entered the United States before 1980. Most women who immigrated here since 1987 are young, under age 26, and married. The foreign-born women aged 35 to 44 years counted in the 1990 Census averaged 2.3 children each. Among foreign-born women aged 25 and over in 1990, 4 in 10 (3.4 million) do not have a high school education and most of these are not citizens (2.0 million). Of the 1.3 million foreign-born women with a college degree (bachelor's degree or higher), almost half are not citizens. Over half of foreign-born women were in the labor force and the majority (58 percent) were employed in service or technical and administrative support jobs. There were 542,000 foreign-born women with children who headed their households and 42 percent were poor. By contrast, 15 percent of the 2.8 million married-couple families (where the householder was foreign born) with children were poor.

A2. BIRTH TRENDS

Typically, the young American women of the late 1980s had intercourse for the first time at about age 17, married for the first time at age 24, and had two babies from ages 26 to 30. These represent averages. Teenagers girls have 13 percent of all births. More than 3 in 10 babies were born to women aged 30 or older. And 3 in 10 births are to unmarried mothers.

Fertility trends can be confusing since the number of births and the rates at which women have babies have been going in opposite directions. The women of the post-World War II Baby Boom and the women of the Baby Bust that followed are all in their prime childbearing ages. A significant number of mothers are 30 years of age or older at the time of childbirth. There has also been a wave of immigrants who tend to have more children than American-born women. As a result, a lot of babies have been born. Nevertheless, women of the Baby Boom, on average, have smaller families than their mothers did.

When the number of births in a year tops 4 million, demographers call it a baby boom. And that is what the United States has experienced since 1989. The children of the post-World War II Baby Boom (1946 to 1964) have been dubbed the "Baby Echo." The annual number of births from 1989 to 1991 was the highest number the United States had experienced since the peak baby boom years from 1954 to 1964. Almost 4.1 million babies were born in 1992. By comparison, there were 4.3 million births in 1957, the high point during the Baby-Boom years. We expect the number of births to decline as the women of the Baby Boom age.

Fertility rates have declined from those of the 1950s and early 1960s. There were about 69 births per 1,000 women aged 15 to 44 years old in 1992 compared with 123 in 1957. Overall, fertility rates were stable during the 1980s and early 1990s, averaging 65 to 70 births per 1,000 women aged 15 to 44.

Fertility rates vary considerably among race and ethnic groups. The rates for White and Black women did not vary much over the decade of the 1980s; for Asian and American Indian women, however, the 1992 rates were 8–9 percent lower than in 1980. Among Hispanic women, the 1990 rate was 108 births per 1,000 Hispanic women, compared with 89 for non-Hispanic Black women, 75 for American Indian women, 67 for Asian women, and 63 for non-Hispanic White women. There is considerable diversity within the Hispanic population: the fertility rate ranged from a high of 119 for women of Mexican origin to a low of 53 for women of Cuban origin. The fertility rates of Hispanic women, especially Mexican women, are the highest of any racial or ethnic group for which rates can be reliably computed. One result of these differences in fertility patterns, along with changes in the population, is more diversity in new American generations. Two-thirds of the "Baby Echo" generation (children under age 6 in 1994) are White non-Hispanic, compared with three-fourths of the Baby-Boom generation (aged 31 to 49 in 1994).

Most women start having babies in their 20s but there was a record number of babies born to women over age 30 in 1994. We have experienced a substantial increase in birth rates, births per 1,000 population, for women past the traditional peak reproductive years since the mid-1970s. Rates for women over age 30 seem to have stabilized and were slowly declining in the early 1990s.

The timing of birth is the most meaningful difference among race and Hispanic origin groups. Among women under age 25, Black women have the highest fertility rates followed by American Indian, White, and Asian or Pacific Islander (API) women. The rates are similar among the races for those aged 25 to 29. After age 30, we see a reversal as Asian and White women make up for postponed childbearing: Asian women have by far the highest fertility rates followed by White women. The rates for older Black and American Indian women are half to two-thirds those of Asian women 30 years or older. In fact, many Asian women wait until past age 35 to have their first child. (There are, of course, differences among Asian nationality groups.)

In colonial times, women averaged about 8 children each. Changes in the average number of children in the American family resembles the curve of a roller coaster. The Total Fertility Rate (TFR), the average number of lifetime births per woman, during the Depression was similar to today's level (2.2 lifetime births per woman in 1936 compared with 2.1 in 1992). In less technical language that means most women of the 1990s have two children, many have one, and very few have more than three. The TFR increased during the postwar years until 1957 when women averaged 3.8 children over their lifetime. After that, the TFR started a downhill ride and in 1976, women averaged 1.7 lifetime births each. Since then, the upward curve in the averages has been less drastic than mid-century.

There are significant differences in the TFR among race and Hispanic origin groups. In 1992, non-Hispanic White women averaged 1.8 children each in their lifetime, similar to the 1.9 for API women. The average number of children was higher for other groups: 2.2 for American Indian women, 2.5 for non-Hispanic Black women, and the highest, 3.0 for Hispanic women (although Cuban women averaged less than 1.5 children each).

The Baby-Boom generation is aging and most will reach the end of their childbearing years in the 1990s. Barring a sensational increase in fertility or an enormous expansion in young female immigrants, the numbers of births will likely continue a slow decline through the end of this century. Then, we will probably see a slow increase in the number of births as the women of the Baby Echo generation start to reach their 20s. Birth trends are projected to differ substantially by race and Hispanic origin, partly because of differing age structures and partly because of historical differences in levels of fertility.

Many social and economic factors reduce the fertility rate of women and affect the age when they have their babies. These include higher levels of educational attainment and labor force participation, the cost and difficulty of obtaining child care, and the cost of living.

In 1994, about 2 million women with newborns were in the labor force, and two-thirds were full-time workers. That is a labor force participation rate of 53 percent, up from 38 percent in 1980 and 31 percent in 1976. Such increases were the case among both White and Black mothers. Most women with infants now return to work within the first year. Labor force rates are highest for more educated, older first-time mothers. One-third of recent mothers with less than a high school education were in the labor force compared with 70 percent of recent mothers with a bachelor's degree and above. Work experience, greater long-term commitment to a particular job, higher salaries, and more resources for purchasing child care are likely factors.

A3. BIRTH EXPECTATIONS AND CHILDLESSNESS

Levels of childbearing are closely related to our social and economic history. For example, 1 in 5 women who spent most of their childbearing years during the Great Depression and World War II were childless, while only 8 percent of women born in 1935 were childless. In 1992, 1 in 6 women aged 40 to 44 were childless compared with 1 in 10 in 1982. Even though women in their 30s have higher fertility rates than a decade ago, a higher proportion have also remained childless than was the case a decade ago. Based on what childless women in their 30s are saying and current first-childbearing patterns, it appears some 15 to 20 percent will remain childless throughout their lives.

Younger women, those aged 18 to 34 in 1992, reported they expected to average 2.1 children in their lifetime. About 9 percent said they expected to remain childless and 29 percent said they expected to have three or more children. Young married couples once rushed into parenthood, but now many women delay having children into their late 20s and 30s. Today's women in their 30s often want a child. This reflects a fundamental shift in thinking about the question, "How old is too old to be a mother?" In 1990, 41 percent of childless 30- to 34-year-olds said they expected to have at least one child compared with about half that proportion in 1976. Despite the desires contemporary women express, as they delay marriage and childbearing, more will be physically unable to have the children they say the want.

Data from Forrest and Singh at the Alan Guttmacher Institute indicate that of all births, only about 6 in 10 were intended. Nearly 3 in 10 were mistimed according to the mothers. About 1 in 10 were unwanted births. In the early 1960s, over half of all births to married women were unintended (mistimed or unwanted). The proportion of such births dropped to 29 percent in the 1977 to 1982 period. Data for 1983 to 1988 show an increase in unwanted births; as a result, 33 percent of births in this period were unintended. Mistimed and unwanted births are highest among women with lower levels of education. Over half of all births in 1988 to women under 150 percent of the poverty level were unintended.

A4. BIRTHS TO UNMARRIED WOMEN

Many of the numbers, proportions, and rates concerning unwed mothers seem disturbing, but there is much misunderstanding of the trends as well. Unmarried women had 1.2 million babies in 1992, compared to about 90,000 in 1940; in 1977, the number topped half a million for the first time. The number and proportion of births to unmarried women tripled from 1970 to 1992. Of course, the number of women of childbearing age also increased during that time. More importantly, the increasing proportion of births that are to unmarried women is partly because there has been a significant decrease in births to married couples. Additionally, marriage, abortions, and adoptions have all declined. Today's women are more likely to have a baby and keep it without marrying.

Married families, especially Black married families, have fewer children than in the 1970s (in 1992, White married-couple families averaged 1.5 children compared to 0.8 children in Black married-couple families). As a result, children with unwed mothers are a greater proportion of all births. The research of demographers and economists indicate that hard economic times for young men is an important factor in the declining likelihood of the poor to marry. In 1970, 6 percent of White births and 38 percent of Black births were to unwed mothers. In 1992, 1 in 5 new White mothers, 2 in 3 new Black mothers, and half of new American Indian mothers were not married. Among women of Asian descent, the percentage of births to unmarried mothers ranged from 6 percent for Chinese mothers to 17 percent for Filipino mothers. In addition, there is large variation among women of Hispanic origin, ranging from 20 percent of Cuban mothers to 58 percent of Puerto Rican mothers.

Overall, the birth rate of unmarried women has increased from 26 births per 1,000 unmarried women in 1970 to 45 in 1992. Some argue this is not the immense change that has been portrayed and does not indicate irresponsible, promiscuous behavior among unmarried

women. It is the case that the birth rate of unmarried Black women is higher than that of unmarried White women. Contrary to what many believe, however, the birth rate is decreasing among unmarried Black women and increasing steadily among White women (among Black unmarried women, there were 96 births per 1,000 unmarried women in 1980, 79 in 1985, 94 in 1990, and 87 in 1992; among unmarried White women, the birth rate was 14 in 1970 and 35 in 1992).

Of all births to unmarried women in 1992, about 2 in 5 births were to White non-Hispanic mothers, 2 in 5 to Black non-Hispanic mothers, and 1 in 5 to Hispanic-origin mothers.

Premarital childbearing among teenagers is a matter of concern as the mothers and the children born out of wedlock tend to face health and economic hardships. In 1992, about 95 percent of American teenage girls were childless, while 5 percent had borne a child. Girls aged 15 to 17 had nearly 188,000 babies, and their birth rates increased 27 percent from 1986 (31 births per 1,000) to 1991. In 1992, however, there was the hopeful sign of a 2 percent decline among these young girls (to 38 births per 1,000 which was still higher than what we experienced in the early 1970s). Additionally, in 1990 13 percent of all births were to teenagers, a decrease from 16 percent in 1980.

Older teens, those aged 18 and 19, had almost 318,000 births in 1992. Their birth rates increased continuously and sharply from 1988 to 1992—from 84 to 95 births per 1,000. The rate for older teens was stable at 81 or less from 1976 to 1988. The 1992 rate is an improvement over 1970 when the rate was 115 per 1,000.

Birth rates are relatively higher for Black 18- to 19-year-old girls. They had 149 births to unmarried mothers per 1,000 unmarried Black women that age. The rate for Puerto Rican 18- to 19-year-olds was 122 compared with 24 for Cuban girls and 37 for non-Hispanic White girls. While the birth rate of Black teenagers is higher than for White teenagers, growth in out-of-wedlock births since the 1970s has been highest among White teenagers; the birthrate for unmarried Black teens in 1990 was about the same as in 1970.

A5. DEATH AND LIFE EXPECTANCY

Most women should plan for the fact that they will probably live at least into their mid-80s. Even though many more married women will be celebrating their golden wedding anniversaries, most will probably live their final years of life without a husband: half of White women live beyond age 86, and half of White men die before they are 77 years old; for Black women, half die after age 78, and half of Black men die before they are 68 years old. For all groups, this is an extraordinary difference from the beginning of the century when half of Black women died by age 34, Black men by age 30, White men by age 57, and White women by age 61.

It isn't just miracle drugs that brought about such change. Much of the improvement is because of reduced infant and maternal deaths and deaths from infectious diseases. In the early part of the century, a significant increase in life expectancy was achieved by convincing doctors about the role of germs and then, through a major public education project, women were taught to wash their hands before cooking and to have their families wash before eating. Now we have more people living to the oldest ages.

Life expectancy at birth has reached record levels. Based on the mortality experience of 1990, a White baby girl can expect to live to age 79, and a Black baby girl to age 74. White men have increased their life expectancy at birth from 71 years in 1980 to 73 years in 1990. Black men, in that same period, improved their life expectancy by only 0.4 of a year to 64.5 years. Improving the life expectancy of men will generally improve the economic circumstances of elderly women. For those who were 65 years old in 1990, White women could expect to live an additional 19 years, Black women 17 years, White men 15 years, and Black men 13 years.

Nearly 2.2 million people died in 1992, a record high and a sign of our aging population. The age-adjusted death rate, which eliminates the distorting effects of the aging of the population, was at a record low in 1992—505 deaths per 100,000 population (14 percent less than in 1980). Death rates have been decreasing for women of all ages except in the age group 35 to 44 years; the major reason was the increase in deaths from Human Immunodeficiency Virus (HIV) infection.

There are numerous implications of longer life expectancy for women. The lives they lead as younger women have an impact on them as they age. Whether and when they married and had children, how far they went in school, how they cared for their mental and physical health, and how they planned for their financial futures have far-reaching effects. It means new challenges.

Also, it has only been in this century that most men and women live long enough to experience married life after their children leave home. Improvements in mortality have not necessarily meant improved health, however, especially for women at the oldest ages. Women have traditionally been the ones who cared for the frail elderly. More women in their 50s, 60s, and even 70s will face the physical, mental, and financial stress of caring for their most elderly relatives. For many, this will come at a time when they are trying to prepare for their own retirement.

A6. CAUSES OF DEATH

At the beginning of the century, women usually died in childbirth or from an infectious or parasitic disease. Death, and its reasons, have changed dramatically. Two in three women die of heart disease, cancer, or cerebrovascular diseases (stroke). Death rates for women from heart disease and stroke have steadily decreased in the last two decades, but cancer deaths have increased. Death from heart disease was 64 percent greater for Black women than for White women in 1991. Death from strokes are also much higher for Black than for White women. Death rates from lung cancer have increased dramatically among White and Black women.

Both Black and White women have experienced significant increases in HIV-related deaths, although their death rates are much lower than those for men. Men are also more likely than women to die a violent death. White women are much less likely to be murdered than Black women, but White women are more likely to kill themselves than are Black women. In 1991, 40 percent of suicides committed by women were with guns compared to 30 percent in 1970. Poisoning (by solids, liquids, and gases) was the second most frequent method of suicide in 1991. Middle-aged women (35 to 64 years of age) are the most likely to kill themselves.

Women tend to get diseases from which they become chronically ill. Men tend to get diseases from which they die. For women, death is likely to be long in coming, and women often experience significant decreases in the quality of their lives because of this.

A1. POPULATION CHANGE AND IMMIGRATION

A1-1. Estimated Resident Population, by Age, Sex, Race, and Hispanic Origin: July 1, 1994

(Numbers in thousands. Consistent with the 1990 Census, as enumerated.)

Date and age	Total: Total	Total: Male	Total: Female	White: Total	White: Male	White: Female	Black: Total	Black: Male	Black: Female	Am. Indian, Eskimo, Aleut: Total	AI: Male	AI: Female	Asian/Pacific Islander: Total	API: Male	API: Female
July 1, 1994															
All ages	260,341	127,076	133,265	216,470	106,139	110,331	32,672	15,491	17,181	2,210	1,094	1,116	8,989	4,352	4,637
Under 5 years	19,727	10,094	9,633	15,592	7,995	7,597	3,119	1,581	1,538	212	108	105	804	411	393
Under 1 year	3,870	1,981	1,889	3,041	1,560	1,481	619	314	305	42	21	21	168	86	82
1 year	3,878	1,985	1,893	3,060	1,569	1,491	616	313	303	41	21	20	161	83	79
2 years	3,956	2,023	1,933	3,132	1,604	1,528	619	314	305	41	21	20	163	84	80
3 years	3,990	2,041	1,949	3,163	1,622	1,541	623	315	308	42	21	21	163	83	80
4 years	4,032	2,064	1,968	3,195	1,640	1,556	642	325	317	47	24	23	148	76	72
5 to 9 years	18,859	9,657	9,201	14,997	7,695	7,302	2,939	1,491	1,448	223	113	109	700	358	342
5 years	3,884	1,989	1,894	3,063	1,572	1,491	630	319	311	47	24	23	144	74	70
6 years	3,792	1,940	1,852	3,011	1,544	1,468	595	302	293	45	23	22	141	72	69
7 years	3,747	1,917	1,830	2,985	1,531	1,454	582	294	287	43	22	21	136	70	66
8 years	3,595	1,841	1,754	2,874	1,475	1,399	544	276	268	43	22	21	135	69	66
9 years	3,841	1,969	1,872	3,063	1,574	1,490	588	299	289	45	23	22	144	73	71
10 to 14 years	18,753	9,602	9,150	14,921	7,661	7,260	2,864	1,452	1,412	229	116	113	739	374	365
10 years	3,744	1,920	1,824	2,984	1,535	1,450	567	288	279	46	23	22	147	75	72
11 years	3,770	1,931	1,840	3,010	1,545	1,465	566	287	279	46	23	23	148	75	73
12 years	3,768	1,927	1,841	2,994	1,535	1,459	580	294	286	46	23	23	149	75	74
13 years	3,722	1,903	1,818	2,962	1,519	1,443	562	285	278	47	23	23	151	76	75
14 years	3,748	1,921	1,828	2,971	1,526	1,444	588	298	289	45	23	22	145	73	71
15 to 19 years	17,816	9,036	8,580	14,035	7,222	6,814	2,733	1,385	1,349	193	98	95	655	332	323
15 years	3,602	1,848	1,754	2,849	1,466	1,383	572	291	281	43	22	21	138	70	68
16 years	3,515	1,808	1,707	2,802	1,444	1,357	544	277	267	40	20	20	129	66	64
17 years	3,562	1,836	1,727	2,837	1,466	1,372	555	283	272	39	20	19	131	67	64
18 years	3,349	1,714	1,635	2,677	1,375	1,302	515	259	255	35	18	17	122	62	60
19 years	3,588	1,831	1,757	2,870	1,471	1,399	547	274	273	37	18	18	133	67	66
20 to 24 years	18,326	9,311	9,015	14,722	7,527	7,195	2,668	1,313	1,355	187	96	91	750	375	374
20 years	3,480	1,776	1,704	2,781	1,426	1,354	529	264	265	36	18	18	135	68	67
21 years	3,492	1,782	1,710	2,778	1,425	1,353	533	265	267	37	19	18	144	73	72
22 years	3,605	1,835	1,770	2,891	1,481	1,410	528	260	268	37	19	18	149	75	75
23 years	3,839	1,943	1,897	3,094	1,576	1,518	547	267	281	39	20	18	159	79	79
24 years	3,910	1,976	1,934	3,178	1,619	1,559	531	256	275	39	20	19	163	81	82
25 to 29 years	19,177	9,619	9,558	15,593	7,894	7,699	2,619	1,250	1,369	178	92	87	787	383	404
25 years	3,756	1,894	1,862	3,060	1,557	1,504	501	241	260	36	19	17	158	78	80
26 years	3,680	1,846	1,834	2,984	1,510	1,473	508	243	265	35	18	17	153	75	79
27 years	3,778	1,894	1,884	3,076	1,557	1,519	513	245	269	35	18	17	154	75	79
28 years	3,674	1,837	1,837	2,990	1,509	1,481	503	240	263	33	17	16	148	72	76
29 years	4,289	2,147	2,142	3,483	1,761	1,722	594	282	312	38	20	19	174	84	89
30 to 34 years	22,177	11,058	11,119	18,292	9,218	9,074	2,837	1,330	1,507	187	93	94	861	417	444
30 years	4,354	2,173	2,181	3,573	1,801	1,771	573	270	303	37	19	19	171	83	88
31 years	4,332	2,160	2,172	3,563	1,794	1,769	558	263	295	37	19	19	174	84	90
32 years	4,431	2,209	2,222	3,663	1,845	1,818	563	263	299	37	19	19	169	82	87
33 years	4,433	2,201	2,232	3,677	1,846	1,831	550	255	294	36	18	19	170	82	88
34 years	4,626	2,315	2,311	3,817	1,931	1,886	594	279	315	38	19	19	178	86	91
35 to 39 years	21,961	10,920	11,040	18,237	9,165	9,072	2,733	1,280	1,453	174	85	88	816	390	426
35 years	4,523	2,253	2,270	3,743	1,884	1,859	571	268	303	37	18	19	171	83	89
36 years	4,439	2,208	2,231	3,696	1,857	1,839	545	255	290	35	17	18	163	78	84
37 years	4,472	2,223	2,248	3,713	1,866	1,847	560	262	298	35	17	18	164	78	85
38 years	4,055	2,007	2,048	3,375	1,689	1,686	497	231	265	32	15	16	152	71	80
39 years	4,472	2,229	2,243	3,710	1,869	1,841	560	263	297	35	17	18	167	79	88
40 to 44 years	19,699	9,728	9,970	16,516	8,250	8,266	2,308	1,069	1,239	151	73	78	723	336	388
40 years	4,223	2,090	2,133	3,528	1,765	1,763	507	236	271	33	16	17	155	73	82
41 years	4,013	1,979	2,033	3,366	1,680	1,687	464	214	250	32	15	16	151	71	81
42 years	3,922	1,936	1,986	3,303	1,649	1,653	452	208	243	30	15	15	138	64	74
43 years	3,716	1,825	1,891	3,103	1,543	1,560	438	201	237	30	14	15	146	67	79
44 years	3,825	1,897	1,927	3,217	1,614	1,603	448	210	238	27	13	14	133	61	72
45 to 49 years	16,679	8,181	8,498	14,249	7,064	7,185	1,740	793	946	120	58	62	571	266	306
45 years	3,659	1,801	1,858	3,096	1,541	1,555	407	188	219	26	13	13	130	60	70
46 years	3,550	1,743	1,807	3,036	1,508	1,528	369	168	200	25	12	13	120	55	65
47 years	3,843	1,886	1,957	3,322	1,647	1,675	375	170	205	26	13	13	120	56	64
48 years	2,652	1,292	1,360	2,269	1,117	1,151	267	120	147	20	10	11	96	45	51
49 years	2,974	1,458	1,517	2,525	1,250	1,275	322	147	175	22	11	11	105	50	55
50 to 54 years	13,191	6,410	6,781	11,355	5,572	5,782	1,340	602	738	91	43	47	406	192	214
50 years	2,890	1,409	1,481	2,483	1,223	1,261	293	133	161	21	10	11	93	44	49
51 years	2,931	1,430	1,502	2,549	1,255	1,295	278	126	152	19	9	10	85	40	45
52 years	2,549	1,238	1,312	2,191	1,074	1,116	263	118	145	18	8	9	78	37	41
53 years	2,440	1,182	1,258	2,099	1,027	1,072	250	111	138	17	8	9	75	36	39
54 years	2,381	1,152	1,229	2,033	994	1,039	256	114	141	17	8	9	76	36	40
55 to 59 years	10,936	5,244	5,692	9,436	4,573	4,863	1,110	487	623	71	34	37	318	150	168
55 years	2,283	1,099	1,184	1,950	947	1,003	246	110	136	16	7	8	71	34	37
56 years	2,281	1,095	1,185	1,966	955	1,011	234	102	133	15	7	8	66	31	34
57 years	2,178	1,043	1,134	1,876	908	968	224	98	126	14	7	7	64	30	34
58 years	2,021	966	1,055	1,758	849	909	195	85	110	12	6	7	56	26	30
59 years	2,173	1,041	1,132	1,886	914	972	212	92	119	14	7	7	61	28	33
60 to 64 years	10,082	4,740	5,342	8,773	4,172	4,601	984	424	560	57	26	30	268	117	151
60 years	1,981	934	1,046	1,714	817	897	198	86	111	12	6	6	56	25	31
61 years	1,953	923	1,030	1,693	810	883	194	84	110	12	5	6	54	24	30
62 years	1,965	921	1,044	1,705	809	896	196	84	112	11	5	6	53	23	30
63 years	2,065	971	1,094	1,810	861	949	192	82	110	11	5	6	52	23	29
64 years	2,118	990	1,128	1,850	875	975	204	88	116	11	5	6	54	23	31
65 to 69 years	9,970	4,500	5,471	8,792	3,998	4,794	906	386	520	47	21	26	226	95	132
70 to 74 years	8,741	3,790	4,951	7,840	3,420	4,419	694	279	415	36	16	20	171	75	96
75 to 79 years	6,574	2,655	3,919	5,949	2,414	3,534	499	188	311	24	10	14	102	43	59
80 to 84 years	4,351	1,550	2,801	3,962	1,412	2,550	316	107	210	16	6	10	57	25	32
85 to 89 years	2,274	686	1,588	2,083	624	1,459	161	49	111	8	3	6	22	10	13
90 to 94 years	948	235	713	859	210	649	77	21	56	4	1	3	8	3	5
95 to 99 years	249	50	199	225	44	181	20	5	15	1	-	1	3	1	2
100 years and over	50	9	41	42	7	35	7	2	5	-	-	-	1	-	1
16 years and over	199,400	95,875	103,526	168,111	81,323	86,788	23,179	10,678	12,502	1,502	735	767	6,608	3,139	3,469
18 years and over	192,323	92,231	100,092	162,472	78,413	84,059	22,080	10,117	11,963	1,424	695	729	6,347	3,006	3,341
15 to 44 years	118,956	59,673	59,284	97,397	49,276	48,121	15,898	7,626	8,272	1,070	538	533	4,591	2,233	2,359
65 years and over	33,158	13,475	19,683	29,751	12,130	17,621	2,680	1,036	1,644	137	57	80	591	252	339
85 years and over	3,522	980	2,542	3,209	885	2,324	265	76	188	14	4	9	34	14	21
Median age	34.0	32.9	35.2	35.0	33.9	36.2	29.0	27.2	30.4	26.7	25.8	27.6	30.4	29.3	31.3
Mean age	35.7	34.2	37.0	36.6	35.1	38.0	31.1	29.6	32.5	29.3	28.5	30.1	31.4	30.5	32.3

A1-1. Estimated Resident Population, by Age, Sex, Race, and Hispanic Origin: July 1, 1994 *(continued)*

(Numbers in thousands. Consistent with the 1990 Census, as enumerated.)

Date and age	Hispanic origin[1]			Not of Hispanic origin, by race											
				White			Black			American Indian, Eskimo, and Aleut			Asian and Pacific Islander		
	Total	Male	Female	Total	Male	Female	Total	Male	Female	Total	Male	Female	Total	Male	Female
July 1, 1994															
All ages	26,077	13,219	12,857	192,727	94,091	98,636	31,192	14,748	16,444	1,907	938	969	8,438	4,080	4,358
Under 5 years	3,096	1,583	1,513	12,764	6,549	6,215	2,945	1,492	1,453	179	91	89	743	380	363
Under 1 year	643	330	314	2,453	1,258	1,195	583	295	287	35	18	17	156	80	76
1 year	631	323	308	2,482	1,273	1,209	581	295	286	35	18	17	149	76	73
2 years	636	325	311	2,550	1,307	1,243	584	296	288	35	18	17	151	77	74
3 years	608	311	298	2,607	1,338	1,269	589	298	291	35	18	18	151	77	74
4 years	577	294	283	2,672	1,373	1,299	608	307	300	39	20	19	136	70	67
5 to 9 years	2,527	1,292	1,235	12,707	6,525	6,183	2,791	1,415	1,376	188	96	92	646	330	316
5 years	537	275	262	2,578	1,324	1,254	598	303	295	39	20	19	132	68	64
6 years	523	267	255	2,538	1,302	1,236	564	286	278	38	19	18	130	66	64
7 years	500	256	244	2,532	1,299	1,233	552	279	273	37	19	18	126	64	61
8 years	475	243	232	2,443	1,254	1,188	517	262	255	36	18	18	124	63	61
9 years	492	252	241	2,617	1,345	1,271	560	284	275	38	19	19	134	68	66
10 to 14 years	2,355	1,202	1,153	12,783	6,569	6,214	2,733	1,385	1,348	195	99	96	686	347	339
10 years	480	246	235	2,548	1,312	1,237	541	274	266	39	20	19	136	69	67
11 years	480	245	235	2,574	1,323	1,251	540	274	267	39	20	19	138	70	68
12 years	468	238	229	2,570	1,319	1,251	553	280	273	39	20	19	138	70	68
13 years	469	239	230	2,536	1,302	1,234	537	272	265	40	20	20	140	71	69
14 years	458	234	224	2,555	1,314	1,241	562	285	277	39	19	19	134	68	66
15 to 19 years	2,198	1,128	1,070	12,033	6,193	5,840	2,610	1,322	1,289	166	84	82	609	309	300
15 years	439	225	213	2,452	1,262	1,190	547	278	269	37	19	18	128	65	63
16 years	436	224	212	2,405	1,241	1,164	520	265	255	34	17	17	120	61	59
17 years	441	227	214	2,436	1,259	1,177	530	270	260	33	17	16	122	62	60
18 years	428	219	208	2,287	1,175	1,112	491	247	244	30	15	15	114	58	56
19 years	455	233	221	2,454	1,257	1,197	523	261	261	31	16	16	124	63	62
20 to 24 years	2,338	1,245	1,093	12,592	6,390	6,202	2,539	1,246	1,293	159	81	78	697	348	349
20 years	447	232	215	2,372	1,214	1,158	504	252	253	31	15	15	126	63	62
21 years	461	244	217	2,357	1,202	1,155	508	252	255	31	16	15	135	68	67
22 years	457	245	212	2,474	1,257	1,217	503	248	256	32	16	15	139	69	70
23 years	481	259	222	2,658	1,341	1,317	521	253	268	33	17	16	147	74	74
24 years	492	266	226	2,731	1,377	1,355	504	242	262	33	17	16	151	75	76
25 to 29 years	2,483	1,334	1,149	13,338	6,680	6,657	2,475	1,175	1,301	149	75	74	731	354	377
25 years	489	265	224	2,617	1,315	1,301	474	227	247	31	16	15	146	72	75
26 years	486	262	224	2,542	1,272	1,270	480	228	252	29	15	14	142	69	74
27 years	497	267	230	2,624	1,314	1,310	485	230	255	30	15	15	143	69	74
28 years	480	257	223	2,553	1,275	1,278	475	225	250	28	14	14	138	66	71
29 years	531	283	248	3,002	1,504	1,498	562	265	297	32	16	16	162	79	84
30 to 34 years	2,460	1,291	1,168	16,056	8,042	8,014	2,693	1,255	1,438	159	78	81	809	391	418
30 years	517	273	244	3,103	1,553	1,550	543	254	289	32	16	16	160	77	83
31 years	503	265	238	3,106	1,553	1,552	528	247	281	32	16	16	164	79	85
32 years	480	252	228	3,226	1,616	1,611	535	249	286	32	16	16	158	77	81
33 years	484	253	231	3,236	1,615	1,621	522	241	281	31	15	16	160	77	83
34 years	476	249	227	3,385	1,705	1,680	565	264	301	33	18	17	167	81	86
35 to 39 years	2,060	1,058	1,002	16,371	8,206	8,165	2,608	1,215	1,393	150	73	77	772	368	404
35 years	445	230	215	3,340	1,675	1,665	545	254	290	32	16	16	162	78	84
36 years	427	220	207	3,309	1,657	1,651	520	242	278	30	15	15	154	74	80
37 years	410	211	199	3,342	1,675	1,667	535	249	286	30	15	16	155	74	81
38 years	378	193	185	3,032	1,514	1,518	474	220	254	27	13	14	144	68	76
39 years	400	204	196	3,348	1,684	1,664	535	251	285	30	15	16	158	75	83
40 to 44 years	1,632	818	814	15,038	7,508	7,529	2,210	1,020	1,190	133	64	69	687	318	369
40 years	361	182	179	3,201	1,600	1,601	485	225	260	29	14	15	147	69	78
41 years	341	171	170	3,057	1,524	1,533	443	204	240	28	13	14	144	67	77
42 years	317	159	158	3,015	1,505	1,510	433	199	234	26	13	13	131	61	70
43 years	309	154	155	2,823	1,403	1,420	419	192	227	26	12	14	139	64	75
44 years	303	151	152	2,942	1,476	1,466	429	200	229	24	11	12	127	58	69
45 to 49 years	1,230	603	627	13,130	6,514	6,615	1,669	759	910	107	51	55	544	253	292
45 years	278	137	140	2,844	1,416	1,428	391	180	211	23	11	12	124	57	67
46 years	259	127	132	2,800	1,392	1,408	354	161	193	22	11	12	114	52	62
47 years	258	126	132	3,088	1,533	1,555	360	163	197	23	11	12	115	53	61
48 years	213	104	109	2,074	1,022	1,052	255	114	141	18	9	9	92	43	49
49 years	222	108	114	2,323	1,151	1,172	309	141	168	20	10	10	100	47	52
50 to 54 years	913	438	475	10,522	5,172	5,350	1,287	577	710	82	39	43	387	184	204
50 years	204	98	106	2,298	1,133	1,165	282	127	155	19	9	10	88	42	46
51 years	195	94	102	2,371	1,169	1,202	267	120	146	17	8	9	81	38	43
52 years	174	84	91	2,032	998	1,034	253	114	140	16	8	8	74	35	39
53 years	172	83	89	1,941	951	990	240	107	133	15	7	8	72	34	38
54 years	167	80	87	1,880	921	959	246	110	136	15	7	8	72	34	38
55 to 59 years	738	348	390	8,760	4,254	4,507	1,069	468	601	64	30	34	304	143	161
55 years	157	74	83	1,808	880	928	237	106	131	14	7	8	67	32	35
56 years	154	73	81	1,825	889	937	226	98	128	13	6	7	63	30	33
57 years	147	69	78	1,742	845	897	215	94	121	13	6	7	62	29	32
58 years	137	64	73	1,632	789	843	187	82	106	11	5	6	54	25	29
59 years	144	68	76	1,754	851	903	204	89	115	13	6	7	59	27	32
60 to 64 years	616	285	332	8,208	3,910	4,298	950	409	541	51	24	27	257	112	145
60 years	128	59	68	1,597	763	835	191	83	108	11	5	6	54	24	30
61 years	123	57	66	1,581	758	823	187	81	107	11	5	6	52	23	29
62 years	118	54	64	1,597	759	838	189	81	109	10	5	5	50	22	28
63 years	125	58	67	1,695	808	888	185	79	106	10	5	5	50	22	28
64 years	123	57	67	1,737	823	914	197	85	112	10	5	5	51	22	29
65 to 69 years	521	231	290	8,312	3,784	4,528	878	374	504	42	19	23	217	91	126
70 to 74 years	383	167	216	7,485	3,265	4,220	676	271	404	33	14	19	164	72	92
75 to 79 years	243	96	146	5,724	2,325	3,399	487	183	304	23	9	13	98	42	56
80 to 84 years	162	59	103	3,810	1,357	2,453	309	104	205	15	6	9	54	24	30
85 to 89 years	80	27	53	2,008	599	1,409	158	49	109	8	3	5	21	9	12
90 to 94 years	32	10	22	828	200	628	76	20	55	4	1	3	8	3	5
95 to 99 years	8	2	5	218	42	176	20	5	15	1	-	1	3	1	2
100 years and over	2	1	2	40	6	33	7	2	5	-	-	-	1	-	1
16 years and over	17,661	8,917	8,744	152,020	73,186	78,834	22,176	10,179	11,997	1,308	634	674	6,235	2,958	3,277
18 years and over	16,784	8,467	8,317	147,180	70,687	76,493	21,126	9,643	11,483	1,241	600	641	5,993	2,834	3,159
15 to 44 years	13,171	6,875	6,296	85,428	43,020	42,408	15,136	7,233	7,903	916	455	460	4,305	2,089	2,217
65 years and over	1,431	593	838	28,425	11,578	16,847	2,611	1,009	1,602	125	53	73	565	242	323
85 years and over	122	40	82	3,094	847	2,247	260	75	185	13	4	9	32	13	20
Median age	26.1	25.6	26.6	36.2	35.1	37.4	29.1	27.3	30.6	27.2	26.2	28.3	30.7	29.6	31.6
Mean age	28.2	27.4	29.0	37.8	36.1	39.0	31.2	29.7	32.6	29.8	28.9	30.7	31.7	30.7	32.5

[1] Persons of Hispanic origin may be of any race. The information on the total and Hispanic population shown in this report was collected in the 50 states and the District of Columbia, and therefore, does not include residents of Puerto Rico.

Source: Kevin Deardorff, Frederick Hollmann, and Patricia Montgomery, U.S. Bureau of the Census, *U.S. Population Estimates, by Age, Sex, Race, and Hispanic Origin: 1990 to 1994*, Series PPL-21, available from Population Division, March 1995, Table 1.

A1-2. Projections of the Population, by Age, Sex, Race, and Hispanic Origin, for the United States: 2000 and 2050 (Middle Series)

[Numbers in thousands. Resident population]

Date and age	Total			Race											
				White			Black			American Indian, Eskimo, and Aleut			Asian and Pacific Islander		
	Total	Male	Female	Total	Male	Female	Total	Male	Female	Total	Male	Female	Total	Male	Female
JULY 1, 2000															
All ages	276 241	135 101	141 140	226 267	111 245	115 022	35 469	16 802	18 667	2 380	1 177	1 203	12 125	5 877	6 248
Under 5 years	19 431	9 958	9 473	14 945	7 675	7 270	3 214	1 633	1 581	215	109	107	1 056	541	515
Under 1 year	3 862	1 978	1 884	2 945	1 512	1 433	653	332	321	44	22	22	219	112	107
1 year	3 836	1 965	1 871	2 944	1 512	1 433	639	324	314	43	22	21	210	108	102
2 years	3 862	1 981	1 882	2 973	1 527	1 446	637	324	313	43	22	21	210	108	102
3 years	3 891	1 994	1 897	3 005	1 544	1 462	634	322	312	43	22	21	209	107	102
4 years	3 980	2 040	1 940	3 078	1 581	1 497	652	331	321	43	22	21	208	107	101
5 to 9 years	20 531	10 530	10 002	16 012	8 226	7 787	3 302	1 679	1 623	229	116	113	989	509	480
5 years	4 016	2 060	1 956	3 116	1 601	1 515	650	330	320	43	22	21	207	107	100
6 years	4 047	2 074	1 973	3 158	1 621	1 537	645	328	317	43	22	21	201	104	98
7 years	4 093	2 097	1 996	3 196	1 641	1 555	654	331	322	43	22	21	200	103	97
8 years	4 052	2 078	1 974	3 175	1 631	1 544	646	329	318	48	24	23	183	94	89
9 years	4 324	2 221	2 103	3 368	1 732	1 636	707	360	347	51	26	25	198	102	96
10 to 14 years	19 972	10 237	9 735	15 627	8 025	7 602	3 141	1 597	1 544	248	126	122	955	488	467
10 years	4 157	2 134	2 023	3 240	1 666	1 574	675	343	331	51	26	25	191	98	92
11 years	3 982	2 040	1 942	3 113	1 598	1 515	632	321	312	49	25	24	188	96	91
12 years	3 935	2 015	1 921	3 075	1 577	1 498	623	317	306	49	25	24	189	96	93
13 years	3 942	2 019	1 923	3 094	1 588	1 507	604	307	297	50	25	25	194	99	95
14 years	3 956	2 030	1 926	3 105	1 597	1 509	607	310	298	49	25	24	195	99	96
15 to 19 years	19 819	10 167	9 651	15 581	8 018	7 563	3 057	1 551	1 505	229	115	114	952	483	469
15 years	3 872	1 987	1 885	3 029	1 558	1 471	600	305	294	48	24	24	195	99	96
16 years	3 943	2 030	1 913	3 097	1 597	1 499	604	309	294	48	24	24	194	99	95
17 years	4 040	2 082	1 957	3 178	1 642	1 536	620	317	303	47	24	23	195	100	95
18 years	3 870	1 981	1 888	3 053	1 569	1 484	593	300	294	43	21	21	180	91	89
19 years	4 094	2 087	2 008	3 225	1 652	1 573	639	320	320	43	21	22	187	94	93
20 to 24 years	17 947	9 109	8 838	14 199	7 262	6 937	2 668	1 311	1 356	185	93	93	895	443	452
20 years	3 876	1 974	1 902	3 060	1 568	1 493	595	297	299	40	20	20	180	90	90
21 years	3 669	1 869	1 800	2 900	1 486	1 413	554	275	279	38	19	19	177	89	88
22 years	3 545	1 802	1 743	2 809	1 439	1 370	526	259	267	36	18	18	174	86	88
23 years	3 372	1 706	1 666	2 668	1 362	1 306	492	240	253	35	17	17	176	87	90
24 years	3 485	1 758	1 727	2 762	1 407	1 355	500	242	259	36	18	18	187	91	96
25 to 29 years	18 370	9 179	9 191	14 551	7 347	7 204	2 597	1 238	1 359	183	94	89	1 039	500	539
25 years	3 387	1 699	1 688	2 671	1 354	1 317	488	234	254	35	18	18	192	93	99
26 years	3 426	1 707	1 719	2 692	1 355	1 337	501	239	262	36	18	18	197	94	103
27 years	3 683	1 842	1 840	2 910	1 471	1 439	526	252	274	37	19	18	209	100	109
28 years	3 738	1 865	1 873	2 981	1 503	1 478	516	246	271	36	18	17	205	98	107
29 years	4 137	2 065	2 071	3 296	1 663	1 632	565	267	298	40	21	19	236	114	122
30 to 34 years	19 867	9 880	9 987	15 983	8 047	7 936	2 638	1 228	1 410	173	88	85	1 073	516	557
30 years	3 921	1 950	1 972	3 154	1 587	1 568	511	239	272	35	18	17	220	106	114
31 years	3 781	1 880	1 901	3 028	1 524	1 504	506	236	270	34	17	17	213	102	111
32 years	3 868	1 922	1 946	3 113	1 566	1 546	511	237	274	34	17	17	210	101	109
33 years	3 954	1 959	1 995	3 183	1 597	1 586	529	245	284	33	17	17	208	100	109
34 years	4 343	2 169	2 174	3 505	1 772	1 732	580	271	310	36	19	18	221	108	114
35 to 39 years	22 695	11 307	11 388	18 586	9 364	9 222	2 873	1 340	1 533	181	91	90	1 055	512	543
35 years	4 471	2 230	2 241	3 635	1 833	1 802	579	271	308	37	19	18	219	106	113
36 years	4 443	2 212	2 232	3 637	1 830	1 806	561	261	300	35	18	18	211	102	108
37 years	4 597	2 289	2 308	3 770	1 898	1 872	582	271	311	37	18	18	209	102	107
38 years	4 320	2 145	2 175	3 559	1 787	1 771	531	246	285	34	17	17	197	95	102
39 years	4 863	2 432	2 432	3 986	2 015	1 971	621	292	329	38	19	19	218	106	112
40 to 44 years	22 428	11 118	11 309	18 553	9 300	9 253	2 737	1 272	1 465	171	84	87	968	463	505
40 years	4 654	2 312	2 342	3 833	1 926	1 907	578	268	309	36	18	18	207	100	107
41 years	4 540	2 250	2 290	3 755	1 881	1 874	550	255	295	35	17	18	200	96	104
42 years	4 522	2 242	2 280	3 750	1 879	1 871	549	256	294	34	17	17	189	91	98
43 years	4 293	2 115	2 178	3 539	1 764	1 775	525	242	282	34	16	18	196	92	104
44 years	4 418	2 199	2 219	3 676	1 850	1 826	536	251	285	31	15	16	175	83	92
45 to 49 years	19 530	9 593	9 937	16 339	8 124	8 215	2 248	1 024	1 224	143	69	73	800	375	425
45 years	4 210	2 079	2 131	3 514	1 755	1 760	494	228	265	31	15	16	171	81	90
46 years	3 959	1 946	2 013	3 324	1 654	1 670	444	202	242	29	14	15	162	76	86
47 years	3 930	1 926	2 003	3 281	1 629	1 652	458	207	251	29	14	15	161	76	85
48 years	3 554	1 736	1 819	2 989	1 479	1 511	395	178	218	25	12	13	145	67	77
49 years	3 877	1 906	1 972	3 231	1 607	1 623	457	209	248	28	14	14	162	75	86
50 to 54 years	16 640	8 099	8 540	14 196	6 993	7 202	1 706	763	943	113	55	58	625	288	337
50 years	3 687	1 800	1 886	3 111	1 538	1 573	403	182	221	26	12	13	147	68	78
51 years	3 534	1 723	1 811	3 012	1 486	1 525	366	165	201	24	12	12	133	61	72
52 years	3 760	1 836	1 925	3 265	1 611	1 653	349	156	193	23	11	12	123	56	67
53 years	2 787	1 350	1 438	2 371	1 163	1 209	285	126	159	20	10	10	111	51	59
54 years	2 871	1 390	1 481	2 437	1 195	1 242	303	134	168	20	10	10	112	52	61
55 to 59 years	13 047	6 278	6 769	11 200	5 454	5 745	1 305	571	733	84	40	44	459	212	247
55 years	2 789	1 345	1 444	2 374	1 158	1 217	292	130	162	19	9	10	103	48	55
56 years	2 965	1 430	1 535	2 575	1 258	1 317	278	120	157	18	8	9	95	44	51
57 years	2 627	1 262	1 365	2 246	1 092	1 154	272	120	153	17	8	9	92	42	49
58 years	2 311	1 109	1 203	1 994	968	1 026	221	96	125	14	7	8	81	38	44
59 years	2 355	1 132	1 223	2 010	979	1 032	241	105	136	16	7	8	88	41	47
60 to 64 years	10 643	5 043	5 600	9 139	4 386	4 753	1 065	455	610	65	31	34	374	171	202
60 years	2 258	1 070	1 188	1 935	927	1 007	228	98	130	14	7	8	81	38	43
61 years	2 173	1 035	1 138	1 866	901	966	217	93	124	13	6	7	76	35	41
62 years	2 056	974	1 083	1 760	844	916	209	89	120	13	6	7	75	34	40
63 years	2 045	971	1 074	1 763	848	915	200	85	115	12	6	6	70	32	38
64 years	2 110	993	1 117	1 815	865	950	211	90	121	12	6	7	71	32	40
65 to 69 years	9 594	4 420	5 173	8 297	3 864	4 433	938	401	536	50	23	27	309	132	177
70 to 74 years	8 957	3 965	4 993	7 923	3 537	4 386	748	306	442	40	18	22	246	103	143
75 to 79 years	7 507	3 138	4 369	6 735	2 832	3 904	571	220	351	31	13	18	170	73	97
80 to 84 years	4 931	1 842	3 089	4 484	1 681	2 804	336	115	221	19	8	11	91	39	53
85 to 89 years	2 692	845	1 847	2 452	766	1 686	186	57	128	12	4	8	43	17	25
90 to 94 years	1 193	304	890	1 075	269	807	94	26	68	6	2	4	18	7	10
95 to 99 years	373	77	296	327	65	262	37	9	28	3	1	2	7	2	4
100 years and over	75	12	63	63	9	53	10	2	7	1	0	1	2	0	1
16 years and over	212 435	102 389	110 045	176 654	85 761	90 893	25 212	11 588	13 624	1 639	802	838	8 929	4 239	4 690
18 years and over	204 452	98 277	106 175	170 380	82 522	87 858	23 988	10 961	13 027	1 545	754	791	8 540	4 040	4 500
15 to 44 years	121 126	60 761	60 365	97 452	49 338	48 114	16 569	7 941	8 627	1 122	564	558	5 982	2 917	3 065
65 years and over	35 322	14 603	20 719	31 357	13 023	18 334	2 919	1 138	1 781	161	68	93	884	374	510
85 years and over	4 333	1 238	3 095	3 917	1 109	2 808	326	95	231	21	7	15	69	28	41
Median age	35.5	34.3	36.7	36.7	35.6	37.9	29.6	27.6	31.3	27.3	26.7	28.0	30.8	29.8	31.8
Mean age	36.4	35.0	37.6	37.4	36.0	38.7	31.7	30.1	33.1	30.2	29.4	31.0	32.1	31.1	33.0

A1-2. Projections of the Population, by Age, Sex, Race, and Hispanic Origin, for the United States: 2000 and 2050 (Middle Series) *(continued)*

Hispanic origin[1]			Not of Hispanic origin, by race												Date and age
			White			Black			American Indian, Eskimo, and Aleut			Asian and Pacific Islander			
Total	Male	Female	Total	Male	Female	Total	Male	Female	Total	Male	Female	Total	Male	Female	
															JULY 1, 2000
31 166	15 777	15 388	197 872	96 846	101 025	33 741	15 939	17 802	2 055	1 010	1 045	11 407	5 529	5 879	All ages
3 293	1 683	1 610	11 936	6 137	5 799	3 033	1 540	1 493	185	93	92	984	504	480	Under 5 years
674	345	330	2 329	1 197	1 132	616	313	303	38	19	19	204	104	100	Under 1 year
661	338	323	2 340	1 203	1 137	603	306	297	37	18	18	196	101	95	1 year
655	335	320	2 374	1 221	1 153	601	306	295	37	18	18	195	100	95	2 years
650	332	318	2 411	1 240	1 171	598	304	295	37	18	18	195	100	95	3 years
653	334	319	2 481	1 276	1 205	615	312	303	37	19	18	194	99	94	4 years
3 232	1 655	1 578	13 068	6 719	6 350	3 123	1 587	1 536	194	98	96	913	471	443	5 to 9 years
649	332	317	2 523	1 298	1 225	614	312	302	37	19	18	193	99	93	5 years
644	329	315	2 569	1 320	1 249	610	310	300	37	19	18	188	97	91	6 years
639	326	312	2 612	1 343	1 270	618	313	305	37	19	18	186	96	90	7 years
640	328	312	2 594	1 333	1 261	611	311	301	40	20	20	167	86	81	8 years
661	339	322	2 770	1 425	1 344	670	341	329	43	22	21	181	93	87	9 years
2 846	1 456	1 390	13 060	6 711	6 348	2 972	1 511	1 462	209	106	102	885	452	433	10 to 14 years
633	324	309	2 668	1 373	1 295	637	324	313	43	22	21	175	90	85	10 years
578	296	282	2 592	1 331	1 260	598	303	295	41	21	20	174	89	85	11 years
559	286	273	2 571	1 320	1 252	589	299	290	41	21	20	175	89	86	12 years
540	276	264	2 607	1 339	1 268	572	291	281	42	21	21	180	92	89	13 years
536	274	261	2 622	1 349	1 273	576	294	282	42	21	21	181	92	89	14 years
2 624	1 346	1 278	13 200	6 795	6 405	2 910	1 477	1 433	195	98	97	890	452	438	15 to 19 years
523	268	256	2 556	1 316	1 240	570	290	280	41	21	20	182	93	90	15 years
512	263	249	2 633	1 359	1 274	575	295	280	41	21	20	182	93	89	16 years
531	273	258	2 696	1 394	1 303	591	302	289	40	20	20	182	93	89	17 years
514	263	250	2 586	1 329	1 257	565	285	280	36	18	18	169	86	83	18 years
544	279	265	2 729	1 397	1 332	609	305	305	37	18	19	175	88	87	19 years
2 489	1 282	1 208	11 930	6 090	5 840	2 531	1 243	1 288	159	80	80	837	415	422	20 to 24 years
531	273	258	2 576	1 318	1 258	566	282	284	34	17	17	169	84	84	20 years
501	259	242	2 444	1 250	1 194	526	261	265	33	16	16	165	83	82	21 years
487	251	236	2 365	1 209	1 156	499	245	254	31	16	15	163	81	82	22 years
481	248	234	2 229	1 136	1 093	466	227	239	30	15	15	165	81	84	23 years
488	251	237	2 316	1 177	1 139	474	229	245	31	16	15	175	86	90	24 years
2 488	1 297	1 191	12 286	6 160	6 125	2 462	1 171	1 291	158	81	78	976	470	507	25 to 29 years
486	250	236	2 228	1 125	1 103	462	222	241	31	15	15	180	87	93	25 years
477	245	231	2 258	1 131	1 127	476	227	249	31	16	15	185	88	97	26 years
497	259	238	2 457	1 234	1 223	500	239	261	32	16	16	197	94	103	27 years
477	251	226	2 547	1 273	1 274	491	233	258	31	16	15	193	93	100	28 years
552	293	259	2 796	1 397	1 399	534	251	283	34	17	16	221	107	114	29 years
2 657	1 414	1 244	13 566	6 756	6 810	2 491	1 154	1 338	146	73	73	1 007	484	523	30 to 34 years
538	286	252	2 666	1 326	1 340	481	224	258	30	15	15	206	99	107	30 years
523	279	244	2 552	1 269	1 283	478	222	256	28	14	14	199	95	104	31 years
522	278	244	2 638	1 312	1 326	482	223	259	29	14	14	197	95	102	32 years
525	278	247	2 705	1 343	1 362	501	231	270	28	14	14	196	94	102	33 years
549	292	257	3 005	1 505	1 500	549	255	294	31	15	15	208	101	107	34 years
2 609	1 367	1 242	16 208	8 115	8 093	2 728	1 265	1 463	155	76	78	996	483	512	35 to 39 years
546	288	257	3 138	1 570	1 568	549	255	294	31	16	16	207	100	106	35 years
528	277	251	3 154	1 577	1 578	532	246	286	30	15	15	199	97	102	36 years
529	277	253	3 288	1 646	1 642	552	255	297	31	15	16	197	96	101	37 years
475	247	228	3 126	1 561	1 564	504	233	272	29	14	15	187	90	97	38 years
531	278	253	3 502	1 761	1 741	591	276	315	33	16	17	207	100	106	39 years
2 221	1 139	1 082	16 533	8 263	8 270	2 610	1 207	1 403	147	71	76	918	439	479	40 to 44 years
491	254	237	3 386	1 694	1 692	550	254	296	31	15	16	196	95	102	40 years
452	232	220	3 344	1 670	1 674	524	242	282	30	15	16	190	91	98	41 years
441	226	215	3 348	1 673	1 675	524	243	281	29	14	15	180	86	93	42 years
415	211	204	3 162	1 572	1 590	501	230	271	30	14	16	186	88	98	43 years
421	215	206	3 293	1 654	1 639	511	238	273	27	13	14	167	79	88	44 years
1 725	863	862	14 770	7 338	7 432	2 149	975	1 174	125	60	65	761	357	404	45 to 49 years
392	199	194	3 158	1 574	1 584	471	217	254	27	13	14	162	76	85	45 years
355	178	177	3 001	1 492	1 509	425	192	232	25	12	13	154	72	82	46 years
344	172	173	2 969	1 473	1 496	438	197	241	26	12	13	153	72	81	47 years
306	152	154	2 710	1 340	1 370	378	169	209	22	11	12	138	64	74	48 years
328	163	165	2 933	1 459	1 474	437	199	238	25	12	13	154	72	82	49 years
1 321	644	677	12 990	6 405	6 585	1 632	728	904	100	48	52	596	275	321	50 to 54 years
302	148	153	2 837	1 403	1 434	386	173	212	23	11	12	140	65	75	50 years
273	133	139	2 763	1 365	1 399	351	157	193	21	10	11	127	58	69	51 years
260	127	133	3 027	1 496	1 532	335	150	185	21	10	11	117	54	64	52 years
259	125	134	2 134	1 047	1 087	271	119	151	18	8	9	106	49	57	53 years
228	110	118	2 229	1 094	1 134	290	128	161	18	8	9	107	49	58	54 years
969	461	509	10 313	5 032	5 281	1 251	547	705	75	36	40	438	203	235	55 to 59 years
212	102	110	2 181	1 065	1 116	280	124	156	17	8	9	98	45	53	55 years
204	97	107	2 388	1 169	1 219	267	115	151	16	8	8	90	42	49	56 years
204	96	107	2 060	1 004	1 056	261	114	147	15	7	8	88	40	47	57 years
172	81	91	1 837	893	943	212	92	120	13	6	7	78	36	42	58 years
178	85	93	1 847	901	946	231	101	131	14	7	7	84	39	45	59 years
765	356	409	8 438	4 059	4 379	1 023	436	587	59	28	31	357	164	193	60 to 64 years
166	78	89	1 783	856	926	219	94	125	13	6	7	78	36	41	60 years
158	74	84	1 722	833	889	208	89	119	12	6	6	73	34	39	61 years
151	70	81	1 622	780	842	200	85	115	12	5	6	71	33	38	62 years
144	67	77	1 630	786	844	193	82	111	11	5	6	67	31	37	63 years
146	67	79	1 681	804	878	203	87	117	11	5	6	68	31	38	64 years
627	283	344	7 722	3 604	4 118	903	386	517	46	21	25	296	126	169	65 to 69 years
510	224	285	7 452	3 329	4 123	723	296	427	36	16	20	236	99	137	70 to 74 years
371	158	213	6 390	2 684	3 707	554	213	341	28	12	16	163	70	93	75 to 79 years
215	82	132	4 284	1 604	2 681	326	112	215	18	7	11	88	37	50	80 to 84 years
123	42	81	2 336	727	1 610	181	56	125	11	4	7	41	17	24	85 to 89 years
56	18	38	1 022	251	771	92	25	67	6	2	4	17	7	10	90 to 94 years
20	6	14	308	59	249	36	9	27	3	1	2	6	2	4	95 to 99 years
4	1	3	59	8	50	9	2	7	1	0	1	2	0	1	100 years and over
21 271	10 716	10 555	157 252	75 963	81 289	24 043	11 010	13 032	1 426	692	735	8 443	4 009	4 434	16 years and over
20 228	10 180	10 048	151 923	73 211	78 712	22 877	10 413	12 463	1 346	651	695	8 079	3 823	4 256	18 years and over
15 088	7 844	7 244	83 722	42 178	41 543	15 732	7 516	8 215	961	479	482	5 623	2 743	2 881	15 to 44 years
1 925	816	1 110	29 575	12 266	17 308	2 825	1 099	1 726	148	62	86	849	360	489	65 years and over
203	67	135	3 726	1 046	2 680	319	92	226	20	6	14	66	26	40	85 years and over
27.3	26.9	27.7	38.1	36.9	39.3	29.7	27.7	31.5	27.7	26.9	28.6	31.1	30.0	32.1	Median age
29.3	28.6	30.1	38.5	37.1	39.9	31.8	30.2	33.2	30.6	29.8	31.5	32.3	31.3	33.2	Mean age

A1-2. Projections of the Population, by Age, Sex, Race, and Hispanic Origin, for the United States: 2000 and 2050 (Middle Series) *(continued)*

[Numbers in thousands. Resident population]

Date and age	Total			Race											
				White			Black			American Indian, Eskimo, and Aleut			Asian and Pacific Islander		
	Total	Male	Female	Total	Male	Female	Total	Male	Female	Total	Male	Female	Total	Male	Female
JULY 1, 2050															
All ages	392 031	192 098	199 933	285 591	140 947	144 644	61 586	29 279	32 307	4 346	2 131	2 215	40 508	19 741	20 768
Under 5 years	25 382	13 008	12 374	17 216	8 837	8 379	5 171	2 653	2 518	373	187	186	2 622	1 330	1 291
Under 1 year	5 130	2 627	2 503	3 462	1 776	1 686	1 060	544	516	77	38	38	532	268	263
1 year	5 056	2 591	2 465	3 433	1 762	1 671	1 034	530	504	74	37	37	516	262	253
2 years	5 052	2 591	2 461	3 431	1 762	1 669	1 026	528	499	74	37	37	525	266	259
3 years	5 042	2 584	2 458	3 427	1 760	1 668	1 015	521	495	74	37	37	529	269	260
4 years	5 101	2 615	2 486	3 463	1 778	1 685	1 036	531	504	74	37	37	561	287	275
5 to 9 years	25 222	12 937	12 286	17 146	8 802	8 344	5 031	2 583	2 447	370	187	183	2 677	1 365	1 311
5 years	5 085	2 609	2 476	3 454	1 774	1 680	1 023	525	498	75	38	37	534	273	261
6 years	5 054	2 591	2 463	3 448	1 769	1 679	1 004	516	488	73	37	36	528	269	259
7 years	5 050	2 588	2 462	3 439	1 765	1 674	1 005	515	491	74	37	36	532	272	261
8 years	4 847	2 485	2 362	3 296	1 691	1 605	959	492	466	72	36	36	521	265	256
9 years	5 186	2 663	2 523	3 509	1 803	1 706	1 040	535	505	77	39	38	561	287	275
10 to 14 years	25 650	13 156	12 493	17 277	8 871	8 406	5 038	2 588	2 450	392	198	195	2 942	1 499	1 443
10 years	5 194	2 669	2 525	3 514	1 807	1 707	1 029	529	500	78	39	38	574	294	280
11 years	5 104	2 618	2 485	3 456	1 774	1 681	1 002	514	488	77	39	38	569	291	278
12 years	5 099	2 612	2 487	3 422	1 755	1 667	1 008	518	490	79	40	39	590	299	291
13 years	5 123	2 624	2 499	3 444	1 766	1 678	996	511	485	80	40	40	603	306	297
14 years	5 130	2 633	2 497	3 442	1 768	1 673	1 004	517	487	79	40	39	605	308	297
15 to 19 years	25 897	13 294	12 604	17 550	9 028	8 522	5 028	2 585	2 443	372	186	186	2 948	1 495	1 453
15 years	5 152	2 646	2 506	3 450	1 774	1 676	1 015	523	492	79	40	39	607	309	298
16 years	5 133	2 644	2 489	3 466	1 787	1 680	999	517	482	76	38	38	592	302	290
17 years	5 215	2 691	2 524	3 529	1 823	1 706	1 008	522	486	76	38	38	602	307	295
18 years	5 071	2 598	2 474	3 463	1 779	1 684	982	503	479	69	34	35	557	281	275
19 years	5 326	2 715	2 611	3 641	1 865	1 776	1 023	519	504	72	35	37	590	295	295
20 to 24 years	25 313	12 868	12 445	17 464	8 939	8 525	4 608	2 305	2 302	339	168	170	2 903	1 456	1 447
20 years	5 251	2 678	2 573	3 611	1 851	1 760	991	502	489	69	34	35	579	291	289
21 years	5 135	2 620	2 514	3 526	1 808	1 718	955	483	472	69	34	35	584	295	290
22 years	4 982	2 536	2 446	3 443	1 765	1 678	898	450	448	67	33	34	573	288	286
23 years	4 928	2 499	2 429	3 406	1 741	1 665	883	438	445	66	33	33	573	288	286
24 years	5 018	2 535	2 483	3 478	1 774	1 704	880	432	448	67	33	34	593	296	297
25 to 29 years	24 659	12 348	12 311	17 177	8 689	8 489	4 225	2 047	2 178	319	158	161	2 937	1 454	1 484
25 years	4 959	2 497	2 461	3 438	1 747	1 691	862	421	441	66	33	33	592	296	297
26 years	4 922	2 464	2 457	3 422	1 730	1 693	849	413	436	65	32	33	586	290	296
27 years	4 946	2 477	2 469	3 448	1 744	1 704	843	408	434	64	32	32	591	293	298
28 years	4 670	2 331	2 339	3 280	1 655	1 625	784	379	406	59	29	30	547	269	278
29 years	5 162	2 578	2 584	3 589	1 813	1 776	886	426	460	66	33	33	621	306	314
30 to 34 years	24 803	12 327	12 476	17 494	8 806	8 688	4 078	1 935	2 143	303	149	153	2 928	1 436	1 492
30 years	5 026	2 500	2 526	3 535	1 780	1 755	839	400	439	62	31	31	590	290	300
31 years	4 913	2 441	2 472	3 459	1 741	1 719	810	386	424	61	30	31	583	285	298
32 years	4 921	2 444	2 477	3 472	1 747	1 725	804	381	423	60	30	31	584	287	298
33 years	4 885	2 418	2 466	3 463	1 738	1 725	792	373	419	59	29	30	571	278	292
34 years	5 058	2 523	2 535	3 565	1 801	1 764	833	395	438	61	30	31	600	296	303
35 to 39 years	24 316	12 084	12 232	17 246	8 673	8 573	3 937	1 864	2 073	286	142	144	2 847	1 405	1 442
35 years	4 991	2 483	2 507	3 528	1 776	1 752	813	386	427	60	30	30	589	291	298
36 years	4 846	2 406	2 440	3 449	1 734	1 715	780	368	412	57	28	29	561	276	285
37 years	4 878	2 422	2 456	3 455	1 736	1 719	792	374	418	58	29	29	573	283	290
38 years	4 558	2 259	2 299	3 248	1 629	1 619	727	343	384	53	26	27	530	260	269
39 years	5 043	2 514	2 529	3 567	1 798	1 769	824	392	432	59	29	30	594	295	299
40 to 44 years	23 423	11 597	11 825	16 734	8 381	8 353	3 673	1 728	1 944	263	131	133	2 753	1 358	1 395
40 years	4 847	2 405	2 443	3 445	1 729	1 716	773	365	408	56	28	28	573	283	290
41 years	4 698	2 324	2 373	3 347	1 675	1 671	736	345	391	54	27	27	561	277	284
42 years	4 635	2 294	2 340	3 318	1 661	1 658	723	340	383	52	26	26	542	268	274
43 years	4 576	2 255	2 322	3 250	1 621	1 629	712	333	379	53	26	27	561	275	287
44 years	4 667	2 319	2 347	3 375	1 696	1 679	729	346	383	48	24	24	515	254	261
45 to 49 years	22 266	10 946	11 320	16 144	8 029	8 115	3 355	1 552	1 803	227	112	114	2 540	1 254	1 287
45 years	4 551	2 247	2 303	3 286	1 642	1 644	696	326	371	48	24	24	520	256	264
46 years	4 401	2 166	2 235	3 199	1 594	1 605	657	304	353	45	22	23	500	246	254
47 years	4 465	2 191	2 274	3 208	1 592	1 615	686	315	370	47	23	24	525	260	265
48 years	4 204	2 057	2 147	3 088	1 529	1 559	608	278	330	41	20	21	467	229	237
49 years	4 646	2 286	2 361	3 363	1 672	1 691	708	328	380	46	23	23	529	263	266
50 to 54 years	22 071	10 744	11 327	16 355	8 065	8 290	3 190	1 445	1 745	198	97	101	2 329	1 137	1 191
50 years	4 506	2 205	2 301	3 304	1 635	1 669	661	302	359	43	21	22	498	246	252
51 years	4 345	2 119	2 226	3 208	1 584	1 623	629	287	342	40	19	20	468	229	240
52 years	4 333	2 108	2 225	3 220	1 587	1 633	620	280	339	38	18	20	455	222	233
53 years	4 387	2 130	2 257	3 275	1 611	1 663	630	283	346	38	18	19	446	217	228
54 years	4 501	2 182	2 318	3 349	1 647	1 701	651	292	358	39	19	20	462	223	239
55 to 59 years	22 367	10 808	11 559	16 985	8 334	8 650	3 126	1 384	1 742	187	90	97	2 069	999	1 070
55 years	4 414	2 133	2 281	3 281	1 607	1 674	649	292	358	38	18	19	446	216	230
56 years	4 481	2 162	2 320	3 401	1 668	1 733	626	273	353	36	17	18	418	203	216
57 years	4 552	2 198	2 354	3 451	1 692	1 759	641	284	357	36	17	19	423	205	219
58 years	4 327	2 090	2 238	3 348	1 642	1 706	575	254	321	36	18	19	368	176	192
59 years	4 592	2 225	2 367	3 503	1 725	1 778	634	281	353	41	20	21	413	199	214
60 to 64 years	20 553	9 888	10 665	15 820	7 750	8 070	2 760	1 203	1 557	170	82	88	1 803	853	950
60 years	4 297	2 056	2 241	3 282	1 595	1 687	597	261	336	38	18	19	380	182	198
61 years	4 092	1 971	2 121	3 147	1 544	1 603	550	239	311	34	17	18	361	172	189
62 years	4 046	1 946	2 100	3 102	1 519	1 583	551	239	311	34	16	17	360	171	189
63 years	4 019	1 946	2 073	3 126	1 542	1 584	517	225	291	32	15	17	345	163	182
64 years	4 099	1 970	2 130	3 163	1 550	1 613	546	238	308	33	15	17	357	166	191
65 to 69 years	18 859	9 012	9 847	14 672	7 137	7 535	2 452	1 076	1 376	141	66	75	1 594	734	860
70 to 74 years	15 769	7 540	8 229	12 461	6 072	6 389	1 868	811	1 057	105	49	55	1 335	607	728
75 to 79 years	14 510	6 911	7 599	11 696	5 687	6 009	1 576	667	909	90	43	47	1 148	514	634
80 to 84 years	12 078	5 535	6 542	10 093	4 714	5 378	1 066	412	655	69	33	36	850	376	473
85 to 89 years	9 283	3 908	5 375	7 991	3 421	4 571	666	236	430	54	22	32	571	228	343
90 to 94 years	5 779	2 159	3 620	4 968	1 886	3 082	402	125	277	40	15	25	369	134	235
95 to 99 years	2 623	793	1 831	2 193	665	1 528	202	53	149	25	8	17	203	67	137
100 years and over	1 208	234	974	908	161	747	135	28	107	23	6	16	143	40	103
16 years and over	310 626	150 351	160 275	230 502	112 662	117 839	45 331	20 932	24 399	3 132	1 520	1 612	31 661	15 237	16 424
18 years and over	300 277	145 016	155 261	223 507	109 052	114 454	43 324	19 892	23 432	2 980	1 444	1 536	30 467	14 628	15 839
15 to 44 years	148 411	74 518	73 893	103 666	52 516	51 150	25 547	12 464	13 084	1 882	935	947	17 315	8 603	8 712
65 years and over	80 109	36 092	44 016	64 982	29 742	35 240	8 368	3 407	4 960	547	244	303	6 212	2 699	3 513
85 years and over	18 893	7 094	11 799	16 061	6 132	9 928	1 405	441	964	142	52	90	1 286	469	817
Median age	39.0	37.5	40.3	41.2	39.9	42.6	32.1	29.7	34.3	30.1	29.4	30.8	35.5	34.4	36.6
Mean age	40.9	39.6	42.1	42.6	41.4	43.8	35.3	33.4	37.0	34.2	33.3	35.0	37.9	36.7	39.0

A1-2. Projections of the Population, by Age, Sex, Race, and Hispanic Origin, for the United States: 2000 and 2050 (Middle Series) (continued)

Hispanic origin[1] Total	Male	Female	White Total	Male	Female	Black Total	Male	Female	American Indian, Eskimo, and Aleut Total	Male	Female	Asian and Pacific Islander Total	Male	Female	Date and age
															JULY 1, 2050
88 071	43 878	44 193	205 849	101 122	104 727	56 346	26 716	29 630	3 701	1 808	1 893	38 064	18 573	19 491	All ages
7 429	3 808	3 620	10 495	5 387	5 098	4 723	2 421	2 302	323	162	161	2 422	1 230	1 192	Under 5 years
1 517	777	740	2 088	1 072	1 016	968	496	472	67	33	33	491	248	243	Under 1 year
1 491	764	727	2 081	1 069	1 012	944	484	461	64	32	32	476	242	234	1 year
1 479	759	721	2 090	1 074	1 016	937	481	456	64	32	32	481	244	237	2 years
1 468	752	715	2 097	1 078	1 020	927	475	452	64	32	32	485	246	239	3 years
1 474	756	718	2 128	1 094	1 035	946	485	461	64	32	32	489	249	240	4 years
7 166	3 675	3 491	10 665	5 480	5 185	4 596	2 357	2 238	318	160	158	2 477	1 264	1 213	5 to 9 years
1 461	749	712	2 132	1 096	1 036	934	479	455	64	32	32	494	252	242	5 years
1 448	742	706	2 137	1 097	1 040	917	471	446	63	32	31	489	249	240	6 years
1 436	736	700	2 139	1 099	1 040	918	470	449	63	32	31	493	252	241	7 years
1 369	702	667	2 058	1 057	1 001	876	449	427	62	31	31	482	246	237	8 years
1 451	745	706	2 199	1 131	1 068	950	488	462	66	33	33	520	266	254	9 years
7 022	3 601	3 421	10 954	5 629	5 324	4 607	2 364	2 243	337	169	167	2 730	1 392	1 338	10 to 14 years
1 444	742	702	2 211	1 138	1 073	940	483	457	67	34	33	532	273	260	10 years
1 411	724	687	2 183	1 122	1 061	916	469	447	66	33	33	528	270	258	11 years
1 392	713	679	2 170	1 114	1 056	922	473	449	68	34	34	548	278	270	12 years
1 392	713	679	2 192	1 125	1 067	911	467	444	68	34	34	560	285	275	13 years
1 383	709	673	2 199	1 131	1 068	918	472	446	68	34	34	562	287	275	14 years
6 903	3 548	3 354	11 333	5 831	5 501	4 599	2 362	2 237	318	159	159	2 744	1 393	1 351	15 to 19 years
1 378	708	670	2 213	1 139	1 074	929	478	451	67	34	34	565	288	277	15 years
1 372	707	666	2 231	1 151	1 080	914	473	441	65	33	32	551	281	270	16 years
1 387	716	671	2 280	1 178	1 101	922	477	445	65	33	32	561	287	274	17 years
1 351	693	657	2 245	1 153	1 091	898	459	439	59	29	30	519	262	256	18 years
1 415	725	690	2 365	1 210	1 155	935	474	461	62	30	31	549	275	274	19 years
6 663	3 419	3 243	11 448	5 845	5 603	4 205	2 100	2 105	289	143	146	2 709	1 360	1 349	20 to 24 years
1 396	717	679	2 350	1 202	1 148	906	458	447	59	29	30	540	271	269	20 years
1 357	698	659	2 302	1 177	1 125	872	441	431	59	29	30	545	275	270	21 years
1 313	675	638	2 257	1 154	1 103	820	410	410	57	28	29	535	269	266	22 years
1 290	661	629	2 241	1 143	1 098	805	398	407	56	28	28	535	269	267	23 years
1 307	668	639	2 299	1 169	1 129	802	393	409	57	28	29	553	276	277	24 years
6 274	3 180	3 094	11 517	5 811	5 706	3 849	1 862	1 988	272	135	137	2 746	1 361	1 386	25 to 29 years
1 281	653	628	2 282	1 157	1 125	786	383	403	56	28	28	553	276	277	25 years
1 263	640	623	2 283	1 151	1 132	773	375	398	55	27	28	548	272	276	26 years
1 259	638	621	2 312	1 167	1 145	768	371	397	55	27	28	553	274	279	27 years
1 184	598	586	2 210	1 112	1 098	715	344	370	50	25	25	512	252	260	28 years
1 287	651	637	2 430	1 225	1 205	808	388	420	56	28	28	581	287	294	29 years
6 072	3 052	3 020	12 011	6 039	5 972	3 720	1 761	1 958	256	126	130	2 744	1 348	1 396	30 to 34 years
1 251	630	621	2 405	1 209	1 196	765	364	401	53	26	27	553	272	281	30 years
1 213	610	603	2 364	1 188	1 176	738	351	387	51	25	26	546	267	279	31 years
1 205	605	600	2 384	1 198	1 186	734	347	387	51	25	26	548	269	279	32 years
1 189	595	594	2 388	1 198	1 191	723	340	383	50	24	25	535	261	274	33 years
1 215	612	603	2 469	1 247	1 222	760	360	400	52	26	26	562	278	284	34 years
5 709	2 860	2 849	12 093	6 081	6 011	3 598	1 701	1 898	241	119	122	2 675	1 323	1 352	35 to 39 years
1 190	598	593	2 454	1 235	1 219	743	352	391	51	25	25	553	274	280	35 years
1 151	576	574	2 409	1 211	1 198	713	336	377	48	24	24	527	260	267	36 years
1 144	573	571	2 423	1 218	1 205	724	341	383	49	24	25	538	266	272	37 years
1 064	531	532	2 287	1 147	1 139	665	313	352	45	22	23	498	245	253	38 years
1 161	582	578	2 521	1 271	1 250	754	358	396	50	25	25	559	278	281	39 years
5 273	2 625	2 648	11 970	6 000	5 970	3 362	1 580	1 783	222	110	112	2 595	1 283	1 312	40 to 44 years
1 109	554	555	2 444	1 227	1 217	707	333	374	47	24	24	540	267	272	40 years
1 066	531	535	2 384	1 194	1 190	674	315	358	46	23	23	528	262	267	41 years
1 045	520	525	2 374	1 189	1 185	662	310	351	44	22	22	511	254	257	42 years
1 016	503	512	2 334	1 165	1 169	652	305	348	45	22	23	530	260	270	43 years
1 038	518	520	2 434	1 224	1 210	667	316	351	40	20	20	487	240	246	44 years
4 789	2 362	2 428	11 804	5 880	5 925	3 078	1 421	1 657	192	95	97	2 403	1 189	1 214	45 to 49 years
1 000	496	504	2 380	1 191	1 190	638	298	340	40	20	20	492	243	249	45 years
960	475	486	2 327	1 161	1 166	603	278	324	38	19	19	472	233	239	46 years
955	470	485	2 345	1 166	1 179	629	289	340	40	20	20	496	246	250	47 years
901	442	459	2 269	1 125	1 143	558	255	303	35	17	18	442	218	224	48 years
973	479	494	2 483	1 237	1 246	650	301	349	39	19	20	501	249	252	49 years
4 478	2 183	2 295	12 286	6 073	6 213	2 933	1 326	1 607	168	82	86	2 208	1 081	1 126	50 to 54 years
938	459	478	2 453	1 216	1 236	607	277	330	36	18	18	472	234	238	50 years
894	437	457	2 395	1 186	1 209	578	263	315	34	16	17	444	217	226	51 years
881	429	452	2 418	1 195	1 224	570	257	312	33	16	17	431	211	220	52 years
880	428	452	2 474	1 220	1 254	579	260	319	32	16	16	423	207	216	53 years
885	429	455	2 546	1 256	1 290	599	269	330	33	16	17	439	213	226	54 years
4 229	2 043	2 186	13 139	6 467	6 672	2 883	1 274	1 609	157	76	81	1 958	949	1 010	55 to 59 years
852	411	440	2 509	1 232	1 277	598	268	330	32	16	17	423	206	217	55 years
859	415	444	2 618	1 288	1 330	577	251	326	30	15	16	397	193	204	56 years
855	412	443	2 673	1 314	1 358	591	262	330	31	15	16	402	195	207	57 years
821	396	424	2 600	1 279	1 321	530	234	297	30	14	16	347	167	180	58 years
843	408	435	2 739	1 353	1 386	587	259	327	34	16	17	390	188	201	59 years
3 613	1 732	1 880	12 548	6 171	6 377	2 541	1 105	1 436	141	67	73	1 711	812	899	60 to 64 years
791	377	414	2 566	1 252	1 314	550	240	310	31	15	16	360	173	187	60 years
731	351	379	2 485	1 224	1 261	506	219	287	28	14	15	342	163	179	61 years
710	340	369	2 461	1 210	1 251	506	220	287	28	13	14	342	163	179	62 years
690	333	357	2 499	1 238	1 261	476	207	269	27	13	14	328	155	172	63 years
692	331	361	2 537	1 248	1 289	503	219	284	27	13	14	340	158	181	64 years
3 108	1 473	1 635	11 851	5 792	6 060	2 263	991	1 272	118	55	63	1 518	701	817	65 to 69 years
2 597	1 230	1 367	10 092	4 943	5 148	1 717	743	973	89	42	47	1 274	581	693	70 to 74 years
2 260	1 088	1 172	9 630	4 687	4 943	1 445	606	839	77	37	40	1 097	493	605	75 to 79 years
1 884	906	979	8 363	3 881	4 482	961	362	599	58	27	31	812	360	451	80 to 84 years
1 324	595	728	6 769	2 871	3 899	596	203	392	46	19	27	548	220	328	85 to 89 years
767	317	451	4 261	1 594	2 667	360	106	254	35	13	22	356	129	226	90 to 94 years
350	130	220	1 871	545	1 325	184	46	138	23	7	15	197	65	132	95 to 99 years
161	50	110	760	115	645	126	25	102	22	6	16	140	39	101	100 years and over
65 076	32 086	32 990	171 533	83 487	88 045	41 491	19 095	22 396	2 656	1 283	1 373	29 870	14 399	15 471	16 years and over
62 317	30 664	31 653	167 022	81 158	85 864	39 654	18 145	21 510	2 525	1 218	1 308	28 758	13 831	14 927	18 years and over
36 894	18 685	18 209	70 371	35 608	34 763	23 333	11 365	11 968	1 599	792	806	16 213	8 068	8 146	15 to 44 years
12 452	5 790	6 662	53 597	24 427	29 169	7 652	3 082	4 570	467	205	262	5 941	2 588	3 353	65 years and over
2 602	1 092	1 510	13 661	5 125	8 536	1 266	380	886	125	45	81	1 239	452	787	85 years and over
32.1	31.1	33.1	45.2	43.7	46.7	32.1	29.7	34.4	29.9	29.1	30.7	35.8	34.8	36.9	Median age
35.6	34.7	36.4	45.3	44.0	46.6	35.3	33.4	37.1	34.1	33.1	35.0	38.2	37.0	39.3	Mean age

[1]Persons of Hispanic origin may be of any race

Source: Jennifer Cheeseman Day, U.S. Bureau of the Census, *Population Projections of the United States, by Age, Sex, Race, and Hispanic Origin: 1993 to 2050*, Series P25-1104, Washington, D.C.: Government Printing Office, November 1993, Table 2.

A1-3. Population, by Sex, Race, and Hispanic Origin, for Regions, Divisions, and States: 1993

(Numbers in thousands. Resident population.)

Date, region, division, and State	Total		Race								Hispanic origin[1]	
			White		Black		American Indian, Eskimo, and Aleut		Asian and Pacific Islander			
	Total	Female	Total	Female	Total	Female	Total	Female	Total	Female	Total	Female
JULY 1, 1993												
United States[2]	257,927	132,006	214,779	109,473	32,137	16,907	2,165	1,092	8,846	4,534	25,085	12,329
REGION AND DIVISION												
Northeast	51,227	26,549	43,417	22,443	6,132	3,260	123	63	1,555	784	4,069	2,069
New England	13,200	6,814	12,215	6,307	683	353	33	17	269	137	640	323
Middle Atlantic	38,027	19,735	31,201	16,136	5,449	2,906	90	46	1,286	647	3,429	1,746
Midwest	61,149	31,397	53,769	27,521	6,065	3,207	369	186	946	484	1,956	942
East North Central	43,048	22,132	37,069	18,978	5,118	2,716	161	81	699	357	1,621	780
West North Central	18,101	9,265	16,700	8,543	946	491	207	105	247	127	335	162
South	89,362	45,923	70,506	35,989	16,827	8,889	595	299	1,434	746	7,678	3,817
South Atlantic	45,720	23,527	35,150	17,956	9,586	5,059	181	90	804	422	2,446	1,218
East South Central	15,695	8,137	12,451	6,403	3,096	1,657	43	21	106	56	106	51
West South Central	27,947	14,259	22,905	11,631	4,146	2,173	371	188	525	268	5,126	2,547
West	56,189	28,137	47,087	23,521	3,113	1,551	1,078	544	4,911	2,521	11,382	5,501
Mountain	14,723	7,410	13,449	6,766	416	202	556	283	303	160	2,284	1,131
Pacific	41,466	20,726	33,638	16,755	2,697	1,349	523	261	4,608	2,362	9,099	4,370
STATE												
New England												
Maine	1,236	633	1,217	625	5	2	6	3	7	4	8	4
New Hampshire	1,118	570	1,097	560	7	3	2	1	12	6	13	6
Vermont	573	292	565	288	2	1	2	1	4	2	4	2
Massachusetts	5,992	3,108	5,478	2,844	336	173	12	6	167	85	321	162
Rhode Island	1,004	521	933	485	44	22	4	2	23	11	53	27
Connecticut	3,278	1,689	2,926	1,506	289	152	7	3	57	28	241	122
Middle Atlantic												
New York	18,140	9,426	14,099	7,290	3,185	1,708	61	31	795	397	2,319	1,192
New Jersey	7,836	4,045	6,378	3,284	1,119	589	14	7	324	165	838	419
Pennsylvania	12,050	6,264	10,724	5,562	1,145	610	15	7	167	85	272	134
East North Central												
Ohio	11,080	5,731	9,730	5,016	1,219	648	21	11	110	56	158	79
Indiana	5,717	2,940	5,195	2,666	460	243	14	7	48	25	113	55
Illinois	11,708	6,010	9,543	4,868	1,795	953	23	12	348	177	1,016	481
Michigan	9,485	4,873	7,926	4,048	1,373	730	60	30	127	65	226	112
Wisconsin	5,058	2,578	4,676	2,380	272	142	43	22	67	34	108	52
West North Central												
Minnesota	4,527	2,303	4,272	2,174	101	49	55	28	99	51	63	30
Iowa	2,828	1,454	2,736	1,408	54	27	8	4	30	15	40	20
Missouri	5,224	2,701	4,583	2,361	570	304	20	10	50	26	67	33
North Dakota	636	319	601	301	4	1	27	14	4	2	5	2
South Dakota	719	365	653	332	3	1	58	29	4	2	6	3
Nebraska	1,619	828	1,528	781	61	31	14	7	15	8	46	22
Kansas	2,548	1,296	2,327	1,185	153	76	25	13	43	22	107	51
South Atlantic												
Delaware	699	359	560	286	125	66	2	1	12	6	20	9
Maryland	4,966	2,555	3,476	1,770	1,303	687	13	7	174	91	146	72
District of Columbia	577	305	182	89	383	210	1	1	11	5	30	15
Virginia	6,468	3,295	5,016	2,539	1,240	646	15	7	197	103	181	86
West Virginia	1,816	942	1,749	906	55	29	3	1	9	5	9	5
North Carolina	6,946	3,574	5,243	2,673	1,543	818	86	44	74	39	91	41
South Carolina	3,647	1,880	2,512	1,276	1,099	584	9	4	28	15	37	17
Georgia	6,871	3,532	4,883	2,478	1,879	997	13	6	96	50	130	59
Florida	13,730	7,084	11,530	5,938	1,960	1,021	38	19	202	107	1,803	914
East South Central												
Kentucky	3,787	1,951	3,483	1,791	277	145	6	3	22	12	23	10
Tennessee	5,093	2,638	4,222	2,174	820	438	10	5	40	21	39	19
Alabama	4,182	2,175	3,078	1,582	1,059	570	17	9	28	15	27	13
Mississippi	2,632	1,373	1,668	856	940	504	9	5	15	8	17	9
West South Central												
Arkansas	2,422	1,253	2,009	1,033	382	204	14	7	17	9	24	12
Louisiana	4,312	2,234	2,893	1,480	1,347	718	19	9	53	27	103	52
Oklahoma	3,231	1,655	2,674	1,370	242	124	270	137	45	23	98	47
Texas	17,983	9,117	15,330	7,747	2,175	1,127	69	34	410	209	4,901	2,437
Mountain												
Montana	836	421	776	391	2	1	52	26	5	3	14	7
Idaho	1,097	550	1,063	533	4	2	17	8	13	7	66	31
Wyoming	473	236	455	227	4	2	11	5	4	2	29	14
Colorado	3,551	1,790	3,292	1,660	148	73	33	16	78	41	477	237
New Mexico	1,614	819	1,410	714	32	15	151	78	21	11	645	325
Arizona	3,915	1,982	3,479	1,762	120	58	237	121	78	41	789	390
Utah	1,859	934	1,770	890	13	6	30	15	46	23	97	48
Nevada	1,379	679	1,204	590	92	46	25	12	58	31	167	79
Pacific												
Washington	5,255	2,644	4,723	2,376	159	75	96	48	277	146	261	123
Oregon	3,030	1,537	2,840	1,442	51	25	45	22	95	49	136	62
California	31,399	15,678	25,164	12,511	2,430	1,225	280	140	3,525	1,802	8,585	4,128
Alaska	603	286	457	214	24	11	96	47	26	13	21	10
Hawaii	1,179	581	454	213	33	13	6	3	686	352	96	47

[1] Persons of Hispanic origin may be of any race.
[2] Totals may be different from those in the national population projections report (Current Population Reports, P25-1104) due to rounding.

Source: Paul R. Campbell, U.S. Bureau of the Census, *Population Projections for States, by Age, Sex, Race, and Hispanic Origin: 1993 to 2020*, Series P25-1111, Washington, D.C.: Government Printing Office, March 1994, Table 3.

A1-4. Female Immigrants Admitted, by Age: 1983 to 1993

Age and sex	1983	1984	1985	1986	1987	1988	1989	1990	1991	1992	1993
Female	264,975	269,007	283,868	300,931	301,278	318,504	540,661	717,764	613,166	477,062	479,771
Under 5 years	16,807	16,644	16,862	17,138	16,675	15,729	15,542	16,423	18,086	18,460	19,561
5- 9 years	18,911	18,204	18,330	19,260	18,317	18,633	22,803	25,260	24,370	28,614	30,855
10-14 years	21,697	21,534	21,445	22,904	21,212	21,538	41,657	46,736	32,112	35,416	37,866
15-19 years	25,939	26,073	26,483	27,501	28,220	28,099	48,523	62,077	44,357	45,868	46,838
20-24 years	38,046	37,528	40,834	41,077	40,657	40,424	58,307	85,552	91,576	55,548	54,403
25-29 years	40,264	40,545	44,343	45,320	45,356	46,439	80,880	118,271	111,944	71,129	67,922
30-34 years	28,938	29,624	31,398	34,038	34,390	37,439	81,305	111,959	87,968	58,925	56,962
35-39 years	18,655	19,806	21,019	22,764	23,842	27,455	59,012	78,546	59,910	42,406	41,472
40-44 years	12,628	13,070	13,424	14,670	16,206	19,671	38,684	51,606	40,452	30,258	30,534
45-49 years	9,593	10,322	10,690	11,618	12,338	14,514	25,481	32,816	25,870	21,423	21,986
50-54 years	8,626	9,183	9,793	10,762	11,104	12,578	20,189	25,545	21,058	18,105	17,594
55-59 years	8,299	8,884	9,384	10,699	10,777	11,642	16,455	20,867	17,432	15,867	16,330
60-64 years	6,745	7,199	8,105	9,278	9,240	10,067	12,783	17,042	15,109	13,764	14,438
65-69 years	4,599	4,932	5,344	6,426	6,200	6,694	9,340	12,149	11,278	10,449	11,290
70-74 years	2,825	3,090	3,462	4,009	3,654	3,871	4,997	6,375	6,053	5,639	6,289
75-79 years	1,457	1,524	1,793	2,140	1,929	2,228	2,883	3,846	3,325	3,016	3,063
80 years and over	946	845	1,159	1,327	1,133	1,470	1,746	2,614	2,172	2,132	2,323
Unknown	-	-	-	-	28	13	74	80	94	43	45
Unknown sex	22,822	-	-	-	-	-	87	276	234	191	46
Percent distribution	100.0	100.0	100.0	100.0	100.0	100.0	100.0	100.0	100.0	100.0	100.0
Male	48.6	50.5	50.2	50.0	49.9	50.5	50.4	53.3	66.4	51.0	46.9
Female	47.3	49.5	49.8	50.0	50.1	49.5	49.6	46.7	33.6	49.0	53.1
Unknown	4.1	-	-	-	-	-	Z	Z	Z	Z	Z
Median age	26.1	26.5	26.8	27.3	27.7	28.7	30.1	30.1	28.8	28.5	28.3
Male	25.9	26.3	26.7	27.2	27.6	28.7	30.1	30.1	28.6	28.3	27.8
Female	26.3	26.7	26.9	27.4	27.7	28.7	30.2	30.2	29.3	28.8	28.7

- Represents zero. Z rounds to less than 0.05 percent.

Source: Immigration and Naturalization Service, *Statistical Yearbook of the Immigration and Naturalization Service, 1993*, Washington, D.C.: Government Printing Office, 1994, Table 12.

A1-5. Female Immigrants Admitted, by Marital Status and Age: 1993

Age and sex	Total	Single	Married	Widowed	Divorced	Separated	Unknown
Female	479,771	188,178	264,065	17,083	7,445	1,244	1,756
Under 5 years	19,561	19,561	-	-	-	-	-
5- 9 years	30,855	30,855	-	-	-	-	-
10-14 years	37,866	37,818	17	-	6	-	25
15-19 years	46,838	42,878	3,749	1	26	2	182
20-24 years	54,403	20,849	33,202	26	103	55	168
25-29 years	67,922	12,989	54,028	79	482	129	215
30-34 years	56,962	8,248	47,282	145	906	202	179
35-39 years	41,472	4,633	35,210	239	989	219	182
40-44 years	30,534	2,871	25,818	409	1,099	199	138
45-49 years	21,986	1,787	18,269	648	1,039	135	108
50-54 years	17,594	1,406	13,975	1,182	847	104	80
55-59 years	16,330	1,233	12,185	1,984	723	76	129
60-64 years	14,438	1,103	9,590	3,040	566	54	85
65-69 years	11,290	843	6,547	3,398	360	45	97
70-74 years	6,289	529	2,825	2,676	169	14	76
75-79 years	3,063	313	886	1,732	80	6	46
80 years and over	2,323	238	464	1,524	48	4	45
Unknown age	45	24	18	-	2	-	1
Unknown sex	46	16	22	3	1	-	4
Percent distribution	100.0	100.0	100.0	100.0	100.0	100.0	100.0
Male	46.9	52.9	43.5	13.4	37.6	45.2	50.2
Female	53.1	47.1	56.5	86.5	62.4	54.8	49.7
Unknown	Z	Z	Z	Z	Z	Z	.1
Median age	28.3	16.2	35.6	66.6	44.3	39.9	34.3
Male	27.8	16.5	37.4	68.8	42.5	39.5	31.5
Female	28.7	15.7	34.4	66.3	45.5	40.4	38.0

- Represents zero. Z rounds to less than 0.05 percent.

Source: Immigration and Naturalization Service, *Statistical Yearbook of the Immigration and Naturalization Service, 1993*, Washington, D.C.: Government Printing Office, 1994, Table 14.

A1-6. General Characteristics of Foreign-Born Persons, by Nativity, Citizenship, and Year of Entry: 1990

(Data based on sample and subject to sampling variability)

United States	Total						Not a citizen			
		Year of entry						Year of entry		
	Total	1987 to 1990	1985 or 1986	1982 to 1984	1980 or 1981	Before 1980	Total	1987 to 1990	1985 or 1986	1982 to 1984
AGE AND SEX										
All persons	19 767 316	3 136 930	1 738 594	1 826 581	1 961 522	11 103 689	11 770 318	2 937 462	1 569 336	1 474 301
Under 5 years	261 078	238 257	22 821	–	–	–	223 607	204 632	18 975	–
5 to 9 years	486 854	227 324	135 380	101 747	22 403	–	428 768	207 809	119 946	83 471
10 to 14 years	736 234	213 272	120 065	129 521	153 778	119 598	614 242	197 556	108 139	108 848
15 to 19 years	1 161 997	352 899	149 502	147 077	159 699	352 820	920 022	332 335	133 876	122 869
20 to 24 years	1 797 420	529 393	299 438	241 216	201 826	525 547	1 373 273	500 868	269 063	194 062
25 to 34 years	4 521 666	840 467	555 024	620 878	667 252	1 838 045	3 215 320	800 660	504 132	498 989
35 to 44 years	3 753 307	367 055	248 593	320 178	421 740	2 395 741	2 190 831	347 409	226 012	251 412
45 to 54 years	2 552 359	170 220	104 543	135 953	174 052	1 967 591	1 266 315	160 706	95 205	109 030
55 to 64 years	1 800 803	106 453	55 311	67 675	83 814	1 487 550	766 341	100 626	50 518	54 004
65 to 74 years	1 308 199	63 916	33 547	42 945	50 983	1 116 808	459 310	60 437	30 551	35 311
75 to 84 years	936 530	22 475	11 919	15 811	21 237	865 088	237 031	20 428	10 875	13 309
85 years and over	450 869	5 199	2 451	3 580	4 738	434 901	75 258	3 996	2 044	2 996
3 and 4 years	134 639	111 818	22 821	–	–	–	117 931	98 956	18 975	–
16 years and over	18 103 101	2 411 320	1 435 802	1 567 856	1 754 049	10 934 074	10 359 185	2 283 982	1 300 384	1 259 067
18 years and over	17 674 856	2 286 859	1 382 531	1 512 455	1 692 118	10 800 893	10 017 892	2 166 997	1 252 619	1 212 174
21 years and over	16 791 311	1 994 283	1 261 143	1 410 354	1 590 493	10 535 038	9 327 805	1 890 638	1 143 734	1 129 092
60 years and over	3 555 190	141 728	73 012	92 850	113 344	3 134 256	1 117 556	132 268	66 546	75 852
62 years and over	3 205 728	120 110	62 262	80 334	97 810	2 845 212	970 764	111 748	56 603	65 903
Median age	37.3	25.1	27.3	29.5	31.7	46.5	32.2	25.3	27.4	29.3
Female	10 096 455	1 520 027	810 661	868 593	920 813	5 976 361	5 819 433	1 425 398	732 443	699 556
Under 5 years	126 999	115 988	11 011	–	–	–	109 196	99 986	9 210	–
5 to 9 years	237 416	110 081	66 672	49 853	10 810	–	209 130	100 671	59 051	40 974
10 to 14 years	355 894	102 241	57 080	63 235	74 910	58 428	296 636	95 012	51 357	53 001
15 to 19 years	533 506	154 324	65 826	67 193	75 025	171 138	419 745	145 397	59 321	56 001
20 to 24 years	800 346	242 584	118 023	96 368	88 613	254 758	603 739	230 438	106 684	76 871
25 to 34 years	2 134 818	414 533	260 917	289 141	299 007	871 220	1 500 303	395 501	236 467	231 288
35 to 44 years	1 890 537	178 052	119 755	158 689	198 388	1 235 653	1 076 609	168 354	108 876	123 656
45 to 54 years	1 358 441	85 254	51 129	68 479	83 438	1 070 141	673 248	80 374	46 409	54 841
55 to 64 years	1 015 963	61 717	31 121	37 805	44 109	841 211	437 821	58 480	28 512	30 670
65 to 74 years	759 958	37 596	20 036	25 934	30 560	645 832	281 719	35 669	18 421	21 954
75 to 84 years	577 193	14 128	7 417	9 513	12 787	533 348	157 154	12 806	6 768	8 234
85 years and over	305 384	3 529	1 674	2 383	3 166	294 632	54 133	2 710	1 367	2 066
3 and 4 years	65 301	54 290	11 011	–	–	–	57 308	48 098	9 210	–
16 years and over	9 290 381	1 169 893	664 155	742 616	820 265	5 893 452	5 135 982	1 109 362	602 355	595 114
18 years and over	9 090 274	1 113 895	639 615	716 843	791 134	5 828 787	4 976 971	1 056 794	580 301	573 310
21 years and over	8 695 344	989 208	590 956	671 410	744 076	5 699 694	4 671 560	938 649	536 139	536 314
60 years and over	2 138 493	85 297	43 779	55 686	66 205	1 887 526	695 236	79 712	40 079	46 888
62 years and over	1 940 018	72 674	37 592	48 614	58 013	1 723 125	611 355	67 694	34 405	41 041
Median age	39.3	25.7	28.0	30.5	32.2	48.5	33.5	25.9	28.1	30.3
Male	9 670 861	1 616 903	927 933	957 988	1 040 709	5 127 328	5 950 885	1 512 064	836 893	774 745
Median age	35.3	24.5	26.6	28.8	31.2	44.3	31.0	24.7	26.8	28.6
MARITAL STATUS										
Males 15 years and over	8 907 004	1 266 360	784 430	839 808	950 248	5 066 158	5 299 230	1 197 736	709 451	676 401
Never married	2 599 904	644 236	354 105	327 589	335 586	938 388	1 921 181	609 555	319 423	268 242
Now married, except separated	5 494 878	569 570	388 970	456 746	536 685	3 542 907	2 972 849	539 668	352 573	363 626
Separated	197 750	21 964	17 793	20 657	29 426	107 910	135 967	20 603	16 187	17 031
Widowed	212 928	9 345	5 359	5 993	7 983	184 248	62 987	8 466	5 004	4 755
Divorced	401 544	21 245	18 203	28 823	40 568	292 705	206 246	19 444	16 264	22 747
Females 15 years and over	9 376 146	1 191 717	675 898	755 505	835 093	5 917 933	5 204 471	1 129 729	612 825	605 581
Never married	1 803 787	410 110	197 445	200 074	219 373	776 785	1 273 473	389 269	179 756	163 882
Now married, except separated	5 467 686	654 237	398 625	450 664	488 581	3 475 579	3 019 826	621 972	361 042	355 237
Separated	300 810	32 665	24 120	29 780	36 841	177 404	202 288	30 504	21 859	24 941
Widowed	1 179 212	60 318	30 938	38 838	45 282	1 003 836	409 535	56 393	28 245	32 875
Divorced	624 651	34 387	24 770	36 149	45 016	484 329	299 349	31 591	21 923	28 646
FERTILITY										
Women 15 to 24 years	1 333 852	396 908	183 849	163 561	163 638	425 896	1 023 484	375 835	166 005	132 872
Children ever born	513 138	134 740	92 005	71 967	67 968	146 458	411 656	127 046	82 469	61 092
Per 1,000 women	385	339	500	440	415	344	402	338	497	460
Women ever married	384 741	130 990	64 434	46 335	41 892	101 090	304 448	124 028	57 760	37 537
Children ever born	384 895	103 662	70 362	53 916	49 344	107 611	305 696	97 939	62 846	45 372
Per 1,000 women	1 000	791	1 092	1 164	1 178	1 065	1 004	790	1 088	1 209
Women 25 to 34 years	2 134 818	414 533	260 917	289 141	299 007	871 220	1 500 303	395 501	236 467	231 288
Children ever born	3 129 670	446 523	343 197	415 087	515 455	1 409 408	2 230 226	422 150	308 542	335 386
Per 1,000 women	1 466	1 077	1 315	1 436	1 724	1 618	1 487	1 067	1 305	1 450
Women ever married	1 666 813	306 087	204 696	231 781	237 326	686 923	1 162 864	291 605	184 863	183 875
Children ever born	2 849 588	399 773	308 050	378 140	461 495	1 302 130	2 002 041	378 082	276 534	303 301
Per 1,000 women	1 710	1 306	1 505	1 631	1 945	1 896	1 722	1 297	1 496	1 649
Women 35 to 44 years	1 890 537	178 052	119 755	158 689	198 388	1 235 653	1 076 609	168 354	108 876	123 656
Children ever born	4 260 388	378 839	262 369	340 351	459 351	2 819 478	2 552 782	357 841	239 483	271 173
Per 1,000 women	2 254	2 128	2 191	2 145	2 315	2 282	2 371	2 126	2 200	2 193
No children	280 384	34 170	21 839	26 988	31 255	166 132	160 073	32 129	19 787	20 663
1 child	295 915	31 272	20 742	28 293	32 866	182 742	163 878	29 784	18 698	21 198
2 children	611 893	52 362	34 359	48 789	58 949	417 434	316 706	49 637	31 196	37 617
3 children	376 652	30 791	21 130	29 006	35 937	259 788	214 697	29 033	19 341	22 965
4 children	173 005	14 589	10 834	13 366	19 232	114 984	111 236	13 753	9 945	10 844
5 or more children	152 688	14 868	10 851	12 247	20 149	94 573	110 019	14 018	9 909	10 369
Women ever married	1 724 279	155 869	105 681	142 299	175 366	1 145 064	965 017	147 410	95 972	110 169
Children ever born	4 096 324	358 616	247 595	321 602	429 919	2 738 592	2 423 847	338 762	226 222	255 268
Per 1,000 women	2 376	2 301	2 343	2 260	2 452	2 392	2 512	2 298	2 357	2 317

Source: U.S. Bureau of the Census, *The Foreign-Born Population in the United States*, CP-3-1, Washington, D.C.: Government Printing Office, July 1993, Table 1.

A1-7. Educational Attainment of Foreign-Born Persons, by Nativity, Citizenship, and Year of Entry: 1990

(Data based on sample and subject to sampling variability)

United States	Total						Not a citizen			
		Year of entry						Year of entry		
	Total	1987 to 1990	1985 or 1986	1982 to 1984	1980 or 1981	Before 1980	Total	1987 to 1990	1985 or 1986	1982 to 1984
EDUCATIONAL ATTAINMENT										
Persons 18 to 24 years _____	2 351 123	711 074	371 143	305 435	268 302	695 169	1 807 486	672 735	333 282	247 123
High school graduate (includes equivalency) ___	547 717	153 009	76 695	67 415	65 221	185 377	414 094	144 065	68 476	53 716
Some college or associate degree _____	628 124	160 218	74 669	74 046	67 282	251 909	430 235	151 625	67 715	56 092
Bachelor's degree or higher _____	166 068	53 508	17 966	16 923	12 561	65 110	106 132	51 459	16 686	12 937
Persons 25 years and over _____	15 323 733	1 575 785	1 011 388	1 207 020	1 423 816	10 105 724	8 210 406	1 494 262	919 337	965 051
Less than 5th grade _____	1 745 552	190 273	126 931	138 476	203 396	1 086 476	1 233 068	179 359	115 675	120 569
5th to 8th grade _____	2 287 866	187 893	127 487	150 277	232 712	1 589 497	1 346 987	176 915	115 020	126 930
9th to 12th grade, no diploma _____	2 282 080	203 817	148 328	173 825	235 382	1 520 728	1 271 104	191 673	133 041	142 883
High school graduate (includes equivalency) ___	3 007 301	277 411	187 849	220 776	248 066	2 073 199	1 475 389	259 403	168 383	173 232
Some college, no degree _____	1 979 323	166 998	121 289	156 009	169 541	1 365 486	927 005	156 998	109 426	117 789
Associate degree, occupational program _____	476 623	50 066	31 712	41 613	46 150	307 082	235 886	47 389	28 926	30 848
Associate degree, academic program _____	425 535	42 815	28 724	37 724	38 306	277 966	200 435	40 579	25 866	28 162
Bachelor's degree _____	1 769 356	257 614	135 307	168 247	152 406	1 055 782	859 530	248 853	124 338	125 579
Master's degree _____	768 270	117 714	67 536	72 925	59 109	450 986	391 702	114 539	64 699	60 445
Professional school degree _____	348 258	47 829	22 772	26 762	22 759	228 136	151 433	45 956	21 048	20 410
Doctorate degree_____	233 569	33 355	13 453	20 386	15 989	150 386	117 867	32 598	12 915	18 204
Females 25 years and over _____	8 042 294	794 809	492 049	591 944	671 455	5 492 037	4 180 987	753 894	446 820	472 709
Less than 5th grade _____	941 069	104 751	66 705	74 267	106 276	589 070	658 991	99 207	61 641	66 003
5th to 8th grade_____	1 242 575	97 512	63 541	77 057	112 016	892 449	700 987	92 109	57 861	65 608
9th to 12th grade, no diploma _____	1 222 352	104 366	72 249	86 252	107 649	851 836	644 450	98 401	64 832	70 561
High school graduate (includes equivalency) ___	1 775 578	155 520	99 128	118 361	125 046	1 277 523	827 342	145 764	88 622	92 427
Some college, no degree _____	1 017 248	81 066	56 572	72 850	75 123	731 637	457 695	76 073	50 650	54 378
Associate degree, occupational program _____	261 712	28 510	16 936	21 625	21 955	172 686	129 867	27 135	15 464	16 035
Associate degree, academic program _____	243 780	25 254	15 238	20 486	19 551	163 251	114 444	24 140	13 697	15 246
Bachelor's degree _____	867 278	128 210	67 154	81 207	70 530	520 177	420 942	123 732	61 492	60 174
Master's degree _____	295 305	42 031	22 871	25 748	21 482	183 173	141 873	40 685	21 859	21 060
Professional school degree _____	123 196	19 747	8 649	9 499	8 423	76 878	58 151	19 016	7 856	7 205
Doctorate degree_____	52 201	7 842	3 006	4 592	3 404	33 357	26 245	7 632	2 846	4 012

Source: U.S. Bureau of the Census, *The Foreign-Born Population in the United States*, CP-3-1, Washington, D.C.: Government Printing Office, July 1993, Table 3.

A2. BIRTH TRENDS

A2-1. Average Ages of Women and Men, at Puberty, First Intercourse, Marriage, and First Birth: 1890 and 1988

BIG CHANGES

The interval for women between puberty and marriage rose from 7.2 years in 1890 to 11.8 years in 1988; for men in 1988, it was 12.5 years.

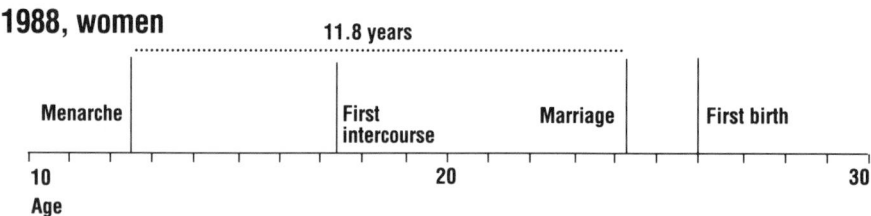

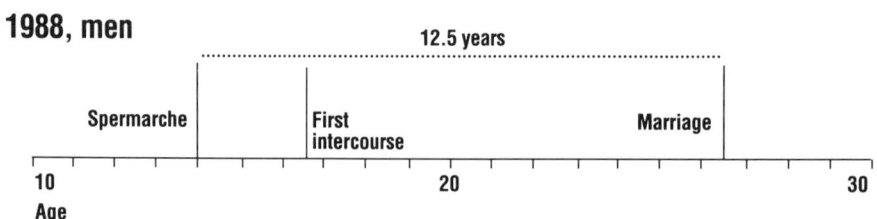

Sources: Menarche, 1890: E. G. Wyshak and R. E. Frisch, "Evidence for a Secular Trend in Age of Menarche," *New England Journal of Medicine*, **306**:1033–1035, 1982. **First marriage, 1890:** U.S. Bureau of the Census, "Marital Status and Living Arrangements: March, 1990," *Current Population Reports*, Series P-20, No. 450, 1991, Table A, p. 1. **First birth, 1890:** National Center for Health Statistics, *Fertility Tables for Birth Cohorts by Color, United States, 1917–73*, Public Health Service, Rockville, Md., 1976, Table 6A, p. 145. **Menarche, first intercourse and first birth and first marriage, 1988:** J. D. Forrest, "Timing of Reproductive Life Stages," *Obstetrics and Gynecology*, **82**:105–111, 1993, Table 3. **Spermarche, 1988:** E. Atwater, *Adolescence*, third ed. Prentice-Hall, Englewood Cliffs, N.J., 1992, p. 63.

Notes: Menarche is the beginning of menstruation in females. **Spermarche** is the beginning of sperm production in males. The data for the different time periods are not total-

ly comparable. For 1890, age at first marriage is calculated in the usual manner as the age by which 50% of the ever-married population had married. (Median age at marriage in 1890 would be higher if it were calculated for the total population.) The 1890 first-birth figure is calculated from the 1917 birth cohort; the 1890 number is unavailable, but it is estimated to be lower. For 1988, the median ages at menarche, spermarche, first intercourse, marriage and first birth are calculated as the age by which 50% of the total female (or male) population in 1988 had experienced the event.

Data points: 1890, women: age at menarche, 14.8; marriage, 22.0; first birth, 23.8. **1988, women:** age at menarche, 12.5; first intercourse, 17.4; marriage, 24.3; first birth, 26.0. **1988, men:** age at spermarche, 14.0; first intercourse, 16.6; marriage, 26.5.

Source: The Alan Guttmacher Institute, *Sex and America's Teenagers*, New York: The Alan Guttmacher Institute, 1994, Figure 1. Reprinted with permission.

A2-2. Typical Ages in Women's Reproductive Lives: 1988

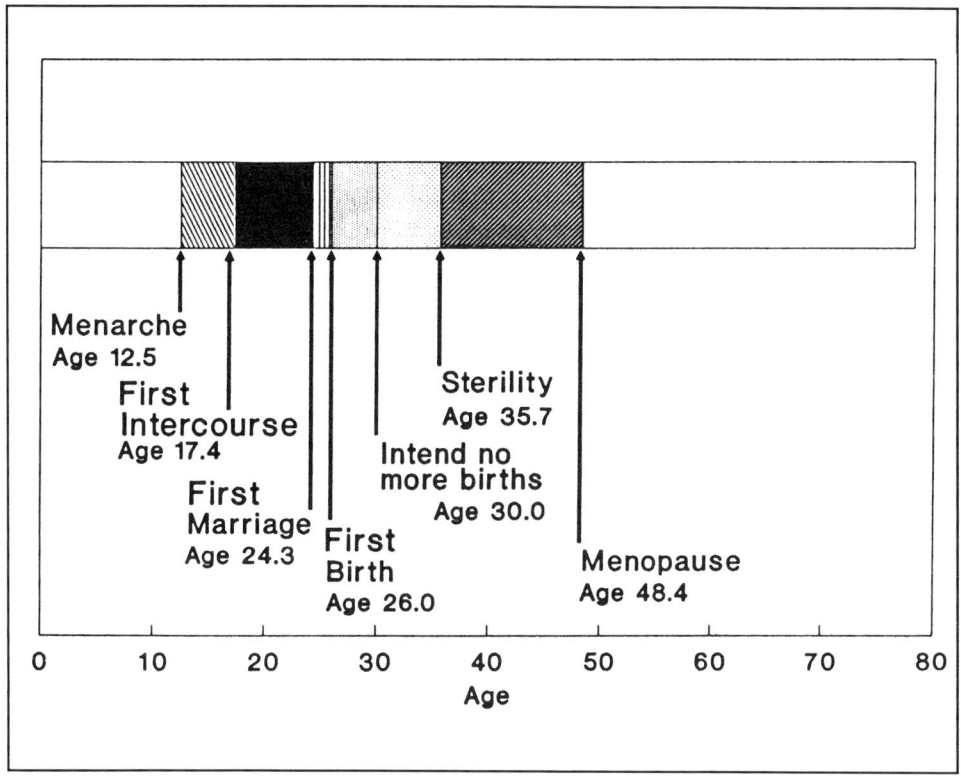

Source: Jacqueline D. Forrest, The Alan Guttmacher Institute, "Levels and Determinants of U.S. Fertility," presentation at The Population and Consumption Task Force of the President's Council on Sustainable Development, October 27, 1994, unpublished.

A2-3. Distribution of Women, by Age at First Birth: 1960 to 1985

(Numbers in thousands)

Year	Number of first births	Percent	Age at first birth			
			Less than 20	20-24	25-29	30 or older
1985	1,555	100.0	23.7	35.6	26.9	13.8
1980	1,546	100.0	28.2	39.2	24.1	8.6
1975	1,319	100.0	35.1	39.2	20.4	5.3
1970	1,431	100.0	35.6	45.6	14.8	4.0
1965	1,157	100.0	38.0	44.6	12.1	5.3
1960	1,090	100.0	37.0	43.2	13.0	6.8

Source: National Center for Health Statistics, Vital Statistics of the United States, annual issues.

Source: U.S. Bureau of the Census, *Work and Family Patterns of American Women*, Current Population Reports, Series P-23, No. 165, Washington, D.C.: U.S. Government Printing Office, 1990, Table A.

A2-4. Completed Fertility Rates and Parity Distribution for Women 50–54 Years Old at the Beginning of Selected Years 1930–1992, by Race of Child and Birth Cohort: Selected Birth Cohorts 1876–80 to 1938–42

[Data are based on the National Vital Statistics System]

Race of child and birth cohort of mother	Age 50–54 as of January 1,–	Completed fertility rate [1]	Parity (number of children born alive)								
			Total	0	1	2	3	4	5	6	7 or more
All races			Distribution of women [2]								
1876–80	1930	3,531.9	1,000.0	216.8	123.2	132.0	114.0	93.0	72.0	64.5	184.5
1886–90	1940	3,136.8	1,000.0	210.4	148.5	153.2	129.7	99.5	68.0	55.4	135.3
1896–1900	1950	2,675.9	1,000.0	194.6	200.7	195.2	136.6	87.8	53.5	41.5	90.1
1906–10	1960	2,285.8	1,000.0	215.6	225.1	218.7	131.4	77.5	44.6	29.2	57.9
1916–20	1970	2,574.0	1,000.0	149.0	179.0	251.7	174.6	102.8	55.8	32.0	55.1
1921–25	1975	2,857.0	1,000.0	108.5	152.1	248.7	197.0	123.5	68.0	39.5	62.7
1926–30	1980	3,079.2	1,000.0	105.5	113.7	226.5	209.6	143.5	81.9	47.6	71.7
1931–35	1985	3,201.4	1,000.0	87.2	96.3	218.8	224.0	160.0	91.4	52.5	69.8
1932–36	1986	3,182.4	1,000.0	84.8	97.0	221.0	226.9	160.8	91.3	51.7	66.5
1933–37	1987	3,146.4	1,000.0	84.0	98.7	224.4	229.5	160.6	90.2	50.2	62.4
1934–38	1988	3,092.6	1,000.0	85.0	100.8	229.7	232.0	159.2	87.7	48.1	57.5
1935–39	1989	3,026.3	1,000.0	86.9	103.8	236.6	234.2	156.6	84.2	45.6	52.1
1936–40	1990	2,949.7	1,000.0	89.6	107.1	245.7	236.1	152.6	79.9	42.4	46.6
1937–41	1991	2,863.8	1,000.0	93.1	111.3	256.5	237.1	147.1	75.1	38.8	41.0
1938–42	1992	2,770.1	1,000.0	97.3	116.1	269.4	236.9	140.4	69.4	35.0	35.5
White											
1876–80	1930	3,444.4	1,000.0	218.2	121.9	136.1	116.9	94.8	74.0	64.2	173.9
1886–90	1940	3,092.9	1,000.0	209.1	144.3	160.3	132.4	100.2	70.3	54.8	128.6
1896–1900	1950	2,631.5	1,000.0	193.1	192.1	205.9	141.4	89.0	55.2	41.1	82.2
1906–10	1960	2,248.9	1,000.0	207.9	218.0	233.2	138.8	79.6	44.7	28.0	49.8
1916–20	1970	2,526.7	1,000.0	134.6	175.9	268.7	185.1	106.5	55.3	30.3	43.6
1921–25	1975	2,793.7	1,000.0	94.2	150.6	264.6	208.8	127.9	67.9	36.9	49.1
1926–30	1980	2,986.0	1,000.0	94.1	114.1	240.2	222.3	148.8	81.2	44.5	54.8
1931–35	1985	3,101.2	1,000.0	78.5	96.8	231.1	236.4	166.0	90.5	48.2	52.5
1932–36	1986	3,080.0	1,000.0	77.9	97.0	232.9	239.2	166.3	89.9	47.3	49.5
1933–37	1987	3,042.3	1,000.0	78.6	98.5	236.2	241.6	165.5	88.1	45.5	46.0
1934–38	1988	2,990.0	1,000.0	80.7	100.6	241.2	243.9	163.3	85.2	43.1	42.0
1935–39	1989	2,926.9	1,000.0	83.2	103.6	248.4	245.7	159.8	81.3	40.3	37.7
1936–40	1990	2,854.7	1,000.0	86.3	107.1	257.6	247.1	154.9	76.5	37.2	33.3
1937–41	1991	2,773.8	1,000.0	90.2	111.5	268.6	247.4	148.5	71.1	33.6	29.1
1938–42	1992	2,685.0	1,000.0	95.0	116.3	281.9	246.2	140.6	65.0	29.9	25.1
All other											
1876–80	1930	4,254.7	1,000.0	207.7	134.0	99.5	87.4	79.9	54.7	64.8	272.0
1886–90	1940	3,451.4	1,000.0	231.9	175.9	105.9	96.6	93.3	52.4	58.0	186.0
1896–1900	1950	2,967.7	1,000.0	227.4	255.0	114.1	97.5	74.3	38.8	42.6	150.3
1906–10	1960	2,529.1	1,000.0	287.5	266.6	114.5	73.2	60.1	43.5	35.6	119.0
1916–20	1970	2,924.2	1,000.0	266.2	202.0	120.9	91.2	72.5	57.8	44.9	144.5
1921–25	1975	3,316.0	1,000.0	217.7	163.5	131.7	108.2	89.0	68.7	56.4	164.8
1926–30	1980	3,718.9	1,000.0	187.4	110.8	130.2	121.0	106.4	85.7	69.3	189.2
1931–35	1985	3,836.2	1,000.0	145.1	93.4	140.8	140.4	121.8	98.2	78.4	181.9
1932–36	1986	3,830.3	1,000.0	131.0	96.4	145.5	145.5	125.9	100.5	79.9	175.3
1933–37	1987	3,805.9	1,000.0	119.4	99.8	150.3	150.2	129.9	102.4	80.6	167.4
1934–38	1988	3,745.8	1,000.0	113.8	102.8	154.9	155.3	132.7	102.7	80.6	157.2
1935–39	1989	3,661.6	1,000.0	111.5	105.4	160.6	160.4	135.3	102.4	79.2	145.2
1936–40	1990	3,556.1	1,000.0	111.8	107.6	168.2	165.6	137.2	101.3	76.9	131.4
1937–41	1991	3,438.0	1,000.0	112.7	110.6	177.6	170.6	139.0	99.5	73.3	116.7
1938–42	1992	3,313.1	1,000.0	113.0	114.9	188.9	175.8	140.3	96.3	69.2	101.6

[1]Number of children born alive to each 1,000 women who have completed their reproductive histories (women 50–54 years of age).
[2]Proportional distribution of each 1,000 women in the cohort by the number of children born alive to them.

NOTES: Example of use of table—For every 1,000 women 50–54 years of age in 1980, an average of 3,079.2 children were born alive (about 3 children per woman). About 10 percent of the women in this cohort reached 50–54 years of age having had no children, about 11 percent had one child, and about 12 percent had six children or more.

SOURCES: Centers for Disease Control and Prevention, National Center for Health Statistics: Fertility Tables for Birth Cohorts by Color, United States, 1917–73 by R. Heuser. DHEW Pub. No. (HRA) 76-1152. Health Resources Administration. Washington. U.S. Government Printing Office, Apr. 1976; Data computed from Vital Statistics of the United States, 1991, Vol. I, Natality. Public Health Service. Washington. U.S. Government Printing Office, 1993.

Source: National Center for Health Statistics, *Health, United States, 1993,* (PHS) 94-1232, Washington, D.C.: U.S. Government Printing Office, 1994, Table 5.

A2-5. Live Births, Birth Rates, and Fertility Rates, for Whites and Blacks: 1909 to 1990

(Birth rates per 1,000 population for specified group. Fertility rates per 1,000 women aged 15–44 years in specified group. Beginning 1970 excluded births to nonresidents of the United States)

Year	Number				Birth Rate[1]				Fertility Rate			
	All races	White	All other		All races	White	All other		All races	White	All other	
			Total	Black			Total	Black			Total	Black
REGISTERED BIRTHS					Race of Mother							
1990	4,158,212	3,290,273	867,939	684,336	16.7	15.8	21.7	22.4	70.9	68.3	83.2	86.8
1989[2]	4,040,958	3,192,355	848,603	673,124	16.4	15.4	21.6	22.3	69.2	66.4	82.7	86.2
					Race of Child							
1990	4,158,212	3,225,343	932,869	724,576	16.7	15.5	23.3	23.8	70.9	66.9	89.4	91.9
1989[2]	4,040,958	3,131,991	908,967	709,395	16.4	15.1	23.1	23.5	69.2	65.1	88.6	90.8
1988[2]	3,909,510	3,046,162	863,348	671,976	16.0	14.8	22.5	22.6	67.3	63.4	85.9	87.0
1987[2]	3,809,394	2,992,488	816,906	641,567	15.7	14.6	21.8	21.9	65.8	62.3	83.1	84.1
1986[2]	3,756,547	2,970,439	786,108	621,221	15.6	14.6	21.4	21.5	65.4	62.1	81.9	82.6
1985[2]	3,760,561	2,991,373	769,188	608,193	15.8	14.8	21.4	21.3	66.3	63.1	82.3	82.4
1984[2][3]	3,669,141	2,923,502	745,639	592,745	15.6	14.6	21.2	21.0	65.5	62.3	81.8	81.5
1983[2][3]	3,638,933	2,904,250	734,683	586,027	15.6	14.6	21.4	21.0	65.7	62.5	82.7	82.0
1982[2][3]	3,680,537	2,942,054	738,483	592,641	15.9	14.9	22.0	21.5	67.3	63.9	85.3	84.3
1981[2][3]	3,629,238	2,908,669	720,569	587,797	15.8	14.8	21.9	21.7	67.3	63.9	85.3	85.3
1980[3]	3,612,258	2,898,732	713,526	589,616	15.9	14.9	22.5	22.1	68.4	64.7	88.6	88.1
1979[3]	3,494,398	2,808,420	685,978	577,855	15.6	14.5	22.2	22.0	67.2	63.4	88.5	88.3
1978[3]	3,333,279	2,681,116	652,163	551,540	15.0	14.0	21.6	21.3	65.5	61.7	87.0	86.7
1977[3]	3,326,632	2,691,070	635,562	544,221	15.1	14.1	21.6	21.4	66.8	63.2	87.7	88.1
1976[3]	3,167,788	2,567,614	600,174	514,479	14.6	13.6	20.8	20.5	65.0	61.5	85.8	85.8
1975[3]	3,144,198	2,551,996	592,202	511,581	14.6	13.6	21.0	20.7	66.0	62.5	87.7	87.9
1974[3]	3,159,958	2,575,792	584,166	507,162	14.8	13.9	21.2	20.8	67.8	64.2	89.8	89.7
1973[3]	3,136,965	2,551,030	585,935	512,597	14.8	13.8	21.7	21.4	68.8	64.9	93.4	93.6
1972[3]	3,258,411	2,655,558	602,853	531,329	15.6	14.5	22.8	22.5	73.1	68.9	99.5	99.9
1971[4]	3,555,970	2,919,746	636,224	564,960	17.2	16.1	24.6	24.4	81.6	77.3	109.1	109.7
1970[4]	3,731,386	3,091,264	640,122	572,362	18.4	17.4	25.1	25.3	87.9	84.1	113.0	115.4
1969[4]	3,600,206	2,993,614	606,592	543,132	17.9	16.9	24.5	24.4	86.1	82.2	111.6	112.1
1968[4]	3,501,564	2,912,224	589,340	531,152	17.6	16.6	24.2	24.2	85.2	81.3	111.9	112.7
1967[5]	3,520,959	2,922,502	598,457	543,976	17.8	16.8	25.0	25.1	87.2	82.8	117.1	118.5
1966[4]	3,606,274	2,993,230	613,044	558,244	18.4	17.4	26.1	26.2	90.8	86.2	123.5	124.7
1965[4]	3,760,358	3,123,860	636,498	581,126	19.4	18.3	27.6	27.7	96.3	91.3	131.9	133.2
1964[4]	4,027,490	3,369,160	658,330	607,556	21.1	20.0	29.2	29.5	104.7	99.8	140.0	142.6
1963[4][6]	4,098,020	3,326,344	638,928	580,658	21.7	20.7	29.7	---	108.3	103.6	143.7	---
1962[4][6]	4,167,362	3,394,068	641,580	584,610	22.4	21.4	30.5	---	112.0	107.5	147.8	---
1961[4]	4,268,326	3,600,864	667,462	611,072	23.3	22.2	31.6	---	117.1	112.3	153.0	---
1960[4]	4,257,850	3,600,744	657,106	602,264	23.7	22.7	32.1	31.9	118.0	113.2	153.6	153.5
1959[4]	4,244,796	3,597,430	647,366	605,962	24.0	22.9	32.9	---	118.8	113.9	156.0	---
BIRTHS ADJUSTED FOR UNDERREGISTRATION[7][8]												
1959[4]	4,286,000	3,619,000	666,000	---	24.2	23.1	33.9	---	119.9	114.5	160.7	---
1958[4]	4,246,000	3,595,000	651,000	---	24.5	23.3	34.0	---	120.0	114.8	159.1	---
1957[4]	4,300,000	3,646,000	654,000	---	25.3	24.0	35.0	---	122.7	117.6	161.7	---
1956[4]	4,210,000	3,570,000	640,000	---	25.2	24.0	35.1	---	121.0	115.9	159.7	---
1955	4,097,000	3,485,000	613,000	---	25.0	23.8	34.5	---	118.3	113.7	154.3	---
1954[4]	4,071,000	3,472,000	599,000	---	25.3	24.2	34.7	---	117.9	113.5	152.2	---
1953[4]	3,959,000	3,387,000	572,000	---	25.1	24.0	33.9	---	115.0	110.9	146.4	---
1952[4]	3,909,000	3,356,000	553,000	---	25.1	24.1	33.4	---	113.8	110.0	142.7	---
1951[4]	3,820,000	3,275,000	545,000	---	24.9	23.9	33.7	---	111.4	107.7	141.7	---
1950	3,632,000	3,108,000	524,000	---	24.1	23.0	33.3	---	106.2	102.3	137.3	---
1949	3,649,000	3,136,000	513,000	---	24.5	23.6	33.0	---	107.1	103.6	135.1	---
1948	3,637,000	3,141,000	495,000	---	24.9	24.0	32.4	---	107.3	104.3	131.6	---
1947	3,817,000	3,347,000	469,000	---	26.6	26.1	31.2	---	113.3	111.8	125.9	---
1946	3,411,000	2,990,000	420,000	---	24.1	23.6	28.4	---	101.9	100.4	113.9	---
1945	2,858,000	2,471,000	388,000	---	20.4	19.7	26.5	---	85.9	83.4	106.0	---
1944	2,939,000	2,545,000	394,000	---	21.2	20.5	27.4	---	88.8	86.3	108.5	---
1943	3,104,000	2,704,000	400,000	---	22.7	22.1	28.3	---	94.3	92.3	111.0	---
1942	2,989,000	2,605,000	384,000	---	22.2	21.5	27.7	---	91.5	89.5	107.6	---
1941	2,703,000	2,330,000	374,000	---	20.3	19.5	27.3	---	83.4	80.7	105.4	---
1940	2,559,000	2,199,000	360,000	---	19.4	18.6	26.7	---	79.9	77.1	102.4	---
1939	2,466,000	2,117,000	349,000	---	18.8	18.0	26.1	---	77.6	74.8	100.1	---
1938	2,496,000	2,148,000	348,000	---	19.2	18.4	26.3	---	79.1	76.5	100.5	---
1937	2,413,000	2,071,000	342,000	---	18.7	17.9	26.0	---	77.1	74.4	99.4	---
1936	2,355,000	2,027,000	328,000	---	18.4	17.6	25.1	---	75.8	73.3	95.9	---
1935	2,377,000	2,042,000	334,000	---	18.7	17.9	25.8	---	77.2	74.5	98.4	---
1934	2,396,000	2,058,000	338,000	---	19.0	18.1	26.3	---	78.5	75.8	100.4	---
1933	2,307,000	1,982,000	325,000	---	18.4	17.6	25.5	---	76.3	73.7	97.3	---
1932	2,440,000	2,099,000	341,000	---	19.5	18.7	26.9	---	81.7	79.0	103.0	---
1931	2,506,000	2,170,000	335,000	---	20.2	19.5	26.6	---	84.6	82.4	102.1	---
1930	2,618,000	2,274,000	344,000	---	21.3	20.6	27.5	---	89.2	87.1	105.9	---
1929	2,582,000	2,244,000	339,000	---	21.2	20.5	27.3	---	89.3	87.3	106.1	---
1928	2,674,000	2,325,000	349,000	---	22.2	21.5	28.5	---	93.8	91.7	111.0	---
1927	2,802,000	2,425,000	377,000	---	23.5	22.7	31.1	---	99.8	97.1	121.7	---
1926	2,839,000	2,441,000	398,000	---	24.2	23.1	33.4	---	102.6	99.2	130.3	---
1925	2,909,000	2,506,000	403,000	---	25.1	24.1	34.2	---	106.6	103.3	134.0	---
1924	2,979,000	2,577,000	401,000	---	26.1	25.1	34.6	---	110.9	107.8	135.6	---
1923	2,910,000	2,531,000	380,000	---	26.0	25.2	33.2	---	110.5	108.0	130.5	---

A2-5. Live Births, Birth Rates, and Fertility Rates, for Whites and Blacks: 1909 to 1990 *(continued)*

(Birth rates per 1,000 population for specified group. Fertility rates per 1,000 women aged 15–44 years in specified group. Beginning 1970 excluded births to nonresidents of the United States)

Year	Number				Birth Rate [1]				Fertility Rate			
	All races	White	All other		All races	White	All other		All races	White	All other	
			Total	Black			Total	Black			Total	Black
	Race of Child—Con.											
BIRTHS ADJUSTED FOR UNDERREGISTRATION [7][8]— Con.												
1922	2,882,000	2,507,000	375,000	- - -	26.2	25.4	33.2	- - -	111.2	108.8	130.8	- - -
1921	3,055,000	2,657,000	398,000	- - -	28.1	27.3	35.8	- - -	119.8	117.2	140.8	- - -
1920	2,950,000	2,566,000	383,000	- - -	27.7	26.9	35.0	- - -	117.9	115.4	137.5	- - -
1919	2,740,000	2,387,000	353,000	- - -	26.1	25.3	32.4	- - -	111.2	- - -	- - -	- - -
1918	2,948,000	2,588,000	360,000	- - -	28.2	27.6	33.0	- - -	119.8	- - -	- - -	- - -
1917	2,944,000	2,587,000	357,000	- - -	28.5	27.9	32.9	- - -	121.0	- - -	- - -	- - -
1916	2,964,000	2,599,000	- - -	- - -	29.1	28.5	- - -	- - -	123.4	121.8	- - -	- - -
1915	2,965,000	2,594,000	- - -	- - -	29.5	28.9	- - -	- - -	125.0	123.2	- - -	- - -
1914	2,966,000	2,588,000	- - -	- - -	29.9	29.3	- - -	- - -	126.6	124.6	- - -	- - -
1913	2,869,000	2,497,000	- - -	- - -	29.5	28.8	- - -	- - -	124.7	122.4	- - -	- - -
1912	2,840,000	2,467,000	- - -	- - -	29.8	29.0	- - -	- - -	125.8	123.3	- - -	- - -
1911	2,809,000	2,435,000	- - -	- - -	29.9	29.1	- - -	- - -	126.3	123.6	- - -	- - -
1910	2,777,000	2,401,000	- - -	- - -	30.1	29.2	- - -	- - -	126.8	123.8	- - -	- - -
1909	2,718,000	2,344,000	- - -	- - -	30.0	29.2	- - -	- - -	126.8	123.6	- - -	- - -

[1]For 1917–19 and 1941–46 based on population including Armed Forces abroad.

[2]Rates are revised and therefore may differ from those published in Vital Statistics of the United States, Volume 1, Natality for 1989 and previous years.

[3]Based on 100 percent of births in selected States and on a 50-percent sample of births in all other States.

[4]Based on a 50-percent sample of births.

[5]Based on a 20- to 50-percent sample of births.

[6]Figures by race exclude data for residents of New Jersey.

[7]Due to rounding to the nearest thousand, figures by race may not add to totals. For 1915–32, figures include adjustments for States not in the registration area; for years prior to 1915, figures are estimates based on the number of registered births in the 10 original registration States for the same period. Estimates for 1909–34 were prepared by P. K. Whelpton. See National Office of Vital Statistics, "Births and Birth Rates in the Entire United Stated, 1909 to 1948," Vital Statistics—Special Reports, Vol. 33, No. 8, 1950.

Source: National Center for Health Statistics, *Vital Statistics of the United States, 1990*, Vol. 1 (Natality), Washington, D.C.: U.S. Government Printing Office, 1994, Table 1-1.

A2-6. Live Births and Fertility Rates: 1930 to 1992

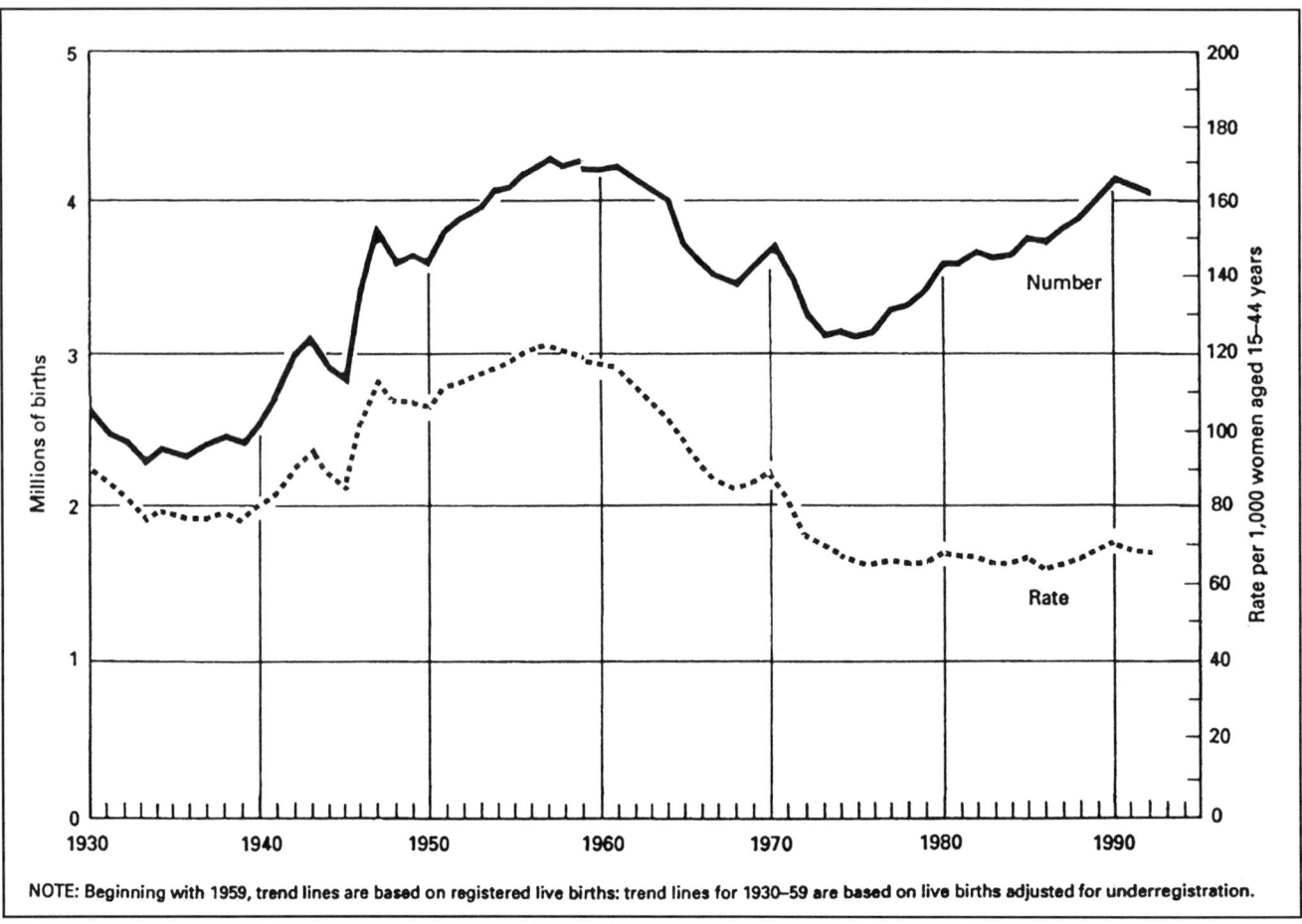

NOTE: Beginning with 1959, trend lines are based on registered live births: trend lines for 1930–59 are based on live births adjusted for underregistration.

Source: S. J. Ventura, J. A. Martin, S. M. Taffel, et. al., National Center for Health Statistics, *Advance Report of Final Natality Statistics, 1992*, Monthly Vital Statistics Report, Vol. 43, No. 5 (suppl.), (PHS) 95-1120 4-0677, Washington, D.C.: U.S. Department of Health and Human Services, October 25, 1994, Figure 1.

A2-7. Live Births, Birth Rates, and Fertility Rates, by Race: 1940 to 1955 and 1960 to 1992

[Birth rates are live births per 1,000 population in specified group. Fertility rates per 1,000 women aged 15–44 years in specified group. Population enumerated as of April 1 for census years and estimated as of July 1 for all other years. Beginning with 1970, excludes births to nonresidents of the United States]

Year	Number					Birth rate					Fertility rate				
	All races[1]	White	Black	American Indian[2]	Asian or Pacific Islander	All races[1]	White	Black	American Indian[2]	Asian or Pacific Islander	All races[1]	White	Black	American Indian[2]	Asian or Pacific Islander
Registered births															
Race of mother:															
1992........	4,065,014	3,201,678	673,633	39,453	150,250	15.9	15.0	21.3	18.4	18.0	68.9	66.5	83.2	75.4	67.2
1991........	4,110,907	3,241,273	682,602	38,841	145,372	16.3	15.4	21.9	18.3	18.2	69.6	67.0	85.2	75.1	67.6
1990........	4,158,212	3,290,273	684,336	39,051	141,635	16.7	15.8	22.4	18.9	19.0	70.9	68.3	86.8	76.2	69.6
1989........	4,040,958	3,192,355	673,124	39,478	133,075	16.4	15.4	22.3	19.7	18.7	69.2	66.4	86.2	79.0	68.2
1988........	3,909,510	3,102,083	638,562	37,088	129,035	16.0	15.0	21.5	19.3	19.2	67.3	64.5	82.6	76.8	70.2
1987........	3,809,394	3,043,828	611,173	35,322	116,560	15.7	14.9	20.8	19.1	18.4	65.8	63.3	80.1	75.6	67.1
1986........	3,756,547	3,019,175	592,910	34,169	107,797	15.6	14.8	20.5	19.2	18.0	65.4	63.1	78.9	75.9	66.0
1985........	3,760,561	3,037,913	581,824	34,037	104,606	15.8	15.0	20.4	19.8	18.7	66.3	64.1	78.8	78.6	68.4
1984[3]........	3,669,141	2,967,100	568,138	33,256	98,926	15.6	14.8	20.1	20.1	18.8	65.5	63.2	78.2	79.8	69.2
1983[3]........	3,638,933	2,946,468	562,624	32,881	95,713	15.6	14.8	20.2	20.6	19.5	65.7	63.4	78.7	81.8	71.7
1982[3]........	3,680,537	2,984,817	568,506	32,436	93,193	15.9	15.1	20.7	21.1	20.3	67.3	64.8	80.9	83.6	74.8
1981[3]........	3,629,238	2,947,679	564,955	29,688	84,553	15.8	15.0	20.8	20.0	20.1	67.3	64.8	82.0	79.6	73.7
1980[3]........	3,612,258	2,936,351	568,080	29,389	74,355	15.9	15.1	21.3	20.7	19.9	68.4	65.6	84.7	82.7	73.2
Race of child:															
1980[3]........	3,612,258	2,898,732	589,616	36,797	- - -	15.9	14.9	22.1	- - -	- - -	68.4	64.7	88.1	- - -	- - -
1979[3]........	3,494,398	2,808,420	577,855	34,269	- - -	15.6	14.5	22.0	- - -	- - -	67.2	63.4	88.3	- - -	- - -
1978[3]........	3,333,279	2,681,116	551,540	33,160	- - -	15.0	14.0	21.3	- - -	- - -	65.5	61.7	86.7	- - -	- - -
1977[3]........	3,326,632	2,691,070	544,221	30,500	- - -	15.1	14.1	21.4	- - -	- - -	66.8	63.2	88.1	- - -	- - -
1976[3]........	3,167,788	2,567,614	514,479	29,009	- - -	14.6	13.6	20.5	- - -	- - -	65.0	61.5	85.8	- - -	- - -
1975[3]........	3,144,198	2,551,996	511,581	27,546	- - -	14.6	13.6	20.7	- - -	- - -	66.0	62.5	87.9	- - -	- - -
1974[3]........	3,159,958	2,575,792	507,162	26,631	- - -	14.8	13.9	20.8	- - -	- - -	67.8	64.2	89.7	- - -	- - -
1973[3]........	3,136,965	2,551,030	512,597	26,464	- - -	14.8	13.8	21.4	- - -	- - -	68.8	64.9	93.6	- - -	- - -
1972[3]........	3,258,411	2,655,558	531,329	27,368	- - -	15.6	14.5	22.5	- - -	- - -	73.1	68.9	99.9	- - -	- - -
1971[4]........	3,555,970	2,919,746	564,960	27,148	- - -	17.2	16.1	24.4	- - -	- - -	81.6	77.3	109.7	- - -	- - -
1970[4]........	3,731,386	3,091,264	572,362	25,864	- - -	18.4	17.4	25.3	- - -	- - -	87.9	84.1	115.4	- - -	- - -
1969[4]........	3,600,206	2,993,614	543,132	24,008	- - -	17.9	16.9	24.4	- - -	- - -	86.1	82.2	112.1	- - -	- - -
1968[4]........	3,501,564	2,912,224	531,152	24,156	- - -	17.6	16.6	24.2	- - -	- - -	85.2	81.3	112.7	- - -	- - -
1967[5]........	3,520,959	2,922,502	543,976	22,665	- - -	17.8	16.8	25.1	- - -	- - -	87.2	82.8	118.5	- - -	- - -
1966[4]........	3,606,274	2,993,230	558,244	23,014	- - -	18.4	17.4	26.2	- - -	- - -	90.8	86.2	124.7	- - -	- - -
1965[4]........	3,760,358	3,123,860	581,126	24,066	- - -	19.4	18.3	27.7	- - -	- - -	96.3	91.3	133.2	- - -	- - -
1964[4]........	4,027,490	3,369,160	607,556	24,382	- - -	21.1	20.0	29.5	- - -	- - -	104.7	99.8	142.6	- - -	- - -
1963[4,6]........	4,098,020	3,326,344	580,658	22,358	- - -	21.7	20.7	- - -	- - -	- - -	108.3	103.6	- - -	- - -	- - -
1962[4,6]........	4,167,362	3,394,068	584,610	21,968	- - -	22.4	21.4	- - -	- - -	- - -	112.0	107.5	- - -	- - -	- - -
1961[4]........	4,268,326	3,600,864	611,072	21,464	- - -	23.3	22.2	- - -	- - -	- - -	117.1	112.3	- - -	- - -	- - -
1960[4]........	4,257,850	3,600,744	602,264	21,114	- - -	23.7	22.7	31.9	- - -	- - -	118.0	113.2	153.5	- - -	- - -
Births adjusted for underregistration															
Race of child:															
1955........	4,097,000	3,485,000	- - -	- - -	- - -	25.0	23.8	- - -	- - -	- - -	118.3	113.7	- - -	- - -	- - -
1950........	3,632,000	3,108,000	- - -	- - -	- - -	24.1	23.0	- - -	- - -	- - -	106.2	102.3	- - -	- - -	- - -
1945........	2,858,000	2,471,000	- - -	- - -	- - -	20.4	19.7	- - -	- - -	- - -	85.9	83.4	- - -	- - -	- - -
1940........	2,559,000	2,199,000	- - -	- - -	- - -	19.4	18.6	- - -	- - -	- - -	79.9	77.1	- - -	- - -	- - -

[1]For 1960–91 includes births to races not shown separately; see Technical notes.
[2]Includes births to Aleuts and Eskimos.
[3]Based on 100 percent of births in selected States and on a 50-percent sample of births in all other States; see Technical notes.
[4]Based on a 50-percent sample of births.
[5]Based on a 20- to 50-percent sample of births.
[6]Figures by race exclude data for New Jersey.

Source: S. J. Ventura, J. A. Martin, S. M. Taffel, et. al., National Center for Health Statistics, *Advance Report of Final Natality Statistics, 1992,* Monthly Vital Statistics Report, Vol. 43, No. 5 (suppl.), (PHS) 95-1120 4-0677, Washington, D.C.: U.S. Department of Health and Human Services, October 25, 1994, Table 1.

A2-8. Number of Births, Rates, and Percent of Births with Selected Demographic Characteristics, by Race of Mother Including Asian National Origins: 1992

Characteristic	All races	White	Black	American Indian [1]	Asian or Pacific Islander					
					Total	Chinese	Japanese	Hawaiian	Filipino	Other
	Number									
Births	4,065,014	3,201,678	673,633	39,453	150,250	25,061	9,098	5,883	28,959	81,249
	Rate									
Birth rate [2]	15.9	15.0	21.3	18.4	18.0	- - -	- - -	- - -	- - -	- - -
Fertility rate [3]	68.9	66.5	83.2	75.4	67.2	- - -	- - -	- - -	- - -	- - -
Total fertility rate [4]	2,065.0	1,993.5	2,442.0	2,190.0	1,942.0	- - -	- - -	- - -	- - -	- - -
Sex ratio [5]	1,050	1,053	1,036	1,034	1,065	1,065	1,049	1,064	1,083	1,062
	Percent									
Births to mothers under 20 years	12.7	10.9	22.7	20.0	5.6	1.0	2.6	18.4	5.6	6.4
Fourth- and higher-order births	10.8	9.6	16.0	22.4	10.4	3.2	3.8	15.4	7.2	14.2
Interval since last live birth of less than 18 months [6]	13.2	11.7	19.6	19.6	15.0	10.3	6.9	18.7	11.7	17.8
Births to unmarried mothers	30.1	22.6	68.1	55.3	14.7	6.1	9.8	45.7	16.8	14.9
Mothers completing 12 years or more of school	76.4	77.7	70.0	64.1	81.0	84.8	97.6	81.4	90.7	74.3
Mothers born in the United States	83.0	84.2	91.8	95.9	14.8	9.1	49.1	97.5	14.3	6.8

[1]Includes births to Aleuts and Eskimos.
[2]Rate per 1,000 population.
[3]Rate per 1,000 women aged 15–44 years.
[4]Rates are sums of birth rates for 5-year age groups multiplied by 5.
[5]Male live births per 1,000 female live births.
[6]Refers only to second- and higher-order births.

Source: S. J. Ventura, J. A. Martin, S. M. Taffel, et. al., National Center for Health Statistics, *Advance Report of Final Natality Statistics, 1992*, Monthly Vital Statistics Report, Vol. 43, No. 5 (suppl.), (PHS) 95-1120 4-0677, Washington, D.C.: U.S. Department of Health and Human Services, October 25, 1994, Figure 1, Table 10.

A2-9. Number of Births, Rates, and Percent of Births with Selected Demographic Characteristics for Hispanic Origin Mothers and Race of Non-Hispanic Mothers: 1992 (49 Reporting States and the District of Columbia)

Characteristic	All origins [1]	Origin of mother								
		Hispanic						Non-Hispanic		
		Total	Mexican	Puerto Rican	Cuban	Central and South American	Other and unknown Hispanic	Total [2]	White	Black
	Number									
Births	4,049,024	643,271	432,047	59,569	11,472	89,031	51,152	3,365,862	2,527,207	657,450
	Rate [3]									
Birth rate [4]	15.9	26.5	27.8	23.2	10.1	27.9		14.8	13.5	21.9
Fertility rate [5]	68.9	108.6	116.0	89.9	50.3	107.0		64.4	60.2	85.5
Total fertility rate [6]	2,065.0	3,043.0	3,196.5	2,644.5	1,485.5	3,076.0		1,941.0	1,810.5	2,514.0
Sex ratio [7]	1,050	1,041	1,040	1,057	1,079	1,040	1,030	1,052	1,056	1,036
	Percent									
Births to mothers under 20 years	12.8	17.1	18.0	21.4	7.1	9.6	20.0	12.0	9.4	22.9
Fourth- and higher-order births	10.8	15.2	16.6	13.3	6.6	12.5	12.1	10.0	8.2	16.0
Interval since last live birth of less than 18 months [8]	13.3	15.8	16.2	17.9	10.6	12.9	15.9	12.8	10.6	19.7
Births to unmarried mothers	30.2	39.1	36.3	57.5	20.2	43.9	37.6	28.5	18.5	68.3
Mothers completing 12 years or more of school	76.4	45.9	38.7	59.0	84.4	56.4	65.3	82.1	85.5	70.2
Mothers born in the United States	82.9	37.5	36.4	58.9	27.7	5.6	80.2	91.6	95.6	93.0

[1]Includes origin not stated.
[2]Includes races other than white and black.
[3]Birth, fertility, and total fertility rates by Hispanic origin are estimated for the United States. Rates for Hispanic women are based on birth data for 49 reporting States and the District of Columbia. Births for New Hampshire, which did not require reporting of Hispanic origin, and births with origin not stated are included in the rates for non-Hispanic women. See Technical notes.
[4]Rate per 1,000 population.
[5]Rate per 1,000 women aged 15–44 years.
[6]Rates are sums of birth rates for 5-year age groups multiplied by 5.
[7]Male live births per 1,000 female live births.
[8]Refers only to second- and higher-order births.

Source: S. J. Ventura, J. A. Martin, S. M. Taffel, et. al., National Center for Health Statistics, *Advance Report of Final Natality Statistics, 1992*, Monthly Vital Statistics Report, Vol. 43, No. 5 (suppl.), (PHS) 95-1120 4-0677, Washington, D.C.: U.S. Department of Health and Human Services, October 25, 1994, Figure 1, Table 11.

A2-10. Live Births, by Age, Place of Birth of Mother, and Hispanic Origin of Mother, and by Race of Mothers of Non-Hispanic Origin: 1990 (48 Reporting States and the District of Columbia)

Age and place of birth of mother	All origins	Origin of mother									Not stated
		Hispanic						Non-Hispanic			
		Total	Mexican	Puerto Rican	Cuban	Central and South American	Other and unknown Hispanic	Total [1]	White	Black	
ALL PLACES OF BIRTH [2]											
All ages	4,092,994	595,073	385,640	58,807	11,311	83,008	56,307	3,457,417	2,626,500	661,701	40,504
Under 15 years	11,535	2,346	1,556	360	16	132	282	9,104	2,602	6,204	85
15-19 years	512,978	97,685	66,615	12,420	851	7,377	10,422	410,841	249,954	147,521	4,452
15 years	27,363	5,790	3,849	837	35	383	686	21,340	8,854	11,736	233
16 years	57,033	12,064	8,112	1,678	87	782	1,405	44,475	22,793	20,227	494
17 years	96,055	19,329	13,222	2,485	165	1,351	2,106	75,867	44,127	29,287	859
18 years	142,503	26,839	18,514	3,333	251	2,009	2,732	114,471	71,752	39,055	1,193
19 years	190,024	33,663	22,918	4,087	313	2,852	3,493	154,688	102,428	47,216	1,673
20-24 years	1,075,072	189,193	127,893	19,811	2,176	22,207	17,106	876,268	631,233	210,491	9,611
25-29 years	1,256,814	166,105	104,560	15,071	4,420	26,704	15,350	1,078,760	863,490	162,091	11,949
30-34 years	873,275	96,079	58,438	7,834	2,680	17,882	9,245	767,560	627,057	95,653	9,636
35-39 years	313,630	36,374	22,113	2,729	1,006	7,249	3,277	273,220	219,811	34,215	4,036
40-44 years	48,067	6,971	4,270	550	156	1,393	602	40,386	31,508	5,341	710
45-49 years	1,623	320	195	32	6	64	23	1,278	845	185	25
U.S. BORN											
All ages	3,442,794	230,587	146,978	33,296	2,324	3,675	44,314	3,178,092	2,512,837	614,123	34,115
Under 15 years	10,462	1,589	1,060	236	11	17	265	8,799	2,549	6,086	74
15-19 years	453,512	53,105	34,041	8,385	436	912	9,331	396,378	244,559	143,620	4,029
15 years	24,695	3,815	2,496	603	15	63	638	20,665	8,708	11,505	215
16 years	50,954	7,444	4,827	1,147	52	125	1,293	43,056	22,364	19,785	454
17 years	85,022	10,874	7,074	1,640	89	180	1,891	73,374	43,257	28,567	774
18 years	125,661	14,032	8,970	2,262	125	230	2,445	110,553	70,297	37,972	1,076
19 years	167,180	16,940	10,674	2,733	155	314	3,064	148,730	99,933	45,791	1,510
20-24 years	907,336	74,677	46,941	11,732	701	1,344	13,959	824,408	609,563	200,440	8,251
25-29 years	1,054,398	58,016	36,857	7,994	805	860	11,500	986,489	825,545	147,235	9,893
30-34 years	726,742	31,168	20,019	3,820	286	402	6,641	687,523	594,572	83,169	8,051
35-39 years	253,176	10,342	6,890	1,018	77	127	2,230	239,567	206,385	29,049	3,267
40-44 years	36,208	1,635	1,134	106	8	13	374	34,038	28,935	4,389	535
45-49 years	960	55	36	5	–	–	14	890	729	135	15
FOREIGN OR PUERTO RICAN BORN											
All ages	642,264	363,684	238,269	25,398	8,983	79,304	11,730	273,271	110,581	44,927	5,309
Under 15 years	1,014	753	492	124	5	115	17	257	39	84	4
15-19 years	57,920	44,423	32,495	4,008	414	6,463	1,043	13,241	4,844	3,268	256
15 years	2,563	1,962	1,345	232	20	320	45	594	121	175	7
16 years	5,861	4,595	3,275	526	35	656	103	1,247	353	351	19
17 years	10,717	8,428	6,134	841	76	1,170	207	2,241	762	583	48
18 years	16,480	12,774	9,525	1,065	126	1,779	279	3,626	1,322	931	80
19 years	22,299	16,664	12,216	1,344	157	2,538	409	5,533	2,286	1,228	102
20-24 years	165,338	114,242	80,823	8,040	1,474	20,849	3,056	50,057	20,792	9,212	1,039
25-29 years	200,408	107,894	67,598	7,052	3,613	25,838	3,793	90,751	37,150	14,220	1,763
30-34 years	145,188	64,784	38,358	3,999	2,394	17,474	2,559	79,014	31,900	12,117	1,390
35-39 years	59,970	25,998	15,212	1,705	929	7,121	1,031	33,280	13,210	5,041	692
40-44 years	11,771	5,326	3,133	443	148	1,380	222	6,287	2,532	937	158
45-49 years	655	264	158	27	6	64	9	384	114	48	7

[1] Includes races other than white and black.
[2] Includes births with place of birth of mother not stated.

Source: National Center for Health Statistics, *Vital Statistics of the United States, 1990*, Vol. 1 (Natality), Washington, D.C.: U.S. Government Printing Office, 1994, Table 1-43.

A2-11. Birth Rates, by Age of Mother: 1960 to 1992

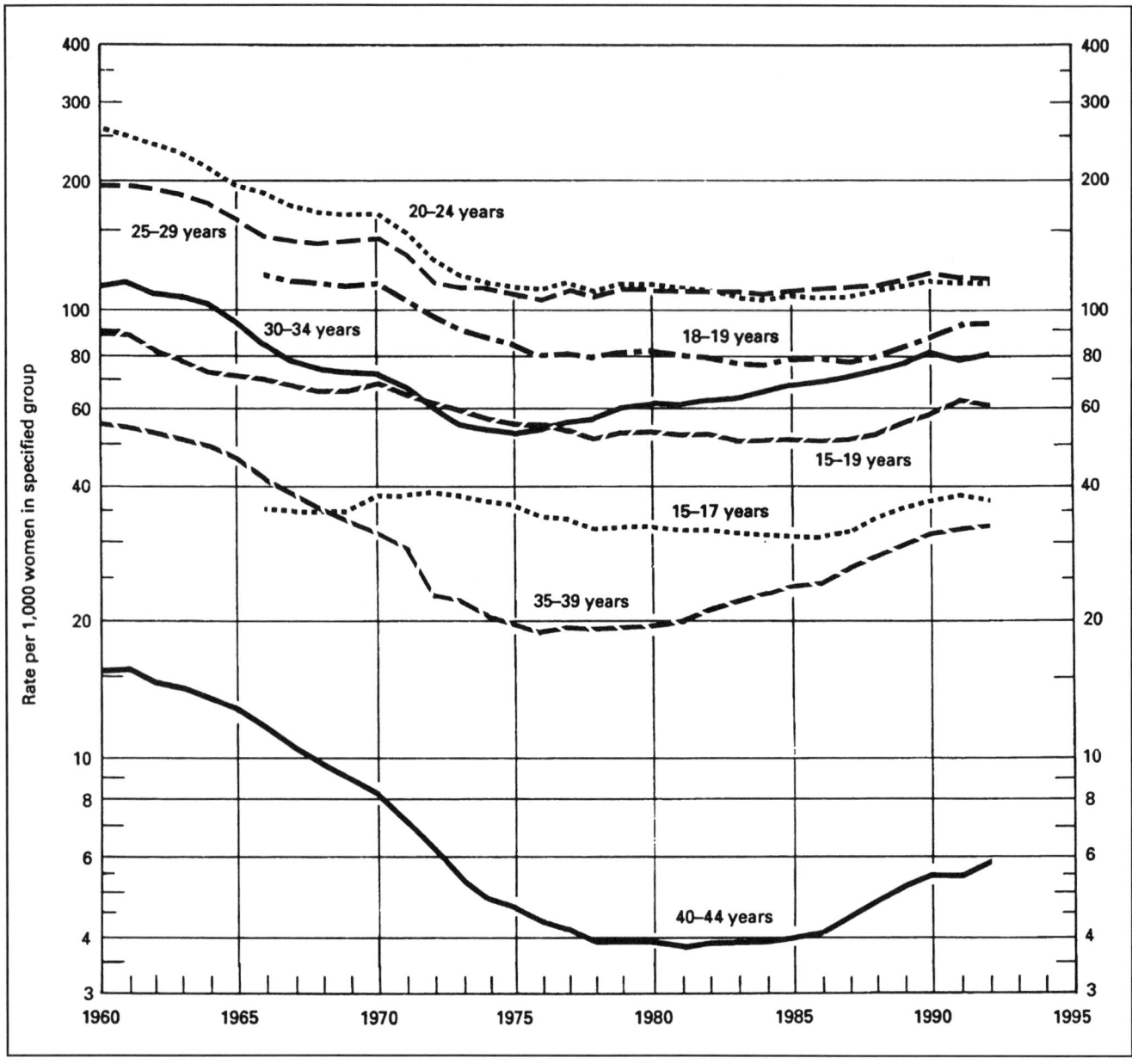

Source: S. J. Ventura, J. A. Martin, S. M. Taffel, et. al., National Center for Health Statistics, *Advance Report of Final Natality Statistics, 1992*, Monthly Vital Statistics Report, Vol. 43, No. 5 (suppl.), (PHS) 95-1120 4-0677, Washington, D.C.: U.S. Department of Health and Human Services, October 25, 1994, Figure 2.

A2-12. Percentage of Pregnancies among Women Aged 15 to 19 Ending in Birth: 1972 to 1990

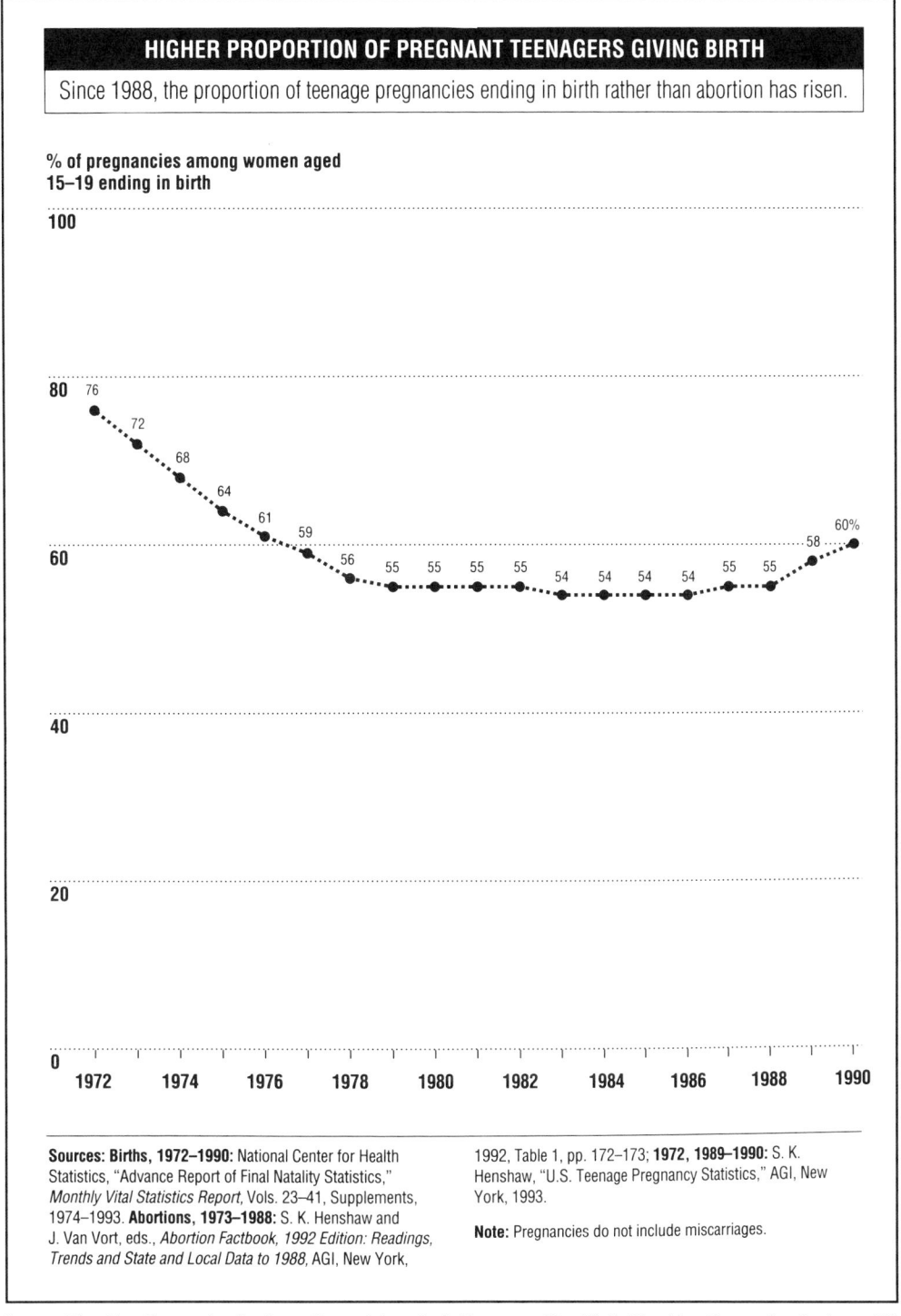

HIGHER PROPORTION OF PREGNANT TEENAGERS GIVING BIRTH

Since 1988, the proportion of teenage pregnancies ending in birth rather than abortion has risen.

% of pregnancies among women aged
15–19 ending in birth

Sources: Births, 1972–1990: National Center for Health Statistics, "Advance Report of Final Natality Statistics," *Monthly Vital Statistics Report*, Vols. 23–41, Supplements, 1974–1993. **Abortions, 1973–1988:** S. K. Henshaw and J. Van Vort, eds., *Abortion Factbook, 1992 Edition: Readings, Trends and State and Local Data to 1988*, AGI, New York, 1992, Table 1, pp. 172–173; **1972, 1989–1990:** S. K. Henshaw, "U.S. Teenage Pregnancy Statistics," AGI, New York, 1993.

Note: Pregnancies do not include miscarriages.

Source: The Alan Guttmacher Institute, *Sex and America's Teenagers*, New York: The Alan Guttmacher Institute, 1994, Figure 33. Reprinted with permission.

A2-13. Projected Fertility Rates, by Age and Race: 1992 and 2010

(The total fertility rate is the number of births that 1,000 women would have in their lifetime if, at each year of age, they experienced the birth rates occurring in the specified year. Birth rates represent live births per 1,000 women in age group indicated. Projections are based on middle fertility assumptions.)

AGE GROUP	ALL RACES [1]		WHITE		BLACK		ASIAN AND PACIFIC ISLANDERS		AMERICAN INDIAN, ESKIMO, ALEUT		HISPANIC [2]	
	1992	2010	1992	2010	1992	2010	1992	2010	1992	2010	1992	2010
Total fertility rate ..	2,054	2,092	1,953	1,981	2,468	2,459	2,335	2,271	2,874	2,855	2,655	2,588
Birth rates:												
10 to 14 years old....	1.4	1.5	0.6	0.7	5.3	5.2	0.6	0.6	1.9	1.9	2.3	2.2
15 to 19 years old....	57.3	58.7	46.7	48.5	113.7	112.7	28.3	27.2	105.9	105.5	86.3	84.1
20 to 24 years old....	118.0	120.0	109.8	112.1	161.6	160.8	95.8	93.1	210.5	209.0	163.2	159.1
25 to 29 years old....	120.0	121.0	119.8	120.0	113.8	113.6	152.2	149.1	142.1	141.1	139.1	135.6
30 to 34 years old....	79.2	80.5	79.7	79.9	66.6	66.6	123.8	120.7	76.2	75.8	88.6	86.4
35 to 39 years old....	29.6	31.0	29.1	29.9	27.2	27.3	53.6	52.2	31.2	31.1	41.3	40.2
40 to 44 years old....	4.9	5.4	4.7	5.0	5.2	5.3	11.3	11.0	6.7	6.8	9.7	9.5
45 to 49 years old....	0.2	0.3	0.2	0.2	0.3	0.3	1.3	1.2	0.4	0.4	0.6	0.6

[1] Includes other races not shown separately.   [2] Persons of Hispanic origin may be of any race.

Source: U.S. Bureau of the Census, *Current Population Reports*, series P25-1092; and unpublished data.

Source: U.S. Bureau of the Census, *Statistical Abstract of the United States: 1993*, (113th edition), Washington, D.C.: U.S. Government Printing Office, 1993, Table 96.

A2-14. Percent Distribution of Births, by Race and Hispanic Origin: 1990 to 2050

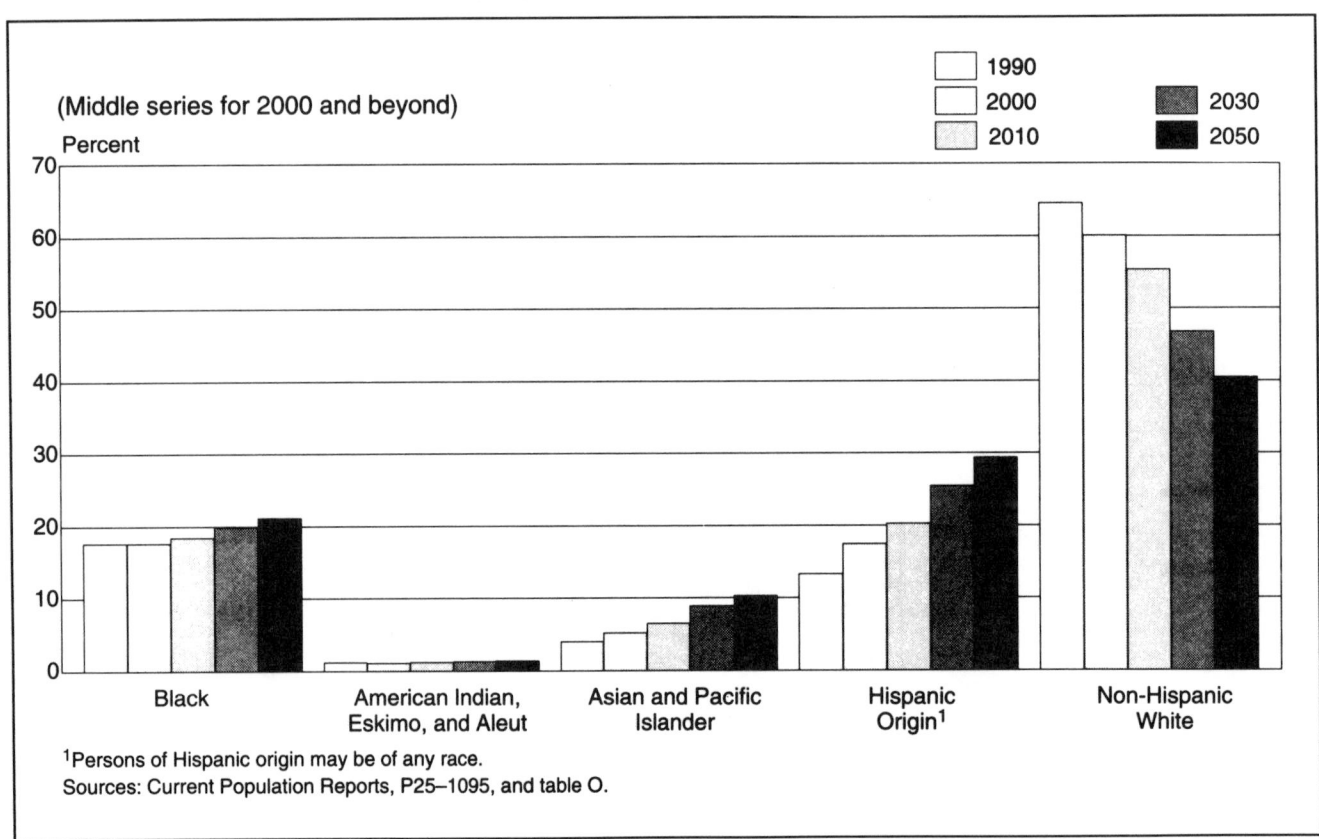

Source: Jennifer Cheeseman Day, U.S. Bureau of the Census, *Population Projections of the United States, by Age, Sex, Race, and Hispanic Origin: 1993 to 2050*, Current Population Reports, Series P25-1104, Washington, D.C.: U.S. Government Printing Office, November 1993, Figure 15.

A2-15. Children Ever Born, by Age, Race, and Hispanic Origin of Mother: 1990

(Data based on sample and subject to sampling variability.)

United States	All persons	Race					Hispanic origin (of any race)	White, not of Hispanic origin
		White	Black	American Indian, Eskimo, or Aleut	Asian or Pacific Islander	Other race		
FERTILITY								
Women 15 to 24 years	**17 769 944**	**13 506 701**	**2 585 136**	**169 637**	**581 261**	**927 209**	**1 938 311**	**12 563 441**
Children ever born	5 420 229	3 425 411	1 334 675	90 637	91 653	477 853	901 379	3 034 019
Per 1,000 women	305	254	516	534	158	515	465	241
Women ever married	3 726 372	3 038 939	303 504	38 482	82 769	262 678	521 219	2 794 858
Children ever born	3 462 487	2 654 608	379 107	49 917	67 530	311 325	601 407	2 380 981
Per 1,000 women	929	874	1 249	1 297	816	1 185	1 154	852
Women 25 to 34 years	**21 757 561**	**17 017 533**	**2 872 381**	**186 646**	**725 215**	**955 786**	**2 076 193**	**15 973 799**
Children ever born	28 942 178	21 391 915	4 634 379	352 449	779 523	1 783 912	3 607 708	19 694 202
Per 1,000 women	1 330	1 257	1 613	1 888	1 075	1 866	1 738	1 233
Women ever married	16 431 453	13 482 011	1 536 979	136 936	550 528	724 999	1 577 448	12 680 774
Children ever born	26 088 416	20 568 607	2 943 447	294 715	749 218	1 532 429	3 151 021	19 047 492
Per 1,000 women	1 588	1 526	1 915	2 152	1 361	2 114	1 998	1 502
Women 35 to 44 years	**19 012 425**	**15 317 704**	**2 255 515**	**150 205**	**672 487**	**616 514**	**1 457 001**	**14 536 139**
Children ever born	37 260 340	28 769 752	5 075 478	372 668	1 299 946	1 742 496	3 769 710	26 883 666
Per 1,000 women	1 960	1 878	2 250	2 481	1 933	2 826	2 587	1 849
No children	3 459 251	2 928 170	326 498	19 659	123 120	61 804	176 433	2 822 064
1 child	3 196 133	2 554 439	435 387	22 464	115 288	68 555	185 369	2 445 965
2 children	6 589 685	5 523 130	628 185	41 220	244 357	152 793	397 944	5 294 225
3 children	3 605 811	2 861 816	443 449	31 929	119 176	149 441	337 560	2 687 114
4 children	1 357 031	978 612	227 256	18 226	41 685	91 252	187 143	889 572
5 or more children	804 514	471 537	194 740	16 707	28 861	92 669	172 552	397 199
Women ever married	17 154 920	14 092 322	1 764 689	134 368	617 501	546 040	1 298 473	13 390 046
Children ever born	36 033 647	28 477 832	4 299 316	351 771	1 285 080	1 619 648	3 548 525	26 676 224
Per 1,000 women	2 100	2 021	2 436	2 618	2 081	2 966	2 733	1 992

Source: U.S. Bureau of the Census, *Social and Economic Characteristics of the United States: 1990 Census of Population*, CP-2-1, Washington, D.C.: U.S. Government Printing Office, 1993, Table 41.

A2-16. Distribution of Women and Average Number of Children Ever Born, by Race, Age, and Marital Status: June 1994

Percent distribution. Numbers in thousands.

Characteristic	Total women	Women by number of children ever born								Children ever born	
		Total	None	One	Two	Three	Four	Five and six	Seven or more	Total number	Per 1,000 women
ALL RACES											
All Marital Classes											
15 to 44 years	60,088	100.0	42.0	17.9	23.0	11.5	3.7	1.6	.3	74,644	1,242
15 to 19 years	8,798	100.0	91.5	6.9	1.3	.2	.1	–	–	913	104
20 to 24 years	9,310	100.0	65.3	20.9	9.5	3.3	.8	.2	–	5,051	542
25 to 29 years	9,785	100.0	43.6	23.2	20.2	9.2	2.8	.9	.1	10,541	1,077
30 to 34 years	11,131	100.0	26.3	21.0	30.4	15.1	4.4	2.4	.4	17,836	1,602
35 to 39 years	11,093	100.0	19.6	16.8	35.5	19.0	5.9	2.5	.6	20,710	1,867
40 to 44 years	9,972	100.0	17.5	17.1	35.3	18.9	7.0	3.3	.8	19,593	1,965
Women Ever Married											
15 to 44 years	37,355	100.0	19.1	22.5	33.8	16.8	5.2	2.2	.5	65,954	1,766
15 to 19 years	393	100.0	49.2	43.5	6.8	.4	–	–	–	230	584
20 to 24 years	3,189	100.0	37.4	36.4	19.2	5.6	1.0	.3	.1	3,120	978
25 to 29 years	6,283	100.0	28.9	29.0	26.7	11.5	3.0	.9	.1	8,420	1,340
30 to 34 years	8,898	100.0	17.5	22.8	34.9	17.3	4.8	2.3	.4	15,912	1,788
35 to 39 years	9,584	100.0	13.3	17.0	39.2	20.9	6.4	2.5	.7	19,408	2,025
40 to 44 years	9,009	100.0	12.1	17.6	38.2	20.5	7.4	3.4	.8	18,863	2,094
Women Never Married											
15 to 44 years	22,733	100.0	79.8	10.3	5.2	2.7	1.2	.7	.1	8,690	382
15 to 19 years	8,405	100.0	93.5	5.2	1.0	.2	.1	–	–	683	81
20 to 24 years	6,121	100.0	79.8	12.9	4.4	2.1	.7	.2	–	1,930	315
25 to 29 years	3,502	100.0	70.0	13.0	8.4	5.2	2.5	.8	.2	2,121	606
30 to 34 years	2,233	100.0	61.4	14.1	12.3	6.4	2.8	2.6	.3	1,924	862
35 to 39 years	1,509	100.0	59.9	15.5	12.3	7.0	2.5	2.4	.3	1,302	863
40 to 44 years	963	100.0	68.4	12.6	7.9	4.4	3.4	1.9	1.3	730	758

Source: Amara Bachu, U.S. Bureau of the Census, *Fertility of American Women: June 1994*, Current Population Reports, P20-482, Washington, D.C.: U.S. Government Printing Office, September, 1995, Table 1.

A2-17. Women Who Had a Child in Year before Survey Date and Their Percentage in the Labor Force, by Selected Characteristics: June 1994 and June 1990

[Numbers in thousands]

Characteristic	July 1993 to June 1994		July 1989 to June 1990	
	Number	Percent in labor force	Number	Percent in labor force
Total	3,890	53.1	3,913	52.8
EDUCATIONAL ATTAINMENT				
Less than high school	832	33.5	816	31.5
High school, 4 years	1,303	48.1	1,588	51.9
College, 1 or more years	1,754	66.2	1,509	65.3
No degree	679	59.9	777	[1]62.8
Associate degree	302	71.1	(NA)	(NA)
Bachelor's degree and above	773	69.7	732	[2]68.0
AGE				
15 to 19 years	397	39.3	338	42.8
20 to 24 years	938	51.0	1,038	45.5
25 to 29 years	1,054	54.5	1,192	55.3
30 to 44 years	1,501	57.1	1,346	58.9
BIRTH ORDER AND AGE OF WOMAN				
First Birth	1,647	59.0	1,540	59.7
15 to 19 years	319	40.1	255	48.0
20 to 24 years	544	56.5	474	56.1
25 to 29 years	429	67.5	491	63.1
30 to 44 years	355	69.2	319	69.1
Second or higher order birth	2,242	48.9	2,374	48.4
15 to 19 years	78	36.1	83	26.9
20 to 24 years	394	43.4	564	36.5
25 to 29 years	624	45.6	701	49.8
30 to 44 years	1,146	53.4	1,026	55.7
RACE				
White	3,107	55.4	3,148	54.5
Black	567	47.0	615	46.9
Asian or Pacific Islander	112	37.7	101	48.0
HISPANIC ORIGIN				
Hispanic[3]	644	37.7	491	43.8
Not Hispanic	3,245	56.2	3,422	54.1
MARITAL STATUS				
Married, husband present	2,798	54.5	2,826	56.4
Widowed, divorced or separated[4]	199	52.0	319	50.9
Never married	892	49.0	769	40.4

[1] 1 to 3 years of college completed.
[2] 4 or more years of college completed.
[3] Persons of Hispanic origin may be of any race.
[4] Includes married, husband absent.

Source: June Current Population Survey, 1990 and 1994.

Source: Amara Bachu, U.S. Bureau of the Census, *Fertility of American Women: June 1994*, Current Population Reports, P20-482, Washington, D.C.: U.S. Government Printing Office, September, 1995, Table I.

A2-18. Live Births, by Educational Attainment of Mother, and by Age and Race of Mother: 1992

Age and race of mother	Total	Years of school completed by mother					
		0–8 years	9–11 years	12 years	13–15 years	16 years or more	Not stated
All races[1]							
All ages	4,065,014	259,238	683,287	1,468,019	834,965	754,963	64,542
Under 15 years	12,220	9,234	2,411	–	–	–	575
15–19 years	505,415	52,889	269,593	153,661	20,015	–	9,257
15 years	29,267	10,202	18,115	–	–	–	950
16 years	60,136	9,270	47,992	1,673	–	–	1,201
17 years	98,146	9,388	73,119	13,519	286	–	1,834
18 years	138,663	10,981	68,477	53,445	3,456	–	2,304
19 years	179,203	13,048	61,890	85,024	16,273	–	2,968
20–24 years	1,070,490	70,776	224,399	500,201	214,541	44,440	16,133
25–29 years	1,179,264	59,409	111,472	440,663	298,458	251,936	17,326
30–34 years	895,271	40,765	53,717	269,541	212,971	304,338	13,939
35–39 years	344,644	20,552	18,508	90,258	77,351	131,992	5,983
40 years and over.	57,710	5,613	3,187	13,695	11,629	22,257	1,329
White							
All ages	3,201,678	218,804	484,604	1,132,244	666.637	654,504	44,885
Under 15 years	5,367	4,083	1,032	–	–	–	252
15–19 years	342,739	42,053	177,118	104,493	13,281	–	5,794
15 years	15,966	6,005	9,468	–	–	–	493
16 years	37,256	6,811	28,771	999	–	–	675
17 years	65,564	7,919	47,436	8,860	210	–	1,139
18 years	95,949	9,625	46,975	35,667	2,191	–	1,491
19 years	128,004	11,693	44,468	58,967	10,880	–	1,996
20–24 years	814,422	63,254	169,061	373,498	161,673	36,000	10,936
25–29 years	964,586	52,524	84,354	353,897	243,304	218,135	12,372
30–34 years	745,510	35,335	38,285	218,873	176,132	266,682	10,203
35–39 years	282,617	17,147	12,589	71,092	62,938	114,455	4,396
40 years and over.	46,437	4,408	2,165	10,391	9,309	19,232	932
Black							
All ages	673,633	23,551	174,010	278,582	132,016	51,202	14,272
Under 15 years	6,448	4,855	1,293	–	–	–	300
15–19 years	146,800	9,204	84,369	44,238	5,997	–	2,992
15 years	12,432	3,939	8,068	–	–	–	425
16 years	20,970	2,210	17,677	616	–	–	467
17 years	29,600	1,208	23,516	4,214	63	–	599
18 years	38,362	988	19,530	16,040	1,104	–	700
19 years	45,436	859	15,578	23,368	4,830	–	801
20–24 years	216,057	3,433	48,231	109,942	44,675	5,852	3,924
25–29 years	157,960	2,511	22,396	69,549	42,708	17,367	3,429
30–34 years	100,339	1,976	12,333	38,395	27,103	18,056	2,476
35–39 years	39,389	1,255	4,635	14,088	9,973	8,482	956
40 years and over.	6,640	317	753	2,370	1,560	1,445	195

[1]Includes races other than white and black.

Source: S. J. Ventura, J. A. Martin, S. M. Taffel, et. al., National Center for Health Statistics, *Advance Report of Final Natality Statistics, 1992,* Monthly Vital Statistics Report, Vol. 43, No. 5 (suppl.), (PHS) 95-1120 4-0677, Washington, D.C.: U.S. Department of Health and Human Services, October 25, 1994, Table 18.

A2-19. Live Births, by Educational Attainment of Mother, by Place of Birth, and by Specified Race or National Origin (Selected Asian Origins) of Mother and of Child: 1990 (48 Reporting States, the District of Columbia, and New York City)

Years of school completed by mother and place of birth of mother	All races [1]	White	Black	American Indian [2]	Chinese	Japanese	Hawaiian	Filipino	Other Asian or Pacific Islander
	Race of Mother								
ALL PLACES OF BIRTH [3]									
Total	3,916,583	3,077,143	664,880	36,856	22,347	8,426	6,046	25,314	72,672
0-8 years	246,481	206,374	22,909	1,790	1,807	75	112	795	12,087
9-11 years	672,563	475,502	173,924	11,368	1,677	221	1,053	1,801	6,600
12 years	1,479,183	1,141,432	282,961	15,292	6,162	2,072	3,409	6,569	20,414
13-15 years	783,275	625,926	125,118	6,124	3,496	2,314	1,049	7,310	11,457
16 years or more	674,043	584,288	47,131	1,595	8,850	3,681	410	8,649	18,918
Not stated	61,038	43,621	12,837	687	355	63	13	190	3,196
Percent Completing 12 Years or More	76.2	77.5	69.8	63.6	84.2	96.5	80.7	89.7	73.1
U.S. BORN									
Total	3,290,168	2,622,670	610,762	35,619	2,308	4,490	5,808	3,885	4,072
0-8 years	84,962	64,702	18,241	1,645	52	30	70	84	120
9-11 years	567,287	387,762	165,977	11,202	69	142	1,025	553	445
12 years	1,313,763	1,028,097	262,941	14,952	272	1,044	3,317	1,678	1,246
13-15 years	697,169	572,101	114,566	5,924	473	1,148	1,012	1,026	820
16 years or more	584,794	538,062	39,580	1,303	1,419	2,121	375	527	1,322
Not stated	42,193	31,946	9,457	593	23	5	9	17	119
Percent Completing 12 Years or More	79.9	82.5	69.4	63.3	94.7	96.2	81.1	83.5	85.7
FOREIGN BORN									
Total	619,373	450,586	51,286	1,113	20,016	3,932	237	21,416	68,460
0-8 years	161,148	141,397	4,587	144	1,754	44	42	709	11,957
9-11 years	104,132	87,201	7,392	131	1,608	79	28	1,246	6,142
12 years	163,502	112,345	19,198	283	5,882	1,028	92	4,888	19,141
13-15 years	85,583	53,511	10,380	192	3,022	1,165	36	6,284	10,614
16 years or more	88,884	45,946	7,493	290	7,424	1,558	35	8,119	17,583
Not stated	16,124	10,186	2,236	73	326	58	4	170	3,023
Percent Completing 12 Years or More	56.0	48.1	75.6	73.6	82.9	96.8	70.0	90.8	72.3
	Race of Child								
ALL PLACES OF BIRTH [3]									
Total	3,916,583	3,016,514	702,537	46,082	23,819	10,141	8,636	26,740	78,422
0-8 years	246,481	204,685	24,035	2,039	1,823	92	131	818	12,283
9-11 years	672,563	463,347	182,319	13,452	1,724	296	1,347	2,128	7,432
12 years	1,479,183	1,116,866	298,852	19,430	6,493	2,458	4,686	7,241	22,014
13-15 years	783,275	612,770	132,923	7,956	3,868	2,838	1,707	7,640	12,904
16 years or more	674,043	575,956	51,046	2,445	9,531	4,377	746	8,719	20,519
Not stated	61,038	42,890	13,362	760	380	80	19	194	3,270
Percent Completing 12 Years or More	76.2	77.5	70.1	65.8	84.9	96.1	82.8	88.9	73.8
U.S. BORN									
Total	3,290,168	2,569,203	641,933	44,381	3,614	5,883	8,081	6,307	9,556
0-8 years	84,962	63,561	18,965	1,861	67	40	83	115	227
9-11 years	567,287	376,799	173,304	13,215	117	198	1,297	923	1,238
12 years	1,313,763	1,006,181	276,217	18,907	558	1,365	4,446	2,605	3,028
13-15 years	697,169	560,514	120,950	7,648	782	1,581	1,572	1,689	2,174
16 years or more	584,794	530,785	42,634	2,097	2,051	2,677	668	943	2,707
Not stated	42,193	31,363	9,863	653	39	22	15	32	182
Percent Completing 12 Years or More	79.9	82.6	69.6	65.5	94.9	95.9	82.9	83.5	84.4
FOREIGN BORN									
Total	619,373	443,476	57,733	1,572	20,181	4,253	553	20,418	68,722
0-8 years	161,148	140,851	4,988	177	1,754	51	48	701	12,046
9-11 years	104,132	86,019	8,451	201	1,607	98	50	1,203	6,181
12 years	163,502	109,706	21,801	466	5,927	1,093	239	4,634	18,958
13-15 years	85,583	51,954	11,791	300	3,086	1,255	134	5,951	10,706
16 years or more	88,884	44,894	8,354	345	7,473	1,698	78	7,772	17,798
Not stated	16,124	10,052	2,348	83	334	58	4	157	3,033
Percent Completing 12 Years or More	56.0	47.7	75.7	74.6	83.1	96.4	82.1	90.6	72.3

[1] Includes births of other races which are not shown separately.
[2] Includes births to Aleuts and Eskimos.
[3] Includes births with place of birth of mother not stated.

Source: National Center for Health Statistics, *Vital Statistics of the United States, 1990*, Vol. 1 (Natality), Washington, D.C.: U.S. Government Printing Office, 1994, Table 1-37.

A2-20. Live Births, by Educational Attainment of Mother, by Place of Birth and Hispanic Origin of Mother, and by Race of Mothers of Non-Hispanic Origin: 1990 (46 Reporting States, the District of Columbia, and New York City)

Years of school completed by mother and place of birth of mother	All origins	Origin of mother									Not stated
		Hispanic						Non-Hispanic			
		Total	Mexican	Puerto Rican	Cuban	Central and South American	Other and unknown Hispanic	Total [1]	White	Black	
ALL PLACES OF BIRTH [2]											
Total	3,851,365	580,142	380,963	55,437	11,121	79,446	53,175	3,235,748	2,431,695	643,178	35,475
0-8 years	244,778	153,363	125,046	4,505	423	19,802	3,587	88,888	52,003	21,115	2,527
9-11 years	661,286	153,644	105,650	18,289	1,546	14,530	13,629	503,098	314,070	168,886	4,544
12 years	1,452,643	168,217	98,365	18,729	3,691	25,862	21,570	1,273,501	949,060	274,798	10,925
13-15 years	770,394	65,230	34,474	8,358	3,123	10,741	8,534	699,760	548,064	121,626	5,404
16 years or more	663,137	28,906	12,206	3,416	2,229	6,655	4,400	627,851	540,868	45,744	6,380
Not stated	59,127	10,782	5,222	2,140	109	1,856	1,455	42,650	27,630	11,009	5,695
Percent Completing 12 Years or More	76.1	46.1	38.6	57.2	82.1	55.8	66.7	81.5	84.8	69.9	76.3
U.S. BORN											
Total	3,228,322	225,076	145,323	31,277	2,240	3,459	42,777	2,973,407	2,326,992	598,053	29,839
0-8 years	83,622	15,289	11,443	1,802	62	123	1,859	66,542	47,077	17,815	1,791
9-11 years	556,382	72,631	48,191	11,174	452	797	12,017	479,553	305,640	162,723	4,198
12 years	1,288,325	87,985	56,956	10,947	694	1,216	18,172	1,190,849	913,837	257,972	9,491
13-15 years	684,913	33,642	20,593	4,699	610	819	6,921	646,497	524,981	112,371	4,774
16 years or more	574,612	11,924	6,664	1,529	401	437	2,893	557,148	511,489	38,918	5,540
Not stated	40,468	3,605	1,476	1,126	21	67	915	32,818	23,968	8,254	4,045
Percent Completing 12 Years or More	79.9	60.3	58.5	57.0	76.8	72.9	66.9	81.4	84.7	69.4	76.8
FOREIGN OR PUERTO RICAN BORN											
Total	616,048	354,313	235,263	24,055	8,877	75,958	10,160	257,073	102,126	42,706	4,662
0-8 years	160,786	137,952	113,516	2,695	361	19,677	1,703	22,171	4,834	3,227	663
9-11 years	103,768	80,880	57,389	7,084	1,093	13,727	1,587	22,573	8,039	5,630	315
12 years	162,412	80,056	41,341	7,746	2,997	24,634	3,338	81,074	34,453	16,115	1,282
13-15 years	84,966	31,544	13,857	3,651	2,511	9,920	1,605	52,810	22,828	9,091	612
16 years or more	88,163	16,964	5,531	1,886	1,827	6,216	1,504	70,373	29,125	6,775	826
Not stated	15,953	6,917	3,629	993	88	1,784	423	8,072	2,847	1,868	964
Percent Completing 12 Years or More	55.9	37.0	26.2	57.6	83.5	55.0	66.2	82.0	87.0	78.3	73.6

[1] Includes races other than white and black.
[2] Includes births with place of birth of mother not stated.

Source: National Center for Health Statistics, *Vital Statistics of the United States, 1990*, Vol. 1 (Natality), Washington, D.C.: U.S. Government Printing Office, 1994, Table 1-45.

A3. BIRTH EXPECTATIONS AND CHILDLESSNESS

A3-1. Children Ever Born per 1,000 Women and Percent Childless, by Selected Characteristics: 1994

Characteristic	Women 15 to 24 years old			Women 25 to 34 years old			Women 35 to 44 years old		
	Number of women	Children ever born Per 1,000 women	Percent childless	Number of women	Children ever born Per 1,000 women	Percent childless	Number of women	Children ever born Per 1,000 women	Percent childless
REGION									
All Marital Classes									
Total	18,108	329	78.0	20,915	1,357	34.4	21,065	1,913	18.6
Northeast	3,378	248	83.8	4,099	1,158	41.7	4,279	1,765	21.6
Midwest	4,372	336	77.6	4,892	1,392	34.2	5,032	1,957	17.1
South	6,369	351	76.5	7,417	1,395	31.8	7,134	1,913	16.6
West	3,989	355	76.1	4,507	1,436	32.2	4,620	2,003	20.9
Women Ever Married									
Total	3,582	935	38.7	15,181	1,603	22.2	18,592	2,058	12.7
Northeast	367	953	41.2	2,640	1,459	25.6	3,643	1,939	14.2
Midwest	820	889	42.9	3,541	1,651	21.9	4,448	2,108	11.1
South	1,483	910	38.9	5,610	1,597	21.2	6,364	2,024	11.7
West	912	1,011	33.5	3,390	1,674	21.5	4,137	2,163	14.7
Women Never Married									
Total	14,526	180	87.7	5,734	705	66.6	2,472	822	63.2
Northeast	3,011	162	89.0	1,459	613	70.8	635	766	63.9
Midwest	3,552	209	85.6	1,351	715	66.5	584	805	62.8
South	4,887	182	87.9	1,808	768	64.6	770	999	56.5
West	3,077	161	88.7	1,117	713	64.6	483	633	73.5
EDUCATIONAL ATTAINMENT									
All Marital Classes									
Total	18,108	329	78.0	20,915	1,357	34.4	21,065	1,913	18.6
Not a high school graduate	7,525	296	82.5	2,610	2,281	13.6	2,234	2,678	9.4
High school, 4 years	4,114	560	61.2	7,180	1,580	24.8	7,248	2,020	14.1
College: 1 or more years	6,469	221	83.5	11,125	996	45.5	11,582	1,699	23.2
Some college, no degree	4,495	237	82.4	4,148	1,289	33.9	4,029	1,890	17.0
Associate degree	686	338	72.6	1,957	1,126	37.0	2,113	1,847	18.2
Bachelors degree	1,224	104	93.1	3,973	729	57.4	3,654	1,576	27.9
Graduate or professional degree	64	(B)	(B)	1,047	605	62.3	1,786	1,342	33.7
Women Ever Married									
Total	3,582	935	38.7	15,181	1,603	22.2	18,592	2,058	12.7
Not a high school graduate	771	1,476	20.4	1,877	2,442	7.2	1,888	2,787	5.8
High school, 4 years	1,336	975	32.4	5,499	1,751	16.4	6,505	2,130	10.1
College: 1 or more years	1,475	616	53.9	7,806	1,297	29.9	10,199	1,878	15.7
Some college, no degree	903	750	45.7	3,060	1,545	22.7	3,592	2,042	10.9
Associate degree	263	624	49.9	1,481	1,347	25.0	1,910	1,979	12.8
Bachelors degree	285	217	80.8	2,615	1,069	38.4	3,195	1,772	19.6
Graduate or professional degree	24	(B)	(B)	649	929	41.5	1,502	1,579	22.4
Women Never Married									
Total	14,526	180	87.7	5,734	705	66.6	2,472	822	63.2
Not a high school graduate	6,754	162	89.6	733	1,870	30.1	346	2,084	29.4
High school, 4 years	2,778	360	75.0	1,682	1,021	52.0	743	1,056	49.7
College: 1 or more years	4,994	105	92.3	3,320	288	82.1	1,383	381	79.0
Some college, no degree	3,592	109	91.7	1,088	567	65.5	437	641	67.1
Associate degree	423	159	86.8	476	437	74.2	202	601	69.9
Bachelors degree	939	69	96.9	1,357	74	94.2	459	217	85.1
Graduate or professional degree	40	(B)	(B)	398	77	96.1	284	87	93.8

A3-1. Children Ever Born per 1,000 Women and Percent Childless, by Selected Characteristics: 1992 (continued)

Characteristic	Women 15 to 24 years old			Women 25 to 34 years old			Women 35 to 44 years old		
	Number of women	Children ever born Per 1,000 women	Percent childless	Number of women	Children ever born Per 1,000 women	Percent childless	Number of women	Children ever born Per 1,000 women	Percent childless
METROPOLITAN RESIDENCE									
All Marital Classes									
Total	18,108	329	78.0	20,915	1,357	34.4	21,065	1,913	18.6
Metropolitan	14,271	326	78.5	17,039	1,296	36.9	16,835	1,866	20.0
In central cities	5,865	399	73.9	6,861	1,368	37.2	6,118	1,792	23.2
Outside central cities	8,407	275	81.7	10,178	1,248	36.7	10,717	1,909	18.2
Nonmetropolitan	3,837	342	76.3	3,876	1,622	23.6	4,230	2,101	13.2
Women Ever Married									
Total	3,582	935	38.7	15,181	1,603	22.2	18,592	2,058	12.7
Metropolitan	2,651	924	40.1	12,039	1,548	24.2	14,689	2,022	13.5
In central cities	1,113	919	39.0	4,319	1,651	22.9	4,953	1,987	14.9
Outside central cities	1,538	928	40.9	7,720	1,491	24.8	9,736	2,040	12.8
Nonmetropolitan	931	967	34.7	3,142	1,811	14.8	3,903	2,196	9.8
Women Never Married									
Total	14,526	180	87.7	5,734	705	66.6	2,472	822	63.2
Metropolitan	11,620	190	87.3	5,000	689	67.5	2,146	800	64.5
In central cities	4,752	277	82.0	2,542	886	61.3	1,164	961	58.5
Outside central cities	6,869	129	90.9	2,458	486	73.8	981	609	71.7
Nonmetropolitan	2,906	141	89.6	735	813	61.1	326	964	54.7
LABOR FORCE STATUS									
All Marital Classes									
Total	18,108	329	78.0	20,915	1,357	34.4	21,065	1,913	18.6
In labor force	11,645	267	81.2	15,357	1,139	41.1	15,995	1,783	21.0
Employed	9,962	246	82.2	14,437	1,105	42.1	15,244	1,775	21.2
Unemployed	1,682	392	74.8	919	1,679	25.8	751	1,941	18.5
Not in labor force	6,464	442	72.4	5,559	1,957	15.9	5,070	2,325	11.0
Women Ever Married									
Total	3,582	935	38.7	15,181	1,603	22.2	18,592	2,058	12.7
In labor force	2,323	745	47.9	10,851	1,413	27.2	14,042	1,944	14.3
Employed	2,072	696	50.0	10,264	1,385	27.8	13,431	1,937	14.4
Unemployed	250	1,150	30.3	587	1,902	16.1	611	2,084	12.8
Not in labor force	1,259	1,287	21.7	4,330	2,080	9.8	4,551	2,412	7.8
Women Never Married									
Total	14,526	180	87.7	5,734	705	66.6	2,472	822	63.2
In labor force	9,322	148	89.5	4,505	482	74.6	1,953	627	69.6
Employed	7,890	128	90.7	4,174	418	77.1	1,814	575	71.6
Unemployed	1,432	260	82.6	332	1,285	43.1	139	1,312	43.5
Not in labor force	5,204	237	84.6	1,229	1,525	37.4	519	1,554	39.2
OCCUPATION									
All Marital Classes									
Total employed	9,962	246	82.2	14,437	1,105	42.1	15,244	1,775	21.2
Managerial and professional	1,183	168	88.0	4,425	821	53.0	5,272	1,536	27.7
Technical, sales, and administrative support	4,857	215	83.2	6,096	1,048	41.8	5,950	1,782	20.1
Service occupations	2,939	265	82.2	2,385	1,466	32.3	2,220	2,051	14.6
Farming, forestry, and fishing	158	213	82.7	143	2,036	17.3	168	2,519	11.8
Precision production, craft, and repair	143	531	63.9	311	1,416	38.1	377	2,017	15.3
Operators, fabricators, and laborers	683	467	69.4	1,077	1,582	25.0	1,257	2,086	14.0
Women Ever Married									
Total employed	2,072	696	50.0	10,264	1,385	27.8	13,431	1,937	14.4
Managerial and professional	368	443	69.2	3,073	1,124	36.5	4,598	1,724	19.0
Technical, sales, and administrative support	988	567	53.8	4,362	1,303	28.5	5,349	1,937	13.8
Service occupations	463	1,000	35.6	1,701	1,747	19.0	1,912	2,188	9.9
Farming, forestry, and fishing	39	(B)	(B)	122	2,146	9.7	162	2,567	10.0
Precision production, craft, and repair	47	(B)	(B)	235	1,681	27.3	326	2,245	6.6
Operators, fabricators, and laborers	168	1,026	35.5	770	1,878	11.8	1,083	2,214	8.7
Women Never Married									
Total employed	7,890	128	90.7	4,174	418	77.1	1,814	575	71.6
Managerial and professional	815	44	96.5	1,351	132	90.6	674	256	87.0
Technical, sales, and administrative support	3,869	125	90.7	1,734	409	75.1	601	399	76.1
Service occupations	2,476	127	91.0	684	765	65.4	308	1,199	43.7
Farming, forestry, and fishing	119	43	95.7	21	(B)	(B)	7	(B)	(B)
Precision production, craft, and repair	96	219	85.9	76	602	71.4	51	(B)	(B)
Operators, fabricators, and laborers	514	284	80.4	307	839	58.0	174	1,291	47.0

Source: Amara Bachu, U.S. Bureau of the Census, *Fertility of American Women: June 1994,* Current Population Reports, P20-482, Washington, D.C.: U.S. Government Printing Office, September, 1995, Table 2.

A3-2. Women in Their Thirties Who Had a Child in Year before the Survey, by Age and Childlessness: Selected Years 1976 to 1994

[Years ending in June. Numbers in thousands]

Year	Number of women 15 to 44 years	30 to 34 years old		Women who had a birth in the last year		35 to 39 years old		Women who had a birth in the last year	
		Number of women	Percent childless	Number of women	Births per 1,000 women	Number of women	Percent childless	Number of women	Births per 1,000 women
1994	60,088	11,131	26.3	1,006	90.4	11,093	19.6	399	36.0
1990	58,381	11,091	25.7	892	80.4	10,111	17.7	377	37.3
1988	¹52,586	10,838	25.1	884	81.6	9,586	17.7	324	33.8
1987	¹52,139	10,612	23.6	786	74.1	9,409	16.7	341	36.2
1986	¹51,581	10,331	23.9	815	78.9	9,401	16.6	285	30.3
1985	¹50,951	10,078	26.2	704	69.9	8,859	16.7	229	25.9
1984	¹50,304	9,745	23.5	703	72.2	8,575	15.4	195	22.7
1983	¹49,486	9,528	22.9	658	69.1	8,181	14.6	225	27.5
1982	¹48,666	9,405	22.5	691	73.5	7,838	14.4	230	29.3
1981	¹47,686	9,318	20.6	628	67.3	7,361	12.3	210	28.6
1980	¹45,652	8,651	19.8	519	60.0	7,144	12.1	192	26.9
1976	¹41,618	7,160	15.6	404	56.4	6,064	10.5	137	22.6

¹18 to 44 years old.
Source: June Current Population Surveys, 1976, 1980 to 1994.

Source: Amara Bachu, U.S. Bureau of the Census, *Fertility of American Women: June 1994*, Current Population Reports, P20-482, Washington, D.C.: U.S. Government Printing Office, September, 1995, Table G.

A3-3. Birth Expectations of Childless Women: June 1976, 1980, 1985, and 1990

(Percent distribution for birth expectations based on all interviewed respondents)

Age and survey year	Percent currently childless	Total	Birth expectations		
			Expects 1+ births	Expects 0 births	Uncertain
18 to 24 years old:					
1990	70.7	100.0	64.9	10.9	24.3
1985	71.4	100.0	66.1	12.1	21.8
1980	70.0	100.0	66.5	13.8	19.8
1976	69.0	100.0	68.4	13.6	18.1
25 to 29 years old:					
1990	42.1	100.0	62.8	17.3	20.0
1985	41.5	100.0	62.9	18.2	19.0
1980	36.8	100.0	55.5	25.5	19.1
1976	30.8	100.0	51.7	30.6	17.6
30 to 34 years old:					
1990	25.7	100.0	40.6	33.8	25.7
1985	26.2	100.0	36.3	44.4	19.3
1980	19.8	100.0	29.5	50.7	19.6
1976	15.6	100.0	22.3	59.1	18.6
35 to 39 years old:					
1990	17.7	100.0	16.0	65.2	18.8
1985	16.7	100.0	13.4	73.9	12.6
1980	12.1	100.0	11.4	75.4	13.1
1976	10.5	100.0	(NA)	(NA)	(NA)

NA Not available.
Note: Population bases are in table 1.

Source: U.S. Bureau of the Census, *Studies in American Fertility*, Current Population Reports, Series P-23, No. 176, Washington, D.C.: U.S. Government Printing Office, 1991, Table A.

A3-4. Lifetime Births Expected by Currently Married Women and Percentage of Expected Births Already Born, by Age and Race: Selected Years 1967 to 1992

[Data are based on household interviews of samples of currently married women of the civilian noninstitutionalized population]

Race and year	All ages 18–34 years	18–19 years	20–21 years	22–24 years	25–29 years	30–34 years
All races	Expected births per currently married woman					
1967	3.1	2.7	2.9	2.9	3.0	3.3
1971	2.6	2.3	2.4	2.4	2.6	3.0
1975	2.3	2.2	2.2	2.2	2.3	2.6
1980	2.2	2.1	2.2	2.1	2.2	2.2
1985	2.2	2.1	2.2	2.2	2.2	2.2
1988	2.2	2.1	2.2	2.2	2.3	2.2
1990	2.3	2.1	2.2	2.3	2.3	2.3
1992	2.2	2.3	2.3	2.3	2.3	2.2
White						
1967	3.0	2.7	3.0	2.8	3.0	3.2
1971	2.6	2.3	2.4	2.4	2.6	2.9
1975	2.3	2.2	2.1	2.1	2.2	2.6
1980	2.2	2.1	2.2	2.1	2.1	2.2
1985	2.2	2.0	2.2	2.2	2.2	2.1
1988	2.2	2.1	2.2	2.2	2.3	2.2
1990	2.3	2.1	2.2	2.3	2.3	2.3
1992	2.2	2.3	2.3	2.3	2.3	2.2
Black						
1967	3.5	*	2.5	3.0	3.4	4.3
1971	3.1	*	2.4	2.8	3.1	3.7
1975	2.8	*	2.6	2.5	2.6	3.2
1980	2.4	*	2.2	2.1	2.4	2.5
1985	2.4	*	*	2.3	2.3	2.5
1988	2.3	*	*	2.2	2.3	2.3
1990	2.5	2.1	2.4	2.6	2.4	2.6
1992	2.4	*	*	2.1	2.4	2.4
All races	Percent of expected births already born					
1967	70.2	26.9	33.2	47.8	76.1	92.7
1971	69.4	25.3	32.5	46.7	74.4	93.7
1975	68.8	27.5	30.7	43.9	70.9	93.0
1980	67.0	29.5	32.9	44.9	64.7	89.7
1985	64.2	27.0	30.9	41.8	60.2	84.4
1988	65.3	25.0	33.4	40.9	58.9	83.6
1990	64.5	29.9	33.1	44.2	57.5	81.1
1992	66.3	27.9	36.1	45.0	59.4	82.2
White						
1967	68.9	24.2	30.1	46.2	75.1	92.9
1971	68.9	23.7	31.4	45.3	74.1	93.8
1975	68.2	24.9	29.4	42.3	70.5	93.2
1980	66.3	28.6	31.8	43.5	64.0	90.0
1985	63.3	25.7	30.6	40.4	59.4	84.1
1988	64.4	24.0	32.6	38.9	58.2	83.2
1990	63.6	26.8	30.0	43.1	56.2	80.8
1992	65.4	27.4	33.6	42.7	58.1	82.2
Black						
1967	82.8	*	65.7	67.9	87.9	92.3
1971	74.8	*	43.0	57.5	81.0	93.4
1975	76.4	*	43.3	61.0	78.2	91.8
1980	74.7	*	46.1	58.9	73.8	90.9
1985	77.1	*	*	62.3	72.8	91.4
1988	75.5	*	*	61.4	70.1	89.9
1990	74.1	49.0	54.8	56.6	71.9	85.0
1992	79.3	*	*	76.1	73.3	85.9

*Estimates based on 50 or fewer subjects are not shown.

NOTE: Data for 1989 and 1991 are not available because surveys were not conducted in those years.

SOURCE: U.S. Bureau of the Census: Population characteristics. Current Population Reports. Series P-20, Nos. 301, 375, 406, 436, 454, and 470. Washington. U.S. Government Printing Office, Nov. 1976, Oct. 1982, June 1986, May 1989, Oct. 1991, and June 1993. Data from the Current Population Survey (CPS).

Source: National Center for Health Statistics, *Health, United States, 1993*, (PHS) 94-1232, Washington, D.C.: U.S. Government Printing Office, 1994, Table 6.

A3-5. Births as of June 1992 and Lifetime Births Expected per 1,000 Wives 18 to 34 Years Old, by Selected Characteristics

(Numbers in thousands. Data limited to "reporting" women.)

Characteristic	Wives 18 to 24 years old			Wives 25 to 29 years old			Wives 30 to 34 years old		
		Rate Per 1,000 wives			Rate Per 1,000 wives			Rate Per 1,000 wives	
	Number of wives	Births to date	Lifetime births expected	Number of wives	Births to date	Lifetime births expected	Number of wives	Births to date	Lifetime births expected
AGE AT FIRST MARRIAGE									
Total	2,078	935	2,300	4,208	1,343	2,268	5,561	1,823	2,218
Under 18 years	321	1,634	2,474	381	2,424	2,761	568	2,415	2,497
18 and 19 years	740	1,027	2,336	757	1,976	2,375	1,116	2,309	2,426
20 and 21 years	636	752	2,214	881	1,616	2,293	1,058	2,066	2,237
22 to 24 years	381	474	2,225	1,420	958	2,168	1,271	1,804	2,199
25 or more years	–	(B)	(B)	770	584	2,075	1,549	1,104	1,968
BIRTHS TO DATE									
Total	2,078	935	2,300	4,208	1,343	2,268	5,561	1,823	2,218
Childless	834	–	2,000	1,213	–	1,815	847	–	1,088
One child	722	1,000	2,208	1,210	1,000	2,023	1,193	1,000	1,689
Two children	383	2,000	2,638	1,145	2,000	2,315	2,153	2,000	2,153
Three children	108	3,000	3,433	473	3,000	3,099	982	3,000	3,081
Four or more children	31	(B)	(B)	167	4,394	4,662	387	4,376	4,491
EDUCATION OF WIFE									
Total	2,078	935	2,300	4,208	1,343	2,268	5,561	1,823	2,218
Not a high school graduate	378	1,631	2,570	487	2,206	2,604	543	2,481	2,628
High school, 4 years	908	926	2,168	1,513	1,603	2,239	2,258	1,919	2,147
College: 1 or more years	791	613	2,321	2,209	975	2,214	2,760	1,615	2,195
Some college, no degree	527	743	2,315	853	1,327	2,305	995	1,843	2,217
Associate degree	128	504	2,180	391	1,128	2,172	445	1,796	2,233
Bachelors degree	131	224	2,496	799	616	2,151	1,028	1,463	2,164
Graduate or professional degree	5	(B)	(B)	166	531	2,146	292	1,091	2,176
EDUCATION OF HUSBAND[1]									
Total	2,078	935	2,300	4,208	1,343	2,268	5,561	1,823	2,218
Not a high school graduate	430	1,362	2,451	563	2,011	2,479	614	2,187	2,364
High school, 4 years	923	947	2,169	1,586	1,520	2,235	2,040	1,946	2,198
College: 1 or more years	725	666	2,375	2,059	1,025	2,235	2,908	1,659	2,200
Some college, no degree	375	856	2,512	802	1,311	2,236	987	1,866	2,205
Associate degree	131	556	2,144	284	1,018	2,129	411	1,816	2,160
Bachelors degree	191	431	2,364	729	777	2,246	1,082	1,482	2,142
Graduate or professional degree	28	(B)	(B)	244	830	2,326	427	1,480	2,377
OCCUPATION OF WIFE									
Total employed	1,279	705	2,176	2,857	1,104	2,164	3,736	1,656	2,095
Managerial and professional	186	429	2,185	819	778	2,134	1,081	1,359	2,019
Technical, sales, and administrative support	650	608	2,141	1,282	1,074	2,130	1,630	1,670	2,097
Service occupations	287	993	2,227	450	1,524	2,288	587	1,982	2,238
Farming, forestry, and fishing	17	(B)	(B)	28	(B)	(B)	59	(B)	(B)
Precision production, craft, and repair	19	(B)	(B)	63	(B)	(B)	93	1,894	2,009
Operators, fabricators, and laborers	120	818	2,054	214	1,561	2,229	285	1,775	1,968
OCCUPATION OF CIVILIAN HUSBAND[1]									
Total employed	1,832	898	2,294	3,869	1,310	2,263	5,117	1,798	2,207
Managerial and professional	200	660	2,336	907	898	2,230	1,372	1,658	2,240
Technical, sales, and administrative support	383	600	2,318	778	1,049	2,244	1,101	1,623	2,158
Service occupations	207	1,023	2,256	280	1,431	2,280	362	1,796	2,148
Farming, forestry, and fishing	76	1,201	2,566	164	1,634	2,418	160	2,227	2,478
Precision production, craft, and repair	439	974	2,161	929	1,584	2,296	1,181	1,976	2,239
Operators, fabricators, and laborers	527	1,048	2,346	812	1,600	2,241	942	1,910	2,150
FAMILY INCOME[1]									
Wife in Labor Force									
Total income	1,404	724	2,185	3,016	1,125	2,175	3,941	1,672	2,109
Under $10,000	155	942	2,473	96	1,683	2,415	129	2,271	2,473
$10,000 to $19,999	332	784	2,175	319	1,708	2,376	374	2,022	2,266
$20,000 to $24,999	225	866	2,017	253	1,583	2,435	287	1,988	2,258
$25,000 to $29,999	171	697	2,184	313	1,324	2,192	338	1,945	2,321
$30,000 to $34,999	138	654	2,126	378	1,220	2,105	376	1,698	1,919
$35,000 to $49,999	240	616	2,216	815	1,035	2,076	1,025	1,672	2,082
$50,000 to $74,999	99	362	2,108	583	703	2,087	905	1,477	2,039
$75,000 and over	21	(B)	(B)	182	470	2,234	389	1,110	1,950
Income not reported	25	(B)	(B)	78	944	2,037	118	1,609	2,135
Wife Not in Labor Force									
Total income	674	1,375	2,538	1,192	1,895	2,504	1,620	2,190	2,483
Under $10,000	169	1,756	2,675	138	2,313	2,672	135	2,350	2,540
$10,000 to $19,999	242	1,277	2,424	289	2,162	2,721	224	2,555	2,733
$20,000 to $24,999	78	1,224	2,428	167	2,027	2,415	134	2,081	2,329
$25,000 to $29,999	63	(B)	(B)	101	1,719	2,460	135	2,238	2,412
$30,000 to $34,999	24	(B)	(B)	137	1,719	2,305	200	1,997	2,231
$35,000 to $49,999	43	(B)	(B)	195	1,672	2,452	375	2,151	2,492
$50,000 to $74,999	27	(B)	(B)	103	1,560	2,405	257	2,100	2,514
$75,000 and over	9	(B)	(B)	31	(B)	(B)	113	2,058	2,588
Income not reported	19	(B)	(B)	32	(B)	(B)	48	(B)	(B)

[1] Limited to wives in married-couple families.

Source: Amara Bachu, U.S. Bureau of the Census, *Fertility of American Women: June 1992*, Current Population Reports, P20-470, Washington, D.C.: U.S. Government Printing Office, 1993, Table 7.

A3-6. Births, by Intention Status: 1988 and 1984–1988

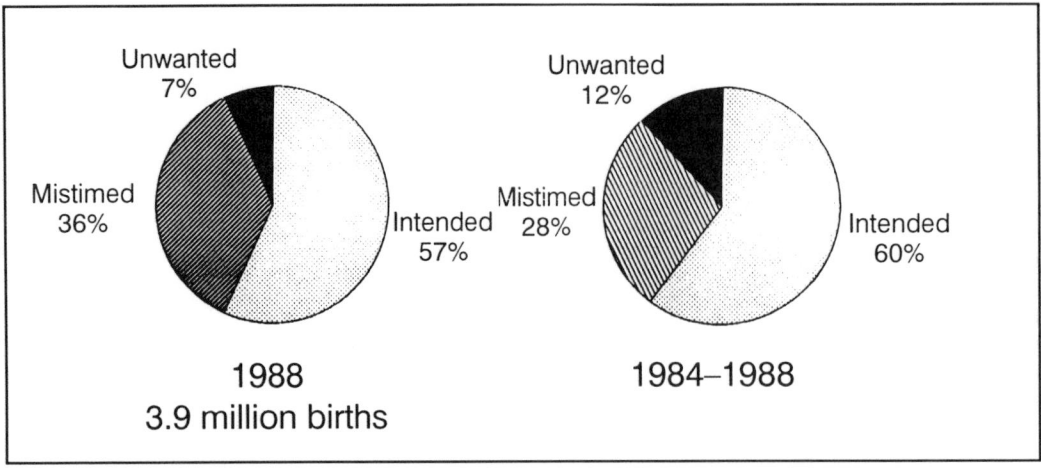

Source: Jacqueline D. Forrest, The Alan Guttmacher Institute, "Levels and Determinants of U.S. Fertility," presentation at The Population and Consumption Task Force of the President's Council on Sustainable Development, October 27, 1994, unpublished.

A3-7. Percentage of Births to Currently Married Women that Are Unintended: Selected Years, 1961–65 to 1983–88

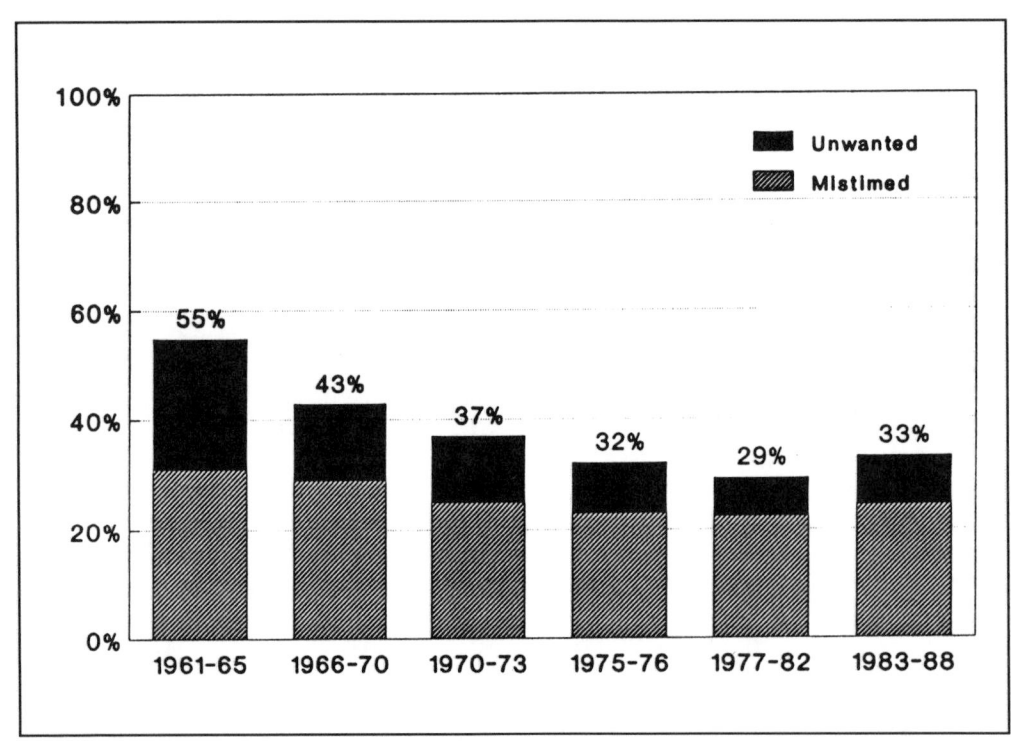

Source: Jacqueline D. Forrest, The Alan Guttmacher Institute, "Levels and Determinants of U.S. Fertility," presentation at The Population and Consumption Task Force of the President's Council on Sustainable Development, October 27, 1994, unpublished.

A3-8. Births, by Intention Status and Mother's Education: 1988

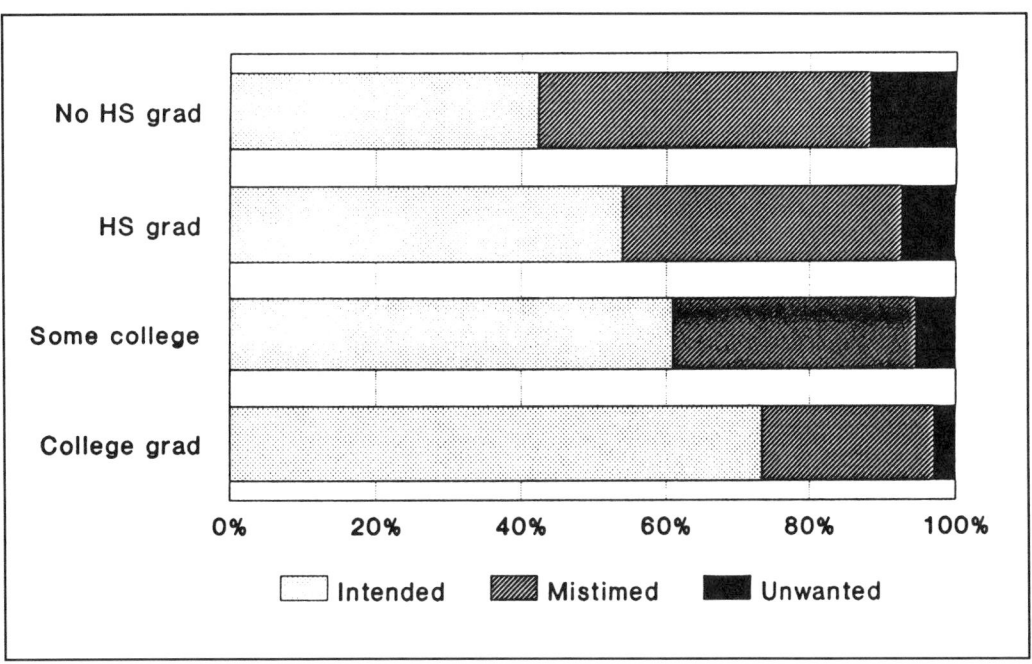

Source: Jacqueline D. Forrest, The Alan Guttmacher Institute, "Levels and Determinants of U.S. Fertility," presentation at The Population and Consumption Task Force of the President's Council on Sustainable Development, October 27, 1994, unpublished.

A3-9. Births, by Intention Status and Mother's Poverty Status*: 1988

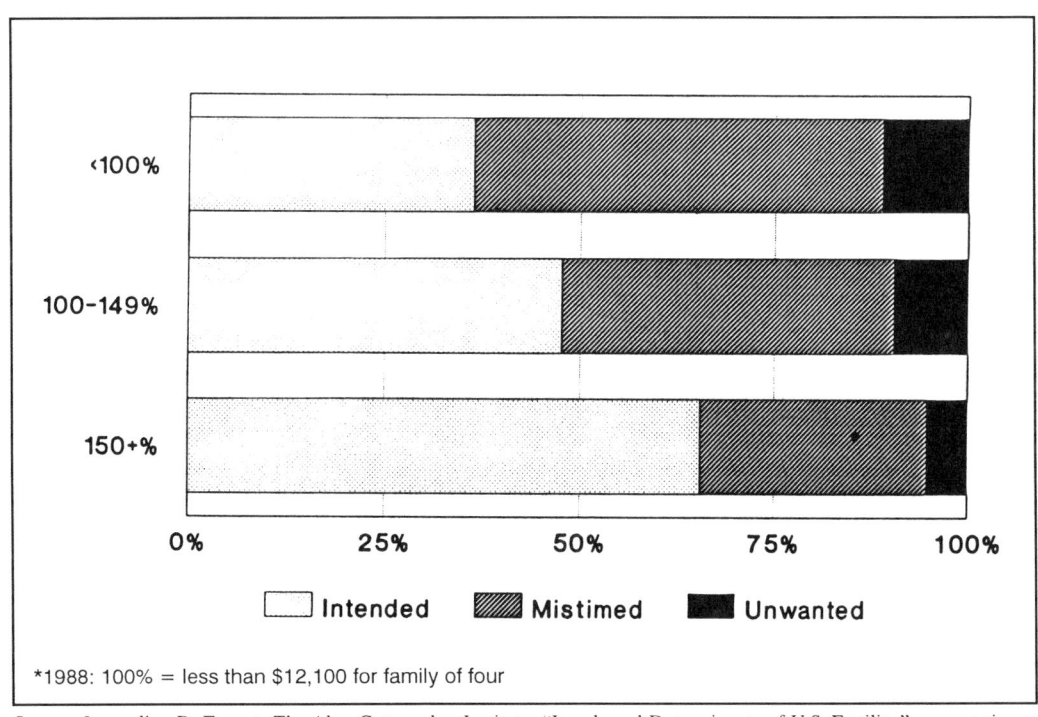

*1988: 100% = less than $12,100 for family of four

Source: Jacqueline D. Forrest, The Alan Guttmacher Institute, "Levels and Determinants of U.S. Fertility," presentation at The Population and Consumption Task Force of the President's Council on Sustainable Development, October 27, 1994, unpublished.

A4. BIRTHS TO UNMARRIED WOMEN

A4-1. Percentage of Live Births to Unmarried Mothers, by Race of Mother: 1970 to 1991

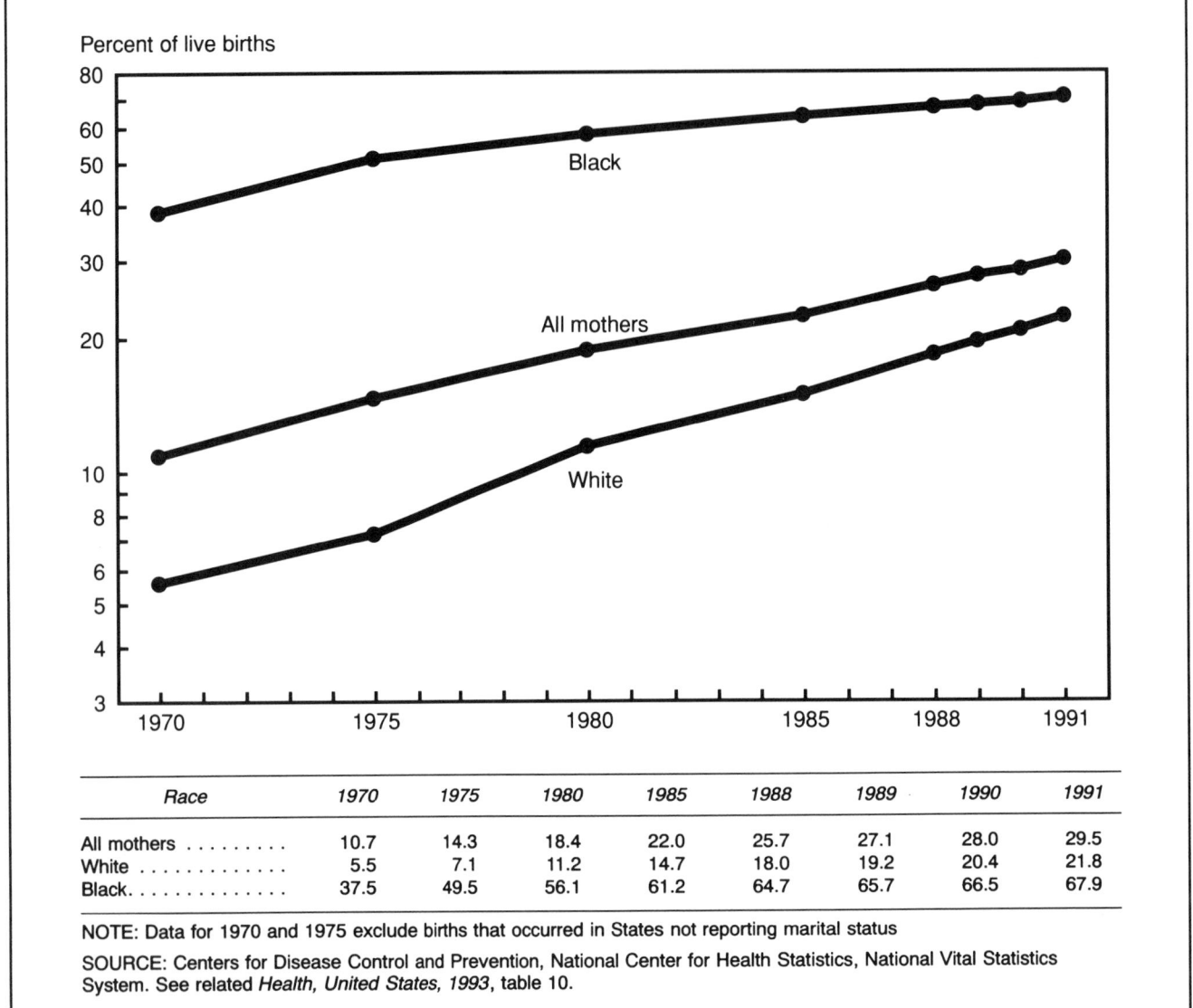

Percent of live births

Race	1970	1975	1980	1985	1988	1989	1990	1991
All mothers	10.7	14.3	18.4	22.0	25.7	27.1	28.0	29.5
White	5.5	7.1	11.2	14.7	18.0	19.2	20.4	21.8
Black.	37.5	49.5	56.1	61.2	64.7	65.7	66.5	67.9

NOTE: Data for 1970 and 1975 exclude births that occurred in States not reporting marital status

SOURCE: Centers for Disease Control and Prevention, National Center for Health Statistics, National Vital Statistics System. See related *Health, United States, 1993*, table 10.

Source: National Center for Health Statistics, *Health, United States, 1993*, (PHS) 94-1232, Washington, D.C.: U.S. Government Printing Office, 1994, Figure 4.

A4-2. Percentage of Live Births to Unmarried Mothers, by Race and Hispanic Origin of Mother: 1991

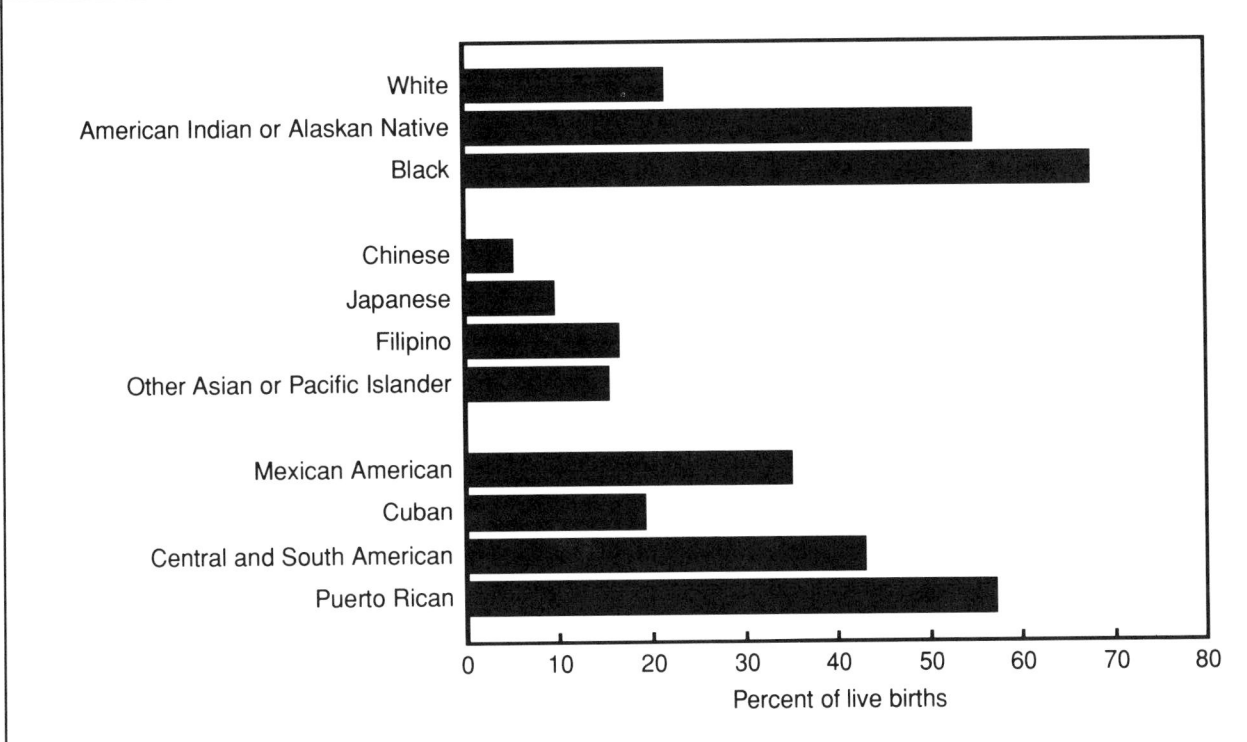

Race and Hispanic origin	Percent
White	21.8
American Indian or Alaskan Native	55.3
Black	67.9
Chinese	5.5
Japanese	9.8
Filipino	16.8
Other Asian or Pacific Islander[1]	15.6
Mexican American	35.3
Cuban	19.5
Central and South American	43.1
Puerto Rican	57.5

[1]Includes Hawaiians and part Hawaiians.

NOTES: The race groups white, black, Asian or Pacific Islander subgroups, and American Indian or Alaskan Native include persons of Hispanic and non-Hispanic origin. Conversely, persons of Hispanic origin may be of any race. Data for Hispanic subgroups exclude data from New Hampshire

SOURCE: Centers for Disease Control and Prevention, National Center for Health Statistics, National Vital Statistics System. See related *Health, United States, 1993*, table 8.

Source: National Center for Health Statistics, *Health, United States, 1993*, (PHS) 94-1232, Washington, D.C.: U.S. Government Printing Office, 1994, Figure 5.

A4-3. Maternal Age and Marital Status for Live Births, by Detailed Race of Mother and Hispanic Origin of Mother: Selected Years 1970 to 1991

[Data are based on the National Vital Statistics System]

Age, marital status, race of mother, and Hispanic origin of mother	1970	1975	1980	1982	1983	1984	1985	1986	1987	1988	1989	1990	1991
Age of mother less than 18 years						Percent of live births							
All mothers	6.3	7.6	5.8	5.2	5.0	4.8	4.7	4.8	4.8	4.8	4.8	4.7	4.9
White	4.8	6.0	4.5	4.1	3.9	3.7	3.7	3.7	3.7	3.7	3.6	3.6	3.8
Black	14.8	16.3	12.5	11.4	11.2	10.8	10.6	10.6	10.7	10.6	10.5	10.1	10.3
American Indian or Alaskan Native	7.5	11.2	9.4	8.5	8.7	7.9	7.6	8.0	7.9	7.8	7.5	7.2	7.9
Asian or Pacific Islander	---	---	1.5	1.7	1.6	1.6	1.6	1.7	1.8	1.8	2.0	2.1	2.1
Chinese	1.1	0.4	0.3	0.3	0.3	0.2	0.3	0.2	0.2	0.3	0.3	0.4	0.3
Japanese	2.0	1.7	1.0	1.3	0.7	0.8	0.9	0.9	0.9	0.8	0.9	0.8	1.0
Filipino	3.7	2.4	1.6	1.6	1.8	2.0	1.6	1.7	1.8	1.7	1.9	2.0	2.0
Other Asian or Pacific Islander [1]	---	---	1.8	2.0	1.9	2.0	2.1	2.2	2.3	2.4	2.6	2.7	2.7
Hispanic origin (selected States) [2,3]	---	---	7.4	7.2	7.0	6.7	6.4	6.5	6.6	6.6	6.7	6.6	6.9
Mexican American	---	---	7.7	7.5	7.5	7.2	6.9	6.9	7.0	7.0	6.9	6.9	7.2
Puerto Rican	---	---	10.0	9.9	9.3	8.5	8.5	8.4	8.7	9.2	9.4	9.1	9.5
Cuban	---	---	3.8	3.2	2.6	2.5	2.2	2.3	2.1	2.2	2.7	2.7	2.6
Central and South American	---	---	2.4	2.6	2.6	2.4	2.4	2.4	2.7	2.7	3.0	3.2	3.5
Other and unknown Hispanic	---	---	6.5	6.9	7.1	7.0	7.0	7.3	7.7	7.6	8.0	8.0	8.3
Non-Hispanic white (selected States) [2]	---	---	4.0	3.6	3.4	3.2	3.2	3.2	3.2	3.2	3.0	3.0	3.1
Non-Hispanic black (selected States) [2]	---	---	12.7	11.6	11.2	10.9	10.7	10.6	10.7	10.8	10.5	10.2	10.3
Age of mother 18–19 years													
All mothers	11.3	11.3	9.8	9.0	8.7	8.3	8.0	7.8	7.6	7.7	8.1	8.1	8.1
White	10.4	10.3	9.0	8.2	7.9	7.4	7.1	7.0	6.8	6.9	7.2	7.3	7.2
Black	16.6	16.9	14.5	13.7	13.6	13.3	12.9	12.6	12.9	12.3	12.8	13.0	12.8
American Indian or Alaskan Native	12.8	15.2	14.6	13.8	13.3	13.1	12.4	12.1	11.8	11.4	12.1	12.3	12.4
Asian or Pacific Islander	---	---	3.9	4.1	3.7	3.4	3.4	3.4	3.3	3.4	3.7	3.7	3.7
Chinese	3.9	1.7	1.0	0.8	0.6	0.5	0.6	0.5	0.6	0.5	0.7	0.8	0.8
Japanese	4.1	3.3	2.3	2.5	2.3	2.3	1.9	1.9	1.6	1.8	1.8	2.0	1.7
Filipino	7.1	5.0	4.0	4.3	3.8	3.5	3.7	3.4	3.4	3.8	4.0	4.1	4.0
Other Asian or Pacific Islander [1]	---	---	4.9	4.9	4.5	4.3	4.2	4.3	4.1	4.3	4.6	4.5	4.6
Hispanic origin (selected States) [2,3]	---	---	11.6	11.1	10.6	10.3	10.1	9.9	9.7	9.8	10.0	10.2	10.3
Mexican American	---	---	12.0	11.5	10.9	10.8	10.6	10.5	10.3	10.3	10.5	10.7	10.9
Puerto Rican	---	---	13.3	13.1	13.2	12.8	12.4	12.5	11.8	12.2	12.6	12.6	12.2
Cuban	---	---	9.2	8.2	6.8	5.7	4.9	4.5	4.1	3.9	4.3	5.0	4.5
Central and South American	---	---	6.0	6.4	6.0	5.7	5.8	5.7	5.3	5.4	5.6	5.9	6.0
Other and unknown Hispanic	---	---	10.8	11.3	11.2	10.9	10.5	10.0	10.5	10.8	11.2	11.1	11.4
Non-Hispanic white (selected States) [2]	---	---	8.5	7.8	7.4	6.8	6.6	6.4	6.2	6.6	6.5	6.6	6.5
Non-Hispanic black (selected States) [2]	---	---	14.7	13.9	13.5	13.4	12.9	12.6	12.2	12.4	13.0	13.0	12.9
Unmarried mothers													
All mothers	10.7	14.3	18.4	19.4	20.3	21.0	22.0	23.4	24.5	25.7	27.1	28.0	29.5
White	5.5	7.1	11.2	12.3	12.9	13.6	14.7	15.9	16.9	18.0	19.2	20.4	21.8
Black	37.5	49.5	56.1	57.7	59.2	60.3	61.2	62.4	63.4	64.7	65.7	66.5	67.9
American Indian or Alaskan Native	22.4	32.7	39.2	42.6	45.3	46.1	46.8	48.8	51.1	51.7	52.7	53.6	55.3
Asian or Pacific Islander	---	---	7.3	7.9	8.6	9.2	9.5	10.0	11.0	11.5	12.4	13.2	13.9
Chinese	3.0	1.6	2.7	2.5	3.3	3.4	3.0	3.5	4.5	3.9	4.2	5.0	5.5
Japanese	4.6	4.6	5.2	7.1	7.2	6.9	7.9	7.9	7.9	8.8	9.4	9.6	9.8
Filipino	9.1	6.9	8.6	9.9	10.3	10.8	11.4	12.0	12.7	13.6	14.8	15.9	16.8
Other Asian or Pacific Islander [1]	---	---	8.5	8.7	9.5	10.4	10.9	11.4	12.4	13.2	14.2	14.9	15.6
Hispanic origin (selected States) [2,3]	---	---	23.6	25.6	27.5	28.3	29.5	31.6	32.6	34.0	35.5	36.7	38.5
Mexican American	---	---	20.3	21.9	23.7	24.2	25.7	27.9	28.9	30.6	31.7	33.3	35.3
Puerto Rican	---	---	46.3	49.0	49.5	50.8	51.1	52.6	53.0	53.3	55.2	55.9	57.5
Cuban	---	---	10.0	15.9	16.1	16.2	16.1	15.8	16.1	16.3	17.5	18.2	19.5
Central and South American	---	---	27.1	30.2	33.0	34.0	34.9	38.0	37.1	36.4	38.9	41.2	43.1
Other and unknown Hispanic	---	---	22.4	26.3	28.2	30.0	31.1	31.9	34.2	35.5	37.0	37.2	37.9
Non-Hispanic white (selected States) [2]	---	---	9.6	10.5	11.0	11.5	12.4	13.5	14.3	15.2	16.1	16.9	18.0
Non-Hispanic black (selected States) [2]	---	---	57.3	59.0	60.5	61.5	62.1	63.3	64.2	64.8	66.0	66.7	68.2

[1] Includes Hawaiians and part Hawaiians.
[2] Trend data for Hispanics and non-Hispanics are affected by expansion of the reporting area for an Hispanic-origin item on the birth certificate and by immigration. These two factors affect numbers of events, composition of the Hispanic population, and maternal and infant health characteristics. The number of States in the reporting area increased from 22 in 1980, to 23 plus the District of Columbia (DC) in 1983, 30 plus DC in 1988, 47 plus DC in 1989, 48 plus DC in 1990, and 49 plus DC in 1991
[3] Includes mothers of all races.

NOTES: Data for 1970 and 1975 exclude births that occurred in States not reporting marital status persons of Hispanic and non-Hispanic origin. Conversely, persons of Hispanic origin may be of any race. The race groups, white and black, include persons of Hispanic and non-Hispanic origin.

SOURCE: Centers for Disease Control and Prevention, National Center for Health Statistics: Data computed by the Division of Analysis from data compiled by the Division of Vital Statistics.

Source: National Center for Health Statistics, *Health, United States, 1993*, (PHS) 94-1232, Washington, D.C.: U.S. Government Printing Office, 1994, Table 10.

A4-4. Number and Ratio of Births to Unmarried Women, by Race: 1940 to 1990

[Prior to 1980, due to rounding estimates to the nearest hundred, figures by race may not add to totals. Ratios per 1,000 live births in specified group. Beginning 1970 excludes births to nonresidents of the United States;

Year	Number				Ratio			
	All races	White	All other Total	Black	All races	White	All other Total	Black
	Race of Mother							
Reported/Inferred [1]								
1990	1,165,384	669,698	495,686	455,304	280.3	203.5	571.1	665.3
1989	1,094,169	613,543	480,626	442,395	270.8	192.2	566.4	657.2
	Race of Child							
1990	1,165,384	647,376	518,008	472,660	280.3	200.7	555.3	652.3
1989	1,094,169	593,911	500,258	457,480	270.8	189.6	550.4	644.9
1988	1,005,299	539,696	465,603	426,665	257.1	177.2	539.3	634.9
1987	933,013	498,645	434,368	399,144	244.9	166.6	531.7	622.1
1986	878,477	466,774	411,703	380,261	233.9	157.1	523.7	612.1
1985	828,174	432,969	395,205	365,527	220.2	144.7	513.8	601.0
1984 [2]	770,355	391,929	378,426	350,896	210.0	134.1	507.5	592.0
1983 [2]	737,893	370,884	367,009	341,077	202.8	127.7	499.5	582.0
1982 [2]	715,227	355,180	360,047	335,927	194.3	120.7	487.5	566.8
1981 [2]	686,605	337,050	349,555	328,879	189.2	115.9	485.1	559.5
1980 [2]	665,747	320,063	345,684	325,737	184.3	110.4	484.5	552.5
Estimated [3]								
1980 [2]	643,400	294,200	349,300	327,000	178.1	101.5	489.5	554.6
1979 [2]	597,800	263,000	334,800	315,800	171.1	93.6	488.1	546.5
1978 [2]	543,900	233,600	310,200	293,400	163.2	87.1	475.6	532.0
1977 [2]	515,700	220,100	295,500	281,600	155.0	81.8	464.9	517.4
1976 [2]	468,100	197,100	271,000	258,800	147.8	76.8	451.5	503.0
1975 [2]	447,900	186,400	261,600	249,600	142.5	73.0	441.7	487.9
1974 [2]	418,100	168,500	249,600	238,800	132.3	65.4	427.3	470.9
1973 [2]	407,300	163,000	244,500	234,500	129.8	63.9	416.9	457.5
1972 [2]	403,200	160,500	242,700	233,300	123.7	60.4	402.6	439.1
1971 [4]	401,400	163,800	237,500	229,000	112.9	56.1	373.3	405.3
1970 [4]	398,700	175,100	223,600	215,100	106.9	56.6	349.3	375.8
1969 [4]	360,800	163,700	197,200	189,400	100.2	54.7	325.1	348.7
1968 [4]	339,200	155,200	183,900	– – –	96.9	53.3	312.0	– – –
1967 [5]	318,100	142,200	175,800	– – –	90.3	48.7	293.8	– – –
1966 [4]	302,400	132,900	169,500	– – –	83.9	44.4	276.5	– – –
1965 [4]	291,200	123,700	167,500	– – –	77.4	39.5	263.2	– – –
1964 [4]	275,700	114,300	161,300	– – –	68.5	33.9	245.0	– – –
1963 [4]	259,400	104,600	154,900	– – –	63.3	30.4	235.5	– – –
1962 [4]	245,100	94,700	150,400	– – –	58.8	27.0	227.8	– – –
1961 [4]	240,200	91,100	149,100	– – –	56.3	25.3	223.4	– – –
1960 [4]	224,300	82,500	141,800	– – –	52.7	22.9	215.8	– – –
1959 [4]	220,600	79,600	141,100	– – –	52.0	22.1	218.0	– – –
1958 [4]	208,700	74,600	134,100	– – –	49.6	20.9	212.3	– – –
1957 [4]	201,700	70,800	130,900	– – –	47.4	19.6	206.7	– – –
1956 [4]	193,500	67,500	126,000	– – –	46.5	19.0	204.0	– – –
1955	183,300	64,200	119,200	– – –	45.3	18.6	202.4	– – –
1954 [4]	176,600	62,700	113,900	– – –	44.0	18.2	198.5	– – –
1953 [4]	160,800	56,600	104,200	– – –	41.2	16.9	191.1	– – –
1952 [4]	150,300	54,100	96,200	– – –	39.1	16.3	183.4	– – –
1951 [4]	146,500	52,600	93,900	– – –	39.1	16.3	182.8	– – –
1950	141,600	53,500	88,100	– – –	39.8	17.5	179.6	– – –
1949	133,200	53,500	79,700	– – –	37.4	17.3	167.5	– – –
1948	129,700	54,800	74,900	– – –	36.7	17.8	164.7	– – –
1947	131,900	60,500	71,500	– – –	35.7	18.5	168.0	– – –
1946	125,200	61,400	63,800	– – –	38.1	21.1	170.1	– – –
1945	117,400	56,400	60,900	– – –	42.9	23.6	179.3	– – –
1944	105,200	49,600	55,600	– – –	37.6	20.2	163.4	– – –
1943	98,100	42,800	55,400	– – –	33.4	16.5	162.8	– – –
1942	95,500	42,000	54,500	– – –	34.3	16.9	169.2	– – –
1941	95,700	41,900	53,800	– – –	38.1	19.0	174.5	– – –
1940	89,500	40,300	49,200	– – –	37.9	19.5	168.3	– – –

[1] Data for States in which marital status was not reported have been inferred from other items on the birth certificate and included with data from the reporting States; see Technical Appendix.
[2] Based on 100 percent of births in selected States and on a 50-percent sample of births in all other States; see Technical Appendix.
[3] Births to unmarried women are estimated for the United States from data for registration areas in which marital status of mother was reported; see Technical Appendix.
[4] Based on a 50-percent sample of births.
[5] Based on a 20- to 50-percent sample of births.

Source: National Center for Health Statistics, *Vital Statistics of the United States, 1990*, Vol. 1 (Natality), Washington, D.C.: U.S. Government Printing Office, 1994, Table 1-76.

A4-5. Birth Rates for Unmarried Mothers, by Age of Mother: 1980 to 1992

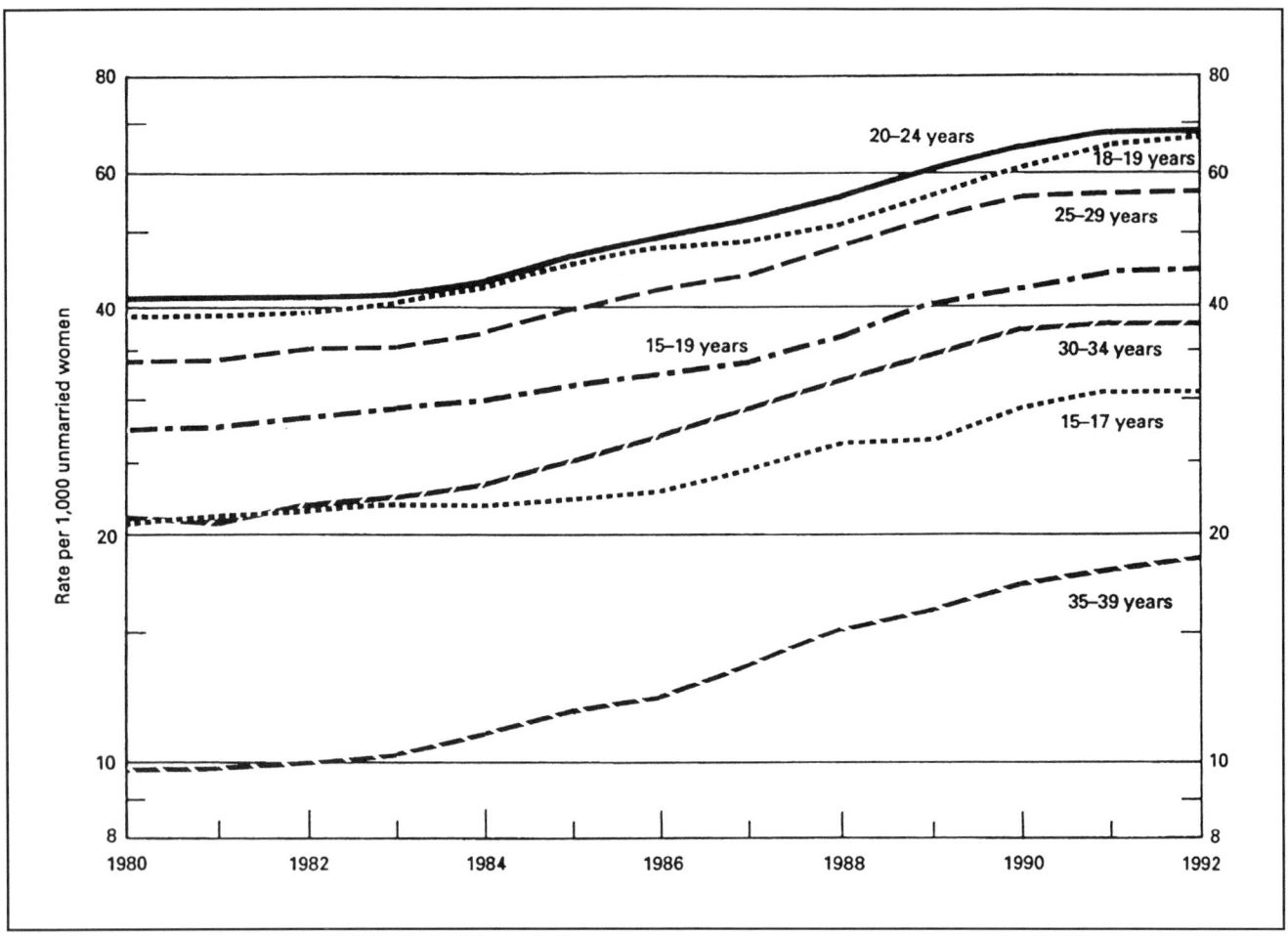

Source: S. J. Ventura, J. A. Martin, S. M. Taffel, et. al., National Center for Health Statistics, *Advance Report of Final Natality Statistics, 1992*, Monthly Vital Statistics Report, Vol. 43, No. 5 (suppl.), (PHS) 95-1120 4-0677, Washington, D.C.: U.S. Department of Health and Human Services, October 25, 1994, Figure 3.

A4-6. Number, Rate, and Ratio of Births to Unmarried Women, by Age and Race of Mother: 1992

Age of mother	Number			Rate per 1,000 unmarried women in specified group			Ratio per 1,000 live births		
	All races [1]	White	Black	All races [1]	White	Black	All races [1]	White	Black
All ages	1,224,876	721,986	458,969	[2]45.2	[2]35.2	[2]86.5	301.3	225.5	681.3
Under 15 years.	11,161	4,553	6,296	- - -	- - -	- - -	913.3	848.3	976.4
15–19 years.	353,878	206,830	135,994	44.6	33.0	105.9	700.2	603.5	926.4
15 years	25,459	12,664	12,059				869.9	793.2	970.0
16 years	49,021	27,323	20,158 }	30.4	21.6	78.0	815.2	733.4	961.3
17 years	74,103	43,861	27,985 ⌡				755.0	669.0	945.4
18 years	96,009	57,566	35,422 }	67.3	51.5	147.8	692.4	600.0	923.4
19 years	109,286	65,416	40,370 ⌡				609.8	511.0	888.5
20–24 years.	435,727	258,268	162,561	68.5	52.7	144.3	407.0	317.1	752.4
25–29 years.	233,467	137,639	86,853	56.5	45.4	98.2	198.0	142.7	549.8
30–34 years.	127,982	75,696	46,860	37.9	31.5	57.7	143.0	101.5	467.0
35–39 years.	52,447	32,218	17,608	18.8	16.2	25.8	152.2	114.0	447.0
40 years and over	10,214	6,782	2,797	[3]4.1	[3]3.6	[3]5.4	177.0	146.0	421.2

[1]Includes races other than white and black.
[2]Rates computed by relating total births to unmarried mothers, regardless of age of mother, to unmarried women aged 15–44 years.
[3]Rates computed by relating births to unmarried mothers aged 40 years and over to unmarried women aged 40–44 years.

NOTE: For 44 States and the District of Columbia, marital status of mother is reported on the birth certificate; for 6 States, mother's marital status is inferred

Source: S. J. Ventura, J. A. Martin, S. M. Taffel, et. al., National Center for Health Statistics, *Advance Report of Final Natality Statistics, 1992*, Monthly Vital Statistics Report, Vol. 43, No. 5 (suppl.), (PHS) 95-1120 4-0677, Washington, D.C.: U.S. Department of Health and Human Services, October 25, 1994, Table 14.

A4-7. Birth Rates for Unmarried Women, by Age of Mother and Race: 1970, 1975, and 1980 to 1992

[Rates are live births to unmarried women per 1,000 unmarried women in specified group, estimated as of July 1]

Year and race	15–44 years [1]	Age of mother							
		15–19 years			20–24 years	25–29 years	30–34 years	35–39 years	40–44 years [2]
		Total	15–17 years	18–19 years					
All races [3]									
1992 [4]	45.2	44.6	30.4	67.3	68.5	56.5	37.9	18.8	4.1
1991 [4]	45.2	44.8	30.9	65.7	68.0	56.5	38.1	18.0	3.8
1990 [4]	43.8	42.5	29.6	60.7	65.1	56.0	37.6	17.3	3.6
1989 [4]	41.6	40.1	28.7	56.0	61.2	52.8	34.9	16.0	3.4
1988 [4]	38.5	36.4	26.4	51.5	56.0	48.5	32.0	15.0	3.2
1987 [4]	36.0	33.8	24.5	48.9	52.6	44.5	29.6	13.5	2.9
1986 [4]	34.2	32.3	22.8	48.0	49.3	42.2	27.2	12.2	2.7
1985 [4]	32.8	31.4	22.4	45.9	46.5	39.9	25.2	11.6	2.5
1984 [4,5]	31.0	30.0	21.9	42.5	43.0	37.1	23.3	10.9	2.5
1983 [4,5]	30.3	29.5	22.0	40.7	41.8	35.5	22.4	10.2	2.6
1982 [4,5]	30.0	28.7	21.5	39.6	41.5	35.1	21.9	10.0	2.7
1981 [4,5]	29.5	27.9	20.9	39.0	41.1	34.5	20.8	9.8	2.6
1980 [4,5]	29.4	27.6	20.6	39.0	40.9	34.0	21.1	9.7	2.6
1980 [5,6]	28.4	27.5	20.7	38.7	39.7	31.4	18.5	8.4	2.3
1975 [5,6]	24.5	23.9	19.3	32.5	31.2	27.5	17.9	9.1	2.6
1970 [6,7]	26.4	22.4	17.1	32.9	38.4	37.0	27.1	13.6	3.5
White									
Race of mother:									
1992 [4]	35.2	33.0	21.6	51.5	52.7	45.4	31.5	16.2	3.6
1991 [4]	34.6	32.8	21.8	49.6	51.5	44.6	31.1	15.2	3.2
1990 [4]	32.9	30.6	20.4	44.9	48.2	43.0	29.9	14.5	3.2
1989 [4]	30.2	28.0	19.3	40.2	43.8	39.1	26.8	13.1	2.9
1988 [4]	27.4	25.3	17.6	36.8	39.2	35.4	24.2	12.1	2.7
1987 [4]	25.3	23.2	16.2	34.5	36.6	32.0	22.3	10.7	2.4
1986 [4]	23.9	21.8	14.9	33.5	34.2	30.5	20.1	9.7	2.2
1985 [4]	22.5	20.8	14.5	31.2	31.7	28.5	18.4	9.0	2.0
1984 [4,5]	20.6	19.3	13.7	27.9	28.5	25.5	16.8	8.4	2.0
1983 [4,5]	19.8	18.7	13.6	26.4	27.1	23.8	15.9	7.8	2.0
1982 [4,5]	19.3	18.0	13.1	25.3	26.5	23.1	15.3	7.4	2.1
1981 [4,5]	18.6	17.2	12.6	24.6	25.8	22.3	14.2	7.2	1.9
1980 [4,5]	18.1	16.5	12.0	24.1	25.1	21.5	14.1	7.1	1.8
Race of child:									
1980 [5,6]	16.2	15.9	11.7	22.8	22.4	17.3	10.5	5.3	1.4
1975 [5,6]	12.4	12.0	9.6	16.5	15.5	14.8	9.8	5.4	1.5
1970 [6,7]	13.9	10.9	7.5	17.6	22.5	21.1	14.2	7.6	2.0

See footnotes at end of table.

A4-7. Birth Rates for Unmarried Women, by Age of Mother and Race: 1970, 1975, and 1980 to 1992 *(continued)*

[Rates are live births to unmarried women per 1,000 unmarried women in specified group, estimated as of July 1]

		Age of mother							
		15–19 years							
Year and race	15–44 years[1]	Total	15–17 years	18–19 years	20–24 years	25–29 years	30–34 years	35–39 years	40–44 years[2]
Black									
Race of mother:									
1992[4]	86.5	105.9	78.0	147.8	144.3	98.2	57.7	25.8	5.4
1991[4]	89.5	108.5	80.4	148.7	147.5	100.9	60.1	25.6	5.4
1990[4]	90.5	106.0	78.8	143.7	144.8	105.3	61.5	25.5	5.1
1989[4]	90.7	104.5	78.9	140.9	142.4	102.9	60.5	24.9	5.0
1988[4]	86.5	96.1	73.5	130.5	133.6	97.2	57.4	24.1	5.0
1987[4]	82.6	90.9	69.9	123.0	126.1	91.6	53.1	22.4	4.7
1986[4]	79.0	88.5	67.0	121.1	118.0	84.6	50.0	20.6	4.4
1985[4]	77.0	87.6	66.8	117.9	113.1	79.3	47.5	20.4	4.3
1984[4,5]	75.2	86.1	66.5	113.6	107.9	77.8	43.8	19.4	4.3
1983[4,5]	76.2	85.5	66.8	111.9	107.2	79.7	43.8	19.4	4.8
1982[4,5]	77.9	85.1	66.3	112.7	109.3	82.7	44.1	19.5	5.2
1981[4,5]	79.4	85.0	65.9	114.2	110.7	83.1	45.5	19.6	5.6
1980[4,5]	81.1	87.9	68.8	118.2	112.3	81.4	46.7	19.0	5.5
Race of child:									
1980[5,6]	83.2	90.3	70.6	121.8	116.0	82.9	47.0	18.5	5.5
1975[5,6]	84.2	93.5	76.8	123.8	108.0	75.7	50.0	20.5	7.2
1970[6,7]	95.5	96.9	77.9	136.4	131.5	100.9	71.8	32.9	10.4

[1]Rates computed by relating total births to unmarried mothers, regardless of age of mother, to unmarried women aged 15–44 years.
[2]Rates computed by relating births to unmarried mothers aged 40 years and over to unmarried women aged 40–44 years.
[3]Includes races other than white and black.
[4]Data for States in which marital status was not reported have been inferred and included with data from the remaining States; see Technical notes.
[5]Based on 100 percent of births in selected States and on a 50-percent sample of births in all other States; see Technical notes.
[6]Births to unmarried women are estimated for the United States from data for registration areas in which marital status of mother was reported; see Technical notes.
[7]Based on a 50-percent sample of births.

Source: S. J. Ventura, J. A. Martin, S. M. Taffel, et. al., National Center for Health Statistics, *Advance Report of Final Natality Statistics, 1992*, Monthly Vital Statistics Report, Vol. 43, No. 5 (suppl.), (PHS) 95-1120 4-0677, Washington, D.C.: U.S. Department of Health and Human Services, October 25, 1994, Table 15.

A4-8. Age-Specific Birth Rates for Unmarried Women, by Hispanic Origin of Mother and Race of Non-Hispanic Mothers: 1990 (48 Reporting States and the District of Columbia)

[Rates are births to unmarried mothers per 1,000 unmarried women residing in area for specified group]

State, Hispanic origin of mother, and race of non-Hispanic mother	15–44 years[1]	Age of mother			20–24 years	25–29 years	30–34 years	35–44 years[2]
		15–19 years						
		Total	15–17 years	18–19 years				
Total of 48 reporting States and the District of Columbia[3]								
All origins[4]	41.7	42.7	29.9	59.3	64.0	53.9	35.8	10.4
Hispanic	83.4	66.2	46.8	96.9	122.5	115.9	82.9	29.1
Mexican	87.1	65.5	45.7	98.3	129.2	124.1	88.9	31.5
Puerto Rican	84.0	86.9	63.1	122.1	132.1	101.8	61.5	19.2
Cuban	20.8	16.8	11.6	24.2	23.4	30.7	28.5	9.1
Other and unknown Hispanic[5]	101.3	62.9	45.0	88.7	116.1	122.2	94.5	34.4
Non-Hispanic[4,6]	37.3	39.9	27.7	55.1	57.6	47.3	31.1	8.8
White[4]	24.4	25.0	16.2	37.0	36.4	30.3	20.5	6.1
Black[4]	88.4	110.5	82.6	148.5	138.9	102.2	61.0	16.8

[1]Rates computed by relating total births to unmarried mothers, regardless of age of mother, to unmarried women 15–44 years of age.
[2]Rates computed by relating births to unmarried mothers aged 35 years and over to unmarried women 35–44 years of age.
[3]Excludes New Hampshire and Oklahoma, which did not report Hispanic origin of the mother on the birth certificate.
[4]Includes origin not stated.
[5]Includes Central and South American and "Other and unknown Hispanic" origin.
[6]Includes races other than white and black.
[7]Rates are births to Mexican and "Other and unknown Hispanic" unmarried mothers per 1,000 unmarried Mexican and "Other and unknown Hispanic" women. See text, page 5.

Source: S. C. Clarke and S. J. Ventura, National Center for Health Statistics, *Birth and Fertility Rates for States: United States, 1990*, Vital and Health Statistics, Series 21, No. 52, (PHS) 95-1930, Washington, D.C.: U.S. Department of Health and Human Services, 1994, Table 8.

A4-9. Live Births, by Mother's Marital Status, Educational Attainment, Age, and Race: 1990 (48 Reporting States, the District of Columbia, and New York City)

(For most States, marital status of mother is reported on the birth certificate, and for the other States, mother's marital status is inferred. Figures for marital status not classifiable are included in births to married women.)

Marital status, age, and race of mother	Total	Years of school completed by mother					
		0-8 years	9-11 years	12 years	13-15 years	16 years or more	Not stated
Births to unmarried women,[1] all ages	1,108,693	102,500	378,808	435,817	135,735	33,587	22,246
Under 15 years	10,318	7,723	2,166	–	–	–	429
15-19 years	334,298	31,549	189,989	96,294	10,706	–	5,760
15 years	23,177	7,816	14,735	–	–	–	626
16 years	44,377	6,270	36,229	1,063	–	–	815
17 years	68,915	5,607	52,809	9,214	121	–	1,164
18 years	91,519	5,861	46,891	35,267	2,078	–	1,422
19 years	106,310	5,995	39,325	50,750	8,507	–	1,733
20-24 years	383,864	26,510	108,966	179,926	55,788	5,772	6,902
25-29 years	218,193	18,633	49,871	96,569	38,081	10,167	4,872
30-34 years	112,003	11,341	20,336	45,936	21,653	9,904	2,833
35-39 years	41,897	5,307	6,328	14,653	8,128	6,296	1,185
40-49 years	8,120	1,437	1,152	2,439	1,379	1,448	265
White, all ages	628,173	79,136	216,785	230,404	69,097	20,614	12,137
Under 15 years	3,972	2,979	825	–	–	–	168
15-19 years	188,376	22,186	105,534	51,692	5,732	–	3,232
15 years	11,070	3,922	6,827	–	–	–	321
16 years	23,740	4,075	18,634	574	–	–	457
17 years	39,144	4,309	29,171	4,916	71	–	677
18 years	52,844	4,865	27,101	18,968	1,145	–	765
19 years	61,578	5,015	23,801	27,234	4,516	–	1,012
20-24 years	217,725	22,822	65,885	93,593	28,421	3,166	3,838
25-29 years	123,434	16,165	29,370	50,918	18,733	5,644	2,604
30-34 years	63,891	9,547	11,152	24,646	10,866	6,180	1,500
35-39 years	25,390	4,310	3,343	8,124	4,466	4,511	636
40-49 years	5,385	1,127	676	1,431	879	1,113	159
Black, all ages	442,338	19,228	150,470	191,041	61,684	10,926	8,989
Under 15 years	6,084	4,566	1,274	–	–	–	244
15-19 years	135,862	8,348	78,826	41,748	4,642	–	2,298
15 years	11,432	3,690	7,454	–	–	–	288
16 years	19,364	2,023	16,554	464	–	–	323
17 years	27,745	1,113	22,107	4,041	46	–	438
18 years	35,948	802	18,393	15,287	866	–	600
19 years	41,373	720	14,318	21,956	3,730	–	649
20-24 years	153,394	2,531	39,849	80,473	25,451	2,366	2,724
25-29 years	86,797	1,635	18,853	42,421	17,936	3,917	2,035
30-34 years	43,488	1,259	8,491	19,614	9,952	3,012	1,160
35-39 years	14,470	704	2,749	5,905	3,276	1,381	455
40-49 years	2,243	185	428	880	427	250	73

[1] Includes races other than white and black.

Source: National Center for Health Statistics, *Vital Statistics of the United States, 1990*, Vol. 1 (Natality), Washington, D.C.: U.S. Government Printing Office, 1994, Table 1-82.

A4-10. Native-Born and Foreign-Born Unmarried Women 18 to 44 Years Old Who Had a Birth in the Year before the Survey Date: 1983, 1986, and 1988

(Numbers in thousands)

Year	Native-born women			Foreign born		
	Total	Unmarried women[1]		Total	Unmarried women[1]	
		Number	Percent		Number	Percent
1988	3,232	835	25.8	390	79	20.3
1986	3,138	642	20.5	379	54	14.2
1983	[2]3,625	[2]582	[2]16.1	[3]271	[3]33	[3]12.2

[1] Women widowed, divorced or never married at the survey date.
[2] Data are for native-born and foreign-born women for June 1983.
[3] Data for foreign-born women refer to April 1983.
Source: Current Population Surveys: April 1983, June 1983, 1986, and 1988.

Source: U.S. Bureau of the Census, *Studies in American Fertility*, Current Population Reports, Series P-23, No. 176, Washington, D.C.: U.S. Government Printing Office, 1991, Table K.

A4-11. Fertility Indicators for Never-Married Women 15 to 44 Years Old, by Selected Characteristics: June 1990 and 1994

[Numbers in thousands]

Characteristics	1994				1990			
	Total	Number of mothers	Mothers as a percent of total	Children ever born per 1,000 women	Total	Number of mothers	Mothers as a percent of total	Children ever born per 1,000 women
Total.........................	22,733	4,603	20.2	378	20,739	3,756	18.1	323
AGE								
15 to 19 years	8,405	544	6.5	81	8,049	451	5.6	68
20 to 24 years	6,121	1,237	20.2	315	5,633	1,086	19.3	312
25 to 29 years	3,502	1,052	30.0	603	3,297	970	29.4	555
30 to 34 years	2,233	861	38.6	842	1,972	650	33.0	668
35 to 39 years	1,509	605	40.1	853	1,076	385	35.8	741
40 to 44 years	963	304	31.6	729	711	213	30.0	644
RACE								
White	16,668	2,158	12.9	210	15,707	1,710	10.9	170
Black	4,855	2,244	46.2	964	4,189	1,955	46.7	929
Asian and Pacifc Islander...........	726	67	9.2	179	653	42	6.4	100
HISPANIC ORIGIN								
Hispanic[1]........................	2,535	687	27.1	531	1,935	505	26.1	507
Not Hispanic.....................	20,198	3,916	19.4	359	18,804	3,251	17.3	305
EDUCATIONAL ATTAINMENT								
Less than high school..............	7,833	1,458	18.6	398	7,229	1,324	18.3	371
High school, 4 years	5,203	1,876	36.1	668	5,959	1,582	26.5	446
College, 1 or more years	9,697	1,268	13.1	206	7,551	850	11.3	181
No degree....................	5,118	819	16.0	251	4,558	[2]638	14.0	229
Associate Degree	1,101	240	21.8	361	(NA)	(NA)	(NA)	(NA)
Bachelor's degree and above	3,478	209	6.0	92	2,993	[3]211	7.0	108
LABOR FORCE STATUS								
In labor force	15,780	2,718	17.2	301	14,472	2,160	14.9	236
Not in labor force..................	6,953	1,885	27.1	553	6,268	1,596	25.5	525
OCCUPATION								
Managerial and professional.........	2,840	243	8.6	136	2,411	214	8.9	135
Other	11,037	1,959	17.7	306	10,484	1,548	14.8	231
REGION OF RESIDENCE								
Northeast........................	5,105	987	19.3	361	4,650	774	16.6	285
Midwest.........................	5,487	1,180	21.5	392	5,020	894	17.8	325
South...........................	7,464	1,565	21.0	403	6,661	1,356	20.4	374
West............................	4,676	871	18.6	339	4,409	731	16.6	285

[1]Persons of Hispanic origin may be of any race.
[2]1 to 3 years of college completed.
[3]4 or more years of college completed.

Source: June Current Population surveys, 1990 and 1994.

Source: Amara Bachu, U.S. Bureau of the Census, *Fertility of American Women: June 1994*, Current Population Reports, P20-482, Washington, D.C.: U.S. Government Printing Office, 1995, Table J.

A5. DEATH AND LIFE EXPECTANCY

A5-1. Life Expectancy, by Sex and Race: 1970 to 1992

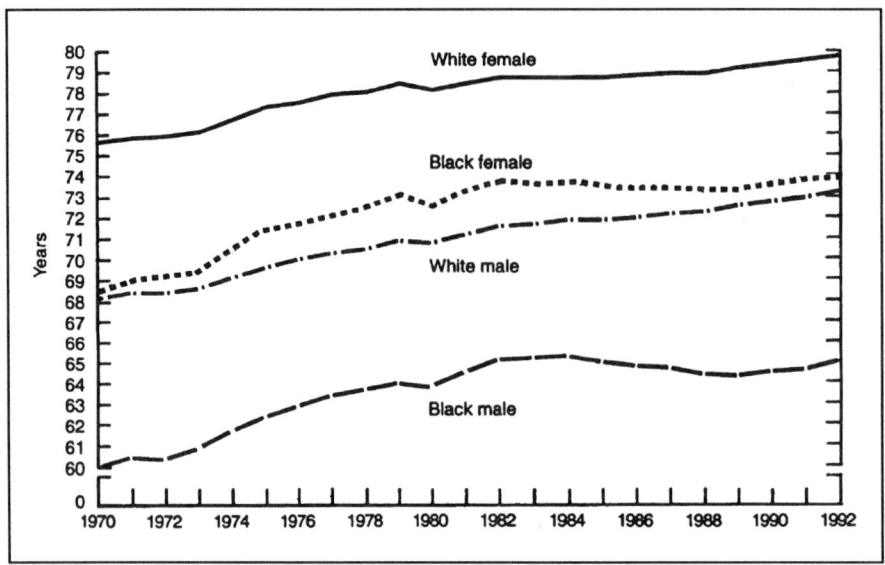

Source: Kenneth D. Kochanek, and Bettie L. Hudson, National Center for Health Statistics, *Advance Report of Final Mortality Statistics, 1992*, Monthly Vital Statistics Report, Vol. 43, No. 6 (suppl.), Washington, D.C.: U.S. Department of Health and Human Services, December 8, 1994, Figure 3.

A5-2. Expectation of Life at Selected Ages, by Race and Sex: Death-Registration States for Selected Years from 1900–02 to 1990

Life table value, period, and age	Total	White		All other			
				Total		Black	
		Male	Female	Male	Female	Male	Female
Expectation of life							
At birth:							
1990	75.4	72.7	79.4	67.0	75.2	64.5	73.6
1989[1]	75.1	72.5	79.2	66.7	74.9	64.3	73.3
1979–81	73.88	70.82	78.22	65.63	74.00	64.10	73.88
1969–71	70.75	67.94	75.49	60.98	69.05	69.00	68.32
1959–61	69.89	67.55	74.19	61.48	66.47	- - -	- - -
1900–1902	49.24	48.23	51.08	- - -	- - -	32.54	35.04
At age 1 year:							
1990	75.1	72.3	78.9	67.2	75.3	65.8	73.8
1989[1]	74.9	72.2	78.8	66.9	75.0	64.6	73.6
1979–81	73.82	70.70	77.98	66.01	74.31	64.60	73.31
1969–71	71.19	68.33	75.66	62.13	70.01	61.24	69.37
1959–61	70.75	68.34	74.68	63.50	68.10	- - -	- - -
1900–1902	55.20	54.61	56.39	- - -	- - -	42.46	43.54
At age 20 years:							
1990	56.6	54.0	60.3	49.0	56.8	46.7	55.3
1989[1]	56.5	53.8	60.2	48.7	56.5	46.5	55.1
1979–81	55.46	52.45	59.44	47.87	55.88	46.48	54.90
1969–71	53.00	50.22	57.24	44.37	51.85	43.49	51.22
1959–61	52.58	50.25	56.29	45.78	50.07	- - -	- - -
1900–1902	42.79	42.19	43.77	- - -	- - -	35.11	36.89
At age 65 years:							
1990	17.2	15.2	19.1	14.0	17.8	13.2	17.2
1989[1]	17.1	15.1	18.9	13.9	17.5	13.0	16.9
1979–81	16.51	14.26	18.55	13.83	17.60	13.29	17.13
1969–71	15.00	13.02	16.93	12.87	15.99	12.53	15.67
1959–61	14.39	12.97	15.88	12.84	15.12	- - -	- - -
1900–1902	11.86	11.51	12.23	- - -	- - -	10.38	11.38

[1]Life table values are revised and, therefore, may differ from those published in *Vital Statistics of the United States, 1989 Life Tables, Volume II, Section 6* and earlier years.

Source: National Center for Health Statistics, *Life Tables*, Vital Statistics of the United States: 1990, Vol. II, Section 6, DHHS Publication No. (PHS) 94-1104, Hyattsville, MD: Public Health Service, September 1994, Table A.

A5-3. Percent Surviving from Birth to Selected Ages and Median Age at Death, by Race and Sex: Death-Registration States for Selected Years from 1900–02 to 1990

Life table value, period, and age	Total	White		All other			
				Total		Black	
		Male	Female	Male	Female	Male	Female
Percent surviving from birth							
To age 1 year:							
1990	99.1	99.1	99.3	98.3	98.6	98.0	98.4
1989[1]	99.0	99.1	99.3	98.2	98.5	98.0	98.3
1979–81	98.7	98.8	99.0	97.9	98.3	97.7	98.1
1969–71	98.0	98.0	98.5	96.6	97.2	96.4	97.1
1959–61	97.4	97.4	98.0	95.3	96.2	- - -	- - -
1900–1902	87.6	86.7	88.9	- - -	- - -	74.7	78.5
To age 20 years:							
1990	98.2	98.1	98.8	96.8	97.9	96.3	97.6
1989[1]	98.1	98.1	98.7	96.8	97.8	96.4	97.5
1979–81	97.7	97.5	98.4	96.4	97.4	96.1	97.2
1969–71	96.7	96.5	97.6	94.3	95.9	94.1	95.7
1959–61	96.1	95.9	97.1	93.1	94.7	- - -	- - -
1900–1902	77.2	76.4	79.0	- - -	- - -	56.7	59.1
To age 65 years:							
1990	79.6	76.0	86.4	62.7	78.3	57.1	75.1
1989[1]	79.5	75.9	86.3	63.6	78.3	57.8	75.3
1979–81	77.1	72.4	84.8	58.5	75.4	55.1	73.3
1969–71	71.9	66.3	81.6	49.6	66.1	47.5	64.7
1959–61	71.1	65.8	80.7	51.4	60.8	- - -	- - -
1900–1902	40.9	39.2	43.8	- - -	- - -	19.0	22.0
Median age at death:							
1990	79.0	76.2	85.8	70.9	79.3	68.3	77.6
1989[1]	78.8	76.0	82.6	70.3	78.8	67.8	77.2
1979–81	77.6	74.2	81.8	69.0	77.8	67.4	76.6
1969–71	74.9	71.5	79.5	64.8	72.8	63.8	72.2
1959–61	74.3	71.4	78.5	65.6	70.6	- - -	- - -
1900–1902	58.4	57.2	60.6	- - -	- - -	29.8	34.3

[1]Life table values are revised and, therefore, may differ from those published in *Vital Statistics of the United States, 1989 Life Tables, Volume II Section 6* and earlier years.

Source: National Center for Health Statistics, *Life Tables*, Vital Statistics of the United States: 1990, Vol. II, Section 6, DHHS Publication No. (PHS) 94-1104, Hyattsville, MD: Public Health Service, September 1994, Table B.

A5-4. Deaths, by Race and Sex: Death-Registration States, 1900–1932, and United States, 1933–1989

(Beginning 1970, excludes deaths of nonresidents of the United States.)

Area and year	All races			White			All other					
							Total			Black		
	Both sexes	Male	Female	Both sexes	Male	Female	Both sexes	Male	Female	Both sexes	Male	Female
UNITED STATES [1]												
1989	2,150,466	1,114,190	1,036,276	1,853,841	950,852	902,989	296,625	163,338	133,287	267,642	146,393	121,249
1988	2,167,999	1,125,540	1,042,459	1,876,906	965,419	911,487	291,093	160,121	130,972	264,019	144,228	119,791
1987	2,123,323	1,107,958	1,015,365	1,843,067	953,382	889,685	280,256	154,576	125,680	254,814	139,551	115,263
1986	2,105,361	1,104,005	1,001,356	1,831,083	952,554	878,529	274,278	151,451	122,827	250,326	137,214	113,112
1985	2,086,440	1,097,758	988,682	1,819,054	950,455	868,599	267,386	147,303	120,083	244,207	133,610	110,597
1984	2,039,369	1,076,514	962,855	1,781,897	934,529	847,368	257,472	141,985	115,487	235,884	129,147	106,737
1983	2,019,201	1,071,923	947,278	1,765,582	931,779	833,803	253,619	140,144	113,475	233,124	127,911	105,213
1982	1,974,797	1,056,440	918,357	1,729,085	919,239	809,846	245,712	137,201	108,511	226,513	125,610	100,903
1981	1,977,981	1,063,772	914,209	1,731,233	925,490	805,743	246,748	138,282	108,466	228,560	127,296	101,264
1980	1,989,841	1,075,078	914,763	1,738,607	933,878	804,729	251,234	141,200	110,034	233,135	130,138	102,997
1979	1,913,841	1,044,959	868,882	1,676,145	910,137	766,008	237,696	135,822	102,874	220,818	124,433	96,385
1978	1,927,788	1,055,290	872,498	1,689,722	920,123	769,599	238,066	135,167	102,899	221,340	124,663	96,677
1977	1,899,597	1,046,243	853,354	1,664,100	912,670	751,430	235,497	133,573	101,924	220,076	123,894	96,182
1976	1,909,440	1,051,983	857,457	1,674,989	918,589	756,400	234,451	133,394	101,057	219,442	123,977	95,465
1975	1,892,879	1,050,819	842,060	1,660,366	917,804	742,562	232,513	133,015	99,498	217,932	123,770	94,162
1974	1,934,388	1,071,627	862,761	1,697,295	936,640	760,655	237,093	134,987	102,106	222,948	126,036	96,912
1973	1,973,003	1,096,795	876,208	1,728,405	957,918	770,487	244,598	138,877	105,721	230,110	129,647	100,463
1972 [2]	1,963,944	1,096,198	867,746	1,721,468	957,518	763,950	242,476	138,680	103,796	228,450	129,740	98,710
1971	1,927,542	1,077,332	850,210	1,689,771	942,337	747,434	237,771	134,995	102,776	224,138	126,362	97,776
1970	1,921,031	1,078,478	842,553	1,682,096	942,437	739,659	238,935	136,041	102,894	225,647	127,540	98,107
1969	1,921,990	1,080,926	841,064	1,683,622	945,380	738,242	238,368	135,546	102,822	225,537	127,145	98,392
1968	1,930,082	1,087,220	842,862	1,689,559	951,154	738,405	240,523	136,066	104,457	227,682	127,793	99,889
1967	1,851,323	1,045,945	805,378	1,627,151	919,514	707,637	224,172	126,431	97,741	212,252	118,689	93,563
1966	1,863,149	1,052,827	810,322	1,634,461	924,342	710,119	228,688	128,485	100,203	216,736	120,843	95,893
1965	1,828,136	1,035,200	792,936	1,605,498	910,511	694,987	222,638	124,689	97,949	211,230	117,328	93,902
1964	1,798,051	1,017,778	780,273	1,578,674	895,518	683,156	219,377	122,260	97,117	209,065	115,717	93,348
1963 [3]	1,813,549	1,027,686	785,863	1,533,015	871,994	661,021	216,662	120,406	96,256	204,888	112,708	92,180
1962 [3]	1,756,720	994,789	761,931	1,488,113	846,458	641,655	206,583	114,262	92,321	195,598	107,105	88,493
1961	1,701,522	966,827	734,695	1,498,332	854,569	643,763	203,190	112,258	90,932	192,791	105,493	87,298
1960	1,711,982	975,648	736,334	1,505,335	860,857	644,478	206,647	114,791	91,856	196,010	107,701	88,309
1959	1,656,814	943,088	713,726	1,460,840	834,651	626,189	195,974	108,437	87,537	187,951	103,126	84,825
1958	1,647,886	936,794	711,092	1,451,077	828,550	622,527	196,809	108,244	88,565	189,341	103,333	86,008
1957	1,633,128	930,728	702,400	1,437,652	823,067	614,585	195,476	107,661	87,815	187,912	102,709	85,203
1956	1,564,476	893,357	671,119	1,380,915	792,364	588,551	183,561	100,993	82,568	176,341	96,140	80,201
1955	1,528,717	872,638	656,079	1,350,869	774,758	576,111	177,848	97,880	79,968	171,021	93,378	77,643
1954	1,481,091	846,124	634,967	1,306,989	750,099	556,890	174,102	96,025	78,077	167,241	91,403	75,838
1953	1,517,541	867,100	650,441	1,335,835	766,703	569,132	181,706	100,397	81,309	174,625	95,739	78,886
1952	1,496,838	853,927	642,911	1,315,022	753,571	561,451	181,816	100,356	81,460	174,695	95,723	78,972
1951	1,482,099	845,233	636,866	1,302,969	747,049	555,920	179,130	98,184	80,946	171,983	93,515	78,468
1950	1,452,454	827,749	624,705	1,276,085	731,366	544,719	176,369	96,383	79,986	169,606	92,004	77,602
1949	1,443,607	821,291	622,316	1,268,848	726,169	542,679	174,759	95,122	79,637	168,067	90,765	77,302
1948	1,444,337	820,931	623,406	1,270,589	725,818	544,771	173,748	95,113	78,635	167,046	90,732	76,314
1947	1,445,370	818,234	627,136	1,274,893	726,104	548,789	170,477	92,130	78,347	163,781	87,760	76,021
1946	1,395,617	785,689	609,928	1,232,337	697,323	535,014	163,280	88,366	74,914	156,493	83,949	72,544
1945	1,401,719	788,063	613,656	1,233,889	697,698	536,191	167,830	90,365	77,465	160,733	85,716	75,017
1944	1,411,338	789,861	621,477	1,238,829	697,731	541,098	172,509	92,130	80,379	165,180	87,488	77,692
1943	1,459,544	817,485	642,059	1,280,887	721,777	559,110	178,657	95,708	82,949	171,247	90,998	80,249
1942	1,385,187	780,454	604,733	1,209,944	685,468	524,476	175,243	94,986	80,257	168,244	90,430	77,814
1941	1,397,642	780,033	612,609	1,213,511	685,672	527,839	184,131	99,361	84,770	176,729	94,697	82,032
1940	1,417,269	791,003	626,266	1,231,223	690,901	540,322	186,046	100,102	85,944	178,743	95,517	83,226
1939	1,387,897	768,877	619,020	1,207,078	672,047	535,031	180,819	96,830	83,989	173,510	92,276	81,234
1938	1,381,391	764,902	616,489	1,195,431	665,559	529,872	185,960	99,343	86,617	178,573	94,659	83,914
1937	1,450,427	808,834	641,593	1,254,787	702,630	552,157	195,640	106,204	89,436	187,594	101,166	86,428
1936	1,479,228	821,439	657,789	1,278,379	712,126	566,253	200,849	109,313	91,536	192,748	104,235	88,513
1935	1,392,752	771,320	621,432	1,207,359	671,298	536,061	185,393	100,022	85,371	177,523	95,033	82,490
1934	1,396,903	772,595	624,308	1,207,197	670,476	536,721	189,706	102,119	87,587	182,075	97,358	84,717
1933	1,342,106	737,312	604,794	1,162,398	641,725	520,673	179,708	95,587	84,121	172,114	90,807	81,307
DEATH-REGISTRATION STATES [4]												
1932	1,293,269	704,506	588,763	1,122,470	614,093	508,377	170,799	90,413	80,386	163,442	85,752	77,690
1931	1,307,273	717,630	589,643	1,125,377	621,120	504,257	181,896	96,510	85,386	174,023	91,587	82,436
1930	1,327,240	726,680	600,560	1,136,884	625,792	511,092	190,356	100,888	89,468	182,021	95,696	86,325
1929	1,369,757	745,491	624,266	1,175,490	642,463	533,027	194,267	103,028	91,239	186,676	98,196	88,480
1928	1,361,987	738,891	623,096	1,168,269	637,063	531,206	193,718	101,828	91,890	186,898	97,627	89,271
1927	1,211,627	656,697	554,930	1,050,358	572,061	478,297	161,269	84,636	76,633	155,462	80,949	74,513
1926	1,257,256	677,032	580,224	1,093,850	590,852	502,998	163,406	86,180	77,226	157,284	82,312	74,972
1925	1,191,809	641,397	550,412	1,035,500	559,356	476,144	156,309	82,041	74,268	150,665	78,462	72,203
1924	1,151,076	619,874	531,202	997,617	539,303	458,314	153,459	80,571	72,888	147,852	76,991	70,861
1923	1,174,065	625,259	548,806	1,028,101	549,623	478,478	145,964	75,636	70,328	140,894	72,379	68,515
1922	1,083,952	575,927	508,025	951,452	507,567	443,885	132,500	68,360	64,140	127,733	65,205	62,528
1921	1,009,673	533,267	476,406	895,593	475,172	420,421	114,080	58,095	55,985	109,597	55,119	54,478
1920	1,118,070	586,136	531,934	990,859	521,440	469,419	127,211	64,696	62,515	121,956	61,332	60,624
1919	1,072,263	567,185	505,078	945,436	502,968	442,468	126,827	64,217	62,610	121,636	60,863	60,773
1918	1,430,079	784,307	645,772	1,282,533	706,613	575,920	147,546	77,694	69,852	- - -	- - -	- - -
1917	981,239	538,523	442,716	882,735	486,208	396,527	98,504	52,315	46,189	- - -	- - -	- - -
1916	924,971	504,887	420,084	842,597	461,432	381,165	82,374	43,455	38,919	78,715	41,002	37,713
1915	815,500	443,928	371,572	762,289	415,476	346,813	53,211	28,452	24,759	49,767	26,111	23,656
1914	810,914	443,622	367,292	758,600	415,493	343,107	52,314	28,129	24,185	49,135	25,950	23,185
1913	802,909	440,347	362,562	752,265	413,225	339,040	50,644	27,122	23,522	- - -	- - -	- - -

A5-4. Deaths, by Race and Sex: Death-Registration States, 1900–1932, and United States, 1933–1989 *(continued)*

	All races			White			All other					
							Total			Black		
Area and year	Both sexes	Male	Female	Both sexes	Male	Female	Both sexes	Male	Female	Both sexes	Male	Female
Beginning 1970 excludes deaths of nonresidents of the United States												
DEATH-REGISTRATION STATES [4] – Con.												
1912	745,771	408,093	337,678	709,531	388,302	321,229	36,240	19,791	16,449	- - -	- - -	- - -
1911	749,918	408,133	341,785	713,244	388,238	325,006	36,674	19,895	16,779	33,722	17,850	15,872
1910	696,856	380,073	316,783	669,475	365,042	304,433	27,381	15,031	12,350	24,908	13,151	11,757
1909	630,057	341,551	288,506	603,551	327,153	276,398	26,506	14,398	12,108	23,579	12,428	11,151
1908	567,245	307,359	259,886	542,800	294,173	248,627	24,445	13,186	11,259	21,700	11,226	10,474
1907	550,245	299,799	250,446	525,259	286,269	238,990	24,986	13,530	11,456	22,482	11,759	10,723
1906	531,005	287,691	243,314	506,553	274,579	231,974	24,452	13,112	11,340	22,120	11,488	10,632
1905	345,863	183,085	162,778	334,344	177,105	157,239	11,519	5,980	5,539	11,103	5,700	5,403
1904	349,855	184,991	164,864	338,301	178,963	159,338	11,554	6,028	5,526	11,129	5,729	5,400
1903	327,295	172,623	154,672	316,650	167,134	149,516	10,645	5,489	5,156	10,273	5,231	5,042
1902	318,636	168,639	149,997	308,550	163,387	145,163	10,086	5,252	4,834	9,718	4,986	4,732
1901	332,203	174,867	157,336	321,948	169,530	152,418	10,255	5,337	4,918	9,834	5,030	4,804
1900	343,217	179,016	164,201	332,810	173,731	159,079	10,407	5,285	5,122	9,954	4,972	4,982

[1] Alaska included in 1959 and Hawaii in 1960.
[2] Deaths based on a 50-percent sample.
[3] Figures by race exclude data for residents of New Jersey
[4] Increased in number from 10 States and the District of Columbia in 1900 to the entire conterminous United States in 1933.

Source: National Center for Health Statistics, *Vital Statistics of the United States, 1989*, Vol. II (Mortality, Part A), DHHS Pub. No. (PHS) 93-1101, Washington, D.C.: U.S. Public Health Service, 1993, Table 1-1.

A5-5. Differences in Life Expectancy at Birth between Males and Females, by Race; and between Whites and Blacks, by Sex: Death-Registration States for Selected Years from 1900–02 to 1990

	Female-Male		White-Black	
Period	White	Black	Male	Female
1990	6.7	9.1	8.2	5.8
1989[1]	6.7	9.0	8.2	5.9
1988[1]	6.7	8.8	7.8	5.7
1987[1]	6.8	8.7	7.4	5.5
1986[1]	6.9	8.6	7.1	5.4
1985[1]	6.9	8.4	6.8	5.3
1984[1]	6.9	8.3	6.5	5.1
1979–81	7.40	8.78	6.72	5.34
1969–71	7.55	8.32	7.94	7.17
1959–61	6.64	- - -	- - -	- - -
1900–1902	2.85	2.50	15.69	16.04

[1] Life table values are revised and, therefore, may differ from those published in *Vital Statistics of the United States, 1989 Life Tables, Volume II, Section 6* and earlier years.

Source: National Center for Health Statistics, *Life Tables*, Vital Statistics of the United States: 1990, Vol. II, Section 6, DHHS Publication No. (PHS) 94-1104, Hyattsville, MD: Public Health Service, September 1994, Table D.

A5-6. Death Rates, by Age and Sex: 1950 to 1992

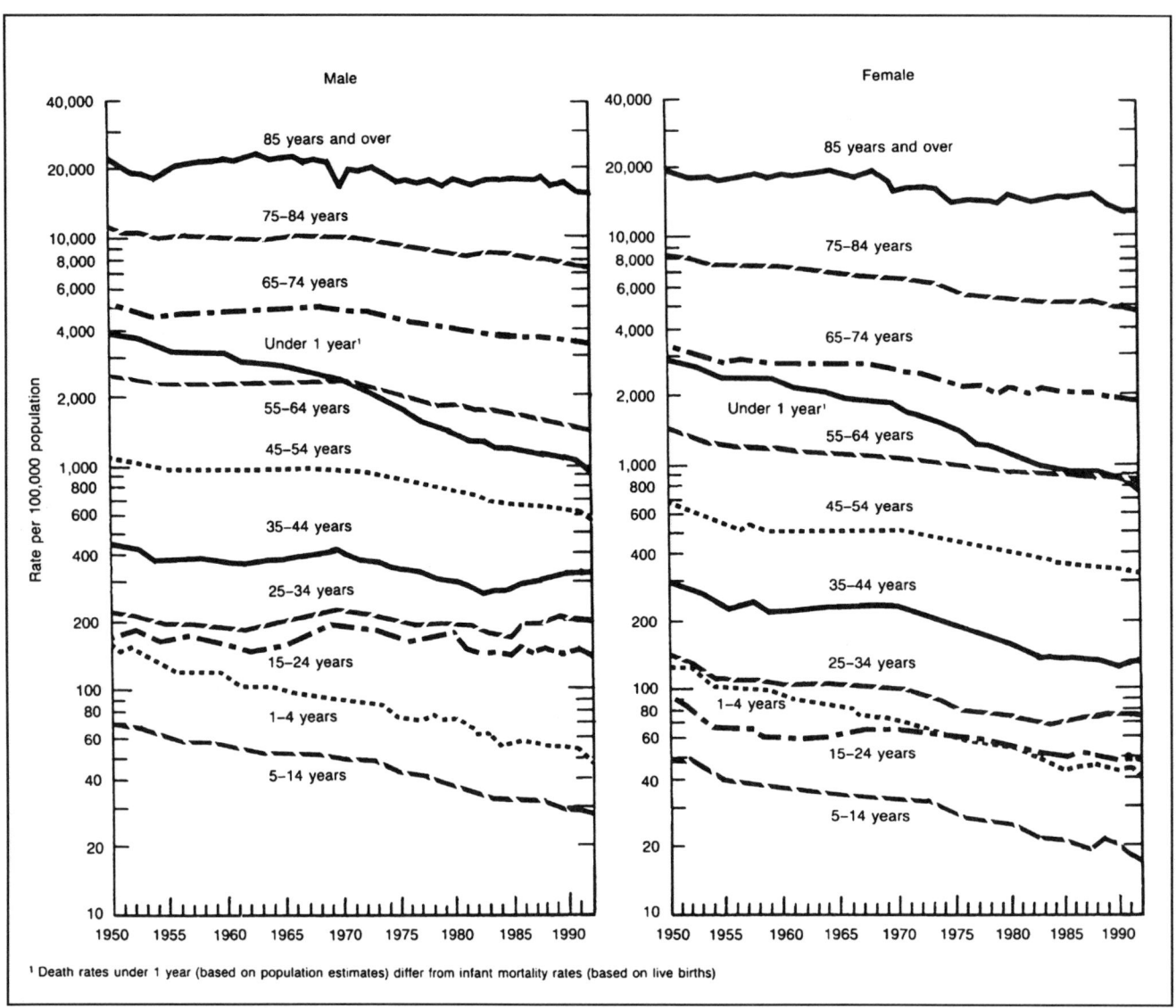

¹ Death rates under 1 year (based on population estimates) differ from infant mortality rates (based on live births)

Source: Kenneth D. Kochanek, and Bettie L. Hudson, National Center for Health Statistics, *Advance Report of Final Mortality Statistics, 1992,* Monthly Vital Statistics Report, Vol. 43, No. 6 (suppl.), Washington, D.C.: U.S. Department of Health and Human Services, December 8, 1994, Figure 2.

A5-7. Deaths and Age-Adjusted Death Rates, by Race and Sex: 1940, 1950, 1960, 1970, and 1975 to 1992

(Crude rates on an annual basis per 100,000 population in specified group; age-adjusted rates per 100,000 U.S. standard million population. Rates are based on populations enumerated as of April 1 for census years and estimated as of July 1 for all other years. Beginning 1970, excludes deaths of nonresidents of the United States. Data for specified races other than White and Black should be interpreted with caution because of inconsistencies in reporting race on the death certificate.)

Number

Year	All races[1] Both sexes	All races[1] Male	All races[1] Female	White Both sexes	White Male	White Female	Black Both sexes	Black Male	Black Female	American Indian[2] Both sexes	American Indian[2] Male	American Indian[2] Female	Asian or Pacific Islander[3] Both sexes	Asian or Pacific Islander[3] Male	Asian or Pacific Islander[3] Female
1992	2,175,613	1,122,336	1,053,277	1,873,781	956,957	916,824	269,219	146,630	122,589	8,953	5,181	3,772	23,660	13,568	10,092
1991	2,169,518	1,121,665	1,047,853	1,868,904	956,497	912,407	269,525	147,331	122,194	8,621	4,948	3,673	22,173	12,727	9,446
1990	2,148,463	1,113,417	1,035,046	1,853,254	950,812	902,442	265,498	145,359	120,139	8,316	4,877	3,439	21,127	12,211	8,916
1989	2,150,466	1,114,190	1,036,276	1,853,841	950,852	902,989	267,642	146,393	121,249	8,614	5,066	3,548	20,042	11,688	8,354
1988	2,167,999	1,125,540	1,042,459	1,876,906	965,419	911,487	264,019	144,228	119,791	7,917	4,617	3,300	18,963	11,155	7,808
1987	2,123,323	1,107,958	1,015,365	1,843,067	953,382	889,685	254,814	139,551	115,263	7,602	4,432	3,170	17,689	10,496	7,193
1986	2,105,361	1,104,005	1,001,356	1,831,083	952,554	878,529	250,326	137,214	113,112	7,301	4,365	2,936	16,514	9,795	6,719
1985	2,086,440	1,097,758	988,682	1,819,054	950,455	868,599	244,207	133,610	110,597	7,154	4,181	2,973	15,887	9,441	6,446
1984	2,039,369	1,076,514	962,855	1,781,897	934,529	847,368	235,884	129,147	106,737	6,949	4,117	2,832	14,483	8,627	5,856
1983	2,019,201	1,071,923	947,278	1,765,582	931,779	833,803	233,124	127,911	105,213	6,839	4,064	2,775	13,554	8,126	5,428
1982	1,974,797	1,056,440	918,357	1,729,085	919,239	809,846	226,513	125,610	100,903	6,679	3,974	2,705	12,430	7,564	4,866
1981	1,977,981	1,063,772	914,209	1,731,233	925,490	805,743	228,560	127,296	101,264	6,608	4,016	2,592	11,475	6,908	4,567
1980	1,989,841	1,075,078	914,763	1,738,607	933,878	804,729	233,135	130,138	102,997	6,923	4,193	2,730	11,071	6,809	4,262
1979	1,913,841	1,044,959	868,882	1,676,145	910,137	766,008	220,818	124,433	96,385	6,728	4,171	2,557	...	...	...
1978	1,927,788	1,055,290	872,498	1,689,722	920,123	769,599	221,340	124,663	96,677	6,959	4,343	2,616	...	...	...
1977	1,899,597	1,046,243	853,354	1,664,100	912,670	751,430	220,076	123,894	96,182	6,454	4,019	2,435	...	...	...
1976	1,909,440	1,051,983	857,457	1,674,989	918,589	756,400	219,442	123,977	95,465	6,300	3,883	2,417	...	...	...
1975	1,892,879	1,050,819	842,060	1,660,366	917,804	742,562	217,932	123,770	94,162	6,166	3,838	2,328	...	...	...
1970	1,921,031	1,078,478	842,553	1,682,096	942,437	739,659	225,647	127,540	98,107	5,675	3,391	2,284	...	...	...
1960	1,711,982	975,648	736,334	1,505,335	860,857	644,478	196,010	107,701	88,309	4,528	2,658	1,870	...	...	...
1950	1,452,454	827,749	624,705	1,276,085	731,366	544,719	169,606	92,004	77,602	4,440	2,497	1,943	...	...	...
1940	1,417,269	791,003	626,266	1,231,223	690,901	540,322	178,743	95,517	83,226	4,791	2,527	2,264	...	...	...

A5-7. Deaths and Age-Adjusted Death Rates, by Race and Sex: 1940, 1950, 1960, 1970, and 1975 to 1992 (continued)

(Crude rates on an annual basis per 100,000 population in specified group; age-adjusted rates per 100,000 U.S. standard million population. Rates are based on populations enumerated as of April 1 for census years and estimated as of July 1 for all other years. Beginning 1970, excludes deaths of nonresidents of the United States. Data for specified races other than White and Black should be interpreted with caution because of inconsistencies in reporting race on the death certificate.)

Year	All races[1]			White			Black			American Indian[2]			Asian or Pacific Islander[3]		
	Both sexes	Male	Female	Both sexes	Male	Female	Both sexes	Male	Female	Both sexes	Male	Female	Both sexes	Male	Female
							Age-adjusted death rate								
1992	504.5	656.0	380.3	477.5	620.9	359.9	767.5	1,026.9	568.4	453.1	579.6	343.1	285.8	364.1	220.5
1991	513.7	669.9	386.5	486.8	634.4	366.3	780.7	1,048.8	575.1	441.8	562.6	335.9	283.2	360.2	218.3
1990	520.2	680.2	390.6	492.8	644.3	369.9	789.2	1,061.3	581.6	445.1	573.1	335.1	297.6	377.8	228.9
1989	528.0	689.3	397.3	499.6	652.2	376.0	805.9	1,082.8	594.3	475.7	622.8	353.4	295.8	378.9	225.2
1988	539.9	706.1	406.1	512.8	671.3	385.3	809.7	1,083.0	601.0	456.3	585.7	343.2	300.2	385.4	226.5
1987	539.2	706.8	404.6	513.7	674.2	384.8	796.4	1,063.6	592.4	456.7	580.8	351.3	297.0	386.2	221.3
1986	544.8	716.2	407.6	520.1	684.9	388.1	796.8	1,061.9	594.1	451.4	591.6	328.4	296.7	385.3	220.3
1985	548.9	723.0	410.3	524.9	693.3	391.0	793.6	1,053.4	594.8	468.2	602.6	353.3	305.7	396.9	228.5
1984	548.1	721.6	410.5	525.2	693.6	391.7	783.3	1,035.9	590.1	476.9	614.2	347.3	299.4	386.0	223.0
1983	552.5	729.4	412.5	529.4	701.6	393.3	787.4	1,037.5	595.3	485.9	634.0	360.1	298.9	388.6	218.0
1982	554.7	734.2	411.9	532.3	706.8	393.6	782.1	1,035.4	585.9	494.3	634.6	371.6	293.6	389.2	212.8
1981	568.6	753.8	420.8	544.8	724.8	401.5	807.0	1,068.8	602.7	514.0	676.7	368.5	293.2	382.3	213.9
1980	585.8	777.2	432.6	559.4	745.3	411.1	842.5	1,112.8	631.1	564.1	732.5	414.1	315.6	416.6	224.6
1979	577.0	768.6	423.1	551.9	738.4	402.5	812.1	1,073.3	605.0	---	---	---	---	---	---
1978	595.0	791.4	437.4	569.5	761.1	416.4	831.8	1,093.9	622.7	---	---	---	---	---	---
1977	602.1	801.3	441.8	575.7	770.6	419.6	849.3	1,112.1	639.6	---	---	---	---	---	---
1976	618.5	820.9	455.0	591.3	789.3	432.5	870.5	1,138.3	654.5	---	---	---	---	---	---
1975	630.4	837.2	462.5	602.2	804.3	439.0	890.8	1,163.0	670.6	---	---	---	---	---	---
1970	714.3	931.6	532.5	679.6	893.4	501.7	1,044.0	1,318.6	814.4	---	---	---	---	---	---
1960	760.9	949.3	590.6	727.0	917.7	555.0	1,073.3	1,246.1	916.9	---	---	---	---	---	---
1950	841.5	1,001.6	688.4	800.4	963.1	645.0	---	---	---	---	---	---	---	---	---
1940	1,076.1	1,213.0	938.9	1,017.2	1,155.1	879.0	---	---	---	---	---	---	---	---	---

[1] For 1940–91 includes deaths among races not shown separately; see Technical notes.
[2] Includes deaths among Aleuts and Eskimos.
[3] Includes deaths among Chinese, Filipino, Hawaiian, Japanese, and other Asian or Pacific Islander.

Source: Kenneth D. Kochanek, and Bettie L. Hudson, National Center for Health Statistics, *Advance Report of Final Mortality Statistics, 1992,* Monthly Vital Statistics Report, Vol. 43, No. 6 (suppl.), Washington, D.C.: U.S. Department of Health and Human Services, December 8, 1994, Table 1.

A5-8. Deaths and Death Rates, by Age, Race, and Sex: 1992

(Rates per 100,000 population in specified group. Data for specified races other than White and Black should be interpreted with caution because of inconsistencies in reporting race on the death certificate.)

Number

Age	All races Both sexes	All races Male	All races Female	White Both sexes	White Male	White Female	Black Both sexes	Black Male	Black Female	American Indian[1] Both sexes	American Indian[1] Male	American Indian[1] Female	Asian or Pacific Islander[2] Both sexes	Asian or Pacific Islander[2] Male	Asian or Pacific Islander[2] Female
All ages	2,175,613	1,122,336	1,053,277	1,873,781	956,957	916,824	269,219	146,630	122,589	8,953	5,181	3,772	23,660	13,568	10,092
Under 1 year	34,628	19,545	15,083	22,164	12,625	9,539	11,348	6,298	5,050	393	221	172	723	401	322
1–4 years	6,764	3,809	2,955	4,685	2,690	1,995	1,799	965	834	127	67	60	153	87	66
5–9 years	3,739	2,231	1,508	2,690	1,605	1,085	894	529	365	54	33	21	101	64	37
10–14 years	4,454	2,849	1,605	3,299	2,093	1,206	982	633	349	61	48	13	112	75	37
15–19 years	14,411	10,747	3,664	10,308	7,440	2,868	3,583	2,923	660	206	155	51	314	229	85
20–24 years	20,137	15,460	4,677	14,033	10,696	3,337	5,399	4,246	1,153	279	212	67	426	306	120
25–29 years	24,314	18,032	6,282	17,051	12,825	4,226	6,559	4,695	1,864	293	228	65	411	284	127
30–34 years	34,167	24,863	9,304	24,450	18,210	6,240	8,836	6,083	2,753	378	253	125	503	317	186
35–39 years	42,089	29,641	12,448	30,127	21,690	8,437	10,965	7,308	3,657	403	272	131	594	371	223
40–44 years	49,201	33,354	15,847	35,886	24,726	11,160	12,213	7,949	4,264	366	246	120	736	433	303
45–49 years	56,533	36,622	19,911	43,451	28,343	15,108	11,753	7,493	4,260	431	280	151	898	506	392
50–54 years	68,497	42,649	25,848	53,689	33,681	20,008	13,252	8,021	5,231	487	308	179	1,069	639	430
55–59 years	94,582	58,083	36,499	75,750	47,042	28,708	16,727	9,824	6,903	668	392	276	1,437	825	612
60–64 years	146,409	88,797	57,612	122,213	74,994	47,219	21,669	12,380	9,289	719	408	311	1,808	1,015	793
65–69 years	211,071	124,228	86,843	180,788	107,427	73,361	27,011	14,946	12,065	818	454	364	2,454	1,401	1,053
70–74 years	266,845	149,937	116,908	234,117	132,273	101,844	29,124	15,580	13,544	849	457	392	2,755	1,627	1,128
75–79 years	301,736	158,257	143,479	270,238	142,422	127,816	27,875	13,782	14,093	799	422	377	2,824	1,631	1,193
80–84 years	308,116	141,640	166,476	279,507	128,484	151,023	25,260	11,253	14,007	721	354	367	2,628	1,549	1,079
85 years and over	487,446	161,236	326,210	448,984	147,419	301,565	33,856	11,646	22,210	900	370	530	3,706	1,801	1,905
Not stated	474	356	118	351	272	79	114	76	38	1	1	–	8	7	1

Death rate

Age	All races Both sexes	All races Male	All races Female	White Both sexes	White Male	White Female	Black Both sexes	Black Male	Black Female	American Indian[1] Both sexes	American Indian[1] Male	American Indian[1] Female	Asian or Pacific Islander[2] Both sexes	Asian or Pacific Islander[2] Male	Asian or Pacific Islander[2] Female
All ages[3]	852.9	901.6	806.5	880.0	917.2	844.3	850.5	977.5	736.2	417.7	487.7	348.9	283.1	332.7	235.8
Under 1 year[4]	865.7	956.6	770.8	701.8	780.9	618.7	1,786.0	1,957.9	1,609.7	939.2	1,057.5	821.2	439.8	477.7	400.2
1–4 years	43.6	48.0	39.0	38.1	42.6	33.3	73.2	77.6	68.7	72.0	74.7	69.3	26.9	29.9	23.8
5–9 years	20.4	23.7	16.8	18.3	21.3	15.2	32.1	37.5	26.6	25.1	30.1	19.8	15.4	19.1	11.5
10–14 years	24.6	30.7	18.2	22.8	28.2	17.2	35.3	44.9	25.4	28.3	44.0	*	16.9	22.2	11.3
15–19 years	84.3	122.4	44.0	75.6	106.0	43.3	135.5	218.4	50.5	110.8	163.7	55.9	49.7	70.6	27.6
20–24 years	105.7	159.4	50.1	91.0	135.4	44.3	200.7	321.0	84.3	149.7	218.0	75.2	57.4	80.8	33.1
25–29 years	120.5	178.0	62.5	103.2	153.3	51.9	241.3	361.7	131.3	160.2	245.2	72.4	53.8	75.4	32.8
30–34 years	153.5	224.0	83.3	132.4	195.8	68.1	316.0	464.4	185.2	203.2	275.3	132.8	61.4	79.9	44.1
35–39 years	199.5	282.8	117.2	171.2	245.5	96.3	427.0	609.6	267.1	240.8	334.0	152.4	77.6	101.5	55.8
40–44 years	261.6	359.1	166.5	226.3	312.2	140.6	570.7	803.2	370.7	257.3	355.9	164.1	110.4	139.6	85.0
45–49 years	368.0	485.7	254.6	328.6	432.5	226.5	762.4	1,065.7	508.0	391.5	522.4	267.3	184.9	219.6	153.5
50–54 years	568.2	728.1	417.1	518.6	663.4	379.3	1,054.9	1,419.3	757.0	577.6	759.7	408.9	295.2	366.5	229.0
55–59 years	902.1	1,156.5	668.2	835.1	1,071.5	613.4	1,579.0	2,103.6	1,165.4	997.2	1,229.3	786.3	500.4	620.6	396.8
60–64 years	1,402.2	1,815.2	1,038.2	1,334.9	1,729.7	979.7	2,204.1	2,924.3	1,659.5	1,303.7	1,574.4	1,063.8	729.6	948.4	563.3
65–69 years	2,114.8	2,775.4	1,577.7	2,042.6	2,688.5	1,511.0	3,075.9	4,029.1	2,378.8	1,819.9	2,219.3	1,486.3	1,189.4	1,576.7	896.4
70–74 years	3,146.8	4,109.3	2,419.9	3,073.0	4,012.4	2,356.4	4,278.6	5,724.9	3,315.3	2,541.5	3,145.9	2,076.5	1,872.3	2,486.2	1,380.5
75–79 years	4,705.9	6,202.4	3,716.8	4,662.2	6,148.8	3,672.7	5,596.3	7,502.0	4,482.7	3,434.9	4,410.5	2,753.2	3,001.3	3,882.7	2,290.5
80–84 years	7,429.1	9,726.0	6,186.1	7,391.0	9,700.5	6,146.1	8,400.8	10,969.8	7,070.5	5,133.1	6,753.1	4,168.6	5,156.3	6,461.7	3,997.0
85 years and over	14,972.9	17,740.4	13,901.0	15,104.2	17,956.2	14,015.9	14,278.6	16,717.1	13,264.1	7,726.0	9,381.3	6,878.7	10,841.3	12,628.8	9,561.8

[1] Includes deaths among Aleuts and Eskimos.
[2] Includes deaths among Chinese, Filipino, Hawaiian, Japanese, and other Asian or Pacific Islander.
[3] Figures for age not stated are included in "All ages" but not distributed among age groups.
[4] Death rates under 1 year (based on population estimates) differ from infant mortality rates (based on live births); see tables E and 24–28 for infant mortality rates, and Technical notes for further discussion of the difference.

Source: Kenneth D. Kochanek, and Bettie L. Hudson, National Center for Health Statistics, Advance Report of Final Mortality Statistics, 1992, Monthly Vital Statistics Report, Vol. 43, No. 6 (suppl.). Washington, D.C.: U.S. Department of Health and Human Services, December 8, 1994, Table 2.

A5-9. Deaths, by Age and Hispanic Origin, Race for Non-Hispanic Origin, and Sex: 1992 (48 States and the District of Columbia; excludes Oklahoma and New Hampshire)

Hispanic origin, race for non-Hispanic origin, and sex	Total	Under 1 year	1–4 years	5–14 years	15–24 years	25–34 years	35–44 years	45–54 years	55–64 years	65–74 years	75–84 years	85 years and over	Not stated
All origins	2,136,558	34,117	6,661	8,061	33,999	57,666	89,941	122,905	236,625	469,370	598,807	477,954	452
Male	1,102,513	19,260	3,753	4,988	25,818	42,307	62,088	77,958	144,215	269,214	294,491	158,079	342
Female	1,034,045	14,857	2,908	3,073	8,181	15,359	27,853	44,947	92,410	200,156	304,316	319,875	110
Hispanic	82,395	4,376	908	943	4,700	6,955	7,558	7,049	10,354	14,436	14,398	10,641	77
Male	49,434	2,420	509	565	3,876	5,556	5,743	4,736	6,303	8,267	7,127	4,259	73
Female	32,961	1,956	399	378	824	1,399	1,815	2,313	4,051	6,169	7,271	6,382	4
Mexican	44,483	2,925	612	599	3,205	3,637	3,563	3,492	5,651	7,965	7,319	5,454	61
Male	26,971	1,621	341	357	2,686	2,997	2,677	2,285	3,395	4,543	3,726	2,285	58
Female	17,512	1,304	271	242	519	640	886	1,207	2,256	3,422	3,593	3,169	3
Puerto Rican	10,481	466	105	104	402	1,164	1,576	1,317	1,436	1,634	1,462	815	–
Male	6,452	237	57	61	317	851	1,224	910	880	955	672	288	–
Female	4,029	229	48	43	85	313	352	407	556	679	790	527	–
Cuban	8,109	71	15	22	66	272	402	529	1,022	1,718	2,287	1,701	4
Male	4,563	44	9	15	53	232	337	375	689	1,085	1,138	583	3
Female	3,546	27	6	7	13	40	65	154	333	633	1,149	1,118	1
Central and South American	6,080	325	58	88	459	881	799	638	714	819	787	510	2
Male	3,524	162	31	51	378	707	580	406	385	358	306	158	2
Female	2,556	163	27	37	81	174	219	232	329	461	481	352	–
Other and unknown Hispanic	13,242	589	118	130	568	1,001	1,218	1,073	1,531	2,300	2,543	2,161	10
Male	7,924	356	71	81	442	769	925	760	954	1,326	1,285	945	10
Female	5,318	233	47	49	126	232	293	313	577	974	1,258	1,216	–
Non-Hispanic[1]	2,026,890	28,921	5,669	7,056	28,930	49,767	80,741	113,908	223,257	449,474	577,475	461,494	198
Male	1,038,336	16,369	3,196	4,390	21,660	36,057	55,140	71,870	135,988	257,803	283,912	151,822	129
Female	988,554	12,552	2,473	2,666	7,270	13,710	25,601	42,038	87,269	191,671	293,563	309,672	69
White	1,734,220	16,996	3,671	4,900	19,024	33,373	56,274	86,895	181,420	388,221	519,071	424,260	115
Male	878,144	9,755	2,115	3,032	13,832	24,634	39,137	55,206	111,853	224,289	255,773	138,442	76
Female	856,076	7,241	1,556	1,868	5,192	8,739	17,137	31,689	69,567	163,932	263,298	285,818	39
Black	262,047	10,903	1,747	1,844	8,784	14,933	22,494	24,288	37,476	54,797	51,826	32,876	79
Male	142,575	6,036	942	1,150	7,011	10,431	14,772	15,029	21,644	29,787	24,401	11,322	50
Female	119,472	4,867	805	694	1,773	4,502	7,722	9,259	15,832	25,010	27,425	21,554	29
Not stated[2]	27,273	820	84	62	369	944	1,642	1,948	3,014	5,460	6,934	5,819	177
Male	14,743	471	48	33	282	694	1,205	1,352	1,924	3,144	3,452	1,998	140
Female	12,530	349	36	29	87	250	437	596	1,090	2,316	3,482	3,821	37

[1] Includes races other than white and black.
[2] Includes deaths that occurred in States that did not report Hispanic origin on the death certificate.

Source: Kenneth D. Kochanek, and Bettie L. Hudson, National Center for Health Statistics, *Advance Report of Final Mortality Statistics, 1992*, Monthly Vital Statistics Report, Vol. 43, No. 6 (suppl.), Washington, D.C.: U.S. Department of Health and Human Services, December 8, 1994, Table 15.

A5-10. Deaths for Those Aged 85 Years and Over, by Single Years of Age, Race, and Sex: 1989

Age	All races			White		All other			
						Total		Black	
	Both sexes	Male	Female	Male	Female	Male	Female	Male	Female
85 years and over	457,358	149,735	307,623	136,813	284,856	12,922	22,767	11,056	20,669
85 years	54,346	22,014	32,332	20,077	29,764	1,937	2,568	1,618	2,330
86 years	51,648	20,124	31,524	18,320	28,978	1,804	2,546	1,563	2,336
87 years	47,661	17,731	29,930	16,281	27,676	1,450	2,254	1,224	2,041
88 years	46,195	16,235	29,960	14,721	27,468	1,514	2,492	1,289	2,267
89 years	42,098	14,196	27,902	12,875	25,688	1,321	2,214	1,141	2,026
90 years	36,003	11,529	24,474	10,687	23,006	842	1,468	707	1,321
91 years	33,310	10,091	23,219	9,361	21,775	730	1,444	605	1,287
92 years	29,167	8,550	20,617	7,910	19,345	640	1,272	558	1,139
93 years	26,144	7,287	18,857	6,679	17,656	608	1,201	538	1,070
94 years	21,629	5,787	15,842	5,313	14,829	474	1,013	412	911
95 years	17,899	4,551	13,348	4,227	12,495	324	853	277	765
96 years	14,419	3,521	10,898	3,236	10,144	285	754	251	679
97 years	10,964	2,555	8,409	2,309	7,789	246	620	222	575
98 years	7,899	1,775	6,124	1,606	5,685	169	439	145	408
99 years	6,033	1,398	4,635	1,227	4,236	171	399	146	365
100 years	4,323	906	3,417	781	3,098	125	319	106	292
101 years	2,766	575	2,191	500	1,954	75	237	64	221
102 years	1,787	358	1,429	310	1,266	48	163	43	152
103 years	1,194	238	956	194	800	44	156	38	148
104 years	742	113	629	84	515	29	114	26	106
105 years	450	68	382	51	311	17	71	15	68
106 years	271	49	222	27	164	22	58	21	56
107 years	191	25	166	16	113	9	53	9	49
108 years	80	22	58	7	34	15	24	14	24
109 years	44	15	29	6	22	9	7	8	7
110 years	38	6	32	6	28	-	4	-	4
111 years	18	3	15	-	9	3	6	3	6
112 years	19	6	13	1	7	5	6	5	6
113 years	6	2	4	-	-	2	4	2	4
114 years	4	1	3	-	-	1	3	1	3
115 years	2	2	-	1	-	1	-	1	-
116 years	1	-	1	-	1	-	-	-	-
117 years	1	1	-	-	-	1	-	1	-
118 years	-	-	-	-	-	-	-	-	-
119 years	3	-	3	-	-	-	3	-	3
120 years	1	-	1	-	-	-	1	-	1
121 years	1	-	1	-	-	-	1	-	1
122 years	-	-	-	-	-	-	-	-	-
123 years	1	1	-	-	-	1	-	1	-
124 years	-	-	-	-	-	-	-	-	-
125 years and over	-	-	-	-	-	-	-	-	-

Source: National Center for Health Statistics, *Vital Statistics of the United States, 1989*, Vol. II (Mortality, Part A), DHHS Pub. No. (PHS) 93-1101, Washington, D.C.: U.S. Public Health Service, 1993, Table 1-5.

A5-11. Deaths and Percent Distribution of Deaths for Ages 15 Years and Over, by Educational Attainment, Race, and Sex: 1992 (42 States and the District of Columbia)

Years of school completed	All races			White			All other					
							Total			Black		
	Both sexes	Male	Female	Both sexes	Male	Female	Both sexes	Male	Female	Both sexes	Male	Female
Number [1]												
Total	1,783,993	920,323	863,670	1,547,201	790,282	756,919	236,792	130,041	106,751	209,710	114,467	95,243
0–8 years	430,537	215,145	215,392	361,705	178,796	182,909	68,832	36,349	32,483	60,914	32,614	28,300
9–11 years	236,577	128,480	108,097	195,494	105,189	90,305	41,083	23,291	17,792	38,112	21,448	16,664
12 years	620,922	307,869	313,053	552,389	269,495	282,894	68,533	38,374	30,159	60,716	33,714	27,002
13–15 years	201,240	102,801	98,439	181,992	92,188	89,804	19,248	10,613	8,635	16,378	8,832	7,546
16 years or more	182,588	109,692	72,896	168,338	101,786	66,552	14,250	7,906	6,344	10,599	5,334	5,265
Not stated	112,129	56,336	55,793	87,283	42,828	44,455	24,846	13,508	11,338	22,991	12,525	10,466
Percent distribution [2]												
Total	100.0	100.0	100.0	100.0	100.0	100.0	100.0	100.0	100.0	100.0	100.0	100.0
0–8 years	25.8	24.9	26.7	24.8	23.9	25.7	32.5	31.2	34.0	32.6	32.0	33.4
9–11 years	14.2	14.9	13.4	13.4	14.1	12.7	19.4	20.0	18.6	20.4	21.0	19.7
12 years	37.1	35.6	38.8	37.8	36.1	39.7	32.3	32.9	31.6	32.5	33.1	31.9
13–15 years	12.0	11.9	12.2	12.5	12.3	12.6	9.1	9.1	9.1	8.8	8.7	8.9
16 years or more	10.9	12.7	9.0	11.5	13.6	9.3	6.7	6.8	6.6	5.7	5.2	6.2

[1]Excludes figures for age not stated.
[2]Denominators of percent distribution exclude deaths of persons of unknown educational attainment.

Source: Kenneth D. Kochanek, and Bettie L. Hudson, National Center for Health Statistics, *Advance Report of Final Mortality Statistics, 1992*, Monthly Vital Statistics Report, Vol. 43, No. 6 (suppl.), Washington, D.C.: U.S. Department of Health and Human Services, December 8, 1994, Table 23.

A6. CAUSES OF DEATH

A6-1. Selected Causes of Death, by Sex and Selected Characteristics: 1991

(**In thousands.** Excludes deaths of nonresidents of the United States. Deaths classified according to ninth revision of *International Classification of Diseases*.)

AGE, SEX, AND RACE	Total[1]	Heart disease	Cancer	Accidents and adverse effects	Cerebrovascular diseases	Chronic obstructive pulmonary diseases[2]	Pneumonia, flu	Suicide	Chronic liver disease, cirrhosis	Diabetes mellitus	Homicide and legal intervention
ALL RACES[3]											
Both sexes, total[4]	2,169.5	720.9	514.7	89.3	143.5	90.7	77.9	30.8	25.4	49.0	26.5
Under 1 year old	36.8	0.7	0.1	1.0	0.2	0.1	0.6	-	(Z)	(Z)	0.4
1 to 4 years old	7.2	0.3	0.5	2.7	0.1	0.1	0.2	-	(Z)	(Z)	0.4
5 to 14 years old	8.5	0.3	1.1	3.7	0.1	0.1	0.1	0.3	(Z)	(Z)	0.5
15 to 24 years old	36.5	1.0	1.8	15.3	0.2	0.2	0.3	4.8	(Z)	0.1	8.2
25 to 34 years old	59.6	3.4	5.3	14.8	0.8	0.3	0.8	6.5	0.9	0.7	7.8
35 to 44 years old	88.1	12.4	16.9	11.8	2.5	0.7	1.4	5.8	3.6	1.6	4.6
45 to 54 years old	120.7	30.4	40.0	7.1	4.7	2.3	1.7	4.0	4.5	3.0	2.1
55 to 64 years old	248.1	75.0	94.2	6.6	9.7	10.4	3.7	3.2	6.0	7.0	1.2
65 to 74 years old	478.6	159.4	159.3	8.1	25.5	28.6	10.2	3.1	6.2	13.8	0.7
75 to 84 years old	607.5	228.9	139.4	10.1	49.4	33.7	24.6	2.4	3.5	14.7	0.4
85 years old and over	477.4	209.0	56.1	8.2	50.2	14.1	34.1	0.8	0.7	8.0	0.1
Male, total[4]	1,121.7	360.0	272.4	59.7	56.7	50.5	36.2	24.8	16.3	21.1	20.8
Under 1 year old	21.0	0.4	(Z)	0.6	0.1	(Z)	0.3	-	(Z)	-	0.2
1 to 4 years old	4.0	0.2	0.3	1.6	(Z)	(Z)	0.1	-	(Z)	(Z)	0.2
5 to 14 years old	5.3	0.2	0.7	2.5	(Z)	0.1	0.1	0.2	(Z)	(Z)	0.3
15 to 24 years old	27.5	0.6	1.1	11.5	0.1	0.1	0.2	4.1	(Z)	0.1	6.9
25 to 34 years old	43.7	2.3	2.6	11.6	0.4	0.2	0.5	5.4	0.5	0.4	6.2
35 to 44 years old	60.6	9.2	7.5	9.0	1.4	0.4	0.9	4.5	2.6	0.9	3.6
45 to 54 years old	76.0	22.5	20.0	5.2	2.6	1.2	1.1	3.0	3.2	1.7	1.6
55 to 64 years old	151.4	51.7	52.2	4.5	5.2	5.7	2.3	2.5	4.1	3.5	0.9
65 to 74 years old	275.9	97.8	89.9	4.9	13.1	16.2	6.0	2.5	3.7	6.4	0.5
75 to 84 years old	299.0	110.8	73.8	5.1	20.6	19.3	12.7	2.1	1.8	6.0	0.2
85 years old and over	156.8	64.0	24.3	3.1	13.1	7.3	12.1	0.6	0.3	2.3	(Z)
Female, total[4]	1,047.9	361.0	242.3	29.6	86.8	40.2	41.6	6.0	9.2	27.9	5.7
Under 1 year old	15.8	0.3	(Z)	0.4	0.1	(Z)	0.3	-	(Z)	(Z)	0.2
1 to 4 years old	3.2	0.2	0.2	1.1	(Z)	(Z)	0.1	-	(Z)	(Z)	0.2
5 to 14 years old	3.2	0.1	0.5	1.2	(Z)	(Z)	0.1	0.1	(Z)	(Z)	0.2
15 to 24 years old	8.9	0.3	0.7	3.7	0.1	0.1	0.1	0.7	(Z)	0.1	1.2
25 to 34 years old	15.9	1.1	2.7	3.2	0.4	0.2	0.3	1.2	0.3	0.3	1.6
35 to 44 years old	27.6	3.2	9.4	2.8	1.2	0.3	0.5	1.3	1.0	0.6	1.0
45 to 54 years old	44.6	7.8	20.0	1.9	2.2	1.2	0.7	1.0	1.3	1.4	0.5
55 to 64 years old	96.6	23.3	42.0	2.0	4.5	4.7	1.4	0.7	1.9	3.5	0.3
65 to 74 years old	202.8	61.6	69.4	3.2	12.4	12.3	4.3	0.6	2.5	7.5	0.2
75 to 84 years old	308.5	118.0	65.6	5.0	28.8	14.5	11.9	0.4	1.7	8.7	0.2
85 years old and over	320.6	145.0	31.8	5.1	37.0	6.8	22.1	0.1	0.4	5.8	0.1
WHITE											
Both sexes, total[4]	1,868.9	636.8	450.0	74.4	123.7	84.0	69.3	28.0	21.4	39.6	12.8
Under 1 year old	23.7	0.5	0.1	0.6	0.1	(Z)	0.3	-	(Z)	(Z)	0.2
1 to 4 years old	5.0	0.2	0.4	1.9	(Z)	(Z)	0.1	-	(Z)	(Z)	0.2
5 to 14 years old	6.3	0.2	0.9	2.7	0.1	0.1	0.1	0.2	(Z)	(Z)	0.3
15 to 24 years old	26.0	0.7	1.5	12.9	0.2	0.1	0.2	4.1	(Z)	0.1	3.2
25 to 34 years old	42.3	2.3	4.3	12.0	0.5	0.2	0.5	5.7	0.6	0.5	3.5
35 to 44 years old	64.0	9.0	13.4	9.2	1.6	0.4	0.9	5.3	2.6	1.1	2.4
45 to 54 years old	93.7	23.7	32.5	5.8	3.1	1.9	1.2	3.7	3.5	2.1	1.3
55 to 64 years old	205.3	61.8	80.2	5.4	7.1	9.3	3.0	3.0	5.1	5.2	0.7
65 to 74 years old	415.8	138.2	140.2	7.0	20.9	26.5	8.8	3.0	5.6	11.1	0.5
75 to 84 years old	546.6	206.6	125.2	9.2	43.8	32.0	22.3	2.3	3.2	12.4	0.3
85 years old and over	439.8	193.7	50.8	7.5	46.2	13.4	31.9	0.7	0.7	7.0	0.1
BLACK											
Both sexes, total[4]	269.5	76.0	57.9	12.5	17.4	5.8	7.4	2.1	3.5	8.5	13.0
Under 1 year old	12.0	2.2	(Z)	0.3	(Z)	(Z)	0.2	-	(Z)	-	0.2
1 to 4 years old	1.9	0.1	0.1	0.6	(Z)	(Z)	0.1	-	-	-	0.2
5 to 14 years old	1.9	0.8	0.2	0.8	(Z)	0.1	(Z)	(Z)	(Z)	(Z)	0.2
15 to 24 years old	9.3	0.3	0.3	1.9	(Z)	0.1	0.1	0.5	(Z)	(Z)	4.8
25 to 34 years old	15.7	1.0	0.9	2.3	0.3	0.1	0.3	0.6	0.2	0.2	4.0
35 to 44 years old	22.1	3.2	3.0	2.2	0.9	0.2	0.5	0.4	0.8	0.4	2.0
45 to 54 years old	24.4	6.2	6.5	1.1	1.4	0.5	0.5	0.2	0.8	0.8	0.7
55 to 64 years old	38.4	12.0	12.5	10.0	2.3	1.0	0.7	0.1	0.8	1.6	0.4
65 to 74 years old	56.4	19.3	17.1	10.0	4.0	1.8	1.2	0.1	0.6	2.5	0.3
75 to 84 years old	54.2	20.0	12.7	8.0	4.9	1.5	1.9	0.1	0.2	2.0	0.1
85 years old and over	33.1	13.6	4.7	0.6	3.4	0.6	1.8	(Z)	(Z)	1.0	(Z)

- Represents zero. Z Fewer than 50. [1] Includes other causes not shown separately. [2] Includes allied conditions. [3] Includes other races not shown separately. [4] Includes those deaths with age not stated.

Source: U.S. National Center for Health Statistics, *Vital Statistics of the United States,* annual.

Source: U.S. Bureau of the Census, *Statistical Abstract of the United States: 1994,* (114th edition), Washington, D.C.: U.S. Government Printing Office, 1994, Table 126.

A6-2. Leading Causes of Death, by Age and Sex: 1991

(Excludes deaths of nonresidents of the United States. Deaths classified according to ninth revision of *International Classification of Diseases*. See also *Historical Statistics, Colonial Times to 1970,* Series B 149–166)

AGE AND LEADING CAUSE OF DEATH	NUMBER OF DEATHS			DEATH RATE PER 100,000 POPULATION		
	Total	Male	Female	Total	Male	Female
ALL AGES [1]						
All races [2]	2,169,518	1,121,665	1,047,853	860.3	912.1	811.0
White	1,868,904	956,497	912,407	886.2	926.2	847.7
Black	269,525	147,331	122,194	864.9	998.7	744.5
Leading causes of death:						
Heart disease	720,862	359,814	361,048	285.9	292.6	279.5
Malignant neoplasms (cancer)	514,657	272,380	242,277	204.1	221.5	187.5
Cerebrovascular disease (stroke)	143,481	56,714	86,767	56.9	46.1	67.2
Chronic obstructive pulmonary disease	90,650	50,485	40,165	35.9	41.1	31.2
Accidents	89,347	59,730	29,617	35.4	48.6	22.9
Motor vehicle	43,536	29,947	13,589	17.3	24.4	10.5
Pneumonia	77,860	36,214	41,646	30.9	29.4	32.2
Diabetes	48,951	21,096	27,855	19.4	17.2	21.6
Suicide [3]	30,810	24,769	(NA)	12.2	20.1	(NA)
HIV infection [3]	29,555	26,046	(NA)	11.7	21.2	(NA)
Homicide and legal intervention	26,513	20,768	(NA)	10.5	16.9	(NA)
1 TO 4 YEARS OLD						
All causes	7,214	4,045	3,169	47.4	52.0	42.7
Leading causes of death:						
Accidents	2,665	1,566	1,099	17.5	20.1	14.8
Motor vehicle	902	491	411	5.9	6.3	5.5
Congenital anomalies	871	469	402	5.7	6.0	5.4
Malignant neoplasms (cancer)	526	288	238	3.5	3.7	3.2
Homicide and legal intervention	428	235	193	2.8	3.0	2.6
Heart disease	332	178	154	2.2	2.3	2.1
Pneumonia and influenza	207	125	82	1.4	1.6	1.1
5 TO 14 YEARS OLD						
All causes	8,479	5,272	3,207	23.6	28.7	18.3
Leading causes of death:						
Accidents	3,660	2,493	1,167	10.2	13.6	6.7
Malignant neoplasms (cancer)	1,106	650	456	3.1	3.5	2.6
Congenital anomalies	487	263	224	1.4	1.4	1.3
Homicide and legal intervention	519	337	182	1.4	1.8	1.0
Heart disease	281	151	130	0.8	0.8	0.7
Pneumonia and influenza	135	69	66	0.4	0.4	0.4
15 TO 24 YEARS OLD						
All causes	36,452	27,549	8,903	100.1	148.0	50.0
Leading causes of death:						
Accidents	15,278	11,534	3,744	42.0	62.0	21.0
Motor vehicle	11,664	8,468	3,196	32.0	45.5	18.0
Homicide and legal intervention	8,159	6,923	1,236	22.4	37.2	6.9
Suicide	4,751	4,073	678	13.1	21.9	3.8
Malignant neoplasms (cancer)	1,814	1,083	731	5.0	5.8	4.1
Heart disease	990	641	349	2.7	3.4	2.0
HIV infection [3]	613	452	161	1.7	2.4	0.9
25 TO 44 YEARS OLD						
All causes	147,750	104,261	43,489	179.9	255.2	105.3
Leading causes of death:						
Accidents	26,526	20,561	5,965	32.3	50.3	14.4
Motor vehicle	15,082	11,142	3,940	18.4	27.3	9.5
Malignant neoplasms (cancer)	22,228	10,164	12,064	27.1	24.9	29.2
HIV infection [3]	21,747	19,263	2,484	26.5	47.1	6.0
Heart disease	15,822	11,497	4,325	19.3	28.1	10.5
Homicide and legal intervention	12,372	9,770	2,602	15.1	23.9	6.3
Suicide	12,281	9,836	2,445	14.9	24.1	5.9
45 TO 64 YEARS OLD						
All causes	368,754	227,464	141,290	788.9	1,011.2	582.6
Leading causes of death:						
Malignant neoplasms (cancer)	134,117	72,193	61,924	286.9	320.9	255.4
Heart disease	105,359	74,258	31,101	225.4	330.1	128.3
Cerebrovascular (stroke)	14,464	7,791	6,673	30.9	34.6	27.5
Accidents	13,693	9,750	3,943	29.3	43.3	16.3
Motor vehicle	6,616	4,458	2,158	14.2	19.8	8.9
Chronic obstructive pulmonary disease	12,769	6,874	5,895	27.3	30.6	24.3
Chronic liver disease and cirrhosis	10,497	7,301	3,196	22.5	32.5	13.2
Diabetes	10,045	5,129	4,916	21.5	22.8	20.3
65 YEARS OLD AND OVER						
All causes	1,563,527	731,629	831,898	4,924.0	5,719.9	4,387.0
Leading causes of death:						
Heart disease	597,267	272,619	324,648	1,881.0	2,131.3	1,712.0
Malignant neoplasms (cancer)	354,768	187,944	166,824	1,117.3	1,469.3	879.7
Cerebrovascular (stroke)	125,139	46,887	78,252	394.1	366.6	412.7
Chronic obstructive pulmonary disease	76,412	42,814	33,598	240.6	334.7	177.2
Pneumonia and influenza	68,962	30,710	38,252	217.2	240.1	201.7
Diabetes	36,528	14,593	21,935	115.0	114.1	115.7
Accidents	26,444	13,163	13,281	83.3	102.9	70.0
Motor vehicle	7,044	3,956	3,088	22.2	30.9	16.3

[1] Includes those deaths with age not stated. [2] Includes other races not shown separately. [3] Human immunodeficiency virus.

Source: U.S. National Center for Health Statistics, *Vital Statistics of the United States,* annual; and unpublished data.

Source: U.S. Bureau of the Census, *Statistical Abstract of the United States: 1994,* (114th edition), Washington, D.C.: U.S. Government Printing Office, 1994, Table 127.

A6-3. Maternal Mortality Rates, by Race: Birth-Registration States or United States, 1915 to 1989

(Beginning in 1989, race for live births is tabulated according to race of mother. Prior to 1933, data are for birth-registration States only. Beginning 1970, excludes deaths of nonresidents of the United States. Rates per 100,000 live births in specified group. Deaths are classified according to the International classification of Diseases in use at the time.)

Year	All races	White	All other		Year	All races	White	All other	
			Total	Black				Total	Black
Race of mother [1]									
1989	7.9	5.6	16.5	18.4	**Race of child-Con.**				
Race of child [2]					1962 [4]	35.2	23.8	95.9	99.4
1989	7.9	5.7	15.4	17.5	1961	36.9	24.9	101.3	105.4
1988	8.4	5.9	17.4	19.5	1960	37.1	26.0	97.9	103.6
1987	6.6	5.1	12.0	14.2	1959	37.4	25.8	102.1	105.0
1986	7.2	4.9	16.0	18.8	1958	37.6	26.3	101.8	104.5
1985	7.8	5.2	18.1	20.4	1957	41.0	27.5	118.3	121.6
1984	7.8	5.4	16.9	19.7	1956	40.9	28.7	110.7	114.3
1983	8.0	5.9	16.3	18.3	1955	47.0	32.8	130.3	134.3
1982	7.9	5.8	16.4	18.2	1954	52.4	37.2	143.8	145.9
1981	8.5	6.3	17.3	20.4	1953	61.1	44.1	166.1	168.3
1980	9.2	6.7	19.8	21.5	1952	67.8	48.9	188.1	189.2
1979	9.6	6.4	22.7	25.1	1951	75.0	54.9	201.3	204.2
1978	9.6	6.4	23.0	25.0	1950	83.3	61.1	221.6	223.0
1977	11.2	7.7	26.0	29.2	1949	90.3	68.1	234.8	237.6
1976	12.3	9.0	26.5	29.5	1948	116.6	89.4	301.0	303.6
1975	12.8	9.1	29.0	31.3	1947	134.5	108.6	334.6	336.2
1974	14.6	10.0	35.1	38.3	1946	156.7	130.7	358.9	363.6
1973	15.2	10.7	34.6	38.4	1945	207.2	172.1	454.8	456.7
1972 [3]	18.8	14.3	38.5	40.7	1944	227.9	189.4	506.0	513.9
1971	18.8	13.0	45.3	48.3	1943	245.2	210.5	509.9	512.8
1970	21.5	14.4	55.9	59.8	1942	258.7	221.8	544.0	549.1
1969	22.2	15.5	55.7	59.5	1941	316.5	266.0	678.1	690.2
1968	24.5	16.6	63.6	65.9	1940	376.0	319.8	773.5	781.7
1967	28.0	19.5	69.5	72.6	1935-39	493.9	439.9	875.5	884.1
1966	29.1	20.2	72.4	74.2	1930-34 [5]	636.0	575.4	1,080.7	1,047.4
1965	31.6	21.0	83.7	88.3	1925-29	668.6	615.0	1,163.7	1,217.3
1964	33.3	22.3	89.9	93.8	1920-24	689.5	649.2	1,134.3	- - -
1963 [4]	35.8	24.0	96.9	101.1	1915-19	727.9	700.3	1,253.5	- - -

[1] Maternal deaths based on race of decedent; live births based on race of mother.
[2] Maternal deaths based on race of decedent; live births based on race of child.
[3] Deaths based on a 50-percent sample.
[4] Figures by race exclude data for residents of New Jersey.
[5] For 1932–34, Mexicans are included with "All other".

Source: National Center for Health Statistics, *Vital Statistics of the United States, 1989*, Vol. II (Mortality, Part A), DHHS Pub. No. (PHS) 93-1101, Washington, D.C.: U.S. Public Health Service, 1993, Table 1-16.

A6-4 Death Rates for Heart Disease, by Race and Sex: 1970 to 1991

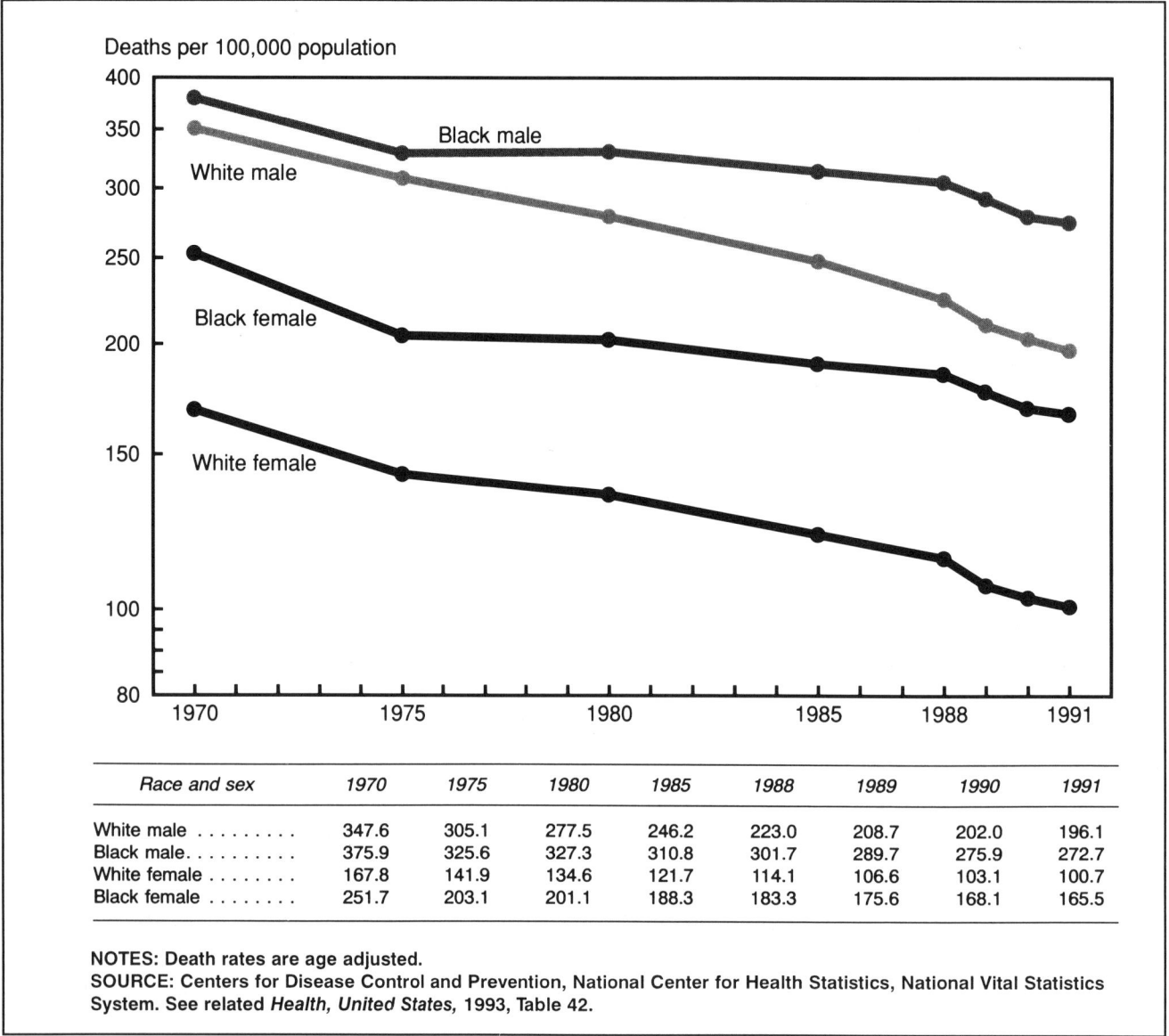

Deaths per 100,000 population

Race and sex	1970	1975	1980	1985	1988	1989	1990	1991
White male	347.6	305.1	277.5	246.2	223.0	208.7	202.0	196.1
Black male.	375.9	325.6	327.3	310.8	301.7	289.7	275.9	272.7
White female	167.8	141.9	134.6	121.7	114.1	106.6	103.1	100.7
Black female	251.7	203.1	201.1	188.3	183.3	175.6	168.1	165.5

NOTES: Death rates are age adjusted.
SOURCE: Centers for Disease Control and Prevention, National Center for Health Statistics, National Vital Statistics System. See related *Health, United States,* 1993, Table 42.

Source: National Center for Health Statistics, *Health, United States, 1993*, (PHS) 94-1232, Washington, D.C.: U.S. Government Printing Office, 1994, Figure 11.

A6-5 Death Rates from Cancer, by Sex and Age: 1970 to 1991

(Deaths per 100,000 population in the specified age groups. See headnote of Table A6-2).

AGE AT DEATH AND SELECTED TYPE OF CANCER	MALE					FEMALE				
	1970	1980	1985	1990	1991	1970	1980	1985	1990	1991
Total [1]	182.1	205.3	213.4	221.3	221.5	144.4	163.6	175.7	186.0	187.5
25 to 34 years	16.3	13.4	13.2	12.6	12.2	16.7	14.0	13.2	12.6	12.6
35 to 44 years	53.0	44.0	42.4	38.5	38.8	65.6	53.1	49.2	48.1	47.2
45 to 54 years	183.5	188.7	175.2	162.5	159.0	181.5	171.8	165.3	155.5	151.3
55 to 64 years	511.8	520.8	536.9	532.9	525.7	343.2	361.7	381.8	375.2	379.1
65 to 74 years	1,006.8	1,093.2	1,105.2	1,122.2	1,120.4	557.9	607.1	645.3	677.4	676.9
75 to 84 years	1,588.3	1,790.5	1,839.7	1,914.4	1,898.4	891.9	903.1	937.8	1,010.3	1,020.7
85 years old and over	1,720.8	2,369.5	2,451.8	2,739.9	2,753.3	1,096.7	1,255.7	1,281.4	1,372.1	1,395.2
Persons, 35 to 44 years old:										
Respiratory, intrathoracic	17.0	12.6	10.6	9.1	8.6	6.5	6.8	5.8	5.4	5.5
Digestive organs, peritoneum . .	11.4	9.5	9.1	8.9	9.2	8.6	6.5	5.8	5.5	5.7
Breast	0.1	-	(B)	(B)	(B)	20.4	17.9	17.5	17.8	16.9
Genital organs	1.4	0.7	0.7	0.6	0.7	13.6	8.3	7.1	7.3	7.1
Lymphatic and hematopoietic tissues, excl. leukemia	5.6	4.3	4.6	4.5	5.1	3.2	2.4	2.3	2.1	2.2
Urinary organs	1.9	1.4	1.6	1.5	1.5	1.0	0.6	0.9	0.6	0.7
Lip, oral cavity, and pharynx . . .	1.7	1.8	1.4	1.3	1.3	0.7	0.5	0.6	0.3	0.3
Leukemia	3.4	3.2	3.0	2.5	2.3	2.8	2.6	2.1	2.2	2.0
Persons, 45 to 54 years old:										
Respiratory, intrathoracic	72.1	79.8	71.0	63.0	60.6	22.2	34.8	36.2	35.3	33.8
Digestive organs, peritoneum . .	45.9	44.3	41.9	40.4	38.2	32.5	27.8	25.9	23.3	22.3
Breast	0.4	0.2	0.3	0.3	(B)	52.6	48.1	47.1	45.4	44.3
Genital organs	3.4	3.4	3.2	2.9	3.0	34.4	24.1	20.6	19.4	18.4
Lymphatic and hematopoietic tissues, excl. leukemia	12.8	10.2	10.0	10.9	11.0	8.3	6.6	6.5	6.0	6.4
Urinary organs	8.0	7.4	7.5	7.2	7.1	3.5	3.3	3.1	2.9	3.0
Lip, oral cavity, and pharynx . . .	7.9	8.2	6.8	5.9	6.1	2.8	2.6	2.0	1.6	1.6
Leukemia	6.6	6.2	5.7	5.6	5.5	4.9	4.4	4.3	4.1	4.0
Persons, 55 to 64 years old:										
Respiratory, intrathoracic	202.3	223.8	233.6	232.6	226.0	38.9	74.5	94.5	107.6	107.0
Digestive organs, peritoneum . .	139.0	129.3	130.8	124.0	125.4	86.0	79.1	75.2	69.3	70.0
Breast	0.6	0.7	0.6	0.6	0.5	77.6	80.5	84.2	78.6	79.1
Genital organs	22.8	23.5	24.6	27.9	26.8	58.2	46.8	43.1	40.1	40.3
Lymphatic and hematopoietic tissues, excl. leukemia	27.1	24.4	25.3	27.2	26.7	17.7	16.8	17.6	16.7	18.1
Urinary organs	26.4	22.9	22.5	23.5	23.2	9.4	8.9	8.6	8.8	9.6
Lip, oral cavity, and pharynx . . .	20.1	17.9	16.0	16.2	14.7	6.2	6.0	5.4	4.7	5.3
Leukemia	15.4	14.7	14.7	14.7	14.6	9.0	9.3	9.2	8.8	9.1
Persons, 65 to 74 years old:										
Respiratory, intrathoracic	340.7	422.0	432.5	447.3	446.0	45.6	106.1	145.3	181.7	185.8
Digestive organs, peritoneum . .	293.3	284.1	277.6	267.4	262.6	185.8	173.6	162.9	153.0	149.7
Breast	1.4	1.1	1.1	1.1	1.1	93.8	101.1	107.8	111.7	108.6
Genital organs	103.7	107.6	110.3	123.5	122.1	85.6	73.6	71.2	71.0	70.2
Lymphatic and hematopoietic tissues, excl. leukemia	50.3	48.1	53.2	56.8	57.9	34.6	34.4	36.6	39.5	41.1
Urinary organs	60.3	56.9	52.0	50.7	52.8	20.1	19.7	19.7	19.8	19.7
Lip, oral cavity, and pharynx . . .	26.8	25.4	24.2	21.5	20.6	6.7	8.8	8.6	8.3	7.8
Leukemia	35.3	35.3	34.7	36.0	36.1	19.3	18.7	19.2	18.8	19.3
Persons, 75 to 84 years old:										
Respiratory, intrathoracic	354.2	511.5	558.9	594.4	593.9	56.5	98.0	135.7	194.5	207.1
Digestive organs, peritoneum . .	507.5	496.6	476.1	468.0	454.1	353.3	326.3	308.7	293.3	290.0
Breast	2.7	2.1	2.3	1.6	1.7	127.4	126.4	136.2	146.3	145.1
Genital organs	299.4	315.4	321.3	358.5	363.5	104.9	95.7	92.7	95.3	94.8
Lymphatic and hematopoietic tissues, excl. leukemia	74.0	80.0	92.8	104.5	104.1	49.4	57.8	63.5	71.2	75.4
Urinary organs	112.2	112.4	106.1	107.5	103.5	44.0	37.4	36.4	38.5	38.5
Lip, oral cavity, and pharynx . . .	36.6	31.4	27.6	26.1	25.7	10.8	10.9	9.8	11.6	11.3
Leukemia	68.3	71.5	70.0	71.9	69.7	39.6	38.5	38.0	38.8	39.8
Persons, 85 years old and over:										
Respiratory, intrathoracic	215.3	386.3	457.3	538.0	552.1	56.5	96.3	104.2	142.8	154.4
Digestive organs, peritoneum . .	583.7	705.8	667.1	699.5	688.2	465.0	504.3	497.6	497.6	495.6
Breast	2.9	2.6	3.9	2.4	4.1	157.1	169.3	178.5	196.8	197.9
Genital organs	434.2	612.3	614.6	750.0	781.0	107.3	115.9	106.1	115.6	117.8
Lymphatic and hematopoietic tissues, excl. leukemia	58.1	93.2	114.8	140.5	140.7	41.7	63.0	73.7	90.0	92.8
Urinary organs	140.5	177.0	185.5	186.3	186.2	59.9	63.8	63.2	68.5	67.7
Lip, oral cavity, and pharynx . . .	47.0	40.2	32.7	37.4	31.9	19.2	16.0	16.0	17.5	17.1
Leukemia	83.3	117.1	114.8	116.0	111.7	50.9	61.1	63.9	65.0	70.0

- Represents zero.
B Base figure too small to meet statistical standards for reliability of a derived figure.
[1] Includes persons under 25 years of age and malignant neoplasms of other and unspecified sites, not shown separately.
Source: U.S. National Center for Health Statistics, *Vital Statistics of the United States,* annual; and unpublished data.

Source: U.S. Bureau of the Census, *Statistical Abstract of the United States: 1994,* (114th edition), Washington, D.C.: U.S. Government Printing Office, 1994, Table 132.

A6-6. Death Rates for Lung Cancer, by Race and Sex: 1970 to 1991

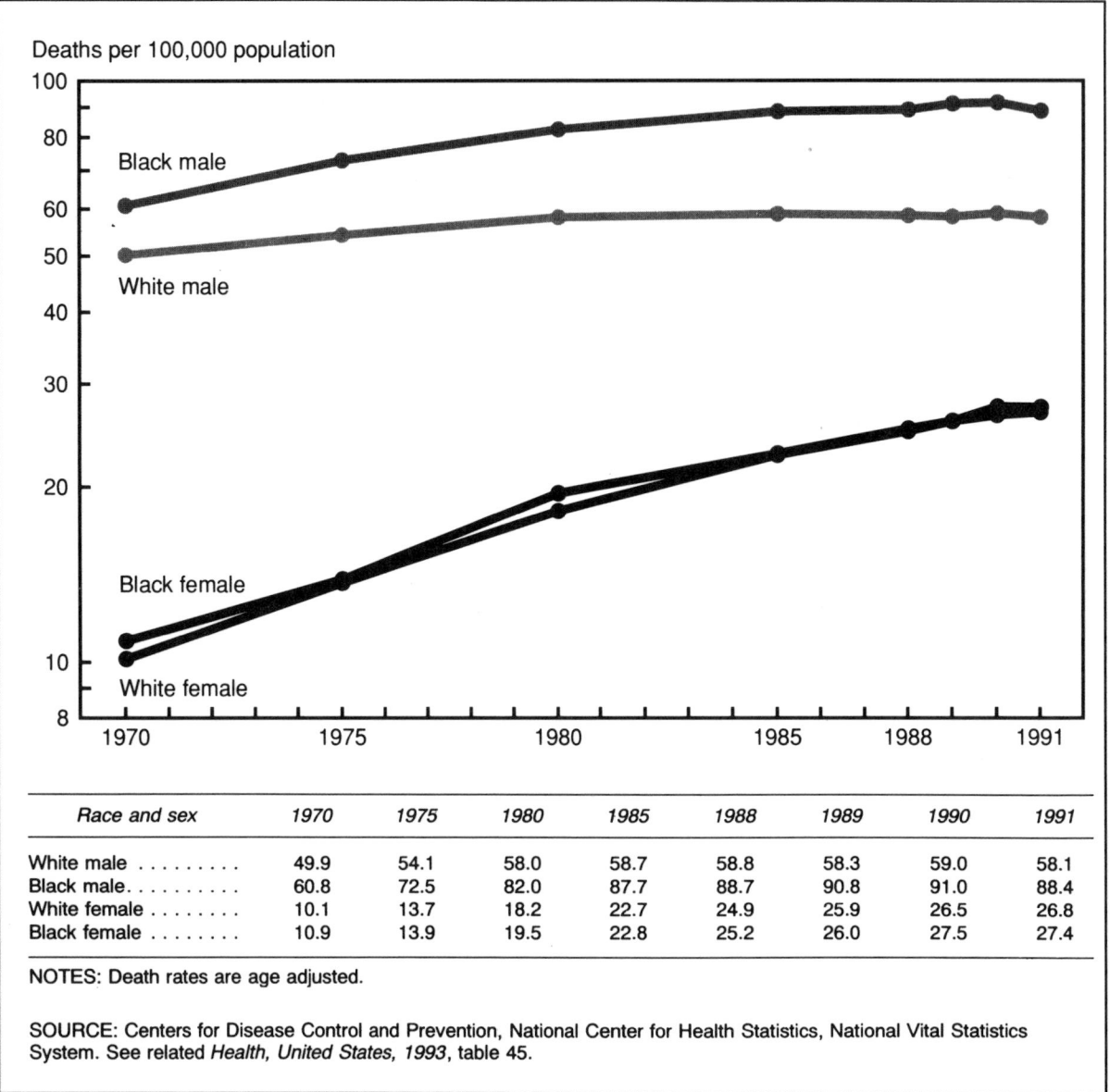

Race and sex	1970	1975	1980	1985	1988	1989	1990	1991
White male	49.9	54.1	58.0	58.7	58.8	58.3	59.0	58.1
Black male.	60.8	72.5	82.0	87.7	88.7	90.8	91.0	88.4
White female	10.1	13.7	18.2	22.7	24.9	25.9	26.5	26.8
Black female	10.9	13.9	19.5	22.8	25.2	26.0	27.5	27.4

NOTES: Death rates are age adjusted.

SOURCE: Centers for Disease Control and Prevention, National Center for Health Statistics, National Vital Statistics System. See related *Health, United States, 1993*, table 45.

Source: National Center for Health Statistics, *Health, United States, 1993*, (PHS) 94-1232, Washington, D.C.: U.S. Government Printing Office, 1994, Figure 13.

A6-7. Death Rates for Stroke, by Race and Sex: 1970 to 1991

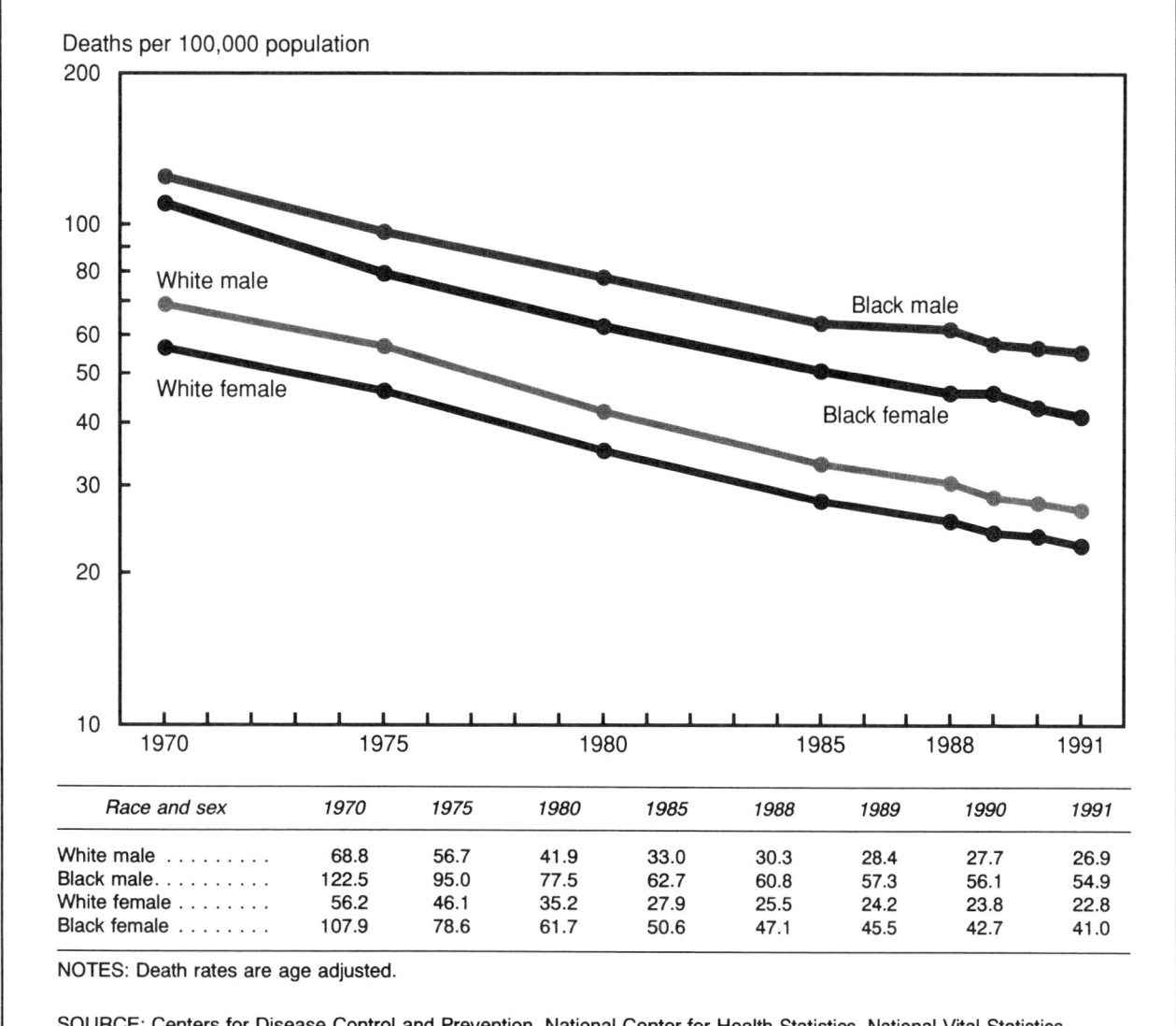

Race and sex	1970	1975	1980	1985	1988	1989	1990	1991
White male	68.8	56.7	41.9	33.0	30.3	28.4	27.7	26.9
Black male.	122.5	95.0	77.5	62.7	60.8	57.3	56.1	54.9
White female	56.2	46.1	35.2	27.9	25.5	24.2	23.8	22.8
Black female	107.9	78.6	61.7	50.6	47.1	45.5	42.7	41.0

NOTES: Death rates are age adjusted.

SOURCE: Centers for Disease Control and Prevention, National Center for Health Statistics, National Vital Statistics System. See related *Health, United States, 1993*, table 43.

Source: National Center for Health Statistics, *Health, United States, 1993*, (PHS) 94-1232, Washington, D.C.: U.S. Government Printing Office, 1994, Figure 12.

A6-8. Death Rates for Human Immunodeficiency Virus (HIV) Infection, by Race and Sex: 1987 to 1991

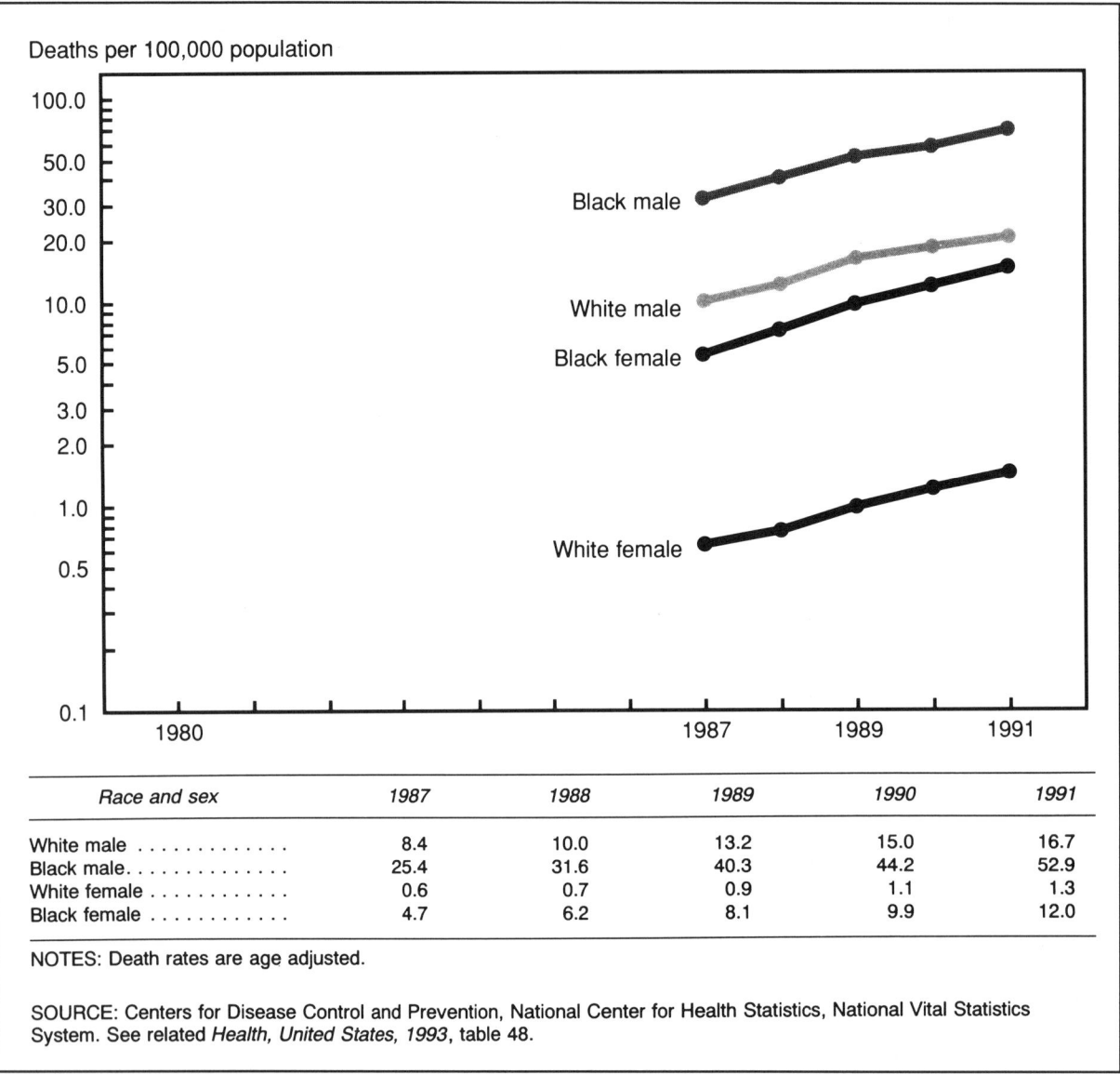

Race and sex	1987	1988	1989	1990	1991
White male	8.4	10.0	13.2	15.0	16.7
Black male.	25.4	31.6	40.3	44.2	52.9
White female	0.6	0.7	0.9	1.1	1.3
Black female	4.7	6.2	8.1	9.9	12.0

NOTES: Death rates are age adjusted.

SOURCE: Centers for Disease Control and Prevention, National Center for Health Statistics, National Vital Statistics System. See related *Health, United States, 1993*, table 48.

Source: National Center for Health Statistics, *Health, United States, 1993*, (PHS)94-1232, Washington, D.C.: U.S. Government Printing Office, 1994, Figure 14.

A6-9. Deaths, by 10-Year Age Groups for Human Immunodeficiency Virus Infection (HIV), by Race and Sex: 1992

Year, race, and sex	All ages [1]	Under 1 year [2]	1–4 years	5–14 years	15–24 years	25–34 years	35–44 years	45–54 years	55–64 years	65–74 years	75–84 years	85 years and over	Age-adjusted rate [3]
Age													
1992						Number							
All races	33,566	100	161	104	578	10,426	14,203	5,575	1,785	519	88	14	...
Male	29,325	47	88	67	419	8,965	12,544	5,104	1,578	431	63	6	...
Female	4,241	53	73	37	159	1,461	1,659	471	207	88	25	8	...
White	21,921	27	60	55	290	6,784	9,189	3,906	1,184	343	65	11	...
Male	20,161	14	32	40	225	6,161	8,577	3,677	1,087	286	50	5	...
Female	1,760	13	28	15	65	623	612	229	97	57	15	6	...
All other	11,645	73	101	49	288	3,642	5,014	1,669	601	176	23	3	...
Male	9,164	33	56	27	194	2,804	3,967	1,427	491	145	13	1	...
Female	2,481	40	45	22	94	838	1,047	242	110	31	10	2	...
Black	11,378	73	100	47	286	3,556	4,900	1,624	589	171	23	3	...
Male	8,925	33	56	26	192	2,724	3,866	1,385	481	142	13	1	...
Female	2,453	40	44	21	94	832	1,034	239	108	29	10	2	...

[1]Figures for age not stated included in "All ages" but not distributed among age groups.
[2]Death rates under 1 year (based on population estimates) differ from infant mortality rates (based on live births).

Source: Kenneth D. Kochanek, and Bettie L. Hudson, National Center for Health Statistics, *Advance Report of Final Mortality Statistics, 1992*, Monthly Vital Statistics Report, Vol. 43, No. 6 (suppl.), Washington, D.C.: U.S. Department of Health and Human Services, December 8, 1994, Table 13.

A6-10. Suicides, by Sex and Method Used: 1970 to 1991

(Excludes deaths of nonresidents of the United States. Beginning 1979, deaths classified according to the ninth revision of the International Classification of Diseases. For earlier years, classified according to the revision in use at the time; see *Historical Statistics, Colonial Times to 1970*, Series H 979–986)

METHOD	MALE						FEMALE					
	1970	1980	1985	1989	1990	1991	1970	1980	1985	1989	1990	1991
Total	**16,629**	**20,505**	**23,145**	**24,102**	**24,724**	**24,769**	**6,851**	**6,364**	**6,308**	**6,130**	**6,182**	**6,041**
Firearms [1]	9,704	12,937	14,809	15,680	16,285	16,120	2,068	2,459	2,554	2,498	2,600	2,406
Percent of total	58	63	64	65	66	65	30	39	41	41	42	40
Poisoning [2]	3,299	2,997	3,319	3,211	3,221	3,316	3,285	2,456	2,385	2,232	2,203	2,228
Hanging and strangulation [3]	2,422	2,997	3,532	3,708	3,688	3,751	831	694	732	776	756	810
Other [4]	1,204	1,574	1,485	1,503	1,530	1,582	667	755	637	624	623	597

[1] Includes explosives in 1970.   [2] Includes solids, liquids, and gases.   [3] Includes suffocation.   [4] Beginning 1980, includes explosives.

Source of tables 133-135: U.S. National Center for Health Statistics, *Vital Statistics of the United States*, annual; and unpublished data.

Source: U.S. Bureau of the Census, *Statistical Abstract of the United States: 1994*, (114th edition), Washington, D.C.: U.S. Government Printing Office, 1994, Table 135.

A6-11. Death Rates for Suicide, by Race and Sex: 1970 to 1991

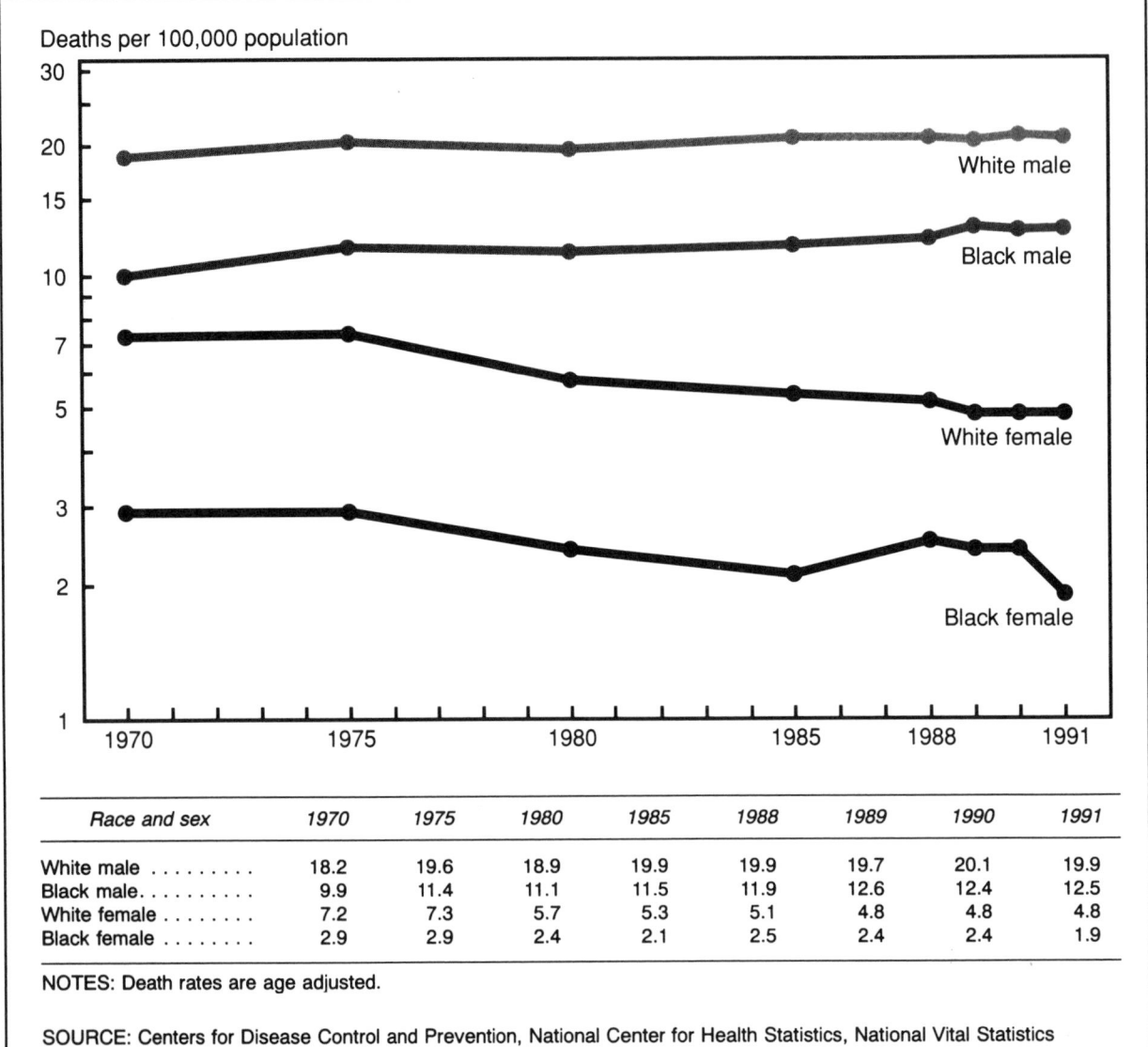

Deaths per 100,000 population

Race and sex	1970	1975	1980	1985	1988	1989	1990	1991
White male	18.2	19.6	18.9	19.9	19.9	19.7	20.1	19.9
Black male	9.9	11.4	11.1	11.5	11.9	12.6	12.4	12.5
White female	7.2	7.3	5.7	5.3	5.1	4.8	4.8	4.8
Black female	2.9	2.9	2.4	2.1	2.5	2.4	2.4	1.9

NOTES: Death rates are age adjusted.

SOURCE: Centers for Disease Control and Prevention, National Center for Health Statistics, National Vital Statistics System. See related *Health, United States, 1993*, table 52.

Source: National Center for Health Statistics, *Health, United States, 1993*, (PHS) 94-1232, Washington, D.C.: U.S. Government Printing Office, 1994, Figure 16.

A6-12. Suicide Rates, by Sex, Race, and Age Group: 1980 to 1991

AGE	TOTAL [1]			MALE						FEMALE					
				White			Black			White			Black		
	1980	1990	1991	1980	1990	1991	1980	1990	1991	1980	1990	1991	1980	1990	1991
All ages [2]	11.9	12.4	12.2	19.9	22.0	21.7	10.3	12.0	12.1	5.9	5.3	5.2	2.2	2.3	1.9
10 to 14 years old	0.8	1.5	1.5	1.4	2.3	2.4	0.5	1.6	2.0	0.3	0.9	0.8	0.1	(B)	(B)
15 to 19 years old	8.5	11.1	11.0	15.0	19.3	19.1	5.6	11.5	12.2	3.3	4.0	4.2	1.6	1.9	(B)
20 to 24 years old	16.1	15.1	14.9	27.8	26.8	26.5	20.0	19.0	20.7	5.9	4.4	4.3	3.1	2.6	1.8
25 to 34 years old	16.0	15.2	15.2	25.6	25.6	26.1	21.8	21.9	21.1	7.5	6.0	5.8	4.1	3.7	3.3
35 to 44 years old	15.4	15.3	14.7	23.5	25.3	24.7	15.6	16.9	15.2	9.1	7.4	7.2	4.6	4.0	2.9
45 to 54 years old	15.9	14.8	15.5	24.2	24.8	25.3	12.0	14.8	14.3	10.2	7.5	8.3	2.8	3.2	3.0
55 to 64 years old	15.9	16.0	15.4	25.8	27.5	26.8	11.7	10.8	13.0	9.1	8.0	7.1	2.3	2.6	2.1
65 to 74 years over . . .	16.9	17.9	16.9	32.5	34.2	32.6	11.1	14.7	13.8	7.0	7.2	6.4	1.7	2.6	2.4
75 to 84 years over . . .	19.1	24.9	23.5	45.5	60.2	56.1	10.5	14.4	21.6	5.7	6.7	6.0	1.4	(B)	(B)
85 years and over	19.2	22.2	24.0	52.8	70.3	75.1	18.9	(B)	(B)	5.8	5.4	6.6	0.1	(B)	(B)

B Base figure too small to meet statistical standards for reliability of a derived figure. [1] Includes other races not shown separately. [2] Includes other age groups not shown separately.

Source: U.S. National Center for Health Statistics, *Monthly Vital Statistics Report;* and unpublished data.

Source: U.S. Bureau of the Census, *Statistical Abstract of the United States: 1994,* (114th edition), Washington, D.C.: U.S. Government Printing Office, 1994, Table 136.

A6-13. Firearm Mortality among Children, Youth, and Adults under Age 35, by Sex and Race: 1991

[**Death rate per 100,000 population.** Deaths classified according to the ninth revision of the *International Classification of Diseases*]

ITEM	Under 5 years old	5 to 9 years old	10 to 14 years old	15 to 19 years old	20 to 24 years old	25 to 29 years old	30 to 34 years old
MALE							
Total: White	0.5	0.5	4.6	29.1	34.6	29.0	26.0
Black	1.4	1.5	11.5	140.5	184.3	129.4	94.8
Accidents: White	0.1	0.3	1.6	2.9	1.6	1.0	0.8
Black	0.2	0.6	2.0	6.3	4.7	2.2	1.2
Suicide: White	(X)	(X)	1.5	13.6	17.7	15.3	14.9
Black	(X)	(X)	1.1	9.0	14.4	13.4	10.5
Homicide: White	0.3	0.3	1.4	11.8	14.9	12.3	10.1
Black	1.1	0.9	8.2	123.6	164.4	113.4	82.9
FEMALE							
Total: White	0.4	0.3	1.0	4.6	5.1	4.9	5.5
Black	1.5	0.5	3.0	12.7	17.7	16.5	13.9
Accidents: White	0.1	0.1	0.1	0.2	0.2	0.1	0.1
Black	0.4	0.1	0.2	0.2	(X)	0.1	0.1
Suicide: White	(X)	(X)	0.4	2.1	2.0	2.4	2.8
Black	(X)	(X)	0.1	0.8	0.7	1.9	0.7
Homicide: White	0.3	0.2	0.5	2.2	2.7	2.3	2.4
Black	1.1	0.4	2.7	11.2	16.8	14.4	13.1
Accidents: White	0.1	0.1	0.1	0.2	0.2	0.1	0.1
Black	0.4	0.1	0.2	0.2	(X)	0.1	0.1

X Not applicable.

Source: U.S. National Center for Health Statistics, *Advance Data from Vital and Health Statistics,* No. 231.

Source: U.S. Bureau of the Census, *Statistical Abstract of the United States: 1994,* (114th edition), Washington, D.C.: U.S. Government Printing Office, 1994, Table 137.

A6-14. Death Rates for Homicide and Legal Intervention, by Race and Sex: 1970 to 1991

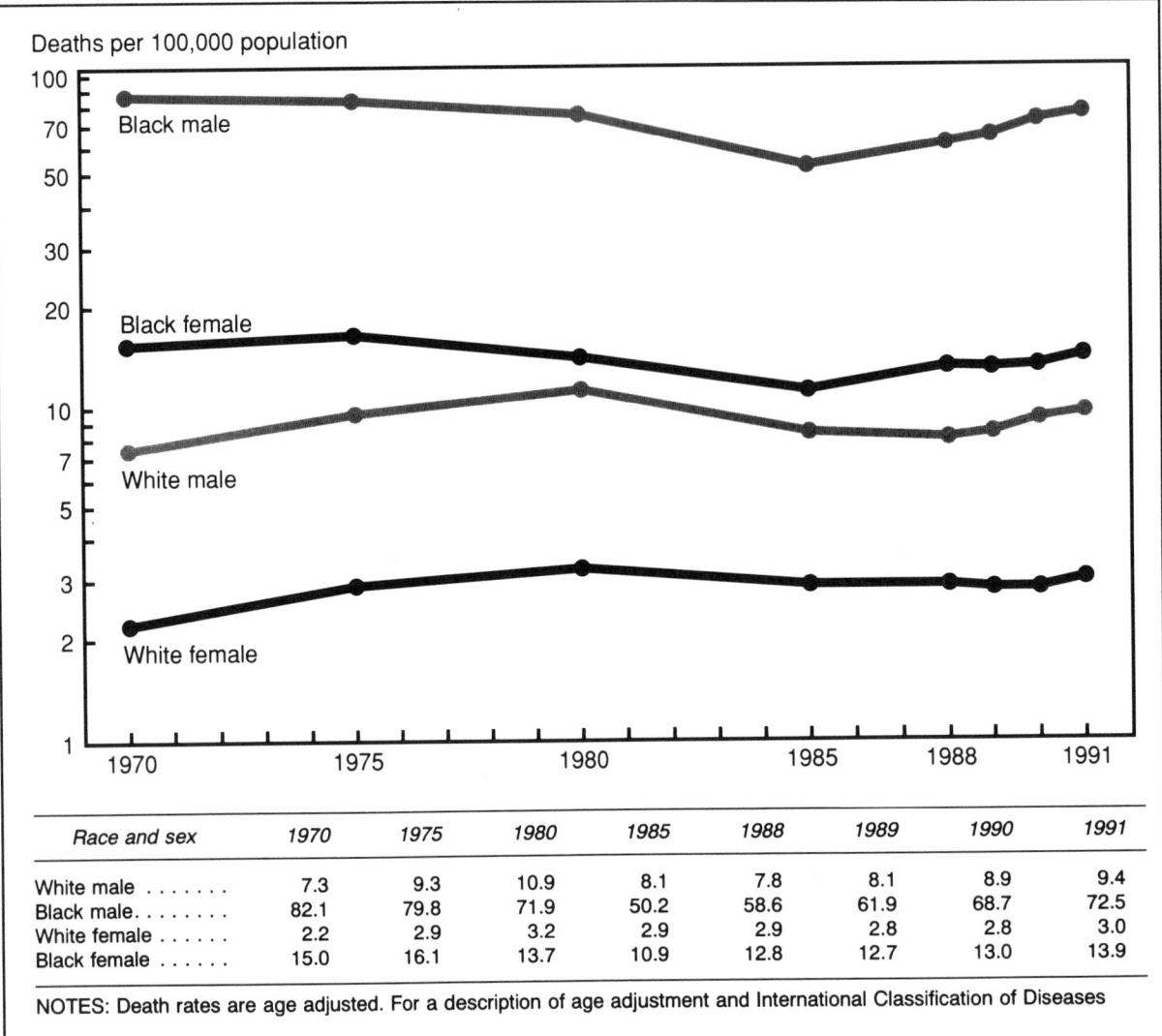

Race and sex	1970	1975	1980	1985	1988	1989	1990	1991
White male	7.3	9.3	10.9	8.1	7.8	8.1	8.9	9.4
Black male	82.1	79.8	71.9	50.2	58.6	61.9	68.7	72.5
White female	2.2	2.9	3.2	2.9	2.9	2.8	2.8	3.0
Black female	15.0	16.1	13.7	10.9	12.8	12.7	13.0	13.9

NOTES: Death rates are age adjusted. For a description of age adjustment and International Classification of Diseases

SOURCE: Centers for Disease Control and Prevention, National Center for Health Statistics, National Vital Statistics System. See related *Health, United States, 1993*, table 51.

Source: National Center for Health Statistics, *Health, United States, 1993*, (PHS) 94-1232, Washington, D.C.: U.S. Government Printing Office, 1994, Figure 17.

Employment and Economic Status

B1. LABOR FORCE PARTICIPATION

Most adult women work. Since the 1970s, it is increasingly likely children will have both parents in the labor force. Almost half (47 percent) of all married couples with children with a wife aged 15 to 44 in 1992 were families with children in which both parents worked, up from 33 percent in 1976. Couples in which only the husband was employed declined from 48 percent in 1976 to 27 percent in 1992. Dual-employed spouses who were childless in 1992 represented 13 percent of all married couples.

In 1994, nearly 3 in 5 women (58 percent) participated in the labor force. In the past, Black women participated in the labor force at a somewhat higher rate than White women; but as delayed marriage and divorce have become more prominent factors in the lives of White women, their rates have become similar.

Black women have been more than twice as likely as White, non-Hispanic women to be unemployed since 1980 (for example, in 1994 the unemployment rates were 12 percent and 5 percent, respectively).

The Bureau of Labor Statistics projects 72 million women will be in the labor force by 2005. That is 63 percent of women 16 years and older. That would be a 24 percent increase in the size of the female labor force since 1992, compared to a projected growth rate of less than 14 percent for men during that time. That is a somewhat slower rate of growth than women experienced in the decade of the 1980s.

Every age group among women is expected to have higher labor force participation rates in 2005 than they had in 1992. The highest rates are for women aged 35 to 44, increasing from 77 percent in 1992 to 86 percent in 2005. In 1987, 3 in 4 women in the labor force were of childbearing age (15 to 44 years). That was the highest proportion it had been since such data started to be collected just after World War II. The Baby Boom is aging. As a result, we expect to see a gradual decrease to about 3 in 5 women of childbearing age in the labor force by 2005. Working women in their late 50s and 60s will be increasingly likely to be thinking about the care of frail, elderly relatives rather than young children.

Women are in the workforce longer than ever before. Among women born before 1930, those who married generally had a tenuous attachment to the labor force and relied on their husbands for economic support. The small minority in that cohort who never married tended to work full time and continuously throughout their lives. A 25-year old woman in 1994 is likely to stay in the labor force even longer over her lifetime than was the case for a woman that age in the early 1980s. On average, a 25-year old woman is expected to work nearly 28 years over her worklife; in 1980, worklife expectancy was only 24 years.

More education also relates to longer worklife expectancy. The average 25-year-old woman in 1994 with a college degree is expected to work 32 years but only 20 years if she is a high school dropout. Accordingly, longer worklife relates to higher lifetime earnings capacity.

B2. EARNINGS AND PENSION COVERAGE

There is a wage gap between men and women but measuring it, and the reasons for it, are complex. Equal educational attainment and job experience do not lead to equal pay for many women. Discrimination is certainly part of the reason, but not the full explanation for the difference. Differences in the productivity of men and women and differences in their occupational distribution (see Section B4) are two additional reasons given in the literature for lack of wage parity. There are, for example, differences in the educational fields of study of men and women (see Section D5), in their hours and weeks worked (see Section B3), and in their family responsibilities. Age is another important factor. Younger women experience less of a wage gap than older women have.

Generally speaking, men earn more than women and White women earn more than Black women. And, generally, during the 1980s, the weekly pay of men was relatively lower than in the 1970s, while pay increased for women—thus significantly decreasing earnings inequity between genders.

The difference between men and women in earnings is greater between Whites than between Blacks. Black women earn about three-fourths of what Black men earn, while there is a differential of about three-fifths in the earnings of White, non-Hispanic men and women. This represents a decline in the gender-pay gap for White workers as well as for Black workers. The pay gap between White and Black women working year round and full time increased during the 1980s. Among women working year round and full time, Black women earned 95 percent as much as White women in 1978; by 1990, Black women earned only 87 percent as much.

Among persons who worked year round and full time, the median earnings of Black women increased from 75 percent of what Black men earned in 1979 to 86 percent in 1993; among White non-Hispanics, the relative increase was from 59 percent to 71 percent. In part, this was because median earnings decreased among men and increased among women.

There has also been a widening in the earnings gap between women who are high school dropouts and women who are more educated. A college degree means earning power for women. Among year-round, full-time workers in 1993, Black women and White, non-Hispanic women with at least a bachelor's degree had median earnings of $31,000 and $33,000 respectively, compared with high school graduates who earned $20,000 and $17,300 respectively.

Among women who are self-employed, median real earnings increased in the years from 1975 to 1990, both absolutely and relative to women who earn salaries. Nevertheless, self-employed women had lower labor-market earnings, on average, than female wage and salary workers.

Both husband and wife are earners in half of White non-Hispanic and of Black married-couple families. The husband is the sole earner in only about 1 in 7 married couples.

During the recessionary period of 1990 to 1992, there were job losses and earnings losses. The proportion of women in full-time jobs with low earnings (less than $208 a week) rose from 29 percent to 44 percent at the time of obtaining a new job. Three in four low-earnings women who got new jobs continued to earn less than $208 a week. Among high-earnings women ($600 or more a week on the job they left), only 1 in 3 maintained their high-earning status when they got a new job.

In addition, the gender gap in pension coverage is narrowing. In 1993, 55 percent of women with wage and salary income had pension coverage compared with 60 percent of men. In 1979, there was an 18-point difference (67 percent of men versus 49 percent of women).

B3. WORKING MOTHERS AND CHILD CARE

In 1940, the mothers of 1 in 10 children were in the labor force. After that, mothers became increasingly qualified for the workforce through higher education; and with more divorce, more women have had to work. As a result of both need and preference, 6 in 10 children had working moms in 1990.

Most married mothers with children work. Almost three in four married mothers, about 18 million women, worked at some time in 1992, compared with just over half of married mothers in 1970. About 9 million married mothers worked year round and full time in 1992. That was 37 percent of all married women, compared to 16 percent in 1970. Another way to view this issue is that most married mothers either do not work or work only part year or part time, especially when their children are very young. These data show that most women juggle work and families. Of all married mothers, 27 percent did not work at all during 1992, compared to 49 percent in 1970. In addition, Hispanic mothers were less likely to work than White or Black mothers.

Two-thirds of mothers with children under six worked at some time in 1992; three in ten of these mothers worked year round and full time. Nearly 8 in 10 mothers with only school-age children worked at some time in 1992; half of these mothers worked year round and full time. Black married mothers, especially those with children under age six, are more likely than White or Hispanic married mothers to work year round and full time.

Women play an increasingly important role as providers of family income and are likely to work during their pregnancy. Most return to work within the first six months after the birth. In the 1960s, only 1 in 8 women returned to work in less than a year, compared with 2 in 3 in the early 1980s. Three in four women work six or more months before the birth of their first child. Half have some maternity benefits. Less than one-fourth of new mothers quit working.

Most preschoolers with working mothers receive care in a home environment. About one-third of preschoolers receive care in their own homes, about one-third in someone else's home, and about one-fourth are placed in organized day care. Over half of children under age five are cared for by a relative. Care by fathers increased in the early 1990s and most (56 percent in 1991) of these fathers were unemployed. Grandparents also help out as sitters for working mothers, especially when the mother is unmarried. Only 2 percent of mothers cared for their children during their working hours in their place of work (other than their home). Among women who paid for child care, the average cost was $63 a week in 1991, or 7 percent of family income. Poor women were less likely to pay for child care than nonpoor women (24 percent and 36 percent, respectively). Among poor women who do pay for child care, however, these costs consumed 27 percent of their family budget on average.

B4. OCCUPATIONS

Overall, the labor force is sharply segregated by sex, and the number of women in high-paying jobs remains small. Some types of jobs, however, are held almost exclusively by women. Women constitute more than 90 percent of all receptionists, child-care workers, bank tellers, nurses, secretaries, bookkeepers, private household workers, and typists.

Women increasingly joined the ranks of managers and professionals during the 1980s, although they remained heavily concentrated in the relatively low-paying professional fields of teaching and nursing. A higher proportion of White (30 percent) than Black (20 percent) women were employed in managerial and professional specialty jobs in March 1994. About 17 percent of Hispanic women are in these fields. Most women who leave jobs in managerial, executive, and professional fields take new jobs in the same broad group, but about 30 percent (in the 1990–92 recession period) entered technical, sales, and administrative support occupations when they returned to the workforce.

White women (43 percent) were more likely than Black women (39 percent) to be employed in technical, sales, and administrative support jobs in 1994. Black women were more likely than White women to be employed in service occupations (27 percent and 17 percent, respectively).

Women owned more than 4.1 million businesses in 1987, an increase of 58 percent from 1982. Receipts increased from $98.3 billion to $278.1 billion over that period. Among firms owned by minority women in 1987, Black women owned the largest share (41 percent) and Asian women had the largest receipts. Data from the 1992 economic censuses will be available in late 1996.

B5. INCOME AND ASSETS

Despite all the economic advances women have experienced in recent decades, they remain in a secondary economic status. Compared to 1970, more are the sole economic support of their families. Making it in today's economy, however, is not the same for all women, and these differences will carry into their elder years. Black and Hispanic women generally face economic problems that are more intense and longer in duration than those of many White women. Also, women with more education tend to have more resources and smaller families to support than women with lower levels of education.

Compared to today's elderly women, a larger proportion of women reaching age 65 in the future will have pensions in their own names. Women are increasingly covered by retirement plans to which they are the primary contributors (lump-sum payment plans commonly known as 401(k) savings plans), even though saving this way has been difficult for most. Median annuity benefits of women are generally half those of men (a gain from 1990 when median benefits were 37 percent of those of men). Married women will have the economic support of a husband for a few years longer than is common today, as more men live into their 70s and 80s.

Married-couple families fare better economically than families headed by women alone. From 1969 to 1993, White married couples experienced a 16-percent increase in median family income compared to a 31-percent increase for Black married-couple families. In that same period however, median family income decreased slightly for both White and Black female householders.

Women who are the financial support of their families face several serious economic problems. Earnings are their chief source of income, but they tend to earn less than men. If they lose their job, there usually is not a second earner in the household. In addition, they frequently receive little or no economic support from the absent father(s) of their children (see Section D1). In 1994, more than 12 million women headed families alone. The median income of such women with children was $16,020 for White and $10,380 for Black women. By contrast, for married-couple households, White median income was $46,380 and the median for Blacks was $36,660. Only 11 percent of families headed by women alone had incomes of $50,000 or more in 1993. Median income in female-headed households in which no husband was present was actually higher in 1979 than in 1993 for both White and Black women.

The wealth of most Americans is in their home. Married-couple households had median net-worth holdings in 1991 of about $60,000 compared to less than $15,000 in households maintained by women. Most of that was equity in a home. When house equity was excluded, median net worth dropped to less than $4,000 for female householders, compared to about $19,000 for married couples. The net worth of married couples was less in 1991 than in 1988 but remained unchanged for female householders. Net worth increases with age, so female householders 65 years and older had a net worth of almost $60,000 in 1991 and just under $13,000 if their home equity was not counted. Female householders under age 35 had total net-worth holdings of less than $1,400.

B6. POVERTY

Women supporting their families alone and elderly women living alone were much more likely to be poor than women in married-couple families. In 1993, poverty was defined as having an income of less than $14,763 for a family of four people and $6,930 for a person 65 years or older living alone.

Half of Black families maintained by women with no husband and 3 in 10 such White families were poor in 1993. By contrast, 12 percent of Black married-couple families were poor as were 6 percent of White married-couple families. These levels and patterns have changed little from what they were in 1979.

Eight in ten poor Black families with children were headed by women alone as were half of such non-Hispanic White families. Poor non-Hispanic White families with children were more likely than were poor Black families with children to be married couples (43 percent and 14 percent, respectively). Some of this poverty is because so many absent fathers contribute little or nothing towards child support (see Section D1).

Female-headed families have significantly longer poverty spells than persons in married-couple households. In the 1990–91 period, 18 percent of persons in female-headed families were poor the entire period compared to 1 percent of persons in married-couple families. Female-householder families are also more likely to have family incomes below half of their respective poverty thresholds (18 percent compared to 2 percent in married-couple families in 1990).

B7. PUBLIC ASSISTANCE

Families maintained by women with no husband have much higher poverty rates than married-couple families. As a result, persons in families maintained by women were six times more likely than those in married-couple families (37 percent versus 6 percent) to have participated in a major government assistance program (lived in public housing or received benefits from Aid to Families with Dependent Children (AFDC), General Assistance, Supplemental Security Income (SSI), Medicaid, Food Stamps, or federal or state rent assistance) in an average month of 1990. Families maintained by women also had longer median spells of receiving major means-tested assistance programs.

One in ten American mothers (aged 15 to 44 with children under 18 years old living in their homes) receive payments from AFDC, a program to provide financial assistance to needy families. Most AFDC mothers have low education, are not married, have no job, and are aged 30 to 34. In 1993, 3.8 million mothers aged 15 to 44 were AFDC recipients. About one-fourth became mothers for the first time when they were teenagers, and they had not married by the time the baby was born. Five percent of mothers on welfare were teens. Nearly half have never been married, and they averaged 2.4 children each. Almost half of AFDC mothers left school before receiving a high school diploma, but about 1 in 7 are enrolled in school. On average, AFDC mothers enrolled in school were 28 years old and had 2 children. Only 11 percent of AFDC recipients enrolled in school were teenagers. In addition, 9 in 10 AFDC mothers were native-born Americans.

B1. LABOR FORCE PARTICIPATION

B1-1. Employment Status of the Civilian Noninstitutional Population, by Sex and Race: 1980 to 1994

[Numbers in thousands. Annual averages except 1994]

Year	Men						Women					
	Civilian noninstitutional population	Civilian labor force					Civilian noninstitutional population	Civilian labor force				
		Total	Percent of population	Employed	Unemployed			Total	Percent of population	Employed	Unemployed	
					Number	Percent of labor force					Number	Percent of labor force
TOTAL												
1980...............	79,398	61,453	77.4	57,186	4,267	6.9	88,348	45,487	51.5	42,117	3,370	7.4
1981...............	80,511	61,974	77.0	57,397	4,577	7.4	89,618	46,696	52.1	43,000	3,696	7.9
1982...............	81,523	62,450	76.6	56,271	6,179	9.9	90,748	47,755	52.6	43,256	4,499	9.4
1983...............	82,531	63,047	76.4	56,787	6,260	9.9	91,684	48,503	52.9	44,047	4,457	9.2
1984...............	83,605	63,835	76.4	59,091	4,744	7.4	92,778	49,709	53.6	45,915	3,794	7.6
1985...............	84,469	64,411	76.3	59,891	4,521	7.0	93,736	51,050	54.5	47,259	3,791	7.4
1986...............	85,798	65,422	76.3	60,892	4,530	6.9	94,789	52,413	55.3	48,706	3,707	7.1
1987...............	86,899	66,207	76.2	62,107	4,101	6.2	95,853	53,658	56.0	50,334	3,324	6.2
1988...............	87,857	66,927	76.2	63,273	3,655	5.5	96,756	54,742	56.6	51,696	3,046	5.6
1989...............	88,762	67,840	76.4	64,315	3,525	5.2	97,630	56,030	57.4	53,027	3,003	5.4
1990...............	89,650	68,234	76.1	64,435	3,799	5.6	98,399	56,544	57.5	53,479	3,075	5.4
1991...............	90,552	68,411	75.5	63,593	4,817	7.0	99,214	56,893	57.3	53,284	3,609	6.3
1992...............	91,541	69,184	75.6	63,805	5,380	7.8	100,035	57,798	57.8	53,793	4,005	6.9
1993...............	92,620	69,633	75.2	64,700	4,932	7.1	100,930	58,407	57.9	54,606	3,801	6.5
1994...............	94,027	69,517	73.9	64,295	5,221	7.5	102,182	59,646	58.4	55,812	3,834	6.4
BLACK												
1980...............	7,945	5,612	70.6	4,798	815	14.5	9,881	5,253	53.2	4,515	737	14.0
1981...............	8,117	5,684	70.0	4,793	891	15.7	10,101	5,401	53.5	4,561	840	15.6
1982...............	8,284	5,804	70.1	4,637	1,167	20.1	10,300	5,527	53.7	4,552	975	17.6
1983...............	8,448	5,966	70.6	4,753	1,213	20.3	10,476	5,681	54.2	4,623	1,058	18.6
1984...............	8,654	6,126	70.8	5,123	1,003	16.4	10,694	5,906	55.2	4,995	911	15.4
1985...............	8,791	6,220	70.8	5,269	951	15.3	10,873	6,145	56.5	5,231	914	14.9
1986...............	8,956	6,374	71.2	5,428	946	14.8	11,033	6,281	56.9	5,386	895	14.2
1987...............	9,128	6,487	71.1	5,661	826	12.7	11,223	6,507	58.0	5,648	859	13.2
1988...............	9,289	6,596	71.0	5,824	771	11.7	11,402	6,609	58.0	5,834	776	11.7
1989...............	9,439	6,701	71.0	5,928	773	11.5	11,582	6,796	58.7	6,025	772	11.4
1990...............	9,567	6,708	70.1	5,915	793	11.8	11,733	6,785	57.8	6,051	734	10.8
1991...............	9,717	6,754	69.5	5,880	874	12.9	11,898	6,788	57.0	5,983	805	11.9
1992...............	9,888	6,892	69.7	5,846	1,046	15.2	12,069	6,999	58.0	6,087	912	13.0
1993...............	10,078	6,911	68.6	5,957	954	13.8	12,251	7,031	57.4	6,189	842	12.0
1994...............	10,203	6,782	66.5	5,836	946	14.0	12,568	7,379	58.7	6,487	892	12.1
WHITE												
1980...............	69,634	54,473	78.2	51,127	3,344	6.1	76,489	39,127	51.2	36,589	2,540	6.5
1981...............	70,480	54,895	77.9	51,315	3,580	6.5	77,428	40,156	51.9	37,394	2,762	6.9
1982...............	71,211	55,132	77.4	50,287	4,845	8.8	78,230	41,009	52.4	37,616	3,396	8.3
1983...............	71,922	55,480	77.1	50,621	4,859	8.8	78,884	41,541	52.7	38,272	3,270	7.9
1984...............	72,723	56,061	77.1	52,462	3,600	6.4	79,624	42,430	53.3	39,658	2,772	6.5
1985...............	73,373	56,472	77.0	53,045	3,426	6.1	80,306	43,455	54.1	40,689	2,765	6.4
1986...............	74,390	57,217	76.9	53,785	3,433	6.0	81,041	44,584	55.0	41,876	2,708	6.1
1987...............	75,190	57,779	76.8	54,646	3,133	5.4	81,769	45,510	55.7	43,142	2,369	5.2
1988...............	75,855	58,317	76.9	55,550	2,766	4.7	82,340	46,439	56.4	44,262	2,177	4.7
1989...............	76,468	58,988	77.1	56,352	2,636	4.5	82,871	47,367	57.2	45,323	2,135	4.5
1990...............	77,082	59,298	76.9	56,432	2,866	4.8	83,332	47,879	57.5	45,654	2,225	4.6
1991...............	77,689	59,332	76.4	55,557	3,775	6.4	83,822	48,154	57.4	45,482	2,672	5.5
1992...............	78,351	59,830	76.4	55,709	4,121	6.9	84,307	48,696	57.8	45,770	2,926	6.0
1993...............	79,080	60,150	76.1	56,397	3,753	6.2	84,841	49,208	58.0	46,415	2,793	5.7
1994...............	79,845	59,818	74.9	55,786	4,033	6.7	85,331	49,849	58.4	47,094	2,754	5.5
WHITE, NOT HISPANIC												
1994...............	71,649	53,420	74.6	50,093	3,327	6.2	77,232	45,679	59.1	43,390	2,289	5.0

Note: Data for 1994 are not annual averages but reflect characteristics of the population for March 1994 and are not adjusted for seasonal changes.

Source: Claudette E. Bennett, U.S. Bureau of Census, *The Black Population in the United States: March 1994 and 1993,* Current Population Reports, Series P20-480, Washington, D.C.: U.S. Government Printing Office, January 1995, Table L.

B1-2. Labor Force Participation Rates (Annual Averages) of Women, by Age: 1965 to 1993

[In percent]

Year	Total, 16 years and older	16 to 19 years	20 to 24 years	25 to 34 years	35 to 44 years	45 to 54 years	55 years and older
1965............	39.3	38.0	49.9	38.5	46.1	50.9	24.6
1966............	40.3	41.4	51.5	39.8	46.8	51.7	24.8
1967............	41.1	41.6	53.3	41.9	48.1	51.8	25.0
1968............	41.6	41.9	54.5	42.6	48.9	52.3	25.0
1969............	42.7	43.2	56.7	43.7	49.9	53.8	25.5
1970............	43.3	44.0	57.7	45.0	51.1	54.4	25.3
1971............	43.4	43.4	57.7	45.6	51.6	54.3	25.1
1972............	43.9	45.8	59.1	47.8	52.0	53.9	24.5
1973............	44.7	47.8	61.1	50.4	53.3	53.7	23.8
1974............	45.7	49.1	63.1	52.6	54.7	54.6	23.0
1975............	46.3	49.1	64.1	54.9	55.8	54.6	23.1
1976............	47.3	49.8	65.0	57.3	57.8	55.0	23.0
1977............	48.4	51.2	66.5	59.7	59.6	55.8	22.9
1978............	50.0	53.7	68.3	62.2	61.6	57.1	23.1
1979............	50.9	54.2	69.0	63.9	63.6	58.3	23.2
1980............	51.5	52.9	68.9	65.5	65.5	59.9	22.8
1981............	52.1	51.8	69.6	66.7	66.8	61.1	22.7
1982............	52.6	51.4	69.8	68.0	68.0	61.6	22.7
1983............	52.9	50.8	69.9	69.0	68.7	61.9	22.4
1984............	53.6	51.8	70.4	69.8	70.1	62.9	22.2
1985............	54.5	52.1	71.8	70.9	71.8	64.4	22.0
1986............	55.3	53.0	72.4	71.6	73.1	65.9	22.1
1987............	56.0	53.3	73.0	72.4	74.5	67.1	22.0
1988............	56.6	53.6	72.7	72.7	75.2	69.0	22.3
1989............	57.4	53.9	72.4	73.5	76.0	70.5	23.0
1990............	57.5	51.8	71.6	73.6	76.5	71.2	23.0
1991............	57.3	50.2	70.4	73.3	76.6	72.0	22.8
1992............	57.8	49.2	71.2	74.1	76.8	72.7	23.0
1993............	57.9	49.9	71.3	73.6	76.7	73.5	23.0

Source: Howard V. Hayghe, "Are Women Leaving the Labor Force?" *Monthly Labor Review*, July 1994, Table 1.

B1-3. Labor Force Status in Urban and Rural Areas, by Age and Sex: 1990

[Data based on sample and subject to sampling variability.]

United States Urban and Rural and Size of Place		Urban						Rural			
			Inside urbanized area			Outside urbanized area					
	United States	Total	Total	Central place	Urban fringe	Place of 10,000 or more	Place of 2,500 to 9,999	Total	Place of 1,000 to 2,499	Place of less than 1,000	Rural farm
LABOR FORCE STATUS											
Persons 16 years and over	191 829 271	145 148 034	123 072 579	61 358 074	61 714 505	10 652 535	11 422 920	46 681 237	5 371 705	2 876 858	3 022 837
In labor force	125 182 378	95 619 567	82 191 894	39 700 480	42 491 414	6 556 740	6 870 933	29 562 811	3 203 946	1 678 490	1 972 394
Percent of persons 16 years and over	65.3	65.9	66.8	64.7	68.9	61.6	60.2	63.3	59.6	58.3	65.2
Armed Forces	1 708 928	1 523 599	1 249 127	599 902	649 225	146 643	127 829	185 329	20 960	5 822	2 263
Civilian labor force	123 473 450	94 095 968	80 942 767	39 100 578	41 842 189	6 410 097	6 743 104	29 377 482	3 182 986	1 672 668	1 970 131
Employed	115 681 202	88 062 103	75 840 926	36 037 995	39 802 931	5 954 560	6 266 617	27 619 099	2 971 545	1 551 830	1 909 060
At work 35 or more hours	89 428 871	68 085 993	58 960 814	27 780 332	31 180 482	4 395 683	4 729 496	21 342 878	2 260 836	1 175 976	1 439 770
Unemployed	7 792 248	6 033 865	5 101 841	3 062 583	2 039 258	455 537	476 487	1 758 383	211 441	120 838	61 071
Percent of civilian labor force	6.3	6.4	6.3	7.8	4.9	7.1	7.1	6.0	6.6	7.2	3.1
Not in labor force	66 646 893	49 528 467	40 880 685	21 657 594	19 223 091	4 095 795	4 551 987	17 118 426	2 167 759	1 198 368	1 050 443
Institutionalized persons	3 232 910	2 396 039	1 773 173	998 912	774 261	295 024	327 842	836 871	127 047	39 297	-
Females 16 years and over	99 803 358	76 252 547	64 493 999	32 374 630	32 119 369	5 649 462	6 109 086	23 550 811	2 867 508	1 521 194	1 460 378
In labor force	56 672 949	43 906 398	37 737 708	18 442 977	19 294 731	3 021 952	3 146 738	12 766 551	1 460 169	750 757	763 049
Percent of females 16 years and over	56.8	57.6	58.5	57.0	60.1	53.5	51.5	54.2	50.9	49.4	52.3
Armed Forces	185 700	167 037	138 001	71 268	66 733	14 414	14 622	18 663	2 199	670	292
Civilian labor force	56 487 249	43 739 361	37 599 707	18 371 709	19 227 998	3 007 538	3 132 116	12 747 888	1 457 970	750 087	762 757
Employed	52 976 623	40 999 342	35 296 308	16 988 210	18 308 098	2 793 752	2 909 282	11 977 281	1 363 036	699 125	734 219
At work 35 or more hours	36 418 960	28 419 931	24 688 286	12 004 463	12 683 823	1 813 368	1 918 277	7 999 029	900 095	457 090	467 034
Unemployed	3 510 626	2 740 019	2 303 399	1 383 499	919 900	213 786	222 834	770 607	94 934	50 962	28 538
Percent of civilian labor force	6.2	6.3	6.1	7.5	4.8	7.1	7.1	6.0	6.5	6.8	3.7
Not in labor force	43 130 409	32 346 149	26 756 291	13 931 653	12 824 638	2 627 510	2 962 348	10 784 260	1 407 339	770 437	697 329
Institutionalized persons	1 487 110	1 219 834	899 096	479 491	419 605	144 025	176 713	267 276	74 967	23 605	-
Males 16 to 19 years	7 342 263	5 443 132	4 515 012	2 314 501	2 200 511	471 723	456 397	1 899 131	203 282	109 702	120 755
Employed	2 962 432	2 181 272	1 815 845	836 992	978 853	183 125	182 302	781 160	79 010	40 590	57 139
Unemployed	670 528	514 350	427 520	245 994	181 526	43 924	42 906	156 178	18 654	9 638	5 369
Not in labor force	3 562 362	2 615 499	2 168 010	1 177 343	990 667	228 088	219 401	946 863	104 525	58 998	57 957
Males 20 to 24 years	9 449 385	7 606 697	6 428 060	3 539 548	2 888 512	654 904	523 733	1 842 688	208 342	103 219	100 895
Employed	6 419 967	5 086 079	4 351 089	2 284 526	2 066 563	395 035	339 955	1 333 888	149 580	76 877	81 259
Unemployed	768 405	607 501	511 221	319 751	191 470	49 941	46 339	160 904	20 326	11 347	5 759
Not in labor force	1 806 836	1 490 149	1 220 267	770 942	449 325	168 042	101 840	316 687	33 356	13 629	13 290
Males 25 to 54 years	52 743 194	39 560 291	34 104 183	16 604 479	17 499 704	2 628 351	2 827 757	13 182 903	1 332 844	709 490	758 978
Employed	44 842 502	33 588 717	29 069 450	13 539 179	15 530 271	2 164 426	2 354 841	11 253 785	1 137 742	599 837	698 895
Unemployed	2 450 753	1 877 099	1 607 808	981 436	626 372	128 320	140 971	573 654	66 486	42 063	17 188
Not in labor force	4 553 238	3 297 464	2 768 922	1 775 836	993 086	262 144	266 398	1 255 774	116 104	64 341	41 817
Males 55 to 64 years	9 957 003	7 148 947	6 061 359	2 829 378	3 231 981	500 326	587 262	2 808 056	297 503	165 009	267 861
Employed	6 377 542	4 666 717	4 005 904	1 772 236	2 233 668	308 792	352 021	1 710 825	178 188	97 181	210 844
Unemployed	294 523	218 602	186 954	97 539	89 415	14 347	17 301	75 921	7 998	5 260	3 161
Not in labor force	3 279 732	2 259 257	1 864 680	957 607	907 073	176 894	217 683	1 020 475	111 241	62 509	53 840
Males 65 to 69 years	4 555 259	3 310 472	2 758 277	1 324 480	1 433 797	251 141	301 054	1 244 787	148 796	83 615	121 521
In labor force	1 269 464	943 164	804 375	372 040	432 335	64 163	74 626	326 300	36 986	21 361	65 433
Not in labor force	3 285 795	2 367 308	1 953 902	952 440	1 001 462	186 978	226 428	918 487	111 810	62 254	56 088
Did not work in 1989	2 675 255	1 944 439	1 605 194	793 730	811 464	153 261	185 984	730 816	90 219	48 856	25 042
Males 70 years and over	7 958 809	5 825 948	4 711 689	2 371 058	2 340 631	496 628	617 631	2 132 861	313 430	184 629	192 449
In labor force	930 288	673 307	563 076	279 285	283 791	50 489	59 742	256 981	30 046	18 429	62 327
Not in labor force	7 028 521	5 152 641	4 148 613	2 091 773	2 056 840	446 139	557 889	1 875 880	283 384	166 200	130 122
Did not work in 1989	6 289 799	4 669 292	3 761 819	1 905 068	1 856 751	403 652	503 821	1 620 507	252 983	143 127	67 308
Females 16 to 19 years	6 973 185	5 271 686	4 356 393	2 287 352	2 069 041	473 306	441 987	1 701 499	193 573	102 242	101 477
Employed	2 880 619	2 208 621	1 832 977	859 756	973 221	196 195	179 449	671 998	75 779	36 370	40 225
Unemployed	541 322	417 379	342 280	202 083	140 197	37 841	37 258	123 943	15 293	7 933	5 018
Not in labor force	3 530 010	2 626 461	2 166 124	1 216 974	949 150	237 350	222 987	903 549	102 322	57 859	56 201
Females 20 to 24 years	9 176 002	7 462 924	6 321 211	3 527 700	2 793 511	628 768	512 945	1 713 078	209 793	104 936	74 466
Employed	5 946 615	4 863 428	4 174 164	2 185 216	1 988 948	377 731	311 533	1 083 187	130 204	63 490	50 079
Unemployed	605 852	483 626	400 680	257 737	142 943	43 895	39 051	122 226	16 520	8 861	3 981
Not in labor force	2 564 310	2 062 394	1 703 109	1 061 345	641 764	202 147	157 138	501 916	62 355	32 363	20 372
Females 25 to 54 years	53 809 217	40 839 784	35 203 923	17 128 125	18 075 798	2 690 955	2 944 906	12 969 433	1 390 946	721 955	728 209
Employed	37 761 559	28 977 347	25 082 053	11 889 534	13 192 519	1 870 873	2 024 421	8 784 212	963 944	491 950	500 304
Unemployed	2 079 910	1 615 507	1 369 590	818 991	550 599	117 154	128 763	464 403	55 030	30 041	16 117
Not in labor force	13 863 239	10 153 206	8 673 066	4 380 565	4 292 501	695 481	784 659	3 710 033	370 673	199 596	211 586
Females 55 to 64 years	11 163 747	8 286 271	6 975 447	3 393 028	3 582 419	605 782	705 042	2 877 476	344 075	187 265	255 286
Employed	4 894 548	3 764 590	3 211 324	1 538 078	1 673 246	260 419	292 847	1 129 958	142 190	78 088	111 259
Unemployed	199 774	155 105	132 254	71 661	60 593	10 554	12 297	44 669	5 752	2 837	2 519
Not in labor force	6 068 702	4 365 973	3 631 361	1 782 997	1 848 364	334 757	399 855	1 702 729	196 126	106 340	141 485
Females 65 to 69 years	5 604 849	4 244 016	3 518 651	1 753 222	1 765 429	332 051	393 314	1 360 833	189 756	104 146	108 508
In labor force	944 717	750 854	637 513	321 479	316 034	53 126	60 215	193 863	29 693	16 856	19 432
Not in labor force	4 660 132	3 493 162	2 881 138	1 431 743	1 449 395	278 925	333 099	1 166 970	160 063	87 290	89 076
Did not work in 1989	4 202 287	3 151 160	2 597 857	1 290 671	1 307 186	251 814	301 489	1 051 127	144 033	77 582	72 563
Females 70 years and over	13 076 358	10 147 866	8 118 374	4 285 203	3 833 171	918 600	1 110 892	2 928 492	539 345	300 650	192 432
In labor force	632 342	502 913	416 881	227 174	189 707	39 750	46 282	129 429	23 565	13 661	13 823
Not in labor force	12 444 016	9 644 953	7 701 493	4 058 029	3 643 464	878 850	1 064 610	2 799 063	515 800	286 989	178 609
Did not work in 1989	11 840 761	9 220 061	7 366 829	3 878 927	3 487 902	838 050	1 015 182	2 620 700	488 266	266 788	140 466
PRESENCE OF OWN CHILDREN IN FAMILIES AND SUBFAMILIES											
Females 16 years and over	99 803 358	76 252 547	64 493 999	32 374 630	32 119 369	5 649 462	6 109 086	23 550 811	2 867 508	1 521 194	1 460 378
With own children under 6 years	15 233 818	11 544 096	9 771 998	4 855 947	4 916 051	849 147	922 951	3 689 722	417 918	223 379	177 537
In labor force	9 095 156	6 884 215	5 800 481	2 828 405	2 972 076	522 059	561 675	2 210 941	257 548	137 838	108 782
With own children 6 to 17 years only	16 490 186	11 856 968	9 933 810	4 647 130	5 286 680	898 842	1 024 316	4 633 218	499 335	270 735	269 235
In labor force	12 367 705	8 951 982	7 481 046	3 424 921	4 056 125	688 795	782 141	3 415 723	380 445	204 259	197 181
Own children under 6 years living with two parents	15 993 967	11 730 677	9 909 778	4 384 018	5 525 760	863 690	957 209	4 263 290	452 639	248 294	234 466
Both parents in labor force	8 874 102	6 521 224	5 481 824	2 417 904	3 063 920	496 176	543 224	2 352 878	260 641	143 409	132 131
Both at work 35 or more hours	4 433 879	3 254 697	2 738 692	1 243 019	1 495 673	250 248	265 757	1 179 182	128 615	71 495	67 238
Own children under 6 years living with one parent	5 279 645	4 387 706	3 713 516	2 475 580	1 237 936	332 226	341 964	891 939	139 426	73 726	23 204
Parent in labor force	3 169 479	2 597 462	2 187 650	1 358 300	829 350	201 293	208 519	572 017	86 133	44 963	15 634
At work 35 or more hours	1 936 665	1 585 593	1 349 093	791 681	557 412	116 147	120 353	351 072	51 107	25 804	10 172
Own children 6 to 17 years living with two parents	29 673 627	20 452 809	17 019 863	7 287 558	9 732 305	1 584 542	1 848 404	9 220 818	931 679	528 964	636 425
Both parents in labor force	19 477 241	13 458 537	11 128 649	4 650 805	6 477 844	1 077 712	1 252 176	6 018 704	632 080	357 181	422 461
Both at work 35 or more hours	10 782 593	7 440 319	6 136 899	2 627 690	3 509 209	609 883	693 537	3 342 274	348 346	195 892	238 963
Own children 6 to 17 years living with one parent	9 931 854	8 097 524	6 839 456	4 241 465	2 597 991	606 326	651 742	1 834 330	281 006	147 520	50 144
Parent in labor force	7 343 393	5 949 612	5 009 872	2 898 574	2 111 298	453 174	486 566	1 393 781	211 328	109 437	39 594
At work 35 or more hours	5 231 410	4 241 271	3 597 241	1 983 974	1 613 267	309 915	334 115	990 139	146 777	74 198	29 864

Source: U.S. Bureau of the Census, *Social and Economic Characteristics of the United States: 1990 Census of Population*, CP-2-1, Washington, D.C.: U.S. Government Printing Office, 1993, Table 19.

B1-4. Labor Force Characteristics, by Race and Hispanic Origin: 1990

[Data based on sample and subject to sampling variability.]

United States	All persons	Race — White	Race — Black	Race — American Indian, Eskimo, or Aleut	Race — Asian or Pacific Islander	Race — Other race	Hispanic origin (of any race)	White, not of Hispanic origin
LABOR FORCE STATUS								
Persons 16 years and over	191 829 271	157 119 373	21 386 343	1 395 009	5 403 615	6 524 931	15 025 902	149 164 557
In labor force	125 182 378	102 800 818	13 413 487	865 703	3 645 946	4 456 424	10 139 070	97 467 714
Percent of persons 16 years and over	65.3	65.4	62.7	62.1	67.5	68.3	67.5	65.3
Armed Forces	1 708 928	1 275 082	318 306	14 391	42 866	58 283	117 347	1 224 593
Civilian labor force	123 473 450	101 525 736	13 095 181	851 312	3 603 080	4 398 141	10 021 723	96 243 121
Employed	115 681 202	96 237 561	11 407 803	728 953	3 411 586	3 895 299	8 981 516	91 447 312
At work 35 or more hours	89 428 871	74 240 108	8 873 999	548 730	2 690 953	3 075 081	7 078 492	70 470 721
Unemployed	7 792 248	5 288 175	1 687 378	122 359	191 494	502 842	1 040 207	4 795 809
Percent of civilian labor force	6.3	5.2	12.9	14.4	5.3	11.4	10.4	5.0
Not in labor force	66 646 893	54 318 555	7 972 856	529 306	1 757 669	2 068 507	4 886 832	51 696 843
Institutionalized persons	3 232 910	2 360 364	722 050	31 375	23 391	95 730	240 572	2 245 385
Females 16 years and over	99 803 358	81 541 169	11 597 691	714 654	2 810 588	3 139 256	7 410 116	77 546 546
In labor force	56 672 949	45 947 179	6 901 351	393 437	1 688 145	1 742 837	4 145 686	43 705 520
Percent of females 16 years and over	56.8	56.3	59.5	55.1	60.1	55.5	55.9	56.4
Armed Forces	185 700	120 552	53 709	2 017	4 063	5 359	12 143	115 037
Civilian labor force	56 487 249	45 826 627	6 847 642	391 420	1 684 082	1 737 478	4 133 543	43 590 483
Employed	52 976 623	43 515 117	6 015 288	340 042	1 590 897	1 515 279	3 669 186	41 499 763
At work 35 or more hours	36 418 960	29 467 638	4 470 242	235 857	1 174 018	1 071 205	2 605 432	28 036 488
Unemployed	3 510 626	2 311 510	832 354	51 378	93 185	222 199	464 357	2 090 720
Percent of civilian labor force	6.2	5.0	12.2	13.1	5.5	12.8	11.2	4.8
Not in labor force	43 130 409	35 593 990	4 696 340	321 217	1 122 443	1 396 419	3 264 430	33 841 026
Institutionalized persons	1 487 110	1 309 391	149 200	7 261	8 954	12 304	39 187	1 285 589
Males 16 to 19 years	7 342 263	5 543 693	1 072 640	74 536	247 569	403 825	848 933	5 127 602
Employed	2 962 432	2 453 192	256 572	21 985	73 407	157 276	327 922	2 290 734
Unemployed	670 528	460 692	137 333	9 190	14 626	48 687	97 373	415 598
Not in labor force	3 562 362	2 521 228	650 894	41 984	157 048	191 208	411 580	2 317 348
Males 20 to 24 years	9 469 385	7 263 216	1 212 585	88 901	311 767	592 916	1 197 579	6 699 767
Employed	6 419 967	5 154 588	611 066	48 798	179 585	425 930	854 007	4 749 099
Unemployed	768 405	507 787	170 514	13 825	16 824	59 455	117 795	453 974
Not in labor force	1 806 836	1 248 963	343 341	21 626	105 474	87 432	189 444	1 158 783
Males 25 to 54 years	52 743 194	42 937 054	5 686 136	411 828	1 630 771	2 077 405	4 590 167	40 590 845
Employed	44 842 502	37 589 632	3 921 380	284 470	1 382 945	1 664 075	3 705 608	35 660 537
Unemployed	2 450 753	1 691 210	501 719	44 164	56 378	157 282	322 083	1 540 404
Not in labor force	4 553 238	2 966 583	1 114 548	76 893	165 205	230 009	505 969	2 726 457
Males 55 to 64 years	9 957 003	8 640 902	869 733	55 995	205 333	185 040	543 449	8 301 214
Employed	6 377 542	5 620 921	471 369	27 507	145 196	112 549	346 982	5 397 856
Unemployed	294 523	236 665	34 837	3 085	7 962	11 974	29 897	219 790
Not in labor force	3 279 732	2 779 018	362 965	25 359	51 987	60 403	166 292	2 679 426
Males 65 to 69 years	4 555 259	4 046 612	356 341	20 108	76 895	55 303	182 651	3 925 161
In labor force	1 269 464	1 141 235	81 965	4 363	26 527	15 374	55 077	1 103 791
Not in labor force	3 285 795	2 905 377	274 376	15 745	50 368	39 929	127 574	2 821 370
Did not work in 1989	2 675 255	2 346 126	239 385	13 416	41 780	34 548	107 631	2 276 120
Males 70 years and over	7 958 809	7 146 727	591 217	28 987	120 692	71 186	253 007	6 973 422
In labor force	930 288	843 331	60 825	2 505	15 548	8 079	31 464	820 989
Not in labor force	7 028 521	6 303 396	530 392	26 482	105 144	63 107	221 543	6 152 433
Did not work in 1989	6 289 799	5 613 410	495 995	24 303	97 104	58 987	205 592	5 473 801
Females 16 to 19 years	6 973 185	5 255 802	1 056 432	69 233	233 428	358 290	751 549	4 887 969
Employed	2 880 619	2 398 515	276 106	20 236	73 165	112 597	245 762	2 272 538
Unemployed	541 322	359 046	128 329	7 523	10 857	35 567	70 667	326 918
Not in labor force	3 530 010	2 484 743	645 828	41 192	149 039	209 208	433 120	2 275 849
Females 20 to 24 years	9 176 002	7 033 354	1 283 452	82 718	294 485	481 993	1 001 048	6 550 571
Employed	5 946 615	4 822 599	662 335	39 895	168 071	253 715	547 862	4 546 923
Unemployed	605 852	368 091	171 765	9 552	13 326	43 118	85 076	329 885
Not in labor force	2 564 310	1 805 452	431 333	32 551	111 968	183 006	363 779	1 638 321
Females 25 to 54 years	53 809 217	43 111 433	6 578 709	431 080	1 777 497	1 910 498	4 414 333	40 777 951
Employed	37 761 559	30 815 968	4 424 857	251 698	1 203 710	1 065 326	2 588 841	29 393 493
Unemployed	2 079 910	1 361 135	494 029	31 853	59 948	132 945	280 510	1 226 933
Not in labor force	13 863 239	10 865 027	1 630 433	146 514	511 318	709 947	1 539 234	10 091 082
Females 55 to 64 years	11 163 747	9 503 847	1 125 815	62 995	260 191	210 899	622 648	9 115 058
Employed	4 894 548	4 173 827	505 641	22 406	121 478	71 196	237 979	4 016 959
Unemployed	199 774	155 951	26 502	1 953	6 890	8 478	21 939	143 442
Not in labor force	6 068 702	5 173 539	593 541	38 636	131 768	131 218	362 666	4 954 178
Females 65 to 69 years	5 604 849	4 904 414	507 624	24 292	98 240	70 279	228 685	4 754 245
In labor force	944 717	822 170	91 626	3 744	18 228	8 949	34 580	797 974
Not in labor force	4 660 132	4 082 244	415 998	20 548	80 012	61 330	194 105	3 956 271
Did not work in 1989	4 202 287	3 675 743	377 408	18 589	73 041	57 506	179 969	3 559 605
Females 70 years and over	13 076 358	11 732 319	1 045 659	44 336	146 747	107 297	391 853	11 460 752
In labor force	632 342	549 334	66 452	2 560	8 409	5 587	20 327	535 427
Not in labor force	12 444 016	11 182 985	979 207	41 776	138 338	101 710	371 526	10 925 325
Did not work in 1989	11 840 761	10 628 686	939 939	39 694	133 512	98 930	359 792	10 379 637

Source: U.S. Bureau of the Census, *Social and Economic Characteristics of the United States: 1990 Census of Population*, CP-2-1, Washington, D.C.: U.S. Government Printing Office, 1993, Table 44.

B1-5. Labor Force Characteristics in Urban and Rural Areas: 1990

[Data based on sample and subject to sampling variability.]

United States Urban and Rural and Size of Place		Urban						Rural			
			Inside urbanized area			Outside urbanized area					
	United States	Total	Total	Central place	Urban fringe	Place of 10,000 or more	Place of 2,500 to 9,999	Total	Place of 1,000 to 2,499	Place of less than 1,000	Rural farm
CLASS OF WORKER											
Employed persons 16 years and over	**115 681 202**	**88 062 103**	**75 840 926**	**36 037 995**	**39 802 931**	**5 954 560**	**6 266 617**	**27 619 099**	**2 971 545**	**1 551 830**	**1 909 060**
Private for profit wage and salary workers	81 781 333	62 757 416	54 348 979	25 174 241	29 174 738	4 074 411	4 334 026	19 023 917	2 045 534	1 038 265	938 170
Employees of own corporation	3 118 578	2 305 296	2 024 948	807 231	1 217 717	130 195	150 153	813 282	69 511	32 787	98 507
Private not-for-profit wage and salary workers	7 760 060	6 276 393	5 466 450	2 824 081	2 642 369	409 419	400 524	1 483 667	183 342	89 770	74 239
Local government workers	8 244 755	6 362 783	5 422 606	2 753 312	2 669 294	440 672	499 505	1 881 972	239 752	128 229	115 993
State government workers	5 381 445	3 960 486	3 157 376	1 801 564	1 355 812	447 567	355 543	1 420 959	162 559	88 783	76 734
Federal government workers	3 940 900	3 160 449	2 794 338	1 326 005	1 468 333	179 641	186 470	780 451	85 473	48 458	42 316
Self-employed workers	8 067 483	5 258 979	4 416 613	2 052 092	2 364 521	380 162	462 204	2 808 504	240 456	148 351	595 145
In agriculture	1 062 778	229 067	170 559	79 441	91 118	23 392	35 116	833 711	25 264	25 627	485 516
Unpaid family workers	505 226	285 597	234 564	106 700	127 864	22 688	28 345	219 629	14 429	9 974	66 463
Employed females 16 years and over	**52 976 623**	**40 999 342**	**35 296 308**	**16 988 210**	**18 308 098**	**2 793 752**	**2 909 282**	**11 977 281**	**1 363 036**	**699 125**	**734 219**
Private for profit wage and salary workers	35 647 886	27 783 576	24 068 380	11 307 235	12 761 145	1 803 797	1 911 399	7 864 310	885 437	440 103	387 073
Employees of own corporation	758 589	561 544	487 461	202 803	284 658	34 442	39 641	197 045	18 794	8 736	21 222
Private not-for-profit wage and salary workers	5 045 116	4 061 441	3 538 652	1 781 660	1 756 992	267 400	255 389	983 675	118 069	56 517	55 359
Local government workers	4 617 771	3 534 405	3 008 870	1 504 114	1 504 756	248 984	276 551	1 083 366	133 981	71 390	75 067
State government workers	3 002 677	2 215 898	1 774 984	1 011 424	763 560	241 183	199 731	786 779	92 272	49 945	44 802
Federal government workers	1 663 488	1 323 601	1 174 284	580 955	593 329	73 518	75 799	339 887	38 049	24 613	21 342
Self-employed workers	2 708 708	1 902 868	1 584 929	739 656	845 273	144 881	173 058	805 840	86 830	50 971	120 857
Unpaid family workers	290 977	177 553	146 209	63 166	83 043	13 989	17 355	113 424	8 398	5 586	29 719
WORK STATUS IN 1989											
Persons 16 years and over, worked in 1989	**134 529 779**	**102 317 200**	**87 491 273**	**42 228 089**	**45 263 184**	**7 305 780**	**7 520 147**	**32 212 579**	**3 499 246**	**1 854 534**	**2 254 898**
50 to 52 weeks	84 533 428	64 302 538	55 574 600	25 657 174	29 917 426	4 233 334	4 494 604	20 230 890	2 141 016	1 100 600	1 479 036
48 and 49 weeks	5 825 217	4 644 872	4 037 029	2 104 565	1 932 464	305 658	302 185	1 180 345	128 344	66 060	67 232
40 to 47 weeks	11 370 482	8 733 256	7 469 752	3 700 044	3 769 708	625 065	638 439	2 637 226	291 873	150 245	154 474
27 to 39 weeks	10 110 388	7 568 649	6 292 627	3 277 645	3 014 982	634 907	641 115	2 541 739	293 494	168 146	158 554
14 to 26 weeks	11 628 106	8 820 585	7 335 329	3 848 060	3 487 269	760 616	724 640	2 807 521	321 326	176 848	178 894
1 to 13 weeks	11 062 158	8 247 300	6 781 936	3 640 601	3 141 335	746 200	719 164	2 814 858	323 193	192 635	216 708
Usually worked 35 or more hours per week	105 361 883	80 043 995	68 748 757	33 042 755	35 706 002	5 501 130	5 794 108	25 317 888	2 715 269	1 434 162	1 692 007
40 or more weeks	87 097 175	66 439 286	57 523 447	26 898 801	30 624 646	4 308 612	4 607 227	20 657 889	2 177 296	1 117 266	1 392 027
50 to 52 weeks	74 660 124	56 853 309	49 269 435	22 693 395	26 576 040	3 664 863	3 919 011	17 806 815	1 865 432	953 069	1 236 786
27 to 39 weeks	6 296 616	4 630 291	3 834 598	2 041 837	1 792 761	382 945	412 748	1 666 325	193 078	113 605	97 817
Usually worked 15 to 34 hours per week	23 491 124	18 052 460	15 250 333	7 491 137	7 759 196	1 443 903	1 358 224	5 438 664	614 678	323 140	407 301
40 or more weeks	12 332 049	9 555 846	8 158 562	3 892 440	4 266 122	716 584	680 700	2 776 203	314 268	158 278	226 742
50 to 52 weeks	8 377 547	6 391 892	5 434 405	2 547 216	2 887 189	480 485	477 002	1 985 655	226 493	116 592	176 251
27 to 39 weeks	3 104 413	2 394 959	2 007 884	1 016 732	991 152	203 769	183 306	709 454	80 137	43 545	46 056
Usually worked 1 to 14 hours per week	5 676 772	4 220 745	3 492 183	1 694 197	1 797 986	360 747	367 815	1 456 027	169 299	97 232	155 590
40 or more weeks	2 299 903	1 685 534	1 399 372	670 542	728 830	138 861	147 301	614 369	69 669	41 361	81 973
50 to 52 weeks	1 495 757	1 057 337	870 760	416 563	454 197	87 986	98 591	438 420	49 091	30 939	65 999
27 to 39 weeks	709 359	543 399	450 145	219 076	231 069	48 193	45 061	165 960	20 279	10 996	14 681
Females 16 years and over, worked in 1989	**61 904 615**	**47 753 167**	**40 831 906**	**19 900 719**	**20 931 187**	**3 418 766**	**3 502 495**	**14 151 448**	**1 624 590**	**846 248**	**892 325**
50 to 52 weeks	35 419 603	27 500 686	23 838 940	11 297 859	12 541 081	1 780 764	1 880 982	7 918 917	895 720	453 266	500 925
48 and 49 weeks	2 692 119	2 178 750	1 895 764	991 572	904 192	143 348	139 638	513 369	58 912	29 598	27 657
40 to 47 weeks	5 996 730	4 670 450	4 001 070	1 929 459	2 071 611	333 280	336 100	1 326 280	151 546	74 773	76 720
27 to 39 weeks	5 569 882	4 184 889	3 466 978	1 754 097	1 712 881	357 373	360 538	1 384 993	165 796	92 299	89 393
14 to 26 weeks	6 241 320	4 741 167	3 938 698	1 995 430	1 943 268	405 771	396 698	1 500 153	176 623	94 682	91 831
1 to 13 weeks	5 984 961	4 477 225	3 690 456	1 932 302	1 758 154	398 230	388 539	1 507 736	175 993	101 630	105 799
Usually worked 35 or more hours per week	42 973 185	33 381 568	28 780 776	14 218 646	14 562 130	2 251 534	2 349 258	9 591 617	1 091 270	561 927	561 537
40 or more weeks	34 274 397	26 847 119	23 380 068	11 316 330	12 063 738	1 685 714	1 781 337	7 427 278	833 446	415 492	423 862
50 to 52 weeks	28 714 940	22 479 573	19 604 275	9 397 801	10 206 474	1 397 971	1 477 327	6 235 367	697 204	346 762	359 852
27 to 39 weeks	3 061 761	2 270 657	1 873 519	982 896	890 623	192 263	204 875	791 104	96 026	54 079	50 301
Usually worked 15 to 34 hours per week	15 324 105	11 688 066	9 832 411	4 646 529	5 185 882	937 999	917 656	3 636 039	422 432	221 157	246 062
40 or more weeks	8 378 004	6 431 754	5 467 766	2 494 569	2 973 197	483 122	480 866	1 946 250	226 581	114 567	140 216
50 to 52 weeks	5 775 176	4 362 008	3 693 148	1 651 419	2 041 729	327 861	340 999	1 413 168	166 171	85 881	109 006
27 to 39 weeks	2 032 961	1 550 277	1 291 947	631 250	660 697	132 742	125 588	482 684	56 022	30 787	30 020
Usually worked 1 to 14 hours per week	3 607 325	2 683 533	2 218 719	1 035 544	1 183 175	229 233	235 581	923 792	110 888	63 164	84 726
40 or more weeks	1 456 051	1 071 013	887 940	407 991	479 949	88 556	94 517	385 038	46 151	27 578	41 224
50 to 52 weeks	929 487	659 105	541 517	248 639	292 878	54 932	62 656	270 382	32 345	20 623	32 067
27 to 39 weeks	475 160	363 955	301 512	139 951	161 561	32 368	30 075	111 205	13 748	7 433	9 072
WORKERS IN FAMILY IN 1989											
Families	**65 049 428**	**47 815 502**	**40 338 661**	**19 111 188**	**21 227 473**	**3 506 713**	**3 970 128**	**17 233 926**	**1 916 297**	**1 042 156**	**1 162 367**
No workers	8 477 151	6 265 202	5 103 339	2 841 302	2 262 037	527 068	634 795	2 211 949	305 410	168 671	76 075
1 worker	18 243 077	13 461 816	11 295 736	5 688 823	5 606 913	1 016 964	1 149 116	4 781 261	544 473	299 329	347 850
2 workers	29 637 580	21 624 425	18 304 443	8 192 748	10 111 695	1 577 540	1 742 442	8 013 155	846 818	458 371	554 113
3 or more workers	8 691 620	6 464 059	5 635 143	2 388 315	3 246 828	385 141	443 775	2 227 561	219 596	115 785	184 329
Married-couple families	**51 718 214**	**36 843 114**	**30 930 889**	**13 503 916**	**17 426 973**	**2 748 735**	**3 163 490**	**14 875 100**	**1 563 963**	**861 257**	**1 070 524**
No workers	6 129 613	4 327 221	3 470 057	1 665 811	1 804 246	380 448	476 716	1 802 392	237 572	132 269	67 147
1 worker	11 870 620	8 275 151	6 925 518	3 107 517	3 818 001	621 535	728 098	3 595 469	360 814	205 839	308 654
2 workers	26 129 451	18 709 257	15 742 243	6 800 519	8 941 724	1 404 690	1 562 324	7 420 194	766 732	417 737	520 637
Husband and wife worked	23 856 655	17 074 077	14 321 764	6 166 478	8 155 286	1 305 963	1 446 350	6 782 578	707 598	386 004	462 436
3 or more workers	7 588 530	5 531 485	4 793 071	1 930 069	2 863 002	342 062	396 352	2 057 045	198 845	105 412	174 086
Husband and wife worked	6 742 469	4 882 328	4 206 474	1 666 720	2 539 754	313 587	362 267	1 860 141	181 976	96 647	155 294
Female householder, no husband present	**10 381 654**	**8 665 622**	**7 405 278**	**4 496 864**	**2 908 414**	**612 346**	**647 998**	**1 716 032**	**277 677**	**138 065**	**50 683**
No workers	2 056 800	1 720 321	1 449 367	1 054 208	395 159	131 334	139 620	336 479	58 636	30 625	6 387
1 worker	4 929 373	4 083 947	3 433 371	2 056 451	1 376 920	315 928	334 648	845 426	142 779	69 976	21 057
2 workers	2 557 262	2 148 169	1 880 864	1 033 302	847 562	131 085	136 220	409 093	59 988	29 415	17 498
3 or more workers	838 219	713 185	641 676	352 903	288 773	33 999	37 510	125 034	16 274	8 049	5 741
LABOR FORCE STATUS OF FAMILY MEMBERS											
Married-couple families	**51 718 214**	**36 843 114**	**30 930 889**	**13 503 916**	**17 426 973**	**2 748 735**	**3 163 490**	**14 875 100**	**1 563 963**	**861 257**	**1 070 524**
Husband employed or in Armed Forces	39 286 822	28 149 602	23 848 177	10 066 813	13 781 364	2 029 304	2 272 121	11 137 220	1 110 824	595 316	847 203
Wife employed or in Armed Forces	25 799 947	18 587 004	15 747 081	6 577 813	9 169 268	1 344 159	1 495 764	7 212 943	736 327	391 540	519 421
Wife unemployed	1 071 291	772 499	639 226	318 037	321 189	63 058	70 215	298 792	31 284	17 413	12 387
Wife not in labor force	12 415 584	8 790 099	7 461 870	3 170 963	4 290 907	622 087	706 142	3 625 485	343 213	186 363	315 395
Husband unemployed	1 364 119	954 470	789 011	417 152	371 859	74 181	91 278	409 649	45 113	29 246	11 887
Wife employed or in Armed Forces	790 277	566 537	476 391	242 136	234 255	40 723	49 423	223 740	24 674	15 808	6 506
Wife unemployed	127 477	88 394	69 142	41 617	27 525	8 539	10 713	39 083	4 773	3 041	1 178
Wife not in labor force	446 365	299 539	243 478	133 399	110 079	24 919	31 142	146 826	15 666	10 397	4 203
Husband not in labor force	11 067 273	7 739 042	6 293 701	3 019 951	3 273 750	645 250	800 091	3 328 231	408 026	236 695	211 434
Wife employed or in Armed Forces	2 383 825	1 671 249	1 389 798	687 669	702 129	127 146	154 305	712 576	80 735	48 132	40 956
Wife unemployed	127 210	86 029	69 995	40 716	29 279	7 030	9 004	41 181	4 496	2 682	1 698
Wife not in labor force	8 556 238	5 981 764	4 833 908	2 291 566	2 542 342	511 074	636 782	2 574 474	322 795	185 881	168 780
Female householder, no husband present	**10 381 654**	**8 665 622**	**7 405 278**	**4 496 864**	**2 908 414**	**612 346**	**647 998**	**1 716 032**	**277 677**	**138 065**	**50 683**
Employed or in Armed Forces	6 031 687	5 088 570	4 383 127	2 449 240	1 933 887	346 373	359 070	943 117	153 578	71 945	21 878
Unemployed	593 069	504 592	420 803	302 362	118 441	40 902	42 887	88 477	16 383	8 252	1 514
Not in labor force	3 756 898	3 072 460	2 601 348	1 745 262	856 086	225 071	246 041	684 438	107 716	57 868	27 291

Source: U.S. Bureau of the Census, *Social and Economic Characteristics of the United States: 1990 Census of Population*, CP-2-1, Washington, D.C.: U.S. Government Printing Office, 1993, Table 22.

B1-6. Class of Worker, Work Status in 1989, and Number of Workers in Families in 1989, by Race and Hispanic Origin: 1990

[Data based on sample and subject to sampling variability.]

United States	All persons	White	Black	American Indian, Eskimo, or Aleut	Asian or Pacific Islander	Other race	Hispanic origin (of any race)	White, not of Hispanic origin
CLASS OF WORKER								
Employed persons 16 years and over	**115 681 202**	**96 237 561**	**11 407 803**	**728 953**	**3 411 586**	**3 895 299**	**8 981 516**	**91 447 312**
Private for profit wage and salary workers	81 781 333	68 136 520	7 610 653	473 852	2 449 328	3 110 980	6 987 883	64 474 694
Employees of own corporation	3 118 578	2 852 857	94 427	9 722	115 399	46 173	147 343	2 754 933
Private not-for-profit wage and salary workers	7 760 060	6 588 643	742 351	44 583	218 930	165 553	410 718	6 362 934
Local government workers	8 244 755	6 552 785	1 231 855	66 172	158 495	235 448	577 730	6 235 102
State government workers	5 381 445	4 278 367	757 734	43 141	184 743	117 460	299 289	4 107 997
Federal government workers	3 940 900	2 914 983	726 293	56 132	147 950	95 542	252 848	2 771 167
Self-employed workers	8 067 483	7 318 612	321 516	42 270	227 250	157 835	421 198	7 066 005
In agriculture	1 062 778	1 005 876	21 944	4 614	11 821	18 523	40 993	983 950
Unpaid family workers	505 226	447 651	17 401	2 803	24 890	12 481	31 850	429 413
Employed females 16 years and over	**52 976 623**	**43 515 117**	**6 015 288**	**340 042**	**1 590 897**	**1 515 279**	**3 669 186**	**41 499 763**
Private for profit wage and salary workers	35 647 886	29 384 344	3 787 782	206 340	1 128 285	1 141 135	2 703 950	27 917 690
Employees of own corporation	758 589	679 538	29 096	3 056	34 512	12 387	38 445	654 438
Private not-for-profit wage and salary workers	5 045 116	4 318 366	488 904	27 579	123 217	87 050	226 983	4 189 909
Local government workers	4 617 771	3 658 838	718 821	34 311	83 981	121 820	306 212	3 487 920
State government workers	3 002 677	2 328 412	492 672	24 691	90 332	66 570	170 398	2 231 115
Federal government workers	1 663 488	1 137 547	394 015	29 755	61 778	40 393	103 373	1 080 975
Self-employed workers	2 708 708	2 427 162	124 580	16 026	87 877	53 063	143 506	2 340 830
Unpaid family workers	290 977	260 448	8 514	1 340	15 427	5 248	14 764	251 324
WORK STATUS IN 1989								
Persons 16 years and over, worked in 1989	**134 529 779**	**111 350 984**	**13 914 568**	**940 172**	**3 824 000**	**4 500 055**	**10 334 670**	**105 876 755**
50 to 52 weeks	84 533 428	71 367 339	8 042 778	472 252	2 309 455	2 341 604	5 647 572	68 256 293
48 and 49 weeks	5 825 217	4 437 724	701 540	39 576	268 951	377 426	765 230	4 075 635
40 to 47 weeks	11 370 482	9 407 780	1 146 309	80 053	321 012	415 328	934 356	8 920 793
27 to 39 weeks	10 110 388	8 200 361	1 135 436	91 517	261 145	421 929	921 507	7 731 591
14 to 26 weeks	11 628 106	9 299 943	1 380 301	117 477	336 256	494 129	1 088 172	8 744 324
1 to 13 weeks	11 062 158	8 637 837	1 508 204	139 297	327 181	449 639	977 833	8 148 119
Usually worked 35 or more hours per week	105 361 883	86 810 887	11 078 912	740 837	3 037 181	3 694 066	8 419 788	82 379 507
40 or more weeks	87 097 175	72 595 660	8 689 678	515 937	2 517 488	2 778 412	6 469 552	69 127 245
50 to 52 weeks	74 660 124	62 809 360	7 239 604	422 031	2 066 573	2 122 556	5 095 863	60 012 196
27 to 39 weeks	6 296 616	5 003 046	762 882	64 503	158 366	307 819	655 046	4 678 059
Usually worked 15 to 34 hours per week	23 491 124	19 822 503	2 235 581	160 366	618 854	653 820	1 559 353	18 967 372
40 or more weeks	12 332 049	10 675 150	975 978	63 650	318 364	298 907	740 363	10 257 858
50 to 52 weeks	8 377 547	7 294 965	651 067	42 253	205 027	184 235	467 792	7 026 526
27 to 39 weeks	3 104 413	2 601 157	305 716	22 452	81 267	93 821	219 994	2 481 609
Usually worked 1 to 14 hours per week	5 676 772	4 717 594	600 075	38 969	167 965	152 169	355 529	4 529 876
40 or more weeks	2 299 903	1 942 033	224 971	12 294	63 566	57 039	137 243	1 867 618
50 to 52 weeks	1 495 757	1 263 014	152 107	7 968	37 855	34 813	83 917	1 217 571
27 to 39 weeks	709 359	596 158	66 838	4 562	21 512	20 289	46 467	571 923
Females 16 years and over, worked in 1989	**61 904 615**	**50 747 988**	**7 137 050**	**433 349**	**1 787 262**	**1 798 966**	**4 304 180**	**48 407 278**
50 to 52 weeks	35 419 603	29 347 758	4 003 406	205 888	1 008 791	853 760	2 169 391	28 117 360
48 and 49 weeks	2 692 119	2 046 442	365 603	16 904	124 904	138 266	294 147	1 902 375
40 to 47 weeks	5 996 730	4 993 075	632 882	38 235	165 324	167 214	402 590	4 772 937
27 to 39 weeks	5 569 882	4 572 964	631 517	45 804	139 430	180 167	418 945	4 349 363
14 to 26 weeks	6 241 320	5 061 450	716 379	56 940	176 036	230 515	519 212	4 791 277
1 to 13 weeks	5 984 961	4 726 299	787 263	69 578	172 777	229 044	499 895	4 473 966
Usually worked 35 or more hours per week	42 973 185	34 579 618	5 418 162	311 436	1 333 277	1 330 692	3 169 835	32 866 204
40 or more weeks	34 274 397	27 802 103	4 232 765	212 942	1 075 894	950 693	2 336 251	26 510 719
50 to 52 weeks	28 714 940	23 459 793	3 489 925	173 875	866 664	724 683	1 833 090	22 425 329
27 to 39 weeks	3 061 761	2 440 145	399 557	28 652	78 645	114 762	260 702	2 304 363
Usually worked 15 to 34 hours per week	15 324 105	13 107 704	1 372 271	99 556	360 554	384 020	931 489	12 590 652
40 or more weeks	8 378 004	7 332 452	636 366	41 247	188 914	179 025	454 921	7 071 489
50 to 52 weeks	5 775 176	5 090 201	424 642	27 584	122 002	110 747	290 141	4 920 036
27 to 39 weeks	2 032 961	1 724 536	191 789	14 302	48 252	54 082	131 073	1 651 438
Usually worked 1 to 14 hours per week	3 607 325	3 060 666	346 617	22 357	93 431	84 254	202 856	2 950 422
40 or more weeks	1 456 051	1 252 720	132 760	6 838	34 211	29 522	74 956	1 210 464
50 to 52 weeks	929 487	797 764	88 839	4 429	20 125	18 330	46 160	771 995
27 to 39 weeks	475 160	408 283	40 171	2 850	12 533	11 323	27 170	393 562
WORKERS IN FAMILY IN 1989								
Families	**65 049 428**	**53 845 200**	**7 055 063**	**463 968**	**1 577 820**	**2 107 377**	**4 776 075**	**51 337 479**
No workers	8 477 151	6 866 496	1 173 808	67 067	131 352	238 428	533 688	6 598 688
1 worker	18 243 077	14 672 797	2 344 189	153 924	413 200	658 967	1 492 336	13 891 781
2 workers	29 637 580	25 306 415	2 595 101	187 916	720 804	827 344	1 914 539	24 275 747
3 or more workers	8 691 620	6 999 492	941 965	55 061	312 464	382 638	835 512	6 571 263
Married-couple families	**51 718 214**	**45 178 672**	**3 521 382**	**305 156**	**1 295 099**	**1 417 905**	**3 339 694**	**43 342 946**
No workers	6 129 613	5 588 666	345 299	29 632	91 301	74 715	219 748	5 449 811
1 worker	11 870 620	10 429 743	692 228	75 213	303 369	370 067	874 426	9 945 895
2 workers	26 129 451	22 829 971	1 832 900	155 414	635 979	675 187	1 579 493	21 967 267
Husband and wife worked	23 856 655	20 926 870	1 642 420	139 524	577 774	570 067	1 339 489	20 194 145
3 or more workers	7 588 530	6 330 292	650 955	44 897	264 450	297 936	666 027	5 979 973
Husband and wife worked	6 742 469	5 686 727	532 299	38 893	226 789	227 761	520 793	5 408 564
Female householder, no husband present	**10 381 654**	**6 540 382**	**3 045 283**	**121 370**	**185 926**	**488 693**	**1 029 646**	**6 058 841**
No workers	2 056 800	1 083 218	759 968	32 080	32 120	149 414	283 838	968 480
1 worker	4 929 373	3 194 979	1 404 530	58 200	74 060	197 604	432 787	2 984 183
2 workers	2 557 262	1 760 764	629 390	23 394	50 952	92 762	210 991	1 652 907
3 or more workers	838 219	501 421	251 395	7 696	28 794	48 913	102 030	453 271

Source: U.S. Bureau of the Census, *Social and Economic Characteristics of the United States: 1990 Census of Population*, CP-2-1, Washington, D.C.: U.S. Government Printing Office, 1993, Table 47.

B1-7. Top 25 County Rankings in Women's Civilian Labor Force Participation Rate: 1990

County	Rate
United States	56.7
Summit, CO	84.1
Routt, CO	78.4
Eagle, CO	78.2
San Miguel, CO	77.7
Pitkin, CO	77.2
Aleutians West, AK	74.8
Grand, CO	74.4
Juneau, AK	74.0
Alexandria, VA (IC)	73.5
Mono, CA	73.3
Teton, WY	73.3
Hinsdale, CO	73.2
Prince Georges, MD	72.8
Dakota, MN	72.5
Anoka, MN	72.4
Prince William, VA	72.3
Howard, MD	72.2
Manassas, VA (IC)	72.0
Gwinnett, GA	71.8
Sitka, AK	71.5
Manassas Park, VA (IC)	71.4
Blaine, ID	70.8
Loudoun, VA	70.6
Fairfax, VA	70.5
Arlington, VA	70.4

NOTE: (IC) indicates an independent city

Source: U.S. Bureau of the Census, *Census and You*, Vol. 29, No. 9, September 1994, pg. 1.

B1-8. Civilian Labor Force and Participation Rates, by Sex, Age, Race, and Hispanic Origin, 1979 and 1992, and Moderate Growth Projections to 2005 of the Bureau of Labor Statistics

Group	Participation rate (thousands)			Level (thousands)			Change (thousands)		Percent change		Annual growth rate (percent)	
	1979	1992	2005	1979	1992	1992–2005	1979–92	1992–2005	1979–92	1992–2005	1979–92	1992–2005
Total, 16 years and older	63 7	66 3	68 8	104.962	126.982	150.516	22.020	23,534	21.0	18.5	1 5	1 3
Men, 16 years and older	77 8	75 6	74 7	60.726	69,184	78,718	8,458	9,534	13.9	13.8	1 0	1 0
16 to 19	61 5	41 1	55 5	5.111	3.547	4.624	−1,564	1,077	−30.6	30.4	−2 8	2.1
20 to 24	86 4	83 3	84 4	8.535	7.242	8.111	−1,293	869	−15.1	12.0	−1 3	9
25 to 34	95 3	93 8	93 5	16.387	19.355	16,509	2,968	−2,846	18.1	−14.7	1 3	−1 2
35 to 44	95 7	93 8	93 5	11.531	18.162	19.645	6,631	1,483	57.5	8.2	3 6	6
45 to 54	91 4	90 8	90 2	10.008	12.101	18.065	2,093	5,964	20.9	49.3	1 5	3 1
55 to 64	72 8	67 0	69 7	7.212	6.701	9.560	−511	2,859	−7.1	42.7	− 6	2 8
65 and over	19 9	16 1	14 7	1.943	2.077	2.203	134	126	6.9	6.1	5	5
Women, 16 years and older	50 9	57 8	63 2	44.235	57.798	71.798	13,563	14,000	30.7	24.2	2.1	1 7
16 to 19	54 2	49 2	52.4	4.527	3.204	4.222	−1,323	1,018	−29.2	31.8	−2 6	2 1
20 to 24	69 0	71 2	73 6	7.234	6.461	7.169	−773	708	−10.7	11.0	− 9	8
25 to 34	63 9	74 1	80 7	11.551	15.748	14.839	4,197	−909	36.3	−5.8	2.4	− 5
35 to 44	63 6	76 8	86 2	8.154	15.441	18.643	7,287	3,202	89.4	20.7	5.0	1 5
45 to 54	58 3	72.7	82.8	6.889	10.290	17.354	3,401	7,064	49.4	68.6	3.1	4 1
55 to 64	41 7	46 6	52.4	4.719	5.169	7.825	450	2,656	9.5	51.4	7	3.2
65 and older	8.3	8 3	8 8	1.161	1.485	1.747	324	262	27.9	17.6	1 9	1 3
White, 16 years and older	63 9	66 7	69.5	91.923	108.526	124.847	16,603	16,321	18.1	15.0	1 3	1 1
Men	78 6	76 4	75 3	53.856	59.830	66.007	5,974	6,177	11.1	10.3	8	8
Women	50 5	57 8	63.6	38.067	48.696	58.840	10,629	10,144	27.9	20.8	1 9	1 5
Black, 16 years and older	61 4	63 3	66.2	10.678	13.891	17.395	3,213	3,504	30.1	25.2	2.0	1 7
Men	71.3	69 7	70.5	5.559	6.892	8.355	1,333	1,463	24.0	21.2	1 7	1 5
Women	53.1	58 0	62.6	5.119	6.999	9.040	1,880	2,041	36.7	29.2	2.4	2.0
Asian and other, 16 years and older[1]	66.1	65 6	66 6	2.361	4.565	8.274	2,204	3,709	93.4	81.2	5.2	4 7
Men	76 6	74 6	74.1	1.311	2.462	4.355	1,151	1,893	87.8	76.9	5.0	4 5
Women	56.4	57 5	59.9	1.049	2.103	3.918	1,054	1,815	100.5	86.3	5.5	4 9
Hispanic, 16 years and older	(²)	66 5	68 4	(²)	10.131	16.581	(²)	6,450	(²)	63.7	³4.3	3 9
Men	(²)	80.5	79.5	(²)	6091	9.628	(²)	3,537	(²)	58.1	³4 0	3.6
Women	(²)	52.6	57.3	(²)	4040	6.953	(²)	2,913	(²)	72.1	³4.7	4 3
Other than Hispanic, 16 years and older	(²)	66.3	68.8	(²)	116,851	133,935	(²)	17,084	(²)	14.6	³1.2	1.1
Men	(²)	75.1	74.1	(²)	63,093	69,090	(²)	5,997	(²)	9.5	³.8	7
Women	(²)	58.2	64.0	(²)	53,758	64,846	(²)	11,088	(²)	20.6	³1.8	1.5
White non-Hispanic, 16 years and older	(²)	66.8	69.4	(²)	98,819	109,753	(²)	10,934	(²)	11.1	³1.0	.8
Men	(²)	75.9	74.7	(²)	53,997	57,218	(²)	3,221	(²)	6.0	³.5	.4
Women	(²)	58.3	64.4	(²)	44,822	52,535	(²)	7,713	(²)	17.2	³1.6	1.2

[1] The "Asian and other" group includes (1) Asians and Pacific Islanders and (2) American Indians and Alaska Natives. The historical data are derived by subtracting "black" from the "black and other" group; projections are made directly, not by subtraction.
² Data for Hispanic origin is not available before 1980.
³ Data are for 1980–92.

Source: Howard N. Fullerton, "Another Look At the Labor Force," *Monthly Labor Review*, November 1993, Table 4.

B1-9. Distribution of Married Couples, by Employment Status and Fertility: Selected Years, June 1976 to 1992

(Numbers in thousands. Limited to married-couple families)

Survey year and characteristic	Number of couples	Husband and wife employed			Husband employed, wife not employed			All other couples
		Total	Wife childless	Wife with one or more children	Total	Wife childless	Wife with one or more children	
1992 Survey								
Total..............................	29,531	17,834	3,910	13,924	7,835	758	7,077	3,861
Age:								
15 to 19 years	286	90	58	32	123	34	89	73
20 to 24 years	2,538	1,329	695	634	719	168	551	491
25 to 29 years	5,514	3,241	1,199	2,042	1,554	184	1,370	718
30 to 34 years	7,268	4,315	895	3,420	2,043	168	1,875	910
35 to 39 years	7,296	4,539	598	3,941	1,916	103	1,813	840
40 to 44 years	6,629	4,321	465	3,856	1,480	102	1,378	829
Race:								
White	26,132	15,893	3,604	12,289	7,071	683	6,388	3,168
Black	2,129	1,292	171	1,121	396	29	367	441
Asian and Pacific Islander	184	94	28	66	52	5	47	37
Hispanic origin:								
Hispanic[1].......................	2,743	1,312	174	1,138	985	84	901	445
Not Hispanic....................	26,788	16,521	3,736	12,785	6,851	675	6,176	3,416
Education:								
Both college graduates...........	4,768	3,162	941	2,221	1,187	120	1,067	417
All other.......................	24,763	14,671	2,969	11,702	6,648	638	6,010	3,444
Occupation:								
Both mangerial-professional	2,831	2,462	631	1,831	(X)	(X)	(X)	368
All other.......................	17,203	15,371	3,279	12,092	(X)	(X)	(X)	11,831
Family income:								
Under $10,000	1,580	383	96	287	527	63	464	671
$10,000 to $19,999.............	3,552	1,360	325	1,035	1,304	149	1,155	887
$20,000 to $24,999.............	2,385	1,251	245	1,006	725	56	669	409
$25,000 to $29,999.............	2,397	1,367	286	1,081	664	56	608	365
$30,000 to $34,999.............	2,723	1,559	303	1,256	849	83	766	315
$35,000 to $49,999.............	6,591	4,490	909	3,581	1,564	142	1,422	538
$50,000 to $74,999.............	5,769	4,367	980	3,387	1,089	97	992	314
$75,000 and over................	3,196	2,257	588	1,669	753	59	694	186
Income not reported	1,337	798	177	621	362	53	309	176
Tenure								
Own home.......................	20,559	13,444	2,571	10,873	5,294	421	4,873	1,822
Rent	8,453	4,134	1,291	2,843	2,365	315	2,050	1,953
No cash rent....................	518	256	48	208	176	23	153	86
Metropolitan residence:								
Metropolitan	22,643	13,576	3,123	10,453	6,074	607	5,467	2,993
Central city	7,585	4,370	1,066	3,304	1,996	238	1,758	1,219
Not central city...............	15,058	9,206	2,057	7,149	4,078	369	3,709	1,774
Nonmetropolitan.................	6,887	4,258	787	3,471	1,763	152	1,611	868
Region of residence:								
Northeast.......................	5,645	3,449	771	2,678	1,592	131	1,461	604
Midwest........................	7,064	4,546	1,002	3,544	1,791	174	1,617	726
South	10,396	6,326	1,380	4,946	2,626	263	2,363	1,444
West...........................	6,427	3,514	758	2,756	1,827	191	1,636	1,087
1987 Survey	29,413	17,596	4,150	13,466	8,941	844	8,097	2,876
1982 Survey	26,777	14,113	3,672	10,441	10,073	1,114	8,959	2,591
1976 Survey	25,420	11,379	3,048	8,331	12,200	1,221	10,979	1,841

Note: Data for 1992 are for families where the wife was 15 to 44 years old; for previous sureys, the data are for women 18 to 44 years old.

[1]Persons of Hispanic origin may be of any race.

Source: June Current Population Surveys, 1976, 1982, 1987 and 1992.

Source: Claudette E. Bennett, U.S. Bureau of Census, *The Black Population in the United States: March 1994 and 1993*, Current Population Reports, Series P20-480, Washington, D.C.: U.S. Government Printing Office, January 1995, Table 1.

B1-10. Labor Force Participation Rates for Women Who Have Had a Child in the Last Year, by Educational Attainment: 1992 and 1982

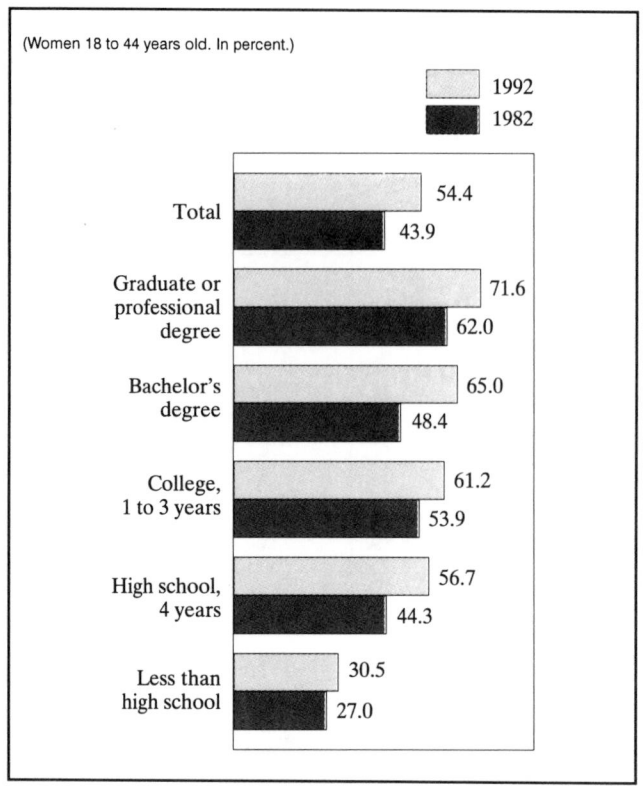

Source: U.S. Bureau of the Census, *How We're Changing—Demographic State of the Nation: 1994*, Current Population Reports, Special Studies, Series P-23, No. 187, January 1994, Figure 1.

B1-11. Changing Patterns of Worklife Expectancy for Women: 1979–80 and 1993–94

25 Year Old Female	1979/1980[1]	1993/1994[2]
Without a High School Diploma	17.9 yrs	20.0 yrs
All Education Levels	24.0 yrs	27.6 yrs
With a College Degree	27.9 yrs	31.7 yrs

[1]U.S. Department of Labor, Bureau of Labor Statistics, *Worklife Estimates: Effects of Race and Education*, Bulletin 2254 (Washington, DC: U.S. Government Printing Office, February, 1986), Tables A-4 and A-6.
[2]Gamboa, A.M. *The New Worklife Expectancy Tables, 1995 Edition*. Vocational Econometrics, Inc., Louisville, Kentucky, January 1995. The data were secured from the U.S. Department of Commerce, Bureau of the Census, Current Population Reports, 1989–1994 by Special Tabulation, Contract Reference Number 33–94–30.

Courtesy of Vocational Econometrics, Inc.
Louisville, Kentucky

Source: A. M. Gamboa, *The New Worklife Expectancy Tables, 1995 Edition*, Vocational Econometrics, Inc., 1 Riverfront Plaza Building, Suite 2100, Louisville, KY, January 1995.

B1-12. Characteristics of Women Workers with Different Work Schedules and Employment Statuses: Calendar Year 1987

WAGE AND SALARY WORKERS

Worker Characteristics	SINGLE EMPLOYER			SIMULTANEOUS PACKAGERS				JOB CHANGERS			
	PT/PY	FT/PY	FT/FY	PT/PY	PT/FY	FT/PY	FT/FY	PT/PY	PT/FY	FT/PY	FT/FY
Number of workers	3,693,000	7,373,000	21,213,000	720,000	1,521,000	211,000	1,803,000	2,639,000	1,224,000	1,690,000	1,990,000
% with children under 6	26.6	23.0	15.1	17.3	16.3	29.9	8.6	24.5	25.0	22.4	18.0
% with FT/FY working spouse	41.5	53.2	42.8	21.0	37.4	27.8	28.5	26.4	36.3	25.8	30.1
% with college diploma	12.0	16.5	23.7	18.0	29.2	15.4	34.7	10.0	17.9	15.4	25.3
Total family earnings	23,958	31,199	34,778	23,772	35,057	18,980	26,938	22,748	29,029	21,918	27,188
Personal earnings as % of family earnings	29.4	40.9	60.2	40.4	41.7	60.9	71.8	35.9	42.8	51.5	63.9
% with means-tested benefits	17.2	5.4	1.6	8.7	5.4	24.0	2.2	16.6	10.4	20.4	0.8

Worker Characteristics	SELF-EMPLOYED WITH SINGLE JOB		MIXED SELF & SALARIED (PRIMARY)		MIXED SELF & SALARIED (SECONDARY)		TWO OR MORE SELF-EMPLOYED JOBS	
	L FT/FY	FT/FY	L FT/FY	FT/FY	L FT/FY	FT/FY	L FT/FY	FT/FY
Number of workers	1,837,000	915,000	648,000	213,000	745,000	682,000	216,000	139,000
% with children under six	24.1	10.5	26.6	18.7	27.5	12.9	38.6	13.5
% with FT/FY working spouse	57.5	57.4	51.0	51.9	55.3	42.8	62.5	46.7
% with college diploma	17.9	15.6	28.5	33.8	34.0	37.7	27.9	35.5
Total family earnings	25,503	27,066	25,962	31,970	31,338	36,736	33,699	30,484
Personal earnings as % of family earnings	29.7	47.0	34.4	52.9	38.8	61.4	27.2	56.2
% with means-tested benefits	4.1	1.0	7.5	0.0	8.3	0.0	2.2	0.9

* Sequential Packagers not shown because categories had less than 30 sample cases.
Source: IWPR calculations based on the 1986 and the 1987 panels of The Survey of Income and Program Participation.

Source: Roberta M. Spalter-Roth, Heidi I. Hartmann, and Lois B. Shaw, Institute for Women's Policy Research (Washington, D.C.), *Exploring the Characteristics of Self-Employment and Part-Time Work Among Women,* unpublished (contract for the U.S. Department of Labor, Women's Bureau), May 1993, Table 5.

B2. EARNINGS AND PENSION COVERAGE

B2-1. Trends in Real Earnings, by Race and Sex for Full-Time Workers: 1969 to 1990

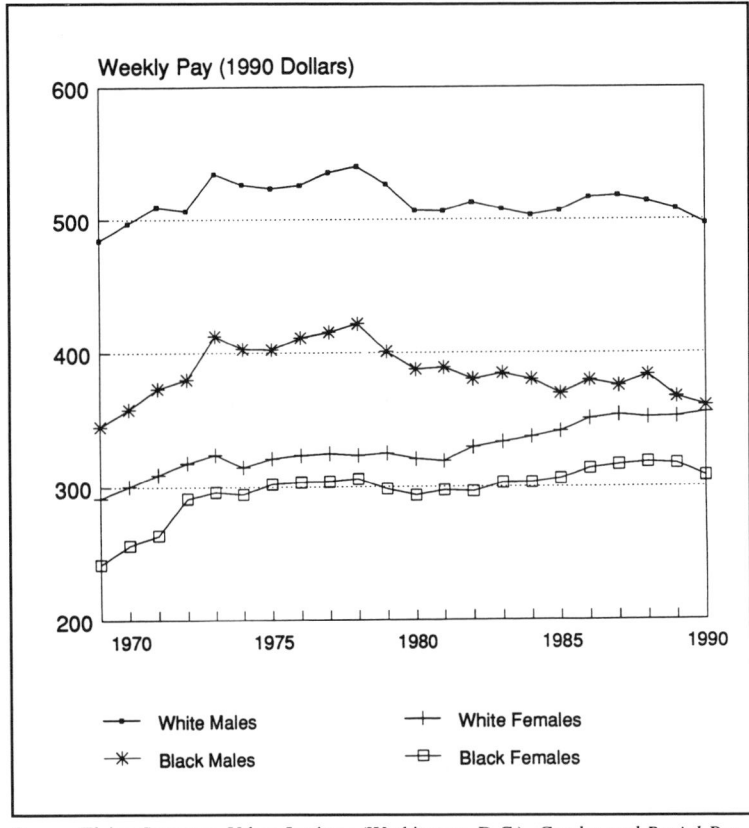

Source: Elaine Sorensen, Urban Institute (Washington, D.C.), *Gender and Racial Pay Gaps in the 1980s: Accounting for Different Trends*, unpublished (contract for the U.S. Department of Labor, Women's Bureau), October 30, 1991, Figure 1.

B2-2. Median Earnings of Year-Round, Full-Time Workers, by Sex and Race: 1979 and 1993

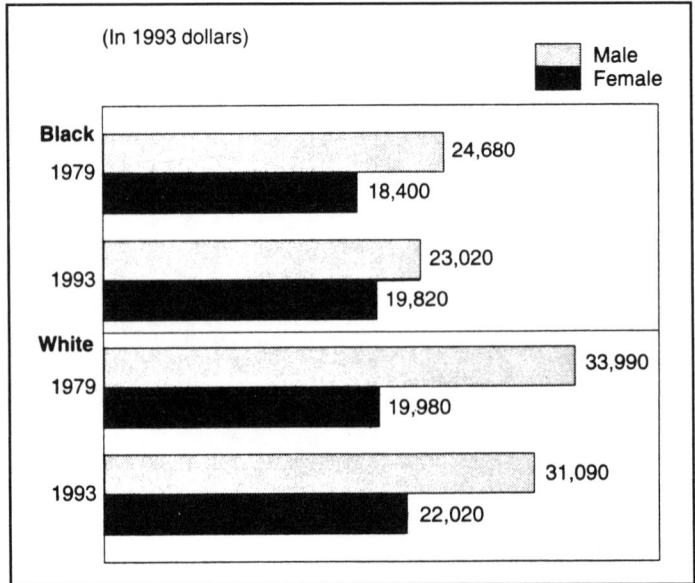

Source: Claudette E. Bennett, U.S. Bureau of the Census, *The Black Population in the United States: March 1994 and 1993*, Current Population Reports, Series P20-480, Washington, D.C.: U.S. Government Printing Office, January 1995, Figure 6.

B2-3. Median Earnings, by Sex and Race: 1993, 1989, 1979, and 1969

[In 1993 dollars. For meaning of symbols, see text]

Income and earnings	1993				1989			1979[r]			1969		
	Black	White	White, not Hispanic	Ratio: Black to White	Black	White	Ratio: Black to White	Black	White	Ratio: Black to White	Black	White	Ratio: Black to White
MEDIAN EARNINGS OF PERSONS[2]													
Male.............(dollars)..	16,753	23,670	25,299	0.71	17,853	25,821	0.69	17,438	26,496	0.66	15,902	26,241	0.61
Standard error......(dollars)..	297	204	137	(X)	352	133	(X)	476	180	(X)	(NA)	(NA)	(X)
Female...........(dollars)..	12,534	14,041	14,561	0.89	13,429	13,662	0.98	11,527	11,710	0.98	7,280	9,704	0.75
Standard error......(dollars)..	301	152	161	(X)	265	100	(X)	301	107	(X)	(NA)	(NA)	(X)
MEDIAN EARNINGS OF YEAR-ROUND, FULL-TIME WORKERS[2]													
Male.............(dollars)..	23,019	31,090	31,971	0.74	23,803	33,259	0.72	24,678	33,985	0.73	21,565	32,040	0.67
Standard error......(dollars)..	609	124	128	(X)	315	261	(X)	490	137	(X)	(NA)	(NA)	(X)
Female...........(dollars)..	19,816	22,023	22,383	0.90	20,264	22,050	0.92	18,402	19,976	0.92	14,703	18,623	0.79
Standard error......(dollars)..	366	105	108	(X)	319	160	(X)	348	107	(X)	(NA)	(NA)	(X)
PER CAPITA MONEY INCOME													
Per capita income......(dollars)..	9,863	16,800	15,777	0.59	10,193	17,359	0.59	8,678	14,790	0.59	6,462	11,641	0.56

[1]The data for families do not include families in group quarters. For March 1994, in some CPS publications the data for families include group quarters.
[2]Persons 15 years and older.

Source: Claudette E. Bennett, U.S. Bureau of the Census, The Black Population in the United States: March 1994 and 1993, Current Population Reports, Series P20-480, Washington, D.C.: U.S. Government Printing Office, January 1995, Table M.

B2-4. Two-Parent Families with Children under Age 18, by Earner Status of Father and Mother: 1987 to 1992

[Numbers in thousands]

Year	Total two-parent families	Father earner, not mother		Father and mother earners		Father not earner[1]	
		Number	Percent of total	Number	Percent of total	Number	Percent of total
1987.......	24,635	6,557	26.6	17,120	69.5	958	3.9
1988.......	24,751	6,474	26.2	17,321	70.0	956	3.9
1989.......	24,552	6,336	25.8	17,299	70.5	917	3.7
1990.......	24,435	6,360	26.0	17,200	70.4	875	3.6
1991.......	24,460	6,020	24.6	17,377	71.0	1,063	4.3
1992.......	24,746	6,281	25.4	17,285	69.8	1,180	4.8

[1] Includes families in which mother and /or other family members are earners,or in which there are no earners.

NOTE: Data on earner status of individuals during a specific calendar year is collected in March of the following year.

Source: Howard V. Hayghe, "Are Women Leaving the Labor Force?" *Monthly Labor Review,* July 1994, Table 2.

B2-5. Total Money Income in 1993 of Families, by Family Type, Earner Status, and Race

[Families as of March 1994. For meanings of symbols, see text]

Total money income	Black						White, not Hispanic					
		Married-couple families			Female house-holder, no spouse present	Male house-holder, no spouse present		Married-couple families			Female house-holder, no spouse present	Male house-holder, no spouse present
	All fami-lies[1]	Total[2]	Hus-band only earner	Hus-band and wife earners			All fami-lies[1]	Total[2]	Hus-band only earner	Hus-band and wife earners		
UNITED STATES												
Total....thousands..	7,989	3,714	450	1,684	3,825	450	52,464	43,742	6,479	20,488	6,796	1,927
Percent..........	100.0	100.0	100.0	100.0	100.0	100.0	100.0	100.0	100.0	100.0	100.0	100.0
Under $5,000............	10.7	2.9	4.6	0.7	18.3	10.8	2.1	1.0	1.4	0.5	8.6	4.1
$5,000 to $9,999..........	15.1	5.8	6.9	1.8	24.2	14.5	4.0	2.3	2.6	1.0	13.8	7.6
$10,000 to $14,999	11.4	6.8	6.8	2.5	15.7	12.8	6.0	4.8	6.1	1.7	12.9	8.7
$15,000 to $19,999	9.9	8.1	14.6	5.6	11.1	13.4	7.0	6.2	8.0	3.2	11.4	9.2
$20,000 to $24,999	8.7	9.4	16.1	7.7	7.9	10.1	7.4	6.9	9.1	4.7	9.7	11.0
$25,000 to $34,999	13.7	16.7	23.2	17.8	10.9	12.6	14.9	14.5	17.4	13.2	16.3	18.2
$35,000 to $49,999	13.0	18.3	16.8	22.2	7.3	16.4	19.3	20.1	20.4	23.7	14.2	18.0
$50,000 to $59,999	5.6	9.3	3.3	13.7	2.3	2.8	10.7	11.7	10.5	14.2	5.4	7.8
$60,000 to $74,999	5.4	9.7	5.4	13.2	1.1	5.4	10.8	12.1	8.5	15.0	3.9	6.2
$75,000 and over	6.6	13.0	2.3	14.7	.1.1	1.2	17.7	20.3	16.0	22.9	3.8	9.2
Median income ..(dollars)..	21,548	35,228	25,429	44,987	11,905	19,476	41,114	45,241	37,839	51,163	21,649	30,168
Standard error .(dollars)..	441	796	1,518	1,250	308	1,171	215	261	667	281	428	902

[1]The data for families do not include families in group quarters. For March 1994, in some CPS publications the data for families include group quarters.
[2]Includes other combinations of earners such as wife only, wife and children, or no earners.

Source: Claudette E. Bennett, U.S. Bureau of the Census, *The Black Population in the United States: March 1994 and 1993,* Current Population Reports, Series P20-480, Washington, D.C.: U.S. Government Printing Office, January 1995, Table 10.

B2-6. Total Money Earnings in 1993 of Persons 15 Years Old and Over, by Sex and Race

[Persons as of March 1994]

Total money earnings and region	All persons						Year-round, full-time workers					
	Black			White, not Hispanic			Black			White, not Hispanic		
	Both sexes	Male	Female	Both sexes	Male	Female	Both sexes	Male	Female	Both sexes	Male	Female
UNITED STATES												
Total.............thousands..	23,499	10,630	12,869	152,045	73,575	78,470	8,724	4,419	4,305	64,921	39,342	25,579
Total with earnings ....thousands..	14,661	7,036	7,625	105,838	56,654	49,183	8,724	4,419	4,305	64,879	39,325	25,554
Percent	100.0	100.0	100.0	100.0	100.0	100.0	100.0	100.0	100.0	100.0	100.0	100.0
$1 to $2,499 or loss	14.5	13.4	15.6	11.3	8.8	14.2	1.5	1.4	1.6	1.6	1.5	1.7
$2,500 to $4,999	6.9	5.7	8.1	6.5	4.9	8.3	0.9	0.5	1.2	0.7	0.4	1.0
$5,000 to $7,499	7.5	6.1	8.7	6.3	4.4	8.4	2.8	2.0	3.7	1.6	1.1	2.3
$7,500 to $9,999	6.5	5.5	7.4	4.8	3.5	6.3	4.7	3.6	6.0	2.4	1.6	3.8
$10,000 to $12,499..............	9.6	9.0	10.1	6.6	5.1	8.4	10.0	9.0	11.1	5.3	3.9	7.5
$12,500 to $14,999..............	5.5	4.6	6.3	4.3	3.5	5.3	6.8	4.9	8.7	4.5	3.4	6.3
$15,000 to $17,499..............	7.6	8.1	7.2	6.3	5.6	7.0	10.6	10.7	10.6	7.2	5.8	9.5
$17,500 to $19,999..............	5.4	5.7	5.1	4.4	3.8	5.1	7.6	7.5	7.7	5.6	4.2	7.6
$20,000 to $22,499..............	6.8	6.8	6.9	6.5	6.1	7.0	10.1	9.5	10.8	8.5	7.0	10.9
$22,500 to $24,999..............	3.5	3.5	3.5	3.8	3.6	4.0	5.0	4.7	5.2	5.3	4.5	6.5
$25,000 to $29,999..............	7.8	8.8	6.9	8.2	8.7	7.6	11.7	12.5	11.0	11.5	10.8	12.5
$30,000 to $34,999..............	5.5	6.2	4.9	7.0	8.3	5.5	8.5	9.0	8.1	10.1	10.7	9.2
$35,000 to $39,999..............	4.2	5.0	3.5	5.4	6.5	4.1	6.7	7.5	5.8	7.8	8.5	6.8
$40,000 to $44,999..............	2.7	3.6	1.8	4.6	6.0	3.0	4.0	5.2	2.6	6.9	8.0	5.1
$45,000 to $49,999..............	1.9	2.1	1.7	2.9	4.0	1.6	2.7	2.9	2.4	4.3	5.4	2.7
$50,000 to $59,999..............	2.0	2.9	1.1	4.3	6.3	2.1	3.1	4.4	1.7	6.5	8.4	3.4
$60,000 to $74,999..............	1.2	1.9	0.6	3.0	4.6	1.1	1.9	3.0	0.8	4.5	6.3	1.7
$75,000 and over	0.9	1.2	0.6	3.9	6.4	0.9	1.3	1.7	0.9	5.7	8.5	1.5
Median earnings ....(dollars)..	14,758	16,753	12,534	19,732	25,299	14,561	21,238	23,019	19,816	27,433	31,971	22,383
Standard error ....(dollars)..	293	297	301	131	137	161	213	609	366	111	128	108

Source: Claudette E. Bennett, U.S. Bureau of the Census, *The Black Population in the United States: March 1994 and 1993*, Current Population Reports, Series P20-480, Washington, D.C.: U.S. Government Printing Office, January 1995, Table 11.

B2-7. Executive, Administrative, and Managerial Occupations, by Race, Educational Attainment, Income, and Gender: 1990

(PRIVATE SECTOR ONLY)

Private Sector refers to Business Services, Communications, Construction, Entertainment, Manufacturing, Public Administration, and Utilities Industries

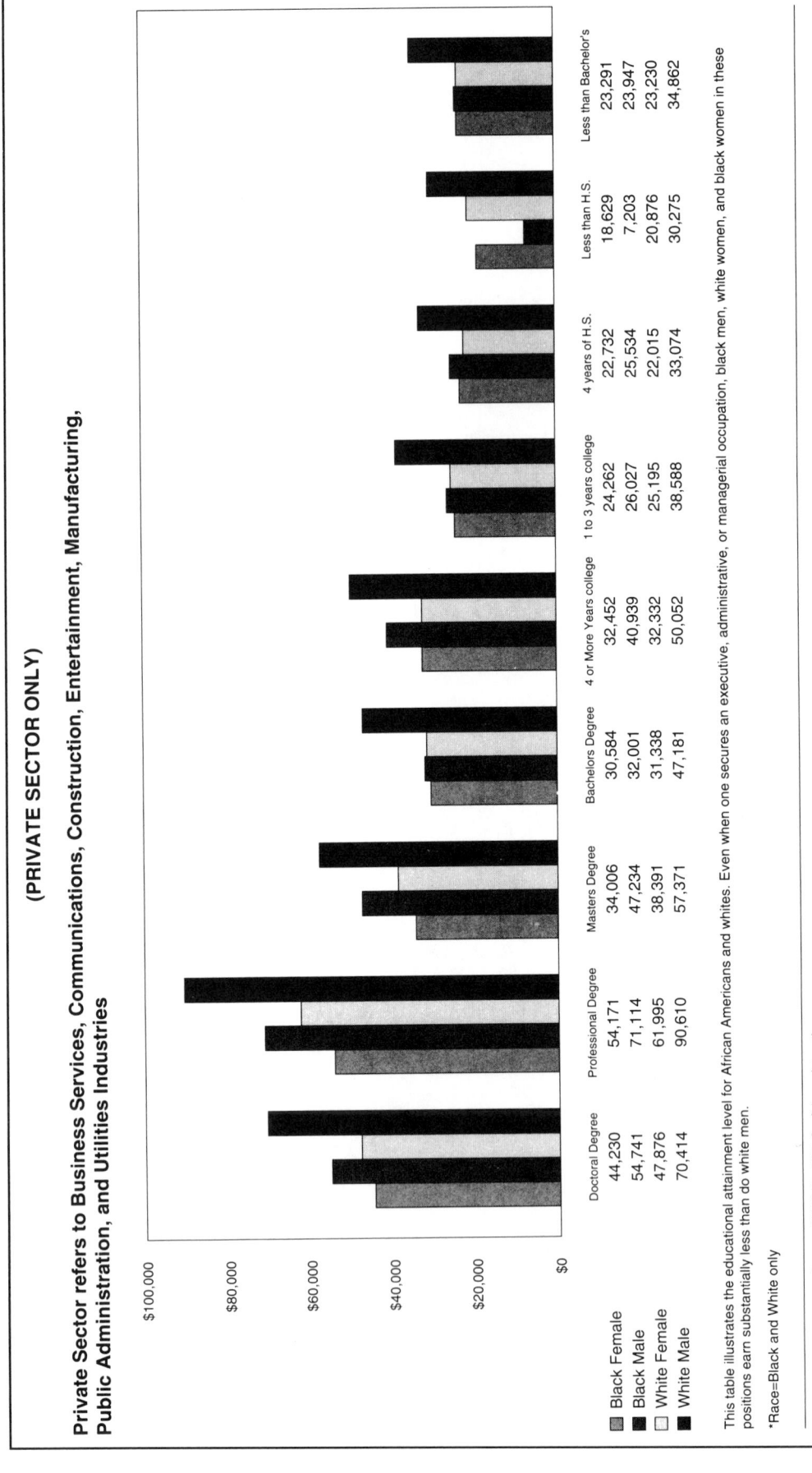

	Doctoral Degree	Professional Degree	Masters Degree	Bachelors Degree	4 or More Years college	1 to 3 years college	4 years of H.S.	Less than H.S.	Less than Bachelor's
Black Female	44,230	54,171	34,006	30,584	32,452	24,262	22,732	18,629	23,291
Black Male	54,741	71,114	47,234	32,001	40,939	26,027	25,534	7,203	23,947
White Female	47,876	61,995	38,391	31,338	32,332	25,195	22,015	20,876	23,230
White Male	70,414	90,610	57,371	47,181	50,052	38,588	33,074	30,275	34,862

This table illustrates the educational attainment level for African Americans and whites. Even when one secures an executive, administrative, or managerial occupation, black men, white women, and black women in these positions earn substantially less than do white men.

*Race=Black and White only

Source: 1990 Bureau of the Census. PUMS file. 95% Confidence Interval
Source: The Impact of the Glass Ceiling on African American Men and Women Prepared for the Glass Ceiling Commission
Source: Congressional Black Caucus Foundation's Institute for Policy Research and Education Prepared for the Glass Ceiling Commission

Source: Glass Ceiling Commission, *Good for Business: Making Full Use of the Nation's Human Capital,* Washington, D.C.: U.S. Government Printing Office, March 1995, Table 4.

B2-8. Changes in Real Earnings of Full-Time, Year-Round Workers: 1973 to 1989

[Difference in averages of logarithms]

Demographic group	1973–89	1973–79	1979–89
All	−0.023	−0.019	−0.004
Men	−.050	−.018	−.032
Women	.137	.047	.091
Years of schooling			
Men:			
0–11	−.247	−.051	−.196
12	−.155	−.041	−.113
13–15	−.071	−.044	−.028
16 or more	−.024	−.073	.049
Women:			
0–11	−.018	.041	−.059
12	.042	.028	.015
13–15	.076	.005	.071
16 or more	.122	−.019	.141
Years of potential experience[1]			
Men:			
0–9	−.082	−.002	−.080
10–19	−.111	−.026	−.085
20–29	−.049	−.033	−.016
30 or more	.034	.029	.005
Women:			
0–9	.107	.055	.051
10–19	.135	.042	.093
20–29	.157	.033	.125
30 or more	.095	.043	.051

[1] Potential labor market experience is defined as age, minus number of years of schooling, minus 6 years, to account for the preschool period. It is used because the Current Population Survey does not measure *actual* labor market experience.

NOTE: Earnings are deflated into 1989 dollars using the gross domestic product deflator for personal consumption expenditures.

Source: Howard V. Hayghe, "Are Women Leaving the Labor Force?" *Monthly Labor Review*, July 1994, Table 1.

B2-9. Median Earnings, by Sex and Educational Attainment of Hispanics: 1991

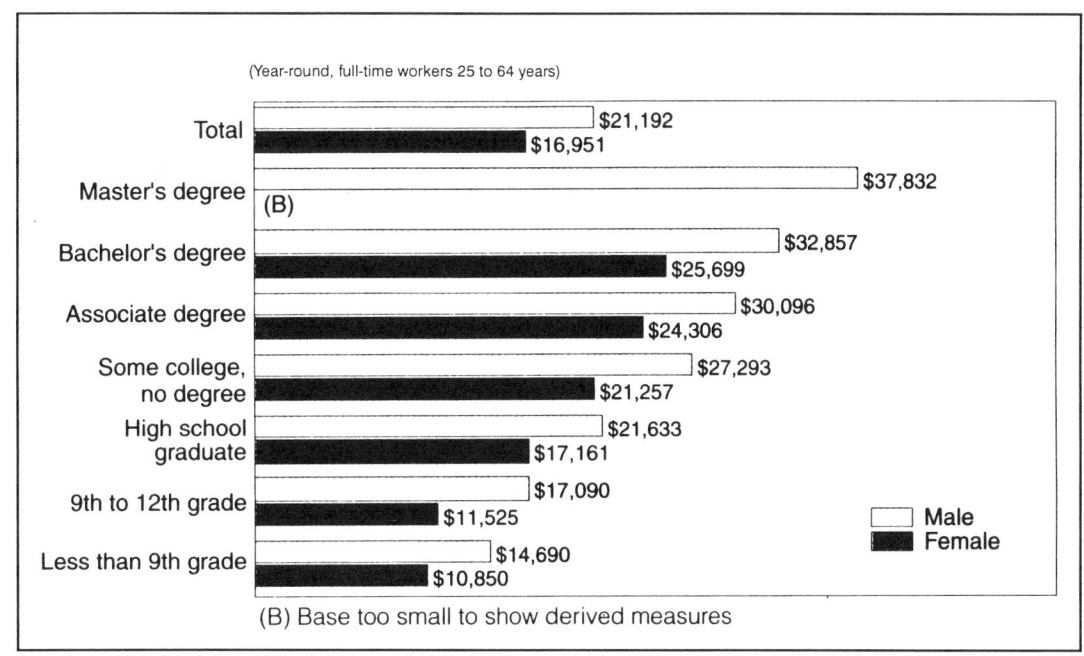

Source: U.S. Bureau of the Census, *Hispanic Americans Today*, Current Population Reports, Series P23-183, Washington, D.C.: U.S. Government Printing Office, 1993, Figure 25.

B2-10. Mean Earnings of All Workers 18 Years Old and Over, by Educational Attainment, Race, Hispanic Origin, and Sex: 1975 to 1992

(Mean annual earnings [dollars])

Earnings Year	Total	Std. Err.	Not a high school graduate	Std. Err.	High school graduate	Std. Err.	Some college/ Associate degree	Std. Err.	Bachelor's degree	Std. Err.	Advanced degree	Std. Err.
TOTAL												
Male												
1992	28,448	158	14,934	212	22,978	173	25,660	169	40,039	456	58,324	478
1991	27,494	148	15,056	187	22,663	163	25,345	183	38,484	432	54,449	474
1990	27,164	151	14,991	155	22,378	158	26,120	288	38,901	505	49,768	751
1989	27,025	155	14,727	150	22,508	172	25,555	278	38,692	510	50,144	777
1988	25,344	146	14,551	163	21,481	166	23,827	285	35,906	479	45,677	689
1987	24,015	138	14,544	188	20,364	150	22,781	268	33,677	472	43,140	663
1986	23,057	120	13,703	217	19,453	131	21,784	229	33,376	406	41,836	583
1985	21,823	111	13,124	185	18,575	125	20,698	208	31,433	386	39,768	548
1984	20,452	92	12,775	170	18,016	116	18,863	178	29,203	301	35,804	403
1983	19,175	89	12,052	160	16,728	108	18,052	187	27,239	295	33,635	388
1982	18,244	85	11,513	144	16,160	107	17,108	172	25,758	285	32,109	390
1981	17,542	79	11,668	146	15,900	101	16,870	168	24,353	273	30,072	376
1980	16,382	73	11,042	129	15,002	92	15,871	158	23,340	272	27,846	360
1979	15,430	70	10,628	102	14,317	87	14,716	145	21,482	260	26,411	358
1978	14,154	67	9,894	93	13,188	85	13,382	137	19,861	250	24,274	351
1977	12,888	56	8,939	81	12,092	70	12,393	122	18,187	210	22,786	311
1976	11,923	52	8,522	79	11,189	65	11,376	122	16,714	186	21,202	301
1975	11,091	49	7,843	71	10,475	64	10,805	112	15,758	188	19,672	283
Female												
1992	17,145	96	9,311	178	14,128	117	16,023	138	23,991	272	33,814	665
1991	16,320	91	8,818	161	13,523	109	15,643	141	22,802	258	32,929	645
1990	15,493	86	8,808	169	12,986	103	15,002	154	21,933	270	28,862	459
1989	14,809	84	8,268	167	12,468	98	14,688	155	21,089	264	26,977	469
1988	13,833	84	7,711	165	11,857	100	14,009	179	19,216	253	25,010	451
1987	13,049	80	7,504	171	11,309	100	13,158	155	18,217	261	24,004	447
1986	12,214	67	7,109	169	10,606	78	12,029	133	17,623	233	22,672	367
1985	11,493	63	6,874	179	10,115	76	11,504	134	16,114	207	21,202	334
1984	10,742	56	6,644	203	9,561	69	10,614	110	14,865	193	20,275	313
1983	10,111	NA	6,292	NA	9,147	NA	9,981	NA	13,808	NA	18,593	NA
1982	9,403	50	5,932	123	8,715	66	9,348	108	12,511	167	17,009	272
1981	8,619	44	5,673	165	8,063	57	8,811	98	11,384	156	15,647	264
1980	7,909	42	5,263	134	7,423	53	8,256	99	10,628	152	14,022	241
1979	7,099	38	4,840	106	6,741	48	7,190	89	9,474	137	12,717	231
1978	6,396	35	4,397	111	6,192	46	6,441	79	8,408	128	11,603	222
1977	5,804	30	4,032	86	5,624	39	5,856	69	7,923	115	10,848	191
1976	5,373	28	3,723	76	5,240	37	5,301	70	7,383	102	10,345	199
1975	4,968	26	3,438	75	4,802	34	5,019	62	6,963	98	9,818	187
WHITE												
Male												
1992	29,515	174	15,414	241	23,844	192	26,387	187	40,893	488	59,329	496
1991	28,516	163	15,499	211	23,475	179	26,090	198	39,547	468	55,257	493
1990	28,105	167	15,319	168	23,135	174	26,841	317	39,780	546	50,385	798
1989	28,013	171	15,217	165	23,291	191	26,260	303	39,654	553	51,031	831
1988	26,184	160	14,943	175	22,216	181	24,462	310	36,637	521	46,181	728
1987	24,898	152	15,303	202	21,012	162	23,310	295	34,865	510	43,440	702
1986	23,892	131	14,168	183	20,128	143	22,303	248	34,273	437	42,480	618
1985	22,604	122	13,579	158	19,203	136	21,240	224	32,165	416	40,358	580
1984	21,174	100	13,248	148	18,681	125	19,344	193	29,781	321	36,219	423
1983	19,812	96	12,573	140	17,281	117	18,388	202	27,726	309	33,981	409
1982	18,859	92	11,952	129	16,662	116	17,571	186	26,404	302	32,266	406
1981	18,141	86	12,094	142	16,352	109	17,303	184	24,943	289	30,396	393
1980	16,945	79	11,539	114	15,382	99	16,313	171	23,803	286	27,991	373
1979	15,971	76	11,127	109	13,916	94	15,043	157	21,785	271	26,645	374
1978	14,627	72	10,358	103	13,534	91	13,589	146	20,085	263	24,635	369
1977	13,329	60	9,366	86	12,377	74	12,657	131	18,521	219	23,093	325
1976	12,342	56	8,867	85	11,497	69	11,616	130	16,995	194	21,490	314
1975	11,448	53	8,110	77	10,726	69	11,028	119	16,079	197	19,858	295

B2-10. Mean Earnings of All Workers 18 Years Old and Over, by Educational Attainment, Race, Hispanic Origin, and Sex: 1975 to 1992 *(continued)*

(Mean annual earnings [dollars])

Earnings Year	Total	Std. Err.	Not a high school graduate	Std. Err.	High school graduate	Std. Err.	Some college/ Associate degree	Std. Err.	Bach- elor's degree	Std. Err.	Advanced degree	Std. Err.
Female												
1992	17,289	106	9,428	207	14,233	129	16,116	149	23,738	295	33,675	720
1991	16,431	98	8,677	174	13,621	118	15,677	155	22,471	276	32,687	678
1990	15,559	94	8,725	186	13,031	113	14,922	165	21,725	294	28,694	486
1989	14,810	91	8,338	182	12,406	107	14,640	170	20,741	272	26,709	510
1988	13,902	93	7,747	184	11,915	110	13,898	198	19,169	274	24,824	488
1987	13,161	89	7,798	190	11,421	110	13,015	167	18,170	289	23,753	482
1986	12,247	72	7,123	181	10,641	84	11,964	140	17,418	245	22,320	397
1985	11,555	70	6,931	172	10,142	82	11,488	148	15,883	229	21,202	357
1984	10,732	61	6,614	175	9,561	74	10,504	119	14,617	209	20,092	332
1983	10,126	NA	6,317	NA	9,150	NA	9,969	NA	13,664	NA	18,230	NA
1982	9,419	55	5,896	135	8,714	72	9,336	117	12,352	181	16,779	287
1981	8,646	48	5,727	148	8,054	61	8,740	107	11,196	167	15,523	279
1980	7,926	45	6,675	127	7,415	57	8,221	108	10,447	159	13,809	253
1979	7,105	41	4,909	110	6,731	51	7,135	96	9,275	145	12,420	243
1978	6,398	38	4,476	138	6,176	49	6,342	85	8,231	131	11,404	235
1977	5,808	32	4,097	95	5,604	41	5,774	73	7,750	123	10,655	203
1976	5,383	31	3,788	86	5,214	40	5,250	74	7,262	109	10,131	207
1975	4,982	28	3,500	80	4,800	36	4,926	65	6,822	105	9,728	199
BLACK												
Male												
1992	19,278	342	12,661	510	16,978	382	22,697	527	30,989	1,489	48,968	4,519
1991	18,607	284	15,714	423	17,352	382	20,548	542	26,075	966	43,927	2,307
1990	18,859	300	13,031	430	17,046	332	21,152	708	29,471	1,291	39,104	2,888
1989	18,108	283	11,827	355	16,658	328	20,253	566	27,493	1,201	38,166	2,655
1988	17,782	326	12,439	529	16,345	404	19,265	818	28,506	1,220	36,452	2,650
1987	16,171	283	11,899	375	14,800	374	18,081	612	23,345	1,091	34,073	2,645
1986	15,441	256	11,248	409	14,214	294	17,419	693	23,412	1,161	31,054	2,035
1985	14,932	254	10,802	396	13,721	308	16,415	628	23,818	1,072	31,947	2,484
1984	13,560	212	10,216	374	12,382	280	14,960	471	21,986	961	27,893	1,670
1983	12,789	205	9,094	339	11,956	265	15,113	500	20,370	1,033	25,466	1,470
1982	12,203	203	9,153	340	11,952	268	12,926	458	17,658	861	26,452	2,006
1981	11,937	174	9,266	318	11,905	261	13,740	432	16,624	776	21,082	1,197
1980	11,085	170	8,421	291	11,563	260	12,393	417	15,616	739	23,346	1,986
1979	10,403	157	7,938	278	10,662	225	11,971	384	16,161	1,071	21,092	1,673
1978	9,651	147	7,423	233	9,869	219	11,197	409	16,009	944	18,083	1,031
1977	8,710	110	6,648	187	9,332	184	10,023	300	12,978	641	16,385	808
1976	7,991	105	6,670	187	8,056	155	8,688	300	12,246	597	17,859	1,388
1975	7,541	89	6,364	173	7,847	138	8,505	267	11,318	572	13,720	702
Female												
1992	15,605	241	8,756	376	13,550	312	15,553	440	24,572	821	34,902	921
1991	15,065	231	9,151	524	12,810	301	15,743	400	25,235	912	32,467	2,413
1990	14,449	221	8,946	402	12,560	269	15,734	466	23,837	827	28,074	1,265
1989	14,122	215	7,827	403	12,701	255	15,044	411	23,541	1,017	27,933	1,290
1988	12,916	203	7,325	391	11,469	255	14,557	419	19,862	804	26,072	1,094
1987	12,106	193	7,452	360	11,030	256	13,123	412	18,815	668	24,383	1,062
1986	11,571	215	6,984	375	10,434	244	12,459	516	19,562	1,129	24,400	1,149
1985	10,904	170	6,879	366	9,918	233	11,488	347	17,779	569	21,502	1,003
1984	10,482	157	6,754	464	9,527	201	11,115	318	17,134	618	21,000	860
1983	9,778	NA	6,154	NA	9,197	NA	10,215	NA	14,738	NA	21,539	NA
1982	9,024	141	6,047	279	8,737	186	9,574	315	13,284	576	19,198	1,077
1981	8,225	129	5,404	252	8,088	183	9,329	285	12,839	527	17,743	1,011
1980	7,684	121	4,685	242	7,508	164	8,544	266	12,389	568	17,278	951
1979	6,940	112	4,448	232	6,866	154	7,735	273	11,555	504	15,766	785
1978	6,219	104	3,993	212	6,417	149	7,207	248	10,122	598	12,459	585
1977	5,704	84	3,793	158	5,837	142	6,576	203	9,604	347	12,896	524
1976	5,283	74	3,486	162	5,541	108	5,801	199	8,910	321	12,501	465
1975	4,732	68	3,145	140	4,825	96	5,908	211	8,180	258	10,934	505

B2-10. Mean Earnings of All Workers 18 Years Old and Over, by Educational Attainment, Race, Hispanic Origin, and Sex: 1975 to 1992 *(continued)*

(Mean annual earnings [dollars])

Earnings Year	Total	Std. Err.	Not a high school graduate	Std. Err.	High school graduate	Std. Err.	Some college/ Associate degree	Std. Err.	Bach- elor's degree	Std. Err.	Advanced degree	Std. Err.
HISPANIC ORIGIN[1]												
Male												
1992	18,842	365	13,313	366	19,357	662	23,033	596	33,430	1,957	53,645	2,748
1991	18,516	316	13,133	263	18,582	471	21,974	693	31,699	1,729	45,873	2,549
1990	18,320	332	13,182	276	18,100	455	22,376	831	31,485	1,966	47,479	4,339
1989	18,087	352	13,167	265	17,579	452	22,374	996	32,767	2,536	49,088	4,778
1988	17,357	361	12,836	316	17,446	475	21,631	1,205	26,935	1,807	40,916	4,602
1987	17,048	372	12,823	369	16,774	523	19,414	773	26,581	1,782	39,014	4,410
1986	15,624	305	11,262	313	15,948	476	19,675	962	27,427	1,975	32,538	2,705
1985	15,293	285	11,671	342	15,602	464	18,168	771	24,723	1,723	32,831	2,792
1984	14,957	344	11,441	385	15,763	549	17,261	1,014	23,835	1,878	30,727	3,231
1983	14,265	324	11,353	400	14,584	549	16,626	864	21,911	2,111	28,680	2,681
1982	13,484	339	10,108	392	13,883	488	15,560	845	22,565	2,632	34,474	3,995
1981	13,052	292	10,447	342	13,513	489	15,432	785	19,201	1,928	27,619	3,427
1980	12,310	303	9,825	394	13,108	526	14,331	890	19,224	1,986	24,642	3,439
1979	11,332	268	9,393	378	11,714	448	12,489	714	18,923	2,113	21,299	2,619
1978	10,473	258	8,836	427	10,940	426	11,545	665	16,898	1,861	20,702	2,730
1977	9,655	198	8,192	281	10,386	372	9,924	501	15,189	1,420	19,025	2,291
1976	8,787	195	7,440	272	9,640	345	8,843	508	13,650	1,299	16,184	2,339
1975	8,162	189	6,745	268	8,546	289	8,807	536	12,881	1,142	17,991	2,535
Female												
1992	13,880	304	8,913	334	13,396	435	16,076	669	22,160	1,343	34,551	2,666
1991	13,069	273	4,809	307	13,043	380	15,721	564	20,791	1,377	30,721	2,392
1990	12,516	254	5,093	309	12,109	354	15,245	629	19,378	1,331	27,184	1,824
1989	12,307	266	8,256	401	11,799	365	14,482	629	22,617	1,379	26,700	2,265
1988	11,573	290	7,597	349	11,284	392	14,012	662	19,707	1,171	24,444	3,675
1987	11,234	286	7,350	354	10,627	417	13,929	688	18,003	1,033	26,584	3,436
1986	10,457	231	7,130	338	10,319	332	12,648	547	16,142	1,165	22,071	2,096
1985	9,865	236	6,699	367	9,784	327	11,791	639	15,503	1,098	22,480	2,173
1984	9,150	252	6,438	436	9,492	380	10,848	619	14,404	1,310	18,706	2,355
1983	8,704	NA	6,305	NA	9,261	NA	9,750	NA	13,507	NA	16,817	NA
1982	8,195	233	5,781	373	8,668	374	9,896	605	13,719	1,235	15,244	2,247
1981	7,723	215	5,486	364	8,292	342	9,483	563	12,292	1,101	15,503	2,767
1980	6,770	199	5,028	358	6,923	287	8,808	576	10,568	1,177	14,668	2,935
1979	6,255	184	4,675	347	6,708	286	7,069	482	9,168	1,001	13,313	1,905
1978	5,501	173	4,135	377	5,834	273	6,686	507	9,684	1,098	10,908	1,872
1977	4,964	137	3,707	276	5,466	236	5,588	367	9,082	691	10,569	2,119
1976	4,548	132	3,537	273	5,124	229	5,075	373	6,884	826	9,218	1,425
1975	4,152	122	3,233	277	4,708	209	4,790	376	6,226	805	8,067	1,536

Note: Prior to 1991, some college/Associate degrees equal 1 to 3 years of college completed; Bachelor's degree equals 4 years of college; Advanced degree equals 5 or more years of college completed.

NA - Not Available

[1] May be of any race.

Source: Robert Kominski and Andrea Adams, U.S. Bureau of the Census, *Educational Attainment in the United States: March 1993 and 1992,* Current Population Reports, P20-476, Washington, D.C.: U.S. Government Printing Office, 1994, Table 19.

B2-11. Total Money Earnings in 1993 of Persons 25 Years Old and Over, by Educational Attainment, Sex, and Race

(Persons as of March 1994)

Total money earnings, race, region, and sex	All persons					Year-round, full-time workers				
	Total	Not a high school graduate	High school graduate	Some college or associate degree	Bachelor's degree or more	Total	Not a high school graduate	High school graduate	Some college or associate degree	Bachelor's degree or more
WHITE, NOT HISPANIC										
Male..............thousands..	61,074	9,079	20,071	14,942	16,981	36,459	2,728	11,570	9,787	12,375
Total with earnings ....thousands..	47,422	4,480	15,541	12,497	14,904	36,443	2,728	11,560	9,782	12,373
Percent	100.0	100.0	100.0	100.0	100.0	100.0	100.0	100.0	100.0	100.0
$1 to $2,499 or loss	4.6	10.6	4.8	4.4	2.9	1.5	3.9	1.6	1.4	0.9
$2,500 to $4,999.................	2.6	5.4	2.9	2.5	1.7	0.3	0.6	0.3	0.5	0.2
$5,000 to $7,499.................	3.2	7.8	3.6	2.7	1.9	0.8	2.5	0.9	0.8	0.4
$7,500 to $9,999.................	2.7	6.1	3.1	2.9	1.2	1.1	4.3	1.1	1.1	0.4
$10,000 to $12,499..............	4.4	8.4	5.4	4.1	2.4	3.0	7.9	3.9	2.5	1.4
$12,500 to $14,999..............	3.1	6.5	3.5	3.3	1.6	2.7	7.0	3.4	2.8	1.1
$15,000 to $17,499..............	5.6	9.5	7.4	5.2	2.7	5.1	10.7	7.4	4.5	2.3
$17,500 to $19,999..............	3.8	4.0	5.2	4.3	1.8	3.9	5.2	5.6	4.4	1.5
$20,000 to $22,499..............	6.5	7.8	8.6	6.9	3.7	6.7	10.0	9.2	7.1	3.3
$22,500 to $24,999..............	4.0	5.0	5.1	4.2	2.3	4.4	6.7	5.8	4.7	2.3
$25,000 to $29,999..............	9.8	10.4	12.2	10.6	6.3	11.0	14.2	14.2	11.8	6.6
$30,000 to $34,999..............	9.6	6.6	11.2	10.9	7.8	11.3	9.4	13.6	12.8	8.3
$35,000 to $39,999..............	7.6	4.0	7.5	9.1	7.4	9.0	5.9	9.0	10.9	8.2
$40,000 to $44,999..............	7.1	3.4	6.5	8.0	8.1	8.6	5.2	8.2	9.6	8.9
$45,000 to $49,999..............	4.8	1.5	3.7	5.3	6.4	5.8	2.2	4.5	6.4	7.3
$50,000 to $59,999..............	7.4	1.5	4.8	6.9	12.3	9.0	2.3	6.0	8.5	13.8
$60,000 to $74,999..............	5.5	0.8	2.6	4.5	10.7	6.7	1.2	3.2	5.4	12.3
$75,000 and over	7.6	0.6	1.8	4.1	18.7	9.2	0.9	2.1	4.8	21.0
Median earnings ....(dollars)..	29,681	16,357	25,140	29,175	42,492	33,776	21,980	28,367	32,425	47,177
Standard error ....(dollars)..	262	297	206	485	515	281	360	335	300	350
Female............thousands..	66,214	10,155	24,942	17,144	13,973	23,405	1,292	8,178	7,103	6,832
Total with earnings ....thousands..	40,565	2,848	14,585	12,202	10,931	23,380	1,292	8,169	7,094	6,826
Percent	100.0	100.0	100.0	100.0	100.0	100.0	100.0	100.0	100.0	100.0
$1 to $2,499 or loss	10.0	20.4	11.1	9.7	6.3	1.7	4.6	2.2	1.5	0.9
$2,500 to $4,999.................	6.4	11.7	7.7	5.9	3.7	0.9	2.5	1.4	0.8	0.2
$5,000 to $7,499.................	7.5	13.9	9.1	7.0	4.3	1.9	7.6	2.2	1.6	0.7
$7,500 to $9,999.................	6.0	9.9	7.9	5.6	3.0	3.1	10.6	4.2	2.7	0.6
$10,000 to $12,499..............	8.6	11.4	10.9	8.3	5.3	6.8	16.5	10.0	5.7	2.3
$12,500 to $14,999..............	5.4	5.7	7.2	5.5	2.7	5.7	9.4	8.5	5.2	2.2
$15,000 to $17,499..............	7.4	8.4	8.8	7.8	4.7	8.9	13.3	12.0	9.1	4.0
$17,500 to $19,999..............	5.6	5.5	6.8	5.9	3.6	7.5	10.5	10.1	7.5	3.7
$20,000 to $22,499..............	7.8	4.7	8.3	9.2	6.3	10.9	9.2	13.0	13.0	6.6
$22,500 to $24,999..............	4.5	1.7	4.3	5.0	5.0	6.6	2.7	7.0	7.4	6.0
$25,000 to $29,999..............	8.9	3.1	7.7	10.4	10.4	13.1	6.7	12.1	15.7	12.9
$30,000 to $34,999..............	6.6	0.9	4.5	7.3	10.2	9.9	1.8	7.7	10.7	13.2
$35,000 to $39,999..............	5.0	1.2	2.8	4.7	9.0	7.4	2.0	4.6	7.4	11.6
$40,000 to $44,999..............	3.6	0.5	1.3	3.2	7.9	5.5	1.1	2.0	5.0	10.9
$45,000 to $49,999..............	1.9	0.2	0.5	1.6	4.6	2.9	0.4	0.8	2.5	6.3
$50,000 to $59,999..............	2.5	0.2	0.7	1.6	6.5	3.8	0.4	1.1	2.5	8.8
$60,000 to $74,999..............	1.3	0.2	0.4	0.6	3.4	1.8	0.2	0.6	0.9	4.7
$75,000 and over	1.1	0.5	0.2	0.6	3.1	1.7	0.4	0.4	0.7	4.4
Median earnings ....(dollars)..	17,061	8,512	13,666	17,589	27,088	23,482	14,653	19,849	23,399	32,919
Standard error ....(dollars)..	126	356	216	264	292	186	525	199	302	532

B2-11. Total Money Earnings in 1993 of Persons 25 Years Old and Over, by Educational Attainment, Sex, and Race *(continued)*

[Persons as of March 1994. For meaning of symbols, see text]

Total money earnings, race, region, and sex	All persons					Year-round, full-time workers				
	Total	Not a high school graduate	High school graduate	Some college or associate degree	Bachelor's degree or more	Total	Not a high school graduate	High school graduate	Some college or associate degree	Bachelor's degree or more
BLACK—Con.										
United States—Con.										
Male . . . . .thousands. .	8,051	2,275	2,971	1,775	1,030	4,063	623	1,582	1,082	776
Total with earnings . . . .thousands. .	5,690	1,065	2,289	1,429	908	4,063	623	1,582	1,082	776
Percent	100.0	100.0	100.0	100.0	100.0	100.0	100.0	100.0	100.0	100.0
$1 to $2,499 or loss	7.2	14.9	6.9	5.6	1.1	1.2	3.3	1.7	0.1	-
$2,500 to $4,999	4.0	8.4	4.0	2.3	1.8	0.4	1.3	0.4	0.3	-
$5,000 to $7,499	4.6	6.1	5.5	3.9	1.7	1.2	2.5	1.2	1.1	-
$7,500 to $9,999	5.6	9.8	6.6	3.3	2.1	3.3	6.8	4.2	1.3	1.2
$10,000 to $12,499	9.1	12.4	10.6	7.4	4.4	8.4	15.6	10.4	5.4	3.0
$12,500 to $14,999	5.0	4.8	6.1	5.3	1.9	4.9	5.6	6.2	5.8	0.6
$15,000 to $17,499	8.9	6.5	12.5	7.5	4.6	10.5	9.8	15.0	8.3	4.6
$17,500 to $19,999	6.5	7.9	6.8	7.4	2.6	7.6	11.8	8.2	7.8	2.5
$20,000 to $22,499	7.6	6.0	8.7	7.3	7.1	9.5	9.6	11.7	7.1	8.3
$22,500 to $24,999	4.1	3.6	3.7	5.5	3.3	4.8	5.3	3.7	7.1	3.6
$25,000 to $29,999	10.3	8.5	9.9	12.1	10.4	12.8	12.1	11.9	15.1	11.8
$30,000 to $34,999	7.2	3.4	6.4	9.5	9.9	9.1	4.6	8.6	11.4	10.7
$35,000 to $39,999	6.1	3.4	4.6	6.9	11.8	8.2	4.6	6.5	8.9	13.5
$40,000 to $44,999	4.3	1.1	3.7	4.9	8.5	5.4	1.9	4.8	6.2	8.5
$45,000 to $49,999	2.4	0.7	0.9	4.3	5.0	3.2	1.0	1.2	5.7	5.5
$50,000 to $59,999	3.5	1.7	1.6	4.0	9.9	4.7	2.9	2.2	5.0	10.7
$60,000 to $74,999	2.4	0.4	1.1	2.0	8.4	3.2	0.6	1.6	2.7	9.4
$75,000 and over	1.3	0.4	0.5	0.6	5.4	1.7	0.7	0.6	0.8	6.1
Median earnings . . . .(dollars). .	19,644	12,170	17,078	22,468	33,957	24,105	18,594	20,584	26,562	35,853
Standard error . . . .(dollars). .	406	623	335	838	1,697	650	683	433	676	684
Female. . . . . .thousands. .	10,053	2,634	3,578	2,534	1,307	4,015	391	1,390	1,419	814
Total with earnings . . . .thousands. .	6,309	863	2,315	2,016	1,114	4,015	391	1,390	1,419	814
Percent	100.0	100.0	100.0	100.0	100.0	100.0	100.0	100.0	100.0	100.0
$1 to $2,499 or loss	10.9	21.7	12.6	8.0	4.3	1.6	2.6	1.3	2.2	0.6
$2,500 to $4,999	6.1	9.1	7.5	5.2	2.4	1.1	2.1	1.4	1.1	-
$5,000 to $7,499	8.0	13.9	9.6	6.4	3.1	3.4	7.3	4.9	2.3	0.6
$7,500 to $9,999	7.2	11.5	9.4	5.1	3.0	5.5	13.9	7.7	3.4	1.3
$10,000 to $12,499	11.0	14.5	13.6	10.8	3.1	10.8	20.3	14.7	9.7	1.7
$12,500 to $14,999	6.4	8.3	8.0	6.3	1.7	8.0	14.4	11.4	6.6	1.5
$15,000 to $17,499	7.9	5.4	9.5	8.7	4.9	10.4	8.8	14.8	10.0	4.5
$17,500 to $19,999	5.8	3.7	4.7	7.4	6.7	7.9	7.5	7.0	9.3	7.3
$20,000 to $22,499	7.9	5.6	7.3	9.9	7.5	11.0	11.4	10.5	12.3	9.6
$22,500 to $24,999	3.9	2.0	3.1	4.6	5.7	5.1	4.3	4.1	6.2	5.4
$25,000 to $29,999	8.2	1.3	7.6	9.9	11.5	11.5	1.9	11.6	13.7	12.1
$30,000 to $34,999	5.8	1.2	3.1	7.6	11.6	8.5	2.0	4.8	10.3	14.8
$35,000 to $39,999	4.2	0.5	2.1	4.4	11.0	6.2	1.2	2.9	6.1	14.3
$40,000 to $44,999	2.1	1.1	0.5	2.6	5.4	2.8	2.2	0.8	3.2	5.9
$45,000 to $49,999	2.0	-	0.5	1.6	7.3	2.6	-	0.8	1.6	8.4
$50,000 to $59,999	1.4	-	0.4	1.1	4.8	1.9	-	0.7	1.4	5.5
$60,000 to $74,999	0.7	0.1	0.2	0.1	3.4	0.9	-	0.2	0.2	3.6
$75,000 and over	0.6	-	0.3	0.3	2.6	0.9	-	0.5	0.3	3.1
Median earnings . . . .(dollars). .	15,146	8,631	12,008	17,373	27,965	20,304	13,148	16,459	21,082	31,157
Standard error . . . .(dollars). .	340	592	307	546	1,159	287	695	364	435	575

Source: Robert Kominski and Andrea Adams, U.S. Bureau of the Census, *Educational Attainment in the United States: March 1993 and 1992*, Current Population Reports, P20-476, Washington, D.C.: U.S. Government Printing Office, 1994, Table 12.

B2-12. Occupation of Longest Job in 1993 of Year-Round, Full-Time Workers 25 Years Old and Over, by Total Money Median Earnings, Educational Attainment, Sex, and Race

[Numbers in thousands. Persons as of March 1994.]

Occupation of longest job	Total		Not a high school graduate		High school graduate		Some college or associate degree		Bachelor's degree or more	
	Male	Female	Male	Female	Male	Female	Male	Female	Male	Female
WHITE, NOT HISPANIC										
Executive, administrative, and managerial workers.......	6,645	4,409	156	88	1,160	1,126	1,677	1,536	3,652	1,658
Median earnings.........................(dollars)..	45,874	29,675	31,265	17,911	34,906	25,826	39,370	26,864	54,681	36,719
Standard error.........................(dollars)..	471	493	851	1,867	1,159	431	1,002	380	1,202	479
Professional specialty workers.........................	5,605	4,307	23	19	289	219	778	749	4,516	3,321
Median earnings.........................(dollars)..	46,442	32,791	25,143	18,941	36,903	22,085	41,294	31,167	49,709	34,435
Standard error.........................(dollars)..	489	525	3,188	8,746	1,646	1,865	752	553	801	666
Technical and related support workers	1,121	1,078	19	15	215	263	503	552	384	248
Median earnings.........................(dollars)..	36,126	27,679	30,471	24,572	32,684	25,362	36,450	27,539	38,636	34,859
Standard error.........................(dollars)..	643	612	8,348	4,828	1,695	1,082	751	773	1,950	1,984
Sales workers..	4,671	2,528	151	161	1,212	1,037	1,453	745	1,856	585
Median earnings.........................(dollars)..	36,211	20,547	25,009	12,089	30,813	16,924	32,145	21,485	46,254	33,102
Standard error.........................(dollars)..	431	389	2,073	790	706	651	988	659	1,025	1,712
Administrative support workers, including clerical	1,967	6,545	81	155	680	3,197	668	2,473	537	720
Median earnings.........................(dollars)..	30,204	21,275	23,000	18,780	26,494	20,794	30,421	21,533	34,298	24,365
Standard error.........................(dollars)..	622	140	2,302	952	710	193	1,094	221	1,525	817
Private household workers...........................	5	64	-	17	3	24	2	17	-	7
Median earnings.........................(dollars)..	(S)	7,287	-	6,193	(S)	10,462	(S)	6,011	-	12,119
Standard error.........................(dollars)..	(S)	1,750	-	617	(S)	4,504	(S)	8,655	-	2,951
Protective service workers	1,074	129	36	3	360	40	463	46	214	40
Median earnings.........................(dollars)..	33,626	29,110	13,072	(S)	27,876	27,529	36,047	28,315	41,903	39,757
Standard error.........................(dollars)..	927	1,335	4,910	(S)	949	1,985	1,392	1,693	2,472	5,620
Service workers, except private household..............	1,228	2,030	202	392	549	1,001	350	504	127	133
Median earnings.........................(dollars)..	19,329	13,501	15,979	11,889	20,279	13,066	20,900	14,756	17,964	17,647
Standard error.........................(dollars)..	574	380	1,083	547	832	587	1,335	688	1,271	1,683
Farming, fishing, and forestry workers	1,197	199	246	32	511	90	292	57	149	20
Median earnings.........................(dollars)..	16,919	9,598	14,121	8,360	17,293	10,010	19,089	8,630	20,559	17,855
Standard error.........................(dollars)..	491	1,568	933	3,899	993	1,789	1,607	3,533	2,167	7,050
Precision production, craft, and repair workers	6,899	615	840	83	3,365	327	2,212	162	482	42
Median earnings.........................(dollars)..	30,339	22,909	22,579	21,042	29,802	21,239	32,248	27,003	37,405	26,965
Standard error.........................(dollars)..	227	1,105	731	2,422	428	994	414	1,340	2,003	8,211
Machine operators, assemblers, and inspectors	2,184	1,090	361	236	1,217	647	517	173	90	34
Median earnings....¨.....................(dollars)..	26,764	16,783	24,108	14,905	27,156	16,834	28,421	20,626	31,562	15,184
Standard error.........................(dollars)..	373	441	1,237	866	656	650	1,466	884	4,350	1,156
Transportation and material moving workers	2,301	145	413	30	1,304	69	458	37	126	8
Median earnings.........................(dollars)..	28,309	19,800	25,289	18,684	28,691	20,115	30,666	22,138	37,758	22,844
Standard error.........................(dollars)..	753	1,517	640	796	1,020	3,279	1,018	7,709	1,876	9,203
Handlers, equipment cleaners, helpers, and laborers.....	1,111	213	197	61	592	120	247	31	74	1
Median earnings.........................(dollars)..	21,796	15,321	17,004	15,577	22,298	15,359	22,661	14,004	24,579	(S)
Standard error.........................(dollars)..	531	917	966	1,181	902	1,670	1,786	2,043	2,621	(S)

B2-12. Occupation of Longest Job in 1993 of Year-Round, Full-Time Workers 25 Years Old and Over, by Total Money Median Earnings, Educational Attainment, Sex, and Race *(continued)*

[Numbers in thousands. Persons as of March 1994.]

Occupation of longest job	Total Male	Total Female	Not a high school graduate Male	Not a high school graduate Female	High school graduate Male	High school graduate Female	Some college or associate degree Male	Some college or associate degree Female	Bachelor's degree or more Male	Bachelor's degree or more Female
BLACK										
Executive, administrative, and managerial workers.......	364	429	10	8	55	56	91	178	209	187
Median earnings..........................(dollars)..	36,806	30,002	22,658	12,200	31,851	24,953	28,245	25,121	46,980	40,494
Standard error..........................(dollars)..	1,853	1,554	6,771	4,849	2,148	3,972	2,815	1,664	3,241	3,077
Professional specialty workers........................	331	543	5	7	22	53	70	124	233	359
Median earnings..........................(dollars)..	32,712	30,942	(S)	13,316	25,401	19,957	28,595	25,950	36,327	32,402
Standard error..........................(dollars)..	2,596	560	(S)	3,734	4,960	2,738	1,943	2,614	881	1,145
Technical and related support workers...............	131	229	-	1	27	50	82	137	22	40
Median earnings..........................(dollars)..	34,553	22,788	-	(S)	26,122	22,178	33,816	23,219	51,693	23,878
Standard error..........................(dollars)..	3,824	1,391	-	(S)	7,379	1,817	3,554	1,923	6,709	2,544
Sales workers.......................................	251	210	12	7	74	85	84	71	81	47
Median earnings..........................(dollars)..	25,694	14,693	25,969	14,635	20,385	11,342	25,109	14,197	31,865	28,482
Standard error..........................(dollars)..	2,285	1,965	25,491	5,764	2,100	617	4,002	2,217	2,904	4,265
Administrative support workers, including clerical.......	316	1,143	31	44	117	406	121	558	47	134
Median earnings..........................(dollars)..	26,774	20,647	21,017	21,390	28,572	19,256	26,379	21,074	32,249	21,609
Standard error..........................(dollars)..	1,934	434	2,900	3,395	2,286	931	2,763	519	5,320	1,282
Private household workers............................	-	24	-	7	-	15	-	2	-	-
Median earnings..........................(dollars)..	-	11,768	-	4,235	-	14,441	-	(S)	-	-
Standard error..........................(dollars)..	-	2,408	-	4,293	-	4,193	-	(S)	-	-
Protective service workers..........................	212	73	24	3	47	22	97	30	44	18
Median earnings..........................(dollars)..	26,853	25,891	19,196	(S)	23,597	26,502	30,391	25,427	29,259	37,033
Standard error..........................(dollars)..	1,841	1,387	747	(S)	4,039	2,888	2,015	2,390	5,449	11,212
Service workers, except private household..............	401	733	77	183	213	356	80	179	31	16
Median earnings..........................(dollars)..	16,774	12,935	14,993	11,637	15,749	13,791	18,017	14,164	22,049	11,574
Standard error..........................(dollars)..	571	567	2,514	457	694	777	1,312	1,432	3,102	9,648
Farming, fishing, and forestry workers..................	67	6	36	4	22	1	6	-	4	-
Median earnings..........................(dollars)..	11,027	11,591	9,477	(S)	12,885	(S)	15,974	-	(S)	-
Standard error..........................(dollars)..	1,594	2,529	1,819	(S)	3,386	(S)	2,416	-	(S)	-
Precision production, craft, and repair workers..........	646	136	93	19	358	71	151	36	44	9
Median earnings..........................(dollars)..	22,960	22,325	21,899	20,751	21,031	22,477	28,943	23,457	25,874	39,419
Standard error..........................(dollars)..	1,359	1,835	2,727	1,594	1,087	2,627	2,291	4,101	7,490	13,593
Machine operators, assemblers, and inspectors.........	450	360	112	83	248	211	85	62	4	4
Median earnings..........................(dollars)..	20,592	14,601	19,864	14,015	20,741	14,476	21,015	16,974	(S)	(S)
Standard error..........................(dollars)..	723	572	1,351	943	1,101	727	1,615	3,169	(S)	(S)
Transportation and material moving workers............	500	42	137	9	239	22	103	11	21	-
Median earnings..........................(dollars)..	22,000	21,650	20,182	20,949	21,839	16,563	26,213	24,354	30,675	-
Standard error..........................(dollars)..	1,195	1,741	1,422	10,996	1,299	6,870	4,550	2,424	2,299	-
Handlers, equipment cleaners, helpers, and laborers.....	290	72	85	15	121	43	71	14	12	-
Median earnings..........................(dollars)..	16,461	16,171	12,188	14,335	16,333	11,854	22,654	31,896	12,091	-
Standard error..........................(dollars)..	836	4,972	1,273	5,470	652	3,112	4,629	4,225	7,435	-

Source: Claudette E. Bennett, U.S. Bureau of the Census, *The Black Population in the United States: March 1994 and 1993*, Current Population Reports, Series P20-480, Washington, D.C.: U.S. Government Printing Office, January 1995, Table 13.

B2-13. Factors that Increase Wages of Working Mothers, by Race and Hispanic Origin: 1986–87

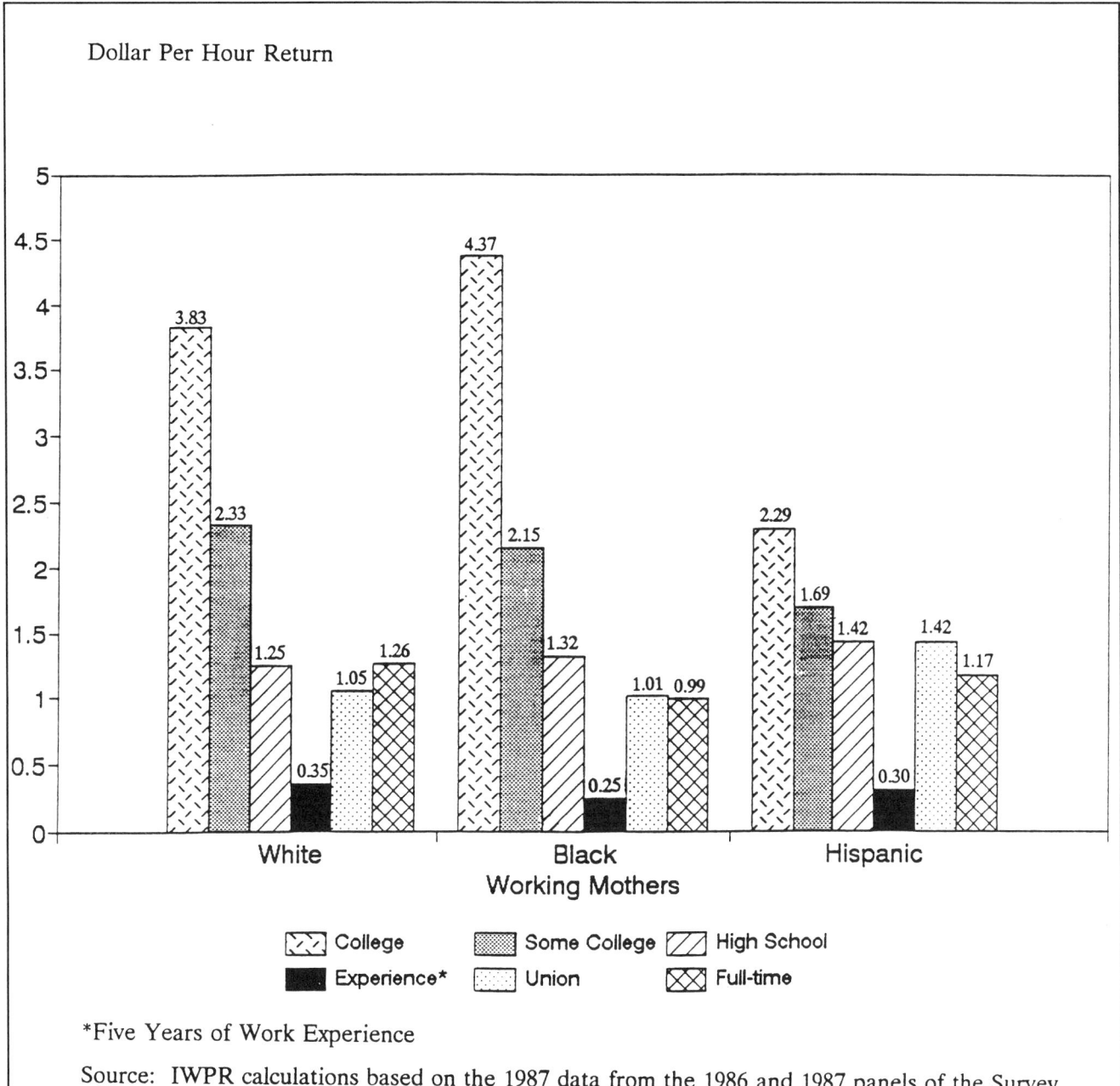

Dollar Per Hour Return

Legend:
- ☒ College
- ■ Experience*
- ▦ Some College
- ▨ Union
- ▨ High School
- ☒ Full-time

*Five Years of Work Experience

Source: IWPR calculations based on the 1987 data from the 1986 and 1987 panels of the Survey of Income and Program Participation.

Note: Although MAREDUC (the interaction variable indicating married with college degree) explained the most variation in the hourly wages of Hispanic mothers in the step-wise regression, it was not significant and is not included in the chart. Therefore, the college variable alone, which was significant, is included in the chart; its smaller effect relative to non-Hispanic black and white mothers is almost certainly due to the large effect of MAREDUC.

Source: Roberta M. Spalter-Roth and Heidi L. Hartmann, Institute for Women's Policy Research (Washington, D.C.), *Increasing Working Mothers' Earnings*, unpublished (contract for the U.S. Department of Labor, Women's Bureau), November 1991, Chart 3.

B2-14. Median Hourly Wages, by Sex, Educational Attainment, and Union Status: 1986–87

(Uncontrolled Results)

Education	Median Hourly Wages in 1987			Union Wage Premium*	Premium as % of Non–Union**	Total Sample Size
	Total	Union	Non–Union			
WOMEN	$6.98	$9.15	$6.65	$2.50	37.6	8,294
Less than High School	$4.99	$6.82	$4.71	$2.11	44.7	987
High School Diploma	$6.29	$8.00	$6.10	$1.90	31.1	3,153
Some College	$7.28	$9.15	$7.11	$2.05	28.8	2,386
College Diploma or More	$10.29	$11.28	$9.92	$1.35	13.6	1,768
MEN	$10.50	$12.03	$9.84	$2.19	22.2	8,939
Less than High School	$7.56	$10.59	$6.66	$3.93	59.0	1,347
High School	$9.67	$11.81	$8.50	$3.31	38.9	3,054
Some College	$10.44	$12.44	$9.77	$2.67	27.3	2,288
College or More	$14.57	$13.69	$14.99	($1.31)	-8.7	2,250

* The difference between union and non–union median hourly wages.
** The union wage premium as a percent of the non–union hourly wage.
Source: IWPR tabulations based on the 1986 and 1987 Panels of the Survey of Income and Program Participation.

Source: Roberta M. Spalter-Roth and Heidi L. Hartmann, Institute for Women's Policy Research (Washington, D.C.), *Increasing Working Mothers' Earnings*, unpublished (contract for the U.S. Department of Labor, Women's Bureau), November 1991, Appendix Table 6.

B2-15. Coverage under Employer or Individual Retirement Plans of Currently Employed Workers 25 to 54 Years Old, by Type of Employment and Sex: April 1993

Type of employment on primary job	Total number of workers (in millions)	Percent covered				
		Current primary job	Current secondary job	From previous job[1]	With active IRA[2]	Total with any coverage
All workers..............	85.9	51	1	7	7	58
Wage and salary............	78.6	55	1	7	6	61
Private.......................	63.9	50	1	7	6	56
Full-time..................	56.6	54	1	7	6	59
Part-time....................	7.3	20	1	5	6	28
Government.................	14.7	80	2	7	6	83
Self-employed..............	7.3	8	1	6	10	22
Men.........................	46.7	53	2	7	7	59
Wage and salary..........	41.7	58	2	8	7	64
Private.......................	35.0	53	1	7	7	59
Full-time..................	33.5	55	1	7	7	61
Part-time....................	1.5	14	1	6	4	20
Government.................	6.6	84	4	9	6	87
Self-employed..............	4.9	10	(3)	7	11	24
Women......................	39.2	50	1	6	6	55
Wage and salary..........	36.9	53	1	6	6	58
Private.......................	28.8	46	1	6	6	52
Full-time..................	23.0	52	1	6	6	58
Part-time....................	5.8	21	1	4	6	30
Government.................	8.0	77	1	5	7	79
Self-employed..............	2.3	4	1	5	8	16

[1] Receiving or expecting pension from a previous job.
[2] Workers who contributed to their own IRA in preceding year.
[3] Less than 0.5 percent.

Source: John R. Woods, "Pension Coverage Among the Baby Boomers: Initial Findings From a 1993 Survey," *Social Security Bulletin*, Vol. 57, No. 3 (Fall 1994), Table 1.

B2-16. Percent Covered by Employer-Sponsored Retirement Plan on Current Primary Job or from Previous Job, by Sector of Employment and Sex of Wage and Salary Workers Aged 25 to 54: 1979, 1983, 1988, and 1993

Sector of employment	1979			1983			1988			1993		
	Current job	Previous job	Either	Current job	Previous job	Either	Current job	Previous job	Either	Current job	Previous job	Either
All workers.......	58	5	60	54	5	56	54	6	57	55	7	58
Private....................	52	4	53	48	5	51	48	6	51	50	7	52
Government...........	83	5	83	78	6	79	82	7	83	80	7	82
Men........................	66	6	67	60	7	62	59	8	62	58	8	60
Private..................	61	6	63	55	6	58	54	8	57	53	7	56
Government.........	90	7	90	84	7	85	87	9	88	84	9	86
Women..................	48	3	49	47	3	49	49	4	51	53	6	55
Private..................	39	2	40	40	3	42	42	4	44	46	6	48
Government.........	75	4	76	72	4	74	77	5	78	77	5	78

[1] Coverage from previous job indicated by current receipt or expected receipt of pension.

Source: John R. Woods, "Pension Coverage Among the Baby Boomers: Initial Findings From a 1993 Survey," *Social Security Bulletin*, Vol. 57, No. 3 (Fall 1994), Table 2.

B2-17. Ratios of Women's Median Earnings to Those of Men by Type of Employment and Full-Time/Part-Time Schedules: 1975 and 1990

Characteristic	1975			1990		
	Annual	Weekly	Hourly	Annual	Weekly	Hourly
Wage-and-salary:						
Total	0.41	0.47	0.58	0.57	0.59	0.71
Full time and full year.....	.58	.58	.61	.69	.69	.75
Part time or part year	.56	.56	.69	.72	.68	.82
Self-employed:						
Total	.15	.17	.38	.28	.33	.46
Full time and full year ...	.32	.33	.36	.47	.47	.48
Part time or part year ...	.20	.21	.45	.33	.33	.48
Unincorporated business ..	.13	.19	.37	.27	.33	.46
Full time and full year ...	.31	.32	.34	.44	.43	.48
Part time or part year ...	.21	.21	.44	.30	.32	.45
Incorporated business	.38	.41	.52	.40	.43	.59
Full time and full year ...	.51	.51	.52	.50	.50	.56
Part time or part year ...	.41	.37	.43	.38	.35	.62

Source: Theresa J. Devine, "Characteristics of Self-Employed Women in the United States," *Monthly Labor Review*, March 1994, Table 10.

B2-18. Percentage of Employed Persons with Health Care Coverage in 1990, by Worker Characteristics and Type of Benefit Plan: 1990

Characteristic	Women				Men			
	Any health plan	Job-related plan	Family plan	Govern-ment plan	Any health plan	Job-related plan	Family plan	Gov-ment plan
All workers:								
Wage-and-salary	87.2	49.9	22.3	10.4	83.9	64.7	41.4	7.1
Self-employed.	83.2	12.6	5.0	14.2	78.7	32.9	24.7	11.5
Full time and full year:								
Wage-and-salary	91.1	72.0	32.1	4.9	89.1	78.5	51.7	3.9
Self-employed	81.8	15.9	6.0	8.6	82.0	38.2	28.9	6.8
Part time or part year:								
Wage-and-salary	83.0	25.3	11.4	16.5	72.3	33.9	18.5	14.4
Self-employed	84.3	9.8	4.1	18.9	70.4	20.0	14.6	23.0
Married with spouse present:								
Wage-and-salary	92.2	48.3	31.5	8.4	91.1	75.3	65.4	8.0
Self-employed	87.6	10.8	5.7	11.6	84.6	36.0	31.6	12.5
Full time and full year:								
Wage-and-salary	94.9	67.1	44.1	5.4	93.6	81.8	71.4	4.4
Self-employed	86.4	13.6	6.9	8.4	86.6	40.6	35.3	7.5
Part time or part year								
Wage-and-salary	89.0	26.9	17.2	11.9	81.4	50.2	42.6	22.0
Self-employed	88.5	8.6	4.9	14.0	78.7	22.8	20.9	27.0
Self-employed in:								
Unincorporated business ..	81.8	9.3	3.8	15.4	73.6	23.2	17.0	13.0
Incorporated business	89.4	27.1	10.5	9.1	89.9	54.6	42.0	8.3

Note: Variables are defined as follows:
- Health plan: Private or government health insurance or group health coverage, in one's own name or through another's coverage.
- Job-related plan: Private health insurance or group health coverage, in one's own name through employment.
- Family plan: Other family or household members covered under own job plan.
- Government plan: A government health plan (Medicare, Medicaid, Champus, or Champva).
Note that coverage may be for all or part of the 1990 calendar year, and also that an individual may be in more than one category during the year.

Source: Theresa J. Devine, "Characteristics of Self-Employed Women in the United States," *Monthly Labor Review*, March 1994, Table 11.

B3. WORKING MOTHERS AND CHILD CARE

B3-1. Proportion of Children with Mothers in the Labor Force: 1940 to 1990

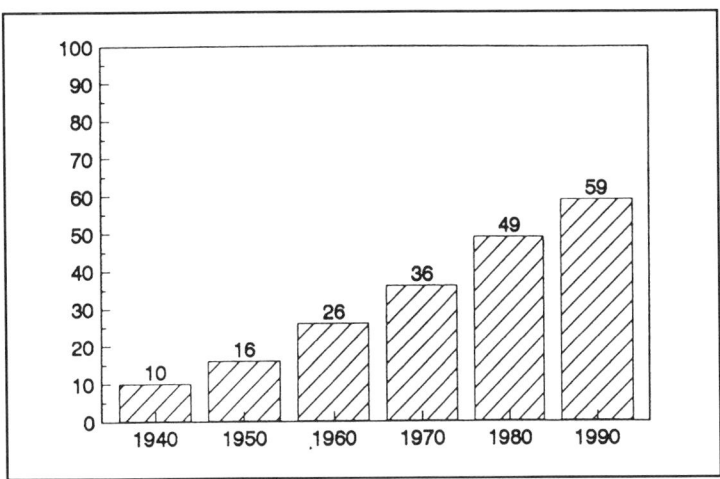

Source: D. J. Hernandez, *The Historical Transformation of Childhood, Children's Statistics, and Social Policy*, Childhood 1993, Vol. 1, Munksgaard, 1993, Figure 4.

B3-2. Work Experience of Married Mothers, by Age of Youngest Child and Race: Selected Years, 1970 to 1992

[Numbers in thousands]

Year and race	With children under 18				With children 6 to 17, none younger				With children under 6			
	Popu-lation	Percent who worked during year		Percent who did not work during year	Popu-lation	Percent who worked during year		Percent who did not work during year	Popu-lation	Percent who worked during year		Percent who did not work during year
		Total	Year round full time[1]	Other[2]			Total	Year round full time[1]	Other[2]			Total	Year round full time[1]	Other[2]	
Total													
1970	24,602	51.3	16.4	34.9	48.7	12,784	57.7	22.8	34.9	42.3	11,919	44.4	9.6	34.8	55.6
1975	25,361	53.7	18.1	35.7	46.3	13,543	59.5	23.4	36.1	40.5	11,819	47.0	11.9	35.2	53.0
1980	25,217	63.4	23.7	39.7	36.6	13,492	68.0	28.9	39.1	32.0	11,725	58.1	17.7	40.4	41.9
1985	25,003	73.9	31.3	42.6	27.1	12,786	72.8	34.6	38.2	27.2	12,217	63.0	22.7	40.3	37.0
1990	24,393	72.8	34.0	38.7	27.2	12,294	77.6	40.0	37.6	22.4	12,099	67.9	28.0	39.9	32.1
1991	24,416	73.5	35.7	37.9	26.5	12,491	79.2	42.2	37.0	20.8	11,925	67.6	28.8	38.7	32.4
1992	24,706	72.9	36.8	36.1	27.1	12,764	78.4	42.6	35.8	21.6	11,942	67.1	30.6	36.5	32.9
White													
1970	22,512	50.2	15.4	34.7	49.8	11,788	56.9	21.8	35.0	43.1	10,723	42.8	8.4	34.4	57.2
1975	22,893	52.8	17.0	35.8	47.2	12,362	58.7	22.3	36.4	41.3	10,531	45.9	10.8	35.1	54.1
1980	22,541	62.8	22.3	40.5	37.2	12,136	67.7	27.7	40.1	32.3	10,405	57.1	16.1	41.0	42.9
1985	22,056	67.3	27.0	40.3	32.7	11,249	72.2	32.7	39.4	27.8	10,808	62.2	20.9	41.3	37.8
1990	21,504	72.7	32.4	40.3	27.3	10,823	77.6	38.3	39.3	22.4	10,686	67.7	26.4	41.3	32.3
1991	21,488	73.4	34.4	39.1	26.6	10,987	79.3	41.0	38.3	20.7	10,501	67.3	27.4	39.9	32.7
1992	21,702	72.6	35.6	37.0	27.4	11,207	78.4	41.7	36.7	21.6	10,495	66.4	29.1	37.3	33.6
Black													
1970	1,910	64.2	27.2	37.0	35.8	861	68.6	34.8	33.8	31.4	1,049	60.6	21.1	39.5	39.4
1975	1,971	64.5	29.8	34.7	35.5	990	69.4	37.0	32.4	30.6	981	59.5	22.5	37.0	40.5
1980	1,924	69.8	36.5	33.3	30.2	1,025	69.8	40.2	29.5	30.2	899	69.7	32.3	37.4	30.3
1985	1,965	76.1	45.0	31.0	23.9	1,038	78.3	50.4	27.9	21.7	926	73.5	39.1	34.4	26.5
1990	1,846	78.9	48.9	30.0	21.1	938	80.5	53.0	27.6	19.5	908	77.3	44.6	32.7	22.7
1991	1,870	78.4	48.7	29.7	21.7	986	79.8	53.3	26.4	20.2	884	76.7	43.3	33.4	23.3
1992	1,863	79.5	49.1	30.4	20.5	992	82.6	52.6	30.0	17.4	871	76.1	44.9	31.2	23.9

[1] Worked full time (35 hours or more a week) 50 to 52 weeks.

[2] Worked either full or part time (less than 35 hours a week) for 1 to 49 weeks.

Source: Howard V. Hayghe and Suzanne M. Bianchi, "Married Mothers' Work Patterns: The Job-Family Compromise," *Monthly Labor Review*, June 1994, Table 5.

B3-3. Work Experience of Persons in 1992, by Selected Characteristics: March 1993

[Numbers in thousands]

Work experience	Parents		Persons 20 to 54 years old		
	Married mothers	All fathers	Women with no children under 18	Men	
				Total	With no children under 18
Total	24,706	26,182	30,616	62,625	36,443
Worked in 1992	18,018	24,784	26,007	57,282	32,498
As percent of total	72.9	94.7	84.9	91.5	89.2
Percent of total who:					
Worked full year in 1992[1] ...	47.9	77.9	63.5	69.2	62.9
Full time[2]	36.8	76.1	54.1	65.6	58.0
Part time[2]	11.1	1.8	9.4	3.6	4.9
Worked part year in 1992[3] ..	25.1	16.8	21.5	22.2	26.2
Full time[2]	12.0	14.5	12.8	17.4	19.4
40 to 49 weeks........	4.4	6.6	4.9	6.9	7.0
27 to 39 weeks........	2.8	3.6	2.9	4.1	4.5
1 to 26 weeks	4.8	4.3	5.0	6.4	7.9
Part time[2]	13.1	2.3	8.7	4.8	6.8
40 to 49 weeks........	3.4	0.6	2.7	1.2	1.6
27 to 39 weeks........	2.7	0.5	1.8	0.9	1.4
1 to 26 weeks	7.0	1.2	4.2	2.7	3.8
Did not work in 1992	27.1	5.3	15.1	8.6	10.8

[1] Fifty to 52 weeks.

[2] Full time is defined as 35 hours a week or more. Part time is less than 35 hours.

[3] One to 49 weeks.

NOTE: Based on the fact that nearly all parents are 20 to 54 years old, data for men and women 20 to 54 years old with no children under 18 were constructed by subtracting parents from estimates for all 20- to 54-year olds.

Source: Howard V. Hayghe and Suzanne M. Bianchi, "Married Mothers' Work Patterns: The Job-Family Compromise," *Monthly Labor Review*, June 1994, Table 1.

B3-4. Work Experience of Married Mothers in 1992, by Age of Youngest Child: March 1993

[Numbers in thousands]

Work experience	With children 6 to 17, none younger	With children under 6	
		Total	Under 3
Marries mothers, total.....................	12,764	11,942	7,168
Worked in 1992	10,004	8,013	4,776
As percent of total	78.4	67.2	66.6
Percent of married mothers who:			
Worked full year in 1992[1].........	55.2	40.0	36.3
Full time[2]	42.6	30.6	27.7
Part time[2]	12.6	9.4	8.6
Worked part year in 1992[3]........	23.1	27.1	30.4
Full time[2]	11.2	12.7	15.2
40 to 49 weeks...............	4.2	4.6	5.6
27 to 39 weeks..............	2.7	2.8	3.4
1 to 26 weeks	4.3	5.3	6.2
Part time[2]	11.9	14.4	15.2
40 to 49 weeks..............	3.6	3.1	3.1
27 to 39 weeks..............	2.8	2.7	2.8
1 to 26 weeks	5.5	8.6	9.4
Did not work in 1992	21.6	32.9	33.4

[1] Fifty to 52 weeks.

[2] Full time is defined as 35 hours a week or more. Part time is less than 35 hours.

[3] One to 49 weeks.

Source: Howard V. Hayghe and Suzanne M. Bianchi, "Married Mothers' Work Patterns: The Job-Family Compromise," *Monthly Labor Review*, June 1994, Table 2.

B3-5. Work Experience of Married Mothers in 1992, by Race and Hispanic Origin of Mother and Age of Youngest Child: March 1993

[Numbers in thousands]

Work experience	White				Black				Hispanic origin			
	Total	With children 6 to 17 only	With children under 6		Total	With children 6 to 17 only	With children under 6		Total	With children 6 to 17 only	With children under 6	
			Total	Under 3			Total	Under 3			Total	Under 3
Married mothers, total..............	21,702	11,207	10,495	6,341	1,863	992	871	495	2,441	1,082	1,359	837
Worked in 1992	15,758	8,786	6,972	4,205	1,481	819	663	357	1,407	704	704	404
As percent of total	72.6	78.4	66.4	66.3	79.5	82.6	76.1	72.1	57.6	65.1	51.8	48.3
Percent of married mothers who:												
Worked full year in 1992[1]........	47.3	55.0	39.1	36.0	55.4	59.8	50.2	41.9	36.2	45.7	28.6	25.2
Full time[2]	35.6	41.7	29.1	26.9	49.1	52.6	44.9	36.0	29.5	37.6	23.2	20.4
Part time[2].....................	11.7	13.3	10.0	9.1	6.3	7.2	5.3	5.9	6.7	8.0	5.5	4.8
Worked part year in 1992[3]	25.2	23.4	27.4	30.4	24.2	22.5	25.9	30.2	21.4	19.3	23.2	23.2
Full time[2]	11.5	10.9	12.3	14.7	15.3	15.1	15.6	19.6	13.6	12.0	14.8	15.6
40 to 49 weeks.............	4.2	4.0	4.4	5.5	5.6	6.0	5.2	5.9	4.2	4.6	3.9	3.7
27 to 39 weeks	2.6	2.6	2.7	3.2	4.3	4.2	4.4	4.8	3.3	3.0	3.5	4.9
1 to 26 weeks	4.7	4.3	5.2	6.0	5.4	4.9	6.1	8.9	6.1	4.4	7.4	7.0
Part time[2]....................	13.7	12.5	15.1	15.7	8.9	7.4	10.3	10.6	7.8	7.3	8.4	7.6
40 to 49 weeks.............	3.5	3.7	3.3	3.1	2.1	1.7	2.5	2.8	1.3	1.5	1.2	1.1
27 to 39 weeks	2.9	3.0	2.9	2.9	1.6	1.4	1.7	3.0	1.8	1.5	2.1	1.8
1 to 26 weeks	7.3	5.8	8.9	9.7	5.2	4.3	6.1	4.8	4.7	4.3	5.1	4.7
Did not work in 1992	27.4	21.6	33.6	33.7	20.5	17.4	23.9	27.9	42.4	35.0	48.2	51.6

[1] Fifty to 52 weeks.

[2] Full time is defined as 35 hours a week or more. Part time is less than 35 hours.

[3] One to 49 weeks.

NOTE: Detail for race and Hispanic-origin groups do not sum to totals because data for the "other races" group are not presented and Hispanics are included in both the white and black population groups.

Source: Howard V. Hayghe and Suzanne M. Bianchi, "Married Mothers' Work Patterns: The Job-Family Compromise," *Monthly Labor Review*, June 1994, Table 3.

B3-6. Work Experience of Fathers and Mothers in Two-Parent Families in 1992, by Age of Youngest Child, Race, and Hispanic Origin: March 1993

[Numbers in thousands]

Parents' work experience	Total	With children 6 to 17, none younger	With children under 6	White	Black	Hispanic origin
Two-parent families, number......................	24,706	12,764	11,942	21,702	1,863	2,441
Percent in which:						
Both parents worked during year	70.1	74.8	65.0	70.0	74.1	54.1
Father only worked during year	25.1	19.6	31.0	25.8	16.6	38.8
Mother only worked during year..............	2.2	3.5	2.1	2.6	5.4	3.6
Two-parent families, percent....................	100.0	100.0	100.0	100.0	100.0	100.0
Father worked year round[1] full time[2]	78.1	78.4	77.7	78.8	71.7	67.3
Mother worked year round[1] full time[2]	29.5	34.3	24.3	28.6	38.0	21.3
Mother worked less than year round full time[3]................................	28.2	27.8	28.6	29.2	21.8	17.9
Mother did not work	20.4	16.2	24.9	21.0	11.9	28.0
Father worked less than year round full time[3]	17.2	16.1	18.3	17.0	19.1	25.6
Mother worked year round[1] full time[2]	5.7	6.3	5.1	5.5	7.8	6.5
Mother worked less than year round full time[3]................................	6.7	6.4	7.0	6.7	6.6	8.4
Mother did not work	4.7	3.4	6.2	4.8	4.7	10.8
Father did not work	4.8	5.5	4.0	4.2	9.2	7.1
Mother worked year round[1] full time[2]	1.6	2.0	1.2	1.5	3.2	1.8
Mother worked less than year round full time[3]................................	1.2	1.5	0.9	1.1	2.1	1.8
Mother did not work	1.9	2.0	1.9	1.6	3.8	3.6

[1] Fifty to 52 weeks.

[2] Full time is defined as 35 hours a week or more. Part time is less than 35 hours.

[3] Worked 1 to 49 weeks, either full or part time.

NOTE: Detail for race and Hispanic-origin groups do not sum to totals because data for the "other races" group are not presented and Hispanics are included in both the white and black population groups.

Source: Howard V. Hayghe and Suzanne M. Bianchi, "Married Mothers' Work Patterns: The Job-Family Compromise," *Monthly Labor Review*, June 1994, Table 4.

B3-7. Work Experience of Mothers and Fathers in Two-Parent Families, by Age of Youngest Child: 1970, 1990, and 1992

[Numbers in thousands]

Parents' work experience	With own children under 18			With children 6 to 17, none younger			With children under 6		
	1970	1990	1992	1970	1990	1992	1970	1990	1992
Two-parent families, total.........	24,703	24,393	24,706	12,784	12,294	12,764	11,919	12,099	11,942
Percent	100.0	100.0	100.0	100.0	100.0	100.0	100.0	100.0	100.0
Both parents had work experience	50.3	70.9	70.1	56.5	75.1	74.8	43.6	66.6	65.0
Both parents worked year round full time[1]..........	13.2	28.0	29.5	18.7	32.9	34.3	7.3	23.0	24.3
One parent worked year round full time[1]..........	29.8	36.0	33.9	31.7	36.1	34.1	27.8	36.0	33.7
Father....................	27.0	31.0	28.2	28.2	30.4	27.8	25.8	31.7	28.6
Mother	2.8	5.0	5.7	3.5	5.7	6.3	2.0	4.2	5.1
Neither parent worked year round full time[1]..........	7.2	6.8	6.7	6.1	6.1	6.4	8.5	7.6	7.0
One parent only had work experience	48.4	27.5	28.0	41.9	23.2	23.2	55.3	31.8	33.1
Father.....................	47.4	25.6	25.1	40.7	20.7	19.6	54.6	30.5	31.0
Worked year round full time[1]...............	39.1	21.0	20.4	34.7	17.1	16.2	43.8	24.9	24.9
Mother	1.0	1.9	2.8	1.3	2.5	3.5	.7	1.3	2.1
Worked year round full time[1]...............	.4	1.0	1.6	.6	1.3	2.0	.2	.8	1.2
Neither parent worked during year.................	1.3	1.7	1.9	1.6	1.7	2.0	1.1	1.6	1.9

[1] Year round full time is defined as 50 to 52 weeks, 35 hours a week or more.

Source: Howard V. Hayghe and Suzanne M. Bianchi, "Married Mothers' Work Patterns: The Job-Family Compromise," *Monthly Labor Review*, June 1994, Table 6.

B3-8. Percentage of Employed Women with Young Children in the Household, by Selected Characteristics: 1975 and 1990

Characteristic	1975		1990	
	Self-employed	Wage-and-salary	Self-employed	Wage-and-salary
Total with children under age 6 in the household ...	17.3	16.7	20.0	18.6
Married with spouse present	21.9	22.3	23.8	24.9
Full time and full year ...	12.1	13.7	16.6	19.7
Part time or part year ...	25.9	28.7	29.4	30.9
Other marital status	4.7	9.0	8.7	11.0
Full time and full year ...	3.2	7.4	5.8	8.2
Part time or part year ...	5.9	10.2	11.7	14.1
Incorporated	6.7	—	13.2	—
Unincorporated..........	18.3	—	21.5	—

NOTE: Dash indicates not applicable.

Source: Theresa J. Devine, "Characteristics of Self-Employed Women in the United States," *Monthly Labor Review*, March 1994, Table 12.

B3-9. Women Who Worked Continuously for Pay Six or More Months before Their First Birth, by Race: 1961–65 to 1981–85

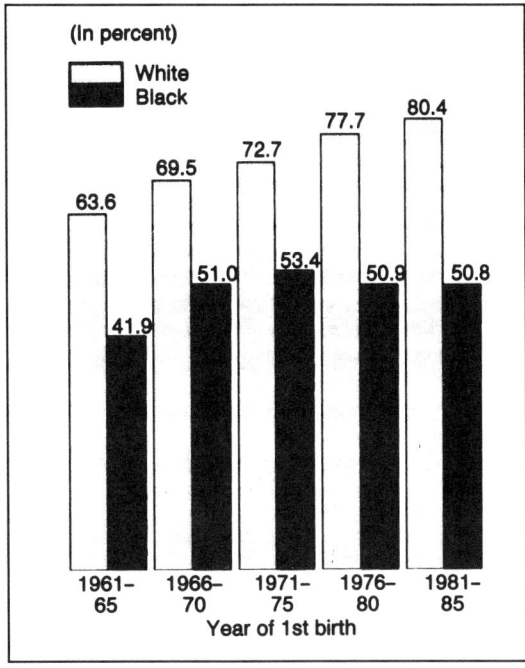

Source: U.S. Bureau of the Census, *Work and Family Patterns of American Women*, Current Population Reports, Series P-23, No. 165, Washington, D.C.: U.S. Government Printing Office, 1990, Figure 2.

B3-10. Women Who Worked during Their First Pregnancy, by Selected Characteristics, 1961–65 to 1981–85

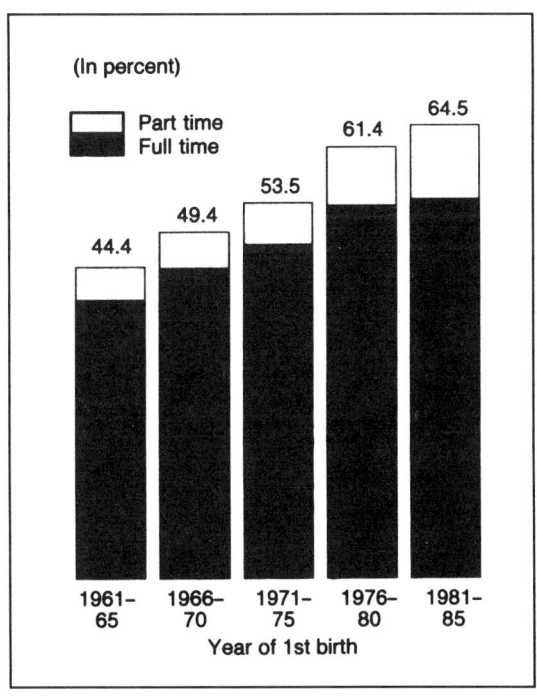

Source: U.S. Bureau of the Census, *Work and Family Patterns of American Women*, Current Population Reports, Series P-23, No. 165, Washington, D.C.: U.S. Government Printing Office, 1990, Figure 3.

B3-11. Percentage of Women Who Quit Their Jobs before Their Child's Birth, by Race: 1961–65 to 1981–85

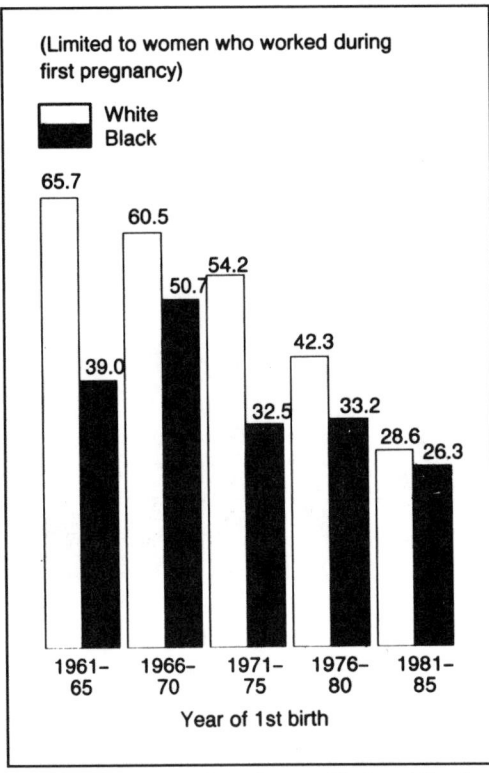

(Limited to women who worked during first pregnancy)

☐ White
■ Black

1961–65: White 65.7, Black 39.0
1966–70: White 60.5, Black 50.7
1971–75: White 54.2, Black 32.5
1976–80: White 42.3, Black 33.2
1981–85: White 28.6, Black 26.3

Year of 1st birth

Source: U.S. Bureau of the Census, *Work and Family Patterns of American Women*, Current Population Reports, Series P-23, No. 165, Washington, D.C.: U.S. Government Printing Office, 1990, Figure 6.

B3-12. Employer Payments for Maternity Leave for the First Birth: 1961–65 to 1981–85

(Numbers in thousands)

Employer payment	Year of first birth				
	1981-85	1976-80	1971-75	1966-70	1961-65
Number of women on maternity leave.....................	2,440	1,502	867	629	449
Percent....................	100.0	100.0	100.0	100.0	100.0
Paid for all leave................	42.0	39.0	29.5	26.3	24.8
Paid for some leave	38.9	33.4	27.8	27.9	24.8
No payment for leave	19.1	27.6	42.8	45.8	50.3

Note: Question asked was "Did your employer pay for all or part of your leave through maternity benefits or sick pay?"

Source: U.S. Bureau of the Census, *Work and Family Patterns of American Women*, Current Population Reports, Series P-23, No. 165, Washington, D.C.: U.S. Government Printing Office, 1990, Table G.

B3-13. Women Working Full Time at First Job after Birth of First Child, by Interval after Birth: 1961–65 to 1981–84

Month returned to work	Year of first birth				
	1981-84	1976-80	1971-75	1966-70	1961-65
Percent working full time:					
Less than 3 months.	76.5	78.8	85.8	76.8	81.2
3 to 5 months	57.1	74.7	75.5	77.4	75.9
6 to 12 months	55.9	69.1	66.4	75.6	73.0
13 to 24 months	(X)	67.0	61.8	70.5	71.2
25 to 36 months	(X)	58.7	66.0	61.3	68.1
37 to 48 months	(X)	52.3	65.0	74.0	67.1
49 to 60 months	(X)	59.8	61.2	70.0	69.0

X Incomplete data for this interval.
Source: Derived from table B-12.

Source: U.S. Bureau of the Census, *Work and Family Patterns of American Women*, Current Population Reports, Series P-23, No. 165, Washington, D.C.: U.S. Government Printing Office, 1990, Tables L.

B3-14. Time Lost before and after First Birth among Women Employed during Their First Pregnancy: 1961–65 to 1981–84

(Numbers in thousands)

Time lost	Year of first birth				
	1981-84	1976-80	1971-75	1966-70	1961-65
Number of women	4,237	4,414	3,700	3,435	2,797
Percent.	100.0	100.0	100.0	100.0	100.0
Less than 3 months.	25.0	16.3	11.5	7.2	6.9
3 to 5 months	22.1	18.6	10.1	9.7	6.9
6 to 8 months	11.7	8.4	8.3	7.4	5.6
9 to 11 months	6.7	4.9	4.4	4.8	4.0
12 or more months	34.6	51.8	65.8	70.9	76.6

Source: U.S. Bureau of the Census, *Work and Family Patterns of American Women*, Current Population Reports, Series P-23, No. 165, Washington, D.C.: U.S. Government Printing Office, 1990, Table L.

B3-15. Primary Child-Care Arrangements Used by Employed Mothers for Children Under 5 Years: Selected Periods, 1977 to 1991

[Numbers in thousands]

Type of arrangement	Fall 1991	Fall 1990	Fall 1988	Fall 1987	Fall 1986	Winter 1985	June 1977[1]
Number of children....................	9,854	9,629	9,483	9,124	8,849	8,168	4,370
Percent..........................	100.0	100.0	100.0	100.0	100.0	100.0	100.0
Care in child's home	35.7	29.7	28.2	29.9	28.7	31.0	33.9
By father............................	20.0	16.5	15.1	15.3	14.5	15.7	14.4
By grandparent	7.2	5.2	5.7	5.1	5.2	5.7	(NA)
By other relative	3.2	2.9	2.2	3.3	3.4	3.7	[2]12.6
By nonrelative	5.4	5.0	5.3	6.2	5.5	5.9	7.0
Care in another home	31.0	35.1	36.8	35.6	40.7	37.0	40.7
By grandparent	8.6	9.1	8.2	8.7	10.2	10.2	(NA)
By relative	4.5	5.9	5.0	4.6	6.5	4.5	18.3
By nonrelative	17.9	20.1	23.6	22.3	24.0	22.3	22.4
Organized child care facilities............	23.0	27.5	25.8	24.4	22.4	23.1	13.0
Day/group care center	15.8	20.6	16.6	16.1	14.9	14.0	(NA)
Nursery school/preschool............	7.3	6.9	9.2	8.3	7.5	9.1	(NA)
School-based activity................	0.5	0.1	0.2	(NA)	(NA)	(NA)	(NA)
Child cares for self.....................	-	0.1	0.1	0.3	-	-	0.4
Mother cares for child at work[3]	8.7	6.4	7.6	8.9	7.4	8.1	11.4
Other arrangements[4]	1.1	1.1	1.3	1.0	0.8	0.8	0.6

- Represents zero.
NA Not available.

[1]Data only for the two youngest children under 5 years of age.
[2]Data for 1977 includes grandparents.
[3]Includes mothers working at home or away from home.
[4]Includes children in kindergarten/grade school.

Source: Tabulations derived from the June 1977 Current Population Survey; Current Population Reports, Series P70-9, table 1; Series P70-20, table 1, Part A and Part B; Series P70-30, table 1; and table 1 of this report.

Source: Lynne M. Casper, Mary Hawkins, and Martin O'Connell, U.S. Bureau of the Census, *Who's Minding the Kids? Child Care Arrangements: Fall 1991*, Current Population Reports, P70-36, Washington, D.C.: U.S. Government Printing Office, 1994, Table C.

B3-16. Predicted Hours of Paid Work for Mothers with Youngest Child Under Age 5, by Predicted Weekly Child Care Expenses: 1990

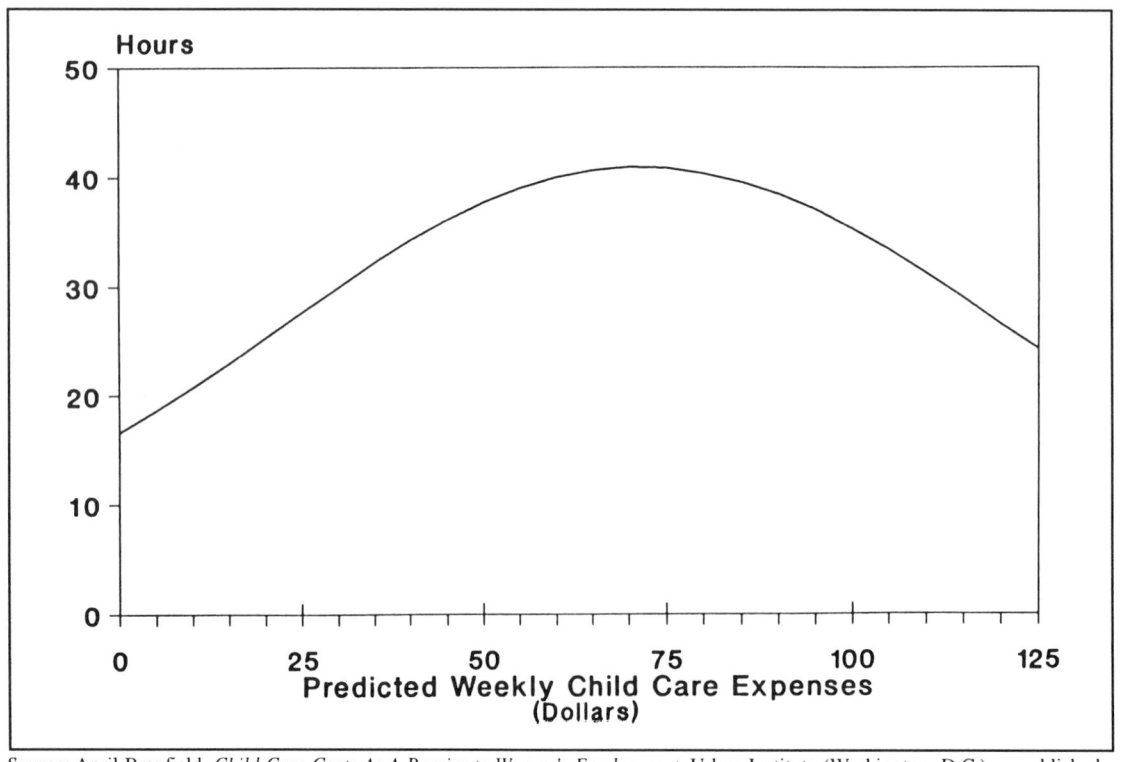

Source: April Brayfield, *Child Care Costs As A Barrier to Women's Employment*, Urban Institute (Washington, D.C.), unpublished (contract for the U.S. Department of Labor, Women's Bureau), September 1992, Figure 6.

B3-17. Percentage of Monthly Family Income Employed Mothers Spent on Child Care, by Income Level and Poverty Status: Fall 1991

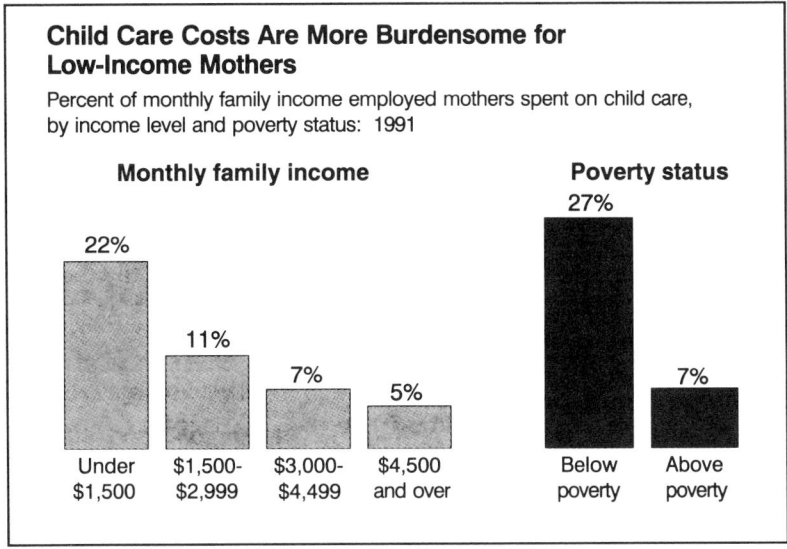

Source: U.S. Bureau of the Census, "Who's Minding the Kids?" *Statistical Brief*, April 1994, Figure 2.

B3-18. Primary Child Care Arrangements Used by Employed Mothers for Children Under 5 Years, by Characteristics of Mothers: Fall 1991

[Numbers in thousands]

Characteristic	Number of children	Care in child's home by — Father	Grand-parent	Other relative	Non-relative	Care in another home by — Grand-parent	Other relative	Non-relative	Day/ group care center	Nursery/ pre-school	School-based activity	Kinder garten/ grade school	Child cares for self	Mother cares for child[1]
Total	9,854	1,974	708	313	527	846	443	1,763	1,553	716	52	105	-	855
Race:														
White.	8,103	1,744	538	210	490	660	297	1,482	1,279	536	35	87	-	747
Black	1,251	170	95	90	13	153	107	224	213	108	17	9	-	52
Hispanic origin:														
Hispanic.	989	187	141	26	88	75	67	99	140	77	5	25	-	58
Non-Hispanic.	8,865	1,787	567	286	439	771	376	1,664	1,412	639	46	80	-	797
Marital status:														
Married, spouse present .	8,048	1,847	454	203	445	652	342	1,379	1,257	568	46	66	-	789
All other marital statuses[2]	1,806	127	254	109	82	194	101	384	295	147	6	39	-	66
Age of child:														
Less than 1 year	1,650	356	144	45	123	237	93	338	161	28	-	-	-	126
1 and 2 years.	4,021	853	323	156	223	346	190	822	612	93	5	-	-	398
3 and 4 years.	4,183	765	241	112	181	263	159	603	780	595	46	105	-	331
Educational attainment:														
Less than high school . . .	1,018	180	153	75	52	124	108	127	87	65	6	9	-	30
High school	3,860	765	249	165	146	355	174	752	615	160	35	50	-	395
College, 1 to 3 years. . . .	2,602	566	210	20	130	254	126	439	443	212	5	31	-	166
College, 4 or more years. .	2,375	462	96	53	199	114	34	445	408	278	6	15	-	264
Employment status:														
Full-time.	6,188	913	405	172	362	555	337	1,274	1,197	525	40	87	-	320
Part-time	3,666	1,061	303	140	165	291	106	489	356	191	12	18	-	535
Occupation:[3]														
Managerial-professional .	2,580	434	136	49	194	183	54	536	470	295	6	22	-	202
Technical, sales, and administrative support . .	4,062	853	303	101	247	360	219	724	668	252	30	58	-	248
Service occupations	2,144	522	176	112	73	136	111	258	295	121	6	21	-	313
Farming, forestry, and fishing	82	7	-	-	-	20	16	10	-	17	-	-	-	12
Precision production, craft, and repair.	216	49	20	5	14	15	7	48	38	6	-	-	-	14
Operators, fabricators, and laborers	720	108	73	47	-	132	37	172	46	25	10	5	-	66
Monthly family income:[4]														
Less than $1,500.	1,618	343	90	114	58	175	93	263	239	90	6	29	-	117
$1,500 to $2,999.	3,173	802	241	100	110	302	191	498	345	209	35	13	-	328
$3,000 to $4,499.	2,594	527	213	58	143	258	99	489	442	128	-	35	-	203
$4,500 and over	2,403	294	158	41	216	94	60	500	526	283	11	28	-	191
Poverty level:[4]														
Below poverty level.	977	261	79	65	42	80	46	106	145	35	6	20	-	93
Above poverty level.	8,811	1,706	623	248	486	748	397	1,644	1,408	674	46	85	-	746
Region of residence:														
Northeast	1,890	518	281	42	154	143	45	227	163	137	-	11	-	169
Midwest.	2,699	609	136	70	144	237	97	580	453	87	-	8	-	279
South.	2,992	444	162	91	75	317	165	623	596	267	40	54	-	158
West	2,273	403	130	110	155	150	136	333	341	224	11	32	-	250
Metropolitan residence:														
Metropolitan	7,419	1,551	610	224	427	587	299	1,249	1,173	551	19	87	-	641
In central cities	2,771	654	211	102	201	196	160	411	452	158	13	26	-	186
Outside central cities . .	4,648	898	400	122	225	391	139	838	721	393	5	61	-	455
Nonmetropolitan	2,436	422	97	89	101	259	144	514	379	165	33	18	-	214

- Represents zero.

[1]Includes mothers working at home or away from home.
[2]Includes married, husband absent (including separated), widowed, divorced, and never-married mothers.
[3]Excludes mothers in the Armed Forces.
[4]Omits persons who did not report family income.

Source: Lynne M. Casper, Mary Hawkins, and Martin O'Connell, U.S. Bureau of the Census, *Who's Minding the Kids? Child Care Arrangements: Fall 1991*, Current Population Reports, P70-36, Washington, D.C.: U.S. Government Printing Office, 1994, Table 2.

B4. OCCUPATIONS

B4-1. Occupation, by Sex and Race: March 1994

(Numbers in thousands.)

Characteristic	All races	Black	White
OCCUPATION[1]			
Employed males, 16 years and over	64,295	5,836	55,786
Percent	100.0	100.0	100.0
Managerial and professional specialty	26.4	14.7	27.5
Technical, sales, and administrative support	20.3	17.6	20.6
Service	10.8	20.0	9.8
Farming, forestry, and fishing	4.0	2.0	4.3
Precision production, craft, and repair	18.0	15.0	18.5
Operators, fabricators, and laborers	20.4	30.7	19.3
Employed females, 16 years and over	55,812	6,487	47,094
Percent	100.0	100.0	100.0
Managerial and professional specialty	28.7	20.1	29.9
Technical, sales, and administrative support	42.6	39.4	43.2
Service	18.1	26.9	16.8
Farming, forestry, and fishing	1.1	0.2	1.2
Precision production, craft, and repair	2.2	2.5	2.1
Operators, fabricators, and laborers	7.3	10.8	6.8

[1]Data for labor force status, occupation, and class of worker shown in this report reflect characteristics of the population for March 1994 and are not adjusted for seasonal changes. Data released by the Department of Labor, Bureau of Labor Statistics, may not agree entirely with data shown in this report due to differences in methodological procedures and seasonal adjustment of the data.

Source: Claudette E. Bennett, U.S. Bureau of the Census, *The Black Population in the United States: March 1994 and 1993*, Current Population Reports, Series P20-480, Washington, D.C.: U.S. Government Printing Office, January 1995, Table 2.

B4-2. Occupations of Hispanic Women: March 1992

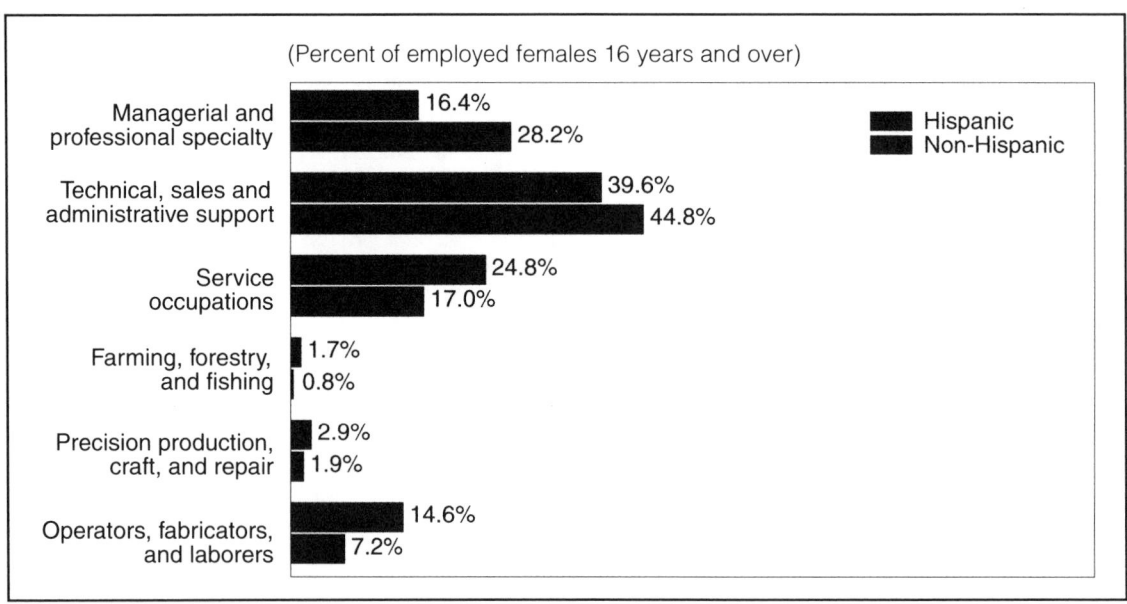

Source: U.S. Bureau of the Census, *Hispanic American Today*, Current Population Reports, Series P23-183, Washington, D.C.: U.S. Government Printing Office, 1993, Figure 24.

B4-3. Percentage of Employed Persons in Managerial and Professional Specialty Occupations, by Race, Hispanic Origin, and Sex: Annual Averages 1983 and 1993

Race and origin	1983	1993
Black:		
Women	16.1	20.5
Men	12.2	14.7
Hispanic origin:		
Women	12.2	16.6
Men	11.5	12.4
White:		
Women	22.6	29.3
Men	25.6	27.1

Source: U.S. Department of Labor, *Employment in Perspective: Women in the Labor Force*, Third Quarter 1994, Report 884, Table A.

B4-4. Occupations of Employed Persons, by Urban and Rural Areas and Size of Place: 1990

[Data based on sample and subject to sampling variability.]

United States Urban and Rural and Size of Place	United States	Urban						Rural			
			Inside urbanized area			Outside urbanized area					
		Total	Total	Central place	Urban fringe	Place of 10,000 or more	Place of 2,500 to 9,999	Total	Place of 1,000 to 2,499	Place of less than 1,000	Rural farm
Employed persons 16 years and over	**115 681 202**	**88 062 103**	**75 840 926**	**36 037 995**	**39 802 931**	**5 954 560**	**6 266 617**	**27 619 099**	**2 971 545**	**1 551 830**	**1 909 060**
Managerial and professional specialty occupations	30 533 582	24 905 394	22 062 651	9 862 657	12 199 994	1 454 504	1 388 239	5 628 188	617 286	272 621	286 715
Executive, administrative, and managerial occupations	14 227 916	11 630 316	10 391 558	4 380 945	6 010 613	623 664	615 094	2 597 600	273 594	120 229	120 670
Officials and administrators, public administration	578 334	448 865	384 852	173 747	211 105	29 572	34 441	129 469	17 032	9 416	8 298
Management and related occupations	4 140 575	3 498 062	3 181 829	1 376 595	1 805 234	162 489	153 744	642 513	66 297	27 146	31 332
Professional specialty occupations	16 305 666	13 275 078	11 671 093	5 481 712	6 189 381	830 840	773 145	3 030 588	343 692	152 392	166 045
Engineers and natural scientists	3 000 976	2 536 282	2 331 867	898 451	1 433 416	110 396	94 019	464 694	39 361	13 119	18 431
Engineers	1 672 559	1 399 111	1 280 067	458 788	821 279	63 774	55 270	273 448	22 836	7 412	9 214
Health diagnosing occupations	869 543	736 586	663 801	297 330	366 471	38 055	34 730	132 957	12 792	3 832	7 814
Health assessment and treating occupations	2 482 553	1 973 238	1 736 911	781 395	955 516	117 837	118 490	509 315	52 675	22 126	28 423
Teachers, librarians, and counselors	5 713 591	4 425 988	3 705 541	1 792 727	1 912 814	373 504	346 943	1 287 603	160 330	77 795	85 088
Teachers, elementary and secondary schools	3 861 446	2 890 545	2 402 543	1 084 833	1 317 710	233 183	254 819	970 901	123 784	62 693	66 530
Technical, sales, and administrative support occupations	36 718 398	29 442 025	25 878 570	11 918 139	13 960 431	1 784 721	1 778 734	7 276 373	804 987	380 165	356 447
Health technologists and technicians	1 397 189	1 092 254	941 834	463 408	478 426	75 409	75 011	304 935	34 042	16 764	13 983
Technologists and technicians, except health	2 860 046	2 339 068	2 095 668	941 026	1 154 642	128 689	114 711	520 978	51 292	20 637	20 611
Sales occupations	13 634 686	10 883 739	9 479 177	4 186 988	5 292 189	705 029	699 533	2 750 947	309 313	141 700	121 360
Supervisors and proprietors, sales occupations	3 352 054	2 599 039	2 237 471	944 940	1 292 531	175 510	186 058	753 015	85 829	42 126	33 099
Sales representatives, commodities and finance	3 941 568	3 266 912	2 951 097	1 203 346	1 747 751	157 465	158 350	674 656	69 484	27 678	31 515
Other sales occupations	6 341 064	5 017 788	4 290 609	2 038 702	2 251 907	372 054	355 125	1 323 276	154 000	71 896	56 746
Cashiers	2 533 639	1 970 275	1 659 246	832 508	826 738	158 071	152 958	563 364	67 873	33 214	22 500
Administrative support occupations, including clerical	18 826 477	15 126 964	13 361 891	6 326 717	7 035 174	875 594	889 479	3 699 513	410 340	201 064	200 493
Computer equipment operators	640 982	522 949	468 265	223 116	245 149	27 663	27 021	118 033	12 831	5 883	5 515
Secretaries, stenographers, and typists	4 582 070	3 619 594	3 168 649	1 425 749	1 742 900	220 948	229 997	962 476	105 563	49 592	52 914
Financial records processing occupations	2 315 205	1 770 857	1 530 402	681 999	848 403	114 061	126 394	544 348	60 422	32 725	39 536
Mail and message distributing occupations	990 423	802 493	729 377	379 139	350 238	35 988	37 128	187 930	19 989	12 969	13 570
Service occupations	15 295 917	11 903 251	10 003 913	5 498 502	4 505 411	936 112	963 226	3 392 666	448 251	244 214	154 003
Private household occupations	521 154	412 074	354 694	217 606	137 088	28 504	28 876	109 080	13 410	7 621	7 324
Protective service occupations	1 992 852	1 587 812	1 368 642	691 741	676 901	107 290	111 880	405 040	48 032	21 600	13 732
Police and firefighters	732 609	586 592	506 159	235 164	270 995	39 211	41 222	146 017	17 303	6 830	4 853
Service occupations, except protective and household	12 781 911	9 903 365	8 280 577	4 589 155	3 691 422	800 318	822 470	2 878 546	386 809	214 993	132 947
Food service occupations	5 167 308	4 047 906	3 380 244	1 839 682	1 540 562	336 346	331 316	1 119 402	151 778	83 441	49 525
Cleaning and building service occupations	3 127 932	2 400 228	2 012 015	1 202 200	809 815	188 889	199 324	727 704	93 807	54 522	31 537
Farming, forestry, and fishing occupations	2 839 010	1 064 252	772 290	388 281	384 009	120 329	171 633	1 774 758	97 040	72 340	687 379
Farm operators and managers	1 066 944	142 250	85 725	39 229	46 496	21 951	34 574	924 694	26 385	29 041	538 002
Farm workers and related occupations	1 590 184	859 113	650 943	331 336	319 607	90 003	118 167	731 071	59 695	35 750	143 464
Precision production, craft, and repair occupations	13 097 963	9 049 606	7 600 511	3 421 328	4 179 183	663 390	785 705	4 048 357	405 618	221 427	168 371
Mechanics and repairers	4 080 305	2 797 671	2 351 406	1 028 013	1 323 393	203 270	242 995	1 282 634	125 894	72 470	55 866
Construction trades	4 793 935	3 298 175	2 798 351	1 260 431	1 537 920	222 001	277 823	1 495 760	142 754	75 421	58 183
Precision production occupations	4 047 043	2 878 824	2 413 789	1 113 174	1 300 615	221 464	243 571	1 168 219	123 947	66 506	50 917
Operators, fabricators, and laborers	17 196 332	11 697 575	9 522 991	4 949 088	4 573 903	995 504	1 179 080	5 498 757	598 363	361 063	256 145
Machine operators and tenders, except precision	4 981 876	3 313 417	2 642 621	1 446 582	1 196 039	303 313	367 483	1 668 459	181 869	104 326	70 134
Fabricators, assemblers, inspectors, and samplers	2 922 321	1 979 275	1 595 531	820 040	775 491	180 040	203 704	943 046	104 118	62 389	43 795
Transportation occupations	3 760 910	2 599 828	2 188 915	1 087 916	1 100 999	186 157	224 756	1 161 082	119 655	77 557	61 340
Motor vehicle operators	3 580 137	2 474 796	2 091 599	1 041 306	1 050 293	174 631	208 566	1 105 341	113 194	74 142	58 948
Material moving equipment operators	968 091	557 564	425 168	201 516	223 652	56 558	75 838	410 527	40 189	26 979	21 780
Handlers, equipment cleaners, helpers, and laborers	4 563 134	3 247 491	2 670 756	1 393 034	1 277 722	269 436	307 299	1 315 643	152 532	89 812	59 096
Construction laborers	948 540	656 502	550 862	287 772	263 090	46 730	58 910	292 038	30 820	18 547	12 801
Freight, stock, and material handlers	1 576 991	1 148 188	945 415	472 854	472 561	96 807	105 966	428 803	49 818	28 324	18 609
Employed females 16 years and over	**52 976 623**	**40 999 342**	**35 296 308**	**16 988 210**	**18 308 098**	**2 793 752**	**2 909 282**	**11 977 281**	**1 363 036**	**699 125**	**734 219**
Managerial and professional specialty occupations	14 752 659	11 938 271	10 543 983	4 877 898	5 666 085	708 952	685 336	2 814 388	310 881	142 938	163 034
Executive, administrative, and managerial occupations	5 993 163	4 940 853	4 434 594	1 977 013	2 457 581	255 869	250 390	1 052 310	113 013	51 686	51 462
Officials and administrators, public administration	251 316	194 455	168 453	79 095	89 358	12 104	13 898	56 861	7 441	4 743	3 647
Management and related occupations	2 156 867	1 818 476	1 660 286	735 869	924 417	81 693	76 497	338 391	33 761	14 058	16 516
Professional specialty occupations	8 759 496	6 997 418	6 109 389	2 900 885	3 208 504	453 083	434 946	1 762 078	197 868	91 252	111 572
Engineers and natural scientists	551 261	477 889	448 485	185 667	262 818	16 158	13 246	73 372	6 001	1 928	3 135
Engineers	151 962	130 877	122 138	48 680	73 458	4 702	4 037	21 085	1 625	556	702
Health diagnosing occupations	171 791	148 269	137 875	66 033	71 842	5 092	5 302	23 522	2 087	733	1 300
Health assessment and treating occupations	2 163 863	1 713 312	1 512 741	670 826	841 915	100 207	100 364	450 551	45 528	19 707	26 507
Teachers, librarians, and counselors	3 977 806	3 058 818	2 569 154	1 205 239	1 363 915	249 176	240 488	918 988	111 089	53 976	65 062
Teachers, elementary and secondary schools	2 946 061	2 216 215	1 853 232	834 152	1 019 080	176 448	186 535	729 846	87 812	43 972	52 669
Technical, sales, and administrative support occupations	23 120 191	18 333 897	16 024 132	7 409 468	8 614 664	1 144 994	1 164 771	4 786 294	531 077	256 338	252 885
Health technologists and technicians	1 133 078	870 195	745 262	359 257	386 005	62 344	62 589	262 883	29 006	14 632	12 752
Technologists and technicians, except health	832 879	692 226	627 440	293 139	334 301	34 430	30 356	140 653	13 760	5 644	6 460
Sales occupations	6 584 290	5 193 283	4 473 886	2 042 837	2 431 049	358 541	360 856	1 391 007	158 881	73 192	64 780
Supervisors and proprietors, sales occupations	1 155 921	890 953	766 744	337 878	428 866	59 835	64 374	264 968	30 352	14 606	12 478
Sales representatives, commodities and finance	1 314 555	1 096 416	997 587	420 468	577 119	48 703	50 126	218 139	21 770	8 425	10 520
Other sales occupations	4 113 814	3 205 914	2 709 555	1 284 491	1 425 064	250 003	246 356	907 900	106 759	50 161	41 782
Cashiers	1 995 673	1 520 185	1 263 235	629 302	633 933	128 253	128 697	475 488	57 617	28 618	19 485
Administrative support occupations, including clerical	14 569 944	11 578 193	10 177 544	4 714 235	5 463 309	689 679	710 970	2 991 751	329 430	162 870	168 893
Computer equipment operators	394 508	312 607	276 325	131 098	145 227	17 993	18 289	81 901	8 844	4 176	4 232
Secretaries, stenographers, and typists	4 490 363	3 538 981	3 095 265	1 380 483	1 714 782	217 198	226 518	951 382	104 088	49 036	52 355
Financial records processing occupations	2 062 414	1 555 732	1 336 754	582 139	754 615	103 282	115 696	506 682	55 678	30 247	37 426
Mail and message distributing occupations	368 423	279 779	253 214	132 573	120 641	12 646	13 919	88 644	8 838	7 052	6 796
Service occupations	8 929 509	6 714 975	5 520 030	2 991 864	2 528 166	576 912	618 033	2 214 534	300 220	171 670	112 727
Private household occupations	494 920	390 364	335 303	205 517	129 786	27 419	27 642	104 556	12 860	7 309	7 147
Protective service occupations	310 463	257 190	224 377	121 087	103 290	16 602	16 211	53 273	6 602	2 853	1 927
Police and firefighters	66 355	56 206	50 605	27 535	23 070	2 727	2 874	10 149	1 154	422	352
Service occupations, except protective and household	8 124 126	6 067 421	4 960 350	2 665 260	2 295 090	532 891	574 180	2 056 705	280 758	161 508	103 653
Food service occupations	3 062 435	2 242 943	1 797 356	924 652	872 704	215 740	229 847	819 492	112 671	66 044	40 210
Cleaning and building service occupations	1 278 437	958 384	790 761	489 031	301 730	79 577	88 046	320 053	42 582	25 457	15 876
Farming, forestry, and fishing occupations	449 506	172 785	125 209	59 788	65 421	20 202	27 374	276 721	13 582	7 842	116 269
Farm operators and managers	149 675	21 696	15 458	6 606	8 852	2 504	3 734	127 979	2 531	2 184	79 610
Farm workers and related occupations	290 041	147 093	107 449	52 041	55 408	17 075	22 569	142 948	10 415	5 274	36 287
Precision production, craft, and repair occupations	1 235 327	891 741	750 318	377 707	372 611	67 848	73 575	343 586	36 942	21 168	17 173
Mechanics and repairers	175 669	132 906	116 511	54 999	61 512	7 808	8 587	42 763	4 111	2 217	1 773
Construction trades	131 124	90 832	76 474	38 426	38 048	6 310	8 048	40 292	4 027	2 162	2 022
Precision production occupations	923 593	665 128	555 314	283 133	272 181	53 282	56 532	258 465	28 498	16 672	13 319
Operators, fabricators, and laborers	4 489 431	2 947 673	2 332 636	1 271 485	1 061 151	274 844	340 193	1 541 758	170 334	99 169	72 131
Machine operators and tenders, except precision	2 018 059	1 282 014	994 817	583 413	411 404	123 685	163 512	736 045	81 065	45 326	30 696
Fabricators, assemblers, inspectors, and samplers	1 082 797	729 544	578 616	307 247	271 369	70 861	80 067	353 253	40 407	23 316	15 665
Transportation occupations	426 426	278 408	234 284	108 306	125 978	19 106	25 018	148 018	12 909	8 041	10 081
Motor vehicle operators	419 603	272 927	229 709	105 801	123 908	18 719	24 499	146 676	12 725	7 968	10 034
Material moving equipment operators	46 995	29 867	23 277	12 260	11 017	3 060	3 530	17 128	1 810	1 108	1 025
Handlers, equipment cleaners, helpers, and laborers	915 154	627 840	501 642	260 259	241 383	58 132	68 066	287 314	34 143	21 378	14 664
Construction laborers	36 177	24 722	20 483	10 520	9 963	1 679	2 560	11 455	1 190	736	493
Freight, stock, and material handlers	359 459	246 942	197 756	95 005	102 751	22 951	26 235	112 517	12 990	8 592	5 551

Source: U.S. Bureau of the Census, *Social and Economic Characteristics of the United States: 1990 Census of Population*, CP-2-1, Washington, D.C.: U.S. Government Printing Office, 1993, Table 20.

B4-5. Occupations of Employed Persons, by Race and Hispanic Origin: 1990

[Data based on sample and subject to sampling variability.]

United States	All persons	Race					Hispanic origin (of any race)	White, not of Hispanic origin
		White	Black	American Indian, Eskimo, or Aleut	Asian or Pacific Islander	Other race		
Employed persons 16 years and over	**115 681 202**	**96 237 561**	**11 407 803**	**728 953**	**3 411 586**	**3 895 299**	**8 981 516**	**91 447 312**
Managerial and professional specialty occupations	30 533 582	26 877 354	2 066 054	133 555	1 045 160	411 459	1 262 178	26 072 188
Executive, administrative, and managerial occupations	14 227 916	12 651 035	875 835	62 825	428 273	209 948	627 693	12 254 816
Officials and administrators, public administration	578 334	484 939	68 142	6 345	10 748	8 160	25 469	468 576
Management and related occupations	4 140 575	3 606 211	303 762	17 191	149 459	63 952	189 088	3 488 813
Professional specialty occupations	16 305 666	14 226 319	1 190 219	70 730	616 887	201 511	634 485	13 817 372
Engineers and natural scientists	3 000 976	2 635 125	126 864	9 274	201 193	28 520	96 970	2 569 523
Engineers	1 672 559	1 475 994	58 041	4 865	117 858	15 801	52 479	1 440 584
Health diagnosing occupations	869 543	754 907	28 401	1 467	77 501	7 267	35 277	728 482
Health assessment and treating occupations	2 482 553	2 124 802	213 393	10 064	110 659	23 635	76 252	2 077 587
Teachers, librarians, and counselors	5 713 591	4 963 417	512 599	28 766	131 237	77 572	238 263	4 809 953
Teachers, elementary and secondary schools	3 861 446	3 358 038	380 073	19 080	49 959	54 296	165 455	3 251 700
Technical, sales, and administrative support occupations	36 718 398	31 121 238	3 354 120	195 096	1 134 130	913 814	2 321 918	29 799 821
Health technologists and technicians	1 397 189	1 123 408	182 904	8 853	52 383	29 641	77 782	1 079 681
Technologists and technicians, except health	2 860 046	2 445 404	190 994	14 113	155 867	53 668	143 367	2 361 025
Sales occupations	13 634 686	11 984 176	875 576	63 582	400 985	310 367	808 785	11 511 646
Supervisors and proprietors, sales occupations	3 352 054	3 012 184	153 862	13 853	109 710	62 445	172 723	2 907 048
Sales representatives, commodities and finance	3 941 568	3 649 726	151 055	11 351	78 905	50 531	157 289	3 547 155
Other sales occupations	6 341 064	5 322 266	570 659	38 378	212 370	197 391	478 773	5 057 443
Cashiers	2 533 639	1 976 839	327 343	20 049	105 851	103 557	232 840	1 856 694
Administrative support occupations, including clerical	18 826 477	15 568 250	2 104 646	108 548	524 895	520 138	1 291 984	14 847 469
Computer equipment operators	640 982	511 106	86 759	3 554	23 640	15 923	40 615	488 214
Secretaries, stenographers, and typists	4 582 070	3 980 228	393 893	25 649	83 460	98 840	258 327	3 830 459
Financial records processing occupations	2 315 205	2 043 830	147 273	11 484	67 517	45 101	123 119	1 970 166
Mail and message distributing occupations	990 423	715 310	197 530	5 198	41 046	31 339	73 208	677 075
Service occupations	15 295 917	11 354 441	2 522 099	134 744	504 688	779 945	1 719 992	10 481 292
Private household occupations	521 154	312 888	136 283	3 856	14 044	54 083	119 588	251 678
Protective service occupations	1 992 852	1 580 054	312 808	17 198	29 083	53 709	134 930	1 504 544
Police and firefighters	732 609	624 642	78 005	5 930	7 596	16 436	43 644	598 591
Service occupations, except protective and household	12 781 911	9 461 499	2 073 008	113 690	461 561	672 153	1 465 474	8 725 070
Food service occupations	5 167 308	3 981 476	609 088	42 233	250 384	284 127	608 350	3 675 719
Cleaning and building service occupations	3 127 932	2 113 844	660 057	32 043	86 854	235 134	491 540	1 876 092
Farming, forestry, and fishing occupations	2 839 010	2 370 802	166 079	24 405	40 718	237 006	446 133	2 168 116
Farm operators and managers	1 066 944	1 022 746	16 660	4 255	7 679	15 604	33 300	1 005 516
Farm workers and related occupations	1 590 184	1 194 090	133 366	15 449	30 175	217 104	403 200	1 013 742
Precision production, craft, and repair occupations	13 097 963	11 257 116	930 011	99 782	273 473	537 581	1 177 553	10 648 470
Mechanics and repairers	4 080 305	3 554 246	286 565	27 650	74 673	137 171	315 039	3 385 520
Construction trades	4 793 935	4 174 722	310 992	42 638	56 341	209 242	452 936	3 942 128
Precision production occupations	4 047 043	3 368 249	324 809	27 530	141 794	184 661	395 605	3 168 249
Operators, fabricators, and laborers	17 196 332	13 256 610	2 369 440	141 371	413 417	1 015 494	2 053 742	12 277 425
Machine operators and tenders, except precision	4 981 876	3 706 366	721 735	35 625	169 521	348 629	684 988	3 389 822
Fabricators, assemblers, inspectors, and samplers	2 922 321	2 235 775	382 571	24 645	95 890	183 440	362 199	2 066 445
Transportation occupations	3 760 910	3 030 438	511 246	28 763	50 674	139 789	314 362	2 867 043
Motor vehicle operators	3 580 137	2 870 272	495 739	27 380	49 126	137 620	307 684	2 711 162
Material moving equipment operators	968 091	785 824	120 269	10 715	8 046	43 237	87 111	743 694
Handlers, equipment cleaners, helpers, and laborers	4 563 134	3 498 207	633 619	41 623	89 286	300 399	605 082	3 210 421
Construction laborers	948 540	727 176	116 549	10 986	11 419	82 410	162 235	651 253
Freight, stock, and material handlers	1 576 991	1 244 126	221 599	12 327	31 370	67 569	145 346	1 170 890
Employed females 16 years and over	**52 976 623**	**43 515 117**	**6 015 288**	**340 042**	**1 590 897**	**1 515 279**	**3 669 186**	**41 499 763**
Managerial and professional specialty occupations	14 752 659	12 741 104	1 283 844	73 848	448 538	205 325	623 927	12 348 409
Executive, administrative, and managerial occupations	5 993 163	5 202 033	484 659	31 884	179 835	94 752	278 720	5 028 901
Officials and administrators, public administration	251 316	201 382	38 849	2 820	4 454	3 811	11 588	194 171
Management and related occupations	2 156 867	1 835 280	192 955	10 586	82 290	35 756	103 345	1 771 995
Professional specialty occupations	8 759 496	7 539 071	799 185	41 964	268 703	110 573	345 207	7 319 508
Engineers and natural scientists	551 261	461 596	42 566	1 980	38 787	6 332	21 209	447 566
Engineers	151 962	125 956	11 185	541	12 264	2 016	6 190	121 964
Health diagnosing occupations	171 791	137 721	9 596	423	22 310	1 741	7 727	132 394
Health assessment and treating occupations	2 163 863	1 853 159	188 300	8 654	94 913	18 837	61 812	1 815 016
Teachers, librarians, and counselors	3 977 806	3 440 715	392 151	20 144	70 241	54 555	169 075	3 331 338
Teachers, elementary and secondary schools	2 946 061	2 541 887	308 959	14 472	38 662	42 081	128 741	2 459 000
Technical, sales, and administrative support occupations	23 120 191	19 454 638	2 330 616	134 493	636 528	563 916	1 434 647	18 638 286
Health technologists and technicians	1 133 078	920 524	148 650	7 017	35 757	21 130	55 644	889 284
Technologists and technicians, except health	832 879	688 505	76 882	4 297	48 025	15 170	41 899	663 359
Sales occupations	6 584 290	5 633 355	551 297	38 479	197 333	163 826	417 587	5 394 135
Supervisors and proprietors, sales occupations	1 155 921	1 025 665	68 822	6 098	35 101	20 235	56 425	991 276
Sales representatives, commodities and finance	1 314 555	1 192 130	67 358	4 753	31 043	19 271	59 102	1 154 046
Other sales occupations	4 113 814	3 415 560	415 117	27 628	131 189	124 320	302 060	3 248 813
Cashiers	1 995 673	1 562 480	268 886	16 528	71 840	75 939	171 625	1 473 643
Administrative support occupations, including clerical	14 569 944	12 212 254	1 553 787	84 700	355 413	363 790	919 517	11 691 508
Computer equipment operators	394 508	316 845	54 886	2 378	11 366	9 033	23 351	303 446
Secretaries, stenographers, and typists	4 490 363	3 909 921	380 866	24 934	78 838	95 804	250 655	3 764 243
Financial records processing occupations	2 062 414	1 837 858	123 890	10 443	52 787	37 436	102 477	1 776 315
Mail and message distributing occupations	368 423	258 492	83 180	2 288	14 313	10 150	22 607	247 099
Service occupations	8 929 509	6 701 294	1 508 458	79 643	259 244	380 870	863 229	6 254 384
Private household occupations	494 920	296 628	130 525	3 556	12 698	51 513	114 019	238 248
Protective service occupations	310 463	224 472	71 413	2 643	3 923	8 012	20 185	213 290
Police and firefighters	66 355	48 652	14 615	652	699	1 737	4 581	45 958
Service occupations, except protective and household	8 124 126	6 180 194	1 306 520	73 444	242 623	321 345	729 025	5 802 846
Food service occupations	3 062 435	2 507 545	325 529	26 436	106 592	96 333	223 035	2 387 604
Cleaning and building service occupations	1 278 437	814 051	308 521	13 895	40 319	101 651	212 298	710 772
Farming, forestry, and fishing occupations	449 506	383 374	21 048	3 740	8 330	33 014	59 747	357 362
Farm operators and managers	149 675	143 343	2 089	772	1 586	1 885	3 646	141 648
Farm workers and related occupations	290 041	232 000	18 074	2 662	6 561	30 744	55 354	208 059
Precision production, craft, and repair occupations	1 235 327	957 420	143 560	10 609	65 307	58 431	128 792	890 922
Mechanics and repairers	175 669	139 398	25 220	1 332	4 492	5 227	11 970	132 964
Construction trades	131 124	110 834	11 938	1 550	2 178	4 624	9 876	105 794
Precision production occupations	923 593	703 036	105 934	7 648	58 598	48 377	106 538	648 197
Operators, fabricators, and laborers	4 489 431	3 277 287	727 762	37 709	172 950	273 723	558 844	3 010 400
Machine operators and tenders, except precision	2 018 059	1 410 339	355 868	15 613	96 039	140 200	283 994	1 276 251
Fabricators, assemblers, inspectors, and samplers	1 082 797	782 067	174 765	9 008	47 664	69 293	140 821	714 412
Transportation occupations	426 426	345 352	63 642	4 650	3 688	9 094	22 356	333 025
Motor vehicle operators	419 603	340 356	62 240	4 538	3 541	8 928	21 943	328 241
Material moving equipment operators	46 995	35 735	8 228	605	507	1 920	4 332	33 544
Handlers, equipment cleaners, helpers, and laborers	915 154	703 794	125 259	7 833	25 052	53 216	107 341	653 168
Construction laborers	36 177	28 614	4 294	497	562	2 210	4 257	26 708
Freight, stock, and material handlers	359 459	294 616	41 876	2 819	8 021	12 127	27 511	280 178

Source: U.S. Bureau of the Census, *Social and Economic Characteristics of the United States: 1990 Census of Population*, CP-2-1, Washington, D.C.: U.S. Government Printing Office, 1993, Table 45.

B4-6. Women Aged 25 to 54 Who Left and Then Entered Jobs, by the Broad Occupation Group of the Job Left and the Job Entered: 1990 to 1992

[Numbers in thousands; data relate only to the person's first spell of joblessness during the period]

Occupation of job left	Occupation of job entered						
	Total	Executive, professional	Technical, sales	Protective service, other service	Farming, forestry, fishing	Precision production, craft	Machine operator, laborer
Total	7,429	1,572	3,055	1,556	153	111	982
Executive, professional	1,734	1,073	511	113	6	9	23
Technical, sales	2,888	349	1,987	317	13	10	211
Protective service, other service	1,529	110	303	947	9	30	130
Farming, forestry, fishing	159	-	32	8	100	-	19
Precision production, craft	152	16	34	23	6	48	24
Machine operator, laborer..............	961	25	188	148	18	14	569

Note: Approximately 5,000 women did not report the occupation they left.

- Represents zero.

Source: Wilfred Masumura and Paul Ryscavage, U.S. Bureau of the Census, *Dynamics of Economic Well-Being: Labor Force and Income, 1990 to 1992,* Current Population Reports, Series P70-40, Washington, D.C.: U.S. Government Printing Office, November 1994, Table I.

B4-7. Female Employees, Median Years of Tenure, and Median Age of Employees, for Selected Occupations: 1987

(Numbers in thousands. Number employed includes both males and females)

Occupation	Number employed	Percent Female	Median years of—	
			Tenure	Age
All employees.......................	112,440	44.8	6.6	35.8
Teachers:				
Secondary school	1,172	54.3	12.5	39.8
Elementary school.....................	1,329	85.3	12.4	39.0
Licensed practical nurses	406	97.0	10.3	36.9
Registered nurses	1,588	95.1	9.3	36.5
Hairdressers	743	89.3	8.9	35.5
Accountants and auditors	1,255	45.7	7.6	35.0
Secretaries	4,107	99.1	7.5	36.1
Bookkeepers, accountants, and auditor clerks ..	2,004	92.4	7.1	38.9
Sewing machine operators	755	91.0	6.6	37.8
Private household cleaners and servants	472	96.0	6.2	45.9
Nursing aides, orderlies, and attendants	1,324	90.4	5.6	36.5
Typists..............................	843	94.6	5.2	32.8
Computer operators.....................	911	66.0	4.8	31.3
Maids and housemen	602	84.6	4.6	38.2
Waiters and waitresses	1,383	85.1	4.2	25.9
Bank tellers..........................	467	90.6	3.8	28.4
Cooks, except short-order.................	1,627	50.1	3.8	29.3
Receptionists.........................	766	97.5	3.3	31.4
Child care workers:				
Private household	405	96.9	2.7	21.9
Not private household	827	96.0	2.7	34.2
Cashiers	2,286	83.0	2.4	24.4

Note: Number of employed persons and percent female refer to monthly averages for 1987. Median years of tenure and age refer to occupations as of January 1987. Tenure refers to the cumulative number of years a person has worked in his or her current occupation, regardless of the number of employers, interruptions in employment, or time spent in other occupations.

Source: Number of employed persons and employed females are from U.S. Bureau of the Census, Statistical Abstract of the United States, 1989, table 642. Occupational tenure and median age are from Max L. Carey, "Occupational Tenure in 1987: Many Workers Have Remained in their Fields," Monthly Labor Review, Vol. 111, No. 10 (October 1988), table 3. Data source is the January 1987 Current Population Survey; standard errors for the medians shown in this table are not available from the published article.

Source: U.S. Bureau of the Census, *Work and Family Patterns of American Women,* Current Population Reports, Series P-23, No. 165, Washington, D.C.: U.S. Government Printing Office, 1990, Table J.

B4-8. Representation of Women in the U.S. Nonagricultural Sector, by Type of Employment: 1975 to 1990

[Numbers in thousands]

Year	All employed		Wage-and-salary		Self-employed	
	Number	Percent	Number	Percent	Number	Percent
1975	95,398	43.2	88,301	44.8	7,097	23.7
1976	98,165	43.8	90,632	45.3	7,534	25.3
1977	101,137	44.0	93,059	45.6	8,078	25.7
1978	104,740	44.7	96,300	46.3	8,440	26.2
1979	106,967	45.0	97,802	46.6	9,164	27.5
1980	110,252	45.3	100,946	46.9	9,306	28.0
1981	111,294	45.4	101,552	47.0	9,741	28.4
1982	110,836	45.5	100,663	47.2	10,173	28.3
1983	112,426	45.9	102,104	47.5	10,322	29.5
1984	115,806	46.3	105,300	48.0	10,506	29.6
1985	118,061	46.3	107,574	47.9	10,487	30.1
1986	120,287	46.5	109,511	48.1	10,777	30.4
1987	122,585	46.8	111,174	48.3	11,410	31.7
1988	124,944	47.1	113,043	48.6	11,902	32.7
1989	126,364	47.1	114,493	48.6	11,871	32.9
1990	127,193	47.2	114,838	48.8	12,355	32.3

Source: Theresa J. Devine, "Characteristics of Self-Employed Women in the United States," *Monthly Labor Review*, March 1994, Table 2.

B4-9. Percent Distribution of Workers, by Gender, Type of Employment, Occupation, and Industry of Employment: 1975 and 1990

Occupation or industry[1]	Women				Men			
	1975[2]		1990		1975[2]		1990	
	Wage-and-salary	Self-employed	Wage-and-salary	Self-employed	Wage-and-salary	Self-employed	Wage-and-salary	Self-employed
Major occupational group								
Executive, administrative, and managerial	4.8	18.1	10.5	16.9	10.4	28.7	11.9	25.4
Professional specialty	14.0	18.1	14.7	14.4	10.4	15.5	11.3	15.5
Technicians and related support	1.5	.7	3.6	.6	2.7	.2	3.3	.9
Sales	11.7	21.1	13.1	20.0	8.7	24.0	9.9	22.9
Administrative support, including clerical	31.8	7.8	28.8	11.5	6.7	.8	6.8	1.0
Private household	3.2	1.1	1.5	(3)	(3)	(3)	(3)	(3)
Protective services	.2	(3)	.7	(3)	2.9	.1	3.2	.1
Other services	17.5	25.7	15.7	29.1	7.7	2.9	8.8	3.5
Farming, forestry, and fishing	.1	(3)	.1	.2	1.3	.8	1.0	.6
Precision production, craft, and repair	1.5	4.9	2.2	4.2	20.6	20.5	19.6	21.4
Machine operators, assemblers, and inspectors	10.4	2.0	6.6	1.3	11.8	1.9	8.9	2.0
Transportation and material moving	.6	.4	.9	.6	8.4	3.9	7.7	5.4
Handlers, equipment cleaners, helpers, and laborers	2.5	.2	1.7	.5	8.1	.4	7.7	1.1
Major industry group								
Construction	.9	1.0	1.2	3.0	9.4	20.4	10.3	22.3
Mining	.2	.1	.3	.1	1.4	.4	1.1	.5
Manufacturing	17.7	3.1	13.3	5.3	30.4	7.3	24.9	6.0
Transportation, communications, and utilities	4.0	1.4	4.4	2.0	10.3	4.1	9.7	5.5
Wholesale trade	2.3	1.2	2.7	2.7	5.0	6.7	5.0	6.5
Retail trade	21.6	31.9	20.2	23.5	14.3	24.2	16.0	16.5
Finance, insurance, and real estate	6.7	4.4	8.6	5.5	4.2	6.7	4.6	7.4
Business and repair services	2.4	8.3	4.9	15.4	3.3	9.9	6.5	14.6
Personal services	7.0	29.6	5.2	22.1	1.8	4.5	2.1	4.1
Professional services	31.8	16.9	33.1	19.0	12.2	14.0	12.6	14.1
Entertainment and recreation services	1.1	2.1	1.3	1.5	1.4	1.7	1.6	2.4
Public administration	4.3	(3)	4.8	(3)	6.3	(3)	5.7	(3)

[1] Occupations are presented in terms of 1980 Major Occupational Groups. Industries are defined in terms of 1980 Major Industry Codes.
[2] See text for discussion of occupation assignments for 1975.
[3] Less than 0.1 percent in the group.

Source: Theresa J. Devine, "Characteristics of Self-Employed Women in the United States," *Monthly Labor Review*, March 1994, Table 7.

B4-10. Percent Increase in Women-Owned Firms and All U.S. Firms, by Legal Form of Organization: 1982 to 1987

Legal form of organization	Percent Increase	
	Women-owned firms	All U.S. firms
Individual proprietorships...............	55.8	28.0
Partnerships	16.1	10.4
Subchapter S corporations	165.5	106.4
Other corporations	(NA)	4.1

Source: U.S. Bureau of the Census, *Women-Owned Businesses: 1987 Economic Censuses*, WB87-1, Washington, D.C.: U.S. Government Printing Office, August 1990, Table A.

B4-11. Ten Largest Major Industry Groups in Receipts for Women-Owned Firms: 1987

SIC code	Major industry group	Firms (number)	Receipts (million dollars)
51	Wholesale trade--nondurable goods	39 514	24 008
59	Miscellaneous retail..............	546 353	21 189
55	Automotive dealers and service stations	20 942	20 224
73	Business services	690 494	18 936
50	Wholesale trade--durable goods...	42 999	18 797
54	Food stores....................	48 469	14 428
58	Eating and drinking places........	90 848	14 167
65	Real estate	335 429	12 641
72	Personal services	561 695	10 289
80	Health services	235 318	9 618

Source: U.S. Bureau of the Census, *Women-Owned Businesses: 1987 Economic Censuses*, WB87-1, Washington, D.C.: U.S. Government Printing Office, August 1990, Table B.

B4-12. Average Receipts per Firm for Women-Owned Firms, by Industry Division: 1987

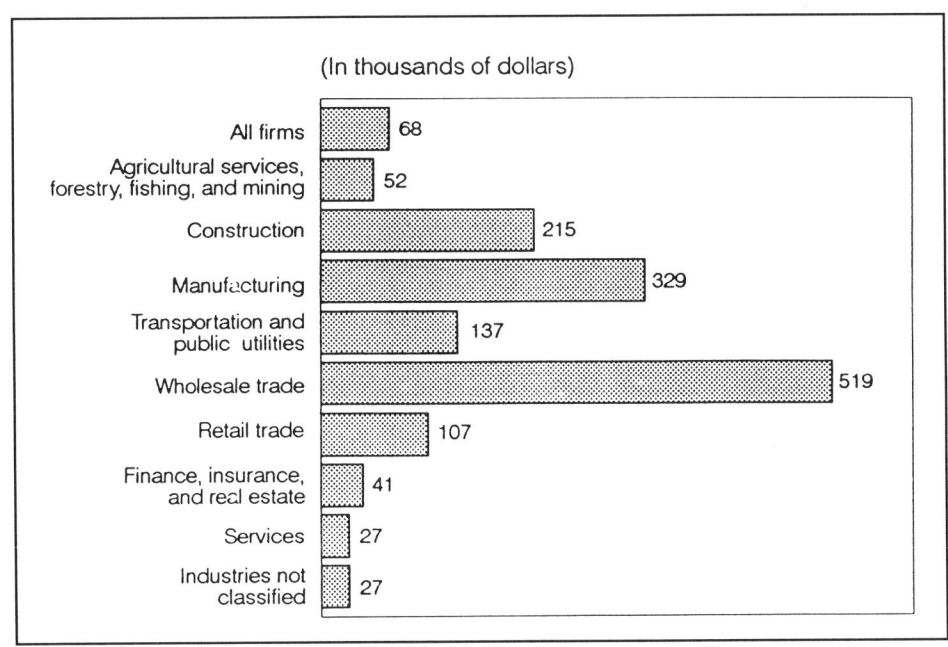

Source: U.S. Bureau of the Census, *Survey of Women-Owned Businesses*, MB92-5PM, Figure 1.

B4-13. Major Industry Groups of Minority-Owned Firms, by Sex and Race: 1987

[Detail may not add to total because of rounding and because a firm may be included in more than one minority groups. This table is based on the 1972 SIC system.]

SIC code	Major industry group and minority	All firms		Firms with paid employees				Relative standard error of estimate (percent)[1] for column—			
		Firms (number)	Sales and receipts ($1,000)	Firms (number)	Sales and receipts ($1,000)	Employees (number)	Annual payroll ($1,000)	A	B	C	D
		A	B	C	D	E	F	A	B	C	D
	All Industries	1 213 750	77 839 943	248 149	56 463 624	836 483	9 508 592	-	-	-	-
	Minority men	825 441	59 846 993	189 521	43 488 036	623 427	7 180 669	-	-	-	-
	Minority women	388 309	17 992 950	58 628	12 975 588	213 056	2 327 923	-	-	1	-
	Black	424 165	19 762 876	70 815	14 130 420	220 467	2 761 105	-	-	-	-
	Men	265 887	13 232 364	51 518	9 289 084	147 520	1 820 396	-	-	-	-
	Women	158 278	6 530 512	19 297	4 841 336	72 947	940 709	-	-	-	-
	Hispanic	422 373	24 731 600	82 908	17 729 432	264 846	3 243 342	-	-	1	-
	Men	307 348	20 403 191	66 907	14 715 111	210 749	2 653 099	-	-	1	-
	Women	115 025	4 328 409	16 001	3 014 321	54 097	590 243	1	1	1	1
	American Indian and Alaska Native	21 380	911 279	3 739	602 789	8 956	109 271	1	1	3	1
	Men	15 072	711 166	2 881	468 016	6 660	85 144	1	1	3	1
	Women	6 308	200 113	858	134 773	2 296	24 127	3	2	5	2
	Asian and Pacific Islander	355 331	33 124 326	92 718	24 501 338	351 345	3 501 917	-	-	-	-
	Men	243 442	25 988 493	69 675	19 370 068	264 873	2 698 681	-	-	-	-
	Women	111 889	7 135 833	23 043	5 131 270	86 472	803 236	1	-	1	-

Source: U.S. Bureau of the Census, *Survey of Minority-Owned Business Enterprises: 1987 Economic Censuses,* WB87-4, Washington, D.C.: U.S. Government Printing Office, August 1991, Table 1.

B4-14. Average Receipts per Firm, by Race, Hispanic Origin, and Sex: 1987

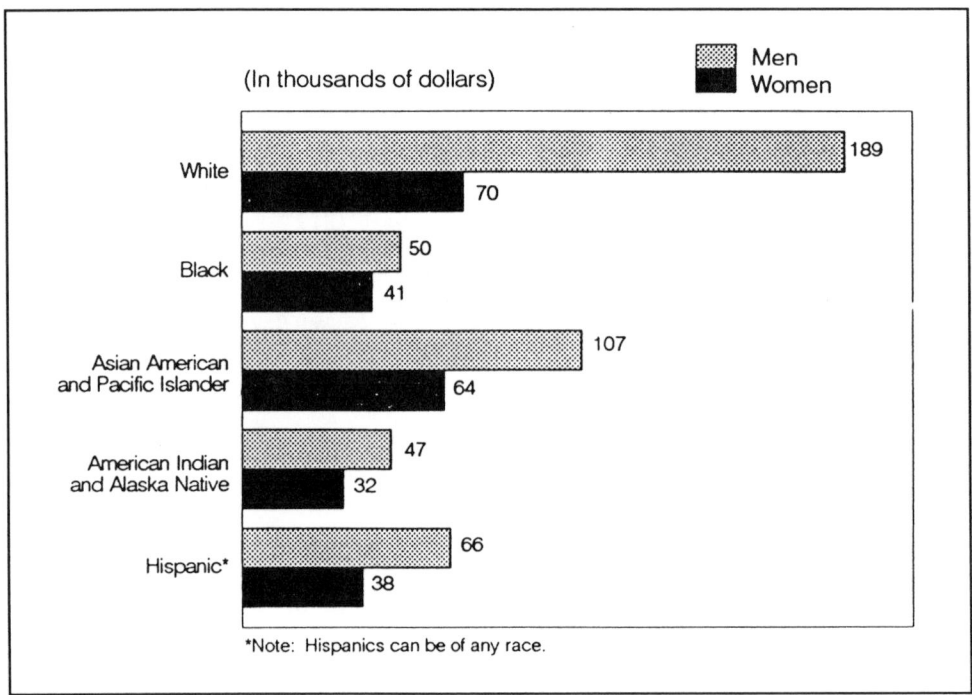

Source: U.S. Bureau of the Census, *Survey of Minority-Owned Business Enterprises,* MB92-6PM, Figure 1.

B4-15. Union and Non-Union Workers, by Occupation and Sex: 1986–87

Occupation	Total		Union*		Non–Union*	
	Workers	Percent	Workers	Percent	Workers	Percent
WOMEN	38,640,000	100.0	6,160,000	100.0	30,780,000	100.0
Executive, Administrative, & Managerial	4,550,000	11.8	310,000	5.0	4,060,000	13.2
Professional Specialty	5,880,000	15.2	1,950,000	31.6	3,690,000	12.0
Technicians & Related Support	1,460,000	3.8	170,000	2.7	1,240,000	4.0
Sales	4,240,000	11.0	310,000	5.1	3,600,000	11.7
Administrative Support	12,060,000	31.2	1,650,000	26.8	9,980,000	32.4
Service	5,980,000	15.5	700,000	11.3	4,910,000	16.0
Private Household Service	460,000	1.2	4,000	0.1	420,000	1.4
Protective Service	180,000	0.5	80,000	1.2	90,000	0.3
Food Preparation & Service	2,180,000	5.6	170,000	2.7	1,890,000	6.1
Health Service	1,560,000	4.0	240,000	3.8	1,220,000	4.0
Cleaning & Building Service (not Household)	910,000	2.3	150,000	2.4	710,000	2.3
Personal Service	700,000	1.8	60,000	1.0	590,000	1.9
Precision Production, Craft, & Repair	950,000	2.5	200,000	3.3	740,000	2.4
Operators, Assemblers, & Fabricators	2,690,000	7.0	680,000	11.1	1,940,000	6.3
Transportation, Handlers, & Laborers	830,000	2.1	190,000	3.1	610,000	2.0
Sample Size	8,294		1,326		6,597	
MEN	43,930,000	100.0	10,030,000	100.0	31,180,000	100.0
Executive, Administrative, & Managerial	6,220,000	14.2	570,000	5.2	5,520,000	17.7
Professional Specialty	5,260,000	12.0	1,120,000	10.2	4,010,000	12.9
Technicians & Related Support	1,630,000	3.7	310,000	2.8	1,260,000	4.1
Sales	4,470,000	10.2	280,000	2.6	3,960,000	12.7
Administrative Support	3,100,000	7.1	970,000	8.8	2,030,000	6.5
Service	4,050,000	9.2	1,180,000	10.7	2,600,000	8.3
Private Household Service	30,000	0.1	0	0.0	30,000	0.1
Protective Service	1,390,000	3.2	670,000	6.0	680,000	2.2
Food Preparation & Service	1,060,000	2.4	120,000	1.0	810,000	2.6
Health Service	130,000	0.3	50,000	0.5	70,000	0.2
Cleaning & Building Service (not Household)	1,290,000	2.9	350,000	3.1	860,000	2.8
Personal Service	150,000	0.3	10,000	0.1	140,000	0.5
Precision Production, Craft, & Repair	9,080,000	20.7	2,910,000	26.4	5,880,000	18.9
Operators, Assemblers, & Fabricators	4,040,000	9.2	1,610,000	14.6	2,270,000	7.3
Transportation, Handlers, & Laborers	6,070,000	13.8	2,070,000	18.8	3,640,000	11.7
Sample Size	8,939		2,277		6,320	

* Union and Non–Union totals do not add to the overall total because of observations with missing union status.
Source: IWPR tabulations based on the 1986 and 1987 Panels of the Survey of Income and Program Participation.

Source: Roberta Spalter-Roth, Heidi Hartmann, and Nancy Collins, Institute For Women's Policy Research (Washington, D.C.), *What Do Unions Do For Women?*, unpublished (contract for the U.S. Department of Labor, Women's Bureau), January 21, 1994, Appendix Table 1.

B4-16. Estimates of Resident Armed Forces, by Age, Sex, Race, and Hispanic Origin: July 1, 1992

Age	Total			Race											
				White			Black			American Indian, Eskimo, and Aleut			Asian and Pacific Islander		
	Total	Male	Female	Total	Male	Female	Total	Male	Female	Total	Male	Female	Total	Male	Female
All ages	1584 873	1411 964	172 909	1225 638	1108 697	116 941	309 101	258 004	51 097	9 963	8 557	1 426	40 151	36 706	3 445
15 to 19 years	111 658	98 467	13 191	89 614	80 034	9 580	19 328	16 113	3 215	844	717	127	1 872	1 603	269
15 years	-	-	-	-	-	-	-	-	-	-	-	-	-	-	-
16 years	-	-	-	-	-	-	-	-	-	-	-	-	-	-	-
17 years	2 900	2 386	514	2 250	1 881	369	560	434	126	35	25	10	55	46	9
18 years	30 603	26 689	3 914	24 654	21 807	2 847	5 230	4 268	962	208	173	35	511	441	70
19 years	78 155	69 392	8 763	62 710	56 346	6 364	13 538	11 411	2 127	601	519	82	1 306	1 116	190
20 to 24 years	512 015	454 355	57 660	397 895	358 892	39 003	101 060	84 101	16 959	3 479	2 943	536	9 581	8 419	1 162
20 years	104 872	93 662	11 210	82 806	74 974	7 832	19 605	16 550	3 055	739	627	112	1 722	1 511	211
21 years	123 478	109 883	13 595	96 536	87 291	9 245	23 907	19 958	3 949	918	783	135	2 117	1 851	266
22 years	111 457	98 914	12 543	86 582	78 076	8 506	22 022	18 382	3 640	775	647	128	2 078	1 809	269
23 years	91 370	80 721	10 649	70 661	63 547	7 114	18 270	15 044	3 226	552	475	77	1 887	1 655	232
24 years	80 838	71 175	9 683	61 310	55 004	6 306	17 256	14 167	3 089	495	411	84	1 777	1 593	184
25 to 29 years	347 745	306 301	41 444	263 947	237 048	26 899	73 568	60 130	13 438	1 683	1 396	285	8 547	7 725	822
25 years	73 933	64 873	9 080	56 088	50 103	5 985	15 655	12 818	2 837	407	339	68	1 803	1 613	190
26 years	71 280	62 724	8 556	53 835	48 327	5 508	15 322	12 504	2 818	340	282	58	1 783	1 611	172
27 years	70 007	61 733	8 274	53 045	47 651	5 394	14 841	12 195	2 646	336	274	62	1 785	1 613	172
28 years	67 951	60 024	7 927	51 707	46 581	5 126	14 375	11 775	2 600	292	246	46	1 577	1 422	155
29 years	64 574	56 947	7 627	49 292	44 386	4 906	13 375	10 838	2 537	308	257	51	1 599	1 466	133
30 to 34 years	272 855	242 328	30 527	207 126	187 279	19 847	57 117	47 222	9 895	1 447	1 242	205	7 165	6 585	580
30 years	61 196	54 109	7 087	46 670	42 093	4 577	12 648	10 328	2 320	279	238	41	1 599	1 450	149
31 years	58 718	52 161	6 557	44 640	40 441	4 199	12 318	10 123	2 195	277	238	39	1 483	1 359	124
32 years	54 091	48 034	6 057	40 815	36 987	3 828	11 549	9 457	2 092	286	256	30	1 441	1 334	107
33 years	50 794	45 121	5 673	38 339	34 552	3 787	10 786	9 042	1 744	312	269	43	1 357	1 258	99
34 years	48 056	42 903	5 153	36 682	33 206	3 456	9 816	8 272	1 544	293	241	52	1 285	1 184	101
35 to 39 years	200 339	180 176	20 163	152 471	138 399	14 072	39 278	33 725	5 553	1 510	1 338	172	7 080	6 714	366
35 years	45 442	40 615	4 827	34 700	31 387	3 313	9 131	7 750	1 381	276	242	34	1 335	1 236	99
36 years	42 796	38 366	4 430	32 562	29 532	3 030	8 590	7 307	1 283	292	259	33	1 352	1 268	84
37 years	41 023	36 946	4 077	31 247	28 406	2 841	8 046	6 922	1 124	379	338	41	1 351	1 280	71
38 years	38 141	34 424	3 717	28 949	26 344	2 605	7 371	6 364	1 007	312	281	31	1 509	1 435	74
39 years	32 937	29 825	3 112	25 013	22 730	2 283	6 140	5 382	758	251	218	33	1 533	1 495	38
40 to 44 years	99 805	92 063	7 742	79 593	73 785	5 808	15 033	13 343	1 690	754	669	85	4 425	4 266	159
40 years	27 440	25 114	2 326	21 037	19 313	1 724	4 762	4 218	544	191	175	16	1 450	1 408	42
41 years	23 108	21 176	1 932	18 071	16 632	1 439	3 833	3 390	443	166	151	15	1 038	1 003	35
42 years	19 491	18 004	1 487	15 658	14 539	1 119	2 797	2 486	311	154	132	22	882	847	35
43 years	16 189	15 062	1 127	13 355	12 492	863	2 109	1 889	220	147	130	17	578	551	27
44 years	13 577	12 707	870	11 472	10 809	663	1 532	1 360	172	96	81	15	477	457	20
45 to 49 years	32 784	31 035	1 749	28 328	26 929	1 399	3 141	2 848	293	219	207	12	1 096	1 051	45
45 years	12 150	11 454	696	10 471	9 922	549	1 186	1 060	126	94	87	7	399	385	14
46 years	7 031	6 643	388	6 039	5 729	310	710	641	69	46	43	3	236	230	6
47 years	5 641	5 362	279	4 884	4 656	228	517	477	40	33	33	-	207	196	11
48 years	4 445	4 236	209	3 847	3 677	170	420	386	34	32	31	1	146	142	4
49 years	3 517	3 340	177	3 087	2 945	142	308	284	24	14	13	1	108	98	10
50 to 54 years	6 255	5 886	369	5 390	5 110	280	528	475	53	36	32	4	301	269	32
50 years	2 272	2 153	119	1 931	1 840	91	229	210	19	14	12	2	98	91	7
51 years	1 583	1 489	94	1 352	1 285	67	135	119	16	11	11	-	85	74	11
52 years	1 172	1 096	76	1 041	961	60	72	64	8	9	7	2	50	44	6
53 years	728	679	49	612	576	36	67	60	7	1	1	-	48	42	6
54 years	500	469	31	454	428	26	25	22	3	1	1	-	20	18	2
55 to 59 years	1 144	1 088	56	1 027	981	46	41	40	1	9	9	-	67	58	9
55 years	388	369	19	346	332	14	19	18	1	2	2	-	21	17	4
56 years	273	260	13	241	229	12	10	10	-	5	5	-	17	16	1
57 years	208	196	12	194	185	9	3	3	-	1	1	-	10	7	3
58 years	166	159	7	146	140	6	3	3	-	-	-	-	17	16	1
59 years	109	104	5	100	95	5	6	6	-	1	1	-	2	2	-
60 to 64 years	273	265	8	247	240	7	7	7	-	2	2	-	17	16	1
60 years	103	100	3	92	89	3	4	4	-	-	-	-	7	7	-
61 years	78	74	4	69	66	3	2	2	-	2	2	-	5	4	1
62 years	45	44	1	42	41	1	-	-	-	-	-	-	3	3	-
63 years	25	25	-	24	24	-	1	1	-	-	-	-	-	-	-
64 years	22	22	-	20	20	-	-	-	-	-	-	-	2	2	-

¹Persons of Hispanic origin may be of any race.

B4-16. Estimates of Resident Armed Forces, by Age, Sex, Race, and Hispanic Origin: July 1, 1992 *(continued)*

| Hispanic origin[1] | | | Not of Hispanic origin, by race | | | | | | | | | | | | Age |
| | | | White | | | Black | | | American Indian, Eskimo, and Aleut | | | Asian and Pacific Islander | | | |
Total	Male	Female	Total	Male	Female	Total	Male	Female	Total	Male	Female	Total	Male	Female	
83 014	74 612	8 402	1151 180	1041 815	109 365	304 583	253 932	50 651	8 522	7 273	1 249	37 574	34 332	3 242	All ages
8 177	7 203	974	82 139	73 446	8 693	18 888	15 726	3 162	715	604	111	1 739	1 488	251	15 to 19 years
-	-	-	-	-	-	-	-	-	-	-	-	-	-	-	15 years
-	-	-	-	-	-	-	-	-	-	-	-	-	-	-	16 years
231	189	42	2 036	1 707	329	549	425	124	32	22	10	52	43	9	17 years
2 359	2 030	329	22 484	19 939	2 545	5 106	4 163	943	178	147	31	476	410	66	18 years
5 587	4 984	603	57 619	51 800	5 819	13 233	11 138	2 095	505	435	70	1 211	1 035	176	19 years
31 773	28 323	3 450	369 141	333 250	35 891	99 344	82 571	16 773	2 901	2 438	463	8 856	7 773	1 083	20 to 24 years
7 241	6 477	764	76 208	69 070	7 138	19 210	16 195	3 015	619	523	96	1 594	1 397	197	20 years
8 126	7 226	900	89 161	80 731	8 430	23 465	19 566	3 899	765	648	117	1 961	1 712	249	21 years
6 845	6 116	729	80 394	72 541	7 853	21 655	18 054	3 601	645	534	111	1 918	1 669	249	22 years
5 265	4 707	578	65 898	59 305	6 593	17 989	14 794	3 195	458	392	66	1 740	1 523	217	23 years
4 276	3 797	479	57 480	51 603	5 877	17 025	13 962	3 063	414	341	73	1 643	1 472	171	24 years
16 417	14 676	1 741	249 276	223 939	25 337	72 672	59 326	13 346	1 427	1 180	247	7 953	7 180	773	25 to 29 years
3 629	3 228	401	52 831	47 225	5 606	15 459	12 643	2 816	344	285	59	1 670	1 492	178	25 years
3 396	3 038	358	50 802	45 615	5 187	15 138	12 339	2 799	287	237	50	1 857	1 495	162	26 years
3 313	2 956	357	50 068	45 013	5 075	14 659	12 032	2 627	285	232	53	1 662	1 500	162	27 years
3 122	2 798	324	48 906	44 071	4 835	14 205	11 622	2 583	249	209	40	1 469	1 324	145	28 years
2 957	2 656	301	46 649	42 015	4 634	13 211	10 690	2 521	262	217	45	1 495	1 369	126	29 years
12 585	11 401	1 184	195 894	177 111	18 783	56 403	46 574	9 829	1 245	1 062	183	6 728	6 180	548	30 to 34 years
2 743	2 466	277	44 223	39 896	4 327	12 494	10 188	2 306	239	202	37	1 497	1 357	140	30 years
2 797	2 538	259	42 133	38 167	3 966	12 159	9 978	2 181	235	201	34	1 394	1 277	117	31 years
2 448	2 212	236	38 634	35 019	3 615	11 410	9 332	2 078	247	220	27	1 352	1 251	101	32 years
2 411	2 190	221	36 188	32 600	3 588	10 650	8 919	1 731	270	231	39	1 275	1 181	94	33 years
2 186	1 995	191	34 716	31 429	3 287	9 690	8 157	1 533	254	208	46	1 210	1 114	96	34 years
9 132	8 416	716	144 438	131 007	13 431	38 773	33 257	5 516	1 318	1 165	153	6 678	6 331	347	35 to 39 years
2 118	1 935	183	32 819	29 670	3 149	9 011	7 641	1 370	239	208	31	1 255	1 161	94	35 years
2 049	1 912	137	30 744	27 835	2 909	8 475	7 199	1 276	254	225	29	1 274	1 195	79	36 years
1 881	1 734	147	29 594	26 885	2 709	7 944	6 827	1 117	330	293	37	1 274	1 207	67	37 years
1 664	1 546	118	27 494	24 995	2 499	7 283	6 281	1 002	274	247	27	1 426	1 355	71	38 years
1 420	1 289	131	23 787	21 622	2 165	6 060	5 309	751	221	192	29	1 449	1 413	36	39 years
3 913	3 637	276	76 191	70 633	5 558	14 828	13 150	1 678	670	593	77	4 203	4 050	153	40 to 44 years
1 204	1 133	71	19 993	18 334	1 659	4 698	4 157	541	168	154	14	1 377	1 336	41	40 years
929	858	71	17 261	15 887	1 374	3 783	3 343	440	148	134	14	987	954	33	41 years
759	697	62	14 999	13 936	1 063	2 758	2 449	309	137	118	19	838	804	34	42 years
592	554	38	12 838	12 009	829	2 080	1 862	218	131	115	16	548	522	26	43 years
429	395	34	11 100	10 467	633	1 509	1 339	170	86	72	14	453	434	19	44 years
858	812	46	27 580	26 226	1 354	3 103	2 810	293	201	190	11	1 042	997	45	45 to 49 years
321	301	20	10 194	9 664	530	1 171	1 045	126	85	79	6	379	365	14	45 years
207	196	11	5 857	5 558	299	701	632	69	42	39	3	224	218	6	46 years
162	156	6	4 743	4 521	222	509	469	40	30	30	-	197	186	11	47 years
91	87	4	3 768	3 602	166	417	383	34	30	29	1	139	135	4	48 years
77	72	5	3 018	2 881	137	305	281	24	14	13	1	103	93	10	49 years
135	124	11	5 271	5 002	269	524	471	53	34	30	4	291	259	32	50 to 54 years
41	36	5	1 896	1 810	86	227	208	19	13	11	2	95	88	7	50 years
38	36	2	1 319	1 254	65	134	118	16	10	10	-	82	71	11	51 years
26	26	-	1 018	958	60	71	63	8	9	7	2	48	42	6	52 years
17	13	4	597	565	32	67	60	7	1	1	-	46	40	6	53 years
13	13	-	441	415	26	25	22	3	1	1	-	20	18	2	54 years
18	14	4	1 009	967	42	41	40	1	9	9	-	67	58	9	55 to 59 years
6	4	2	340	328	12	19	18	1	2	2	-	21	17	4	55 years
1	1	-	240	228	12	10	10	-	5	5	-	17	16	1	56 years
7	5	2	187	180	7	3	3	-	1	1	-	10	7	3	57 years
2	2	-	144	138	6	3	3	-	-	-	-	17	16	-	58 years
2	2	-	98	93	5	6	6	-	1	1	-	2	2	-	59 years
6	6	-	241	234	7	7	7	-	2	2	-	17	16	1	60 to 64 years
3	3	-	89	86	3	4	4	-	-	-	-	7	7	-	60 years
-	-	-	69	66	3	2	2	-	2	2	-	5	4	1	61 years
-	-	-	42	41	1	-	-	-	-	-	-	3	3	-	62 years
1	1	-	23	23	-	1	1	-	-	-	-	-	-	-	63 years
2	2	-	18	18	-	-	-	-	-	-	-	2	2	-	64 years

[1]Persons of Hispanic origin may be of any race.

Source: Jennifer Cheeseman Day, U.S. Bureau of the Census, *Population Projections of the United States, by Age, Sex, Race, and Hispanic Origin: 1993 to 2050,* Series P25-1104, Washington, D.C.: Government Printing Office, November 1993, Table D-2.

B4-17. Estimates of Armed Forces Overseas, by Age, Sex, Race, and Hispanic Origin: July 1, 1992

Age	Total			Race											
				White			Black			American Indian, Eskimo, and Aleut			Asian and Pacific Islander		
	Total	Male	Female	Total	Male	Female	Total	Male	Female	Total	Male	Female	Total	Male	Female
All ages	379 961	332 822	47 139	276 896	247 706	29 190	90 851	74 200	16 651	2 140	1 786	354	10 074	9 130	944
15 to 19 years	18 599	16 360	2 239	14 123	12 627	1 496	4 055	3 371	684	131	109	22	290	253	37
15 years	-	-	-	-	-	-	-	-	-	-	-	-	-	-	-
16 years	-	-	-	-	-	-	-	-	-	-	-	-	-	-	-
17 years	6	5	1	3	3	-	2	1	1	-	-	-	1	1	-
18 years	2 988	2 572	416	2 210	1 939	271	701	572	129	21	16	5	56	45	11
19 years	15 605	13 783	1 822	11 910	10 685	1 225	3 352	2 798	554	110	93	17	233	207	26
20 to 24 years	125 976	110 053	15 923	95 314	84 990	10 324	27 692	22 533	5 159	746	622	124	2 224	1 908	316
20 years	27 773	24 466	3 307	21 499	19 264	2 235	5 670	4 679	991	189	162	27	415	361	54
21 years	30 291	26 564	3 727	23 225	20 775	2 450	6 405	5 221	1 184	178	153	25	483	415	68
22 years	26 042	22 704	3 338	19 749	17 596	2 153	5 674	4 592	1 082	151	123	28	468	393	75
23 years	21 854	19 087	2 767	16 391	14 600	1 791	4 919	4 012	907	109	95	14	435	380	55
24 years	20 016	17 232	2 784	14 450	12 755	1 695	5 024	4 029	995	119	89	30	423	359	64
25 to 29 years	88 522	76 612	11 910	62 983	56 012	6 971	23 015	18 361	4 654	385	319	66	2 139	1 920	219
25 years	19 201	16 550	2 651	13 900	12 288	1 612	4 828	3 843	985	84	72	12	389	347	42
26 years	17 993	15 567	2 426	12 814	11 426	1 388	4 670	3 696	974	95	81	14	414	364	50
27 years	17 567	15 154	2 413	12 416	11 020	1 396	4 610	3 654	956	73	59	14	468	421	47
28 years	17 335	15 081	2 254	12 217	10 922	1 295	4 604	3 704	900	78	64	14	436	391	45
29 years	16 426	14 260	2 166	11 636	10 356	1 280	4 303	3 464	839	55	43	12	432	397	35
30 to 34 years	70 043	60 713	9 330	48 677	43 222	5 455	18 904	15 277	3 627	363	300	63	2 099	1 914	185
30 years	15 767	13 633	2 134	11 064	9 814	1 250	4 133	3 303	830	73	59	14	497	457	40
31 years	15 038	13 015	2 023	10 481	9 314	1 167	4 070	3 273	797	72	64	8	415	364	51
32 years	13 927	11 994	1 933	9 691	8 575	1 116	3 740	2 961	779	74	60	14	422	398	24
33 years	12 928	11 260	1 668	8 854	7 872	982	3 623	2 983	640	74	61	13	377	344	33
34 years	12 383	10 811	1 572	8 587	7 647	940	3 338	2 757	581	70	56	14	388	351	37
35 to 39 years	48 249	42 715	5 534	33 825	30 381	3 444	12 287	10 367	1 920	319	263	56	1 818	1 704	114
35 years	11 684	10 263	1 421	8 167	7 281	886	3 096	2 609	487	73	59	14	348	314	34
36 years	10 690	9 441	1 249	7 451	6 696	755	2 824	2 369	455	65	50	15	350	326	24
37 years	9 932	8 758	1 174	6 926	6 209	717	2 565	2 149	416	70	55	15	371	345	26
38 years	8 517	7 605	912	6 020	5 430	590	2 078	1 778	300	55	50	5	364	347	17
39 years	7 426	6 648	778	5 261	4 765	496	1 724	1 462	262	56	49	7	385	372	13
40 to 44 years	20 964	19 229	1 735	15 638	14 488	1 150	4 068	3 548	520	152	133	19	1 106	1 060	46
40 years	6 104	5 574	530	4 349	4 010	339	1 354	1 182	172	51	45	6	350	337	13
41 years	4 944	4 499	445	3 616	3 335	261	1 042	899	143	42	34	8	244	231	13
42 years	3 942	3 631	311	2 945	2 732	213	731	645	86	25	24	1	241	230	11
43 years	3 295	3 045	250	2 575	2 402	173	533	464	69	22	21	1	165	158	7
44 years	2 679	2 480	199	2 153	2 009	144	408	358	50	12	9	3	106	104	2
45 to 49 years	6 258	5 872	386	5 166	4 884	282	742	660	82	38	34	4	312	294	18
45 years	2 356	2 201	155	1 951	1 835	116	284	254	30	18	16	2	103	96	7
46 years	1 364	1 282	82	1 102	1 047	55	169	145	24	6	5	1	87	85	2
47 years	1 082	1 016	66	900	850	50	127	116	11	9	8	1	46	42	4
48 years	842	792	50	688	653	35	104	94	10	3	3	-	47	42	5
49 years	614	581	33	525	499	26	58	51	7	2	2	-	29	29	-
50 to 54 years	1 093	1 020	73	935	873	62	82	77	5	6	6	-	70	64	6
50 years	393	366	27	335	311	24	37	34	3	2	2	-	19	19	-
51 years	292	275	17	245	230	15	26	24	2	2	2	-	19	19	-
52 years	189	172	17	169	155	14	8	8	-	1	1	-	11	8	3
53 years	137	127	10	116	109	7	9	9	-	-	-	-	12	9	3
54 years	82	80	2	70	68	2	2	2	-	1	1	-	9	9	-
55 to 59 years	222	216	6	204	200	4	5	5	-	-	-	-	13	11	2
55 years	76	76	-	70	70	-	3	3	-	-	-	-	3	3	-
56 years	49	47	2	45	44	1	2	2	-	-	-	-	2	1	1
57 years	44	42	2	40	38	2	-	-	-	-	-	-	4	4	-
58 years	27	26	1	24	24	-	-	-	-	-	-	-	3	2	1
59 years	26	25	1	25	24	1	-	-	-	-	-	-	1	1	-
60 to 64 years	35	32	3	31	29	2	1	1	-	-	-	-	3	2	1
60 years	10	9	1	9	8	1	-	-	-	-	-	-	1	1	-
61 years	13	13	-	12	12	-	1	1	-	-	-	-	-	-	-
62 years	5	4	1	5	4	1	-	-	-	-	-	-	-	-	-
63 years	7	6	1	5	5	-	-	-	-	-	-	-	2	1	1
64 years	-	-	-	-	-	-	-	-	-	-	-	-	-	-	-

¹Persons of Hispanic origin may be of any race.

B4-17. Estimates of Armed Forces Overseas, by Age, Sex, Race, and Hispanic Origin: July 1, 1992 (continued)

| Hispanic origin[1] | | | Not of Hispanic origin, by race | | | | | | | | | | | | Age |
| | | | White | | | Black | | | American Indian, Eskimo, and Aleut | | | Asian and Pacific Islander | | | |
Total	Male	Female	Total	Male	Female	Total	Male	Female	Total	Male	Female	Total	Male	Female	
19 254	17 204	2 050	259 616	232 274	27 342	89 814	73 269	16 545	1 833	1 522	311	9 444	8 553	891	All ages
1 031	915	116	13 188	11 798	1 390	3 998	3 321	677	112	92	20	270	234	36	15 to 19 years
-	-	-	-	-	-	-	-	-	-	-	-	-	-	-	15 years
-	-	-	-	-	-	-	-	-	-	-	-	-	-	-	16 years
-	-	-	3	3	-	2	1	1	-	-	-	1	1	-	17 years
192	168	24	2 035	1 787	248	691	563	128	18	13	5	52	41	11	18 years
839	747	92	11 150	10 008	1 142	3 305	2 757	548	94	79	15	217	192	25	19 years
6 979	6 127	852	88 993	79 438	9 555	27 318	22 205	5 113	629	521	108	2 057	1 762	295	20 to 24 years
1 648	1 456	192	20 002	17 941	2 061	5 581	4 600	981	158	135	23	384	334	50	20 years
1 733	1 536	197	21 648	19 377	2 271	6 311	5 138	1 173	150	128	22	449	385	64	21 years
1 490	1 300	190	18 399	16 418	1 981	5 594	4 522	1 072	127	103	24	432	361	71	22 years
1 145	1 012	133	15 355	13 685	1 670	4 860	3 960	900	93	80	13	401	350	51	23 years
963	823	140	13 589	12 017	1 572	4 972	3 985	987	101	75	26	391	332	59	24 years
3 988	3 551	437	59 420	52 839	6 581	22 803	18 170	4 633	324	268	56	1 967	1 784	203	25 to 29 years
854	775	79	13 135	11 593	1 542	4 782	3 801	981	70	60	10	360	321	39	25 years
814	714	100	12 088	10 789	1 299	4 627	3 658	969	80	68	12	384	338	46	26 years
778	681	97	11 725	10 416	1 309	4 568	3 616	952	61	50	11	435	391	44	27 years
752	676	76	11 546	10 318	1 228	4 565	3 669	896	66	54	12	406	364	42	28 years
790	705	85	10 926	9 723	1 203	4 261	3 426	835	47	36	11	402	370	32	29 years
3 502	3 120	382	45 548	40 435	5 113	18 709	15 102	3 607	311	257	54	1 973	1 799	174	30 to 34 years
750	671	79	10 398	9 216	1 182	4 092	3 267	825	62	51	11	465	428	37	30 years
780	684	96	9 781	8 701	1 080	4 026	3 234	792	61	54	7	390	342	48	31 years
696	621	75	9 067	8 020	1 047	3 703	2 927	776	64	52	12	397	374	23	32 years
668	612	56	8 257	7 325	932	3 585	2 948	637	63	51	12	355	324	31	33 years
608	532	76	8 045	7 173	872	3 303	2 726	577	61	49	12	366	331	35	34 years
2 516	2 327	189	31 587	28 313	3 274	12 147	10 237	1 910	277	226	51	1 722	1 612	110	35 to 39 years
600	541	59	7 630	6 797	833	3 062	2 578	484	63	50	13	329	297	32	35 years
588	543	45	6 923	6 208	715	2 791	2 339	452	57	43	14	331	308	23	36 years
516	474	42	6 469	5 789	680	2 536	2 122	414	60	47	13	351	326	25	37 years
455	433	22	5 616	5 046	570	2 053	1 755	298	48	43	5	345	328	17	38 years
357	336	21	4 949	4 473	478	1 705	1 443	262	49	43	6	368	353	13	39 years
990	927	63	14 767	13 677	1 090	4 017	3 499	518	137	119	18	1 053	1 007	46	40 to 44 years
285	270	15	4 103	3 778	325	1 338	1 167	171	45	39	6	333	320	13	40 years
262	243	19	3 385	3 121	264	1 028	886	142	37	30	7	232	219	13	41 years
183	168	15	2 784	2 586	198	723	637	86	23	22	1	229	218	11	42 years
149	141	8	2 443	2 278	165	525	456	69	20	19	1	158	151	7	43 years
111	105	6	2 052	1 914	138	403	353	50	12	9	3	101	99	2	44 years
209	199	10	4 981	4 709	272	734	652	82	37	33	4	297	279	18	45 to 49 years
85	77	8	1 875	1 767	108	281	251	30	17	15	2	98	91	7	45 years
37	37	-	1 071	1 016	55	167	143	24	6	5	1	83	81	2	46 years
36	35	1	867	818	49	126	115	11	9	8	1	44	40	4	47 years
29	29	-	662	627	35	103	93	10	3	3	-	45	40	5	48 years
22	21	1	506	481	25	57	50	7	2	2	-	27	27	-	49 years
30	29	1	906	845	61	82	77	5	6	6	-	69	63	6	50 to 54 years
13	12	1	323	300	23	37	34	3	2	2	-	18	18	-	50 years
4	4	-	241	226	15	26	24	2	2	2	-	19	19	-	51 years
7	7	-	162	148	14	8	8	-	1	1	-	11	8	3	52 years
4	4	-	112	105	7	9	9	-	-	-	-	12	9	3	53 years
2	2	-	68	66	2	2	2	-	1	1	-	9	9	-	54 years
8	8	-	196	192	4	5	5	-	-	-	-	13	11	2	55 to 59 years
2	2	-	68	68	-	3	3	-	-	-	-	3	3	-	55 years
3	3	-	42	41	1	2	2	-	-	-	-	2	1	1	56 years
1	1	-	39	37	2	-	-	-	-	-	-	4	4	-	57 years
1	1	-	23	23	-	-	-	-	-	-	-	3	2	1	58 years
1	1	-	24	23	1	-	-	-	-	-	-	1	1	-	59 years
1	1	-	30	28	2	1	1	-	-	-	-	3	2	1	60 to 64 years
1	1	-	8	7	1	-	-	-	-	-	-	1	1	-	60 years
-	-	-	12	12	-	1	1	-	-	-	-	-	-	-	61 years
-	-	-	5	4	1	-	-	-	-	-	-	-	-	-	62 years
-	-	-	5	5	-	-	-	-	-	-	-	2	1	1	63 years
-	-	-	-	-	-	-	-	-	-	-	-	-	-	-	64 years

[1]Persons of Hispanic origin may be of any race.

Source: Jennifer Cheeseman Day, U.S. Bureau of the Census, *Population Projections of the United States, by Age, Sex, Race, and Hispanic Origin: 1993 to 2050*, Series P25-1104, Washington, D.C.: Government Printing Office, November 1993, Table D-1.

B5. INCOME AND ASSETS

B5-1. Median Family Income, by Type of Family: 1947 to 1990 (in 1990 Dollars)

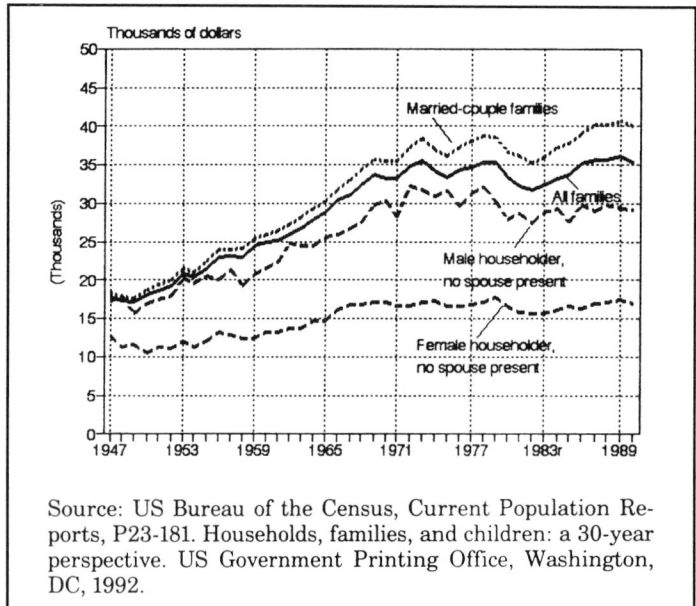

Source: US Bureau of the Census, Current Population Reports, P23-181. Households, families, and children: a 30-year perspective. US Government Printing Office, Washington, DC, 1992.

Source: D. J. Hernandez, *The Historical Transformation of Childhood, Children's Statistics, and Social Policy,* Childhood 1993, Vol. 1, Munksgaard, 1993, Figure 11.

B5-2 Type of Household, by Total Money Income in 1993

[Numbers in thousands. Households as of March of the following year. For meaning of symbols, see text]

Characteristic	Total	Less than $5,000	$5,000 to $9,999	$10,000 to $14,999	$15,000 to $24,999	$25,000 to $34,999	$35,000 to $49,999	$50,000 to $74,999	$75,000 to $99,999	$100,000 and over	Median income Value (dol.)	Median income Standard error (dol.)	Mean income Value (dol.)	Mean income Standard error (dol.)
All households _____	97 107	4 407	9 467	8 956	16 422	14 318	15 792	15 632	6 485	5 628	31 241	146	41 428	224
TYPE OF HOUSEHOLD														
Family households _____	68 490	2 176	4 002	4 873	10 490	10 261	12 467	13 428	5 738	5 054	37 484	208	47 724	292
Married-couple families _____	53 171	708	1 594	2 895	7 440	7 920	10 417	12 084	5 296	4 816	43 129	262	53 603	353
Male householder, no wife present _____	2 913	102	228	283	582	540	550	376	147	106	29 849	715	36 760	876
Female householder, no husband present _____	12 406	1 366	2 180	1 695	2 468	1 801	1 500	968	295	133	18 545	285	25 102	395
Nonfamily households _____	28 617	2 230	5 464	4 083	5 932	4 057	3 325	2 204	747	574	18 880	224	26 358	258
Male householder _____	12 462	783	1 340	1 531	2 642	2 137	1 861	1 296	477	395	24 728	332	32 477	471
Living alone _____	9 440	704	1 257	1 324	2 185	1 639	1 216	699	209	206	21 372	291	27 738	478
Female householder _____	16 155	1 447	4 125	2 552	3 290	1 920	1 464	908	270	179	14 883	228	21 638	265
Living alone _____	14 171	1 386	4 013	2 439	2 958	1 578	1 083	519	115	80	12 995	228	18 539	227

Source: U.S. Bureau of the Census, *Income, Poverty, and Valuation of Noncash Benefits: 1993,* Current Population Reports, P60-188, Washington, D.C.: U.S. Government Printing Office, February 1995, Table 2.

B5-3. Median Income of Families without Children, by Type of Family and Race of Householder: 1979 and 1993

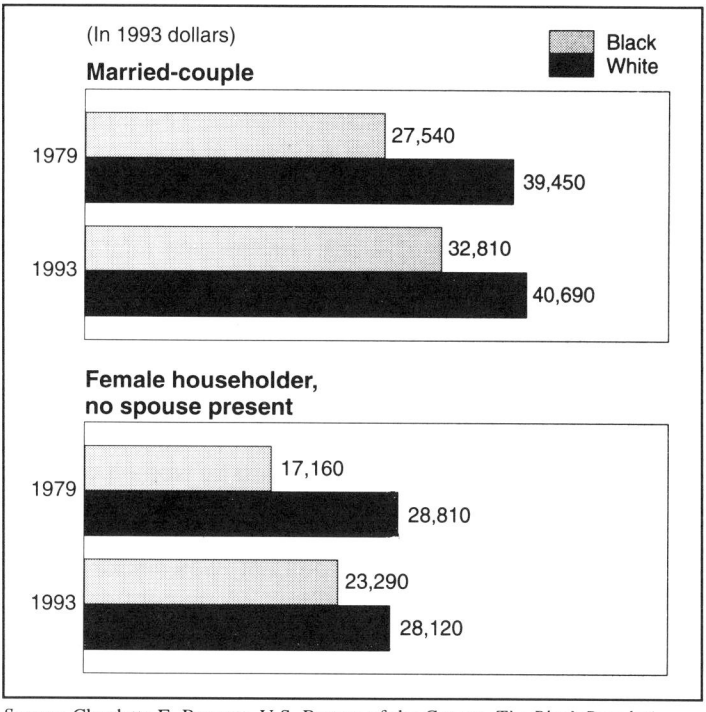

Source: Claudette E. Bennett, U.S. Bureau of the Census, *The Black Population in the United States: March 1994 and 1993*, Current Population Reports, Series P20-480, Washington, D.C.: U.S. Government Printing Office, January 1995, Figure 9.

B5-4. Median Income of Families with Children, by Type of Family and Race of Householder: 1979 and 1993

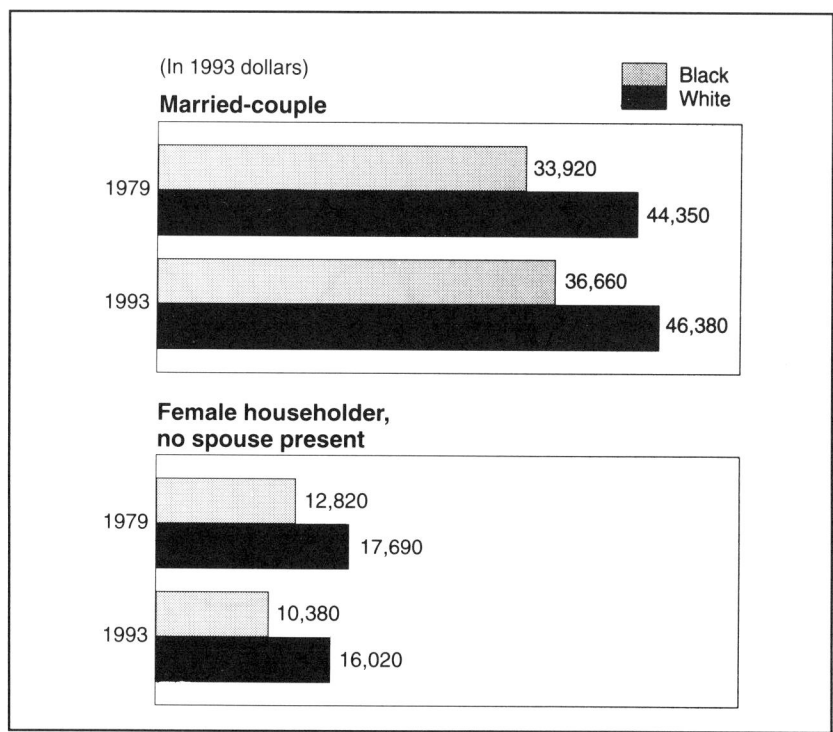

Source: Claudette E. Bennett, U.S. Bureau of the Census, *The Black Population in the United States: March 1994 and 1993*, Current Population Reports, Series P20-480, Washington, D.C.: U.S. Government Printing Office, January 1995, Figure 10.

B5-5 Median Income, by Type of Family, Age of Children, and Race of Householder: 1993

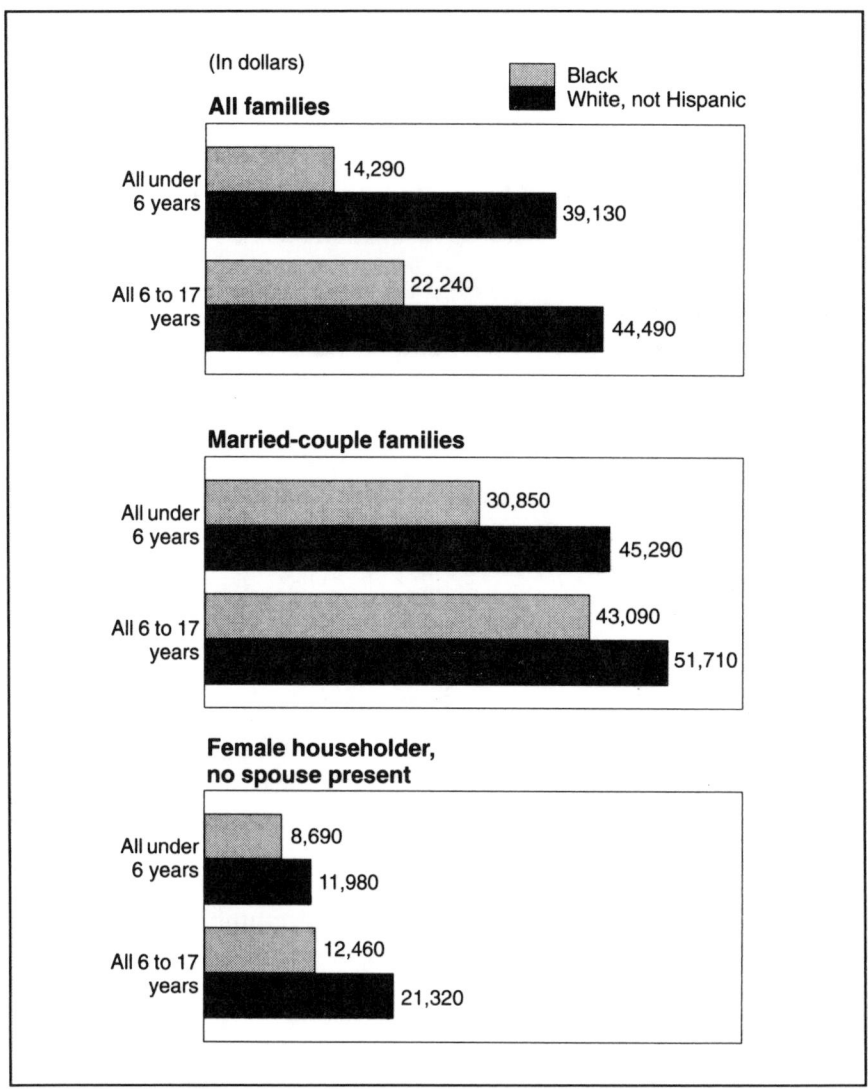

Source: Claudette E. Bennett, U.S. Bureau of the Census, *The Black Population in the United States: March 1994 and 1993*, Current Population Reports, Series P20-480, Washington, D.C.: U.S. Government Printing Office, January 1995, Figure 11.

B5-6. Median Income of Persons and Families, by Sex and Race: 1993, 1989, 1979, and 1969

(In 1993 dollars)

Income and earnings	1993				1989			1979ʳ			1969		
	Black	White	White, not Hispanic	Ratio: Black to White	Black	White	Ratio: Black to White	Black	White	Ratio: Black to White	Black	White	Ratio: Black to White
MEDIAN INCOME[1]													
Households........(dollars)...	19,533	32,960	34,173	0.59	21,073	35,433	0.59	19,787	33,702	0.59	19,408	32,109	0.60
Standard error.....(dollars)...	386	192	200	(X)	429	171	(X)	361	160	(X)	286	117	(X)
Families...........(dollars)...	21,548	39,308	41,114	0.55	23,550	41,922	0.56	22,601	39,911	0.57	22,001	35,920	0.61
Standard error.....(dollars)...	441	242	215	(X)	517	211	(X)	412	174	(X)	(NA)	(NA)	(X)
Persons-													
Male.............(dollars)...	14,605	21,981	23,171	0.66	14,694	24,312	0.60	14,874	24,028	0.62	14,432	24,811	0.58
Standard error...(dollars)...	449	115	173	(X)	354	129	(X)	303	125	(X)	(NA)	(NA)	(X)
Female...........(dollars)...	9,508	11,266	11,599	0.84	9,177	11,434	0.80	7,807	8,578	0.91	6,748	8,003	0.84
Standard error...(dollars)...	207	77	82	(X)	277	85	(X)	174	74	(X)	(NA)	(NA)	(X)
MEDIAN INCOME BY TYPE OF FAMILY[1]													
Married couple......(dollars)...	35,228	43,683	45,241	0.81	35,717	45,690	0.78	32,807	42,479	0.77	26,879	37,559	0.72
Standard error.....(dollars)...	796	276	261	(X)	768	259	(X)	629	180	(X)	(NA)	(NA)	(X)
Female householder, no spouse present........(dollars)...	11,905	20,003	21,649	0.60	13,553	22,078	0.61	13,405	22,323	0.60	12,253	20,171	0.61
Standard error.....(dollars)...	308	351	428	(X)	415	437	(X)	363	330	(X)	(NA)	(NA)	(X)
Male householder, no spouse present........(dollars)...	19,476	28,274	30,168	0.69	21,436	35,527	0.60	24,243	34,487	0.70	22,823	32,340	0.71
Standard error.....(dollars)...	1,171	931	902	(X)	923	851	(X)	1,822	1,088	(X)	(NA)	(NA)	(X)

[1]The data for families do not include families in group quarters. For March 1994, in some CPS publications the data for families include group quarters.

Source: Claudette E. Bennett, U.S. Bureau of the Census, The Black Population in the United States: March 1994 and 1993, Current Population Reports, Series P20-480, Washington, D.C.: U.S. Government Printing Office, January 1995, Table M.

B5-7. Median Income of All Women and Women Who Work Year Round and Full Time, by Selected Characteristics: 1993

[Persons 15 years old and over as of March of the following year. An asterisk (*) preceding percent change indicates statistically significant change at the 90-percent confidence level.]

Characteristic	Number with income (thous.)	Median income Value (dollars)	Median income Standard error (dollars)
TOTAL			
Female			
All females	94 417	11 046	70
Region			
Northeast	19 547	11 375	149
Midwest	22 887	11 031	139
South	32 423	10 557	120
West	19 560	11 568	152
Race and Hispanic Origin			
White	79 484	11 266	77
Black	11 267	9 508	207
Hispanic origin[1]	7 053	8 100	232
Relationship to Family Householder			
In families	74 498	10 350	84
Householder	18 022	12 492	186
Spouse of householder	43 184	11 314	114
Other relative of householder	13 291	5 864	99
In unrelated subfamilies	774	9 056	743
Unrelated individuals	19 145	13 646	199
Age			
Under 65 years	76 762	12 054	84
15 to 24 years	13 519	5 351	111
25 to 34 years	19 572	13 988	218
35 to 44 years	19 667	15 844	212
45 to 54 years	13 999	16 324	239
55 to 64 years	10 005	10 829	227
65 years and over	17 655	8 499	89
65 to 74 years	9 930	8 647	141
75 years and over	7 724	8 365	112
Occupation Group of Longest Job[2] (Earnings)			
Total with earnings[3]	63 660	13 896	136
Executive, administrators, and managerial	7 402	25 282	260
Professional specialty	9 629	25 865	320
Technical and related support	2 429	21 583	334
Sales	8 653	8 238	246
Administrative support, including clerical	16 233	15 733	136
Precision production, craft, and repair	1 414	17 340	687
Machine operators, assemblers, and inspectors	3 273	12 046	244
Transportation and material moving	560	12 125	727
Handlers, equipment cleaners, helpers, and laborers	1 070	7 465	450
Service workers	12 118	6 684	118
Private household	1 045	2 446	173
Service workers, except private household	11 073	7 127	122
Farming, forestry, and fishing	794	3 106	586
Educational Attainment			
Total, 25 years and over	80 898	12 234	75
Less than 9th grade	6 423	6 480	80
9th to 12th grade (no diploma)	8 152	7 187	88
High school graduate (includes equivalency)	29 171	11 089	102
Some college, no degree	14 390	14 489	237
Associate degree	6 282	18 346	471
Bachelor's degree or more	16 480	25 246	272
Bachelor's degree	11 447	22 452	312
Master's degree	4 003	31 389	508
Professional degree	583	32 742	1 772
Doctorate degree	447	42 736	2 005

Characteristic	Number with income (thous.)	Median income Value (dollars)	Median income Standard error (dollars)
YEAR-ROUND, FULL-TIME WORKERS			
Female			
All females	33 544	22 469	121
Region			
Northeast	6 679	25 320	273
Midwest	8 097	21 841	190
South	11 977	21 014	181
West	6 791	24 720	338
Race and Hispanic Origin			
White	27 767	22 979	170
Black	4 305	20 315	285
Hispanic origin[1]	2 440	17 112	314
Relationship to Family Householder			
In families	26 482	22 071	114
Householder	7 295	23 505	332
Spouse of householder	16 147	22 544	199
Other relative of householder	3 040	16 937	261
In unrelated subfamilies	292	17 836	1 528
Unrelated individuals	6 770	24 846	302
Age			
Under 65 years	33 039	22 442	114
15 to 24 years	2 861	15 227	233
25 to 34 years	9 531	21 949	174
35 to 44 years	9 998	25 282	255
45 to 54 years	7 395	24 412	325
55 to 64 years	3 254	22 587	457
65 years and over	505	24 875	1 175
65 to 74 years	424	25 319	1 228
75 years and over	80	19 786	3 863
Occupation Group of Longest Job[2] (Earnings)			
Total with earnings[3]	33 524	21 747	95
Executive, administrators, and managerial	5 503	28 876	507
Professional specialty	5 521	31 906	232
Technical and related support	1 533	26 324	378
Sales	3 514	18 743	438
Administrative support, including clerical	9 456	20 683	125
Precision production, craft, and repair	956	21 357	535
Machine operators, assemblers, and inspectors	1 955	15 379	282
Transportation and material moving	218	19 652	1 195
Handlers, equipment cleaners, helpers, and laborers	397	14 826	871
Service workers	4 165	13 126	284
Private household	190	8 460	814
Service workers, except private household	3 976	13 419	287
Farming, forestry, and fishing	237	10 581	903
Educational Attainment			
Total, 25 years and over	30 683	23 629	166
Less than 9th grade	765	12 415	420
9th to 12th grade (no diploma)	1 576	15 386	330
High school graduate (includes equivalency)	10 513	19 963	173
Some college, no degree	6 279	23 056	342
Associate degree	3 067	25 883	335
Bachelor's degree or more	8 483	34 307	469
Bachelor's degree	5 735	31 197	310
Master's degree	2 166	38 612	717
Professional degree	323	50 211	2 586
Doctorate degree	260	47 248	2 147

[1]Persons of Hispanic origin may be of any race.
[2]Amounts shown are median earnings.
[3]Includes persons whose longest job was in the Armed Forces.

Source: U.S. Bureau of the Census, *Income, Poverty, and Valuation of Noncash Benefits: 1993,* Current Population Reports, P60-188, Washington, D.C.: U.S. Government Printing Office, February 1995, Table 5.

B5-8. Persons, by Total Money Income, Race, Hispanic Origin, and Sex: 1967 to 1993

[Income in 1993 CPI-U-X1 adjusted dollars. Persons 15 years old and over beginning with March 1980, and persons 14 years old and over as of March of the following year for previous years.]

| | Number (thous.) | Number with income (thous.) | With income | | | | | | | | | | | | |
| | | | Percent distribution | | | | | | | | | Median income | | Mean income | |
			Total	$1 to $2,499 or loss	$2,500 to $4,999	$5,000 to $9,999	$10,000 to $14,999	$15,000 to $24,999	$25,000 to $49,999	$50,000 to $74,999	$75,000 and over	Value (dollars)	Standard error (dollars)	Value (dollars)	Standard error (dollars)
ALL RACES															
Male															
1993[7]	96 768	90 194	100.0	7.0	4.9	12.1	12.4	20.8	28.8	8.7	5.2	21 102	106	28 939	205
1992[6]	95 652	90 175	100.0	6.9	5.1	12.9	12.3	20.6	29.0	8.4	4.8	21 067	110	27 613	143
1991	93 760	88 653	100.0	6.4	5.1	12.5	12.4	20.3	30.2	8.4	4.8	21 716	111	27 976	142
1990	92 840	88 220	100.0	6.4	4.7	12.3	11.5	20.9	30.4	9.0	5.0	22 436	113	28 791	151
1989	91 955	87 454	100.0	6.3	4.7	11.6	11.2	20.5	30.7	9.4	5.5	23 182	143	30 002	164
1988	91 034	86 584	100.0	6.7	4.9	11.7	11.0	20.1	31.1	9.5	5.0	23 096	160	29 381	161
1987[1]	90 256	85 713	100.0	6.7	5.1	11.6	11.1	19.7	31.0	9.8	5.0	22 624	156	28 999	146
1986	89 368	84 471	100.0	7.0	5.1	11.8	11.1	19.3	31.3	9.6	4.8	22 564	121	28 771	142
1985	88 478	83 631	100.0	7.3	5.5	12.0	11.6	19.8	30.6	8.9	4.3	21 905	122	27 734	134
1984	87 304	82 183	100.0	7.6	5.5	12.6	11.1	19.0	31.3	8.7	4.1	21 696	125	27 034	120
1983[2]	86 014	80 795	100.0	8.3	5.6	12.1	11.7	20.1	30.1	8.4	3.8	21 270	(NA)	26 379	(NA)
1982	84 955	79 722	100.0	8.2	5.6	12.2	10.6	21.1	30.6	7.6	4.0	21 086	138	26 271	118
1981	83 958	79 688	100.0	7.6	5.8	12.1	10.9	20.1	32.1	7.8	3.6	21 608	146	26 486	117
1980	82 949	78 661	100.0	7.2	5.1	11.9	11.1	20.0	32.9	8.1	3.6	22 000	137	26 934	119
1979[3]	81 947	78 129	100.0	6.8	5.4	11.9	10.1	19.7	33.8	8.3	4.1	23 001	117	27 945	127
1978	80 969	75 609	100.0	7.3	5.2	11.5	10.5	18.6	33.8	8.9	4.0	23 409	135	28 072	131
1977	79 863	74 015	100.0	7.6	5.4	11.6	10.7	18.5	33.7	8.6	3.8	23 145	107	27 581	119
1976	78 782	72 775	100.0	7.8	5.3	11.7	10.7	19.5	33.6	8.1	3.4	22 930	129	27 161	117
1975	77 560	71 234	100.0	7.4	5.2	11.8	10.7	19.4	34.4	7.9	3.3	22 763	118	26 815	118
1974[4]	76 363	70 863	100.0	7.5	5.3	11.3	10.2	18.6	35.0	8.5	3.6	23 532	(NA)	27 455	(NA)
1973	75 040	69 387	100.0	7.5	5.3	10.6	9.1	19.2	35.8	8.4	4.1	24 663	(NA)	28 438	(NA)
1972	73 572	67 474	100.0	7.5	5.6	10.9	9.3	18.6	36.2	8.0	3.9	24 246	(NA)	28 103	(NA)
1971	72 469	66 486	100.0	8.1	5.6	10.9	10.0	19.6	35.0	7.5	3.2	23 143	(NA)	26 459	(NA)
1970	70 592	65 008	100.0	8.3	5.9	10.8	9.8	19.5	35.6	7.1	3.1	23 337	(NA)	26 370	(NA)
1969	69 027	63 882	100.0	8.1	6.4	11.0	9.4	18.6	36.6	7.0	3.0	23 578	(NA)	26 413	(NA)
1968	67 611	62 501	100.0	8.5	6.5	10.6	8.9	21.7	35.6	5.4	2.8	22 921	(NA)	25 397	(NA)
1967	66 519	61 444	100.0	8.7	6.9	11.4	9.0	22.5	34.0	4.9	2.6	22 105	(NA)	24 099	(NA)
Female															
1993[7]	104 032	94 417	100.0	14.1	10.9	21.4	14.4	19.1	16.5	2.6	.9	11 046	71	15 761	105
1992[6]	102 954	93 517	100.0	14.6	10.9	21.3	14.7	18.7	16.7	2.2	.8	11 035	72	15 369	80
1991	101 483	92 569	100.0	14.3	10.8	21.7	14.9	19.0	16.3	2.2	.8	11 114	74	15 330	79
1990	100 680	92 245	100.0	14.9	11.2	20.9	14.4	19.1	16.4	2.3	.8	11 133	78	15 382	81
1989	99 838	91 399	100.0	15.1	11.1	20.6	13.9	19.6	16.6	2.2	.8	11 215	80	15 413	80
1988	99 019	90 593	100.0	15.9	11.1	21.3	14.0	18.9	16.1	2.1	.7	10 852	93	15 038	84
1987[1]	98 225	89 661	100.0	16.0	11.4	21.2	13.8	19.1	15.8	1.9	.7	10 551	85	14 676	76
1986	97 320	87 822	100.0	17.1	11.6	21.6	13.7	18.4	15.2	1.7	.6	10 033	73	14 161	73
1985	96 354	86 531	100.0	17.7	12.0	21.7	14.0	18.1	14.4	1.5	.5	9 692	73	13 662	70
1984	95 282	85 555	100.0	18.1	11.9	22.0	14.1	18.2	13.9	1.4	.5	9 552	63	13 329	65
1983[2]	94 269	83 781	100.0	18.9	12.1	21.7	14.6	18.4	12.7	1.2	.4	9 292	(NA)	12 911	(NA)
1982	93 145	82 505	100.0	19.8	12.2	22.4	13.6	18.9	11.7	1.0	.4	8 898	57	12 387	62
1981	92 228	82 139	100.0	19.9	12.6	22.8	14.1	18.6	11.0	.8	.2	8 753	61	11 932	58
1980	91 133	80 826	100.0	20.3	12.8	22.3	14.4	18.3	10.8	.8	.3	8 638	58	11 890	60
1979[3]	89 914	79 921	100.0	21.4	13.0	21.6	13.9	18.5	10.6	.8	.3	8 498	68	11 767	61
1978	88 617	71 864	100.0	18.4	14.2	22.3	14.7	18.4	10.8	.8	.3	8 709	77	11 986	62
1977	87 399	65 407	100.0	16.3	14.7	23.3	15.4	18.5	10.9	.7	.3	9 011	64	12 097	57
1976	86 157	63 170	100.0	16.9	15.0	23.7	15.0	18.7	10.0	.6	.3	8 699	68	11 859	58
1975	84 982	60 807	100.0	16.6	14.7	23.6	15.6	18.6	10.1	.6	.1	8 703	54	11 604	54
1974[4]	83 599	59 642	100.0	17.3	14.8	23.8	15.3	17.9	10.1	.6	.2	8 581	(NA)	11 585	(NA)
1973	82 244	57 029	100.0	17.8	15.6	22.7	14.0	19.2	9.8	.6	.2	8 560	(NA)	11 630	(NA)
1972	80 896	54 487	100.0	18.3	15.8	22.3	14.1	18.7	10.1	.6	.2	8 458	(NA)	11 641	(NA)
1971	79 565	52 603	100.0	19.0	16.3	21.0	15.2	18.7	9.0	.5	.2	8 073	(NA)	11 174	(NA)
1970	77 649	51 647	100.0	20.8	16.3	20.4	15.0	18.0	8.9	.5	.2	7 827	(NA)	10 979	(NA)
1969	76 277	50 224	100.0	21.3	16.8	19.8	15.1	18.2	8.1	.4	.2	7 819	(NA)	10 801	(NA)
1968	74 889	48 544	100.0	22.0	17.1	19.7	14.6	18.7	7.3	.4	.2	7 739	(NA)	10 471	(NA)
1967	73 584	46 843	100.0	24.0	17.5	19.4	14.3	17.8	6.1	.7	.3	7 169	(NA)	9 884	(NA)

[1]Implementation of a new March CPS processing system.
[2]Implementation of Hispanic population controls.
[3]Implementation of 1980 census population controls.
[4]Implementation of a new March CPS processing system.

Source: U.S. Bureau of the Census, *Income, Poverty, and Valuation of Noncash Benefits: 1993,* Current Population Reports, P60-188, Washington, D.C.: U.S. Government Printing Office, February 1995, Tables 2, 5, D-3.

B5-9. Total Money Income in 1993 of Persons 15 Years and Over, by Sex and Race

[Persons as of March 1994]

Total money income and region	All persons						Year-round, full-time workers					
	Black			White, not Hispanic			Black			White, not Hispanic		
	Both sexes	Male	Female	Both sexes	Male	Female	Both sexes	Male	Female	Both sexes	Male	Female
UNITED STATES												
Total................thousands..	23,499	10,630	12,869	152,045	73,575	78,470	8,724	4,419	4,305	64,921	39,342	25,579
Total with income ....thousands..	20,214	8,947	11,267	143,307	70,179	73,128	8,724	4,419	4,305	64,906	39,333	25,573
Percent	100.0	100.0	100.0	100.0	100.0	100.0	100.0	100.0	100.0	100.0	100.0	100.0
$1 to $2,499 or loss	11.5	11.1	11.8	10.3	6.4	14.1	1.3	1.3	1.3	1.3	1.1	1.4
$2,500 to $4,999	11.5	7.5	14.7	7.2	4.2	10.0	0.9	0.5	1.3	0.5	0.4	0.8
$5,000 to $7,499	13.8	10.8	16.2	8.6	5.3	11.8	2.6	1.9	3.3	1.4	1.0	2.0
$7,500 to $9,999	8.3	7.1	9.1	6.9	5.1	8.6	4.3	3.5	5.2	2.2	1.5	3.4
$10,000 to $12,499...................	9.3	9.5	9.1	7.5	6.4	8.5	9.5	8.5	10.4	4.8	3.6	6.6
$12,500 to $14,999...................	5.1	4.6	5.6	5.5	5.1	5.9	6.6	4.9	8.4	4.4	3.3	6.2
$15,000 to $17,499...................	6.6	7.6	5.8	6.0	5.9	6.1	10.6	10.5	10.7	6.7	5.3	8.8
$17,500 to $19,999...................	4.6	5.1	4.2	4.6	4.5	4.7	7.7	7.5	8.0	5.6	4.2	7.7
$20,000 to $22,499...................	5.3	6.0	4.8	5.5	5.8	5.2	10.1	9.5	10.7	8.1	6.7	10.1
$22,500 to $24,999...................	2.9	3.1	2.8	3.8	4.1	3.6	5.0	4.4	5.6	5.4	4.6	6.7
$25,000 to $29,999...................	6.3	7.6	5.2	7.2	8.4	6.1	11.9	12.4	11.4	11.5	10.6	12.8
$30,000 to $34,999...................	4.5	5.5	3.7	6.0	7.7	4.4	8.9	9.3	8.4	10.2	10.7	9.5
$35,000 to $39,999...................	3.2	4.1	2.5	4.5	5.8	3.3	6.8	7.6	6.0	7.9	8.4	7.2
$40,000 to $44,999...................	2.2	3.4	1.2	3.8	5.3	2.4	4.1	5.6	2.6	7.0	7.9	5.5
$45,000 to $49,999...................	1.4	1.7	1.2	2.5	3.8	1.4	2.7	3.0	2.5	4.7	5.7	3.1
$50,000 to $59,999...................	1.6	2.4	1.0	3.7	5.7	1.8	3.3	4.5	2.1	6.9	8.8	4.0
$60,000 to $74,999...................	1.0	1.7	0.5	2.6	4.2	1.0	2.0	3.0	0.9	4.8	6.6	2.1
$75,000 and over	0.8	1.2	0.5	3.5	6.2	1.0	1.6	2.2	1.0	6.6	9.7	2.0
Median income............(dollars)..	11,324	14,605	9,508	16,631	23,171	11,599	21,593	23,566	20,315	28,916	33,071	23,579
Standard error ....(dollars)..	152	449	207	82	173	82	213	684	285	171	252	175

Source: Claudette E. Bennett, U.S. Bureau of the Census, *The Black Population in the United States: March 1994 and 1993,* Current Population Reports, Series P20-480, Washington, D.C.: U.S. Government Printing Office, January 1995, Table 8.

B5-10. Total Money Income in 1993 of Persons 25 Years and Over, by Educational Attainment, Sex, and Race

Persons as of March 1994.

Total money income, race, region, and sex	Total	Elementary		High school		College	
		Less than 9th grade	9th to 12th grade (no diploma)	High school graduate	Some college or associate degree	Bachelor's degree or more
WHITE, NOT HISPANIC-							
United States-							
Male........................thousands..	61,074	3,850	5,229	20,071	14,942	16,981
Total with income ....thousands..	60,065	3,769	5,043	19,691	14,733	16,829
Percent	100.0	100.0	100.0	100.0	100.0	100.0
$1 to $2,499 or loss	2.7	4.2	4.7	2.9	2.7	1.6
$2,500 to $4,999............................	2.4	7.8	4.3	2.4	1.7	1.3
$5,000 to $7,499	4.2	16.7	8.4	4.2	2.8	1.4
$7,500 to $9,999	4.6	13.1	10.1	5.0	3.6	1.5
$10,000 to $12,499...........................	5.9	11.3	10.8	7.1	4.7	2.9
$12,500 to $14,999...........................	5.1	11.5	9.5	5.7	4.4	2.3
$15,000 to $17,499...........................	5.9	8.6	10.0	7.4	5.7	2.6
$17,500 to $19,999...........................	4.6	4.8	5.9	6.1	5.0	2.2
$20,000 to $22,499...........................	6.1	4.9	6.7	8.0	6.6	3.7
$22,500 to $24,999...........................	4.5	3.5	5.0	5.6	4.7	3.0
$25,000 to $29,999...........................	9.3	5.7	8.8	11.1	10.8	6.8
$30,000 to $34,999...........................	8.7	2.7	5.6	10.0	10.7	7.9
$35,000 to $39,999...........................	6.6	1.4	3.2	6.7	8.4	7.3
$40,000 to $44,999...........................	6.2	1.0	2.7	5.7	7.5	7.7
$45,000 to $49,999...........................	4.4	1.0	1.2	3.7	4.9	6.6
$50,000 to $59,999...........................	6.6	1.0	1.6	4.3	7.0	11.7
$60,000 to $74,999...........................	4.8	0.4	0.6	2.5	4.6	10.1
$75,000 and over	7.2	0.4	0.8	1.8	4.3	19.4
Median income....................(dollars)..	26,652	11,811	15,540	23,080	28,307	43,063
Standard error ....(dollars)..	132	271	264	238	389	498
Female......................thousands..	66,214	4,015	6,141	24,942	17,144	13,973
Total with income ....thousands..	63,307	3,727	5,554	23,642	16,646	13,738
Percent	100.0	100.0	100.0	100.0	100.0	100.0
$1 to $2,499 or loss	11.6	9.2	12.6	13.0	11.8	9.0
$2,500 to $4,999............................	9.1	20.2	16.6	9.9	7.0	4.2
$5,000 to $7,499	11.4	29.0	22.4	11.9	8.4	4.8
$7,500 to $9,999	8.6	16.9	13.8	9.9	7.1	3.8
$10,000 to $12,499...........................	8.5	9.4	10.9	10.5	7.9	4.9
$12,500 to $14,999...........................	6.0	5.4	6.2	7.1	6.4	3.8
$15,000 to $17,499...........................	6.2	3.4	5.5	7.5	6.7	4.7
$17,500 to $19,999...........................	5.0	2.4	3.6	5.8	5.6	4.0
$20,000 to $22,499...........................	5.5	1.3	2.7	6.0	7.2	5.1
$22,500 to $24,999...........................	3.8	0.7	1.0	3.7	4.6	5.1
$25,000 to $29,999...........................	6.7	0.9	2.2	5.6	9.1	9.1
$30,000 to $34,999...........................	5.1	0.5	0.7	3.8	6.3	8.8
$35,000 to $39,999...........................	3.7	0.3	0.6	2.1	4.1	8.1
$40,000 to $44,999...........................	2.7	0.1	0.4	1.0	3.0	7.0
$45,000 to $49,999...........................	1.5	0.2	0.3	0.6	1.5	4.1
$50,000 to $59,999...........................	2.1	0.1	0.2	0.7	1.8	6.2
$60,000 to $74,999...........................	1.2	-	0.1	0.6	0.7	3.5
$75,000 and over	1.2	-	0.3	0.3	0.9	3.8
Median income....................(dollars)..	12,839	6,772	7,314	11,251	15,532	25,298
Standard error ....(dollars)..	124	106	112	117	218	315

B5-10. Total Money Income in 1993 of Persons 25 Years and Over, by Educational Attainment, Sex, and Race *(continued)*

Persons as of March 1994.

Total money income, race, region, and sex	Total	Elementary		High school		College	
		Less than 9th grade	9th to 12th grade (no diploma)	High school graduate	Some college or associate degree	Bachelor's degree or more
BLACK							
United States							
Male........................thousands..	8,051	962	1,313	2,971	1,775	1,030
Total with income ....thousands..	7,370	846	1,144	2,717	1,657	1,006
Percent	100.0	100.0	100.0	100.0	100.0	100.0
$1 to $2,499 or loss	6.0	7.5	9.6	5.9	5.4	1.7
$2,500 to $4,999	5.9	14.5	11.3	4.0	3.7	1.4
$5,000 to $7,499	9.8	27.9	13.3	8.5	4.7	2.4
$7,500 to $9,999	7.4	15.0	8.9	7.7	4.9	2.5
$10,000 to $12,499	9.8	12.2	13.7	10.5	7.7	5.1
$12,500 to $14,999	5.1	3.8	4.9	6.8	5.6	1.2
$15,000 to $17,499	8.2	4.4	6.0	12.2	7.3	4.7
$17,500 to $19,999	5.8	4.2	6.2	6.7	6.2	3.5
$20,000 to $22,499	6.6	1.9	6.5	7.4	7.2	7.4
$22,500 to $24,999	3.5	2.7	2.9	3.5	5.0	2.3
$25,000 to $29,999	8.7	2.3	7.1	9.6	11.0	9.5
$30,000 to $34,999	6.3	1.4	3.0	5.9	8.9	11.1
$35,000 to $39,999	4.9	1.3	2.5	4.1	6.7	10.1
$40,000 to $44,999	4.0	0.4	1.5	3.3	5.4	9.3
$45,000 to $49,999	1.9	-	0.7	0.8	4.2	3.9
$50,000 to $59,999	2.9	0.2	1.4	1.7	3.2	9.3
$60,000 to $74,999	2.0	-	0.5	0.8	2.1	8.4
$75,000 and over	1.3	0.3	0.1	0.6	0.9	6.2
Median income...................(dollars)..	16,823	7,512	11,264	16,349	21,552	32,865
Standard error ....(dollars)..	285	356	435	316	682	1,480
Female......................thousands..	10,053	898	1,736	3,578	2,534	1,307
Total with income ....thousands..	9,388	818	1,582	3,311	2,389	1,289
Percent	100.0	100.0	100.0	100.0	100.0	100.0
$1 to $2,499 or loss	7.8	8.2	10.7	9.2	6.1	3.3
$2,500 to $4,999	12.7	32.1	18.6	12.9	6.8	3.4
$5,000 to $7,499	16.9	35.5	28.3	16.7	9.8	4.6
$7,500 to $9,999	9.2	10.0	12.3	10.3	7.7	4.4
$10,000 to $12,499	9.6	6.0	9.9	12.3	9.7	4.1
$12,500 to $14,999	5.7	3.3	5.6	7.1	6.7	2.1
$15,000 to $17,499	6.5	1.4	4.8	7.7	8.3	5.3
$17,500 to $19,999	4.6	1.0	2.4	4.5	6.6	6.4
$20,000 to $22,499	5.5	1.8	3.2	5.0	8.1	6.9
$22,500 to $24,999	3.0	0.5	1.1	2.5	5.0	4.6
$25,000 to $29,999	6.2	-	1.0	5.9	9.1	11.8
$30,000 to $34,999	4.3	-	1.2	2.7	6.3	11.1
$35,000 to $39,999	3.0	-	0.3	1.5	4.1	9.9
$40,000 to $44,999	1.4	0.2	0.6	0.5	1.9	4.8
$45,000 to $49,999	1.4	-	-	0.4	1.6	5.9
$50,000 to $59,999	1.2	-	-	0.3	1.6	5.4
$60,000 to $74,999	0.6	-	-	0.2	0.1	3.7
$75,000 and over	0.5	-	-	0.2	0.5	2.4
Median income...................(dollars)..	10,918	5,684	6,824	10,169	15,970	26,765
Standard error ....(dollars)..	217	198	178	294	494	812

Source: Claudette E. Bennett, U.S. Bureau of the Census, *The Black Population in the United States: March 1994 and 1993*, Current Population Reports, Series P20-480, Washington, D.C.: U.S. Government Printing Office, January 1995, Table 9.

B5-11. Income in 1989 of Households, Families, and Persons, by Urban and Rural Areas and Size of Place: 1990

[Data based on sample and subject to sampling variability.]

United States Urban and Rural and Size of Place	United States	Total	Urban: Inside urbanized area — Total	Central place	Urban fringe	Urban: Outside urbanized area — Place of 10,000 or more	Place of 2,500 to 9,999	Rural — Total	Place of 1,000 to 2,499	Place of less than 1,000	Rural farm
INCOME IN 1989											
Households	91 993 582	70 071 026	59 267 094	30 141 647	29 125 447	5 172 959	5 630 973	21 922 556	2 676 206	1 461 898	1 374 713
Less than $5,000	5 684 517	4 288 845	3 410 451	2 435 729	974 722	426 635	451 759	1 395 672	209 328	130 133	69 844
$5,000 to $9,999	8 529 980	6 363 284	4 990 302	3 258 993	1 731 309	649 659	723 323	2 166 696	347 224	216 016	103 546
$10,000 to $14,999	8 133 273	5 961 202	4 747 633	2 875 623	1 872 010	575 786	637 783	2 172 071	309 030	186 423	127 491
$15,000 to $24,999	16 123 742	11 924 080	9 773 935	5 526 074	4 247 861	1 024 394	1 125 751	4 199 662	542 831	320 341	272 033
$25,000 to $34,999	14 575 125	10 868 183	9 132 558	4 709 442	4 423 116	827 134	908 491	3 706 942	439 571	244 450	242 725
$35,000 to $49,999	16 428 455	12 478 084	10 740 294	4 958 181	5 782 113	831 672	906 118	3 950 371	432 841	212 483	248 915
$50,000 to $74,999	13 777 883	10 909 264	9 730 848	3 919 629	5 811 219	574 416	604 000	2 868 619	277 744	112 329	190 303
$75,000 to $99,999	4 704 808	3 892 291	3 581 967	1 298 456	2 283 511	152 969	157 355	812 517	68 970	23 067	59 743
$100,000 or more	4 035 799	3 385 793	3 159 106	1 159 520	1 999 586	110 294	116 393	650 006	48 667	16 656	60 113
Median (dollars)	30 056	30 782	32 002	26 784	37 944	23 989	23 741	27 460	23 503	20 917	29 505
Mean (dollars)	38 453	39 689	41 393	35 573	47 416	30 501	30 188	34 505	29 605	26 071	38 441
Families	65 049 428	47 815 502	40 338 661	19 111 188	21 227 473	3 506 713	3 970 128	17 233 926	1 916 297	1 042 156	1 162 367
Less than $5,000	2 582 206	1 958 402	1 588 982	1 143 669	445 313	178 737	190 683	623 804	82 467	48 058	39 553
$5,000 to $9,999	3 636 361	2 536 427	1 986 622	1 351 693	634 929	252 348	297 457	1 099 934	142 620	92 423	62 758
$10,000 to $14,999	4 676 092	3 188 837	2 494 338	1 514 950	979 388	315 799	378 700	1 487 255	188 452	118 521	94 737
$15,000 to $24,999	10 658 345	7 370 615	5 898 008	3 251 255	2 646 753	674 776	797 831	3 287 730	397 252	243 501	226 532
$25,000 to $34,999	10 729 951	7 560 103	6 199 679	3 079 993	3 119 686	631 270	729 154	3 169 848	362 698	208 580	217 319
$35,000 to $49,999	13 270 930	9 708 668	8 218 964	3 646 283	4 572 681	703 244	786 460	3 562 262	382 870	191 978	230 383
$50,000 to $74,999	11 857 079	9 199 865	8 141 307	3 130 153	5 011 154	513 804	544 754	2 657 214	253 963	103 336	179 187
$75,000 to $99,999	4 115 468	3 364 113	3 084 089	1 055 637	2 028 452	138 367	141 657	751 355	62 572	20 994	56 169
$100,000 or more	3 522 996	2 928 472	2 726 672	937 555	1 789 117	98 368	103 432	594 524	43 403	14 765	55 729
Median (dollars)	35 225	36 672	38 233	32 146	43 680	30 149	29 192	31 463	28 872	25 785	31 971
Mean (dollars)	43 803	45 758	47 654	41 095	53 560	36 023	35 089	38 379	34 428	30 436	41 208
Married-couple families	51 718 214	36 843 114	30 930 889	13 503 916	17 426 973	2 748 735	3 163 490	14 875 100	1 563 963	861 257	1 070 524
Less than $15,000	5 619 528	3 446 462	2 624 578	1 566 947	1 057 631	364 274	457 610	2 173 066	239 068	164 414	168 125
$15,000 to $24,999	7 734 791	5 015 523	3 904 613	2 061 365	1 843 248	500 463	610 447	2 719 268	313 318	199 386	205 997
$25,000 to $34,999	8 660 211	5 834 123	4 678 404	2 265 603	2 412 801	529 907	625 812	2 826 088	315 427	186 369	202 261
$35,000 to $49,999	11 566 753	8 248 062	6 889 847	2 987 575	3 902 272	639 080	719 135	3 318 691	353 266	178 744	217 261
$50,000 to $74,999	10 895 423	8 355 754	7 352 886	2 771 846	4 581 040	487 220	515 648	2 539 669	241 299	98 282	170 163
$75,000 or more	7 241 508	5 943 190	5 480 561	1 850 580	3 629 981	227 791	234 838	1 298 318	101 585	34 062	106 717
Female householder, no husband present	10 381 654	8 665 622	7 405 278	4 496 864	2 908 414	612 346	647 998	1 716 032	277 677	138 065	50 683
Less than $5,000	1 530 177	1 271 256	1 033 654	786 184	247 470	117 498	120 104	258 921	47 925	24 489	5 059
$5,000 to $9,999	1 636 764	1 331 911	1 080 894	773 689	307 205	121 767	129 250	304 853	55 262	29 635	6 629
$10,000 to $14,999	1 379 635	1 099 476	892 343	583 382	308 961	97 139	109 994	280 159	47 863	24 826	7 128
$15,000 to $24,999	2 286 235	1 875 170	1 589 719	946 391	643 328	138 117	147 334	411 065	64 390	32 348	11 683
$25,000 to $49,999	2 718 497	2 343 514	2 106 889	1 085 950	1 020 939	117 626	118 999	374 983	52 345	22 901	14 224
$50,000 or more	830 346	744 295	701 779	321 268	380 511	20 199	22 317	86 551	9 892	3 866	5 960
Males 15 years and over, with income	86 674 947	64 820 538	55 067 459	26 767 807	28 299 652	4 722 686	5 030 393	21 854 409	2 378 364	1 291 787	1 501 294
Median income (dollars)	20 409	20 926	21 552	18 198	25 418	16 956	17 479	18 802	17 575	15 987	18 663
Percent year-round full-time workers	53.0	53.0	53.8	49.6	57.8	48.0	48.5	52.9	49.1	46.9	57.9
Median income (dollars)	29 237	30 302	30 855	27 172	33 374	25 965	25 751	26 338	25 356	22 559	23 341
Females 15 years and over, with income	84 560 106	65 214 199	55 083 562	27 693 068	27 390 494	4 889 016	5 241 621	19 345 907	2 450 958	1 296 895	1 154 090
Median income (dollars)	10 371	10 917	11 475	10 558	12 430	8 212	8 161	8 632	8 071	7 272	7 869
Percent year-round full-time workers	33.9	34.4	35.5	33.9	37.2	28.5	28.1	32.1	28.4	26.6	30.4
Median income (dollars)	19 570	20 461	21 042	20 122	21 840	16 534	16 167	16 473	15 867	14 672	15 189
Per capita income (dollars)	14 420	15 064	15 707	13 838	17 562	11 724	11 602	12 408	11 393	10 128	13 672
Persons in households (dollars)	14 649	15 355	15 956	14 108	17 766	12 117	11 848	12 529	11 551	10 180	13 672
Persons in group quarters (dollars)	6 094	6 053	6 277	5 858	6 992	5 188	5 658	6 281	5 317	6 333	–
MEDIAN INCOME IN 1989 BY SELECTED CHARACTERISTICS											
Family type and presence of own children:											
Families (dollars)	35 225	36 672	38 233	32 146	43 680	30 149	29 192	31 463	28 872	25 785	31 971
With own children under 18 years (dollars)	34 627	35 494	36 750	29 601	43 204	29 817	29 190	32 436	29 578	26 805	32 991
With own children under 6 years (dollars)	31 580	32 285	33 844	26 818	40 383	26 405	25 965	29 764	26 493	24 191	29 137
Married-couple families (dollars)	39 584	41 908	43 783	38 849	47 786	34 581	32 956	33 870	32 029	28 340	32 669
With own children under 18 years (dollars)	40 693	42 609	44 457	38 901	48 751	36 278	34 968	35 884	34 274	30 709	34 143
With own children under 6 years (dollars)	36 490	38 346	40 172	35 245	43 725	30 912	30 056	31 563	29 868	26 425	29 469
Female householder, no husband present (dollars)	17 414	17 993	19 083	15 944	24 095	13 259	13 192	15 273	13 572	12 746	20 183
With own children under 18 years (dollars)	12 485	12 693	13 459	11 010	18 211	10 160	10 286	11 794	10 532	10 025	12 628
With own children under 6 years (dollars)	7 775	7 866	8 357	7 134	11 715	6 138	6 105	7 226	6 251	5 960	8 475
Workers in family in 1989:											
No workers (dollars)	14 622	15 137	15 402	11 694	19 943	14 342	14 152	13 521	13 874	12 273	14 725
1 worker (dollars)	25 517	26 370	27 333	22 825	32 117	21 698	21 266	23 133	21 299	19 712	24 721
2 or more workers (dollars)	44 500	46 486	48 116	42 946	52 197	38 608	37 884	39 629	37 320	33 483	37 507
Husband and wife worked (dollars)	46 340	48 899	50 798	45 977	54 234	40 469	39 562	40 667	38 672	34 477	37 853
Nonfamily households (dollars)	17 240	18 406	19 812	17 683	22 399	12 704	11 890	12 635	11 278	9 871	14 924
Male householder (dollars)	22 630	24 056	25 293	22 023	29 814	17 540	17 734	18 097	16 950	14 414	17 986
Living alone (dollars)	20 193	21 179	21 999	19 608	26 134	16 108	15 888	16 000	15 091	12 793	16 787
65 years and over (dollars)	11 688	12 475	13 136	11 633	15 301	10 374	10 020	9 418	9 484	8 359	13 990
Female householder (dollars)	13 729	14 878	16 123	14 738	18 015	10 560	9 641	9 588	9 015	7 950	11 849
Living alone (dollars)	12 226	13 233	14 388	13 016	16 062	9 880	9 032	8 772	8 499	7 663	11 436
65 years and over (dollars)	8 639	9 134	9 585	8 728	10 757	8 016	7 613	7 148	7 351	6 950	10 510

Source: U.S. Bureau of the Census, *Social and Economic Characteristics of the United States: 1990 Census of Population*, CP-2-1, Washington, D.C.: U.S. Government Printing Office, 1993, Table 23.

B5-12. Income in 1989 of Families and Persons, by Race and Hispanic Origin: 1990

[Data based on sample and subject to sampling variability.]

United States	All persons	White	Black	American Indian, Eskimo, or Aleut	Asian or Pacific Islander	Other race	Hispanic origin (of any race)	White, not of Hispanic origin
INCOME IN 1989								
Households	91 993 582	76 906 980	9 941 850	625 367	2 020 498	2 498 887	5 872 040	73 747 747
Less than $5,000	5 684 517	3 726 768	1 513 647	78 140	136 261	229 701	519 528	3 465 190
$5,000 to $9,999	8 529 980	6 610 505	1 412 467	91 731	126 479	288 798	653 488	6 274 975
$10,000 to $14,999	8 133 273	6 540 094	1 089 626	75 537	140 146	287 870	644 179	6 205 647
$15,000 to $24,999	16 123 742	13 295 239	1 878 449	126 456	279 541	544 057	1 205 131	12 675 640
$25,000 to $34,999	14 575 125	12 374 793	1 407 642	91 267	276 512	424 911	963 489	11 867 672
$35,000 to $49,999	16 428 455	14 274 052	1 324 225	83 967	353 574	392 637	937 461	13 758 950
$50,000 to $74,999	13 777 883	12 162 367	928 232	54 774	388 276	244 234	653 931	11 774 378
$75,000 to $99,999	4 704 808	4 203 619	260 092	14 595	168 542	57 960	180 396	4 087 521
$100,000 or more	4 035 799	3 719 543	127 470	8 900	151 167	28 719	114 437	3 637 774
Median (dollars)	30 056	31 435	19 758	20 025	36 784	22 813	24 156	31 672
Mean (dollars)	38 453	40 308	25 872	26 206	46 695	27 843	30 301	40 646
Families	65 049 428	53 845 200	7 055 063	463 968	1 577 820	2 107 377	4 776 075	51 337 479
Less than $5,000	2 582 206	1 419 771	862 062	49 114	70 522	180 737	365 222	1 254 559
$5,000 to $9,999	3 636 361	2 415 421	850 577	60 426	75 072	234 865	483 067	2 186 825
$10,000 to $14,999	4 676 092	3 507 128	762 216	54 908	99 551	252 289	535 520	3 240 989
$15,000 to $24,999	10 658 345	8 549 776	1 341 930	94 195	205 470	466 974	998 207	8 049 852
$25,000 to $34,999	10 729 951	9 043 670	1 043 831	71 009	210 640	360 801	798 318	8 629 800
$35,000 to $49,999	13 270 930	11 519 137	1 060 248	68 493	288 913	334 139	789 353	11 087 614
$50,000 to $74,999	11 857 079	10 467 357	797 643	46 094	339 835	206 150	557 096	10 134 128
$75,000 to $99,999	4 115 468	3 675 722	228 130	12 370	151 611	47 635	152 405	3 576 462
$100,000 or more	3 522 996	3 247 218	108 426	7 359	136 206	23 787	96 887	3 177 250
Median (dollars)	35 225	37 152	22 429	21 750	41 251	22 949	25 064	37 628
Mean (dollars)	43 803	46 330	28 659	28 025	51 102	27 943	31 195	46 930
Married-couple families	51 718 214	45 178 672	3 521 382	305 156	1 295 099	1 417 905	3 339 694	43 342 946
Less than $15,000	5 619 528	4 486 426	601 094	70 912	158 906	302 190	664 507	4 139 565
$15,000 to $24,999	7 734 791	6 575 092	621 592	62 551	154 424	321 132	692 958	6 220 151
$25,000 to $34,999	8 660 211	7 544 938	616 289	54 742	167 491	276 751	612 960	7 223 464
$35,000 to $49,999	11 566 753	10 243 307	745 545	57 587	244 189	276 125	653 998	9 882 640
$50,000 to $74,999	10 895 423	9 726 294	646 514	41 439	302 697	178 479	489 380	9 429 713
$75,000 or more	7 241 508	6 602 615	290 348	17 925	267 392	63 228	225 891	6 447 413
Female householder, no husband present	10 381 654	6 540 382	3 045 283	121 370	185 926	488 693	1 029 646	6 058 841
Less than $5,000	1 530 177	679 291	696 002	28 076	20 848	105 960	206 345	592 849
$5,000 to $9,999	1 636 764	883 985	582 809	29 368	23 576	117 026	224 843	789 442
$10,000 to $14,999	1 379 635	844 016	424 271	18 718	20 000	72 630	151 134	773 575
$15,000 to $24,999	2 286 235	1 531 229	603 978	23 312	34 272	93 444	202 370	1 432 881
$25,000 to $49,999	2 718 497	1 973 670	591 036	18 180	54 590	81 021	194 382	1 870 903
$50,000 or more	830 346	628 191	147 187	3 716	32 640	18 612	50 572	599 191
Males 15 years and over, with income	86 674 947	72 504 525	8 337 527	605 578	2 285 437	2 941 880	6 688 401	68 980 277
Median income (dollars)	20 409	21 695	12 950	12 180	19 396	12 493	13 501	22 065
Percent year-round full-time workers	53.0	54.2	44.9	40.9	52.4	47.5	48.7	54.4
Median income (dollars)	29 237	30 468	21 647	22 080	30 075	18 627	20 316	30 764
Females 15 years and over, with income	84 560 106	69 613 017	9 965 635	587 568	2 125 535	2 268 351	5 473 121	66 627 911
Median income (dollars)	10 371	10 652	8 825	7 310	11 986	7 876	8 354	10 747
Percent year-round full-time workers	33.9	33.6	35.0	29.5	40.6	31.9	33.4	33.6
Median income (dollars)	19 570	19 916	18 005	16 680	21 335	15 362	16 307	20 048
Per capita income (dollars)	14 420	15 687	8 859	8 328	13 638	7 340	8 400	16 074
Persons in households (dollars)	14 649	15 926	9 019	8 367	13 815	7 366	8 444	16 326
Persons in group quarters (dollars)	6 094	6 319	5 226	7 107	5 465	6 162	6 449	6 330
MEDIAN INCOME IN 1989 BY SELECTED CHARACTERISTICS								
Family type and presence of own children:								
Families (dollars)	35 225	37 152	22 429	21 750	41 251	22 949	25 064	37 628
With own children under 18 years (dollars)	34 627	37 303	20 292	20 221	41 025	21 789	23 417	38 074
With own children under 6 years (dollars)	31 580	34 547	16 924	16 856	37 325	20 007	21 230	35 352
Married-couple families (dollars)	39 584	40 396	33 538	28 287	44 965	27 731	29 930	40 723
With own children under 18 years (dollars)	40 693	41 686	35 162	28 124	44 966	27 219	29 208	42 172
With own children under 6 years (dollars)	36 490	37 369	31 268	22 901	40 210	24 138	25 918	37 908
Female householder, no husband present (dollars)	17 414	20 340	12 522	10 742	22 983	11 262	12 406	20 807
With own children under 18 years (dollars)	12 485	15 011	9 539	8 692	15 791	8 915	9 586	15 444
With own children under 6 years (dollars)	7 775	8 942	6 330	6 279	10 838	6 502	6 823	9 117
Workers in family in 1989:								
No workers (dollars)	14 622	17 311	5 308	6 069	9 050	5 431	5 976	17 781
1 worker (dollars)	25 517	27 998	15 764	15 526	27 860	15 776	16 914	28 714
2 or more workers (dollars)	44 500	45 738	36 955	32 978	50 706	32 272	34 879	46 122
Husband and wife worked (dollars)	46 340	47 005	41 557	35 390	52 729	34 166	37 007	47 273
Nonfamily households (dollars)	17 240	17 991	11 624	12 183	21 336	14 905	15 243	18 067
Male householder (dollars)	22 630	24 115	15 368	15 059	23 807	18 095	19 144	24 283
Living alone (dollars)	20 193	21 219	13 160	11 775	21 958	14 185	15 484	21 353
65 years and over (dollars)	11 688	12 574	6 676	6 792	9 295	6 519	7 159	12 726
Female householder (dollars)	13 729	14 294	9 060	9 939	18 405	9 904	10 624	14 369
Living alone (dollars)	12 226	12 737	8 042	8 142	16 190	7 828	8 517	12 837
65 years and over (dollars)	8 639	9 185	5 358	6 179	7 731	5 436	5 721	9 276

Source: U.S. Bureau of the Census, *Social and Economic Characteristics of the United States: 1990 Census of Population*, CP-2-1, Washington, D.C.: U.S. Government Printing Office, 1993, Table 48.

B5-13. Income in 1989 of Households, Families, and Persons for Selected Hispanic Origin Groups: 1990

[Data based on sample and subject to sampling variability.]

United States	All persons	Hispanic origin (of any race)										
		Total	Mexican	Puerto Rican	Cuban	Other Hispanic — Total	Dominican (Dominican Republic)	Central American — Total	Costa Rican	Guatemalan	Honduran	Nicaraguan
INCOME IN 1989												
Households	91 993 582	5 872 040	3 302 126	797 809	392 200	1 379 905	147 716	336 531	17 071	66 397	33 426	49 197
Less than $5,000	5 684 517	519 528	268 253	104 495	36 309	110 471	19 391	21 767	1 026	4 052	3 343	2 810
$5,000 to $9,999	8 529 980	653 488	355 255	122 111	40 231	135 891	23 187	29 677	1 398	5 325	3 286	4 148
$10,000 to $14,999	8 133 273	644 179	388 806	79 704	36 039	139 630	15 821	39 380	1 549	7 981	4 095	5 653
$15,000 to $24,999	16 123 742	1 205 131	717 597	147 107	65 469	274 958	29 365	79 499	2 884	16 454	7 993	11 214
$25,000 to $34,999	14 575 125	963 489	561 475	116 505	57 557	227 952	22 415	60 332	3 005	12 243	5 709	8 882
$35,000 to $49,999	16 428 455	937 461	526 955	114 224	65 921	230 361	19 871	55 078	3 426	11 573	4 613	7 748
$50,000 to $74,999	13 777 883	653 931	348 884	81 330	54 647	169 070	12 668	35 427	2 532	6 177	3 132	6 000
$75,000 to $99,999	4 704 808	180 396	87 451	21 249	19 470	52 226	3 165	9 443	675	1 513	736	1 746
$100,000 or more	4 035 799	114 437	47 450	11 084	16 557	39 346	1 833	5 928	576	1 079	519	996
Median (dollars)	30 056	24 156	23 694	21 056	27 741	26 067	20 006	24 695	30 785	24 569	22 109	25 717
Mean (dollars)	38 453	30 301	29 151	26 903	36 944	33 130	25 579	30 359	36 282	30 152	27 671	31 758
Families	65 049 428	4 776 075	2 776 147	627 527	295 380	1 077 021	126 991	284 787	13 279	56 978	27 445	42 608
Less than $5,000	2 582 206	365 222	199 635	78 436	12 846	74 305	16 664	18 475	613	3 554	2 641	2 413
$5,000 to $9,999	3 636 361	483 067	278 974	89 878	22 186	92 029	19 542	25 799	938	5 007	2 879	3 391
$10,000 to $14,999	4 676 092	535 520	338 065	62 805	25 707	108 943	14 433	36 410	1 057	7 760	3 493	5 227
$15,000 to $24,999	10 658 345	998 207	617 115	113 724	50 386	216 982	25 333	69 700	2 165	14 802	6 557	10 151
$25,000 to $34,999	10 729 951	798 318	477 513	91 417	47 215	182 173	19 352	50 221	2 496	10 093	4 765	7 635
$35,000 to $49,999	13 270 930	789 353	451 378	94 947	56 414	186 614	17 088	44 362	2 803	9 190	3 542	6 439
$50,000 to $74,999	11 857 079	557 096	299 323	68 976	48 597	140 200	10 671	27 721	2 159	4 584	2 517	5 099
$75,000 to $99,999	4 115 468	152 405	73 997	18 227	17 436	42 745	2 398	7 334	553	1 103	604	1 453
$100,000 or more	3 522 996	96 887	40 147	9 117	14 593	33 030	1 510	4 765	495	885	447	800
Median (dollars)	35 225	25 064	24 119	21 941	32 417	27 151	19 726	23 619	32 072	22 862	21 761	25 136
Mean (dollars)	43 803	31 195	29 564	27 869	41 619	34 480	25 236	29 451	38 409	28 581	27 351	31 277
Married-couple families	51 718 214	3 339 694	2 027 520	353 483	230 617	728 074	63 556	180 231	9 279	36 976	16 240	28 534
Less than $15,000	5 619 528	664 507	447 890	62 393	36 673	117 551	13 587	34 771	1 169	7 599	3 373	5 143
$15,000 to $24,999	7 734 791	692 958	450 734	66 058	36 160	140 006	13 721	43 793	1 313	9 575	3 901	6 629
$25,000 to $34,999	8 660 211	612 960	378 177	65 007	36 904	132 872	12 664	35 299	1 706	7 239	3 299	5 522
$35,000 to $49,999	11 566 753	653 998	381 436	75 672	47 450	149 440	12 386	33 392	2 204	7 070	2 700	4 947
$50,000 to $74,999	10 895 423	489 380	265 563	59 979	43 749	120 089	8 067	22 669	1 879	3 761	2 080	4 291
$75,000 or more	7 241 508	225 891	103 720	24 374	29 681	68 116	3 131	10 307	1 008	1 732	887	2 002
Female householder, no husband present	10 381 654	1 029 646	505 042	229 639	48 072	246 893	52 333	64 344	3 104	10 846	8 080	8 851
Less than $5,000	1 530 177	206 345	98 058	59 125	6 113	43 049	12 268	9 028	335	1 612	1 404	1 082
$5,000 to $9,999	1 636 764	224 843	106 113	64 394	6 850	47 486	14 363	11 816	509	1 964	1 739	1 364
$10,000 to $14,999	1 379 635	151 134	80 382	29 216	6 093	35 443	6 797	10 668	422	1 930	1 203	1 484
$15,000 to $24,999	2 286 235	202 370	104 174	36 937	10 043	51 216	8 716	14 719	619	2 630	1 852	2 046
$25,000 to $49,999	2 718 497	194 382	94 236	32 170	14 087	53 889	7 992	14 579	1 023	2 298	1 611	2 233
$50,000 or more	830 346	50 572	22 079	7 797	4 886	15 810	2 197	3 534	196	412	271	642
Males 15 years and over, with income	86 674 947	6 688 401	4 054 638	738 492	396 199	1 499 072	136 297	414 786	17 956	90 481	36 630	59 170
Median income (dollars)	20 409	13 501	12 456	15 290	16 506	15 079	13 410	12 294	18 423	11 883	12 171	12 776
Percent year-round full-time workers	53.0	48.7	47.5	49.4	53.3	50.5	49.9	50.3	54.4	49.3	47.9	50.9
Median (dollars)	29 237	20 316	18 847	22 197	24 671	21 331	18 954	16 515	24 300	15 772	17 574	17 489
Females 15 years and over, with income	84 560 106	5 473 121	2 990 119	743 796	370 213	1 368 993	151 831	353 589	17 646	66 824	37 983	55 035
Median income (dollars)	10 371	8 354	7 975	7 769	9 469	9 220	7 722	8 807	10 227		8 293	8 773
Percent year-round full-time workers	33.9	33.4	32.7	30.3	37.4	35.6	30.5	37.9	37.6	37.6	36.1	38.0
Median (dollars)	19 570	16 307	15 478	18 717	18 283	16 415	15 001	12 831	17 344	11 903	13 607	13 822
Per capita income (dollars)	14 420	8 400	7 447	8 403	13 786	9 873	7 381	8 005	11 019	7 761	7 650	7 995
Persons in households (dollars)	14 649	8 444	7 472	8 470	13 965	9 938	7 393	8 027	11 126	7 785	7 581	8 030
Persons in group quarters (dollars)	6 094	6 449	6 229	6 468	6 328	7 003	6 683	6 432	5 625	6 000	11 918	4 938
MEDIAN INCOME IN 1989 BY SELECTED CHARACTERISTICS												
Family type and presence of own children:												
Families (dollars)	35 225	25 064	24 119	21 941	32 417	27 151	19 726	23 619	32 072	22 862	21 761	25 136
With own children under 18 years (dollars)	34 627	23 417	22 917	19 587	34 464	25 428	17 311	22 403	31 250	22 070	20 304	23 867
With own children under 6 years (dollars)	31 580	21 230	20 827	17 089	34 893	23 049	15 701	21 274	29 511	20 382	18 689	23 362
Married-couple families (dollars)	39 584	29 930	27 664	32 111	36 471	32 568	28 252	27 706	37 592	26 531	26 788	29 294
With own children under 18 years (dollars)	40 693	29 208	27 129	32 068	40 211	31 825	27 921	26 991	37 033	26 043	26 260	27 798
With own children under 6 years (dollars)	36 490	25 918	23 687	29 483	39 326	28 175	26 365	24 335	33 333	22 871	23 361	28 086
Female householder, no husband present (dollars)	17 414	12 406	12 714	8 912	19 511	14 576	9 724	15 358	19 323	14 715	13 482	17 177
With own children under 18 years (dollars)	12 485	9 586	10 276	7 366	14 645	10 816	7 568	12 042	13 060	11 673	10 583	14 413
With own children under 6 years (dollars)	7 775	6 823	6 820	6 045	11 340	7 839	6 684	9 471	9 553	8 834	9 928	12 290
Workers in family in 1989:												
No workers (dollars)	14 622	5 976	6 120	5 477	7 883	6 072	5 124	5 000–	6 463	5 000–	5 000–	5 000–
1 worker (dollars)	25 517	16 914	15 973	18 057	21 997	18 023	15 672	14 548	21 679	14 441	14 841	15 260
2 or more workers (dollars)	44 500	34 879	32 646	38 486	43 025	36 547	33 187	30 740	40 210	29 695	29 659	31 278
Husband and wife worked (dollars)	46 340	37 007	34 658	40 825	45 252	39 503	35 910	32 814	43 131	31 608	32 459	33 520
Nonfamily households (dollars)	17 240	15 243	15 355	13 193	11 870	16 834	11 921	16 983	19 397	17 434	15 441	16 482
Male householder (dollars)	22 630	19 144	18 930	17 327	16 758	21 063	17 026	20 197	24 232	20 034	18 103	20 521
Living alone (dollars)	20 193	15 484	15 153	14 234	13 530	17 229	13 011	15 662	22 059	15 783	14 847	16 862
65 years and over (dollars)	11 688	7 159	6 972	6 672	6 331	8 977	6 611	8 683	27 946	9 491	11 667	11 250
Female householder (dollars)	13 729	10 624	10 352	9 306	8 204	12 480	8 299	13 022	14 595	13 160	12 562	11 975
Living alone (dollars)	12 226	8 517	8 185	7 896	6 919	10 373	7 016	10 451	12 349	9 927	9 403	10 025
65 years and over (dollars)	8 639	5 721	5 490	5 783	5 000–	6 575	5 651	6 578	7 577	6 090	5 199	6 643

B5-13. Income in 1989 of Households, Families, and Persons for Selected Hispanic Origin Groups: 1990 (continued)

[Data based on sample and subject to sampling variability.]

United States	Central American—Con.			South American								All other Hispanic origin	Not of Hispanic origin
	Panamanian	Salvadoran	Other Central American	Total	Argentinean	Chilean	Colombian	Ecuadorian	Peruvian	Venezuelan	Other South American		
INCOME IN 1989													
Households	**30 288**	**137 946**	**2 206**	**320 450**	**38 717**	**22 399**	**112 227**	**56 384**	**52 735**	**15 036**	**22 952**	**575 208**	**86 121 542**
Less than $5,000	2 243	8 002	291	19 405	2 004	1 032	6 964	3 741	2 999	1 448	1 217	49 908	5 164 989
$5,000 to $9,999	2 682	12 607	231	22 444	2 206	1 516	8 172	4 580	3 480	1 122	1 368	60 583	7 876 492
$10,000 to $14,999	2 671	17 196	235	26 521	2 865	1 516	10 082	4 499	4 496	1 228	1 835	57 908	7 489 094
$15,000 to $24,999	5 703	34 754	497	58 617	6 121	3 996	21 772	9 947	10 107	2 534	4 140	107 477	14 918 611
$25,000 to $34,999	4 985	25 198	310	56 217	6 039	3 630	20 420	9 896	9 575	2 465	4 192	88 988	13 611 636
$35,000 to $49,999	5 051	22 315	352	60 918	7 596	4 349	21 300	10 956	9 723	2 820	4 174	94 494	15 490 994
$50,000 to $74,999	4 544	12 835	207	47 735	6 606	3 934	15 295	8 413	7 851	2 041	3 595	73 240	13 123 952
$75,000 to $99,999	1 398	3 305	70	15 732	2 373	1 166	4 639	2 822	2 545	778	1 409	23 886	4 524 412
$100,000 or more	1 011	1 734	13	12 861	2 907	1 260	3 583	1 530	1 959	600	1 022	18 724	3 921 362
Median (dollars)	27 872	23 729	22 304	30 716	35 202	33 391	29 171	30 383	30 453	29 686	31 394	26 121	30 447
Mean (dollars)	35 206	28 832	29 229	38 254	45 881	41 448	36 102	35 718	38 065	37 652	39 857	33 836	39 009
Families	**21 622**	**121 115**	**1 740**	**251 987**	**28 463**	**17 167**	**88 617**	**47 058**	**41 918**	**10 634**	**18 130**	**413 256**	**60 273 353**
Less than $5,000	1 237	7 811	206	11 922	1 020	444	4 398	2 644	1 846	874	696	27 244	2 216 984
$5,000 to $9,999	1 366	12 042	176	13 989	1 072	840	5 525	3 110	2 206	539	697	32 699	3 153 294
$10,000 to $14,999	1 696	16 950	227	19 605	1 551	980	7 845	3 780	3 273	829	1 347	38 495	4 140 572
$15,000 to $24,999	3 827	31 822	376	46 140	4 238	2 999	17 107	8 465	8 291	1 793	3 247	75 809	9 660 138
$25,000 to $34,999	3 455	21 560	217	45 858	4 612	3 035	16 657	8 691	7 571	1 723	3 569	66 742	9 931 633
$35,000 to $49,999	4 167	17 900	321	50 755	6 014	3 591	17 673	9 421	8 518	2 070	3 468	74 409	12 481 577
$50,000 to $74,999	3 798	9 407	157	40 007	5 432	3 260	12 549	7 310	6 564	1 771	3 121	61 801	11 299 983
$75,000 to $99,999	1 222	2 352	47	12 731	2 014	968	3 719	2 343	1 983	561	1 143	20 282	3 963 063
$100,000 or more	854	1 271	13	10 980	2 510	1 050	3 144	1 294	1 666	474	842	15 775	3 426 109
Median (dollars)	32 185	22 006	21 415	32 087	39 044	36 128	30 384	31 074	31 828	32 078	33 162	29 683	36 028
Mean (dollars)	38 934	27 014	29 763	40 251	50 690	44 228	37 761	36 517	39 922	41 483	41 996	37 267	44 802
Married-couple families	**13 027**	**75 170**	**1 005**	**183 855**	**23 810**	**13 589**	**60 828**	**32 957**	**30 418**	**8 201**	**14 052**	**300 432**	**48 378 520**
Less than $15,000	1 188	16 075	224	22 308	2 335	1 232	7 731	4 185	3 998	1 290	1 537	46 885	4 955 021
$15,000 to $24,999	1 805	20 362	208	30 359	3 227	2 208	10 793	5 408	5 121	1 222	2 229	52 133	7 041 833
$25,000 to $34,999	2 111	15 300	122	33 993	3 752	2 336	11 744	6 387	5 539	1 393	2 842	50 916	8 047 251
$35,000 to $49,999	2 989	13 200	282	41 384	5 243	3 077	14 035	7 479	6 842	1 782	2 926	62 278	10 912 755
$50,000 to $74,999	3 194	7 355	109	34 349	4 983	2 905	10 362	6 244	5 518	1 586	2 751	55 004	10 406 043
$75,000 or more	1 740	2 878	60	21 462	4 270	1 831	6 163	3 254	3 249	928	1 767	33 216	7 015 617
Female householder, no husband present	**7 270**	**25 684**	**509**	**45 334**	**3 084**	**2 230**	**19 004**	**9 742**	**6 989**	**1 763**	**2 522**	**84 882**	**9 352 008**
Less than $5,000	883	3 588	124	5 671	391	187	2 191	1 463	792	385	262	16 082	1 323 832
$5,000 to $9,999	959	5 219	62	6 314	284	305	2 654	1 785	845	161	280	14 993	1 411 921
$10,000 to $14,999	849	4 690	90	6 100	327	250	2 925	1 241	855	164	338	11 878	1 228 501
$15,000 to $24,999	1 819	5 637	116	10 213	608	483	4 260	1 974	1 789	451	648	17 568	2 083 865
$25,000 to $49,999	1 983	5 353	79	12 586	1 069	682	5 249	2 512	1 983	389	702	18 732	2 524 115
$50,000 or more	777	1 198	38	4 450	405	323	1 725	767	725	213	292	5 629	779 774
Males 15 years and over, with income	**25 970**	**182 412**	**2 167**	**353 735**	**39 302**	**24 193**	**121 427**	**67 044**	**60 796**	**15 353**	**25 620**	**594 254**	**79 986 546**
Median income (dollars)	18 568	11 874	12 509	17 469	22 329	20 224	16 991	16 304	16 587	18 860	19 117	16 183	21 028
Percent year-round full-time workers	53.9	50.1	50.9	54.4	56.8	56.0	54.7	53.4	52.6	53.7	54.3	48.5	53.3
Median (dollars)	25 660	14 954	19 447	23 857	30 708	26 609	22 347	21 677	22 325	26 446	25 722	25 021	30 090
Females 15 years and over, with income	**34 352**	**139 814**	**1 935**	**306 549**	**30 811**	**20 541**	**115 913**	**55 768**	**49 922**	**12 528**	**21 066**	**557 024**	**79 086 985**
Median income (dollars)	12 011	8 554	9 362	10 495	11 716	10 975	10 246	10 156	10 450	11 187	10 812	9 396	10 533
Percent year-round full-time workers	40.7	37.8	38.3	38.3	37.5	39.0	38.4	38.4	38.3	38.3	37.9	34.2	33.9
Median (dollars)	20 472	12 840	17 132	17 610	21 190	19 296	16 835	17 219	17 219	20 050	18 243	18 183	19 809
Per capita income (dollars)	**12 223**	**7 201**	**9 191**	**12 119**	**17 447**	**13 663**	**11 150**	**10 889**	**11 640**	**12 168**	**12 662**	**10 623**	**15 002**
Persons in households (dollars)	12 427	7 222	9 213	12 196	17 721	13 800	11 215	10 809	11 733	12 334	12 796	10 747	15 252
Persons in group quarters (dollars)	6 947	5 035	7 016	8 249	4 845	4 524	8 713	17 488	5 501	5 282	4 851	6 803	6 066
MEDIAN INCOME IN 1989 BY SELECTED CHARACTERISTICS													
Family type and presence of own children:													
Families (dollars)	32 185	22 006	21 415	32 087	39 044	36 128	30 384	31 074	31 828	32 078	33 162	29 683	36 028
With own children under 18 years (dollars)	30 821	21 291	21 006	30 910	37 481	35 766	28 613	29 226	30 903	31 544	32 230	27 773	35 856
With own children under 6 years (dollars)	28 155	20 665	20 172	28 619	35 296	32 985	26 471	26 850	28 945	31 151	30 280	25 020	32 837
Married-couple families (dollars)	41 500	25 585	30 687	36 515	41 665	40 141	35 124	35 782	35 610	36 339	36 722	35 058	40 284
With own children under 18 years (dollars)	41 602	25 365	31 125	35 639	41 021	40 216	33 778	34 664	35 006	36 041	36 495	35 421	41 646
With own children under 6 years (dollars)	32 072	23 056	24 625	31 304	36 808	32 715	29 799	29 786	31 705	35 331	31 418	31 092	37 389
Female householder, no husband present (dollars)	20 214	14 061	13 464	19 272	24 000	22 523	18 696	16 670	20 481	20 069	20 254	14 760	18 022
With own children under 18 years (dollars)	16 844	11 555	11 193	13 992	17 777	16 845	16 247	10 850	15 623	15 833	16 489	10 941	13 027
With own children under 6 years (dollars)	10 046	8 739	9 507	10 940	21 161	12 031	10 712	8 190	11 723	14 336	10 833	6 917	7 942
Workers in family in 1989:													
No workers (dollars)	7 559	5 000–	5 000–	5 283	7 620	6 548	5 153	5 191	5 000–	5 000–	5 150	8 676	15 406
1 worker (dollars)	21 011	12 970	15 087	21 477	29 052	23 956	19 744	20 522	20 524	23 102	23 877	20 421	26 385
2 or more workers (dollars)	42 799	28 641	30 833	39 655	45 866	42 784	37 707	39 142	38 217	40 960	40 794	40 529	45 284
Husband and wife worked (dollars)	46 514	30 216	37 572	41 878	47 471	44 138	40 238	41 769	40 774	42 166	42 657	42 884	46 910
Nonfamily households (dollars)	**19 599**	**15 945**	**17 386**	**19 633**	**22 325**	**20 998**	**19 027**	**17 298**	**19 327**	**20 398**	**19 500**	**16 310**	**17 322**
Male householder (dollars)	22 754	18 746	20 789	23 147	25 193	26 585	22 773	21 367	21 962	24 583	23 103	21 052	22 894
Living alone (dollars)	21 173	12 983	15 208	19 047	21 260	21 656	18 323	16 711	17 516	22 354	18 776	17 516	20 401
65 years and over (dollars)	7 987	6 340	–	9 469	13 510	8 698	7 597	7 626	10 962	13 750	15 909	9 166	11 847
Female householder (dollars)	16 431	11 285	15 750	15 495	18 884	16 493	14 969	12 936	15 676	15 029	15 018	12 128	13 834
Living alone (dollars)	14 560	7 986	7 109	12 270	16 070	12 235	11 888	9 584	12 163	12 450	12 363	10 313	12 331
65 years and over (dollars)	7 284	6 297	8 077	6 331	8 326	6 752	5 866	5 718	6 130	7 222	6 784	6 767	8 747

Source: U.S. Bureau of the Census, *Social and Economic Characteristics of the United States: 1990 Census of Population*, CP-2-1, Washington, D.C.: U.S. Government Printing Office, 1993, Table 120.

B5-14. Number and Percentage Distribution of Persons 15 Years and Over with Social Security Benefits or with Supplemental Security Income, by Age, Sex, and Race: March 1993 and Median Amount in 1992

[Based on data from the Current Population Survey (CPS); civilian noninstitutionalized population]

Age and median amount	Total Number (in thousands)	Total[2] percent	White	Black	Men Number (in thousands)	Total[2] percent	White	Black	Women Number (in thousands)	Total[2] percent	White	Black
					With Social Security							
Total	36,764	100.0	88.2	9.9	15,658	100.0	88.4	9.6	21,106	100.0	88.0	10.2
Under 55	3,872	100.0	78.8	18.7	1,906	100.0	81.0	16.3	1,966	100.0	76.6	21.1
55-64	4,591	100.0	85.1	12.8	2,082	100.0	86.4	11.5	2,509	100.0	84.0	13.8
65-74	16,515	100.0	89.2	8.9	7,211	100.0	89.3	8.8	9,303	100.0	89.2	8.9
75 or older	11,786	100.0	91.0	7.5	4,458	100.0	90.9	7.0	7,328	100.0	91.0	7.8
Median amount	...	$6,257	$6,439	$5,199	...	$7,648	$7,880	$5,852	...	$5,374	$5,488	$4,699
					With Supplemental Security Income							
Total	4,695	100.0	66.1	28.9	1,745	100.0	66.3	27.4	2,950	100.0	66.0	29.8
Under 55	2,265	100.0	67.9	27.9	1,050	100.0	67.9	27.1	1,215	100.0	67.9	28.5
55-64	706	100.0	65.6	32.0	230	100.0	67.6	28.9	476	100.0	64.6	33.5
65-74	896	100.0	63.0	30.8	281	100.0	63.7	27.5	615	100.0	62.6	32.3
75 or older	828	100.0	65.1	27.1	183	100.0	59.6	26.8	645	100.0	66.6	27.1
Median amount	...	$3,185	$3,159	$2,944	...	$3,594	$3,613	$3,160	...	$2,925	$2,861	$2,871

[1]Includes noninstitutionalized civilian population residing in the 50 States and the District of Columbia.
[2]Includes other races.
Source: Public use file of the March 1993 Income Supplement, Current Population Survey, Bureau of the Census. For a discussion of standard errors of estimated numbers and percentages, see Bureau of the Census, Current Population Reports, P-60 series.

Source: Social Security Administration, *Social Security Bulletin, 1994 Annual Statistical Supplement*, Washington, D.C.: U.S. Government Printing Office, 1994, Table 3.C7.

B5-15. Number of Persons 15 Years and Over with Social Security Benefits or with Supplemental Security Income and Percent of Spanish Origin, by Age and Sex: March 1993 and Median Amount 1992

[Based on data from the Current Population Survey (CPS); civilian noninstitutionalized population]

Age and median amount	Number (in thousands) Total	Men	Women	Percent of Spanish origin[2] Total	Men	Women
			With Social Security			
Total	36,764	15,658	21,106	4.2	4.5	4.0
Under 55	3,872	1,906	1,966	8.9	9.4	8.4
55-64	4,591	2,082	2,509	5.3	4.9	5.6
65-74	16,515	7,211	9,303	3.8	4.0	3.8
75 or older	11,786	4,458	7,328	2.8	3.1	2.7
Median amount	$6,257	$7,648	$5,374	$5,113	$6,247	$4,329
			With Supplemental Security Income			
Total	4,695	1,745	2,950	12.2	14.2	11.0
Under 55	2,265	1,050	1,215	9.9	12.6	7.5
55-64	706	230	476	14.0	15.4	13.3
65-74	896	281	615	15.3	16.4	14.8
75 or older	828	183	645	13.5	18.1	12.2
Median amount	$3,185	$3,594	$2,925	$4,002	$4,436	$3,794

[1]Includes noninstitutionalized civilian population residing in the 50 States and the District of Columbia.
[2]Persons of Spanish origin may be of any race.
Source: Public use file of the March 1993 Income Supplement, Current Population Survey, Bureau of the Census. For a discussion of standard errors of estimated numbers and percentages, see Bureau of the Census, Current Population Reports, P-60 series.

Source: Social Security Administration, *Social Security Bulletin, 1994 Annual Statistical Supplement*, Washington, D.C.: U.S. Government Printing Office, 1994, Table 3.C8.

B5-16. Number and Average Monthly Benefit for Women Beneficiaries of the Old Age Security and Disability Insurance (OASDI) Program, by Type of Benefit and Race: December 1993

[Numbers in thousands. Based on 10-percent sample]

Type of benefit	Total [2] Number	Total [2] Average monthly benefit	White Number	White Average monthly benefit	Black Number	Black Average monthly benefit	Other Number	Other Average monthly benefit
Total	22,600	$549.30	20,137	$558.50	2,000	$475.70	352	$453.30
Workers	13,819	574.40	12,243	582.70	1,300	507.60	200	506.90
Retired	12,447	580.70	11,188	588.60	1,033	508.50	170	511.30
Full benefit	3,418	737.10	3,005	753.20	345	611.40	49	642.60
Reduced benefit, claimed before age 65	9,029	521.50	8,183	528.10	689	457.00	121	458.00
Disabled	1,371	516.40	1,055	520.20	267	504.20	29	481.30
Wives of retired and disabled workers	3,333	333.70	3,056	341.10	193	248.80	67	251.20
Entitlement based on care of children	287	165.00	225	171.70	45	143.40	12	130.90
Husband retired	81	235.40	63	247.80	12	200.60	5	168.00
Husband disabled	206	137.30	162	141.90	33	122.40	7	106.90
Entitlement based on age (aged 62 or older)	3,046	349.60	2,831	354.60	147	281.50	55	278.10
Husband retired	2,988	351.90	2,779	356.90	142	284.00	54	279.10
Full benefit	541	441.50	491	453.00	34	328.30	13	318.70
Reduced benefit, claimed before age 65	2,447	332.10	2,289	336.30	108	270.10	41	266.90
Husband disabled	59	229.40	52	231.90	5	208.30	1	208.70
Widows	5,442	618.00	4,833	634.90	506	480.30	84	487.00
Entitlement based on care of children	273	455.10	197	484.40	55	374.90	15	366.90
Nondisabled, aged 60 or older	5,024	632.10	4,525	645.90	420	501.40	67	516.70
Disabled, aged 50-64	145	437.50	111	454.50	31	380.60	3	396.20
Mothers of deceased workers	4	556.10	3	586.00	1	484.40	(3)	517.80
Special age-72 beneficiaries	2	183.30	1	183.40	(3)	183.40	(3)	183.40

[1] See table 5.A1 for description of race data.
[2] Includes persons of unknown race.
[3] Fewer than 500 beneficiaries.

Source: Social Security Administration, *Social Security Bulletin, 1994 Annual Statistical Supplement*, Washington, D.C.: U.S. Government Printing Office, 1994, Tables 5.A7.

B5-17. Median Net Worth, by Type of Household and Age of Householder: 1991 and 1988

[Excludes group quarters]

Type of household by age of householder	1991 Number of households (thousands)	1991 Median net worth Total	1991 Median net worth Excluding equity in own home	1988 dollars (in 1991 dollars) Number of households (thousands)	1988 dollars (in 1991 dollars) Median net worth Total	1988 dollars (in 1991 dollars) Median net worth Excluding equity in own home
Married-couple households	52,216	$60,065	$18,606	51,697	$66,275	$18,900
Less than 35 years	12,247	12,036	5,235	13,357	13,968	5,458
35 to 54 years	23,080	60,505	18,689	21,437	70,309	19,630
55 to 64 years	7,849	128,782	44,827	8,186	139,383	49,575
65 years and over	9,040	147,904	56,080	8,736	144,326	53,232
Male householders	15,297	$11,986	$5,661	14,383	$15,141	$6,327
Less than 35 years	5,746	5,014	3,507	5,592	5,752	3,938
35 to 54 years	5,409	17,740	7,101	4,857	19,784	7,075
55 to 64 years	1,514	30,857	5,860	1,586	40,278	12,391
65 years and over	2,627	64,381	17,322	2,346	56,704	18,460
Female householders	27,179	$14,762	$3,596	25,437	$15,742	$4,214
Less than 35 years	7,038	1,360	930	6,430	1,598	1,134
35 to 54 years	7,959	10,684	3,224	7,236	12,696	3,406
55 to 64 years	3,211	39,591	6,048	3,336	47,323	8,125
65 years and over	8,972	59,521	12,689	8,471	54,790	12,404

Source: T. J. Eller, *Household Wealth and Asset Ownership: 1991 Survey of Income and Program Participation*, Current Population Reports, P70-34, Washington, D.C.: U.S. Government Printing Office, January 1994, Table J.

B5-18. Households Owning Assets, by Age of Householder: 1991

[Excludes persons in group quarters.]

Characteristic	Number of households (thousands)	Percent owning— Interest earning assets at financial institutions[1]	Other interest-earning assets[2]	Regular checking accounts	Stocks and mutual fund shares	Own business or profession
Total	94 692	73.17	8.98	46.03	20.74	11.70
TYPE OF HOUSEHOLD BY AGE OF HOUSEHOLDER						
Married-couple households	52 216	80.24	10.97	51.50	25.17	16.30
Less than 35 years	12 247	74.10	4.31	46.87	15.22	12.67
35 to 54 years	23 080	81.26	10.77	56.20	27.05	20.46
55 to 64 years	7 849	81.43	14.25	54.55	28.96	19.22
65 years and over	9 040	84.92	17.66	43.13	30.56	8.05
Male householder	15 297	68.17	6.65	39.53	17.15	9.20
Less than 35 years	5 746	68.71	4.69	40.69	13.68	7.90
35 to 54 years	5 409	68.79	6.30	41.62	19.72	13.29
55 to 64 years	1 514	58.63	5.89	40.57	17.38	7.40
65 years and over	2 627	71.17	12.12	32.11	19.30	4.68
Female householder	27 179	62.42	6.48	39.17	14.23	4.27
Less than 35 years	7 038	52.43	1.85	35.24	8.08	3.56
35 to 54 years	7 959	59.15	5.49	41.44	13.41	6.47
55 to 64 years	3 211	62.48	6.07	43.77	19.35	5.05
65 years and over	8 972	73.12	11.13	38.61	17.95	2.61

Charactersitic	Percent owning— Motor vehicles	Own home	Rental property	Other real estate	Mortgages	U.S. savings bonds	IRA or KEOGH accounts	Other assets[3]
Total	86.40	64.71	9.04	10.67	2.03	18.06	22.90	2.76
TYPE OF HOUSEHOLD BY AGE OF HOUSEHOLDER								
Married-couple households	96.26	78.63	11.24	14.18	2.54	23.23	30.23	3.21
Less than 35 years	96.29	56.35	4.69	6.27	.35	21.17	14.83	.91
35 to 54 years	96.71	82.94	12.72	14.97	2.10	26.75	33.49	3.18
55 to 64 years	97.12	88.83	16.00	21.78	4.14	23.78	47.65	5.37
65 years and over	94.31	88.96	12.19	16.26	5.26	16.57	27.63	4.51
Male householder	83.69	46.00	7.62	8.07	1.28	13.10	16.04	2.71
Less than 35 years	85.92	27.45	4.44	3.64	.30	12.51	8.41	1.66
35 to 54 years	85.73	52.53	9.87	11.88	1.21	15.91	24.60	3.49
55 to 64 years	81.90	57.13	9.49	11.03	2.41	9.51	21.65	3.18
65 years and over	75.65	66.73	8.88	8.23	2.93	10.65	11.88	3.14
Female householder	68.99	48.51	5.62	5.40	1.45	10.92	12.69	1.92
Less than 35 years	67.83	17.38	1.25	2.00	.06	9.36	5.55	1.08
35 to 54 years	80.06	49.54	5.14	6.72	1.09	13.82	17.52	1.69
55 to 64 years	72.82	62.62	8.45	7.90	1.92	13.08	25.25	2.65
65 years and over	58.70	66.95	8.45	6.00	2.69	8.80	9.50	2.52

[1]Includes passbook savings accounts, money market deposit accounts, certificates of deposit, and interest-earning checking accounts.
[2]Includes money market funds, U.S. Government securities, municipal and corporate bonds, and other interest-earning assets.
[3]Includes unit trusts and other financial investments.

Source: T. J. Eller, *Household Wealth and Asset Ownership: 1991 Survey of Income and Program Participation*, Current Population Reports, P70-34, Washington, D.C.: U.S. Government Printing Office, January 1994, Tables 2.

B5-19. Distribution of Household Net Worth, by Age of Householder: 1991

[Excludes persons in group quarters.]

Characteristic	Number of households (thousands)	Zero or negative	$1 to $4,999	$5,000 to $9,999	$10,000 to $24,999	$25,000 to $49,999	$50,000 to $99,999	$100,000 to $249,999	$250,000 to $499,999	$500,000 or over
Total	94 692	12.00	13.96	6.52	11.18	12.24	15.58	17.76	7.06	3.64
TYPE OF HOUSEHOLD BY AGE OF HOUSEHOLDER										
Married-couple households	52 216	7.21	8.85	5.30	10.93	13.46	17.44	22.27	9.39	5.12
Less than 35 years	12 247	15.85	19.92	10.65	18.55	13.97	11.29	7.77	1.27	.68
35 to 54 years	23 080	6.14	7.34	4.70	11.32	15.55	19.59	22.84	8.18	4.30
55 to 64 years	7 849	3.39	3.34	2.68	5.35	10.61	18.63	31.03	16.09	8.81
65 years and over	9 040	1.57	2.48	1.84	4.45	9.88	19.26	32.83	17.63	10.01
Male householder	15 297	15.05	21.62	10.26	12.28	10.65	11.20	12.33	4.45	2.11
Less than 35 years	5 746	20.84	29.07	13.74	15.49	8.31	6.50	4.23	1.46	.31
35 to 54 years	5 409	13.71	18.69	10.56	11.55	12.04	13.22	13.84	3.94	2.40
55 to 64 years	1 514	9.65	19.33	6.32	9.83	14.18	13.71	17.04	6.00	3.88
65 years and over	2 627	8.23	12.70	4.33	8.19	10.84	15.85	24.24	11.17	4.40
Female householder	27 179	19.50	19.48	6.78	11.04	10.82	14.46	12.16	4.06	1.67
Less than 35 years	7 038	35.17	32.86	9.96	9.59	6.11	4.26	1.60	.22	.19
35 to 54 years	7 959	20.32	19.86	8.90	13.54	12.38	12.09	9.79	2.23	.86
55 to 64 years	3 211	14.78	12.40	4.19	11.13	12.98	17.76	18.59	5.66	2.45
65 years and over	8 972	8.17	11.19	3.33	9.92	12.35	23.38	20.24	8.11	3.27

Source: T. J. Eller, *Household Wealth and Asset Ownership: 1991 Survey of Income and Program Participation*, Current Population Reports, P70-34, Washington, D.C.: U.S. Government Printing Office, January 1994, Table 4.

B6. POVERTY

B6-1. Persons and Families below Poverty Level, by Race: 1989, 1992, and 1993

[Numbers in thousands]

Characteristic	Below poverty						1993-92 difference		1993-89 difference	
	1993		1992ʳ		1989ʳ		Number of poor	Poverty rate	Number of poor	Poverty rate
	Number	Percent	Number	Percent	Number	Percent				
PERSONS										
Total	39,265	15.1	38,014	14.8	32,415	13.1	*1,251	0.3	*6,850	*2.0
White	26,226	12.2	25,259	11.9	21,294	10.2	*967	0.3	*4,932	*2.0
Not of Hispanic origin	18,883	9.9	18,202	9.6	15,499	8.3	681	0.3	*3,384	*1.6
Black	10,877	33.1	10,827	33.4	9,525	30.8	50	-0.4	*1,352	*2.3
Other races	2,162	18.8	1,928	17.4	1,596	16.6	234	1.4	*566	2.2
Asian and Pacific Islander	1,134	15.3	985	12.7	1,032	14.2	149	2.6	102	1.1
Hispanic origin¹	8,126	30.6	7,592	29.6	6,086	26.3	*534	1.0	*2,040	*4.3
Family Status										
In families	29,927	13.6	28,961	13.3	24,882	11.8	*966	0.3	*5,045	*1.8
Householder	8,393	12.3	8,144	11.9	6,895	10.4	249	0.3	*1,498	*1.9
Related children under 18	14,961	22.0	14,521	21.6	12,541	19.4	440	0.4	*2,420	*2.6
Related children under 6	6,097	25.6	6,082	25.7	5,116	22.5	15	-0.1	*981	*3.1
In unrelated subfamilies	950	54.3	978	55.2	727	54.6	-28	-1.0	*223	-0.3
Children under 18	554	57.2	578	60.4	430	60.5	-24	-3.2	*124	-3.3
Unrelated individual	8,388	22.1	8,075	21.9	6,807	19.3	*313	0.2	*1,581	*2.8
Male	3,281	18.1	3,164	18.2	2,577	15.8	117	-0.1	*704	*2.3
Female	5,107	25.7	4,911	25.3	4,230	22.3	196	0.4	*877	*3.4
Age										
Under 18 years	15,727	22.7	15,294	22.3	13,154	20.1	433	0.4	*2,573	*2.6
18 to 24 years	4,854	19.1	4,665	18.1	4,132	15.4	189	0.9	*722	*3.7
25 to 44 years	10,220	12.2	9,786	11.8	7,988	9.9	*434	*0.5	*2,232	*2.3
45 to 54 years	2,522	8.5	2,262	8.0	1,873	7.5	*260	*0.6	*649	*1.0
55 to 59 years	1,057	9.9	1,008	9.8	971	9.5	49	0.1	86	0.4
60 to 64 years	1,129	11.3	1,072	10.5	986	9.4	57	0.8	*143	*1.9
65 years and over	3,755	12.2	3,928	12.9	3,312	11.4	-173	*-0.7	*443	*0.8
Residence										
Inside metropolitan areas	29,615	14.6	28,380	14.2	23,726	12.3	*1,235	0.4	*5,889	*2.3
Inside central cities	16,805	21.5	16,346	20.9	14,151	18.5	459	0.5	*2,654	*3.0
Outside central cities	12,810	10.3	12,034	9.9	9,574	8.2	*776	0.4	*3,236	*2.1
Outside metropolitan areas	9,650	17.2	9,634	16.9	8,690	15.9	16	0.3	*960	*1.3
Region										
Northeast	6,839	13.3	6,414	12.6	5,213	10.2	*425	0.7	*1,626	*3.1
Midwest	8,172	13.4	8,060	13.3	7,088	12.0	112	0.1	*1,084	*1.4
South	15,375	17.1	15,198	17.1	13,277	15.6	177	0.0	*2,098	*1.5
West	8,879	15.6	8,343	14.8	6,838	12.8	*536	0.7	*2,041	*2.8
FAMILIES										
Total	8,393	12.3	8,144	11.9	6,895	10.4	249	0.3	*1,498	*1.9
White	5,452	9.4	5,255	9.1	4,457	7.9	197	0.3	*995	*1.5
Not of Hispanic origin	3,988	7.6	3,840	7.3	3,287	6.4	148	0.3	*701	*1.2
Black	2,499	31.3	2,484	31.1	2,108	27.9	15	0.1	*391	*3.4
Other races	442	16.8	405	15.8	330	15.1	37	1.0	*112	1.7
Asian and Pacific Islander	235	13.5	215	12.2	201	12.2	20	1.3	34	1.3
Hispanic origin¹	1,625	27.3	1,529	26.7	1,227	23.7	*96	0.7	*398	*3.6
Type of Family										
Married-couple	3,481	6.5	3,385	6.4	2,965	5.7	96	0.1	*516	*0.8
White	2,757	5.8	2,677	5.6	2,347	5.0	80	0.1	*410	*0.8
Black	458	12.3	490	13.0	444	11.7	-32	-0.7	14	0.6
Hispanic origin¹	770	19.1	743	18.9	592	16.4	27	0.3	*178	*2.7
Female householder, no husband present	4,424	35.6	4,275	35.4	3,575	32.6	149	0.2	*849	*3.0
White	2,376	29.2	2,245	28.5	1,886	25.8	131	0.7	*490	*3.4
Black	1,908	49.9	1,878	50.2	1,553	46.7	30	-0.3	*355	3.2
Hispanic origin¹	772	51.6	664	49.3	576	48.0	*108	2.3	*196	3.6

*Statistically significant change at the 90-percent confidence level.

¹Persons of Hispanic origin may be of any race.

ʳRevised, based on 1990 census population controls.

Source: U.S. Bureau of the Census, *Income, Poverty, and Valuation of Noncash Benefits: 1993,* Current Population Reports, P60-188, Washington, D.C.: U.S. Government Printing Office, February 1995, Table C.

B6-2. Poverty Rates, by Type of Family and Race of Householder: 1979 and 1993

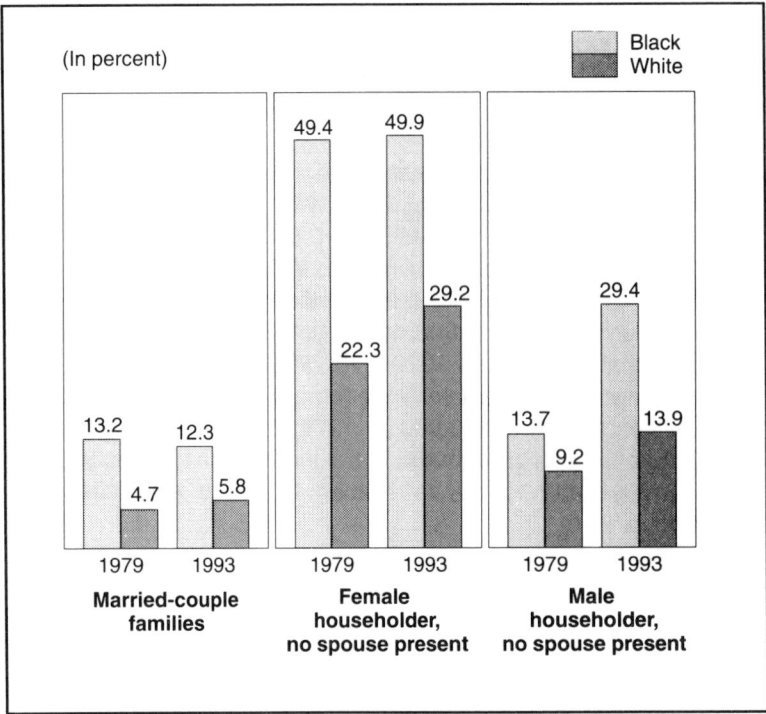

Source: Claudette E. Bennett, U.S. Bureau of the Census, *The Black Population in the United States: March 1994 and 1993*, Current Population Reports, Series P20-480, Washington, D.C.: U.S. Government Printing Office, January 1995, Table N.

B6-3. Selected Characteristics of Families below the Poverty Level: Selected Years, 1974 to 1993

[Numbers in thousands. Families as of March of the following year. For meaning of symbols, see text]

Characteristic	1993 Black	1993 White	1993 White, not His-panic	1989 Black	1989 White	1982 Black	1982 White	1979[r] Black	1979[r] White	1974 Black	1974 White
TYPE OF FAMILY[1]											
All families	7,993	57,881	52,470	7,470	56,590	6,530	53,407	6,184	52,243	5,491	49,440
Number below poverty level	2,499	5,452	3,988	2,077	4,409	2,158	5,118	1,722	3,581	1,479	3,352
Percent below poverty level	31.3	9.4	7.6	27.8	7.8	33.0	9.6	27.8	6.9	26.9	6.8
Married couple	3,715	47,452	43,745	3,750	46,981	3,486	45,252	3,433	44,751	3,357	43,049
Number below poverty level	458	2,757	2,042	443	2,329	543	3,104	453	2,099	435	1,977
Percent below poverty level	12.3	5.8	4.7	11.8	5.0	15.6	6.9	13.2	4.7	13.0	4.6
Female householder, no spouse present	3,828	8,131	6,798	3,275	7,306	2,734	6,507	2,495	6,052	1,934	5,208
Number below poverty level	1,908	2,376	1,699	1,524	1,858	1,535	1,813	1,234	1,350	1,010	1,289
Percent below poverty level	49.9	29.2	25.0	46.5	25.4	56.2	27.9	49.4	22.3	52.2	24.8
Male householder, no spouse present	450	2,298	1,927	446	2,303	309	1,648	256	1,441	200	1,182
Number below poverty level	132	319	248	110	223	79	201	35	132	35	86
Percent below poverty level	29.4	13.9	12.9	24.7	9.7	25.6	12.2	13.7	9.2	17.4	7.3
Families with related children under 18 years	5,525	29,234	25,477	5,031	27,977	4,470	27,118	4,297	27,329	3,915	26,890
Number below poverty level	2,171	4,226	2,946	1,783	3,290	1,819	3,709	1,441	2,619	1,293	2,430
Percent below poverty level	39.3	14.5	11.6	35.4	11.8	40.7	13.7	33.5	9.2	33.0	9.0
Married couple	2,147	22,670	20,166	2,179	22,271	2,093	22,390	2,095	22,878	2,187	(NA)
Number below poverty level	298	1,868	1,263	291	1,457	360	2,005	286	1,216	317	(NA)
Percent below poverty level	13.9	8.2	6.3	13.3	6.5	17.2	9.0	13.7	5.3	14.5	(NA)
Female householder, no spouse present	3,084	5,361	4,330	2,624	4,627	2,199	4,037	2,063	3,866	1,623	3,244
Number below poverty level	1,780	2,123	1,506	1,415	1,671	1,401	1,584	1,129	1,211	949	1,180
Percent below poverty level	57.7	39.6	34.8	53.9	36.1	63.7	39.3	54.7	31.3	58.5	36.4
Male householder, no spouse present	295	1,203	981	228	1,079	178	692	139	584	105	(NA)
Number below poverty level	93	235	177	77	162	58	120	26	82	27	(NA)
Percent below poverty level	31.5	19.6	18.1	33.8	15.0	32.7	17.4	18.4	14.1	26.2	(NA)
Householder 65 years old and over	944	10,054	9,584	880	9,643	813	8,635	807	8,107	641	7,319
Number below poverty level	213	525	445	173	510	239	632	213	602	177	567
Percent below poverty level	22.6	5.2	4.6	19.6	5.3	29.4	7.3	26.4	7.4	27.7	7.7

[1]For March 1994, data for families include families in group quarters.

Source: Claudette E. Bennett, U.S. Bureau of the Census, *The Black Population in the United States: March 1994 and 1993*, Current Population Reports, Series P20-480, Washington, D.C.: U.S. Government Printing Office, January 1995, Table N.

B6-4. Poverty Rates of Hispanic Families, by Family Type and Presence of Children: 1991

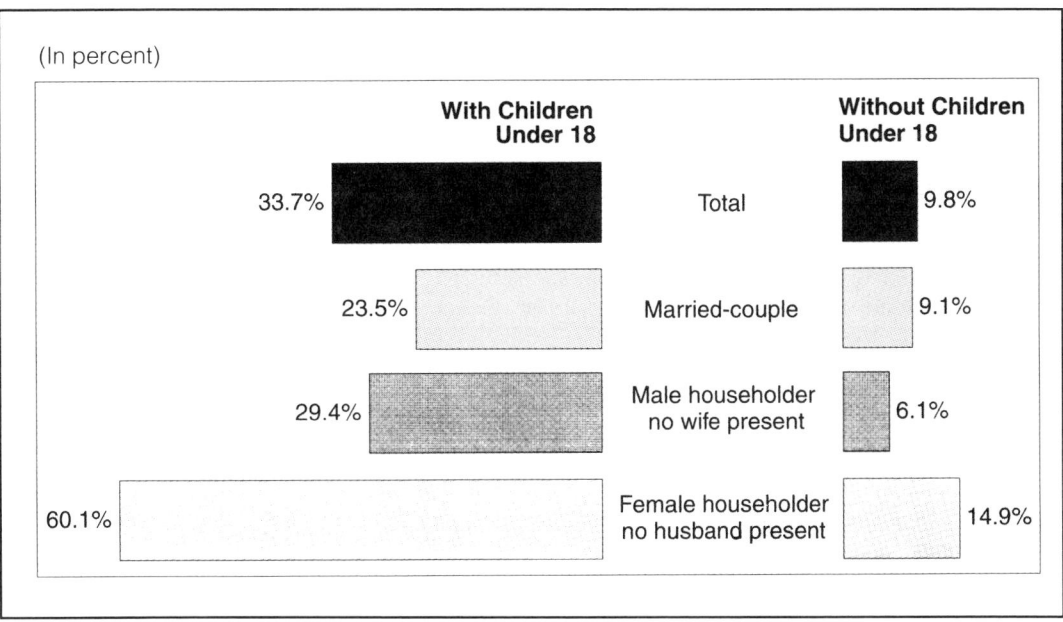

Source: U.S. Bureau of the Census, *Hispanic Americans Today*, Current Population Reports, Series P23-183, Washington, D.C.: U.S. Government Printing Office, 1993, Figure 33.

B6-5. Poverty Status of Persons, by Family Relationship: 1959 to 1993

[Numbers in thousands.Persons as of March of the following year]

Year and characteristic	All persons			Persons in families						Unrelated individuals		
				All families			Families with female householder, no husband present					
		Below poverty level			Below poverty level			Below poverty level			Below poverty level	
	Total	Number	Percent	Total	Number	Percent	Total	Number	Percent	Total	Number	Percent
ALL RACES												
1993...............	259,278	39,265	15.1	219,489	29,927	13.6	37,861	14,636	38.7	38,038	8,388	22.1
1992ʳ...............	256,549	38,014	14.8	217,936	28,961	13.3	36,446	14,205	39.0	36,842	8,075	21.9
1991...............	251,179	35,708	14.2	212,716	27,143	12.8	34,790	13,824	39.7	36,839	7,773	21.1
1990...............	248,644	33,585	13.5	210,967	25,232	12.0	33,795	12,578	37.2	36,056	7,446	20.7
1989...............	245,992	31,528	12.8	209,515	24,066	11.5	32,525	11,668	35.9	35,185	6,760	19.2
1988ʳ...............	243,530	31,745	13.0	208,056	24,048	11.6	32,164	11,972	37.2	34,340	7,070	20.6
1987ʳ...............	240,982	32,221	13.4	206,877	24,725	12.0	31,893	12,148	38.1	32,992	6,857	20.8
1986...............	238,554	32,370	13.6	205,459	24,754	12.0	31,152	11,944	38.3	31,679	6,846	21.6
1985...............	236,594	33,064	14.0	203,963	25,729	12.6	30,878	11,600	37.6	31,351	6,725	21.5
1984...............	233,816	33,700	14.4	202,288	26,458	13.1	30,844	11,831	38.4	30,268	6,609	21.8
1983...............	231,700	35,303	15.2	201,338	27,933	13.9	30,049	12,072	40.2	29,158	6,740	23.1
1982...............	229,412	34,398	15.0	200,385	27,349	13.6	28,834	11,701	40.6	27,908	6,458	23.1
1981...............	227,157	31,822	14.0	198,541	24,850	12.5	28,587	11,051	38.7	27,714	6,490	23.4
1980...............	225,027	29,272	13.0	196,963	22,601	11.5	27,565	10,120	36.7	27,133	6,227	22.9
1979...............	222,903	26,072	11.7	195,860	19,964	10.2	26,927	9,400	34.9	26,170	5,743	21.9
1978...............	215,656	24,497	11.4	191,071	19,062	10.0	26,032	9,269	35.6	24,585	5,435	22.1
1977...............	213,867	24,720	11.6	190,757	19,505	10.2	25,404	9,205	36.2	23,110	5,216	22.6
1976...............	212,303	24,975	11.8	190,844	19,632	10.3	24,204	9,029	37.3	21,459	5,344	24.9
1975...............	210,864	25,877	12.3	190,630	20,789	10.9	23,580	8,846	37.5	20,234	5,088	25.1
1974...............	209,362	23,370	11.2	190,436	18,817	9.9	23,165	8,462	36.5	18,926	4,553	24.1
1973...............	207,621	22,973	11.1	189,361	18,299	9.7	21,823	8,178	37.5	18,260	4,674	25.6
1972...............	206,004	24,460	11.9	189,193	19,577	10.3	21,264	8,114	38.2	16,811	4,883	29.0
1971...............	204,554	25,559	12.5	188,242	20,405	10.8	20,153	7,797	38.7	16,311	5,154	31.6
1970...............	202,183	25,420	12.6	186,692	20,330	10.9	19,673	7,503	38.1	15,491	5,090	32.9
1969...............	199,517	24,147	12.1	184,891	19,175	10.4	17,995	6,879	38.2	14,626	4,972	34.0
1968...............	197,628	25,389	12.8	183,825	20,695	11.3	18,048	6,990	38.7	13,803	4,694	34.0
1967...............	195,672	27,769	14.2	182,558	22,771	12.5	17,788	6,898	38.8	13,114	4,998	38.1
1966...............	193,388	28,510	14.7	181,117	23,809	13.1	17,240	6,861	39.8	12,271	4,701	38.3
1965...............	191,413	33,185	17.3	179,281	28,358	15.8	16,371	7,524	46.0	12,132	4,827	39.8
1964...............	189,710	36,055	19.0	177,653	30,912	17.4	(NA)	7,297	44.4	12,057	5,143	42.7
1963...............	187,258	36,436	19.5	176,076	31,498	17.9	(NA)	7,646	47.7	11,182	4,938	44.2
1962...............	184,276	38,625	21.0	173,263	33,623	19.4	(NA)	7,781	50.3	11,013	5,002	45.4
1961...............	181,277	39,628	21.9	170,131	34,509	20.3	(NA)	7,252	48.1	11,146	5,119	45.9
1960...............	179,503	39,851	22.2	168,615	34,925	20.7	(NA)	7,247	48.9	10,888	4,926	45.2
1959...............	176,557	39,490	22.4	165,858	34,562	20.8	(NA)	7,014	49.4	10,699	4,928	46.1

ʳFor 1992, figures are based on 1990 census population controls. For 1987 and 1988, figures are based on new processing procedures and are also revised to reflect corrections to the files after publication of the 1988 advance report, *Money Income and Poverty Status in the United States: 1988,* P-60, No. 166.

¹Persons of Hispanic origin may be of any race.
NA Not available.

Note: Prior to 1979 persons in unrelated subfamilies were included in persons in families. Beginning in 1979 persons in unrelated subfamilies are included in all persons but are excluded from persons in families.

Source: U.S. Bureau of the Census, *Income, Poverty, and Valuation of Noncash Benefits: 1993,* Current Population Reports, P60-188, Washington, D.C.: U.S. Government Printing Office, February 1995, Table D-4.

B6-6. Poverty Status of Families with Related Children, by Type of Family: 1959 to 1993

[Numbers in thousands. Families as of March of the following year]

Year and characteristic	All families			Married-couple families			Male householder, no wife present			Female householder, no husband present		
	Total	Below poverty level		Total	Below poverty level		Total	Below poverty level		Total	Below poverty level	
		Number	Percent		Number	Percent		Number	Percent		Number	Percent
ALL RACES–												
With Children Under 18 Years												
1993...............	36,456	6,751	18.5	26,121	2,363	9.0	1,577	354	22.5	8,758	4,034	46.1
1992ʳ	35,851	6,457	18.0	25,907	2,237	8.6	1,569	353	22.5	8,375	3,867	46.2
1991...............	34,861	6,170	17.7	25,357	2,106	8.3	1,513	297	19.6	7,991	3,767	47.1
1990...............	34,503	5,676	16.4	25,410	1,990	7.8	1,386	260	18.8	7,707	3,426	44.5
1989...............	34,279	5,308	15.5	25,476	1,872	7.3	1,358	246	18.1	7,445	3,190	42.8
1988ʳ	34,251	5,373	15.7	25,598	1,847	7.2	1,292	232	18.0	7,361	3,294	44.7
1987ʳ	33,996	5,465	16.1	25,464	1,963	7.7	1,316	221	16.8	7,216	3,281	45.5
1986...............	33,801	5,516	16.3	25,571	2,050	8.0	1,136	202	17.8	7,094	3,264	46.0
1985...............	33,536	5,586	16.7	25,496	2,258	8.9	1,147	197	17.1	6,892	3,131	45.4
1984...............	32,942	5,662	17.2	25,038	2,344	9.4	1,072	194	18.1	6,832	3,124	45.7
1983...............	32,787	5,871	17.9	25,216	2,557	10.1	949	192	20.2	6,622	3,122	47.1
1982...............	32,565	5,712	17.5	25,276	2,470	9.8	892	184	20.6	6,397	3,059	47.8
1981...............	32,587	5,191	15.9	25,278	2,199	8.7	822	115	14.0	6,488	2,877	44.3
1980...............	32,773	4,822	14.7	25,671	1,974	7.7	802	144	18.0	6,299	2,703	42.9
1979...............	32,397	4,081	12.6	25,615	1,573	6.1	747	116	15.5	6,035	2,392	39.6
1978...............	31,735	4,060	12.8	25,199	1,495	5.9	699	103	14.7	5,837	2,462	42.2
1977...............	31,637	4,081	12.9	25,284	1,602	6.3	644	95	14.8	5,709	2,384	41.8
1976...............	31,434	4,060	12.9	25,515	1,623	6.4	609	94	15.4	5,310	2,343	44.1
1975...............	31,377	4,172	13.3	25,704	1,855	7.2	554	65	11.7	5,119	2,252	44.0
1974...............	31,319	3,789	12.1	25,857	1,558	6.0	545	84	15.4	4,917	2,147	43.7
1973...............	30,977	3,520	11.4	25,983	(NA)	(NA)	397	(NA)	(NA)	4,597	1,987	43.2
1972...............	30,807	3,621	11.8	26,085	(NA)	(NA)	401	(NA)	(NA)	4,321	1,925	44.5
1971...............	30,725	3,683	12.0	26,201	(NA)	(NA)	447	(NA)	(NA)	4,077	1,830	44.9
1970...............	30,070	3,491	11.6	25,789	(NA)	(NA)	444	(NA)	(NA)	3,837	1,680	43.8
1969...............	29,827	3,226	10.8	26,083	(NA)	(NA)	360	(NA)	(NA)	3,384	1,519	44.9
1968...............	29,325	3,347	11.4	25,684	(NA)	(NA)	372	(NA)	(NA)	3,269	1,459	44.6
1967...............	29,032	3,586	12.4	25,482	(NA)	(NA)	360	(NA)	(NA)	3,190	1,418	44.5
1966...............	28,592	3,734	13.4	25,197	(NA)	(NA)	436	(NA)	(NA)	2,959	1,410	47.1
1965...............	28,100	4,379	15.6	24,829	(NA)	(NA)	398	(NA)	(NA)	2,873	1,499	52.2
1964...............	28,277	4,771	16.9	25,017	(NA)	(NA)	367	(NA)	(NA)	2,893	1,439	49.7
1963...............	28,317	4,991	17.6	25,084	(NA)	(NA)	400	(NA)	(NA)	2,833	1,578	55.7
1962...............	28,174	5,460	19.4	24,990	(NA)	(NA)	483	(NA)	(NA)	2,701	1,613	59.7
1961...............	27,600	5,500	19.9	24,509	(NA)	(NA)	404	(NA)	(NA)	2,687	1,505	56.0
1960...............	27,102	5,328	19.7	24,164	(NA)	(NA)	319	(NA)	(NA)	2,619	1,476	56.3
1959...............	26,992	5,443	20.3	24,099	(NA)	(NA)	349	(NA)	(NA)	2,544	1,525	59.9

ʳFor 1992, figures are based on 1990 census population controls. For 1987 and 1988, figures are based on new processing procedures and are also revised to reflect corrections to the files after publication of the 1988 advance report, *Money Income and Poverty Status in the United States: 1988,* P-60, No. 166.

¹Persons of Hispanic origin may be of any race.
NA Not available.

Note: Prior to 1979, unrelated subfamiles were included in all families. Beginning in 1979, unrelated subfamilies are excluded from all families.

Source: U.S. Bureau of the Census, *Income, Poverty, and Valuation of Noncash Benefits: 1993,* Current Population Reports, P60-188, Washington, D.C.: U.S. Government Printing Office, February 1995, Table D-6.

B6-7. Ratio of Income to Poverty Level of Persons and Persons in Households that Received Means-Tested Assistance, by Age, Sex, and Household Relationship: 1993

(Numbers in thousands. Persons, families and unrelated individuals as of March of the following year.)

Characteristic	Total	Under .50 Number	Under .50 Percent of total	Under 1.00 Number	Under 1.00 Percent of total	Under 1.25 Number	Under 1.25 Percent of total	Under 1.50 Number	Under 1.50 Percent of total	Under 1.75 Number	Under 1.75 Percent of total	Under 2.00 Number	Under 2.00 Percent of total
ALL PERSONS													
Both Sexes													
Total	259 278	15 971	6.2	39 265	15.1	51 801	20.0	64 872	25.0	78 665	30.3	91 390	35.2
Under 18 years	69 292	7 017	10.1	15 727	22.7	19 706	28.4	23 591	34.0	27 586	39.8	31 163	45.0
18 to 24 years	25 475	2 082	8.2	4 854	19.1	6 133	24.1	7 591	29.8	9 086	35.7	10 446	41.0
25 to 34 years	41 946	2 511	6.0	5 804	13.8	7 696	18.3	9 701	23.1	12 069	28.8	14 205	33.9
35 to 44 years	41 528	1 804	4.3	4 415	10.6	5 857	14.1	7 450	17.9	9 129	22.0	10 871	26.2
45 to 54 years	29 522	1 045	3.5	2 522	8.5	3 320	11.2	4 248	14.4	5 095	17.3	6 092	20.6
55 to 59 years	10 732	408	3.8	1 057	9.9	1 464	13.6	1 842	17.2	2 291	21.3	2 653	24.7
60 to 64 years	10 005	357	3.6	1 129	11.3	1 548	15.5	2 007	20.1	2 577	25.8	3 040	30.4
65 years and over	30 779	747	2.4	3 755	12.2	6 077	19.7	8 443	27.4	10 831	35.2	12 920	42.0
65 to 74 years	18 087	365	2.0	1 802	10.0	2 867	15.8	4 127	22.8	5 382	29.8	6 517	36.0
75 years and over	12 692	383	3.0	1 953	15.4	3 210	25.3	4 316	34.0	5 449	42.9	6 403	50.4
Male													
Total	126 668	6 883	5.4	16 900	13.3	22 440	17.7	28 520	22.5	35 133	27.7	41 257	32.6
Under 18 years	35 446	3 590	10.1	8 036	22.7	10 003	28.2	11 978	33.8	14 070	39.7	15 851	44.7
18 to 24 years	12 683	691	5.4	1 875	14.8	2 475	19.5	3 196	25.2	3 944	31.1	4 618	36.4
25 to 34 years	20 872	815	3.9	2 148	10.3	3 043	14.6	4 050	19.4	5 242	25.1	6 291	30.1
35 to 44 years	20 544	746	3.6	1 805	8.8	2 494	12.1	3 273	15.9	4 089	19.9	4 989	24.3
45 to 54 years	14 454	471	3.3	1 134	7.8	1 497	10.4	1 919	13.3	2 286	15.8	2 750	19.0
55 to 59 years	5 140	178	3.5	448	8.7	623	12.1	777	15.1	988	19.2	1 158	22.5
60 to 64 years	4 793	183	3.8	449	9.4	618	12.9	823	17.2	1 069	22.3	1 266	26.4
65 years and over	12 736	209	1.6	1 004	7.9	1 688	13.3	2 504	19.7	3 445	27.1	4 333	34.0
65 to 74 years	7 924	105	1.3	549	6.9	948	12.0	1 395	17.6	1 900	24.0	2 398	30.3
75 years and over	4 812	104	2.2	455	9.5	740	15.4	1 109	23.0	1 545	32.1	1 935	40.2
Female													
Total	132 610	9 088	6.9	22 365	16.9	29 361	22.1	36 352	27.4	43 532	32.8	50 133	37.8
Under 18 years	33 846	3 427	10.1	7 691	22.7	9 703	28.7	11 613	34.3	13 517	39.9	15 312	45.2
18 to 24 years	12 792	1 392	10.9	2 979	23.3	3 659	28.6	4 395	34.4	5 142	40.2	5 829	45.6
25 to 34 years	21 073	1 696	8.0	3 656	17.4	4 653	22.1	5 652	26.8	6 827	32.4	7 914	37.6
35 to 44 years	20 984	1 058	5.0	2 610	12.4	3 363	16.0	4 177	19.9	5 040	24.0	5 882	28.0
45 to 54 years	15 068	574	3.8	1 388	9.2	1 823	12.1	2 329	15.5	2 809	18.6	3 341	22.2
55 to 59 years	5 593	229	4.1	609	10.9	841	15.0	1 065	19.0	1 303	23.3	1 495	26.7
60 to 64 years	5 212	174	3.3	680	13.0	930	17.8	1 183	22.7	1 508	28.9	1 774	34.0
65 years and over	18 043	539	3.0	2 750	15.2	4 388	24.3	5 939	32.9	7 386	40.9	8 587	47.6
65 to 74 years	10 163	260	2.6	1 252	12.3	1 918	18.9	2 733	26.9	3 482	34.3	4 119	40.5
75 years and over	7 880	279	3.5	1 498	19.0	2 470	31.3	3 207	40.7	3 904	49.5	4 468	56.7
Household Relationship													
Total	259 278	15 971	6.2	39 265	15.1	51 801	20.0	64 872	25.0	78 665	30.3	91 390	35.2
65 years and over	30 779	747	2.4	3 755	12.2	6 077	19.7	8 443	27.4	10 831	35.2	12 920	42.0
In families	219 489	11 996	5.5	29 947	13.6	39 547	18.0	50 006	22.8	61 137	27.9	71 720	32.7
Householder	68 506	3 387	4.9	8 393	12.3	11 203	16.4	14 238	20.8	17 564	25.6	20 772	30.3
Under 65 years	57 289	3 224	5.6	7 621	13.3	9 925	17.3	12 247	21.4	14 815	25.9	17 272	30.1
65 years and over	11 217	163	1.5	772	6.9	1 278	11.4	1 991	17.7	2 749	24.5	3 500	31.2
Related children under 18 years	68 040	6 534	9.6	14 961	22.0	18 843	27.7	22 659	33.3	26 584	39.1	30 099	44.2
Under 6 years	23 850	2 818	11.8	6 097	25.6	7 562	31.7	8 977	37.6	10 468	43.9	11 693	49.0
6 to 17 years	44 189	3 716	8.4	8 865	20.1	11 281	25.5	13 682	31.0	16 116	36.5	18 406	41.7
Own children 18 years and over	21 985	694	3.2	2 079	9.5	2 889	13.1	3 887	17.7	4 759	21.6	5 700	25.9
In married-couple families	173 497	4 151	2.4	13 858	8.0	20 187	11.6	27 626	15.9	35 853	20.7	43 972	25.3
Husbands	53 181	1 067	2.0	3 481	6.5	5 179	9.7	7 238	13.6	9 633	18.1	11 996	22.6
Under 65 years	43 731	948	2.2	2 940	6.7	4 268	9.8	5 746	13.1	7 500	17.2	9 201	21.0
65 years and over	9 451	119	1.3	541	5.7	911	9.6	1 491	15.8	2 133	22.6	2 794	29.6
Wives	53 181	1 067	2.0	3 481	6.5	5 179	9.7	7 238	13.6	9 633	18.1	11 996	22.6
Under 65 years	45 868	984	2.1	3 086	6.7	4 519	9.9	6 086	13.3	7 970	17.4	9 796	21.4
65 years and over	7 313	83	1.1	394	5.4	661	9.0	1 151	15.7	1 663	22.7	2 199	30.1
Related children under 18 years	49 767	1 710	3.4	5 845	11.7	8 238	16.6	10 869	21.8	13 691	27.5	16 325	32.8
Under 6 years	17 530	711	4.1	2 355	13.4	3 320	18.9	4 337	24.7	5 443	31.0	6 389	36.4
6 to 17 years	32 236	999	3.1	3 491	10.8	4 918	15.3	6 532	20.3	8 248	25.6	9 935	30.8
Own children 18 years and over	14 431	225	1.6	756	5.2	1 134	7.9	1 640	11.4	2 049	14.2	2 638	18.3
In families with female householder, no spouse present	37 861	7 266	19.2	14 636	38.7	17 426	46.0	19 970	52.7	22 292	58.9	24 224	64.0
Householder	12 411	2 134	17.2	4 424	35.6	5 368	43.3	6 189	49.9	6 916	55.7	7 580	61.1
Under 65 years	10 823	2 085	19.3	4 206	38.9	5 027	46.4	5 704	52.7	6 328	58.5	6 903	63.8
65 years and over	1 588	49	3.1	218	13.7	341	21.5	486	30.6	588	37.0	677	42.6
Related children under 18 years	15 844	4 534	28.6	8 503	53.7	9 766	61.6	10 764	67.9	11 657	73.6	12 382	78.1
Under 6 years	5 412	1 962	36.2	3 446	63.7	3 858	71.3	4 167	77.0	4 456	82.3	4 667	86.2
6 to 17 years	10 432	2 573	24.7	5 056	48.5	5 909	56.6	6 597	63.2	7 201	69.0	7 715	74.0
Own children 18 years and over	6 504	431	6.6	1 196	18.4	1 585	24.4	2 038	31.3	2 450	37.7	2 750	42.3
In unrelated subfamilies	1 751	507	28.9	950	54.3	1 103	63.0	1 198	68.4	1 316	75.1	1 418	81.0
Under 18 years	977	303	31.1	560	57.3	649	66.4	705	72.2	770	78.8	822	84.2
Under 6 years	368	163	44.3	255	69.3	286	77.7	301	81.8	311	84.4	328	89.0
6 to 17 years	608	140	23.0	304	50.0	363	59.6	404	66.4	459	75.5	494	81.3
18 years and over	774	203	26.3	390	50.4	454	58.6	493	63.7	546	70.5	596	77.0
Unrelated individuals	38 038	3 469	9.1	8 388	22.1	11 152	29.3	13 668	35.9	16 212	42.6	18 252	48.0
Male	18 137	1 574	8.7	3 281	18.1	4 283	23.6	5 311	29.3	6 439	35.5	7 370	40.6
Under 65 years	15 757	1 504	9.5	2 901	18.4	3 635	23.1	4 470	28.4	5 372	34.1	6 131	38.9
Living alone	7 444	477	6.4	1 008	13.5	1 288	17.3	1 646	22.1	1 961	26.3	2 310	31.0
65 years and over	2 380	70	2.9	381	16.0	648	27.2	841	35.3	1 066	44.8	1 239	52.1
Living alone	2 046	43	2.1	283	13.9	515	25.2	684	33.4	880	43.0	1 042	50.9
Female	19 901	1 895	9.5	5 107	25.7	6 868	34.5	8 357	42.0	9 773	49.1	10 882	54.7
Under 65 years	12 293	1 517	12.3	3 076	25.0	3 666	29.8	4 330	35.2	5 011	40.8	5 647	45.9
Living alone	6 963	553	7.9	1 388	19.9	1 687	24.2	2 018	29.0	2 377	34.1	2 711	38.9
65 years and over	7 608	378	5.0	2 031	26.7	3 202	42.1	4 027	52.9	4 762	62.6	5 235	68.8
Living alone	7 273	308	4.2	1 902	26.2	3 041	41.8	3 843	52.8	4 552	62.6	5 004	68.8

B6-7. Ratio of Income to Poverty Level of Persons and Persons in Households that Received Means-Tested Assistance, by Age, Sex, and Household Relationship: 1993 (continued)

(Numbers in thousands. Persons, families and unrelated individuals as of March of the following year.)

Characteristic	Total	Under .50 Number	Under .50 Percent of total	Under 1.00 Number	Under 1.00 Percent of total	Under 1.25 Number	Under 1.25 Percent of total	Under 1.50 Number	Under 1.50 Percent of total	Under 1.75 Number	Under 1.75 Percent of total	Under 2.00 Number	Under 2.00 Percent of total
PERSONS IN HOUSEHOLDS THAT RECEIVED MEANS-TESTED ASSISTANCE													
Both Sexes													
Total	67 514	11 805	17.5	28 795	42.7	36 083	53.4	42 539	63.0	48 115	71.3	51 942	76.9
Under 18 years	27 509	6 308	22.9	13 822	50.2	16 774	61.0	19 329	70.3	21 537	78.3	22 940	83.4
18 to 24 years	7 151	1 327	18.6	3 095	43.3	3 822	53.4	4 445	62.2	5 002	70.0	5 409	75.6
25 to 34 years	10 803	1 800	16.7	4 271	39.5	5 390	49.9	6 485	60.0	7 521	69.6	8 202	75.9
35 to 44 years	8 852	1 238	14.0	3 151	35.6	4 077	46.1	4 899	55.3	5 716	64.6	6 275	70.9
45 to 54 years	4 659	581	12.5	1 593	34.2	2 027	43.5	2 460	52.8	2 737	58.7	3 023	64.9
55 to 59 years	1 565	162	10.4	575	36.7	733	46.9	842	53.8	938	59.9	1 017	65.0
60 to 64 years	1 548	144	9.3	566	36.6	716	46.3	853	55.1	971	62.7	1 059	68.4
65 years and over	5 428	245	4.5	1 722	31.7	2 544	46.9	3 227	59.5	3 693	68.0	4 018	74.0
65 to 74 years	2 972	120	4.0	916	30.8	1 301	43.8	1 700	57.2	1 962	66.0	2 144	72.1
75 years and over	2 456	125	5.1	807	32.8	1 243	50.6	1 528	62.2	1 731	70.5	1 874	76.3
Male													
Total	30 926	4 998	16.2	12 281	39.7	15 564	50.3	18 550	60.0	21 312	68.9	23 105	74.7
Under 18 years	14 052	3 226	23.0	7 097	50.5	8 594	61.2	9 875	70.3	11 053	78.7	11 727	83.5
18 to 24 years	3 107	383	12.3	1 111	35.7	1 433	46.1	1 728	55.6	2 005	64.5	2 203	70.9
25 to 34 years	4 537	465	10.3	1 369	30.2	1 831	40.4	2 338	51.5	2 831	62.4	3 140	69.2
35 to 44 years	3 982	459	11.5	1 180	29.6	1 607	40.3	1 995	50.1	2 393	60.1	2 667	67.0
45 to 54 years	2 147	247	11.5	661	30.8	867	40.4	1 052	49.0	1 194	55.6	1 320	61.5
55 to 59 years	698	66	9.4	236	33.8	307	44.0	360	51.6	398	57.0	437	62.6
60 to 64 years	630	76	12.1	182	28.9	238	37.8	291	46.2	341	54.1	382	60.6
65 years and over	1 773	75	4.2	445	25.1	689	38.9	911	51.4	1 099	62.0	1 228	69.3
65 to 74 years	1 065	29	2.7	263	24.7	409	38.4	536	50.3	633	59.5	712	66.9
75 years and over	708	46	6.5	182	25.7	280	39.5	375	53.0	465	65.7	517	72.9
Female													
Total	36 588	6 807	18.6	16 515	45.1	20 519	56.1	23 989	65.6	26 803	73.3	28 838	78.8
Under 18 years	13 456	3 082	22.9	6 725	50.0	8 179	60.8	9 454	70.3	10 484	77.9	11 212	83.3
18 to 24 years	4 043	944	23.3	1 984	49.1	2 389	59.1	2 717	67.2	2 997	74.1	3 206	79.3
25 to 34 years	6 266	1 335	21.3	2 902	46.3	3 559	56.8	4 147	66.2	4 691	74.9	5 062	80.8
35 to 44 years	4 870	779	16.0	1 970	40.5	2 471	50.7	2 904	59.6	3 324	68.3	3 607	74.1
45 to 54 years	2 512	334	13.3	933	37.1	1 161	46.2	1 408	56.1	1 543	61.4	1 703	67.8
55 to 59 years	867	96	11.1	339	39.1	426	49.2	481	55.5	540	62.3	581	67.0
60 to 64 years	918	67	7.3	385	41.9	479	52.1	561	61.2	630	68.6	677	73.7
65 years and over	3 655	170	4.7	1 277	34.9	1 855	50.7	2 316	63.4	2 594	71.0	2 790	76.3
65 to 74 years	1 908	91	4.8	652	34.2	892	46.7	1 163	61.0	1 329	69.7	1 432	75.1
75 years and over	1 748	79	4.5	625	35.7	963	55.1	1 152	65.9	1 266	72.4	1 358	77.7
Household Relationship													
Total	67 514	11 805	17.5	28 795	42.7	36 083	53.4	42 539	63.0	48 115	71.3	51 942	76.9
65 years and over	5 428	245	4.5	1 722	31.7	2 544	46.9	3 227	59.5	3 693	68.0	4 018	74.0
In families	59 261	10 096	17.0	24 443	41.2	30 737	51.9	36 547	61.7	41 580	70.2	45 059	76.0
Householder	15 745	2 720	17.3	6 558	41.6	8 219	52.2	9 691	61.6	10 973	69.7	11 906	75.6
Under 65 years	14 098	2 648	18.8	6 187	43.9	7 656	54.3	8 887	63.0	10 017	71.0	10 822	76.8
65 years and over	1 647	72	4.4	371	22.5	563	34.2	805	48.8	957	58.1	1 084	65.8
Related children under 18 years	26 745	5 972	22.3	13 266	49.6	16 160	60.4	18 668	69.8	20 833	77.9	22 214	83.1
Under 6 years	9 943	2 565	25.8	5 423	54.5	6 443	64.8	7 334	73.8	8 085	81.3	8 550	86.0
6 to 17 years	16 802	3 406	20.3	7 843	46.7	9 717	57.8	11 334	67.5	12 748	75.9	13 664	81.3
Own children 18 years and over	5 747	540	9.4	1 627	28.3	2 187	38.1	2 814	49.0	3 219	56.0	3 604	62.7
In married-couple families	33 490	2 827	8.4	9 823	29.3	13 649	40.8	17 354	51.8	20 735	61.9	23 099	69.0
Husbands	7 902	624	7.9	2 199	27.8	3 069	38.8	3 909	49.5	4 711	59.6	5 275	66.8
Under 65 years	6 931	586	8.5	1 986	28.6	2 753	39.7	3 448	49.7	4 142	59.8	4 631	66.8
65 years and over	970	38	3.9	214	22.0	316	32.5	461	47.5	569	58.6	644	66.4
Wives	7 902	624	7.9	2 199	27.8	3 069	38.8	3 909	49.5	4 711	59.6	5 275	66.8
Under 65 years	7 210	600	8.3	2 069	28.7	2 877	39.9	3 606	50.0	4 321	59.9	4 835	67.1
65 years and over	692	24	3.5	131	18.9	192	27.8	303	43.8	390	56.4	440	63.6
Related children under 18 years	13 800	1 376	10.0	4 682	33.9	6 382	46.2	7 989	57.9	9 461	68.6	10 397	75.3
Under 6 years	5 047	569	11.3	1 897	37.6	2 532	50.2	3 130	62.0	3 632	72.0	3 954	78.4
6 to 17 years	8 753	807	9.2	2 785	31.8	3 851	44.0	4 859	55.5	5 830	66.6	6 443	73.6
Own children 18 years and over	2 746	142	5.2	516	18.8	789	28.7	1 088	39.6	1 260	45.9	1 478	53.8
In families with female householder, no spouse present	22 756	6 839	30.1	13 538	59.5	15 713	69.0	17 544	77.1	18 863	82.9	19 748	86.8
Householder	6 858	1 968	28.7	4 009	58.5	4 709	68.7	5 260	76.7	5 637	82.2	5 928	86.4
Under 65 years	6 255	1 932	30.9	3 861	61.7	4 485	71.7	4 928	78.8	5 269	84.2	5 516	88.2
65 years and over	603	36	6.0	148	24.5	224	37.2	332	55.0	368	60.9	411	68.2
Related children under 18 years	11 723	4 358	37.2	8 075	68.9	9 117	77.8	9 889	84.4	10 448	89.1	10 814	92.2
Under 6 years	4 369	1 890	43.3	3 290	75.3	3 618	82.8	3 850	88.1	4 033	92.3	4 138	94.7
6 to 17 years	7 354	2 468	33.6	4 785	65.1	5 499	74.8	6 039	82.1	6 415	87.2	6 675	90.8
Own children 18 years and over	2 707	374	13.8	1 035	38.2	1 305	48.2	1 614	59.6	1 819	67.2	1 954	72.2
In unrelated subfamilies	1 055	391	37.0	737	69.9	831	78.7	893	84.6	960	91.0	992	94.0
Under 18 years	620	236	38.2	438	70.7	494	79.7	531	85.7	569	91.8	587	94.6
Under 6 years	239	128	53.6	197	82.4	211	88.1	221	92.5	227	94.8	234	98.0
6 to 17 years	381	108	28.4	241	63.3	283	74.4	310	81.4	342	89.9	352	92.5
18 years and over	435	154	35.4	299	68.7	337	77.3	361	83.0	391	89.9	405	93.0
Unrelated individuals	7 198	1 319	18.3	3 615	50.2	4 516	62.7	5 099	70.8	5 575	77.5	5 891	81.8
Male	3 261	650	19.9	1 360	41.7	1 709	52.4	1 963	60.2	2 222	68.1	2 395	73.4
Under 65 years	2 768	628	22.7	1 190	43.0	1 431	51.7	1 635	59.1	1 858	67.1	2 002	72.3
Living alone	776	144	18.5	377	48.6	448	57.8	505	65.2	561	72.3	590	76.1
65 years and over	492	23	4.6	170	34.6	279	56.6	328	66.6	364	73.9	393	79.7
Living alone	380	13	3.3	118	31.0	208	54.7	252	66.3	280	73.8	309	81.3
Female	3 937	669	17.0	2 255	57.3	2 806	71.3	3 136	79.7	3 353	85.2	3 496	88.8
Under 65 years	2 093	575	27.5	1 328	63.5	1 490	71.2	1 641	78.4	1 743	83.3	1 830	87.4
Living alone	1 033	199	19.3	687	66.5	779	75.4	855	82.7	906	87.7	933	90.4
65 years and over	1 844	93	5.1	927	50.3	1 317	71.4	1 495	81.1	1 610	87.3	1 667	90.4
Living alone	1 782	81	4.6	895	50.2	1 280	71.8	1 457	81.7	1 570	88.1	1 624	91.1

Source: U.S. Bureau of the Census, *Income, Poverty, and Valuation of Noncash Benefits: 1993*, Current Population Reports, P60-188, Washington, D.C.: U.S. Government Printing Office, February 1995, Table 8.

B6-8. Living Arrangements of Persons 65 Years and Over, by Poverty Status: March 1993

[Based on data from the Current Population Survey (CPS). Civilian noninstitutionalized population.]

Living arrangement and sex	Population (in thousands)			Percentage distribution			Percent officially poor
	Total	Poor	Nonpoor	Total	Poor	Nonpoor	
Total	30,870	3,983	26,887	100.0	100.0	100.0	12.9
Unrelated individuals.................................	10,041	2,498	7,543	32.5	62.7	28.1	24.9
Family members..	20,829	1,484	19,344	67.5	37.3	71.9	7.1
Householder or spouse	18,842	1,334	17,508	61.0	33.5	65.1	7.1
Other relative [2]	1,987	151	1,836	6.4	3.8	6.8	7.6
Poor by own income	783	127	656	2.5	3.2	2.4	16.2
Not poor by own income	1,203	24	1,180	3.9	.6	4.4	2.0
Men..	12,832	1,142	11,689	41.6	28.7	43.5	8.9
Unrelated individuals.................................	2,355	438	1,917	7.6	11.0	7.1	18.6
Family members..	10,477	705	9,772	33.9	17.7	36.3	6.7
Householder..	9,232	604	8,628	29.9	15.2	32.1	6.5
Spouse of householder...........................	698	54	644	2.3	1.3	2.4	7.7
Other relative [2]	547	47	499	1.8	1.2	1.9	8.7
Poor by own income	148	36	113	.5	.9	.4	24.0
Not poor by own income	399	12	387	1.3	.3	1.4	3.0
Women..	18,038	2,840	15,198	58.4	71.3	56.5	15.7
Unrelated individuals.................................	7,686	2,061	5,625	24.9	51.7	20.9	26.8
Family members..	10,352	780	9,573	33.5	19.6	35.6	7.5
Householder, no husband present.....................	1,594	248	1,346	5.2	6.2	5.0	15.6
Householder with husband present.....................	551	34	517	1.8	.9	1.9	6.2
Wife of householder.................................	6,768	394	6,374	21.9	9.9	23.7	5.8
Other relative [2]	1,440	103	1,336	4.7	2.6	5.0	7.2
Poor by own income	635	91	543	2.1	2.3	2.0	14.4
Not poor by own income	805	12	793	2.6	.3	2.9	1.5

[1] Living arrangements as of March 1993. Poverty status in 1992 as reflected by income of unrelated individual or family money income for year compared with official poverty income criterion for families of appropriate size and composition.

[2] Aged family members who are neither the family householder nor the spouse of the householder. Official poverty classification is based on combined income of all related persons living together. Persons in this group are classified here on the basis of official poverty criteria for family income and on a comparison of their own income with official poverty criteria for elderly persons maintaining their own households. The hidden poor are other relatives in nonpoor households whose own income is below the official poverty line for unrelated individuals or married couples.

Source: Public use file of the March 1993 Income Supplement, Current Population Survey, Bureau of the Census. For a discussion of standard errors of estimated numbers and percentages, see Bureau of the Census, Current Population Reports, P-60 series.

Source: Social Security Administration, *Social Security Bulletin, 1994 Annual Statistical Supplement*, Washington, D.C.: U.S. Government Printing Office, 1994, Table 3.E4.

B6-9. Poverty Status in 1989 of Families and Persons, by Urban and Rural Areas and Size of Place: 1990

[Data based on sample and subject to sampling variability.]

United States Urban and Rural and Size of Place	United States	Urban						Rural			
			Inside urbanized area			Outside urbanized area					
		Total	Total	Central place	Urban fringe	Place of 10,000 or more	Place of 2,500 to 9,999	Total	Place of 1,000 to 2,499	Place of less than 1,000	Rural farm
ALL INCOME LEVELS IN 1989											
Families	**65 049 428**	**47 815 502**	**40 338 661**	**19 111 188**	**21 227 473**	**3 506 713**	**3 970 128**	**17 233 926**	**1 916 297**	**1 042 156**	**1 162 367**
In owner-occupied housing unit	47 221 605	32 739 760	27 482 786	11 289 385	16 193 401	2 382 294	2 874 680	14 481 845	1 480 959	832 692	1 007 755
With related children under 18 years	33 536 660	24 738 738	20 819 261	10 121 874	10 697 387	1 853 442	2 066 035	8 797 922	973 715	526 043	469 566
With related children under 5 years	14 250 048	10 851 738	9 196 168	4 640 290	4 555 878	792 964	862 606	3 398 310	388 629	207 972	160 557
Householder worked in 1989	51 357 521	37 652 847	31 916 249	14 478 526	17 437 723	2 716 519	3 020 079	13 704 674	1 453 821	785 049	1 031 099
Householder worked year round full time in 1989	36 318 276	26 648 950	22 736 829	9 763 058	12 973 771	1 861 316	2 050 805	9 669 326	992 644	517 372	709 952
Householder under 65 years with work disability	4 817 701	3 329 491	2 722 307	1 470 461	1 251 846	277 372	329 812	1 488 210	164 015	93 904	75 970
Householder foreign born	5 888 505	5 503 254	5 200 787	2 822 214	2 378 573	161 929	140 538	385 251	49 886	12 568	17 312
Householder under 25 years	2 554 838	2 003 839	1 620 084	975 468	644 616	196 118	187 637	550 999	77 783	41 157	14 695
Householder 65 years and over	10 796 925	7 864 440	6 455 356	3 143 453	3 311 903	633 766	775 318	2 932 485	388 499	227 484	281 991
Householder high school graduate or higher	49 435 732	37 113 383	31 572 392	13 980 214	17 592 178	2 639 727	2 901 264	12 322 349	1 380 496	717 771	830 477
With public assistance income in 1989	5 024 146	3 908 153	3 244 428	2 196 620	1 047 808	313 841	349 884	1 115 993	155 551	90 473	50 690
With Social Security income in 1989	14 633 024	10 530 796	8 648 586	4 188 943	4 459 643	847 475	1 034 735	4 102 228	519 022	298 210	342 308
Married-couple families	**51 718 214**	**36 843 114**	**30 930 889**	**13 503 916**	**17 426 973**	**2 748 735**	**3 163 490**	**14 875 100**	**1 563 963**	**861 257**	**1 070 524**
With related children under 18 years	25 258 549	17 906 022	15 040 740	6 530 932	8 509 808	1 340 835	1 524 447	7 352 527	744 057	410 068	433 979
With related children under 5 years	11 134 320	8 217 927	6 964 150	3 137 503	3 826 647	595 354	658 423	2 916 393	307 891	166 820	150 108
Householder worked in 1989	42 105 587	30 007 973	25 343 012	10 783 597	14 559 415	2 192 691	2 472 270	12 097 614	1 216 715	667 068	962 338
Householder worked year round full time in 1989	30 876 792	22 124 213	18 793 035	7 659 386	11 133 649	1 577 595	1 753 583	8 752 579	861 690	455 651	672 934
Householder high school graduate or higher	40 340 133	29 510 646	25 001 133	10 331 463	14 669 670	2 132 891	2 376 622	10 829 487	1 151 143	603 745	775 117
Householder 65 years and over	8 856 941	6 353 919	5 175 157	2 402 102	2 773 055	527 820	650 942	2 503 022	327 858	192 396	250 060
With public assistance income in 1989	2 196 987	1 549 956	1 267 663	738 783	528 880	128 565	153 728	647 031	74 222	46 034	38 847
With Social Security income in 1989	11 580 548	8 155 880	6 643 294	3 041 758	3 601 536	675 641	836 945	3 424 668	424 145	244 792	299 883
Female householder, no husband present	**10 381 654**	**8 665 622**	**7 405 278**	**4 496 864**	**2 908 414**	**612 346**	**647 998**	**1 716 032**	**277 677**	**138 065**	**50 683**
With related children under 18 years	6 783 155	5 690 651	4 809 644	3 048 135	1 761 509	430 593	450 414	1 092 504	187 082	91 738	20 874
With related children under 5 years	2 532 331	2 175 289	1 841 414	1 269 382	572 032	165 461	168 414	357 042	64 961	31 939	6 401
Householder worked in 1989	6 889 101	5 786 872	4 956 716	2 823 840	2 132 876	406 968	423 188	1 102 229	179 411	85 546	32 995
Householder worked year round full time in 1989	3 876 706	3 290 707	2 864 262	1 550 811	1 313 451	209 288	217 157	585 999	93 615	42 041	13 304
Householder high school graduate or higher	7 088 336	5 994 342	5 163 942	2 917 683	2 246 259	409 067	421 333	1 093 994	181 174	87 889	29 628
Householder 65 years and over	1 549 529	1 217 693	1 027 997	599 051	428 946	87 491	102 205	331 836	49 369	27 904	20 824
With public assistance income in 1989	2 541 129	2 139 107	1 789 692	1 331 772	457 920	170 462	178 953	402 022	73 234	38 900	8 447
With Social Security income in 1989	2 380 686	1 872 701	1 575 690	909 260	666 430	139 082	157 929	507 985	75 514	41 574	25 036
Unrelated individuals for whom poverty status is determined	**36 672 001**	**30 579 452**	**26 273 057**	**15 443 390**	**10 829 667**	**2 220 724**	**2 085 671**	**6 092 549**	**933 010**	**500 277**	**256 726**
Nonfamily householder	26 944 154	22 255 524	18 928 433	11 030 459	7 897 974	1 666 246	1 660 845	4 688 630	759 909	419 742	212 346
In owner-occupied housing unit	12 782 991	9 466 368	7 850 914	3 896 450	3 954 464	734 219	881 235	3 316 623	459 154	285 693	175 146
65 years and over	9 752 744	7 643 570	6 129 628	3 469 368	2 660 260	690 466	823 476	2 109 174	404 519	240 367	113 683
Persons for whom poverty status is determined	**241 977 859**	**181 564 174**	**154 161 189**	**76 351 190**	**77 809 999**	**13 042 125**	**14 360 860**	**60 413 685**	**6 860 074**	**3 744 567**	**3 863 659**
Persons 18 years and over	179 372 340	135 582 686	115 567 627	57 258 158	58 309 469	9 560 709	10 454 350	43 789 654	5 006 769	2 718 233	2 899 289
Persons 65 years and over	29 562 647	22 189 142	18 138 084	9 224 091	8 913 993	1 834 342	2 216 716	7 373 505	1 099 683	643 192	614 910
Related children under 18 years	62 278 655	45 738 538	38 393 291	18 975 868	19 417 423	3 460 094	3 885 153	16 540 117	1 843 161	1 021 109	961 020
Related children under 6 years	21 604 123	16 379 808	13 850 113	7 010 215	6 839 898	1 212 160	1 317 535	5 224 315	600 415	326 650	260 514
Related children 5 to 17 years	44 300 630	32 058 569	26 810 389	13 096 326	13 714 063	2 453 740	2 794 440	12 242 061	1 346 302	752 068	750 257
INCOME IN 1989 BELOW POVERTY LEVEL											
Families	**6 487 515**	**4 750 259**	**3 813 972**	**2 682 266**	**1 131 706**	**442 065**	**494 222**	**1 737 256**	**223 772**	**137 441**	**104 415**
Percent below poverty level	10.0	9.9	9.5	14.0	5.3	12.6	12.4	10.1	11.7	13.2	9.0
In owner-occupied housing unit	2 307 947	1 249 432	942 899	542 776	400 123	124 557	181 976	1 058 515	101 272	75 230	78 990
With related children under 18 years	4 992 845	3 792 713	3 059 391	2 181 963	877 428	349 969	383 353	1 200 132	167 254	98 150	61 684
With related children under 5 years	2 613 626	2 046 262	1 659 512	1 200 245	459 267	186 702	200 048	567 364	82 793	47 779	27 516
Householder worked in 1989	3 215 463	2 280 500	1 775 863	1 193 414	582 449	240 969	263 668	934 963	118 344	73 505	79 306
Householder worked year round full time in 1989	853 067	541 370	416 890	272 527	144 363	56 604	67 876	311 697	32 935	21 599	48 621
Householder under 65 years with work disability	1 073 192	742 377	581 086	415 180	165 906	73 568	87 723	330 815	41 187	24 787	11 103
Householder foreign born	876 281	815 494	750 034	526 593	223 441	35 145	30 315	60 787	9 758	2 440	2 844
Householder under 25 years	763 410	627 957	494 498	366 528	127 970	69 412	64 047	135 453	24 866	12 904	2 712
Householder 65 years and over	762 939	470 004	359 988	239 102	120 886	46 926	63 090	292 935	32 958	23 904	20 335
Householder high school graduate or higher	3 265 377	2 457 376	1 979 106	1 315 787	663 319	232 668	245 602	808 001	111 274	69 129	58 418
With public assistance income in 1989	2 286 388	1 814 599	1 471 665	1 137 439	334 226	165 361	177 573	471 789	75 529	43 689	10 839
With Social Security income in 1989	1 094 068	682 586	515 963	355 621	160 342	72 434	94 189	411 482	47 945	33 199	23 046
Mean income deficit (dollars)	5 379	5 540	5 631	5 796	5 243	5 206	5 130	4 940	4 940	4 797	5 324
Married-couple families	**2 849 984**	**1 776 741**	**1 381 891**	**885 132**	**496 759**	**177 132**	**217 718**	**1 073 243**	**108 802**	**75 678**	**88 420**
With related children under 18 years	1 834 332	1 187 674	931 851	609 580	322 271	116 062	139 761	646 658	67 145	45 357	50 595
With related children under 5 years	1 011 812	688 186	542 317	358 259	184 058	67 567	78 302	323 626	36 237	23 659	23 209
Householder worked in 1989	1 581 202	973 665	747 168	473 249	273 919	103 813	122 684	607 537	59 749	41 976	70 000
Householder worked year round full time in 1989	549 131	307 800	236 577	144 602	91 975	31 382	39 841	241 331	20 383	15 102	45 280
Householder high school graduate or higher	1 351 051	879 230	694 793	414 497	280 296	86 048	98 389	471 821	48 858	35 553	51 048
Householder 65 years and over	506 426	288 221	216 462	132 077	84 385	29 776	41 983	218 205	22 813	17 422	17 008
With public assistance income in 1989	554 412	357 245	271 502	197 988	73 514	38 804	46 939	197 167	23 004	15 815	6 360
With Social Security income in 1989	635 487	348 175	253 172	160 777	92 395	39 150	55 853	287 312	29 977	22 271	18 664
Mean income deficit (dollars)	4 994	5 180	5 321	5 423	5 140	4 731	4 645	4 686	4 505	4 363	5 319
Female householder, no husband present	**3 230 201**	**2 672 180**	**2 183 127**	**1 620 298**	**562 829**	**239 364**	**249 689**	**558 021**	**102 403**	**53 163**	**11 157**
With related children under 18 years	2 866 941	2 390 081	1 951 721	1 448 847	502 874	214 972	223 388	476 860	90 555	46 271	8 280
With related children under 5 years	1 452 618	1 244 253	1 024 585	775 484	249 101	108 670	110 998	208 365	41 915	20 809	3 172
Householder worked in 1989	1 403 435	1 136 995	890 790	624 820	265 970	121 050	125 155	266 440	51 316	26 451	5 654
Householder worked year round full time in 1989	248 472	194 673	148 453	106 314	42 139	21 795	24 425	53 799	10 816	5 284	1 389
Householder high school graduate or higher	1 721 637	1 429 782	1 160 805	816 857	343 948	133 948	135 029	291 855	56 811	29 664	5 131
Householder 65 years and over	215 978	155 499	122 528	91 615	30 913	14 820	18 151	60 479	8 684	5 366	2 410
With public assistance income in 1989	1 642 582	1 392 649	1 147 324	898 603	248 721	121 111	124 214	249 933	49 559	25 676	3 831
With Social Security income in 1989	390 389	289 015	227 094	169 063	58 031	29 128	32 793	101 374	15 471	9 111	3 100
Mean income deficit (dollars)	5 764	5 829	5 881	6 058	5 368	5 609	5 587	5 454	5 423	5 413	5 612
Unrelated individuals	**8 873 475**	**7 109 647**	**5 793 996**	**4 020 210**	**1 773 786**	**712 886**	**602 765**	**1 763 828**	**270 179**	**161 980**	**64 013**
Percent below poverty level	24.2	23.2	22.1	26.0	16.4	32.1	28.9	29.0	29.0	32.4	24.9
Nonfamily householder	5 210 297	4 033 157	3 182 897	2 245 263	937 634	431 530	418 730	1 177 140	197 804	125 049	43 888
In owner-occupied housing unit	1 957 191	1 186 865	882 053	505 094	376 959	128 373	176 439	770 326	101 900	77 283	35 187
65 years and over	2 494 332	1 789 379	1 347 852	887 514	460 338	192 869	248 658	704 953	127 485	85 039	27 065
Mean income deficit (dollars)	3 311	3 377	3 464	3 463	3 466	3 115	2 850	3 045	2 730	2 631	3 230
Persons	**31 742 864**	**23 912 156**	**19 370 094**	**13 685 715**	**5 684 379**	**2 229 346**	**2 312 716**	**7 830 708**	**1 042 760**	**639 875**	**446 418**
Percent below poverty level	13.1	13.2	12.6	17.9	7.3	17.1	16.1	13.0	15.2	17.1	11.6
Persons 18 years and over	20 313 948	15 255 279	12 355 782	8 642 559	3 713 223	1 447 886	1 451 611	5 058 669	663 092	412 678	286 386
Persons 65 years and over	3 780 585	2 581 889	1 958 498	1 283 840	674 658	270 255	353 136	1 198 696	182 193	124 999	62 247
Related children under 18 years	11 161 836	8 459 939	6 852 215	4 948 078	1 904 137	764 089	843 635	2 701 897	371 197	222 820	157 225
Related children under 6 years	4 331 825	3 379 678	2 741 270	1 992 623	748 647	309 673	328 735	952 147	138 652	81 594	49 227
Related children 5 to 17 years	7 544 737	5 628 817	4 555 394	3 274 368	1 281 026	504 401	569 022	1 915 920	255 719	154 981	117 426
Persons below 125 percent of poverty level	42 246 073	31 423 113	25 382 920	17 514 975	7 867 945	2 925 937	3 114 256	10 822 960	1 431 262	885 691	630 045
Persons below 200 percent of poverty level	74 909 296	54 462 691	43 964 375	28 387 368	15 577 007	4 978 945	5 519 371	20 446 605	2 618 305	1 635 480	1 232 441

Source: U.S. Bureau of the Census, *Social and Economic Characteristics of the United States: 1990 Census of Population*, CP-2-1, Washington, D.C.: U.S. Government Printing Office, 1993, Table 24.

B6-10. Poverty Status in 1989 of Families and Persons, by Race and Hispanic Origin: 1990

[Data based on sample and subject to sampling variability.]

United States	All persons	Race White	Race Black	Race American Indian, Eskimo, or Aleut	Race Asian or Pacific Islander	Race Other race	Hispanic origin (of any race)	White, not of Hispanic origin
ALL INCOME LEVELS IN 1989								
Families	65 049 428	53 845 200	7 055 063	463 968	1 577 820	2 107 377	4 776 075	51 337 479
In owner-occupied housing unit	47 221 605	41 666 428	3 488 403	270 377	949 558	846 839	2 234 435	39 843 104
With related children under 18 years	33 536 660	25 929 135	4 699 116	313 592	996 789	1 598 028	3 353 568	24 811 845
With related children under 5 years	14 250 048	10 777 426	2 064 961	144 727	427 763	835 171	1 673 629	10 194 315
Householder worked in 1989	51 357 521	42 948 299	5 055 636	348 200	1 324 838	1 680 548	3 811 513	40 898 459
Householder worked year round full time in 1989	36 318 276	31 057 625	3 169 072	197 646	908 573	985 360	2 344 303	29 625 967
Householder under 65 years with work disability	4 817 701	3 799 301	714 682	64 327	69 169	170 222	364 823	3 600 592
Householder foreign born	5 888 505	3 147 700	441 553	11 812	1 239 508	1 047 932	2 273 032	2 764 656
Householder under 25 years	2 554 838	1 877 270	412 679	31 542	43 244	190 103	352 154	1 722 160
Householder 65 years and over	10 796 925	9 618 752	883 302	44 476	140 075	110 320	375 526	9 058 625
Householder high school graduate or higher	49 435 732	42 422 515	4 519 185	305 619	1 273 900	914 513	2 366 580	40 841 487
With public assistance income in 1989	5 024 146	2 943 001	1 483 805	88 762	171 172	337 406	679 482	2 829 398
With Social Security income in 1989	14 633 024	12 826 264	1 332 865	75 315	183 312	215 268	621 140	12 096 143
Married-couple families	51 718 214	45 178 672	3 521 382	305 156	1 295 099	1 417 905	3 339 694	42 785 906
With related children under 18 years	25 258 549	21 032 242	2 105 944	192 449	846 351	1 081 563	2 329 405	19 979 328
With related children under 5 years	11 134 320	9 165 153	919 135	89 027	377 487	583 518	1 201 491	8 599 942
Householder worked in 1989	42 105 587	36 703 966	2 799 960	245 868	1 116 840	1 238 953	2 867 065	34 802 995
Householder worked year round full time in 1989	30 876 792	27 241 494	1 935 675	151 004	784 751	763 868	1 847 835	25 896 695
Householder high school graduate or higher	40 340 133	36 071 856	2 350 687	207 764	1 069 747	640 079	1 726 727	34 562 667
Householder 65 years and over	8 856 941	8 150 180	492 633	29 148	113 452	71 528	267 232	7 680 962
With public assistance income in 1989	2 196 987	1 595 184	327 404	34 530	116 160	123 709	271 493	1 500 428
With Social Security income in 1989	11 580 548	10 551 848	702 515	48 378	141 343	136 464	423 083	9 945 243
Female householder, no husband present	10 381 654	6 540 382	3 045 283	121 370	185 926	488 693	1 029 646	6 415 256
With related children under 18 years	6 783 155	3 868 218	2 315 622	95 511	111 206	392 598	782 487	3 870 845
With related children under 5 years	2 532 331	1 245 846	1 023 650	42 989	37 058	182 788	345 235	1 260 399
Householder worked in 1989	6 889 101	4 520 231	1 899 466	73 683	127 662	268 059	596 021	4 494 482
Householder worked year round full time in 1989	3 876 706	2 640 115	1 005 228	32 741	73 571	125 051	296 656	2 627 999
Householder high school graduate or higher	7 088 336	4 815 394	1 875 252	75 312	128 201	194 177	461 745	4 808 024
Householder 65 years and over	1 549 529	1 167 361	321 013	12 115	18 962	30 078	84 741	1 095 393
With public assistance income in 1989	2 541 129	1 180 751	1 078 071	47 625	41 385	193 297	366 937	1 169 372
With Social Security income in 1989	2 380 686	1 748 397	522 774	20 903	28 903	59 709	151 265	1 659 943
Unrelated individuals for whom poverty status is determined	36 672 001	30 375 562	4 208 285	278 246	793 413	1 016 495	2 423 197	28 367 481
Nonfamily householder	26 944 154	23 061 780	2 886 787	161 399	442 678	391 510	1 095 965	21 669 520
In owner-occupied housing unit	12 782 991	11 539 278	961 781	64 930	129 766	87 236	309 934	10 919 678
65 years and over	9 752 744	8 681 911	892 690	37 681	70 525	69 937	260 283	8 124 536
Persons for whom poverty status is determined	241 977 859	194 811 704	28 663 173	1 950 915	7 068 454	9 483 613	21 388 017	182 800 924
Persons 18 years and over	179 372 340	147 704 667	19 327 265	1 279 684	5 042 079	6 018 645	13 915 101	139 393 591
Persons 65 years and over	29 562 647	26 333 010	2 385 907	113 052	434 119	296 559	1 027 755	24 950 136
Related children under 18 years	62 278 655	46 880 667	9 284 053	664 454	2 015 646	3 433 835	7 411 310	43 206 797
Related children under 6 years	21 604 123	16 204 013	3 216 863	231 655	683 890	1 267 702	2 717 165	14 863 865
Related children 5 to 17 years	44 300 630	33 408 002	6 599 196	471 750	1 449 657	2 372 025	5 139 867	30 853 463
INCOME IN 1989 BELOW POVERTY LEVEL								
Families	6 487 515	3 787 586	1 852 014	125 432	182 507	539 976	1 067 179	3 572 683
Percent below poverty level	10.0	7.0	26.3	27.0	11.6	25.6	22.3	7.0
In owner-occupied housing unit	2 307 947	1 660 991	454 432	51 562	34 949	106 013	246 971	1 582 305
With related children under 18 years	4 992 845	2 720 709	1 550 105	104 796	138 221	479 014	920 524	2 562 708
With related children under 5 years	2 613 626	1 388 096	817 253	58 315	69 476	280 486	523 812	1 288 796
Householder worked in 1989	3 215 463	2 003 509	777 559	63 196	84 290	286 909	568 434	1 871 711
Householder worked year round full time in 1989	853 067	559 479	179 343	12 167	20 163	81 915	165 164	511 950
Householder under 65 years with work disability	1 073 192	664 549	296 653	23 948	18 003	70 039	136 770	631 518
Householder foreign born	876 281	374 154	73 281	2 515	162 490	263 841	523 594	221 355
Householder under 25 years	763 410	430 358	231 362	15 017	14 894	71 779	128 678	407 022
Householder 65 years and over	762 939	516 038	197 481	11 211	14 090	24 119	67 961	490 610
Householder high school graduate or higher	3 265 377	2 050 477	895 837	62 109	105 940	151 014	318 379	2 045 143
With public assistance income in 1989	2 286 388	1 094 183	888 048	54 404	58 794	190 959	358 515	1 067 904
With Social Security income in 1989	1 094 068	709 269	306 718	18 332	11 910	47 839	112 495	676 032
Mean income deficit (dollars)	5 379	4 856	6 156	5 938	6 099	6 012	5 942	4 875
Married-couple families	2 849 984	2 042 584	387 992	51 812	120 010	247 586	510 211	1 845 055
With related children under 18 years	1 834 332	1 232 264	256 927	39 646	90 804	214 691	424 054	1 085 474
With related children under 5 years	1 011 812	673 129	132 854	23 123	49 199	133 507	256 143	579 634
Householder worked in 1989	1 581 202	1 139 655	178 572	29 345	60 611	173 019	344 303	1 003 200
Householder worked year round full time in 1989	549 131	412 041	56 183	7 005	16 546	57 356	116 186	361 713
Householder high school graduate or higher	1 351 051	1 032 170	161 223	23 835	72 158	61 665	135 971	990 676
Householder 65 years and over	506 426	390 165	85 691	5 732	11 150	13 688	41 868	366 688
With public assistance income in 1989	554 412	356 651	102 309	16 184	34 647	44 621	92 347	329 613
With Social Security income in 1989	635 487	481 923	112 272	9 170	8 076	24 046	60 852	449 875
Mean income deficit (dollars)	4 994	4 720	5 313	5 977	6 266	5 926	5 817	4 669
Female householder, no husband present	3 230 201	1 517 746	1 356 384	61 131	47 873	247 067	470 419	1 517 708
With related children under 18 years	2 866 941	1 327 810	1 216 660	55 054	39 608	227 809	428 177	1 330 290
With related children under 5 years	1 452 618	636 307	645 676	29 124	17 660	123 851	226 184	639 943
Householder worked in 1989	1 403 435	727 287	549 447	26 600	16 518	83 583	166 736	746 303
Householder worked year round full time in 1989	248 472	115 458	110 452	3 922	2 467	16 173	32 943	122 591
Householder high school graduate or higher	1 721 637	902 046	686 327	32 129	24 192	76 943	157 238	938 748
Householder 65 years and over	215 978	104 759	96 037	4 531	2 111	8 540	21 428	103 323
With public assistance income in 1989	1 642 582	692 869	755 527	34 480	21 009	138 697	251 953	694 564
With Social Security income in 1989	390 389	188 630	171 162	7 631	2 967	19 999	43 205	189 180
Mean income deficit (dollars)	5 764	5 068	6 453	5 922	5 786	6 215	6 176	5 155
Unrelated individuals	8 873 475	6 492 447	1 593 404	113 823	258 514	415 287	927 545	6 003 223
Percent below poverty level	24.2	21.4	37.9	40.9	32.6	40.9	38.3	21.2
Nonfamily householder	5 210 297	3 956 178	980 884	53 431	104 308	115 496	307 943	3 734 887
In owner-occupied housing unit	1 957 191	1 607 889	295 158	21 090	12 380	20 674	68 033	1 533 703
65 years and over	2 494 332	1 959 075	460 486	16 360	22 688	35 723	124 455	1 836 613
Mean income deficit (dollars)	3 311	3 166	3 471	3 714	4 014	4 113	3 969	3 150
Persons	31 742 864	19 025 235	8 441 429	603 188	997 196	2 675 816	5 403 492	16 774 507
Percent below poverty level	13.1	9.8	29.5	30.9	14.1	28.2	25.3	9.2
Persons 18 years and over	20 313 948	13 148 968	4 724 301	342 785	650 705	1 447 189	2 996 026	11 950 741
Persons 65 years and over	3 780 585	2 854 161	761 623	33 219	52 129	79 453	246 362	2 673 031
Related children under 18 years	11 161 836	5 695 183	3 671 536	254 431	337 128	1 203 558	2 356 825	4 663 625
Related children under 6 years	4 331 825	2 231 488	1 410 273	102 229	120 474	467 361	909 240	1 840 047
Related children 5 to 17 years	7 544 737	3 836 033	2 489 090	168 816	237 862	812 936	1 598 712	3 129 318
Persons below 125 percent of poverty level	42 246 073	26 422 974	10 325 165	747 713	1 274 873	3 475 348	7 028 410	23 368 486
Persons below 200 percent of poverty level	74 909 296	50 983 766	15 137 833	1 099 251	2 151 021	5 537 425	11 306 861	45 758 478

Source: U.S. Bureau of the Census, *Social and Economic Characteristics of the United States: 1990 Census of Population*, CP-2-1, Washington, D.C.: U.S. Government Printing Office, 1993, Table 49.

B6-11. Poverty Status in 1989 of Families and Persons for Selected Hispanic Origin Groups: 1990

[Data based on sample and subject to sampling variability.]

United States	All persons	Hispanic origin (of any race)										
						Other Hispanic						
								Central American				
		Total	Mexican	Puerto Rican	Cuban	Total	Dominican (Dominican Republic)	Total	Costa Rican	Guatemalan	Honduran	Nicaraguan
ALL INCOME LEVELS IN 1989												
Families	**65 049 428**	**4 776 075**	**2 776 147**	**627 527**	**295 380**	**1 077 021**	**126 991**	**284 787**	**13 279**	**56 978**	**27 445**	**42 608**
In owner-occupied housing unit	47 221 605	2 234 435	1 415 359	188 870	176 222	453 984	19 490	70 764	5 601	13 141	7 413	11 302
With related children under 18 years	33 536 660	3 353 568	2 051 177	447 015	137 970	717 406	96 234	213 408	9 063	43 071	19 997	32 073
With related children under 5 years	14 250 048	1 673 629	1 067 258	207 577	57 615	341 179	48 410	111 521	4 020	23 050	10 684	14 842
Householder worked in 1989	51 357 521	3 811 513	2 283 364	413 234	235 618	879 297	83 485	250 909	11 444	50 874	22 715	37 859
Householder worked year round full time in 1989	36 318 276	2 344 303	1 362 661	271 839	164 584	545 219	49 275	144 169	7 273	28 597	12 872	22 813
Householder under 65 years with work disability	4 817 701	364 823	202 419	75 850	16 439	70 115	10 749	12 371	774	2 474	1 417	1 730
Householder foreign born	5 888 505	2 273 032	1 270 594	6 191	265 316	730 931	119 613	269 792	11 865	54 933	25 712	39 581
Householder under 25 years	2 554 838	352 154	226 746	54 368	8 060	62 980	7 486	23 045	606	4 577	1 974	2 958
Householder 65 years and over	10 796 925	375 526	203 981	38 321	53 547	79 677	6 173	8 737	749	1 265	1 087	1 843
Householder high school graduate or higher	49 435 732	2 366 580	1 215 666	328 238	174 523	648 153	53 632	135 386	9 085	23 136	14 032	27 164
With public assistance income in 1989	5 024 146	679 482	344 357	173 572	40 320	121 233	35 154	22 508	1 189	4 563	3 073	3 296
With Social Security income in 1989	14 633 024	621 140	345 965	81 223	67 024	126 928	10 817	17 644	1 272	2 879	2 193	3 014
Married-couple families	**51 718 214**	**3 339 694**	**2 027 520**	**353 483**	**230 617**	**728 074**	**63 556**	**180 231**	**9 279**	**36 976**	**16 240**	**28 534**
With related children under 18 years	25 258 549	2 329 405	1 510 320	231 408	106 951	480 726	47 286	140 987	6 518	29 670	11 950	22 193
With related children under 5 years	11 134 320	1 201 491	808 031	109 000	47 246	237 214	24 552	77 063	3 108	16 161	6 663	10 767
Householder worked in 1989	42 105 587	2 867 065	1 760 690	286 608	190 964	628 803	51 720	164 962	8 415	34 169	14 270	26 235
Householder worked year round full time in 1989	30 876 792	1 847 835	1 095 102	202 960	137 073	412 700	33 138	100 601	5 623	20 133	8 878	16 839
Householder high school graduate or higher	40 340 133	1 726 727	913 510	208 406	137 722	467 089	30 649	92 278	6 651	16 446	8 707	19 606
Householder 65 years and over	8 856 941	267 232	142 609	24 215	43 081	57 327	2 962	5 158	431	861	645	1 048
With public assistance income in 1989	2 196 987	271 493	159 650	43 658	23 014	45 171	8 553	8 969	451	1 933	978	1 396
With Social Security income in 1989	11 580 548	423 083	234 506	49 313	51 434	87 830	5 543	10 679	753	1 818	1 288	1 784
Female householder, no husband present	**10 381 654**	**1 029 646**	**505 042**	**229 639**	**48 072**	**246 893**	**52 333**	**64 344**	**3 104**	**10 846**	**8 080**	**8 851**
With related children under 18 years	6 783 155	782 487	392 662	187 065	24 116	178 644	42 185	47 949	2 135	8 088	6 178	6 529
With related children under 5 years	2 532 331	345 235	178 410	85 244	7 645	73 936	20 226	20 415	735	3 631	2 932	2 424
Householder worked in 1989	6 889 101	596 021	311 152	92 918	31 151	160 800	22 750	48 882	2 230	8 217	5 752	6 794
Householder worked year round full time in 1989	3 876 706	296 656	149 397	47 570	18 468	81 221	10 893	23 520	1 161	3 853	2 617	3 396
Householder high school graduate or higher	7 088 336	461 745	208 323	98 576	27 463	127 383	18 192	27 771	1 913	3 499	3 935	4 656
Householder 65 years and over	1 549 529	84 741	47 130	11 349	8 248	18 014	2 743	3 053	278	287	385	687
With public assistance income in 1989	2 541 129	366 937	163 782	121 161	14 113	67 881	24 919	11 582	668	2 169	1 864	1 611
With Social Security income in 1989	2 380 686	151 265	83 863	25 600	11 656	30 146	4 308	5 201	436	702	688	942
Unrelated individuals for whom poverty status is determined	**36 672 001**	**2 423 197**	**1 309 279**	**312 746**	**139 991**	**661 181**	**52 000**	**198 674**	**7 764**	**47 523**	**21 121**	**22 157**
Nonfamily householder	26 944 154	1 095 965	525 979	170 282	96 820	302 884	20 725	51 744	3 792	9 419	5 981	6 589
In owner-occupied housing unit	12 782 991	309 934	169 301	25 756	26 149	88 728	1 896	7 960	877	1 281	830	1 349
65 years and over	9 752 744	260 283	118 794	35 386	38 811	67 292	4 581	8 398	679	1 356	824	1 376
Persons for whom poverty status is determined	**241 977 859**	**21 388 017**	**13 110 843**	**2 564 659**	**1 029 619**	**4 682 896**	**509 786**	**1 298 677**	**56 092**	**264 295**	**128 322**	**199 169**
Persons 18 years and over	179 372 340	13 915 101	8 135 095	1 639 887	840 573	3 299 546	348 930	935 117	41 490	193 715	92 612	138 487
Persons 65 years and over	29 562 647	1 027 755	508 299	110 079	163 523	245 854	19 247	37 926	2 782	5 794	3 746	7 835
Related children under 18 years	62 278 655	7 411 310	4 934 858	917 968	187 917	1 370 567	160 013	358 189	14 514	69 451	35 376	59 823
Related children under 6 years	21 604 123	2 717 165	1 827 310	328 062	67 759	494 034	58 685	125 305	4 630	24 443	12 530	17 884
Related children 5 to 17 years	44 300 630	5 139 867	3 407 886	643 574	131 096	957 311	110 807	253 223	10 721	48 990	24 779	45 304
INCOME IN 1989 BELOW POVERTY LEVEL												
Families	**6 487 515**	**1 067 179**	**649 920**	**185 631**	**33 607**	**198 021**	**42 446**	**59 652**	**1 785**	**12 029**	**6 986**	**8 551**
Percent below poverty level	10.0	22.3	23.4	29.6	11.4	18.4	33.4	20.9	13.4	21.1	25.5	20.1
In owner-occupied housing unit	2 307 947	246 971	191 438	13 331	8 253	33 949	2 085	5 324	195	1 090	803	667
With related children under 18 years	4 992 845	920 524	569 554	163 577	19 662	167 731	38 068	52 336	1 542	10 738	5 981	7 692
With related children under 5 years	2 613 626	523 812	338 531	86 008	8 665	90 608	20 817	29 600	689	6 445	3 503	3 893
Householder worked in 1989	3 215 463	568 434	404 627	46 779	13 939	103 089	12 762	41 141	1 036	8 500	4 269	6 311
Householder worked year round full time in 1989	853 067	165 164	123 123	9 773	4 026	28 242	3 296	12 882	153	2 663	1 191	2 076
Householder under 65 years with work disability	1 073 192	136 770	74 500	35 455	4 271	22 544	5 019	3 899	209	794	577	548
Householder foreign born	876 281	523 594	348 259	1 685	30 571	143 079	40 555	57 746	1 718	11 731	6 692	8 182
Householder under 25 years	763 410	128 678	81 464	26 867	1 480	18 867	2 937	6 122	85	1 290	662	760
Householder 65 years and over	762 939	67 961	41 617	7 546	8 137	10 661	1 761	1 300	138	170	161	307
Householder high school graduate or higher	3 265 377	318 379	164 379	61 555	11 729	80 716	14 443	18 972	911	3 167	2 565	3 945
With public assistance income in 1989	2 286 388	358 515	177 003	112 252	11 334	57 926	21 384	8 662	480	1 772	1 429	1 077
With Social Security income in 1989	1 094 068	112 495	69 884	18 769	7 032	16 810	2 863	2 125	145	341	332	322
Mean income deficit (dollars)	5 379	5 942	5 947	6 294	4 570	5 825	6 237	5 644	5 401	5 682	5 862	5 978
Married-couple families	**2 849 984**	**510 211**	**366 615**	**43 094**	**18 899**	**81 603**	**11 130**	**27 256**	**832**	**6 095**	**2 673**	**4 265**
With related children under 18 years	1 834 332	424 054	316 350	33 144	8 826	65 734	9 341	24 147	657	5 508	2 196	3 890
With related children under 5 years	1 011 812	256 143	196 466	17 843	4 139	37 695	5 115	14 729	341	3 531	1 466	2 073
Householder worked in 1989	1 581 202	344 303	266 512	18 072	8 156	51 563	5 490	20 707	589	4 793	1 850	3 398
Householder worked year round full time in 1989	549 131	116 186	91 534	5 350	2 669	16 633	1 683	7 341	94	1 666	695	1 201
Householder high school graduate or higher	1 351 051	135 971	80 490	15 442	6 073	33 966	4 032	8 786	453	1 768	844	2 187
Householder 65 years and over	506 426	41 868	25 832	3 466	6 552	6 018	779	622	84	76	102	120
With public assistance income in 1989	554 412	92 347	59 311	16 345	5 062	11 629	2 880	2 082	91	484	265	311
With Social Security income in 1989	635 487	60 852	39 764	7 618	4 935	8 535	1 042	1 037	70	166	149	139
Mean income deficit (dollars)	4 994	5 817	5 905	5 974	4 028	5 754	6 254	5 704	5 393	5 784	5 972	5 794
Female householder, no husband present	**3 230 201**	**470 419**	**229 153**	**131 634**	**12 184**	**97 448**	**28 936**	**23 779**	**867**	**4 103**	**3 483**	**2 928**
With related children under 18 years	2 866 941	428 177	209 591	121 845	9 238	87 503	26 867	21 424	822	3 768	3 149	2 625
With related children under 5 years	1 452 618	226 184	114 445	63 612	3 717	44 410	14 523	10 714	322	2 019	1 674	1 172
Householder worked in 1989	1 403 435	166 736	99 549	24 123	4 291	38 773	6 012	13 765	392	2 284	1 834	1 815
Householder worked year round full time in 1989	248 472	32 943	20 418	3 465	837	8 223	1 246	3 604	38	563	365	504
Householder high school graduate or higher	1 721 637	157 238	70 118	42 938	4 719	39 463	9 443	7 785	444	944	1 396	1 213
Householder 65 years and over	215 978	21 428	12 794	3 459	1 291	3 884	862	599	54	62	59	173
With public assistance income in 1989	1 642 582	251 953	110 501	91 829	5 707	43 916	17 872	6 180	378	1 204	1 113	671
With Social Security income in 1989	390 389	43 205	24 777	9 658	1 735	7 035	1 630	955	69	157	144	155
Mean income deficit (dollars)	5 764	6 176	6 161	6 433	5 377	5 965	6 244	5 746	5 407	5 792	5 859	6 320
Unrelated individuals	**8 873 475**	**927 545**	**513 171**	**125 128**	**52 799**	**236 447**	**22 568**	**84 198**	**2 352**	**21 080**	**9 662**	**9 740**
Percent below poverty level	24.2	38.3	39.2	40.0	37.7	35.8	43.4	42.4	30.3	44.4	45.7	44.0
Nonfamily householder	5 210 297	307 943	139 302	59 560	34 343	74 738	7 745	12 440	800	2 317	1 736	1 544
In owner-occupied housing unit	1 957 191	68 033	42 450	4 217	4 727	16 639	337	942	108	143	57	139
65 years and over	2 494 332	124 455	54 295	20 212	22 904	27 044	2 911	3 444	248	564	323	606
Mean income deficit (dollars)	3 311	3 969	4 063	3 667	2 985	4 147	4 167	4 473	4 165	4 495	4 374	4 507
Persons	**31 742 864**	**5 403 492**	**3 447 149**	**812 798**	**149 825**	**993 720**	**168 277**	**309 028**	**8 452**	**66 806**	**34 897**	**45 654**
Percent below poverty level	13.1	25.3	26.3	31.7	14.6	21.2	33.0	23.8	15.1	25.3	27.2	22.9
Persons 18 years and over	20 313 948	2 996 026	1 836 019	424 389	117 121	618 497	97 599	207 690	5 744	45 968	23 820	28 661
Persons 65 years and over	3 780 585	246 362	125 659	32 701	39 522	48 480	6 372	7 361	442	1 175	797	1 401
Related children under 18 years	11 161 836	2 356 825	1 577 800	382 665	31 898	364 462	69 984	96 939	2 648	19 851	10 784	16 248
Related children under 6 years	4 331 825	909 240	614 744	144 298	11 916	138 282	26 615	34 354	822	7 015	3 812	5 021
Related children 5 to 17 years	7 544 737	1 598 712	1 064 558	262 112	22 240	249 802	48 051	68 344	2 038	13 983	7 607	12 198
Persons below 125 percent of poverty level	42 246 073	7 028 410	4 559 235	965 021	198 673	1 305 481	206 614	422 909	10 922	91 740	45 591	63 793
Persons below 200 percent of poverty level	74 909 296	11 306 861	7 411 141	1 365 093	345 208	2 185 419	307 317	729 840	20 112	156 083	73 618	108 468

B6-11. Poverty Status in 1989 of Families and Persons for Selected Hispanic Origin Groups: 1990 *(continued)*

[Data based on sample and subject to sampling variability.]

United States	Hispanic origin (of any race)—Con.												
	Other Hispanic—Con.												
	Central American—Con.			South American									
	Panamanian	Salvadoran	Other Central American	Total	Argentinean	Chilean	Colombian	Ecuadorian	Peruvian	Venezuelan	Other South American	All other Hispanic origin	Not of Hispanic origin
ALL INCOME LEVELS IN 1989													
Families	**21 622**	**121 115**	**1 740**	**251 987**	**28 463**	**17 167**	**88 617**	**47 058**	**41 918**	**10 634**	**18 130**	**413 256**	**60 273 353**
In owner-occupied housing unit	9 103	23 751	453	106 202	15 867	8 718	35 424	16 896	16 190	4 543	8 564	257 528	44 987 170
With related children under 18 years	14 482	93 392	1 330	163 316	16 103	10 693	58 449	31 620	27 599	6 954	11 898	244 448	30 183 092
With related children under 5 years	5 899	52 358	668	73 218	6 512	4 117	26 809	14 077	12 707	3 737	5 259	108 030	12 576 419
Householder worked in 1989	18 566	108 097	1 354	222 716	25 622	15 753	78 256	39 844	37 869	8 953	16 419	322 187	47 546 008
Householder worked year round full time in 1989	12 041	59 650	923	142 651	17 412	10 315	49 804	25 091	23 721	5 589	10 719	209 124	33 973 973
Householder under 65 years with work disability	1 179	4 742	55	10 771	1 063	603	3 969	2 593	1 518	386	639	36 224	4 452 878
Householder foreign born	18 186	117 977	1 538	235 885	26 659	15 784	83 244	44 418	39 364	9 288	17 128	105 641	3 615 473
Householder under 25 years	1 117	11 734	79	9 979	672	480	3 710	2 211	1 580	618	708	22 470	2 202 684
Householder 65 years and over	1 503	2 219	71	11 149	1 662	749	3 693	2 363	1 719	364	599	53 618	10 421 399
Householder high school graduate or higher	17 860	43 115	994	182 957	21 576	13 837	60 900	29 298	34 218	9 332	13 796	276 178	47 069 152
With public assistance income in 1989	1 987	8 186	214	17 892	1 282	819	6 548	5 278	2 577	427	961	45 679	4 344 664
With Social Security income in 1989	2 047	6 092	147	21 202	2 997	1 438	7 198	4 325	3 257	636	1 351	77 265	14 011 884
Married-couple families	**13 027**	**75 170**	**1 005**	**183 855**	**23 810**	**13 589**	**60 828**	**32 957**	**30 418**	**8 201**	**14 052**	**300 432**	**48 378 520**
With related children under 18 years	8 814	61 073	769	123 085	13 691	8 563	41 671	23 110	21 104	5 480	9 466	169 368	22 929 144
With related children under 5 years	3 990	35 958	416	58 267	5 753	3 475	20 461	10 622	10 264	3 232	4 460	77 332	9 932 829
Householder worked in 1989	11 684	69 333	856	167 928	21 851	12 658	55 667	29 452	28 124	7 188	12 988	244 193	39 238 522
Householder worked year round full time in 1989	8 027	40 485	616	112 372	15 154	8 618	37 523	19 417	18 329	4 653	8 678	166 589	29 028 957
Householder high school graduate or higher	11 237	29 013	618	137 529	18 064	11 180	43 528	21 394	25 226	7 355	10 782	206 633	38 613 406
Householder 65 years and over	894	1 234	45	7 965	1 413	548	2 451	1 611	1 201	273	468	41 242	8 589 709
With public assistance income in 1989	587	3 564	60	8 344	848	493	2 729	2 297	1 288	165	524	19 305	1 925 494
With Social Security income in 1989	1 236	3 716	84	14 556	2 344	1 023	4 555	2 939	2 268	442	985	57 052	11 157 465
Female householder, no husband present	**7 270**	**25 684**	**509**	**45 334**	**3 084**	**2 230**	**19 004**	**9 742**	**6 989**	**1 763**	**2 522**	**84 882**	**9 352 008**
With related children under 18 years	4 938	19 674	407	29 241	1 739	1 446	12 264	6 587	4 367	1 141	1 697	59 269	6 000 668
With related children under 5 years	1 640	8 904	149	9 688	505	339	4 122	2 495	1 423	364	440	23 607	2 187 096
Householder worked in 1989	5 682	19 889	318	34 039	2 375	1 844	14 602	6 395	5 591	1 197	2 035	55 129	6 293 080
Householder worked year round full time in 1989	3 221	9 116	156	18 124	1 369	1 003	7 549	3 424	2 942	615	1 222	28 684	3 580 050
Householder high school graduate or higher	5 589	7 911	268	29 711	2 344	1 653	11 606	5 371	5 373	1 417	1 947	51 709	6 626 591
Householder 65 years and over	552	852	12	2 578	192	176	1 007	616	411	91	85	9 640	1 464 788
With public assistance income in 1989	1 257	3 872	141	7 874	355	252	3 053	2 672	985	233	324	23 506	2 174 192
With Social Security income in 1989	685	1 705	43	5 022	485	322	2 024	1 076	704	165	246	15 615	2 229 421
Unrelated individuals for whom poverty status is determined	**13 546**	**85 549**	**1 014**	**142 233**	**15 630**	**9 489**	**53 149**	**22 016**	**23 661**	**8 121**	**10 167**	**268 274**	**34 248 804**
Nonfamily householder	8 666	16 831	466	68 463	10 254	5 232	23 610	9 326	10 817	4 402	4 822	161 952	25 848 189
In owner-occupied housing unit	1 869	1 645	109	14 827	2 765	1 300	4 943	1 710	1 965	965	1 179	64 045	12 473 057
65 years and over	1 832	2 236	95	10 076	1 595	800	3 469	1 839	1 298	391	684	44 237	9 492 461
Persons for whom poverty status is determined	**88 580**	**555 293**	**6 926**	**1 013 910**	**98 844**	**67 700**	**368 169**	**188 760**	**172 290**	**46 774**	**71 373**	**1 860 523**	**220 589 842**
Persons 18 years and over	66 901	396 976	4 936	764 784	79 164	50 656	274 632	143 177	129 363	33 964	53 828	1 250 715	165 457 239
Persons 65 years and over	5 671	11 847	251	42 006	5 880	3 015	14 063	8 266	6 981	1 191	2 610	146 675	28 534 892
Related children under 18 years	21 532	155 518	1 975	247 432	19 561	16 946	92 868	45 270	42 691	12 758	17 338	604 933	54 867 345
Related children under 6 years	7 417	57 681	720	85 663	5 750	6 010	32 842	15 228	15 390	4 532	5 911	224 381	18 886 958
Related children 5 to 17 years	15 389	106 693	1 347	175 258	14 790	11 862	65 181	32 621	29 502	9 036	12 266	418 023	39 160 763
INCOME IN 1989 BELOW POVERTY LEVEL													
Families	**2 837**	**26 969**	**495**	**30 353**	**2 206**	**1 409**	**11 617**	**6 851**	**4 913**	**1 639**	**1 718**	**65 570**	**5 420 336**
Percent below poverty level	13.1	22.3	28.4	12.0	7.8	8.2	13.1	14.6	11.7	15.4	9.5	15.9	9.0
In owner-occupied housing unit	300	2 216	53	5 016	444	328	2 198	759	785	252	250	21 524	2 060 976
With related children under 18 years	2 353	23 654	376	24 705	1 502	1 060	9 425	5 992	4 097	1 297	1 332	52 622	4 072 321
With related children under 5 years	1 109	13 799	162	12 425	776	498	4 731	2 984	2 031	661	744	27 766	2 089 814
Householder worked in 1989	1 591	19 170	264	17 147	1 278	857	6 908	3 069	3 160	871	1 004	32 039	2 647 029
Householder worked year round full time in 1989	285	6 436	78	4 329	195	233	1 921	766	806	147	261	7 735	687 903
Householder under 65 years with work disability	232	1 512	27	2 595	178	114	927	798	326	140	112	11 031	936 422
Householder foreign born	2 530	26 459	434	28 712	2 047	1 334	11 008	6 558	4 688	1 465	1 612	16 066	352 687
Householder under 25 years	410	2 915	–	1 882	120	72	713	340	358	162	117	7 926	634 732
Householder 65 years and over	137	358	29	1 305	178	106	507	264	174	13	63	6 295	694 978
Householder high school graduate or higher	2 019	6 145	220	18 010	1 350	944	6 355	3 274	3 596	1 311	1 180	29 291	2 946 998
With public assistance income in 1989	686	3 104	114	5 815	290	220	2 157	2 217	526	179	226	22 065	1 927 873
With Social Security income in 1989	110	838	37	1 967	242	132	743	433	230	58	129	9 855	981 573
Mean income deficit (dollars)	5 668	5 475	5 809	5 740	5 922	5 006	5 464	6 126	5 800	6 606	5 431	5 764	5 268
Married-couple families	**699**	**12 496**	**196**	**14 810**	**1 352**	**808**	**5 139**	**2 970**	**2 660**	**941**	**940**	**28 407**	**2 339 773**
With related children under 18 years	574	11 188	134	11 869	873	578	4 135	2 551	2 239	779	714	20 377	1 410 278
With related children under 5 years	326	6 924	68	6 768	457	299	2 408	1 410	1 249	485	460	11 083	755 669
Householder worked in 1989	451	9 510	116	9 556	913	547	3 459	1 594	1 883	563	597	15 810	1 236 899
Householder worked year round full time in 1989	95	3 557	33	2 728	146	175	1 181	437	539	113	137	4 881	432 945
Householder high school graduate or higher	475	2 963	96	9 225	758	582	2 963	1 432	2 045	751	694	11 923	1 215 080
Householder 65 years and over	55	156	29	797	141	67	264	186	93	13	33	3 820	464 558
With public assistance income in 1989	71	825	35	1 416	141	76	408	532	158	38	63	5 251	462 065
With Social Security income in 1989	33	451	29	981	126	68	320	266	128	17	56	5 475	574 635
Mean income deficit (dollars)	5 670	5 607	5 264	5 825	5 542	4 805	5 620	6 221	5 913	6 885	5 658	5 570	4 814
Female householder, no husband present	**1 961**	**10 214**	**223**	**12 601**	**653**	**471**	**5 167**	**3 411**	**1 782**	**538**	**579**	**32 132**	**2 759 782**
With related children under 18 years	1 705	9 171	184	10 846	540	408	4 376	3 090	1 521	410	501	28 366	2 438 764
With related children under 5 years	749	4 718	60	4 676	264	138	1 887	1 411	614	137	225	14 497	1 226 434
Householder worked in 1989	1 051	6 292	97	5 765	279	228	2 607	1 159	991	217	284	13 231	1 236 699
Householder worked year round full time in 1989	178	1 942	14	1 204	44	51	549	217	230	13	100	2 169	215 529
Householder high school graduate or higher	1 432	2 267	89	7 133	452	290	2 776	1 593	1 195	427	400	15 102	1 564 399
Householder 65 years and over	82	169	–	419	37	39	185	66	67	–	25	2 004	194 550
With public assistance income in 1989	573	2 162	79	4 033	144	122	1 519	1 623	338	141	146	15 831	1 390 629
With Social Security income in 1989	77	345	8	816	110	64	347	157	72	29	37	3 634	347 184
Mean income deficit (dollars)	5 699	5 546	6 485	5 635	6 377	5 233	5 361	6 025	5 480	6 361	5 062	6 005	5 694
Unrelated individuals	**3 771**	**37 161**	**432**	**43 837**	**3 987**	**2 668**	**17 258**	**6 972**	**6 997**	**2 724**	**3 231**	**85 844**	**7 945 930**
Percent below poverty level	27.8	43.4	42.6	30.8	25.5	28.1	32.5	31.7	29.6	33.5	31.8	32.0	23.2
Nonfamily householder	1 742	4 165	136	14 887	1 824	981	5 595	2 312	2 187	945	1 043	39 666	4 902 354
In owner-occupied housing unit	274	182	39	1 887	253	151	659	188	267	202	167	13 473	1 889 158
65 years and over	721	933	49	4 644	545	275	1 754	1 028	586	172	284	16 045	2 369 877
Mean income deficit (dollars)	4 061	4 539	4 408	4 131	4 088	4 076	4 137	4 037	4 068	4 438	4 283	3 830	3 234
Persons	**13 248**	**137 813**	**2 158**	**145 867**	**10 838**	**6 966**	**55 737**	**30 053**	**24 216**	**9 117**	**8 940**	**370 548**	**26 339 372**
Percent below poverty level	15.0	24.8	31.2	14.4	11.0	10.3	15.1	15.9	14.1	19.5	12.5	19.9	11.9
Persons 18 years and over	9 152	92 913	1 432	103 140	8 332	5 364	39 385	19 905	17 284	6 178	6 692	210 068	17 317 922
Persons 65 years and over	998	2 444	104	7 682	942	498	2 872	1 547	1 130	230	463	27 065	3 534 223
Related children under 18 years	3 994	42 703	711	41 283	2 407	1 512	15 800	9 873	6 725	2 891	2 075	156 256	8 805 011
Related children under 6 years	1 553	15 905	226	15 071	868	580	6 110	3 528	2 347	870	768	62 242	3 422 585
Related children 5 to 17 years	2 697	29 304	517	28 885	1 644	1 026	10 777	7 034	4 734	2 214	1 456	104 522	5 946 025
Persons below 125 percent of poverty level	17 546	190 550	2 767	197 333	14 628	9 397	75 643	39 807	33 876	11 717	12 265	478 625	35 217 663
Persons below 200 percent of poverty level	31 765	335 741	4 053	361 749	26 841	19 285	136 774	73 102	63 806	18 002	23 939	786 513	63 602 435

Source: U.S. Bureau of the Census, *Social and Economic Characteristics of the United States: 1990 Census of Population*, CP-2-1, Washington, D.C.: U.S. Government Printing Office, 1993, Table 121.

B6-12. Poverty Status, by Family and Marital Status: 1991, 1990, and 1987

[In thousands]

Family and marital status	Persons poor in an average month						Persons poor 2 or more months					
	1991		1990		1987		1991		1990		1987	
	Number	Percent	Number	Percent	Number	Percent	Number	Percent	Number	Percent	Number	Percent
Total..................	33,866	13.6	31,818	12.9	31,980	13.3	48,477	19.8	45,638	18.9	44,811	19.1
Family Status												
In families...............	26,488	12.4	24,494	11.6	25,350	12.2	39,343	18.7	36,507	17.5	36,831	17.9
In married-couple families	12,624	7.4	11,852	7.0	13,211	7.9	22,682	13.3	21,509	12.7	21,666	13.0
In families with a female house- holder, no spouse present	12,989	36.7	11,960	35.2	11,495	35.0	15,410	45.4	14,044	43.1	14,014	43.4
Unrelated individuals	7,378	20.4	7,324	20.4	6,630	20.5	9,134	26.9	9,131	27.6	7,980	27.0
Marital Status (persons 18 years and over)												
Married	6,595	6.1	6,298	5.8	7,171	6.8	11,993	11.1	11,563	10.7	12,003	11.3
Separated, divorced, or widowed	6,665	19.4	6,404	18.8	6,508	20.1	8,476	26.3	8,067	25.3	8,523	28.0
Never married	6,645	16.1	6,090	15.1	5,347	14.1	9,134	23.1	8,336	21.9	6,858	19.4

Source: Martina Shea, U.S. Bureau of the Census, *Dynamics of Economic Well-Being: Poverty 1990 to 1992*, Current Population Reports, P70-42, Washington, D.C.: U.S. Government Printing Office, January 1995, Table A.

B6-13. The Chronically Poor and Median Spell Durations, by Family and Marital Status: 1990–91 and 1987–88

[In thousands.]

Family and marital status	Persons poor all 24 months of 2-year period				Median duration of poverty spells in the 1990 panel (in months)
	1990-91		1987-88		
	Number	Percent	Number	Percent	
Total	10,619	4.5	10,162	4.4	4.0
Family Status					
In families	8,031	3.9	7,975	3.9	4.0
In married-couple families	2,299	1.4	2,976	1.8	3.8
In families with a female householder, no spouse present...........................	5,571	17.6	4,872	15.6	6.5
Unrelated individuals	2,589	8.1	2,187	7.7	4.1
Marital Status (persons 18 years and over)					
Married.......................................	1,290	1.2	1,598	1.5	3.8
Separated, divorced, or widowed	2,675	8.8	2,311	8.0	4.9
Never married..................................	1,835	4.9	1,455	4.2	4.4

Source: Martina Shea, U.S. Bureau of the Census, *Dynamics of Economic Well-Being: Poverty 1990 to 1992*, Current Population Reports, P70-42, Washington, D.C.: U.S. Government Printing Office, January 1995, Table B.

B7. PUBLIC ASSISTANCE

B7-1. Program Participation Status, by Family Status: 1990 and 1987

[Numbers in thousands.]

Participation and family status	1990								1987							
	Major means-tested assistance programs[1]		AFDC or General Assistance		Food stamps		Housing assistance		Major means-tested assistance programs[1]		AFDC or General Assistance		Food stamps		Housing assistance	
	Number	Percent	Number	Percent	Number	Percent	Number	Percent	Number	Percent	Number	Percent	Number	Percent	Number	Percent
Average Monthly Participation																
Total	28,461	11.5	10,573	4.3	17,136	6.9	10,694	4.3	27,412	11.4	10,385	4.3	17,365	7.2	9,222	3.8
In families.	23,951	11.3	10,329	4.9	15,576	7.4	8,461	4.0	23,323	11.2	10,052	4.8	15,822	7.6	7,384	3.6
In married-couple families	10,405	6.1	2,495	1.5	5,817	3.4	2,876	1.7	10,350	6.2	2,544	1.5	6,528	3.9	2,426	1.4
In families with a female householder, no spouse present . .	12,640	37.2	7,576	22.3	9,358	27.6	5,270	15.5	12,277	37.4	7,366	22.5	9,065	27.6	4,703	14.3
Unrelated individuals . . .	4,510	12.6	245	0.7	1,561	4.4	2,232	6.2	4,089	12.6	332	1.0	1,543	4.8	1,838	5.7
Persons Ever Participating																
Total	35,663	14.8	12,847	5.3	21,941	9.1	13,745	5.7	34,856	14.8	13,432	5.7	24,221	10.3	11,424	4.9
In families.	30,405	14.6	12,469	6.0	19,923	9.6	11,052	5.3	30,190	14.7	12,890	6.3	22,242	10.8	9,260	4.5
In married-couple families	15,571	9.2	3,874	2.3	8,971	5.3	4,450	2.6	15,230	9.1	3,758	2.2	10,480	6.3	3,297	2.0
In families with a female householder, no spouse present . .	13,799	42.4	8,233	25.3	10,461	32.1	6,289	19.3	14,102	43.7	8,889	27.5	11,341	35.1	5,698	17.6
Unrelated individuals . . .	5,258	15.9	378	1.1	2,018	6.1	2,693	8.2	4,666	15.8	542	1.8	1,979	6.7	2,164	7.3

[1]Major means-tested assistance programs include AFDC or General Assistance, SSI, food stamps, Medicaid, and housing assistance.

Source: Martina Shea, U.S. Bureau of the Census, *Dynamics of Economic Well-Being: Program Participation, 1990 to 1992*, Current Population Reports, P70-41, Washington, D.C.: U.S. Government Printing Office, January 1995, Table B.

B7-2. Median-Spell Durations, by Family Status: 1990 and 1987

[Numbers in months]

Family status	Major means-tested assistance programs[1]		AFDC or General Assistance		Food stamps		Medicaid		Housing assistance	
	1990 panel	1987 panel	1990 panel	1987 panel	1990 panel	1987 panel	1990 panel	1987 panel	1990 panel	1987 panel
Total	7.9	6.4	10.4	7.5	8.8	6.9	10.6	7.4	15.6	12.6
In families....................	7.8	6.0	10.9	7.5	8.6	6.6	9.9	7.2	16.2	12.5
In married-couple families....	7.3	5.4	5.8	5.4	7.0	4.9	7.9	5.4	7.8	7.9
In families with a female householder, no spouse present	11.4	6.8	18.2	11.7	11.5	13.7	15.5	10.5	(X)	(X)
Unrelated individuals	8.6	8.1	5.7	9.6	10.5	9.6	17.5	15.1	11.9	12.7

[1]Major means-tested assistance programs include AFDC or General Assistance, SSI, food stamps, Medicaid, and housing assistance.

Source: Martina Shea, U.S. Bureau of the Census, *Dynamics of Economic Well-Being: Program Participation, 1990 to 1992*, Current Population Reports, P70-41, Washington, D.C.: U.S. Government Printing Office, January 1995, Table B3.

B7-3. AFDC Mothers Compared with Non-AFDC Mothers: Summer 1993

AFDC Mothers Versus Non-AFDC Mothers

Mothers 15 to 44 years old, by AFDC status and selected fertility and socioeconomic characteristics: summer 1993

Characteristic	Receiving AFDC					Not receiving AFDC				
	Mothers		Births per 1,000 mothers	Mean age of mother in years ...		Mothers		Births per 1,000 mothers	Mean age of mother in years ...	
	Number (in thousands)	Percent		at time of survey	at first birth	Number (in thousands)	Percent		at time of survey	at first birth
Total	**3,754**	**100.0**	**2,586**	**29.5**	**20.3**	**32,022**	**100.0**	**2,123**	**34.0**	**22.9**
Age										
15 to 19 years	191	5.1	1,407	18.1	17.0	554	1.7	1,094	18.1	16.9
20 to 24 years	866	23.1	1,964	22.2	18.5	2,615	8.2	1,481	22.3	19.4
25 to 29 years	865	23.0	2,464	27.3	20.1	5,020	15.7	1,891	27.2	21.8
30 to 34 years	921	24.5	2,837	31.9	20.7	7,508	23.4	2,150	32.1	23.3
35 to 39 years	604	16.1	3,226	36.9	21.8	8,389	26.2	2,267	37.0	24.0
40 to 44 years	307	8.2	3,405	41.5	23.2	7,936	24.8	2,375	42.0	23.6
Race										
White	2,074	55.2	2,536	29.9	20.8	26,352	82.3	2,108	34.1	23.1
Black	1,471	39.2	2,694	29.0	19.5	4,258	13.3	2,165	33.4	20.9
Hispanic Origin										
Hispanic[1]	784	20.9	3,114	30.2	20.3	3,406	10.6	2,408	32.9	21.7
Not Hispanic	2,970	79.1	2,447	29.3	20.3	28,616	89.4	2,089	34.2	23.0
Marital Status										
Currently married	1,120	29.8	2,827	31.0	20.7	25,322	79.1	2,185	34.4	23.3
Married, husband present	472	12.6	2,929	31.1	20.6	23,827	74.4	2,175	34.5	23.4
Married, husband absent[2]	648	17.3	2,753	30.9	20.8	1,495	4.7	2,352	33.7	21.3
Widowed or divorced	851	22.7	2,728	32.9	21.0	4,009	12.5	2,078	36.2	21.7
Never married	1,783	47.5	2,366	26.9	19.6	2,691	8.4	1,598	27.1	20.5
Educational Attainment										
Not a high school graduate	1,633	43.5	2,890	28.8	19.2	4,631	14.5	2,464	31.9	19.8
High school, 4 years	1,422	37.9	2,361	29.6	20.8	12,900	40.3	2,094	33.8	21.9
College: 1 or more years	698	18.6	2,333	30.7	21.6	14,490	45.3	2,040	34.9	24.8
Enrollment in School										
Enrolled in school	527	14.0	2,128	28.3	20.1	2,682	8.4	1,950	31.8	21.7
Not enrolled in school	3,226	85.9	2,661	29.7	20.3	29,340	91.6	2,138	34.2	23.0
Labor Force Status										
Worked all or some weeks	474	12.6	2,372	31.3	20.4	21,889	68.4	2,061	34.7	23.0
No job last month	3,280	87.4	2,617	29.2	20.2	10,133	31.6	2,255	32.5	22.6
Monthly Family Income[3]										
Less than $500	1,351	36.1	2,574	29.7	20.3	889	2.8	2,045	31.2	21.0
$500 to $999	1,360	36.3	2,770	29.7	20.2	2,190	6.9	2,308	31.9	21.0
$1,000 to $1,499	479	12.8	2,431	29.8	20.5	3,159	10.0	2,153	32.3	21.5
$1,500 and over	552	14.8	2,293	28.0	20.0	25,309	80.2	2,107	34.6	23.3
Poverty Level[3]										
Below poverty level	3,004	80.3	2,696	29.6	20.2	4,178	13.2	2,489	31.5	20.8
Above poverty level	737	19.7	2,135	29.0	20.5	27,368	86.8	2,068	34.5	23.2
Division										
New England	185	4.9	(B)	(B)	(B)	1,496	4.7	2,022	34.8	24.3
Mid Atlantic	542	14.4	2,689	29.9	20.4	4,388	13.7	2,023	34.2	23.7
East North Central	748	19.9	2,537	29.0	20.6	5,669	17.7	2,107	33.8	22.8
West North Central	222	5.9	3,027	29.1	19.5	2,363	7.4	2,168	34.2	23.1
South Atlantic	591	15.7	2,472	28.9	19.6	5,720	17.9	2,025	34.1	22.7
East South Central	191	5.1	(B)	(B)	(B)	2,006	6.3	2,026	34.0	21.7
West South Central	369	9.8	2,744	29.8	20.3	3,512	11.0	2,220	33.9	22.2
Mountain	119	3.2	(B)	(B)	(B)	1,634	5.1	2,400	34.2	22.8
Pacific	787	21.0	2,596	30.2	20.9	5,234	16.3	2,223	33.7	23.0
Metropolitan Residence										
Metropolitan	3,039	81.0	2,595	29.4	20.3	24,519	76.6	2,101	34.1	23.1
In central cities	2,117	56.4	2,697	29.7	20.0	8,688	27.1	2,125	33.5	22.5
Suburbs	922	24.6	2,362	28.8	20.8	15,830	49.4	2,088	34.4	23.5
Nonmetropolitan	715	19.0	2,547	29.8	20.2	7,503	23.4	2,194	33.8	22.0
Place of Birth										
Native born	3,362	89.6	2,536	29.2	20.0	28,171	88.0	2,095	34.0	22.8
Foreign born	392	10.4	3,014	31.8	22.4	3,850	12.0	2,328	33.9	23.4

(B)Base too small to show derived measure. [1]Persons of Hispanic origin may be of any race. [2]Includes separated women. [3]Excludes those who did not report income.

Source: U.S. Bureau of the Census, *Mothers Who Receive AFDC Payments — Fertility and Socioeconomic Characteristics*, Statistical Brief, SB95/2, March 1995, Table 1.

B7-4. Percent Distribution of Mothers Currently Receiving Aid to Families with Dependent Children (AFDC), by Marital Status: Summer 1993

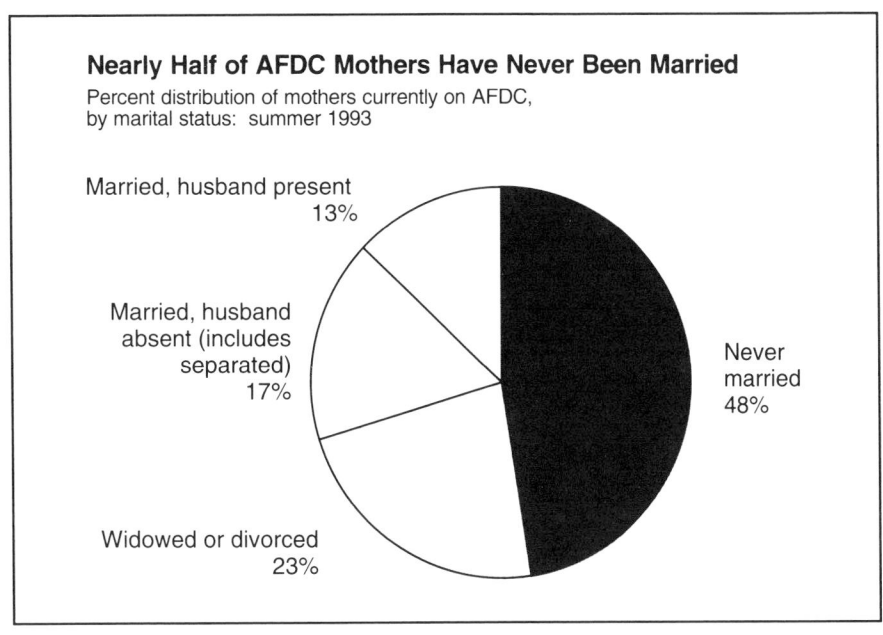

Source: U.S. Bureau of the Census, *Mothers Who Receive AFDC Payments — Fertility and Socioeconomic Characteristics*, Statistical Brief, SB95/2, March 1995, Figure 1.

B7-5. Mean Age at First Birth among Mothers, by Current AFDC Status and Current Age: Summer 1993

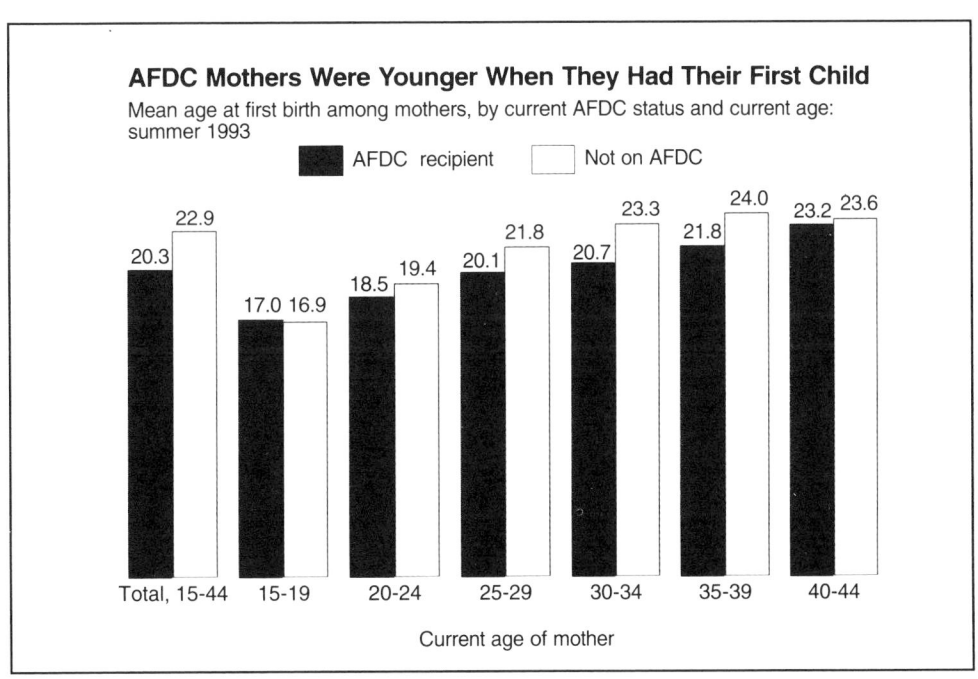

Source: U.S. Bureau of the Census, *Mothers Who Receive AFDC Payments — Fertility and Socioeconomic Characteristics*, Statistical Brief, SB95/2, March 1995, Figure 2.

B7-6. Mothers Aged 15 to 44 Receiving Aid to Families with Dependent Children (AFDC): 1993

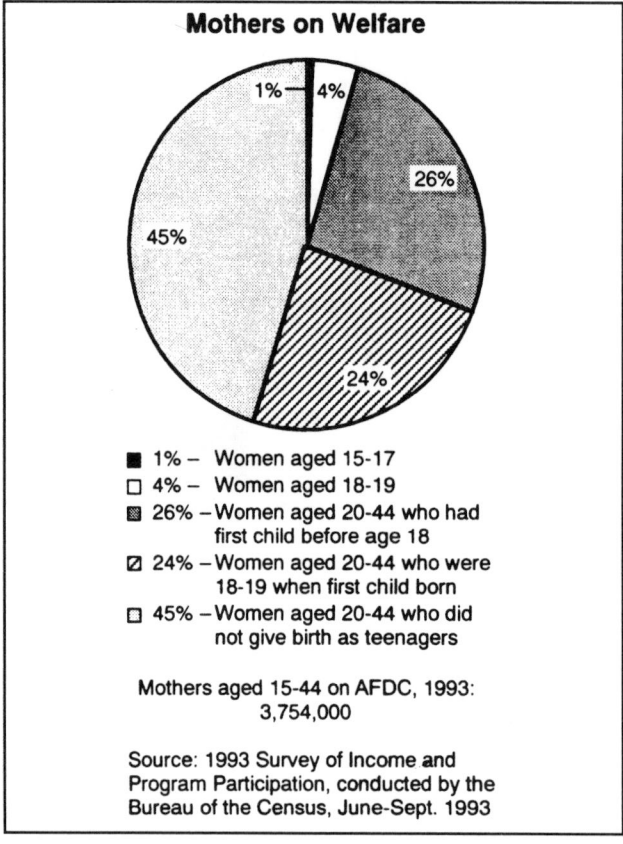

Mothers on Welfare

■ 1% – Women aged 15-17
□ 4% – Women aged 18-19
▦ 26% – Women aged 20-44 who had first child before age 18
▨ 24% – Women aged 20-44 who were 18-19 when first child born
□ 45% – Women aged 20-44 who did not give birth as teenagers

Mothers aged 15-44 on AFDC, 1993:
3,754,000

Source: 1993 Survey of Income and Program Participation, conducted by the Bureau of the Census, June-Sept. 1993

Source: The Alan Guttmacher Institute, *Teenage Pregnancy and the Welfare Reform Debate*, Issues in Brief, February 1995, Figure 3.

Health Characteristics

C1. HEALTH AND DISABILITY STATUS

Most women in America are healthy. Nearly 9 in 10 women report that their health is good or has improved in the last year. Even a majority of elderly women (72 percent of those 65 and over), whom we would think are more often in poor health, say their health is good or better. In reality, poor health and severe disabilities are not a serious problem for the majority of women until they reach at least their mid-70s and beyond.

Women are less likely than men to suffer from acute conditions (those that last less than three months), but when they do, women are likely to lose more days of work because of the conditions. Women suffer most frequently from flu, colds, infectious diseases, and injuries.

Conversely, women tend to suffer more often than men from chronic diseases, many of which are not lethal but are long-lasting, limiting, and involve many trips to the offices of doctors. The chronic diseases most prevalent among women include arthritis and respiratory conditions such as chronic sinusitis. Among women 45 years old and over, the most prevalent chronic diseases are heart disease, high blood pressure, back impairments, hearing impairments, and cataracts. Arthritis is the most commonly reported condition that causes a limiting disability among women; chronic back problems are second.

Has the health of women improved along with increasing life expectancy? In some respects, yes, and in some respects, no. Industry has given more attention to mechanical devices that help men and women overcome limitations of their bodies. And yet, while more women live to older ages, they aren't necessarily more healthy. We see more aged women with multiple, long-lasting, expensive, and complex diseases.

One-fifth of adult women suffer from hypertension, a significant improvement from a decade ago when one-third of women had elevated blood pressure. Nevertheless, 3 in 4 women 75 years and over suffer from this potentially life-threatening disease.

Unlike the improvement in hypertension, new cancer cases increased overall, about 1 percent a year among women from 1973 to 1991. Breast cancer represents one-third of the cancers from which women suffer, and the number of new cases has increased 1.8 percent annually since 1973. Four in five women survive breast cancer for at least five years compared to about three in four women in the mid-1970s. The chances of five-year survival are much better among White women than among Black women (89 percent versus 78 percent, respectively).

In addition, many young women began smoking in the 1950s and now are dying prematurely of lung cancer—the second most frequent type of cancer among women. Less than one in six women survive lung cancer for five years; this survival rate is no different from what it was in the mid-1970s. The incidence of lung and bronchus cancers increased nearly 5 percent a year from 1973 to 1991.

Of the 49 million noninstitutionalized Americans living with a disability, defined in the 1991–92 household survey data as a limitation in a functional activity or in a socially defined role or task, 26 million are women. That is 1 in 5 women. About 2.4 million of these women had no health insurance. The prevalence of disability is lowest among Asian women (less than 11 percent have a disability, and only 6 percent have a severe disability). In addition, half of women who had dropped out of high school had a limiting disability compared with only 14 percent of women with four or more years of college. Also, more than 1 in 4 poor women had a disability, and about 6 million received some kind of public assistance.

About 1 percent of women under age 65 regularly use a wheelchair, cane, crutches, or a walker. Among the 26 million with a limiting disability, less than 6 million, most of whom were elderly, needed significant personal assistance. In fact, women with a disability, unless it is severe, were almost as likely as women with no disability to be in the labor force. Conversely, less than one in four women with a severe disability had a job or business.

There is a strong relationship between gender, age, and the likelihood of a disability. Disability rates are somewhat higher among women than men. Among women living in the community (that is, the civilian noninstitutional population), only 4 percent of girls under 18 and 14 percent of women aged 18 to 44 years have a disability. Among women aged 75 to 84, two-thirds have a limiting disability and nearly half have a severe disability. For women 85 years and older living outside of nursing homes, 86 percent suffer some type of limiting disability; for 72 percent, this disability is severe. These data underline the need for personal assistance among very old women. Much of that care is provided by women in their late 50s and early 60s.

With the aging of the Baby-Boom generation into adulthood and the increased number of very old persons with dementia, the absolute number of persons with serious mental illness (SMI) has been increasing. The SMI population is a heterogeneous group with different diagnoses, levels of disability, and duration of disability. As a result of this heterogeneity, service needs differ. More than 3.3 million women 15 years and over who lived in their homes and outside institutional settings suffered from a mental or emotional disability that caused limitations in their lives. Women report negative moods more than men and had a higher rate of serious mental illness. Women are about as likely as men to see mental health professionals and be admitted to inpatient psychiatric facilities. About 11 percent of women reported they often felt depressed compared with 6 percent of men. Women who often experience negative moods are more likely to smoke and drink than are women who are usually not depressed, bored, or lonely.

C2. PERSONAL HEALTH PRACTICES AND SPORTS

One reason women live longer than men is because they care for themselves better than men do. They don't smoke, drink, or use other detrimental drugs to the extent that men do, and they wear their seat belts with more regularity than five years ago. Between the years 1985 and 1990, however, there was no change in the proportion of women likely to exercise regularly.

During their childbearing years, women see doctors more often than men. There is little or no difference in the average number of visits at younger ages and among the elderly. Women see their doctors more frequently now, however, than they did in the 1960s. In 1992, only 8 percent of women had not seen their doctor in 2 or more years, compared to 17 percent in 1964.

More women are overweight than men. One-third of White, non-Hispanic women and half of Black and of Mexican-American women aged 20 to 74 are overweight. These proportions have increased considerably in recent decades. The problem is most prevalent among women in the 45–64 age range.

The good news on smoking is that it is decreasing among women. In 1965, one-third of women smoked;

in 1992, about one-fourth of women were smokers. The bad news is that 17 percent of 8th grade girls smoked in 1993 as did 29 percent of girls who were seniors in high school. More education greatly decreases the likelihood that women will smoke. Only 15 percent of women with four or more years of college smoke, compared to one-third of women who are high school dropouts. Cigarette smoking during pregnancy is strongly associated with low birthweight and other serious natal complications. Low birthweight is a major predictor of infant mortality and illness during infancy and childhood. Less than 18 percent of women giving birth in 1991 smoked during their pregnancy. Eleven percent of smoking mothers had a low-birthweight baby compared to 6 percent of mothers who did not smoke. Also, smoking at older ages greatly increased the likelihood of giving birth to a low-birthweight baby. White mothers are more likely than Black mothers to smoke during pregnancy. Among those who smoke, White mothers are more likely to be heavy smokers. The National Center for Health Statistics estimates that there would have been 13 percent fewer low-birthweight babies in 1991 if women had not smoked during their pregnancies.

Most women do not drink at all (42 percent) or drink lightly. About one-fifth of women who drink do so moderately and only 3 percent are heavy drinkers (compared with 14 percent of men). The likelihood of drinking decreases with age, but among women who do drink, heavy drinking increases with age. Less than one-third of elderly women drink anything at all but nearly 6 percent are heavy drinkers.

Alcohol is a serious problem among teenage girls. Nearly half of girls who were high school seniors in 1993 drank. One in five senior girls were binge drinkers (five or more drinks in a row). More than one in four girls in the 8th grade drink, and 12 percent of 8th grade girls were binge drinkers.

Alcohol use during pregnancy is a serious risk factor for an unborn baby, especially when combined with smoking. Less than 3 percent of women reported on their baby's birth certificate that they had used alcohol during their pregnancy. From surveys, we believe alcohol use is actually closer to 20 percent or more. Often times, women who have one or two drinks a month tend to report this as not drinking. More than one-fifth of pregnant women who reported on the birth certificate that they drink, also reported having three or more drinks a week.

As shown in Section C3, the number of AIDS cases reported among women is increasing rapidly. In 1990, an estimated 20.4 million women aged 15 to 44 had been tested at some time in their lives for antibodies to human immunodeficiency virus (HIV), the virus that causes AIDS. This is about one-third of women in that age group; there was no significant difference by race or Hispanic origin. Education, however, did make a difference. Forty percent of women with at least some college had been tested.

Breast cancer rates are increasing, which has, in turn, increased women's education about the value of early detection. About half of women had had a recent breast exam by a professional, and 43 percent did monthly self-examinations. Among women 35 years old and older, half had had a mammogram within three years of a 1990 survey.

Exercise walking, swimming, and bicycle riding were the most frequently reported fitness activities of women in 1994 and 1989. Fishing was the sport that interested the most men, followed by swimming and bicycle riding.

C3. REPRODUCTIVE HEALTH

Sexual Activity. The proportion of women who had ever had sexual intercourse rose little in the 1980s. Sexual activity increased rapidly, however, among teenagers, especially among young teens and among Whites and girls from families with incomes above the poverty threshold. By the close of the decade, more than half of America's teenage girls were sexually active, and nearly 1 in 4 girls aged 14 had had intercourse. By age 20, 8 in 10 women have had intercourse. Sexual intercourse among teenagers was common regardless of race, income, religion, or whether the girls lived in urban or rural areas.

Use of Contraceptives. Among women 15 to 44 years old, surgical sterilization increased from 26 percent of women in 1982 to 30 percent in 1990. Among women aged 15 to 34 who use nonsurgical contraceptives, about half use the pill and one-fourth use condoms with their sexual partners. Among women aged 35 to 44, 3 in 5 are sterile. Of the women this age who use contraceptives, a wider variety of methods are used, with condoms being the most popular. Since the early 1980s, women have increasingly used condoms with their sexual partners. In 1990, however, half of women aged 15 to 44 who used condoms did not use them consistently, which has implications both for disease and for unintended pregnancies. Also, use of the pill has declined.

Two-thirds of nonsterile women aged 15 to 44 are sexually active but don't want a baby. Among women in this age group, 12 percent did not use a contraceptive in 1990 (up from 7 percent in 1988). This is risky behavior—9 in 10 of such women become pregnant within a year. They represent over half of all unintended pregnancies; the other half are to women who use contraceptive methods ineffectively.

Overall, about 1 in 3 teenage girls (15 to 19 years old) used contraception. In 1990, 52 percent of teenaged contraceptive users chose the pill, and 44 percent chose the condom. Risk-taking is up among these girls. Among the sexually active, 58 percent used contraceptives in 1990, down from 61 percent in 1988. Only 40 percent of teenagers go to a doctor or medical clinic for contraceptive services within the first year after they have begun intercourse.

Abortions. There were 1.5 million induced abortions in the United States in 1992, a decrease in number from the 1990 high of 1.6 million. In 1975, there were 1 million induced abortions. Less than 3 in 100 women had an abortion in 1992 (the rate of 2.6 abortions per 100 women is the lowest experienced in the United States since 1975 when the rate was 2.1). The ratio of abortions per 100 live births is also decreasing; in 1992, it was 38 compared to a high of 44 in 1983 and a low of 33 in 1975. Among those who have an abortion, over half are under age 25. And yet, teenagers were less likely in 1990 than in 1980 to have an abortion. In 1990, 40 percent of pregnant teens aged 15 to 19 had an abortion compared to 45 percent in 1980. In addition, about 4 in 5 women having an abortion were unmarried. About half of unintended pregnancies are aborted.

Prenatal Care, Health Behavior During Pregnancy, and Deliveries. Doctors and the popular press have been telling women the health of their babies is partly related to their own actions during pregnancy. Currently, there is a particular focus on getting early prenatal care, and completely avoiding smoking and drinking during pregnancy. More than three in four women begin prenatal care in the critical first trimester. In 1992, for the first time, 78 percent of mothers received early care; since 1979, the percentage had remained stable at about 76 percent. Conversely, about 5 percent of women in 1992 did not begin prenatal care until the third trimester or had no prenatal care at all.

There are large differences among race groups in the likelihood of getting early care, however. This difference was reduced somewhat from 1970 to 1980, but since then, there has been no improvement in the large gap in the likelihood of getting care. Early prenatal care has remained stable since 1980 at around 79 percent of White mothers and 60 to 62 percent of Black mothers. In 1992, the percentages increased to 81 percent of White mothers and 64 percent of Black mothers. Less than 3 in 5 American Indian and Mexican-American mothers received early prenatal care in 1991; by contrast, 85 percent of Cuban mothers and 88 percent of Japanese mothers had early care in 1991.

Pregnant women are warned that smoking during pregnancy is associated with reduced infant birthweight, preterm delivery, intrauterine growth retardation, and poorer health among babies and children. This is a public education effort that seems to be having an effect. Cigarette smoking by pregnant women declined in 1992 for the third consecutive year. Only 5 in 100 Asian and Hispanic women smoked during pregnancy; by contrast, 14 Black women and 20 non-Hispanic White women in 100 smoked. The likelihood of smoking during pregnancy decreases notably as education increases.

About 3 percent of women drink during pregnancy. Doctors say it takes very little alcohol to harm a fetus. Drinking during pregnancy occurs more frequently among American Indian mothers (7 percent in 1990 compared to 4 percent of Black mothers, 3 percent of White mothers, and 1 percent of Asian mothers). Mothers 25 years and older were more likely than younger mothers to drink when pregnant (4 percent versus about 2 percent).

Adoption. Just as unmarried women were less likely to have an abortion when they became pregnant in the 1980s than in the 1970s, they were also less likely to put the baby up for adoption. In 1973, 9 percent of single women placed their babies up for adoption compared with 2 percent in 1988. The decrease was dramatic among single White women (19 percent in 1973 and 3 percent in the 1980s). The rates remained stable at 2 percent among single Black women. In 1990, less than 1 million children (84 percent were White) lived with adoptive parents compared with 1.4 million in 1980.

Sexually Transmitted Diseases (STDs). Women and infants disproportionately bear the long-term consequences of STDs. Women infected with gonorrhea or chlamydia can develop pelvic inflammatory disease (PID), which can then lead to infertility and ectopic pregnancies. In 1993, the reported rate of chlamydial infections in women was 244 per 100,000 population. Gonorrhea rates, on the other hand, have declined steadily since the 1980s. In most cases, women are not aware they are infected as symptoms tend to be vague; this leads to delay in seeking medical care, which increases the risk of infertility and ectopic pregnancy. Early prenatal care often results in essential screening and treatment for syphilis and HIV infections that can save the infants from infection. In most industrialized countries other than the United States, syphilis has nearly been eliminated.

Increased premarital sexual experience among young women has put a larger pool at risk of contracting STDs. Rates of gonorrhea in teenagers has been declining since the mid-1980s, but their rates are considerably higher than for other age groups. In addition, the 1993 rate for adolescent women (868 per 100,000 population) significantly exceeded the rate for young men (623).

There were also nearly 39,000 American women with reported cases of Acquired Immunodeficiency Syndrome (AIDS) through September 30, 1993. Women make up about 12 percent of the total AIDS population. The increase in the number of women diagnosed with AIDS has been rapid: in 1985, there were 522 new cases reported; in 1992, 5,942 new cases were reported. From January to September 1993, nearly 13,000 new cases were reported.

Blacks and American Indians have higher rates of STDs than Whites, Asians, and Hispanics, according to surveillance data collected by the Centers for Disease Control and Prevention (CDC). Data and studies by CDC show race and ethnicity are risk markers correlated with fundamental determinants of health status such as poverty, access to quality health care, health-care seeking behavior, illicit drug use, and living in communities with high prevalence of STDs.

C4. HEALTH INSURANCE

Whether a woman is covered by health insurance is associated with employment, occupation, retirement, and participation in federal support programs. As a result, coverage changes over time for many people. During the 1991 calendar year, 82 percent of women had health insurance coverage all year while 18 percent lacked coverage at least one month during the year. Six percent of women (compared with 8 percent of men) had no coverage at all in 1991.

Those in married-couple families are more likely than other family types to have long-term health insurance coverage. Women who head households alone rely more heavily on Medicaid than do married couples. Four in ten persons who lived in a female-headed household with children from 1990 to 1992 were covered by Medicaid for at least one month; one-fourth used Medicaid the entire time. Less than 2 percent of those who lived in married-couple families used Medicaid for one or more months.

About one in eight women who worked year round and full time from 1990 to 1992 had no private or government health insurance. Women were also less likely than men to have employer-provided insurance. In addition, women with more than a high school education were more likely than other women to have insurance coverage. Three in five women who worked full time had employer-provided insurance and less than one in five of those who worked part-time had employer-provided insurance. Of the nearly 23 million women who lost their job in the recessionary period of 1990–1992, less than one in four (23 percent) had employer-provided insurance in their own name before separation from their job. In the month following the loss of their job, only 14 percent received coverage through their employer. Nearly 2 million women either had no coverage or had to get it some other way.

Not surprisingly, the lack of health insurance coverage directly relates to the likelihood of preventive health care measures being taken. For example, cancer screening (mammograms and Pap tests) occurred less frequently among uninsured women.

C1. HEALTH AND DISABILITY STATUS

C1-1. Self-Assessment of Health Status, by Age and Sex: 1993

(Data are based on household interviews of the civilian noninstitutionalized population.)

Characteristic	All persons[1]	All health statuses[2]	Respondent-assessed health status			
			Excellent	Very good	Good	Fair	Poor
	Number in thousands	Percent distribution					
All persons[3]	254,281	100.0	37.6	28.3	23.7	7.7	2.8
Sex and age							
Male:							
All ages	123,706	100.0	40.3	28.2	22.2	6.8	2.6
Under 5 years	10,194	100.0	52.6	27.1	16.9	3.1	*0.3
5–17 years	24,334	100.0	52.1	27.3	17.8	2.4	0.4
18–24 years	11,896	100.0	45.6	30.4	20.7	2.8	0.5
25–44 years	40,200	100.0	41.9	30.7	20.7	5.2	1.5
45–64 years	23,951	100.0	30.9	27.0	26.2	10.9	5.1
65 years and over	13,130	100.0	16.7	23.0	32.6	18.7	9.1
Female:							
All ages	130,576	100.0	35.0	28.4	25.1	8.6	2.9
Under 5 years	9,721	100.0	52.6	27.5	16.7	2.8	0.4
5–17 years	23,209	100.0	50.2	27.8	19.0	2.6	0.4
18–24 years	12,243	100.0	37.3	31.9	24.5	5.3	1.0
25–44 years	41,426	100.0	35.4	31.4	24.9	6.6	1.7
45–64 years	25,837	100.0	26.0	27.1	28.7	12.8	5.4
65 years and over	18,140	100.0	16.2	22.2	33.4	20.0	8.1

Source: V. Benson and M. A. Marano, National Center for Health Statistics, Current Estimates From the National Health Interview Survey, 1993, Vital Health Statistics, Series 10, No. 190, Hyattsville, MD: National Center for Health Statistics, 1994, Table 70.

C1-2. Self-Assessment of Health Status, by Age and Sex: 1987 to 1992

(Data are based on household interviews of a sample of the civilian noninstitutionalized population.)

Characteristic	Percent with fair or poor health					
	1987	1988	1989	1990	1991	1992
Total [1,2].............................	9.5	9.4	9.1	8.9	9.3	9.7
Sex and age						
Male [1].............................	9.0	8.9	8.6	8.4	8.9	9.4
Under 15 years	2.5	2.7	2.6	2.6	2.5	2.9
15–44 years..........................	4.5	4.6	4.6	4.5	5.0	5.7
45–64 years..........................	16.6	16.5	15.4	15.5	16.1	16.5
65–74 years..........................	28.9	27.0	27.2	25.0	26.7	26.8
75 years and over	36.0	33.0	33.0	31.7	33.7	33.5
Female [1]............................	9.9	9.9	9.5	9.3	9.7	10.1
Under 15 years	2.3	2.8	2.3	2.2	2.4	2.7
15–44 years..........................	6.3	6.4	6.6	6.3	6.6	7.2
45–64 years..........................	18.1	17.6	16.8	16.5	17.2	17.8
65–74 years..........................	27.7	26.4	25.6	25.1	25.5	24.7
75 years and over	34.2	34.3	31.5	31.6	33.5	33.0

[1]Age adjusted.
[2]Includes all other races not shown separately and unknown family income.

Source: National Center for Health Statistics, *Health, United States, 1993*, (PHS) 94-1232, Washington, D.C.: U.S. Government Printing Office, 1994,Table 71.

C1-3. Number of Acute Conditions per 100 Persons per Year, by Sex, Age, and Type of Condition: 1993

(Data are based on household interviews of a sample of the civilian noninstitutionalized population.)

Type of acute condition	Male					Female				
	All ages	Under 5 years	5–17 years	18–44 years	45 years and over	All ages	Under 5 years	5–17 years	18–44 years	45 years and over
	Number of acute conditions per 100 persons per year									
All acute conditions	174.4	409.8	250.7	146.1	99.5	205.6	388.6	272.0	199.5	137.4
Infective and parasitic diseases	19.3	52.2	41.6	9.9	8.9	23.2	56.8	42.7	18.7	11.0
Common childhood diseases	1.5	8.0	4.3	*–	*–	2.4	14.6	6.4	*0.5	*–
Intestinal virus, unspecified	4.2	*5.7	8.4	3.3	2.4	4.7	12.1	7.5	4.4	2.0
Viral infections, unspecified	6.3	19.6	11.9	3.2	3.4	7.9	14.8	11.5	6.9	5.7
Other	7.3	18.9	17.0	3.4	3.2	8.2	15.4	17.3	6.9	3.4
Respiratory conditions	92.4	189.0	131.4	84.3	51.8	105.1	176.4	145.4	106.7	66.2
Common cold	25.5	70.0	36.5	19.7	14.1	28.1	62.3	43.2	25.9	15.2
Other acute upper respiratory infections . . .	10.1	22.0	19.8	6.7	5.3	12.4	26.2	15.4	11.8	8.5
Influenza	48.4	67.1	66.4	51.8	26.7	55.7	63.6	81.4	61.3	33.7
Acute bronchitis	4.7	14.7	5.4	4.2	2.1	4.8	14.7	*2.5	4.4	4.2
Pneumonia	1.9	*7.2	*1.6	*1.0	*1.8	2.1	*5.5	*1.3	1.7	2.2
Other respiratory conditions	1.9	8.1	*1.8	*0.9	*1.8	2.0	*4.2	*1.5	1.7	2.3
Digestive system conditions	5.5	11.5	7.5	4.9	3.2	7.1	8.3	9.3	7.8	5.0
Dental conditions	1.3	*4.9	*1.1	*1.5	*0.3	1.2	*3.1	*0.9	1.7	*0.5
Indigestion, nausea, and vomiting	2.1	*2.1	4.3	1.9	*1.0	3.6	*1.4	7.7	3.8	*1.7
Other digestive conditions	2.0	*4.5	*2.1	1.6	*1.9	2.3	*3.8	*0.7	2.3	2.8
Injuries	27.0	26.6	31.0	32.0	17.4	22.0	23.1	21.2	23.2	20.7
Fractures and dislocations	3.5	*0.9	4.3	4.7	*2.0	2.8	*0.3	*2.6	2.7	3.4
Sprains and strains	6.0	*1.1	6.7	7.5	4.8	5.2	*0.5	4.1	7.3	4.2
Open wounds and lacerations	7.0	9.5	7.5	8.2	4.2	3.0	8.5	4.9	2.0	2.0
Contusions and superficial injuries	5.0	*6.3	6.0	6.1	2.5	4.5	*5.4	6.3	3.7	4.3
Other current injuries	5.5	8.8	6.6	5.5	4.0	6.5	8.4	3.4	7.4	6.7
Selected other acute conditions	22.0	110.2	31.7	9.5	9.1	36.4	108.5	42.7	32.4	22.1
Eye conditions	1.0	*4.9	*1.0	*0.6	*0.6	1.4	*6.0	*0.8	*0.6	*1.7
Acute ear infections	10.2	76.0	13.8	2.0	*1.3	11.7	72.1	17.9	4.5	3.8
Other ear conditions	1.1	*3.2	*1.8	*0.6	*0.8	1.6	*7.3	*2.1	*0.9	*0.8
Acute urinary conditions	0.7	*1.1	*0.2	*0.2	*1.6	5.1	*4.2	*2.8	5.7	5.7
Disorders of menstruation	. . .	. . .	. . .	. . .	. . .	0.6	. . .	*1.0	*0.7	*0.5
Other disorders of female genital tract	. . .	. . .	. . .	. . .	. . .	1.4	*–	*1.2	2.6	*0.3
Delivery and other conditions of pregnancy and puerperium	. . .	. . .	. . .	. . .	. . .	3.0	. . .	*0.8	6.9	*–
Skin conditions	1.9	*7.4	3.7	*1.1	*0.4	3.2	11.0	4.0	2.5	1.8
Acute musculoskeletal conditions	3.1	*0.3	*2.3	3.5	3.8	4.5	*–	*2.2	5.0	6.0
Headache, excluding migraine	1.3	*0.6	4.2	*1.0	*0.1	2.0	*–	3.8	2.3	*1.1
Fever, unspecified	2.7	16.7	4.7	*0.5	*0.4	2.1	*7.8	6.1	*0.7	*0.5
All other acute conditions	8.2	20.4	7.5	5.4	9.1	11.7	15.5	10.7	10.8	12.4

NOTES: Excluded from these estimates are conditions involving neither medical attention nor activity restriction. Estimates for which the numerator has an RSE of more than 30 percent are indicated with an asterisk.

Source: V. Benson and M. A. Marano, National Center for Health Statistics, *Current Estimates From the National Health Interview Survey, 1993*, Vital Health Statistics, Series 10, No. 190, Hyattsville, MD: National Center for Health Statistics, 1994, Table 2.

C1-4. Number of Work-Loss Days Associated with Acute Conditions per 100 Currently Employed Persons 18 Years of Age and Over per Year, by Sex, Age, and Type of Condition: 1993

(Data are based on household interviews of the civilian noninstitutionalized population.)

Type of acute condition	Male			Female		
	All ages 18 years and over	18–44 years	45 years and over	All ages 18 years and over	18–44 years	45 years and over
	Number of work-loss days per 100 currently employed persons per year					
All acute conditions	274.0	292.9	233.6	374.8	410.5	299.2
Infective and parasitic diseases	18.4	18.4	*18.2	28.5	33.2	*18.4
Common childhood diseases	*1.5	*2.3	*–	*3.7	*5.5	*–
Intestinal virus, unspecified	*4.3	*4.6	*3.6	*6.4	*7.7	*3.6
Viral infections, unspecified	8.0	*6.2	*11.9	10.1	*10.4	*9.3
Other	*4.5	*5.3	*2.7	*8.3	*9.6	*5.5
Respiratory conditions	106.8	114.8	89.5	163.3	179.3	129.4
Common cold	15.6	17.8	*11.1	27.7	28.7	*25.6
Other acute upper respiratory infections	*6.1	*7.1	*4.0	18.5	19.2	*17.2
Influenza	73.4	78.0	63.6	95.0	106.2	71.1
Acute bronchitis	*6.7	*6.4	*7.4	12.2	13.1	*10.3
Pneumonia	*2.8	*3.1	*2.0	*5.3	*6.9	*2.0
Other respiratory conditions	*2.1	*2.4	*1.4	*4.5	*5.2	*3.1
Digestive system conditions	15.7	14.5	*18.2	15.9	16.9	*13.9
Dental conditions	*2.2	*3.0	*0.6	*4.0	*4.5	*3.0
Indigestion, nausea, and vomiting	*2.4	*1.6	*4.2	*3.6	*4.9	*0.7
Other digestive conditions	11.0	*9.9	*13.5	*8.4	*7.5	*10.2
Injuries	104.7	116.7	78.8	68.2	71.2	61.9
Fractures and dislocations	35.7	39.2	28.2	19.1	16.0	*25.7
Sprains and strains	34.9	45.0	*13.5	27.3	31.1	*19.3
Open wounds and lacerations	10.0	11.4	*7.0	*4.2	*4.0	*4.6
Contusions and superficial injuries	*6.9	*6.5	*7.9	*5.6	*5.7	*5.1
Other current injuries	17.1	14.7	*22.2	12.1	14.4	*7.2
Selected other acute conditions	21.4	25.9	*11.9	78.1	92.0	48.5
Eye conditions	*1.9	*2.8	*–	*0.2	*–	*0.6
Acute ear infections	*0.9	*0.8	*1.0	*2.5	*3.0	*1.5
Other ear conditions	*1.1	*1.5	*0.3	*0.5	*0.8	*–
Acute urinary conditions	*3.6	*3.3	*4.3	*5.9	*8.2	*1.1
Disorders of menstruation	...	...	...	*1.6	*0.8	*3.4
Other disorders of female genital tract	...	...	...	*6.4	*7.9	*3.2
Delivery and other conditions of pregnancy and puerperium	...	...	...	40.3	59.4	*–
Skin conditions	*1.6	*2.2	*0.3	*2.0	*1.8	*2.4
Acute musculoskeletal conditions	10.9	13.9	*4.6	16.5	*7.6	35.3
Headache, excluding migraine	*0.5	*0.6	*0.2	*1.9	*2.3	*1.0
Fever, unspecified	*0.9	*0.8	*1.1	*0.2	*0.3	*–
All other acute conditions	*7.1	*2.5	*17.0	20.8	17.9	27.2

NOTES: Estimates for which the numerator has an RSE of more than 30 percent are indicated with an asterisk.

Source: V. Benson and M. A. Marano, National Center for Health Statistics, *Current Estimates From the National Health Interview Survey, 1993,* Vital Health Statistics, Series 10, No. 190, Hyattsville, MD: National Center for Health Statistics, 1994, Table 37.

C1-5. Number of Selected Reported Chronic Conditions per 1,000 Persons, by Sex and Age: 1993

(Data are based on household interviews of the civilian noninstitutionalized population.)

	Male					Female				
			65 years and over					65 years and over		
Type of chronic condition	*Under 45 years*	*45–64 years*	*Total*	*65–74 years*	*75 years and over*	*Under 45 years*	*45–64 years*	*Total*	*65–74 years*	*75 years and over*
Selected skin and musculoskeletal conditions				Number of chronic conditions per 1,000 persons						
Arthritis	28.0	182.7	407.8	373.8	467.2	36.6	280.6	555.0	533.3	583.2
Gout, including gouty arthritis	4.4	27.1	44.4	54.7	*26.2	*0.4	10.0	21.9	25.6	*17.0
Intervertebral disc disorders	19.0	54.2	33.0	35.6	*28.3	12.6	37.8	35.0	42.1	25.9
Bone spur or tendinitis, unspecified	3.5	11.8	12.6	*13.3	*11.5	6.4	25.7	24.3	36.5	*8.4
Disorders of bone or cartilage	3.2	8.5	*3.5	*4.3	*2.1	2.8	13.9	29.9	23.0	38.8
Trouble with bunions	2.2	*4.8	16.5	*12.9	*23.1	8.3	34.1	47.4	50.0	43.9
Bursitis, unclassified	5.6	35.9	26.9	27.0	*26.6	10.3	42.6	35.6	36.0	35.3
Sebaceous skin cyst	4.3	14.1	*4.3	*1.4	*9.2	5.0	8.7	*6.4	*7.3	*5.2
Trouble with acne	23.8	6.3	*2.3	*3.6	*–	36.7	8.6	*1.2	*1.2	*1.3
Psoriasis	6.4	14.1	12.6	*13.0	*11.9	9.1	16.3	9.4	*8.2	*10.9
Dermatitis	30.1	34.0	20.5	21.4	*18.9	49.0	44.3	44.9	48.3	40.5
Trouble with dry (itching) skin, unclassified	11.7	20.0	41.7	49.9	*27.2	20.2	27.4	36.9	42.9	29.0
Trouble with ingrown nails	18.0	27.4	34.0	23.3	52.8	17.4	37.6	60.6	48.1	77.0
Trouble with corns and calluses	9.2	16.3	28.9	25.0	35.8	14.0	50.2	57.3	54.6	60.9
Impairments										
Visual impairment	31.4	67.3	113.0	89.6	154.1	13.1	32.9	83.1	44.6	133.3
Color blindness	20.0	29.3	39.2	27.5	59.9	*0.8	*2.2	*5.1	*3.5	*7.2
Cataracts	2.5	13.7	106.1	87.1	139.4	*1.3	25.9	184.5	135.9	247.6
Glaucoma	*1.3	17.3	50.4	36.0	75.7	*0.7	14.0	63.6	44.1	89.0
Hearing impairment	48.7	189.3	370.8	320.5	458.8	34.3	101.1	273.1	206.0	360.4
Tinnitus	17.3	68.2	99.2	110.5	79.4	15.1	52.1	96.9	93.5	101.3
Speech impairment	16.7	11.6	15.4	*13.2	*19.3	9.8	*5.1	10.3	*9.9	*10.8
Absence of extremities (excludes tips of fingers or toes only)	4.4	19.9	35.3	27.5	49.0	*0.8	*2.8	*4.8	*6.7	*2.3
Paralysis of extremities, complete or partial	2.9	11.6	28.9	33.1	*21.6	3.6	7.6	18.1	13.9	23.3
Deformity or orthopedic impairment	101.1	183.1	159.6	146.4	183.0	95.5	162.4	192.0	178.0	210.2
Back	52.5	98.7	86.1	74.9	105.8	64.2	104.2	116.4	108.4	126.7
Upper extremities	11.6	42.4	28.3	26.7	31.0	10.0	24.9	28.9	29.6	27.9
Lower extremities	45.9	70.1	70.4	70.1	70.8	31.3	56.0	78.9	76.1	82.7
Selected digestive conditions										
Ulcer	11.2	18.9	32.5	29.3	38.1	14.2	30.5	38.7	41.5	35.0
Hernia of abdominal cavity	7.2	38.1	75.8	69.0	87.6	4.8	27.8	68.4	63.0	75.5
Gastritis or duodenitis	6.7	15.1	26.0	25.4	*27.0	9.7	27.5	29.6	35.6	21.8
Frequent indigestion	19.1	31.1	31.7	21.3	49.9	17.1	39.8	51.1	52.7	49.0
Enteritis or colitis	5.8	9.6	13.7	*12.8	*15.3	8.5	23.0	23.3	22.0	24.9
Spastic colon	*1.1	*4.3	*4.7	*4.3	*5.4	8.0	20.6	16.9	20.6	*12.0
Diverticula of intestines	*0.4	6.5	21.1	17.9	*26.4	*1.0	11.2	64.9	63.3	67.0
Frequent constipation	4.7	8.6	40.8	29.4	60.8	12.2	38.9	69.1	43.4	102.6

See notes at end of table.

C1-5. Number of Selected Reported Chronic Conditions per 1,000 Persons, by Sex and Age: 1993 *(continued)*

(Data are based on household interviews of the civilian noninstitutionalized population.)

	Male					Female				
			65 years and over					65 years and over		
Type of chronic condition	Under 45 years	45–64 years	Total	65–74 years	75 years and over	Under 45 years	45–64 years	Total	65–74 years	75 years and over
Selected conditions of the genitourinary, nervous, endocrine, metabolic, and blood and blood-forming systems					Number of chronic conditions per 1,000 persons					
Goiter or other disorders of the thyroid	*1.6	9.3	*10.5	*9.7	*11.9	17.1	42.8	58.9	60.1	57.3
Diabetes	8.8	64.8	100.5	99.6	102.1	8.5	59.1	105.7	103.7	108.3
Anemias	5.4	*4.8	13.2	*9.7	*19.3	24.5	20.7	27.5	25.4	30.1
Epilepsy	4.6	*3.8	*4.9	*4.5	*5.4	5.9	7.0	*5.4	*7.1	*3.2
Migraine headache	22.1	23.4	*6.6	*8.7	*2.7	63.9	93.2	28.5	29.3	27.4
Neuralgia or neuritis, unspecified	*1.0	*1.5	*2.3	*2.0	*2.7	*0.8	6.9	15.4	*11.4	20.7
Kidney trouble	8.3	17.3	27.6	32.1	*19.9	14.6	23.5	26.4	18.5	36.7
Bladder disorders	2.6	8.8	30.7	28.0	35.4	17.0	34.7	45.0	29.3	65.6
Diseases of prostate	1.9	28.3	89.7	64.0	134.8	. . .	. . .	. . .	. . .	. . .
Disease of female genital organs	. . .	. . .	. . .	. . .	. . .	42.1	51.9	19.3	17.0	22.5
Selected circulatory conditions										
Rheumatic fever with or without heart disease	2.3	7.7	*7.3	*7.2	*7.5	8.1	19.7	17.2	21.5	*11.5
Heart disease	27.9	131.3	357.2	346.8	375.6	38.1	107.6	271.2	223.8	332.8
Ischemic heart disease	5.0	65.6	176.2	179.1	171.0	2.2	26.8	107.9	93.3	127.0
Heart rhythm disorders	17.9	30.3	93.8	92.1	96.8	27.3	57.4	97.2	92.6	103.4
Tachycardia or rapid heart	2.1	10.9	29.1	30.6	*26.4	4.2	19.6	29.0	31.7	25.5
Heart murmurs	14.1	10.1	25.5	33.0	*12.2	20.2	26.3	40.7	38.4	43.8
Other and unspecified heart rhythm disorders . .	1.8	9.2	39.2	28.5	58.1	2.8	11.5	27.6	22.5	34.1
Other selected diseases of heart, excluding hypertension	5.1	35.4	87.3	75.6	107.7	8.6	23.4	65.9	37.8	102.6
High blood pressure (hypertension)	35.1	210.6	316.5	323.3	304.5	32.4	223.1	371.7	359.4	387.7
Cerebrovascular disease	*1.3	18.8	84.8	53.3	140.2	*0.9	19.4	60.7	41.7	85.5
Hardening of the arteries	*0.3	9.6	56.0	49.3	67.9	*0.3	*5.0	35.4	25.1	49.0
Varicose veins of lower extremities	4.6	19.2	36.9	39.0	33.1	26.5	87.0	96.9	93.9	100.7
Hemorrhoids	21.3	66.3	66.0	79.7	42.1	30.2	67.1	80.2	72.2	90.7
Selected respiratory conditions										
Chronic bronchitis	43.8	49.0	54.0	58.6	45.9	58.3	72.6	67.3	78.2	53.1
Asthma	53.9	30.1	42.7	51.9	*26.4	53.8	58.9	52.1	53.8	50.0
Hay fever or allergic rhinitis without asthma	87.4	98.9	63.4	75.6	41.9	99.1	113.4	80.5	87.4	71.7
Chronic sinusitis	119.3	174.7	157.0	174.5	126.4	150.6	195.2	144.9	167.9	115.0
Deviated nasal septum	6.3	9.6	12.4	*12.7	*11.9	5.7	9.7	*5.5	*7.4	*2.9
Chronic disease of tonsils or adenoids	13.9	*1.2	*1.3	*2.0	*–	16.7	*2.5	*2.0	*3.5	*–
Emphysema	*1.0	18.9	40.1	27.3	62.5	*1.6	12.5	22.4	27.5	*15.9

NOTES: Estimates for which the numerator has an RSE of more than 30 percent are indicated with an asterisk.

Source: V. Benson and M. A. Marano, National Center for Health Statistics, *Current Estimates From the National Health Interview Survey, 1993,* Vital Health Statistics, Series 10, No. 190, Hyattsville, MD: National Center for Health Statistics, 1994, Table 58.

C1-6. Persons with a Disability, by Sex and Age: 1991–92

[Numbers in thousands]

Sex and age	Total	With a disability		With a severe disability	
		Number	Percent	Number	Percent
MALES					
Total	122,692	22,916	18.7	9,929	8.1
Less than 3 years	6,000	133	2.2	32	0.5
3 to 5 years	5,946	370	6.2	54	0.9
6 to 14 years	16,761	1,373	8.2	250	1.5
15 to 17 years	5,172	558	10.8	159	3.1
18 to 24 years	12,184	1,271	10.4	416	3.4
25 to 34 years	21,358	2,598	12.2	1,004	4.7
35 to 44 years	19,492	3,297	16.9	1,123	5.8
45 to 54 years	12,961	2,988	23.1	1,167	9.0
55 to 59 years	5,092	1,669	32.8	821	16.1
60 to 64 years	4,894	2,123	43.4	1,173	23.9
65 to 69 years	4,614	1,961	42.5	1,056	22.9
70 to 74 years	3,585	1,614	45.0	851	23.7
75 to 79 years	2,461	1,404	57.0	759	30.8
80 to 84 years	1,425	958	67.2	613	43.1
85 years and over	746	600	80.4	452	60.7
Less than 18 years	33,879	2,434	7.2	495	1.5
18 to 44 years	53,034	7,166	13.5	2,543	4.8
45 to 64 years	22,947	6,780	29.5	3,161	13.8
65 to 74 years	8,199	3,575	43.6	1,907	23.3
75 to 84 years	3,886	2,362	60.8	1,372	35.3
85 years and over	746	600	80.4	452	60.7
FEMALES					
Total	129,104	26,020	20.2	14,187	11.0
Less than 3 years	5,791	121	2.1	8	0.1
3 to 5 years	5,565	228	4.1	21	0.4
6 to 14 years	16,005	689	4.3	163	1.0
15 to 17 years	4,895	374	7.7	150	3.1
18 to 24 years	12,511	1,266	10.1	428	3.4
25 to 34 years	21,581	2,762	12.8	1,088	5.0
35 to 44 years	20,020	3,372	16.8	1,503	7.5
45 to 54 years	13,752	3,225	23.5	1,674	12.2
55 to 59 years	5,502	1,749	31.8	999	18.2
60 to 64 years	5,626	2,229	39.6	1,466	26.1
65 to 69 years	5,571	2,462	44.2	1,505	27.0
70 to 74 years	4,585	2,145	46.8	1,234	26.9
75 to 79 years	3,554	2,126	59.8	1,472	41.4
80 to 84 years	2,448	1,813	74.1	1,256	51.3
85 years and over	1,699	1,458	85.8	1,219	71.8
Less than 18 years	32,256	1,412	4.4	342	1.1
18 to 44 years	54,112	7,400	13.7	3,019	5.6
45 to 64 years	24,880	7,203	29.0	4,139	16.6
65 to 74 years	10,156	4,608	45.4	2,739	27.0
75 to 84 years	6,002	3,939	65.6	2,728	45.5
85 years and over	1,699	1,458	85.8	1,219	71.8

Source: John M. McNeil, U.S. Bureau of the Census, *Americans With Disabilities: 1991–92 (Data from the Survey of Income and Program Participation),* Current Population Reports, Series P70-33, Washington, D.C.: U.S. Government Printing Office, December 1993, Table 7.

C1-7. Selected Measures of Disability Status, by Age and Sex: 1991–92

(Numbers in thousands.)

Age and disability measure	Both Sexes		Males		Females	
	Number	Percent distribution	Number	Percent distribution	Nunber	Percent
PERSONS 15 YEARS OLD AND OVER						
Total	195,729	100.0	93,985	100.0	101,744	100.0
Needs personal assistance with an ADL or IADL	9,211	4.7	3,383	3.6	5,828	5.7
Uses a wheelchair	1,494	0.8	575	0.6	919	0.9
Does not use a wheelchair but has used a cane, crutches, or a walker for six months or longer	3,962	2.0	1,547	1.7	2,415	2.4
With a mental or emotional disability	6,879	3.5	3,534	3.8	3,345	3.3
PERSONS 15 TO 64 YEARS OLD						
Total	165,040	100.0	81,154	100.0	83,886	100.0
Needs personal assistance with an ADL or IADL	3,876	2.4	1,665	2.1	2,211	2.6
Uses a wheelchair	529	0.3	263	0.3	266	0.3
Does not use a wheelchair but has used a cane, crutches, or a walker for six months or longer	1,115	0.7	567	0.7	548	0.7
With a mental or emotional disability	5,746	3.5	3,162	3.9	2,584	3.1
PERSONS 65 YEARS OLD AND OVER						
Total	30,688	100.0	12,831	100.0	17,857	100.0
Needs personal assistance with an ADL or IADL	5,336	17.4	1,718	13.4	3,617	20.3
Uses a wheelchair	965	3.1	311	2.4	653	3.7
Does not use a wheelchair but has used a cane, crutches, or a walker for six months or longer	2,847	9.3	980	7.6	1,867	10.5
With a mental or emotional disability	1,133	3.7	372	2.9	760	4.3
PERSONS 16 TO 67 YEARS OLD						
Total	167,899	100.0	82,261	100.0	85,638	100.0
With a work disability	19,544	11.6	9,620	11.7	9,924	11.6
Prevented from working	8,632	5.1	3,922	4.8	4,710	5.5
PERSONS 16 YEARS OLD AND OVER						
Total	192,348	100.0	92,220	100.0	100,128	100.0
With a housework disability	18,088	9.4	7,477	8.1	10,611	10.6
Unable to do housework	3,591	1.9	1,691	1.8	1,900	1.9

Source: John M. McNeil, U.S. Bureau of the Census, *Americans With Disabilities: 1991–92 (Data from the Survey of Income and Program Participation),* Current Population Reports, Series P70-33, Washington, D.C.: U.S. Government Printing Office, December 1993, Table E.

C1-8. Persons with Disabilities, by Sex: 1991–92

(Covers the civilian noninstitutional resident population and members of the Armed Forces living off post or with their families on post. The criteria for presence of disability varied by age. In general, a disability is considered a reduced ability to perform tasks one would normally do at a given stage in life. Based on the Survey of Income and Program Participation.)

CHARACTERISTIC	PERSONS (1,000)			PERCENT DISTRIBUTION		
	Total	Male	Female	Total	Male	Female
All ages.	**251,796**	**122,692**	**129,104**	**100.0**	**100.0**	**100.0**
With a disability	48,936	22,916	26,020	19.4	18.7	20.2
Severe.	24,117	9,929	14,187	9.6	8.1	11.0
Not severe	24,819	12,987	11,833	9.9	10.6	9.2
PERSONS 15 YEARS OLD AND OVER						
Total	195,729	93,985	101,744	100.0	100.0	100.0
With a disability	46,023	21,040	24,982	23.5	22.4	24.6
Severe.	23,588	9,593	13,995	12.1	10.2	13.8
Not severe	22,435	11,447	10,987	11.5	12.2	10.8
With functional limitations	34,163	14,774	19,389	17.5	15.7	19.1
Has difficulty—						
Seeing words and letters	9,685	4,006	5,679	5.0	4.3	5.6
Hearing normal conversation	10,928	6,421	4,506	5.6	6.8	4.4
Having speech understood	2,284	1,316	968	1.2	1.4	1.0
Lifting or carrying 10 lbs..	16,205	5,218	10,987	8.3	5.6	10.8
Climbing stairs without resting	17,469	6,465	11,003	8.9	6.9	10.8
Walking three city blocks	17,319	6,653	10,665	8.9	7.1	10.5
Is unable to—						
See words and letters	1,590	661	929	0.8	0.7	0.9
Hear normal conversation	924	529	396	0.5	0.6	0.4
Have speech understood	237	141	95	0.1	0.2	0.1
Lift or carry 10 lbs..	7,734	2,375	5,359	4.0	2.5	5.3
Climb stairs without resting	9,116	3,277	5,839	4.7	3.5	5.7
Walk three city blocks	8,972	3,236	5,736	4.6	3.4	5.6
With limitations of activities of daily living	7,919	3,013	4,907	4.1	3.2	4.8
Has difficulty—						
Getting around inside the house.	3,664	1,376	2,288	1.9	1.5	2.3
Getting in/out of bed or a chair	5,280	2,006	3,274	2.7	2.1	3.2
Taking a bath or shower.	4,501	1,550	2,951	2.3	1.7	2.9
Dressing	3,234	1,262	1,971	1.7	1.3	1.9
Eating	1,077	437	640	0.6	0.5	0.6
Getting to or using the toilet	2,084	767	1,317	1.1	0.8	1.3
Needs personal assistance with—						
Getting around inside the house.	1,706	698	1,008	0.9	0.7	1.0
Getting in/out of bed or a chair	2,022	796	1,227	1.0	0.9	1.2
Taking a bath or shower.	2,718	1,028	1,691	1.4	1.1	1.7
Dressing	2,060	866	1,193	1.1	0.9	1.2
Eating	487	226	261	0.3	0.2	0.3
Getting to or using the toilet	1,157	477	680	0.6	0.5	0.7
With limitations of instrumental activities of daily living	11,694	4,601	7,093	6.0	4.9	7.0
Has difficulty—						
Going outside the home	7,809	2,759	5,050	4.0	2.9	5.0
Keeping track of money and bills	3,901	1,621	2,280	2.0	1.7	2.2
Preparing meals	4,530	1,699	2,831	2.3	1.8	2.8
Doing light housework	6,313	2,191	4,122	3.2	2.3	4.1
Using the telephone.	3,130	1,749	1,381	1.6	1.9	1.4
Needs personal assistance with—						
Going outside the home	6,011	2,017	3,994	3.1	2.2	3.9
Keeping track of money and bills	3,425	1,460	1,965	1.8	1.6	1.9
Preparing meals	3,685	1,447	2,238	1.9	1.5	2.2
Doing light housework	4,745	1,626	3,119	2.4	1.7	3.1
Using the telephone.	933	509	424	0.5	0.5	0.4

Source: U.S. Bureau of the Census, *Current Population Reports*, P70-33.

Source: U.S. Bureau of the Census, *Statistical Abstract of the United States: 1994*, (114th edition), Washington, D.C.: U.S. Government Printing Office, 1994, Table 202.

C1-9. Characteristics of Women with a Disability: 1991–92

(Numbers in thousands.)

Sex and age	Total	With a disability		With a severe disability	
		Number	Percent	Number	Percent
FEMALES, ALL AGES					
Total	129,104	26,020	20.2	14,187	11.0
RACE AND HISPANIC ORIGIN					
White	107,586	21,791	20.3	11,613	10.8
Not of Hispanic origin	98,322	20,326	20.7	10,737	10.9
Black	16,656	3,622	21.7	2,253	13.5
American Indian, Eskimo, or Aleut	797	174	21.8	85	10.7
Asian or Pacific Islander	4,066	434	10.7	236	5.8
Hispanic origin	10,948	1,775	16.2	1,082	9.9
FAMILY RELATIONSHIP					
Family householder or spouse	64,084	14,167	22.1	7,435	11.6
With children under 18 years	30,946	4,688	15.2	2,001	6.5
Married, spouse present	52,328	10,548	20.2	5,370	10.3
With children under 18 years	24,216	3,024	12.5	1,186	4.9
No spouse present	11,756	3,618	30.8	2,065	17.6
With children under 18 years	6,730	1,665	24.7	816	12.1
Nonfamily householder	16,269	6,991	43.0	4,331	26.6
Lives alone	14,819	6,731	45.4	4,239	28.6
Child of householder	38,564	2,512	6.5	925	2.4
Other relative of householder	5,899	1,608	27.3	1,129	19.1
Member of secondary family	924	93	10.1	46	5.0
Secondary individual	3,364	651	19.3	321	9.6
YEARS OF SCHOOL COMPLETED					
Persons 25 years old and over	84,338	23,342	27.7	13,417	15.9
Less than 12	18,900	9,275	49.1	6,522	34.5
12	32,931	8,422	25.6	4,346	13.2
13 to 15	16,602	3,440	20.7	1,622	9.8
16 and over	15,905	2,206	13.9	928	5.8
REGION					
Northeast	26,290	5,002	19.0	2,946	11.2
Midwest	32,528	6,465	19.9	3,231	9.9
South	43,919	9,461	21.5	5,410	12.3
West	26,367	5,092	19.3	2,601	9.9
RESIDENCE					
In central city	40,996	8,587	20.9	5,032	12.3
In metro area, not central city	58,181	10,373	17.8	5,492	9.4
Not in metro area	29,927	7,061	23.6	3,664	12.2
RATIO OF INCOME TO LOW-INCOME THRESHOLD					
Less than 1.00	23,386	6,159	26.3	3,875	16.6
1.00 to 1.49	14,201	4,132	29.1	2,562	18.0
1.50 to 1.99	13,847	3,260	23.5	1,848	13.4
2.00 to 2.99	25,427	5,031	19.8	2,566	10.1
3.00 to 3.99	18,658	2,971	15.9	1,377	7.4
4.00 and over	33,547	4,463	13.3	1,956	5.8

C1-9. Characteristics of Women with a Disability: 1991–92 *(continued)*

(Numbers in thousands.)

Sex and age	Total	With a disability		With a severe disability	
		Number	Percent	Number	Percent
HEALTH INSURANCE COVERAGE STATUS					
Covered by private insurance	96,861	17,023	17.6	8,270	8.5
Not covered by private insurance..................	32,243	8,998	27.9	5,918	18.4
Covered by Medicaid..........................	12,346	4,403	35.7	3,319	26.9
Covered by Medicare	18,613	10,945	58.8	7,687	41.3
Covered by Medicaid...........................	14,118	5,110	36.2	3,795	26.9
Not covered by health insurance	15,104	2,441	16.2	1,032	6.8
MEANS-TESTED ASSISTANCE					
Received cash assistance	6,615	3,778	57.1	3,092	46.7
Received food stamps	6,175	2,799	45.3	2,023	32.8
Received housing assistance	6,777	2,362	34.9	1,599	23.6
Received both cash assistance and food stamps....	4,283	2,032	47.4	1,550	36.2
Received all 3 benefits..........................	1,481	716	48.4	573	36.3
Received food stamps only	1,547	602	38.9	383	24.7
Did not receive assistance.......................	116,072	20,325	17.5	9,953	8.6
TENURE OF HOUSING UNIT					
Owner occupied................................	83,406	16,497	19.8	8,817	10.6
Renter occupied................................	45,698	9,523	20.8	5,370	11.8

Source: John M. McNeil, U.S. Bureau of the Census, *Americans With Disabilities: 1991–92 (Data from the Survey of Income and Program Participation)*, Current Population Reports, Series P70-33, Washington, D.C.: U.S. Government Printing Office, December 1993, Table 17.

C1-10. Percentage of Persons 21 to 64 Years Old with a Job or Business, by Sex and Disability Status: 1991–92

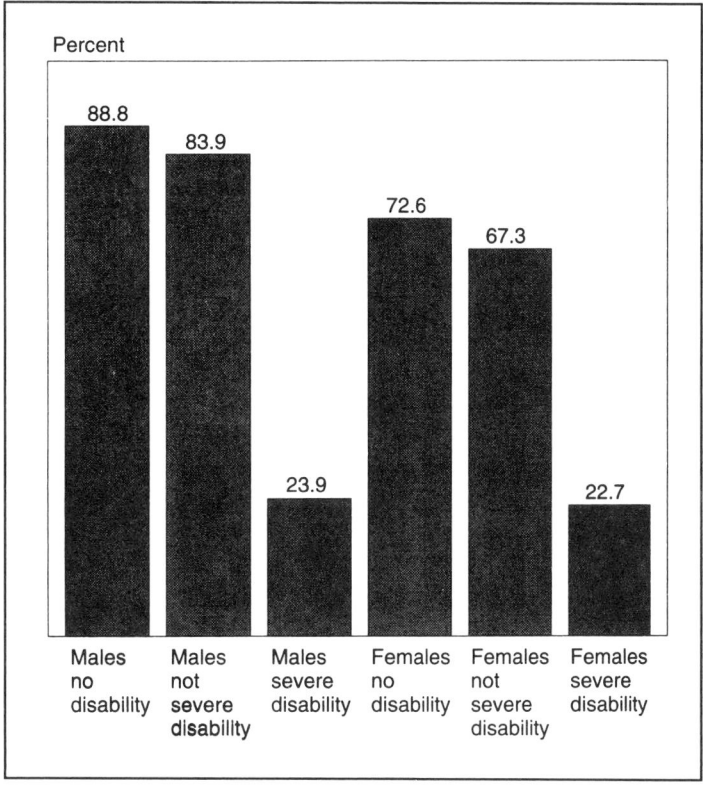

Source: John M. McNeil, U.S. Bureau of the Census, *Americans With Disabilities: 1991–92 (Data from the Survey of Income and Program Participation),* Current Population Reports, Series P70-33, Washington, D.C.: U.S. Government Printing Office, December 1993, Figure 6.

C1-11. Conditions Reported as Cause of Limitations among Women 15 Years Old and Over: 1991–92

(Numbers in thousands.)

Condition	Number of times reported as –							
	First, second or third condition		First condition		Second condition		Third condition	
	Number	Percent distribution	Number	Percent distribution	Number	Percent distribution	Number	Percent distribution
TOTAL..........................	26,088	100.0	16,872	100.0	6,309	100.0	2,907	100.0
Alcohol or drug problem or disorder ..	184	0.7	137	0.8	38	0.6	9	0.3
AIDS or AIDS Related Condition (ARC)............................	25	0.1	22	0.1	–	–	3	0.1
Arthritis or rheumatism	5,384	20.6	4,536	26.9	698	11.1	150	5.2
Back or spine problems (including chronic stiffness or deformity of the back or spine)....................	3,501	13.4	2,583	15.3	837	13.3	81	2.8
Blindness or vision problems (difficulty seeing well enough to read a newspaper, even with glasses on)	923	3.5	462	2.7	295	4.7	166	5.7
Broken bone/fracture	551	2.1	346	2.1	146	2.3	59	2.0
Cancer...........................	464	1.8	301	1.8	114	1.8	49	1.7
Cerebral Palsy	120	0.5	110	0.7	8	0.1	2	0.1
Deafness or serious trouble hearing ..	539	2.1	279	1.7	183	2.9	77	2.6
Diabetes..........................	1,013	3.9	417	2.5	414	6.6	182	6.3
Epilepsy	115	0.4	67	0.4	40	0.6	8	0.3
Head or spinal cord injury	271	1.0	152	0.9	75	1.2	44	1.5
Heart trouble (including heart attack (coronary), hardening of the arteries (arteriosclerosis))	2,666	10.2	1,635	9.7	730	11.6	301	10.4
Hernia or rupture	205	0.8	82	0.5	70	1.1	53	1.8
High blood pressure (hypertension)...	1,524	5.8	385	2.3	697	11.0	442	15.2
Kidney stones or chronic kidney trouble	250	1.0	106	0.6	94	1.5	50	1.7
Learning disability	106	0.4	68	0.4	31	0.5	7	0.2
Lung or respiratory trouble (asthma, bronchitis, emphysema, respiratory allergies, tuberculosis or other lung trouble).........................	1,542	5.9	1,020	6.0	343	5.4	179	6.2
Mental or emotional problem or disorder	487	1.9	259	1.5	140	2.2	88	3.0
Mental retardation	225	0.9	169	1.0	25	0.4	31	1.1
Missing legs, feet, arms, hands, or fingers	62	0.2	40	0.2	16	0.3	6	0.2
Paralysis of any kind...............	390	1.5	275	1.6	80	1.3	35	1.2
Senility/Dementia/Alzheimer's Disease	233	0.9	153	0.9	48	0.8	32	1.1
Speech disorder...................	76	0.3	31	0.2	23	0.4	22	0.8
Stiffness or deformity of the foot, leg, arm, or hand......................	1,142	4.4	665	3.9	291	4.6	186	6.4
Stomach trouble (including ulcers, gallbladder or liver conditions)	368	1.4	61	0.4	117	1.9	190	6.5
Stroke...........................	573	2.2	377	2.2	140	2.2	56	1.9
Thyroid trouble or goiter............	129	0.5	12	0.1	57	0.9	60	2.1
Tumor, cyst or growth..............	120	0.5	66	0.4	33	0.5	21	0.7
Other	2,900	11.1	2,056	12.2	526	8.3	318	10.9

– Represents zero.

Source: John M. McNeil, U.S. Bureau of the Census, *Americans With Disabilities: 1991–92 (Data from the Survey of Income and Program Participation),* Current Population Reports, Series P70-33, Washington, D.C.: U.S. Government Printing Office, December 1993, Table 33.

C1-12. Mean Earnings, by Sex, Age, Years of School Completed, and Disability Status: 1991–92

Sex, age, and years of school completed	With no disability			With a disability, not severe			With a severe disability		
	With earnings (thousands)	Mean earnings		With earnings (thousands)	Mean earnings		With earnings (thousands)	Mean earnings	
		Value	Standard error		Value	Standard error		Value	Standard error
ALL WORKERS									
Total	106,153	$1,962	$13	12,840	$1,771	$47	3,374	$1,422	$169
MALE WORKERS									
Total	57,311	2,405	23	7,443	2,170	77	1,544	1,890	368
Less than 35 years old	26,782	1,715	22	2,133	1,513	70	473	2,027	1,140
Less than 12 years	4,955	947	28	525	958	83	121	(B)	(B)
12 years	10,401	1,610	24	943	1,441	74	227	2,894	2,500
13 to 15 years	6,129	7,613	61	450	1,688	191	72	(B)	(B)
16 years and over	5,296	2,760	54	215	2,820	346	53	(B)	(B)
35 to 54 years old	24,413	3,078	42	3,596	2,407	71	653	2,009	152
Less than 12 years	2,802	1,796	53	661	1,526	110	203	1,177	125
12 years	8,371	2,371	37	1,280	2,220	115	190	1,794	210
13 to 15 years	5,066	2,861	61	911	2,282	89	152	2,403	244
16 years and over	8,175	4,377	106	744	3,664	203	108	(B)	(B)
55 years old and over	6,116	2,738	77	1,714	2,492	287	417	1,547	226
Less than 12 years	1,308	1,657	58	539	1,406	109	204	1,150	182
12 years	2,092	2,278	115	571	2,591	790	112	(B)	(B)
13 to 15 years	1,008	2,605	143	265	2,311	240	51	(B)	(B)
16 years and over	1,708	4,208	196	339	4,196	517	50	(B)	(B)
FEMALE WORKERS									
Total	48,842	1,441	11	5,397	1,220	29	1,831	1,028	42
Less than 35 years old	22,981	1,208	13	1,768	1,001	42	481	862	66
Less than 12 years	3,274	543	16	291	567	56	118	(B)	(B)
12 years	8,560	1,065	16	707	924	62	207	737	73
13 to 15 years	6,254	1,138	20	562	1,093	67	107	(B)	(B)
16 years and over	4,893	1,992	36	207	1,622	169	49	(B)	(B)
35 to 54 years old	20,991	1,710	19	2,619	1,456	44	878	1,228	66
Less than 12 years	2,082	1,072	55	394	883	56	195	848	74
12 years	8,178	1,369	19	1,098	1,264	53	332	1,085	88
13 to 15 years	5,142	1,728	34	637	1,533	101	183	1,437	156
16 years and over	5,589	2,431	47	491	2,243	124	167	1,726	216
55 years old and over	4,870	1,382	36	1,010	993	58	472	825	70
Less than 12 years	1,034	973	56	284	675	67	139	(B)	(B)
12 years	2,143	1,184	36	452	977	85	179	729	107
13 to 15 years	797	1,506	80	149	(B)	(B)	102	(B)	(B)
16 years and over	895	2,219	126	126	(B)	(B)	52	(B)	(B)

B Base less than 150,000.

Source: John M. McNeil, U.S. Bureau of the Census, *Americans With Disabilities: 1991–92 (Data from the Survey of Income and Program Participation)*, Current Population Reports, Series P70-33, Washington, D.C.: U.S. Government Printing Office, December 1993, Table 26.

C1-13. Disability Status of Civilian Noninstitutionalized Persons, by Age, Sex, and Urban/Rural Status: 1990

(Data based on sample and subject to sampling variability.)

United States Urban and Rural and Size of Place	United States	Urban Total	Inside urbanized area Total	Central place	Urban fringe	Outside urbanized area Place of 10,000 or more	Place of 2,500 to 9,999	Rural Total	Place of 1,000 to 2,499	Place of less than 1,000	Rural farm
DISABILITY STATUS OF CIVILIAN NONINSTITUTIONALIZED PERSONS											
Males 16 to 64 years	76 669 407	57 568 740	49 367 936	24 374 046	24 993 890	4 015 518	4 185 286	19 100 667	1 995 857	1 075 117	1 246 518
With a mobility or self-care limitation	3 421 889	2 597 847	2 250 135	1 370 214	879 921	164 343	183 369	824 042	86 735	49 816	48 244
With a mobility limitation	1 565 915	1 135 835	960 320	577 345	382 975	81 790	93 725	430 080	46 300	26 290	20 490
In labor force	412 111	324 114	282 783	166 043	116 740	20 217	21 114	87 997	9 282	5 060	5 967
With a self-care limitation	2 637 472	2 038 232	1 778 832	1 094 211	684 621	123 621	135 779	599 240	63 377	36 087	37 335
With a work disability	6 705 899	4 740 213	3 926 874	2 190 902	1 735 972	380 682	432 657	1 965 686	214 744	124 426	104 372
In labor force	3 084 402	2 229 451	1 865 694	959 821	905 873	173 476	190 281	854 951	91 010	51 443	58 709
Prevented from working	3 158 993	2 175 761	1 781 730	1 070 341	711 389	179 755	214 276	983 232	109 955	64 764	39 167
No work disability	69 963 508	52 828 527	45 441 062	22 183 144	23 257 918	3 634 836	3 752 629	17 134 981	1 781 113	950 691	1 142 146
In labor force	61 702 250	46 510 886	40 110 097	19 117 832	20 992 265	3 114 434	3 286 355	15 191 364	1 566 974	831 350	1 020 905
Females 16 to 64 years	80 654 515	61 469 746	52 543 675	26 160 625	26 383 050	4 360 897	4 565 174	19 184 769	2 128 146	1 113 428	1 159 146
With a mobility or self-care limitation	3 792 873	2 975 760	2 571 213	1 581 415	989 798	193 203	211 344	817 113	95 965	52 479	45 358
With a mobility limitation	1 886 716	1 437 960	1 220 501	728 985	491 516	103 523	113 936	448 756	53 909	28 574	20 644
In labor force	377 913	304 960	266 084	152 473	113 611	19 529	19 347	72 953	8 509	4 350	4 154
With a self-care limitation	2 746 467	2 184 049	1 901 353	1 194 136	707 217	135 291	147 405	562 418	66 097	36 448	33 899
With a work disability	6 120 550	4 543 466	3 762 984	2 147 168	1 615 816	371 077	409 405	1 577 084	193 724	104 024	73 633
In labor force	1 959 588	1 505 880	1 265 662	670 715	594 947	118 191	122 027	453 708	55 514	28 657	23 960
Prevented from working	3 435 036	2 511 628	2 060 407	1 240 179	820 228	210 243	240 978	923 408	115 933	62 926	37 770
No work disability	74 533 965	56 926 280	48 780 691	24 013 457	24 767 234	3 989 820	4 155 769	17 607 685	1 934 422	1 009 404	1 085 513
In labor force	52 950 611	40 979 723	35 279 660	17 152 341	18 127 319	2 796 471	2 903 592	11 970 888	1 349 198	690 913	705 542
Males 65 to 74 years	7 871 539	5 715 545	4 738 813	2 281 448	2 457 365	441 153	535 579	2 155 994	266 195	152 390	210 887
With a mobility or self-care limitation	924 691	668 299	552 507	305 276	247 231	52 741	63 051	256 392	30 953	19 050	19 226
With a mobility limitation	589 834	417 493	341 189	188 104	153 085	34 389	41 915	172 341	20 816	12 983	10 667
With a self-care limitation	633 166	464 163	385 530	214 887	170 643	36 100	42 533	169 003	20 698	12 485	13 742
Females 65 to 74 years	10 062 013	7 633 271	6 287 149	3 163 258	3 123 891	614 013	732 109	2 428 742	356 715	199 021	189 660
With a mobility or self-care limitation	1 467 398	1 125 034	931 870	530 829	401 041	88 182	104 982	342 364	49 371	27 762	21 453
With a mobility limitation	1 041 816	791 093	653 180	371 741	281 439	62 589	75 324	250 723	35 590	20 029	14 331
With a self-care limitation	876 053	676 931	560 804	324 021	236 783	53 492	62 635	199 122	28 815	16 191	13 332
Males 75 years and ever	4 215 939	3 078 435	2 486 628	1 279 895	1 206 733	263 174	328 633	1 137 504	171 304	107 313	103 083
With a mobility or self-care limitation	1 021 930	743 043	600 781	330 616	270 165	63 201	79 061	278 887	39 317	25 454	21 708
With a mobility limitation	796 959	570 021	458 192	251 851	206 341	49 566	62 263	226 938	31 713	20 629	16 605
With a self-care limitation	649 092	476 557	385 703	215 026	170 677	40 685	50 169	172 535	24 693	15 498	13 754
Females 75 years and ever	7 414 020	5 762 659	4 626 078	2 499 988	2 126 090	516 113	620 468	1 651 361	305 481	184 470	111 280
With a mobility or self-care limitation	2 529 422	1 962 087	1 586 383	892 740	693 643	170 991	204 713	567 335	98 005	58 674	36 506
With a mobility limitation	2 183 311	1 681 945	1 357 611	761 323	596 288	146 725	177 609	501 366	85 404	51 339	31 797
With a self-care limitation	1 365 773	1 065 673	865 647	497 524	368 123	92 289	107 737	300 100	50 489	29 586	19 891

Source: U.S. Bureau of the Census, *Social and Economic Characteristics of the United States: 1990 Census of Population*, CP-2-1, Washington, D.C.: U.S. Government Printing Office, 1993, Table 15.

C1-14. Disability Status of Civilian Noninstitutionalized Persons, by Age, Sex, Race, and Hispanic Origin: 1990

(Data based on sample and subject to sampling variability.)

United States	All persons	Race White	Black	American Indian, Eskimo, or Aleut	Asian or Pacific Islander	Other race	Hispanic origin (of any race)	White, not of Hispanic origin
DISABILITY STATUS OF CIVILIAN NONINSTITUTIONALIZED PERSONS								
Males 16 to 64 years	76 669 407	62 558 308	8 043 162	596 490	2 345 354	3 126 093	6 884 794	59 021 646
With a mobility or self-care limitation	3 421 889	2 258 730	771 523	44 526	140 796	206 314	445 987	2 041 812
With a mobility limitation	1 565 915	1 145 473	283 620	20 642	42 130	74 050	167 763	1 059 483
In labor force	412 111	292 919	65 746	5 135	18 942	29 369	65 944	259 694
With a self-care limitation	2 637 472	1 659 977	646 931	34 652	123 424	172 488	369 377	1 482 783
With a work disability	6 705 899	5 372 745	936 599	86 393	98 088	212 074	480 648	5 122 754
In labor force	3 084 402	2 594 567	313 386	37 442	47 301	91 706	207 120	2 486 871
Prevented from working	3 158 993	2 411 001	555 266	42 949	42 009	107 768	243 703	2 284 452
No work disability	69 963 508	57 185 563	7 106 563	510 097	2 247 266	2 914 019	6 404 146	53 898 892
In labor force	61 702 250	51 120 120	5 791 404	415 582	1 829 622	2 545 522	5 594 547	48 241 121
Females 16 to 64 years	80 654 515	64 591 783	9 916 909	639 701	2 557 858	2 948 264	6 755 403	61 035 815
With a mobility or self-care limitation	3 792 873	2 395 678	986 090	50 370	156 843	203 892	447 922	2 177 387
With a mobility limitation	1 886 716	1 346 099	376 463	25 431	54 083	84 640	192 885	1 248 506
In labor force	377 913	265 978	71 176	4 823	16 377	19 559	45 915	242 154
With a self-care limitation	2 746 467	1 612 160	805 810	36 745	131 581	160 171	348 793	1 444 298
With a work disability	6 120 550	4 677 967	1 049 814	81 873	107 524	203 372	455 520	4 448 858
In labor force	1 959 588	1 579 008	272 134	25 239	34 339	48 868	118 146	1 515 967
Prevented from working	3 435 036	2 515 794	679 582	47 533	58 754	133 373	289 037	2 374 468
No work disability	74 533 965	59 913 816	8 867 095	557 828	2 450 334	2 744 892	6 299 883	56 586 957
In labor force	52 950 611	42 876 124	6 417 430	359 877	1 623 106	1 674 074	3 960 490	40 741 124
Males 65 to 74 years	7 871 539	7 030 646	595 410	32 295	129 251	83 937	286 026	6 837 502
With a mobility or self-care limitation	924 691	756 966	126 143	6 814	19 675	15 093	46 830	727 198
With a mobility limitation	589 834	486 632	77 345	4 921	10 883	10 053	30 086	467 657
With a self-care limitation	633 166	511 089	92 867	4 419	14 603	10 188	32 611	490 206
Females 65 to 74 years	10 062 013	8 862 482	881 761	40 569	163 946	113 255	377 840	8 611 400
With a mobility or self-care limitation	1 467 398	1 175 213	226 766	9 282	29 251	26 886	80 052	1 126 011
With a mobility limitation	1 041 816	835 172	160 167	7 214	18 780	20 483	58 737	799 718
With a self-care limitation	876 053	689 269	147 099	5 402	18 900	15 383	47 050	660 033
Males 75 years and over	4 215 939	3 783 747	312 633	15 082	65 182	39 295	138 377	3 689 511
With a mobility or self-care limitation	1 021 930	878 921	106 907	5 021	18 211	12 870	42 980	850 410
With a mobility limitation	796 959	684 954	83 550	4 092	13 825	10 538	34 234	662 465
With a self-care limitation	649 092	552 092	73 382	3 336	11 860	8 422	28 108	533 538
Females 75 years and over	7 414 020	6 656 961	596 112	25 106	75 767	60 074	225 543	6 498 705
With a mobility or self-care limitation	2 529 422	2 203 167	261 704	10 188	27 320	27 043	96 349	2 136 927
With a mobility limitation	2 183 311	1 904 321	223 076	8 787	23 108	24 019	83 985	1 847 013
With a self-care limitation	1 365 773	1 165 353	162 428	5 844	15 531	16 617	58 100	1 126 009

Source: U.S. Bureau of the Census, *Social and Economic Characteristics of the United States: 1990 Census of Population*, CP-2-1, Washington, D.C.: U.S. Government Printing Office, 1993, Table 40.

C1-15. Hypertension among Persons 20 Years of Age and Over, by Sex, Age, Race, and Hispanic Origin: 1960–62, 1971–74, 1976–80, and 1988–91

[Data are based on physical examinations of a sample of the civilian noninstitutionalized population]

Sex, age, race, and Hispanic origin [1]	1960–62	1971–74	1976–80 [2]	1988–91
20–74 years, age adjusted [3]		Percent of population		
Both sexes [4]	36.9	38.3	39.0	23.4
Male	40.0	42.4	44.0	26.3
Female [4]	33.7	34.3	34.0	20.3
White male	39.3	41.7	43.5	25.1
White female [4]	31.7	32.4	32.3	19.0
Black male	48.1	51.8	48.7	37.4
Black female [4]	50.8	50.3	47.5	31.3
White, non-Hispanic male	---	---	43.9	25.4
White, non-Hispanic female [4]	---	---	32.1	18.9
Black, non-Hispanic male	---	---	48.7	37.3
Black, non-Hispanic female [4]	---	---	47.6	31.4
Mexican-American male	---	---	25.0	26.9
Mexican-American female [4]	---	---	21.8	20.8
20–74 years, crude				
Both sexes [4]	39.0	39.7	39.7	23.5
Male	41.7	43.3	44.0	25.7
Female [4]	36.6	36.5	35.6	21.3
White male	41.0	42.8	43.8	25.0
White female [4]	34.9	34.9	34.2	20.4
Black male	50.5	52.1	47.4	34.3
Black female [4]	52.0	50.2	46.1	28.7
White, non-Hispanic male	---	---	44.3	25.8
White, non-Hispanic female [4]	---	---	34.4	20.7
Black, non-Hispanic male	---	---	47.5	34.2
Black, non-Hispanic female [4]	---	---	46.1	29.0
Mexican-American male	---	---	18.8	19.6
Mexican-American female [4]	---	---	16.7	14.9
Male				
20–34 years	22.8	24.8	28.9	9.2
35–44 years	37.7	39.1	40.5	20.0
45–54 years	47.6	55.0	53.6	35.7
55–64 years	60.3	62.5	61.8	46.7
65–74 years	68.8	67.2	67.1	59.0
75 years and over	---	---	---	63.7
Female [4]				
20–34 years	9.3	11.2	11.1	3.0
35–44 years	24.0	28.2	28.8	12.3
45–54 years	43.4	43.6	47.1	23.2
55–64 years	66.4	62.5	61.1	46.5
65–74 years	81.5	78.3	71.8	57.8
75 years and over	---	---	---	75.2

[1]The race groups, white and black, include persons of both Hispanic and non-Hispanic origin. Conversely, persons of Hispanic origin may be of any race.
[2]Data for Mexican-Americans are for 1982–84. See Appendix I.
[3]Age adjusted.
[4]Excludes pregnant women.

NOTE: A person with hypertension is defined by either having elevated blood pressure (systolic pressure of at least 140 mmHg or diastolic pressure of at least 90 mmHg) or taking antihypertensive medication. Percents are based on a single measurement of blood pressure to provide comparable data across the 4 time periods. In 1976–80, 31.3 percent of persons 20–74 years of age had hypertension, based on the average of 3 blood pressure measurements, in contrast to 39.7 percent when a single measurement is used.

SOURCE: Centers for Disease Control and Prevention, National Center for Health Statistics, Division of Health Examination Statistics: Unpublished data.

Source: National Center for Health Statistics, *Health, United States, 1993*, (PHS) 94-1232, Washington, D.C.: U.S. Government Printing Office, 1994, Table 78.

C1-16. Age-Adjusted Cancer Incidence Rates for Selected Cancer Sites in Selected Geographic Areas, by Sex and Race: Selected Years, 1973–91

[Data are based on the Surveillance, Epidemiology, and End Results Program's population-based registries in Atlanta, Detroit, Seattle-Puget Sound, San Francisco-Oakland, Connecticut, Iowa, New Mexico, Utah, and Hawaii]

Race, sex, and site	1973	1975	1980	1985	1987	1988	1989	1990	1991	Estimated annual percent change [1]
White male	Number of new cases per 100,000 population [2]									
All sites	363.2	378.6	405.7	428.3	452.3	448.1	453.7	470.2	494.5	1.4
Oral cavity and pharynx	17.5	18.2	16.8	16.7	17.2	15.4	15.3	15.9	15.3	−0.8
Esophagus	4.8	4.8	4.9	5.3	5.4	5.3	5.1	6.1	5.6	1.0
Stomach	13.9	12.5	12.3	10.5	10.4	10.6	10.7	9.3	9.5	−1.8
Colon and rectum	54.1	55.0	58.4	63.3	61.0	59.3	58.7	58.4	56.3	0.3
Colon	34.7	36.1	39.2	43.3	41.8	40.8	40.1	39.9	39.3	0.7
Rectum	19.4	19.0	19.3	20.0	19.2	18.4	18.6	18.5	17.0	−0.4
Pancreas	12.7	12.4	11.0	10.7	10.5	10.5	10.1	9.9	9.6	−1.1
Lung and bronchus	72.2	75.7	82.1	81.8	83.8	81.7	80.4	79.7	77.9	0.4
Prostate gland	62.3	68.8	78.4	86.3	101.6	104.4	110.0	129.2	159.2	4.0
Urinary bladder	27.2	28.6	31.3	30.9	33.4	32.8	32.0	31.8	31.6	0.9
Non-Hodgkin's lymphoma	10.3	11.4	12.6	15.8	18.2	18.0	18.3	19.1	19.5	3.9
Leukemia	14.3	14.2	14.5	14.3	14.1	13.7	13.9	12.9	12.5	−0.5
Black male										
All sites	441.6	437.8	509.6	529.9	546.1	538.7	536.8	564.6	597.9	1.6
Oral cavity and pharynx	16.8	17.3	23.1	22.5	26.0	23.0	24.1	24.8	20.7	1.8
Esophagus	13.0	17.4	16.4	19.4	18.1	16.7	15.7	19.9	15.1	0.3
Stomach	25.9	19.9	21.4	18.4	20.7	20.0	18.3	18.0	20.2	−0.9
Colon and rectum	42.6	47.5	63.7	60.4	61.3	57.8	64.1	59.9	61.7	1.7
Colon	31.5	34.5	46.0	46.6	47.5	42.8	48.9	46.2	45.9	1.9
Rectum	11.1	13.0	17.7	13.8	13.7	15.0	15.1	13.7	15.7	1.0
Pancreas	15.8	15.4	17.6	19.8	16.0	16.9	13.1	15.5	14.4	−0.6
Lung and bronchus	105.1	101.2	131.2	131.3	124.0	125.9	122.1	118.2	122.0	1.2
Prostate gland	106.4	111.3	126.0	132.6	145.7	146.0	145.4	166.6	209.6	2.8
Urinary bladder	10.7	13.7	14.5	15.8	17.4	14.2	14.1	14.9	14.7	1.0
Non-Hodgkin's lymphoma	9.0	7.1	9.3	9.9	9.4	13.3	11.6	13.8	15.6	3.8
Leukemia	12.0	12.5	13.1	12.9	13.8	10.8	13.0	10.7	9.5	−0.4
White female										
All sites	294.0	309.2	309.7	341.3	350.0	346.4	345.3	350.2	347.8	0.9
Colon and rectum	41.6	42.8	44.6	45.7	41.0	39.9	40.7	39.8	38.0	−0.4
Colon	30.2	30.8	32.8	33.8	30.1	29.3	29.9	29.8	28.2	−0.3
Rectum	11.4	12.0	11.7	11.9	10.9	10.6	10.8	10.0	9.8	−0.8
Pancreas	7.4	7.1	7.3	8.1	7.5	7.6	7.4	7.7	7.3	0.2
Lung and bronchus	17.8	21.8	28.2	35.8	39.5	41.3	40.7	41.9	42.8	4.8
Melanoma of skin	5.9	6.9	9.2	10.3	11.1	10.5	10.8	10.6	11.5	3.5
Breast	84.1	89.3	87.1	106.3	116.8	113.3	109.2	112.8	113.6	1.8
Cervix uteri	12.8	11.1	9.1	7.6	7.4	7.9	8.1	8.3	7.5	−2.5
Corpus uteri	29.4	33.5	25.2	23.1	22.6	21.2	22.1	22.9	22.0	−2.3
Ovary	14.6	14.4	13.9	15.0	14.5	15.5	16.1	15.9	15.7	0.5
Non-Hodgkin's lymphoma	7.5	8.4	9.2	11.3	11.4	12.1	11.8	12.6	12.0	2.7
Black female										
All sites	282.6	295.8	304.8	323.5	327.0	335.6	322.5	339.0	334.0	1.1
Colon and rectum	41.1	43.1	49.5	45.9	48.2	45.8	44.4	49.3	45.5	0.9
Colon	29.5	32.5	40.9	36.0	37.3	36.4	34.1	38.8	37.2	1.2
Rectum	11.6	10.6	8.6	10.0	10.9	9.5	10.3	10.4	8.3	−0.3
Pancreas	11.6	11.8	13.0	11.3	14.9	14.4	11.0	10.6	12.4	0.5
Lung and bronchus	20.9	20.6	34.0	40.7	38.5	42.8	45.4	46.3	49.0	4.9
Breast	68.8	78.3	74.1	92.6	90.3	98.4	88.6	97.2	95.1	1.9
Cervix uteri	29.7	27.9	19.0	15.9	15.2	15.2	13.2	13.6	12.9	−4.3
Corpus uteri	15.0	17.2	14.2	15.2	13.3	14.0	16.4	14.5	14.2	−0.3
Ovary	10.4	10.1	10.0	10.1	10.2	10.7	10.7	10.3	10.0	0.2
Non-Hodgkin's lymphoma	5.5	4.1	6.0	7.0	8.0	7.1	7.7	9.1	8.3	4.0

[1]The estimated annual percent change has been calculated by fitting a linear regression model to the natural logarithm of the yearly rates from 1973–91.
[2]Age adjusted by the direct method to the 1970 U.S. population.

SOURCE: National Cancer Institute, National Institutes of Health, Cancer Statistics Branch, Bethesda, Md. 20892.

Source: National Center for Health Statistics, *Health, United States, 1993,* (PHS) 94-1232, Washington, D.C.: U.S. Government Printing Office, 1994, Table 67.

C1-17. Five-Year Relative Cancer Survival Rates for Selected Cancer Sites in Selected Geographic Areas, by Race and Sex: Selected Years: 1974–76 to 1983–90

[Data are based on the Surveillance, Epidemiology, and End Results Program's population-based registries in Atlanta, Detroit, Seattle-Puget Sound, San Francisco-Oakland, Connecticut, Iowa, New Mexico, Utah, and Hawaii]

Sex and site	All races				White				Black			
	1974–76	1977–79	1980–82	1983–90	1974–76	1977–79	1980–82	1983–90	1974–76	1977–79	1980–82	1983–90
Male	Percent of patients											
All sites	40.8	43.1	45.0	49.0	41.9	44.3	46.3	50.8	31.3	32.1	34.0	35.7
Oral cavity and pharynx	52.2	51.1	50.6	49.5	54.3	53.4	53.8	52.5	31.2	30.8	25.8	28.5
Esophagus	3.6	4.7	6.0	8.6	4.3	5.6	6.7	9.9	2.1	2.4	4.6	5.5
Stomach	13.9	15.3	16.3	16.6	13.2	14.4	15.2	15.5	15.5	14.6	18.5	16.9
Colon	49.4	51.4	55.4	60.9	49.8	51.7	55.8	62.0	44.1	45.4	46.5	49.2
Rectum	47.4	48.6	50.1	57.3	47.8	49.6	51.2	58.2	34.1	38.0	36.1	46.7
Pancreas	3.0	2.3	2.7	2.7	3.1	2.3	2.6	2.4	1.4	2.8	3.7	4.5
Lung and bronchus	11.1	11.8	12.0	12.0	11.0	12.0	12.2	12.1	11.0	8.9	10.9	10.6
Prostate gland	66.7	70.9	73.1	79.6	67.7	71.9	74.3	81.3	58.0	62.1	64.4	66.4
Urinary bladder	73.7	76.4	79.1	82.0	74.5	76.9	79.8	82.6	54.1	62.4	62.3	66.0
Non-Hodgkin's lymphoma	46.9	45.6	49.9	49.9	47.7	46.2	50.6	50.6	43.1	43.2	47.5	42.1
Leukemia	33.1	35.9	37.1	38.4	33.5	36.8	38.3	39.9	32.6	29.0	29.8	29.3
Female												
All sites	56.7	56.0	56.0	58.6	57.4	56.8	56.8	59.8	46.8	46.3	45.6	45.5
Colon	50.6	53.6	55.0	59.0	50.8	53.7	55.3	59.9	46.6	49.8	50.7	50.1
Rectum	49.4	50.8	53.9	58.0	49.7	51.4	54.6	58.7	49.3	38.6	40.7	50.6
Pancreas	2.1	2.7	3.4	3.8	2.1	2.4	3.0	3.5	3.1	4.8	5.9	5.3
Lung and bronchus	15.6	17.0	16.0	15.8	15.8	17.1	16.1	16.2	13.1	17.0	15.4	12.3
Melanoma of skin	84.7	85.8	87.6	89.3	84.8	86.1	87.6	89.4	- - -	- - -	- - -	77.9
Breast	74.3	74.5	76.2	80.4	74.9	75.2	76.9	81.6	62.9	62.8	65.7	65.8
Cervix uteri	68.5	67.7	66.9	67.4	69.2	68.8	67.7	69.9	63.5	61.9	60.4	56.4
Corpus uteri	87.7	84.9	81.4	83.2	88.6	86.2	82.7	84.9	60.4	57.5	53.7	55.2
Ovary	36.5	38.1	38.9	41.8	36.3	37.5	38.7	41.6	40.1	39.8	37.6	38.4
Non-Hodgkin's lymphoma	47.3	50.6	52.4	54.6	47.3	50.5	52.7	55.0	54.1	59.2	53.3	49.5

NOTES: Rates are based on followup of patients through 1991. The rate is the ratio of the observed survival rate for the patient group to the expected survival rate for persons in the general population similar to the patient group with respect to age, sex, race, and calendar year of observation. It estimates the chance of surviving the effects of cancer.

SOURCE: National Cancer Institute, National Institutes of Health, Cancer Statistics Branch, Bethesda, Md. 20892.

Source: National Center for Health Statistics, *Health, United States, 1993,* (PHS) 94-1232, Washington, D.C.: U.S. Government Printing Office, 1994, Table 68.

C1-18. Percentage of Children 3 to 17 Years of Age with Developmental Disabilities, Learning Disabilities, or Behavioral Problems, by Age and Sex: 1988

Selected family characteristic	All ages	3–4 years	5–11 years	12–17 years
All children	19.5	8.0	18.1	25.2
Sex				
Male	22.9	8.7	21.4	29.2
Female	16.0	7.3	14.7	20.8

Source: M. J. Coiro, N. Zill, and B. Bloom, National Center for Health Statistics, *Health of Our Nation's Children,* Vital Health Statistics, Series 10, No. 191, Hyattsville, MD: National Center for Health Statistics, 1994, Table 6.

C1-19. Persons 18 Years and Over with Serious Mental Illness, by Sex: 1989

Characteristic	Adult household population		All adults with serious mental illness			Adults currently limited by serious mental illness		
	Number in thousands	Percent distribution	Number in thousands	Percent distribution	Rate per thousand	Number in thousands	Percent distribution	Percent
Total[1]	179,529	100.0	3,264	100.0	18.2	2,571	100.0	78.8
Sex[1]								
Male	85,257	47.5	1,320	40.4	15.5	1,105	43.0	83.7
Female	94,272	52.5	1,944	59.6	20.6	1,466	57.0	75.4

[1]Includes persons with unknown poverty status, education, and/or self-assessed health status.

Source: Peggy Barker, et. al., National Center for Health Statistics, *Serious Mental Illness and Disability in the Adult Household Population: United States, 1989*, Advance Data, No. 218, September 16, 1992, Table 1.

C1-20. Persons 18 Years and Over with Serious Mental Illness Who Have Ever Seen a Mental Health Professional, by Sex: 1989

Characteristic	Number in thousands	Percent[1]
Total[2]	2,380	77.3
Sex		
Male	959	77.9
Female	1,421	76.8

[1]All percent denominators exclude persons with unknown time since last saw a mental health professional (194,000, or 5.6 percent of total adults with serious mental illness).
[2]Percent denominator for total includes persons with unknown poverty status, education, health status, prescription drug use, and/or disability pay.

Source: Peggy Barker, et. al., National Center for Health Statistics, *Serious Mental Illness and Disability in the Adult Household Population: United States, 1989*, Advance Data, No. 218, September 16, 1992, Table 11.

C1-21. Additions to Selected Inpatient Psychiatric Organizations and Rate per 100,000 Civilian Population, by Sex, Age, and Race: 1975, 1980, and 1986

[Data are based on a sample survey of patients]

Sex, age, and race	State and county mental hospitals			Private psychiatric hospitals			Nonfederal general hospitals [1]		
	1975	1980	1986	1975	1980	1986	1975	1980	1986
Both sexes				Number in thousands					
Total	385	369	326	130	141	207	516	564	794
Under 18 years	25	17	16	15	17	42	43	44	46
18–24 years	72	77	58	19	23	22	93	98	120
25–44 years	166	177	189	47	56	91	220	249	405
45–64 years	102	78	48	35	32	34	121	123	142
65 years and over	21	20	15	13	14	18	38	50	82
White	296	265	217	119	123	177	451	469	607
All other	89	104	109	10	18	30	65	95	187
Male									
Total	249	239	205	56	67	107	212	255	379
Under 18 years	16	11	10	8	9	23	20	20	21
18–24 years	52	56	39	10	13	14	45	52	57
25–44 years	107	119	125	20	27	50	85	115	215
45–64 years	61	43	25	14	13	14	48	46	60
65 years and over	13	11	7	5	5	6	14	21	26
White	191	171	135	51	58	89	184	213	274
All other	58	68	69	5	9	18	27	42	105
Female									
Total	136	130	121	74	74	101	304	309	415
Under 18 years	9	5	6	8	7	20	23	23	25
18–24 years	20	22	19	9	10	8	48	45	63
25–44 years	59	58	64	28	29	41	135	135	190
45–64 years	41	35	24	21	18	20	74	77	81
65 years and over	8	9	8	8	9	12	24	29	56
White	105	94	82	69	65	88	267	256	333
All other	31	36	40	5	9	13	37	53	82
Both sexes				Rate per 100,000 civilian population					
Total	182.2	163.6	136.1	61.4	62.6	86.7	243.8	250.0	331.7
Under 18 years	38.1	26.1	25.2	23.3	26.3	67.1	64.4	68.5	72.0
18–24 years	271.8	264.6	215.5	73.7	79.6	81.3	352.8	334.2	443.7
25–44 years	314.1	282.9	251.9	89.3	89.1	121.6	416.8	399.0	540.4
45–64 years	233.5	175.7	107.0	80.1	71.0	75.2	278.5	276.4	314.9
65 years and over	91.8	78.0	50.9	57.7	54.1	61.9	170.3	195.4	281.5
White	161.1	136.8	106.7	64.9	63.4	87.3	245.4	241.8	299.0
All other	321.9	328.0	299.8	37.9	57.5	83.1	233.3	300.0	514.3
Male									
Total	243.7	219.8	176.6	54.5	61.9	92.1	207.1	233.8	327.6
Under 18 years	48.3	35.4	30.1	22.5	28.9	69.8	59.1	62.6	63.7
18–24 years	409.0	387.9	292.6	78.0	92.2	103.2	350.8	365.3	428.5
25–44 years	418.4	388.1	338.4	76.6	86.8	136.1	332.8	374.7	584.2
45–64 years	291.5	202.3	114.4	66.8	63.2	65.5	228.6	219.1	281.1
65 years and over	136.4	105.3	57.1	50.3	47.3	52.1	152.0	203.4	223.1
White	214.2	182.2	137.1	57.0	61.7	90.3	206.9	226.3	278.3
All other	444.5	457.8	403.0	38.1	62.7	102.8	209.1	281.1	610.3
Female									
Total	124.7	111.1	98.1	67.8	63.3	81.5	278.1	265.1	335.5
Under 18 years	27.5	16.4	20.0	24.1	23.6	64.3	70.0	74.6	80.7
18–24 years	143.1	145.8	141.0	69.6	67.4	60.2	354.6	304.4	458.3
25–44 years	215.9	182.3	168.1	101.2	91.2	107.6	495.8	422.2	498.1
45–64 years	180.5	151.7	100.2	92.3	78.1	84.0	324.3	328.2	345.8
65 years and over	60.8	59.6	46.7	62.8	58.8	68.6	182.9	190.0	321.3
White	111.2	94.1	78.1	72.5	65.0	84.5	281.7	256.4	318.6
All other	212.0	212.6	207.2	37.7	52.8	65.5	254.9	316.7	428.0

[1]Non-Federal general hospitals include public and nonpublic facilities.

SOURCES: National Institute of Mental Health: C. A. Taube and S. A. Barrett: Mental Health, United States, 1985. DHHS Pub. No. (ADM) 85-1378. U.S. Government Printing Office, 1985; R. W. Manderscheid and M. A. Sonnenschein: Mental Health, United States, 1990. DHHS Pub. No. (ADM) 90-1708. U.S. Government Printing Office, 1990; Unpublished data.

Source: National Center for Health Statistics, *Health, United States, 1993,* (PHS) 94-1232, Washington, D.C.: U.S. Government Printing Office, 1994, Table 105.

C1-22. Percentage of Men and Women Who Often or Very Often Felt Negative Moods the Two Weeks before the Survey: 1991

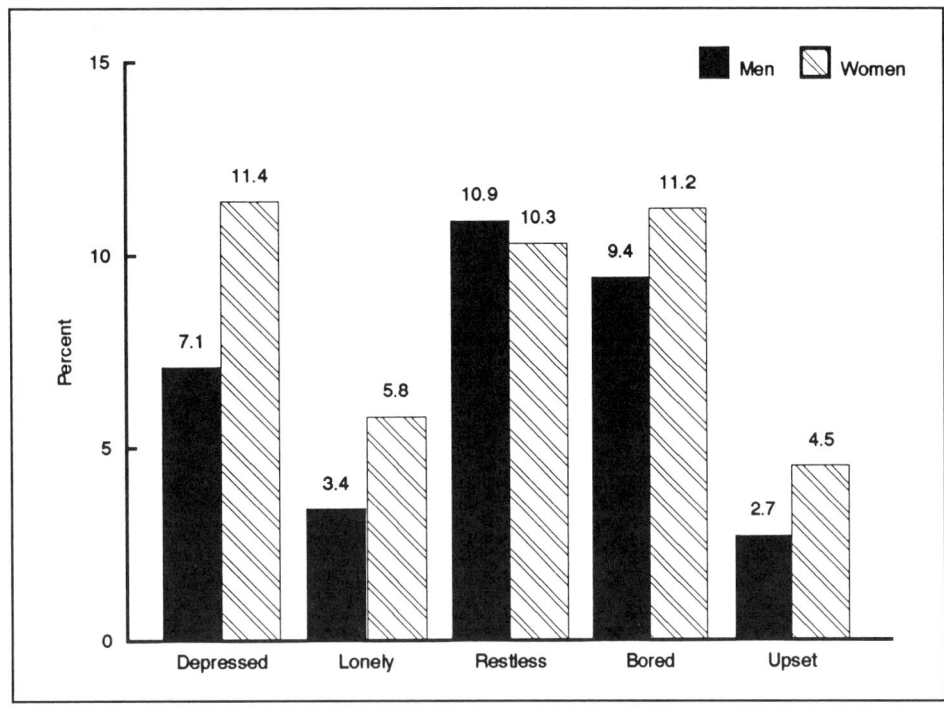

Source: Charlotte A. Schoenborn and John Horm, National Center for Health Statistics, *Negative Mood As Correlates of Smoking and Heavier Drinking: Implications for Health Promotion*, Advance Data, No. 236, November 4, 1993, Hyattsville, MD: National Center for Health Statistics. Figure 1.

C1-23. Number of Men and Women Who Often or Very Often Felt Negative Moods the Two Weeks before the Survey: 1991

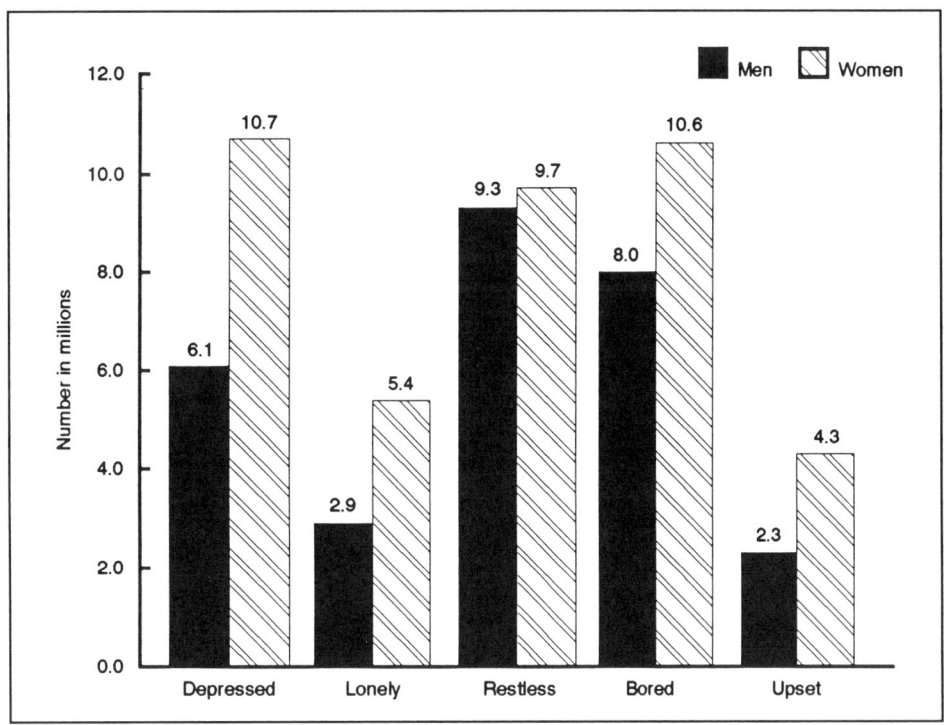

Source: Charlotte A. Schoenborn and John Horm, National Center for Health Statistics, *Negative Mood As Correlates of Smoking and Heavier Drinking: Implications for Health Promotion*, Advance Data, No. 236, November 4, 1993, Hyattsville, MD: National Center for Health Statistics. Figure 2.

C1-24. Prevalence (Unadjusted) of Cigarette Smoking for Men and Women, by Selected Negative Moods and Odds Ratios Adjusted for Age, Race, Education, Income, Marital Status, and Health Status: 1991

Negative moods	Men				Women			
	Population (in thousands)	Prevalence	Odds ratio	95-percent confidence limits	Population (in thousands)	Prevalence	Odds ratio	95-percent confidence limits
Depressed								
Very often or often.	6,006	41.5	1.4	1.2,1.7	10,639	33.3	1.5	1.4,1.7
Sometimes	12,824	31.8	1.1	1.0,1.2	20,423	27.2	1.3	1.2,1.4
Rarely or never.	65,514	26.9	1.0	. . .	62,379	21.4	1.0	. . .
Lonely								
Very often or often.	2,842	44.9	1.7	1.4,2.1	5,405	35.7	1.6	1.4,1.9
Sometimes	5,479	36.2	1.2	1.0,1.4	9,868	28.0	1.2	1.1,1.3
Rarely or never.	76,090	27.5	1.0	. . .	78,182	22.7	1.0	. . .
Restless								
Very often or often.	9,220	39.2	1.3	1.1,1.5	9,637	35.8	1.7	1.5,1.9
Sometimes	13,040	29.9	1.0	0.9,1.2	13,977	28.1	1.3	1.1,1.4
Rarely or never.	61,956	26.8	1.0	. . .	69,708	21.6	1.0	. . .
Bored								
Very often or often.	7,886	42.8	1.6	1.4,1.9	10,455	36.4	1.7	1.5,1.9
Sometimes	16,810	32.3	1.2	1.1,1.4	19,169	26.6	1.2	1.1,1.3
Rarely or never.	59,479	25.8	1.0	. . .	63,660	21.3	1.0	. . .
Upset								
Very often or often.	2,271	38.0	1.2	0.9,1.6	4,215	34.2	1.3	1.1,1.5
Sometimes	7,506	31.8	1.0	0.9,1.2	10,840	24.0	0.9	0.8,1.0
Rarely or never.	74,504	28.1	1.0	. . .	78,225	23.5	1.0	. . .

NOTES: The population columns represent the number of men or women with specified levels of selected negative moods. Population estimates for smoking among these individuals can be derived by multiplying the population estimate for a particular negative mood category by the prevalence estimates.

Source: Charlotte A. Schoenborn and John Horm, National Center for Health Statistics, *Negative Mood As Correlates of Smoking and Heavier Drinking: Implications for Health Promotion*, Advance Data, No. 236, November 4, 1993, Hyattsville, MD: National Center for Health Statistics. Table 1.

C1-25. Prevalence (Unadjusted) of Heavy Drinking for Men and Women, by Selected Negative Moods and Odds Ratios Adjusted for Age, Race, Education, Income, Marital Status, and Health Status: 1991

Negative moods	Men				Women			
	Population	Prevalence	Odds ratio	95-percent confidence limits	Population	Prevalence	Odds ratio	95-percent confidence limits
Depressed								
Very often or often.	5,960	7.1	1.6	1.2,2.1	10,618	2.5	1.1	0.8,1.5
Sometimes	12,788	5.4	1.2	0.9,1.5	20,456	2.3	1.1	0.8,1.4
Rarely or never.	65,594	4.7	1.0	. . .	62,570	2.3	1.0	. . .
Lonely								
Very often or often.	2,819	9.4	1.9	1.3,2.7	5,409	2.8	1.3	0.9,2.1
Sometimes	5,499	6.0	1.2	0.9,1.6	9,870	1.9	1.0	0.7,1.4
Rarely or never.	76,092	4.8	1.0	. . .	78,383	2.3	1.0	. . .
Restless								
Very often or often.	9,186	7.7	1.7	1.3,2.1	9,625	2.9	1.4	1.0,1.8
Sometimes	13,004	4.8	1.1	0.9,1.4	14,074	1.9	0.9	0.7,1.2
Rarely or never.	62,029	4.6	1.0	. . .	69,824	2.3	1.0	. . .
Bored								
Very often or often.	7,840	8.2	1.9	1.5,2.4	10,452	2.9	1.4	1.0,1.8
Sometimes	16,742	5.3	1.2	1.0,1.5	19,227	1.9	0.8	0.6,1.1
Rarely or never.	59,600	4.5	1.0	. . .	63,804	2.3	1.0	. . .
Upset								
Very often or often.	2,256	6.8	1.4	0.9,2.2	4,223	2.6	1.3	0.8,2.0
Sometimes	7,487	6.4	1.3	1.0,1.7	10,891	2.2	1.1	0.8,1.5
Rarely or never.	74,543	4.8	1.0	. . .	78,379	2.3	1.0	. . .

NOTES: The population columns represent the number of persons with specified levels of negative moods. Population estimates for heavier drinking (men: three or more drinks per day; women: 2 or more drinks per day) among these individuals can be derived by multiplying the population in a particular negative mood category by the prevalence estimates.

Source: Charlotte A. Schoenborn and John Horm, National Center for Health Statistics, *Negative Mood As Correlates of Smoking and Heavier Drinking: Implications for Health Promotion*, Advance Data, No. 236, November 4, 1993, Hyattsville, MD: National Center for Health Statistics. Table 2.

C2. PERSONAL HEALTH PRACTICES AND SPORTS

C2-1. Physician Contacts, by Sex and Age of Patient: 1992

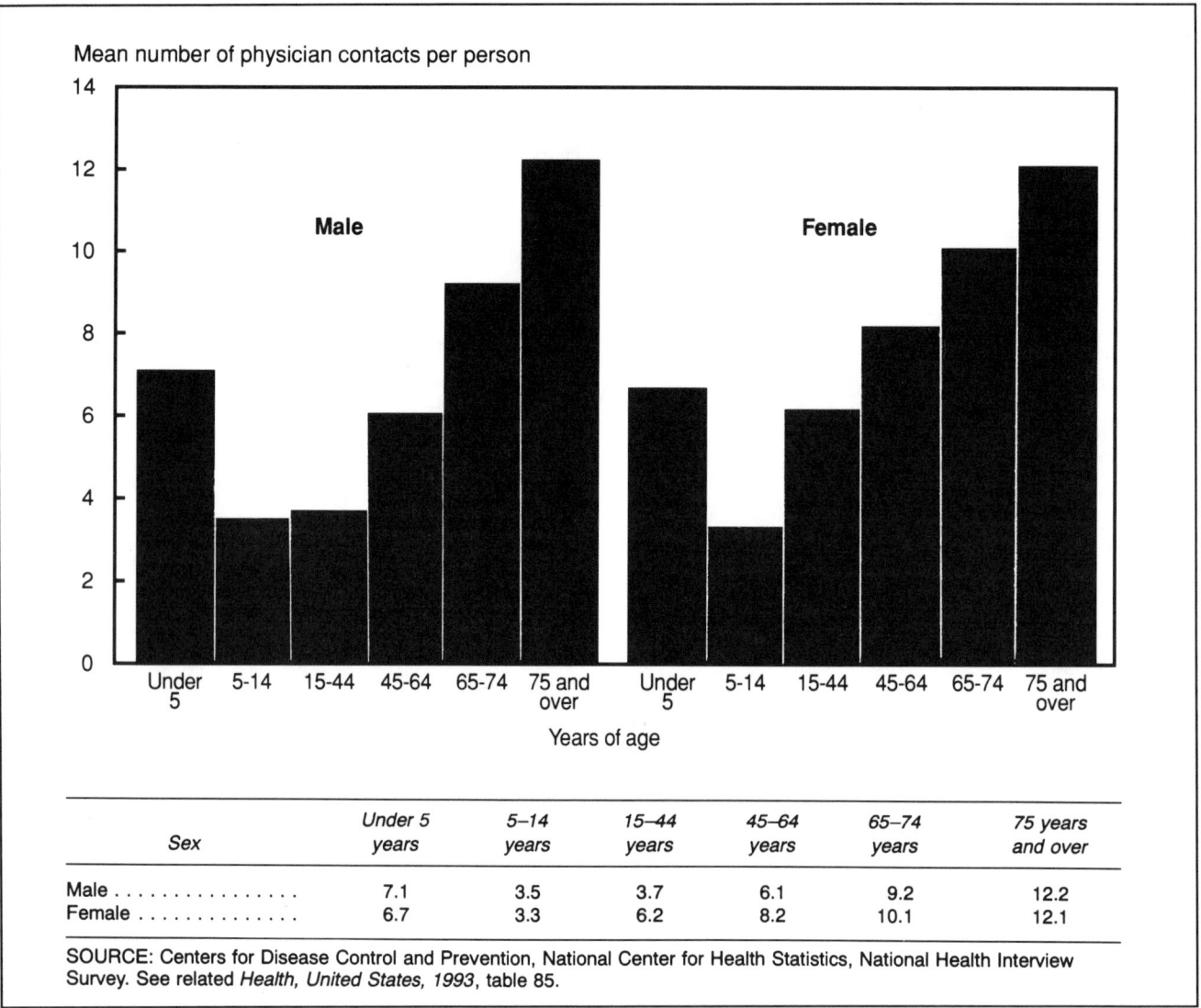

Mean number of physician contacts per person

Sex	Under 5 years	5–14 years	15–44 years	45–64 years	65–74 years	75 years and over
Male	7.1	3.5	3.7	6.1	9.2	12.2
Female	6.7	3.3	6.2	8.2	10.1	12.1

SOURCE: Centers for Disease Control and Prevention, National Center for Health Statistics, National Health Interview Survey. See related *Health, United States, 1993*, table 85.

Source: National Center for Health Statistics, *Health, United States, 1993*, (PHS) 94-1232, Washington, D.C.: U.S. Government Printing Office, 1994, Figure 25.

C2-2. Interval since Last Physician Contact, by Age and Sex: 1964, 1987, and 1992

[Data are based on household interviews of a sample of the civilian noninstitutionalized population]

Characteristic	Total	Less than 1 year			1 year–less than 2 years			2 years or more [1]		
		1964	1987	1992	1964	1987	1992	1964	1987	1992
					Percent distribution [2]					
Total [3,4]	100.0	66.9	76.6	78.4	14.0	10.6	10.1	19.1	12.8	11.4
Sex and age										
Male [3]	100.0	63.5	71.9	73.2	15.0	11.5	11.4	21.5	16.6	15.4
Under 15 years	100.0	- - -	81.6	83.9	- - -	10.8	10.0	- - -	7.6	6.1
15–44 years.	100.0	- - -	63.2	63.0	- - -	14.0	14.6	- - -	22.9	22.4
45–64 years.	100.0	- - -	70.4	72.3	- - -	10.2	10.3	- - -	19.4	17.4
65–74 years.	100.0	- - -	81.0	84.8	- - -	6.5	4.8	- - -	12.5	10.4
75 years and over	100.0	- - -	86.9	89.4	- - -	5.1	3.4	- - -	8.0	7.2
Female [3]	100.0	69.9	81.0	83.3	13.1	9.7	8.9	17.0	9.3	7.7
Under 15 years	100.0	- - -	81.6	83.3	- - -	11.5	10.4	- - -	7.0	6.3
15–44 years.	100.0	- - -	80.4	81.8	- - -	10.1	9.8	- - -	9.5	8.3
45–64 years.	100.0	- - -	79.1	83.3	- - -	8.5	7.3	- - -	12.4	9.4
65–74 years.	100.0	- - -	85.0	87.5	- - -	5.3	4.8	- - -	9.8	7.7
75 years and over	100.0	- - -	88.3	92.1	- - -	5.1	3.6	- - -	6.6	4.3

[1]Includes persons who never visited a physician.
[2]Denominator excludes persons with unknown interval.
[3]Age adjusted.
[4]Includes all other races not shown separately and unknown family income.
*Relative standard error greater than 30 percent.

Source: National Center for Health Statistics, *Health, United States, 1993,* (PHS) 94-1232, Washington, D.C.: U.S. Government Printing Office, 1994, Table 88.

C2-3. Percentage of Overweight Persons 20 Years and Over, by Sex, Age, Race, and Hispanic Origin: Selected Periods from 1960–62 to 1988–91

[Data are based on physical examinations of a sample of the civilian noninstitutionalized population]

Sex, age, race, and Hispanic origin [1]	1960–62	1971–74	1976–80 [2]	1988–91
20–74 years, age adjusted [3]		Percent of population		
Both sexes	24.4	24.9	25.4	33.3
Male	22.9	23.6	24.0	31.6
Female [4]	25.6	25.9	26.5	35.0
White male	23.1	23.8	24.2	32.0
White female [4]	23.5	24.0	24.4	33.5
Black male	22.2	24.3	25.7	31.5
Black female [4]	41.7	42.9	44.3	49.6
White, non-Hispanic male	- - -	- - -	24.1	32.1
White, non-Hispanic female [4]	- - -	- - -	23.9	32.4
Black, non-Hispanic male	- - -	- - -	25.6	31.5
Black, non-Hispanic female [4]	- - -	- - -	44.1	49.5
Mexican-American male	- - -	- - -	31.0	39.5
Mexican-American female [4]	- - -	- - -	41.4	47.9
20–74 years, crude				
Both sexes	25.5	25.5	25.7	33.7
Male	23.4	24.0	24.2	31.7
Female [4]	27.4	27.0	27.1	35.6
White male	23.7	24.2	24.4	32.4
White female [4]	25.4	25.2	25.1	34.3
Black male	22.5	24.5	25.7	31.2
Black female [4]	43.0	43.2	43.7	49.1
White, non-Hispanic male	- - -	- - -	24.4	32.7
White, non-Hispanic female [4]	- - -	- - -	24.8	33.3
Black, non-Hispanic male	- - -	- - -	25.6	31.2
Black, non-Hispanic female [4]	- - -	- - -	43.4	49.1
Mexican-American male	- - -	- - -	29.5	35.6
Mexican-American female [4]	- - -	- - -	39.1	47.1
Male				
20–34 years	19.6	19.2	17.3	22.2
35–44 years	22.8	29.4	28.9	35.3
45–54 years	28.1	27.6	31.0	35.6
55–64 years	26.9	24.8	28.1	40.1
65–74 years	21.8	23.0	25.2	42.9
75 years and over	- - -	- - -	- - -	26.4
Female [4]				
20–34 years	13.2	14.8	16.8	25.1
35–44 years	24.1	27.3	27.0	36.9
45–54 years	30.7	32.3	32.5	41.6
55–64 years	43.2	38.5	37.0	48.5
65–74 years	42.9	38.0	38.4	39.8
75 years and over	- - -	- - -	- - -	30.9

[1]The race groups, white and black, include persons of both Hispanic and non-Hispanic origin. Conversely, persons of Hispanic origin may be of any race.
[2]Data for Mexican-Americans are for 1982–84. See Appendix I.
[3]Age adjusted.
[4]Excludes pregnant women.

NOTES: Overweight is defined for men as body mass index greater than or equal to 27.8 kilograms/meter ^{2}, and for women as body mass index greater than or equal to 27.3 kilograms/meter ^{2}. These cut points were used because they represent the sex-specific 85th percentiles for persons 20–29 years of age in the 1976–80 National Health and Nutrition Examination Survey. Height was measured without shoes; two pounds are deducted from data for 1960–62 to allow for weight of clothing.

SOURCE: Centers for Disease Control and Prevention, National Center for Health Statistics, Division of Health Examination Statistics: Unpublished data.

Source: National Center for Health Statistics, *Health, United States, 1993,* (PHS) 94-1232, Washington, D.C.: U.S. Government Printing Office, 1994, Table 80.

C2-4. Use of Selected Substances in the Month before the Survey by Persons 12 Years Old and Over, by Age, Sex, Race, and Hispanic Origin: Selected Years 1974 to 1992

[Data are based on household interviews of a sample of the population 12 years of age and over in the coterminous United States]

Substance, age, sex, race, and Hispanic origin	1974	1976	1977	1979	1982	1985	1988	1990	1991	1992
Cigarettes					Percent of population					
12–17 years.................	25	23	22	(^{1})	15	15	12	12	11	10
12–13 years.................	13	11	10	(^{1})	*3	6	3	2	3	2
14–15 years.................	25	20	22	(^{1})	10	14	11	14	9	10
16–17 years.................	38	39	35	(^{1})	30	25	20	18	21	18
12–17 years:										
Male	27	21	23	(^{1})	16	16	12	12	12	10
Female...................	24	26	22	(^{1})	13	15	11	11	10	10
White, non-Hispanic	- - -	- - -	- - -	- - -	- - -	17	14	14	13	12
Black, non-Hispanic	- - -	- - -	- - -	- - -	- - -	9	5	4	4	3
Hispanic...................	- - -	- - -	- - -	- - -	- - -	11	8	11	9	7
Alcohol [2]										
12 years and over	54	52	54	60	55	59	53	51	51	48
12–17 years.................	34	32	31	37	27	31	25	25	20	16
12–13 years.................	19	19	13	20	10	11	7	8	7	4
14–15 years.................	32	31	28	36	23	35	23	26	19	15
16–17 years.................	51	47	52	55	45	46	42	38	35	30
18–25 years.................	69	69	70	76	68	71	65	63	64	59
26–34 years.................	68	68	70	70	71	70	64	63	62	61
35 years and over...........	49	52	50	58	52	57	52	49	49	46
12–17 years:										
Male	39	36	37	39	27	34	27	25	22	17
Female...................	29	29	25	36	27	29	23	24	18	15
White, non-Hispanic	- - -	- - -	- - -	- - -	- - -	35	27	28	20	17
Black, non-Hispanic	- - -	- - -	- - -	- - -	- - -	21	16	15	20	13
Hispanic...................	- - -	- - -	- - -	- - -	- - -	23	25	19	23	16
18–25 years:										
Male	- - -	79	82	84	75	78	75	74	70	66
Female...................	- - -	58	59	68	61	65	57	53	58	53
White, non-Hispanic	- - -	- - -	- - -	- - -	- - -	76	69	66	67	63
Black, non-Hispanic	- - -	- - -	- - -	- - -	- - -	58	50	59	56	51
Hispanic...................	- - -	- - -	- - -	- - -	- - -	58	61	57	53	53
Marijuana										
12 years and over	8	9	10	13	11	9	6	5	5	4
12–17 years.................	12	12	17	17	12	12	6	5	4	4
12–13 years.................	*2	*3	*4	4	*2	*4	1	*	*	1
14–15 years.................	12	13	16	17	8	11	5	5	4	4
16–17 years.................	20	21	30	28	23	21	12	10	9	8
18–25 years.................	25	25	27	35	27	22	15	13	13	11
26–34 years.................	8	11	12	17	17	17	11	9	7	8
35 years and over...........	*	1	1	2	3	2	1	2	2	2
12–17 years:										
Male	12	14	20	19	13	13	6	6	5	5
Female...................	11	11	13	14	10	11	7	4	4	3
White, non-Hispanic	- - -	- - -	- - -	- - -	- - -	13	7	6	4	4
Black, non-Hispanic	- - -	- - -	- - -	- - -	- - -	8	4	3	4	3
Hispanic...................	- - -	- - -	- - -	- - -	- - -	10	5	4	5	5
18–25 years:										
Male	- - -	31	35	45	36	27	20	17	16	15
Female...................	- - -	19	20	26	19	17	11	9	10	8
White, non-Hispanic	- - -	- - -	- - -	- - -	- - -	22	16	14	14	12
Black, non-Hispanic	- - -	- - -	- - -	- - -	- - -	24	15	13	15	11
Hispanic...................	- - -	- - -	- - -	- - -	- - -	15	14	8	9	8
Cocaine										
12 years and over	0.2	0.7	1.0	2.4	2.3	2.9	1.5	0.8	0.9	0.6
12–17 years.................	*1.0	*1.0	*0.8	1.4	1.6	1.5	1.1	0.6	0.4	0.3
18–25 years.................	3.1	2.0	3.7	9.3	6.8	7.6	4.5	2.2	2.0	1.8
26–34 years.................	- - -	- - -	- - -	- - -	3.3	6.1	2.6	1.7	1.8	1.4
35 years and over...........	- - -	- - -	- - -	- - -	0.5	0.5	0.4	0.2	0.5	0.2

See footnotes at end of table.

C2-4. Use of Selected Substances in the Month before the Survey by Persons 12 Years Old and Over, by Age, Sex, Race, and Hispanic Origin: Selected Years 1974 to 1992 *(continued)*

[Data are based on household interviews of a sample of the population 12 years of age and over in the coterminous United States]

Substance, age, sex, race, and Hispanic origin	1974	1976	1977	1979	1982	1985	1988	1990	1991	1992
Cocaine—Con.					Percent of population					
12–17 years:										
Male	- - -	- - -	- - -	- - -	1.8	2.0	0.9	0.7	0.5	0.2
Female	- - -	- - -	- - -	- - -	*1.5	*1.4	1.4	0.4	0.3	0.3
White, non-Hispanic	- - -	- - -	- - -	- - -	- - -	1.7	1.3	0.4	*0.3	0.1
Black, non-Hispanic	- - -	- - -	- - -	- - -	- - -	1.1	0.5	0.7	*0.5	0.2
Hispanic	- - -	- - -	- - -	- - -	- - -	2.7	1.3	1.9	1.3	1.2
18–25 years:										
Male	- - -	- - -	- - -	- - -	9.1	9.0	6.0	2.8	2.8	2.9
Female	- - -	- - -	- - -	- - -	4.7	6.2	3.0	1.6	1.3	0.8
White, non-Hispanic	- - -	- - -	- - -	- - -	- - -	8.0	4.1	1.9	1.7	2.0
Black, non-Hispanic	- - -	- - -	- - -	- - -	- - -	6.5	4.3	3.6	3.1	1.4
Hispanic	- - -	- - -	- - -	- - -	- - -	6.4	6.7	3.1	2.7	1.8

[1]Data not comparable because definitions differ.

[2]In surveys conducted in 1979 and later years, private answer sheets were used for alcohol questions; prior to 1979 respondents answered questions aloud.

*Relative standard error greater than 30 percent. Estimates with relative standard error greater than 50 percent are not shown.

NOTES: Estimates of the use of substances from the National Household Survey on Drug Abuse and the Monitoring the Future Study differ because of different methodologies, sampling frames, and tabulation categories. See Appendix I.

SOURCES: National Institute on Drug Abuse: National Household Survey on Drug Abuse: Main Findings, 1979, by P. M. Fishburne, H. I. Abelson, and I. Cisin. DHHS Pub. No. (ADM) 80-976. Alcohol, Drug Abuse, and Mental Health Administration. Washington. U.S. Government Printing Office, 1980; National Household Survey on Drug Abuse: Main Findings, 1982, by J. D. Miller et al. DHHS Pub. No. (ADM) 83-1263. Alcohol, Drug Abuse, and Mental Health Administration. Washington. U.S. Government Printing Office, 1983; National Household Survey on Drug Abuse: Main Findings, 1985. DHHS Pub. No. (ADM) 88-1586. National Household Survey on Drug Abuse: Main Findings, 1988; National Household Survey on Drug Abuse: Main Findings, 1990; National Household Survey on Drug Abuse: Main Findings, 1991; and Preliminary Estimates from the 1992 National Household Survey on Drug Abuse: Advance Report Number 3.

Source: National Center for Health Statistics, *Health, United States, 1993*, (PHS) 94-1232, Washington, D.C.: U.S. Government Printing Office, 1994, Table 74.

C2-5. Use of Selected Substances by High School Seniors and Eighth-Graders in the Month before the Survey and Binge Drinking in the Two Weeks before the Survey, by Sex and Race: Selected Years 1980 to 1993

[Data are based on a survey of high school seniors and eighth-graders in the coterminous United States]

Substance, sex, race, and grade in school	1980	1983	1984	1985	1986	1987	1988	1989	1990	1991	1992	1993
Cigarettes	Percent using substance in the past month											
All seniors	30.5	30.3	29.3	30.1	29.6	29.4	28.7	28.6	29.4	28.3	27.8	29.9
Male	26.8	28.0	25.9	28.2	27.9	27.0	28.0	27.7	29.1	29.0	29.2	30.7
Female	33.4	31.6	31.9	31.4	30.6	31.4	28.9	29.0	29.2	27.5	26.1	28.7
White	31.0	31.3	31.0	31.7	32.0	32.2	32.3	32.1	32.5	31.8	31.8	34.6
Black	25.2	21.2	17.6	18.7	14.6	13.9	12.8	12.4	12.0	9.4	8.2	10.9
All eighth-graders	---	---	---	---	---	---	---	---	---	14.3	15.5	16.7
Male	---	---	---	---	---	---	---	---	---	15.5	14.9	17.2
Female	---	---	---	---	---	---	---	---	---	13.1	15.9	16.3
White	---	---	---	---	---	---	---	---	---	15.0	17.4	18.1
Black	---	---	---	---	---	---	---	---	---	5.3	5.3	7.7
Marijuana												
All seniors	33.7	27.0	25.2	25.7	23.4	21.0	18.0	16.7	14.0	13.8	11.9	15.5
Male	37.8	31.0	28.2	28.7	26.8	23.1	20.7	19.5	16.1	16.1	13.4	18.2
Female	29.1	22.2	21.1	22.4	20.0	18.6	15.2	13.8	11.5	11.2	10.2	12.5
White	34.2	26.6	25.3	26.4	24.6	22.3	19.9	18.6	15.6	15.0	13.1	16.7
Black	26.5	26.9	22.8	21.7	16.6	12.4	9.8	9.4	5.2	6.5	5.6	10.8
All eighth-graders	---	---	---	---	---	---	---	---	---	3.2	3.7	5.1
Male	---	---	---	---	---	---	---	---	---	3.8	3.8	6.1
Female	---	---	---	---	---	---	---	---	---	2.6	3.5	4.1
White	---	---	---	---	---	---	---	---	---	3.0	3.5	4.6
Black	---	---	---	---	---	---	---	---	---	2.1	1.9	3.7
Cocaine												
All seniors	5.2	4.9	5.8	6.7	6.2	4.3	3.4	2.8	1.9	1.4	1.3	1.3
Male	6.0	5.7	7.0	7.7	7.2	4.9	4.2	3.6	2.3	1.7	1.5	1.7
Female	4.3	4.1	4.4	5.6	5.1	3.7	2.6	2.0	1.3	0.9	0.9	0.9
White	5.4	4.9	6.0	7.0	6.4	4.4	3.7	2.9	1.8	1.3	1.2	1.2
Black	2.0	3.0	2.4	2.7	2.7	1.8	1.4	1.2	0.5	0.8	0.5	0.4
All eighth-graders	---	---	---	---	---	---	---	---	---	0.5	0.7	0.7
Male	---	---	---	---	---	---	---	---	---	0.7	0.6	0.9
Female	---	---	---	---	---	---	---	---	---	0.4	0.8	0.6
White	---	---	---	---	---	---	---	---	---	0.4	0.6	0.5
Black	---	---	---	---	---	---	---	---	---	0.4	0.4	0.3
Inhalants												
All seniors	1.4	1.7	1.9	2.2	2.5	2.8	2.6	2.3	2.7	2.4	2.3	2.5
Male	1.8	2.4	2.5	2.8	3.2	3.4	3.2	3.1	3.5	3.3	3.0	3.2
Female	1.0	0.9	1.2	1.7	1.9	2.2	2.0	1.5	2.0	1.6	1.6	1.7
White	1.4	1.8	2.0	2.4	2.7	3.0	2.9	2.4	3.0	2.4	2.4	2.7
Black	1.0	1.0	1.2	0.8	1.5	1.8	1.8	1.1	1.5	1.5	1.5	1.3
All eighth-graders	---	---	---	---	---	---	---	---	---	4.4	4.7	5.4
Male	---	---	---	---	---	---	---	---	---	4.1	4.4	4.9
Female	---	---	---	---	---	---	---	---	---	4.7	4.9	6.0
White	---	---	---	---	---	---	---	---	---	4.5	5.0	5.8
Black	---	---	---	---	---	---	---	---	---	2.3	2.4	2.9

See footnotes at end of table.

C2-5. Use of Selected Substances by High School Seniors and Eighth-Graders in the Month before the Survey and Binge Drinking in the Two Weeks before the Survey, by Sex and Race: Selected Years 1980 to 1993 *(continued)*

[Data are based on a survey of high school seniors and eighth-graders in the coterminous United States]

Substance, sex, race, and grade in school	1980	1983	1984	1985	1986	1987	1988	1989	1990	1991	1992	1993
Alcohol	Percent using substance in the past month											
All seniors	72.0	69.4	67.2	65.9	65.3	66.4	63.9	60.0	57.1	54.0	51.3	51.0
Male	77.4	74.4	71.4	69.8	69.0	69.9	68.0	65.1	61.3	58.4	55.8	54.9
Female	66.8	64.3	62.8	62.1	61.9	63.1	59.9	54.9	52.3	49.0	46.8	46.7
White	75.8	73.5	72.1	70.2	70.2	71.8	69.5	65.3	62.2	57.7	56.0	54.8
Black	47.7	49.3	42.1	43.6	40.4	38.5	40.9	38.1	32.9	34.4	29.5	38.9
All eighth-graders	---	---	---	---	---	---	---	---	---	25.1	26.1	26.2
Male	---	---	---	---	---	---	---	---	---	26.3	26.3	26.7
Female	---	---	---	---	---	---	---	---	---	23.8	25.9	26.1
White	---	---	---	---	---	---	---	---	---	26.0	27.3	26.7
Black	---	---	---	---	---	---	---	---	---	17.8	19.2	20.6
Binge drinking [1]	Percent in last 2 weeks											
All seniors	41.2	40.8	38.7	36.7	36.8	37.5	34.7	33.0	32.2	29.8	27.9	27.5
Male	52.1	50.4	47.5	45.3	46.1	46.1	43.0	41.2	39.1	37.8	35.6	34.6
Female	30.5	31.0	29.6	28.2	28.1	29.2	26.5	24.9	24.4	21.2	20.3	20.7
White	44.6	44.4	42.9	40.1	40.5	41.2	38.8	36.9	36.2	32.9	31.3	31.3
Black	17.0	19.8	14.8	16.7	16.1	15.5	14.9	16.6	11.6	11.8	10.8	14.6
All eighth-graders	---	---	---	---	---	---	---	---	---	12.9	13.4	13.5
Male	---	---	---	---	---	---	---	---	---	14.3	13.9	14.8
Female	---	---	---	---	---	---	---	---	---	11.4	12.8	12.3
White	---	---	---	---	---	---	---	---	---	12.6	12.9	12.4
Black	---	---	---	---	---	---	---	---	---	9.9	9.3	11.9

[1]Five or more drinks in a row at least once in the prior 2-week period.

NOTES: Monitoring the Future Study excludes high school dropouts (about 15 percent of the age group during the 1980's) and absentees (about 16–19 percent of high school students). High school dropouts and absentees have higher drug usage than those included in the survey. Estimates of the use of substances from the National Household Survey on Drug Abuse and the Monitoring the Future Study differ because of different methodologies, sampling frames, and tabulation categories.

SOURCE: National Institute on Drug Abuse: Monitoring the Future Study: Annual surveys.

Source: National Center for Health Statistics, *Health, United States, 1993,* (PHS) 94-1232, Washington, D.C.: U.S. Government Printing Office, 1994, Table 75.

C2-6. Current Cigarette Smoking by Persons 18 Years of Age and Over, by Sex, Race, and Age: Selected Years 1965 to 1992

[Data are based on household interviews of a sample of the civilian noninstitutionalized population]

Sex, race, and age	1965	1974	1979	1983	1985	1987	1988	1990	1991	1992 [1]
All persons					Percent of persons 18 years of age and over					
18 years and over, age adjusted........	42.3	37.2	33.5	32.2	30.0	28.7	27.9	25.4	25.4	26.4
18 years and over, crude	42.4	37.1	33.5	32.1	30.1	28.8	28.1	25.5	25.6	26.5
All males										
18 years and over, age adjusted........	51.6	42.9	37.2	34.7	32.1	31.0	30.1	28.0	27.5	28.2
18 years and over, crude	51.9	43.1	37.5	35.1	32.6	31.2	30.8	28.4	28.1	28.6
18–24 years	54.1	42.1	35.0	32.9	28.0	28.2	25.5	26.6	23.5	28.0
25–34 years	60.7	50.5	43.9	38.8	38.2	34.8	36.2	31.6	32.8	32.8
35–44 years	58.2	51.0	41.8	41.0	37.6	36.6	36.5	34.5	33.1	32.9
45–64 years	51.9	42.6	39.3	35.9	33.4	33.5	31.3	29.3	29.3	28.6
65 years and over	28.5	24.8	20.9	22.0	19.6	17.2	18.0	14.6	15.1	16.1
White:										
18 years and over, age adjusted	50.8	41.7	36.5	34.1	31.3	30.4	29.5	27.6	27.0	28.0
18 years and over, crude...........	51.1	41.9	36.8	34.5	31.7	30.5	30.1	28.0	27.4	28.2
18–24 years	53.0	40.8	34.3	32.5	28.4	29.2	26.7	27.4	25.1	30.0
25–34 years	60.1	49.5	43.6	38.6	37.3	33.8	35.4	31.6	32.1	33.5
35–44 years	57.3	50.1	41.3	40.8	36.6	36.2	35.8	33.5	32.1	30.9
45–64 years	51.3	41.2	38.3	35.0	32.1	32.4	30.0	28.7	28.0	28.1
65 years and over	27.7	24.3	20.5	20.6	18.9	16.0	16.9	13.7	14.2	14.9
Black:										
18 years and over, age adjusted	59.2	54.0	44.1	41.3	39.9	39.0	36.5	32.2	34.7	32.0
18 years and over, crude...........	60.4	54.3	44.1	40.6	39.9	39.0	36.5	32.5	35.0	32.2
18–24 years	62.8	54.9	40.2	34.2	27.2	24.9	18.6	21.3	15.0	16.2
25–34 years	68.4	58.5	47.5	39.9	45.6	44.9	41.6	33.8	39.4	29.5
35–44 years	67.3	61.5	48.6	45.5	45.0	44.0	42.5	42.0	44.4	47.5
45–64 years	57.9	57.8	50.0	44.8	46.1	44.3	43.2	36.7	42.0	35.4
65 years and over	36.4	29.7	26.2	38.9	27.7	30.3	29.8	21.5	24.3	28.3
All females										
18 years and over, age adjusted........	34.0	32.5	30.3	29.9	28.2	26.7	26.0	23.1	23.6	24.8
18 years and over, crude	33.9	32.1	29.9	29.5	27.9	26.5	25.7	22.8	23.5	24.6
18–24 years	38.1	34.1	33.8	35.5	30.4	26.1	26.3	22.5	22.4	24.9
25–34 years	43.7	38.8	33.7	32.6	32.0	31.8	31.3	28.2	28.4	30.1
35–44 years	43.7	39.8	37.0	33.8	31.5	29.6	27.8	24.8	27.6	27.3
45–64 years	32.0	33.4	30.7	31.0	29.9	28.6	27.7	24.8	24.6	26.1
65 years and over	9.6	12.0	13.2	13.1	13.5	13.7	12.8	11.5	12.0	12.4
White:										
18 years and over, age adjusted	34.3	32.3	30.6	30.1	28.3	27.2	26.2	23.9	24.2	25.7
18 years and over, crude...........	34.0	31.7	30.1	29.4	27.7	26.7	25.7	23.4	23.7	25.1
18–24 years	38.4	34.0	34.5	36.5	31.8	27.8	27.5	25.4	25.1	28.5
25–34 years	43.4	38.6	34.1	32.2	32.0	31.9	31.0	28.5	28.4	31.5
35–44 years	43.9	39.3	37.2	34.8	31.0	29.2	28.3	25.0	27.0	27.6
45–64 years	32.7	33.0	30.6	30.6	29.7	29.0	27.7	25.4	25.3	25.8
65 years and over	9.8	12.3	13.8	13.2	13.3	13.9	12.6	11.5	12.1	12.6
Black:										
18 years and over, age adjusted	32.1	35.9	30.8	31.8	30.7	27.2	27.1	20.4	23.1	23.9
18 years and over, crude...........	33.7	36.4	31.1	32.2	31.0	28.0	27.8	21.2	24.4	24.2
18–24 years	37.1	35.6	31.8	32.0	23.7	20.4	21.8	10.0	11.8	10.3
25–34 years	47.8	42.2	35.2	38.0	36.2	35.8	37.2	29.1	32.4	26.9
35–44 years	42.8	46.4	37.7	32.7	40.2	35.3	27.6	25.5	35.3	32.4
45–64 years	25.7	38.9	34.2	36.3	33.4	28.4	29.5	22.6	23.4	30.9
65 years and over	7.1	8.9	8.5	13.1	14.5	11.7	14.8	11.1	9.6	11.1

[1]Data for 1992 are not strictly comparable with data for earlier years. Beginning in 1992 the definition of current smoker was modified to specifically include persons who smoked only "some days." Prior to 1992, a current smoker was defined by the questions "Have you ever smoked 100 cigarettes in your lifetime?" and "Do you smoke now?" (traditional definition). In 1992, data were collected for half the respondents using the traditional smoking questions, and for the other half of respondents using a revised smoking question ("Do you smoke everyday, some days, or not at all?"). An unpublished analysis of the 1992 traditional smoking measure revealed that the crude percent of current smokers age 18 and over remained the same as 1991. The figures shown for 1992 in this table combine data collected using the traditional and the revised questions. Future estimates of smoking prevalence will be based on the revised definition which is considered a more complete estimate of smoking prevalence.

SOURCE: Centers for Disease Control and Prevention, National Center for Health Statistics, Division of Health Interview Statistics: Data from the National Health Interview Survey; data computed by the Division of Epidemiology and Health Promotion from data compiled by the Division of Health Interview Statistics.

Source: National Center for Health Statistics, *Health, United States, 1993,* (PHS) 94-1232, Washington, D.C.: U.S. Government Printing Office, 1994, Table 72.

C2-7. Percentage of Children under 18 Years Old Who Lived in a Household with a Smoker in the Year before the Survey, by Age and Sex of Child: 1988

Selected family characteristic	All ages	Less than 1 year	1–2 years	3–4 years	5–11 years	12–17 years
All children	43.8	38.5	42.9	41.2	44.5	45.2
Sex						
Male	44.1	39.2	42.8	42.0	44.7	45.6
Female	43.4	37.7	42.9	40.3	44.2	44.7

Source: M. J. Coiro, N. Zill, and B. Bloom, National Center for Health Statistics, *Health of Our Nation's Children*, Vital Health Statistics, Series 10, No. 191, Hyattsville, MD: National Center for Health Statistics, 1994, Table 17.

C2-8. Age-Adjusted Prevalence of Current Cigarette Smoking of Persons 25 Years and Over, by Sex, Race, and Education: Selected Years 1974 to 1992

[Data are based on household interviews of a sample of the civilian noninstitutionalized population]

Sex, race, and education	1974	1979	1983	1985	1987	1988	1990	1991	1992 [1]
	Percent of persons 25 years of age and over, age adjusted								
All persons [2]	37.1	33.3	31.7	30.2	29.1	28.4	25.6	26.0	26.5
Less than 12 years	43.8	41.1	40.8	41.0	40.6	39.4	36.7	37.4	36.7
12 years	36.4	33.7	33.6	32.1	31.8	31.8	29.3	29.7	30.7
13–15 years	35.8	33.2	30.3	29.7	27.2	26.4	23.5	24.7	24.6
16 or more years	27.5	22.8	20.7	18.6	16.7	16.3	14.1	13.9	15.3
All males [2]	43.0	37.6	35.1	32.9	31.5	31.1	28.3	28.4	28.2
Less than 12 years	52.4	48.1	47.2	46.0	45.7	44.9	41.8	42.4	41.2
12 years	42.6	39.1	37.4	35.6	35.2	35.2	33.2	32.9	33.3
13–15 years	41.6	36.5	33.0	33.0	28.4	29.0	25.9	27.2	26.1
16 or more years	28.6	23.1	21.8	19.7	17.3	17.2	14.6	14.8	15.8
White males [2]	41.9	36.9	34.5	31.9	30.6	30.1	27.7	27.3	27.6
Less than 12 years	51.6	48.0	47.9	45.2	45.3	44.8	41.7	41.8	41.4
12 years	42.2	38.6	37.1	34.8	34.6	34.2	33.0	32.4	32.9
13–15 years	41.4	36.4	32.6	32.3	28.0	28.2	25.4	26.0	25.9
16 or more years	28.1	22.8	21.1	19.2	17.4	17.1	14.5	14.7	15.0
Black males [2]	53.8	44.9	42.8	42.5	41.9	40.3	34.5	38.8	35.3
Less than 12 years	58.3	50.1	46.0	51.1	49.4	45.3	41.4	47.8	44.5
12 years	*51.2	48.4	47.2	41.9	43.6	48.3	37.4	39.6	38.7
13–15 years	*45.7	39.3	44.7	42.3	32.4	34.8	28.3	32.7	27.0
16 or more years	*41.8	*37.9	*31.3	*32.0	20.9	21.5	20.6	18.3	*26.9
All females [2]	32.2	29.6	28.8	27.8	26.9	25.9	23.2	23.9	24.8
Less than 12 years	36.8	35.0	35.3	36.7	36.1	34.5	32.1	33.0	32.4
12 years	32.5	29.9	30.9	29.6	29.2	29.1	26.3	27.1	28.7
13–15 years	30.2	30.0	27.5	26.7	26.0	24.1	21.1	22.5	23.3
16 or more years	26.1	22.5	19.2	17.4	16.1	15.3	13.6	12.8	14.6
White females [2]	31.9	29.8	28.8	27.6	27.0	25.9	23.6	24.0	25.1
Less than 12 years	37.0	36.1	35.5	37.1	37.0	35.2	33.6	33.7	33.1
12 years	32.1	29.9	30.9	29.4	29.4	29.3	26.8	27.5	29.5
13–15 years	30.5	30.6	28.0	27.1	26.2	23.8	21.4	22.3	23.6
16 or more years	25.8	21.9	18.9	16.8	16.4	15.1	13.7	13.3	14.2
Black females [2]	35.9	30.6	31.8	32.1	28.6	28.2	22.6	25.5	26.8
Less than 12 years	36.4	31.9	36.9	39.2	35.0	33.9	26.8	33.3	33.2
12 years	41.9	33.0	35.2	32.3	28.1	30.1	24.0	26.0	25.9
13–15 years	33.2	*28.8	26.5	23.7	27.2	26.8	23.1	24.8	27.0
16 or more years	*35.2	*43.4	*38.7	27.5	19.5	22.2	16.9	14.4	*25.8

[1] Data for 1992 are not strictly comparable with data for earlier years. Beginning in 1992 the definition of current smoker was modified to specifically include persons who smoked only "some days." Prior to 1992, a current smoker was defined by the questions "Have you ever smoked 100 cigarettes in your lifetime?" and "Do you smoke now?" (traditional definition). In 1992, data were collected for half the respondents using the traditional smoking questions, and for the other half of respondents using a revised smoking question ("Do you smoke everyday, some days, or not at all?"). An unpublished analysis of the 1992 traditional smoking measure revealed that the crude percent of current smokers age 18 and over remained the same as 1991. The figures shown for 1992 in this table combine data collected using the traditional and the revised questions. Future estimates of smoking prevalence will be based on the revised definition which is considered a more complete estimate of smoking prevalence.
[2] Includes unknown education.

*These age-adjusted percents should be considered unreliable because of small sample size. For age groups where percent smoking was 0 or 100 the age-adjustment procedure was modified to substitute the percent from the next lower education group.

SOURCE: Data computed by the Centers for Disease Control and Prevention, National Center for Health Statistics, Division of Epidemiology and Health Promotion from data compiled by the Division of Health Interview Statistics.

Source: National Center for Health Statistics, *Health, United States, 1993*, (PHS)94-1232, Washington, D.C.: U.S. Government Printing Office, 1994, Table 73.

C2-9. Number of Live Births by Smoking Status of Mother, Percent Smokers, and Percent Distribution, by Average Number of Cigarettes Smoked per Day by Mothers, According to Age and Race of Mother: 1991 (46 Reporting States and the District of Columbia)

Smoking status, smoking measure, and race of mother	All ages	Under 15 years	Age of mother							
			15–19 years			20–24 years	25–29 years	30–34 years	35–39 years	40–49 years
			Total	15–17 years	18–19 years					
All races [1]					Number					
Total	3,111,544	9,720	409,564	148,200	261,364	837,451	921,862	658,395	238,127	36,425
Smoker	531,683	705	77,869	23,641	54,228	170,870	152,176	95,538	30,368	4,157
Nonsmoker	2,461,074	8,619	316,911	119,070	197,841	636,607	734,930	535,885	197,438	30,684
Not stated	118,787	396	14,784	5,489	9,295	29,974	34,756	26,972	10,321	1,584
White										
Total	2,439,406	3,718	267,183	88,880	178,303	626,992	758,240	554,765	198,936	29,572
Smoker	441,529	557	67,471	20,354	47,117	143,914	124,703	77,396	24,204	3,284
Nonsmoker	1,905,945	2,982	189,974	65,147	124,827	461,149	605,622	455,041	166,159	25,018
Not stated	91,932	179	9,738	3,379	6,359	21,929	27,915	22,328	8,573	1,270
Black										
Total	563,205	5,739	130,715	55,100	75,615	184,569	130,874	78,026	28,589	4,693
Smoker	79,143	119	8,431	2,593	5,838	23,434	24,636	16,346	5,434	743
Nonsmoker	462,165	5,411	117,724	50,578	67,146	154,145	100,858	58,331	21,951	3,745
Not stated	21,897	209	4,560	1,929	2,631	6,990	5,380	3,349	1,204	205
					Percent					
Smoker [1]	17.8	7.6	19.7	16.6	21.5	21.2	17.2	15.1	13.3	11.9
White	18.8	15.7	26.2	23.8	27.4	23.8	17.1	14.5	12.7	11.6
Black	14.6	2.2	6.7	4.9	8.0	13.2	19.6	21.9	19.8	16.6
All races [1]					Percent distribution					
Smoker	100.0	100.0	100.0	100.0	100.0	100.0	100.0	100.0	100.0	100.0
1–5 cigarettes	20.7	36.7	26.2	30.1	24.5	20.8	19.5	18.7	18.0	17.7
6–10 cigarettes	39.8	42.6	43.0	43.5	42.8	40.9	39.1	37.9	36.2	34.8
11–15 cigarettes	6.4	*	5.0	4.4	5.3	6.2	7.0	7.0	6.2	6.2
16–20 cigarettes	27.4	16.2	22.4	19.2	23.8	27.1	28.5	29.1	30.1	30.6
21–30 cigarettes	4.0	*	2.4	2.0	2.6	3.5	4.2	5.0	6.0	6.7
31–40 cigarettes	1.5	*	0.8	0.7	0.8	1.2	1.5	2.1	3.1	3.4
41 cigarettes or more	0.2	*	0.2	0.2	0.2	0.2	0.2	0.3	0.4	0.6
White										
Smoker	100.0	100.0	100.0	100.0	100.0	100.0	100.0	100.0	100.0	100.0
1–5 cigarettes	18.0	30.3	23.3	27.0	21.7	17.8	16.9	16.5	16.0	15.5
6–10 cigarettes	39.2	47.3	43.6	44.6	43.1	40.5	38.0	36.6	34.5	33.6
11–15 cigarettes	7.0	*	5.5	4.8	5.7	6.9	7.7	7.7	6.8	6.5
16–20 cigarettes	29.5	17.6	24.1	20.6	25.6	29.4	30.9	31.1	32.0	32.4
21–30 cigarettes	4.4	*	2.6	2.2	2.8	3.9	4.7	5.6	6.9	7.3
31–40 cigarettes	1.6	*	0.8	0.7	0.9	1.3	1.7	2.2	3.5	3.9
41 cigarettes or more	0.2	*	0.2	0.2	0.2	0.2	0.2	0.3	0.4	0.6
Black										
Smoker	100.0	100.0	100.0	100.0	100.0	100.0	100.0	100.0	100.0	100.0
1–5 cigarettes	33.8	63.2	46.4	51.8	44.0	37.4	31.6	28.4	25.9	26.2
6–10 cigarettes	43.0	25.5	39.2	35.7	40.8	43.3	44.1	43.4	42.9	38.6
11–15 cigarettes	3.2	*	2.0	1.9	2.1	2.7	3.4	3.9	3.8	4.7
16–20 cigarettes	16.8	*	10.7	9.1	11.4	14.2	17.6	20.4	22.8	24.1
21–30 cigarettes	1.9	*	0.9	*	1.0	1.5	1.9	2.4	2.5	4.4
31–40 cigarettes	1.0	*	0.6	*	0.6	0.7	1.1	1.3	1.7	*
41 cigarettes or more	0.2	*	*	*	*	0.2	0.2	0.2	*	*

[1] Includes races other than white and black.

NOTE: Excludes data for California, Indiana, New York, and South Dakota, which did not require reporting of tobacco use during pregnancy.

Source: S. J. Ventura, S. M. Taffel, and T. J. Mathews, National Center for Health Statistics, *Advance Report of Maternal and Infant Health Data from the Birth Certificate, 1991*, Monthly Vital Statistics Report, Vol. 42, No. 11 (suppl.), Washington, D.C.: U.S. Department of Health and Human Services, May 11, 1994, Table 2.

C2-10. Number of Live Births, Percentage of Mothers Who Smoked Cigarettes during Pregnancy, and Percent Distribution of Average Number of Cigarettes Smoked per Day by Mothers, According to Educational Attainment and Race of Mother: 1991 (45 Reporting States and the District of Columbia)

Smoking measure and race of mother	Total	0–8 years	9–11 years	12 years	13–15 years	16 years or more	Not stated
				All births			
All races[1]	3,031,833	138,435	522,705	1,156,115	622,388	550,802	41,388
White	2,368,796	110,811	353,621	886,101	502,083	487,932	28,248
Black	560,122	19,902	152,742	235,811	102,608	39,009	10,050
				Percent			
Smoker[1]	17.7	18.3	31.9	20.6	12.4	4.2	16.2
White	18.8	20.2	37.4	22.6	12.8	4.2	16.3
Black	14.6	12.0	20.1	14.2	11.0	5.2	19.5
All races[1]				Percent distribution			
Smoker	100.0	100.0	100.0	100.0	100.0	100.0	100.0
10 cigarettes or less	60.4	54.7	59.0	59.9	63.4	72.4	60.5
11–20 cigarettes	33.8	36.4	34.6	34.7	31.6	24.0	33.6
21 cigarettes or more	5.8	9.0	6.4	5.4	5.0	3.6	5.9
White							
Smoker	100.0	100.0	100.0	100.0	100.0	100.0	100.0
10 cigarettes or less	57.1	52.3	54.6	56.6	60.7	71.7	55.5
11–20 cigarettes	36.6	38.2	38.2	37.4	33.9	24.6	37.5
21 cigarettes or more	6.3	9.5	7.1	5.9	5.4	3.7	7.0
Black							
Smoker	100.0	100.0	100.0	100.0	100.0	100.0	100.0
10 cigarettes or less	76.8	72.7	76.1	77.6	77.7	78.5	71.9
11–20 cigarettes	20.1	22.1	20.3	19.7	19.6	19.7	24.6
21 cigarettes or more	3.1	5.2	3.7	2.6	2.7	1.8	3.5

[1]Includes races other than white and black.

NOTE: Excludes data for California, Indiana, New York, South Dakota, and Washington, which did not require reporting of either tobacco use during pregnancy or educational attainment of mother.

Source: S. J. Ventura, S. M. Taffel, and T. J. Mathews, National Center for Health Statistics, *Advance Report of Maternal and Infant Health Data from the Birth Certificate, 1991*, Monthly Vital Statistics Report, Vol. 42, No. 11 (suppl.), Washington, D.C.: U.S. Department of Health and Human Services, May 11, 1994, Table 4.

C2-11. Percent Low Birthweight by Smoking Status, Age, and Race of Mother: Total of 46 Reporting States and the District of Columbia, 1991

[Low birthweight is defined as weight of less than 2,500 grams (5 lb 8 oz)]

Smoking status and race of mother	All ages	Under 15 years	15–19 years			20–24 years	25–29 years	30–34 years	35–39 years	40–49 years
			Total	15–17 years	18–19 years					
All races[1]	7.3	14.3	9.7	10.6	9.2	7.5	6.4	6.6	7.7	8.7
Smoker	11.4	15.5	10.8	11.6	10.5	10.2	11.3	12.8	15.1	17.1
Nonsmoker	6.4	14.1	9.3	10.4	8.7	6.7	5.3	5.5	6.5	7.4
Not stated	8.9	16.5	11.2	12.3	10.6	9.4	7.8	8.2	9.3	10.6
White	5.9	11.7	7.9	8.7	7.4	6.0	5.2	5.4	6.5	7.3
Smoker	9.6	14.1	10.2	11.2	9.8	8.9	9.2	10.0	12.5	14.7
Nonsmoker	5.0	11.3	7.0	7.9	6.5	5.0	4.3	4.6	5.6	6.3
Not stated	7.1	*	9.3	10.5	8.6	7.4	6.2	6.8	7.7	9.4
Black	13.6	16.2	13.6	13.8	13.4	12.7	13.4	15.1	16.0	17.0
Smoker	21.8	22.7	16.9	15.6	17.5	18.9	22.3	25.9	27.2	27.5
Nonsmoker	12.1	15.8	13.3	13.7	12.9	11.7	11.0	11.9	12.9	14.8
Not stated	16.6	22.2	15.5	15.6	15.5	15.7	16.5	18.3	20.7	19.3

[1]Includes races other than white and black.

NOTE: Excludes data for California, Indiana, New York, and South Dakota, which did not require reporting of tobacco use during pregnancy.

Source: S. J. Ventura, S. M. Taffel, and T. J. Mathews, National Center for Health Statistics, *Advance Report of Maternal and Infant Health Data from the Birth Certificate, 1991*, Monthly Vital Statistics Report, Vol. 42, No. 11 (suppl.), Washington, D.C.: U.S. Department of Health and Human Services, May 11, 1994, Table 5.

C2-12. Alcohol Consumption by Persons 18 Years of Age and Over, by Sex, Race, Hispanic Origin, and Age, 1985 and 1990

[Data are based on household interviews of a sample of the civilian noninstitutionalized population]

Alcohol consumption, race, Hispanic origin, and age	Both sexes		Male		Female	
	1985	1990	1985	1990	1985	1990
Drinking status	Percent distribution					
All	100.0	100.0	100.0	100.0	100.0	100.0
Abstainer	26.9	29.7	14.4	16.6	38.0	41.5
Former drinker	7.5	9.6	9.2	11.6	6.1	7.8
Current drinker	65.6	60.7	76.4	71.8	55.9	50.7
	Percent current drinkers among all persons					
All races:						
18–44 years.	72.8	67.5	82.4	77.1	63.8	58.3
18–24 years	71.8	63.7	79.5	71.7	64.5	56.1
25–44 years	73.2	68.8	83.5	78.9	63.5	59.0
45 years and over	55.5	51.3	67.4	63.8	45.6	40.8
45–64 years	62.2	57.6	72.2	68.4	53.0	47.6
65 years and over	44.3	41.4	58.2	55.6	34.7	31.3
White, non-Hispanic:						
18–44 years.	76.9	72.7	85.0	80.4	68.9	65.1
18–24 years	77.9	71.5	84.9	77.5	71.0	65.7
25–44 years	76.5	73.1	85.0	81.2	68.2	65.0
45 years and over	57.6	53.8	69.0	65.5	48.2	44.0
45–64 years	65.2	61.0	74.1	70.6	56.9	52.2
65 years and over	45.8	43.3	59.6	57.1	36.2	33.3
Black, non-Hispanic:						
18–44 years.	59.0	51.5	72.2	68.1	48.2	37.9
45 years and over	41.5	36.0	57.1	51.3	29.9	24.5
Hispanic:						
18–44 years.	58.7	55.7	73.2	71.3	45.6	42.0
45 years and over	48.5	43.4	64.3	63.3	35.4	27.8
Level of alcohol consumption in past 2 weeks for current drinkers	Percent distribution of current drinkers					
All drinking levels	100.0	100.0	100.0	100.0	100.0	100.0
None	21.6	24.1	18.0	20.3	26.1	29.1
Light.	37.1	39.4	30.9	33.9	44.7	46.4
Moderate	29.5	27.4	34.0	32.3	24.0	21.1
Heavier.	11.8	9.1	17.2	13.6	5.3	3.4
	Percent heavier drinkers among current drinkers					
All races:						
18–44 years.	11.0	8.5	16.6	13.0	4.2	2.8
18–24 years	12.2	8.8	18.3	13.8	5.0	2.7
25–44 years	10.6	8.4	16.0	12.7	3.8	2.9
45 years and over	13.3	10.3	18.2	14.7	7.4	4.6
45–64 years	13.2	9.9	18.1	14.4	7.2	4.1
65 years and over	13.6	11.0	18.4	15.3	7.9	5.5
White, non-Hispanic:						
18–44 years.	11.2	8.5	17.1	13.2	4.0	2.8
18–24 years	13.3	9.9	20.4	16.0	5.2	3.0
25–44 years	10.4	8.1	16.0	12.4	3.6	2.7
45 years and over	13.4	10.4	18.2	15.0	7.6	4.7
45–64 years	13.2	10.0	18.0	14.6	7.3	4.2
65 years and over	13.9	11.3	18.7	15.8	8.3	5.7
Black, non-Hispanic:						
18–44 years.	9.6	10.3	13.4	14.7	5.1	3.9
45 years and over	10.3	7.7	16.2	10.1	*	*
Hispanic:						
18–44 years.	10.6	7.9	15.2	11.3	*	*
45 years and over	15.7	12.1	*	17.2	*	*

*Estimates based on fewer than 30 subjects are not shown.

NOTES: Abstainers consumed less than 12 drinks in any single year. Former drinkers consumed 12 or more drinks in any single year, but no drinks in the past year. Current drinkers consumed 12 or more drinks in a single year and at least 1 drink in the past year. For current drinkers, drinking levels are classified according to the average daily consumption of absolute alcohol (ethanol), in ounces, in the previous 2-week period, assuming 0.5 ounce ethanol per drink, as follows: none; light, .01–.21; moderate, .22–.99; and heavier, 1.00 or more. This corresponds to up to 3, 4–13, and 14 or more drinks per week for light, moderate, and heavier drinkers.

SOURCE: Data computed by the Alcohol Epidemiologic Data System of the National Institute on Alcohol Abuse and Alcoholism from data in the National Health Interview Survey compiled by the Division of Health Interview Statistics, National Center for Health Statistics, Centers for Disease Control and Prevention.

Source: National Center for Health Statistics, *Health, United States, 1993*, (PHS) 94-1232, Washington, D.C.: U.S. Government Printing Office, 1994, Table 77.

C2-13. Number of Live Births by Drinking Status of Mother, Percent Drinkers, and Percent Distribution, by Average Numbers of Drinks per Week, According to Age and Race of Mother 1991 (47 Reporting States and the District of Columbia)

Drinking status, drinking measure, and race of mother	All ages	Under 15 years	Age of mother							
			15–19 years			20–24 years	25–29 years	30–34 years	35–39 years	40–49 years
			Total	15–17 years	18–19 years					
All races[1]					Number					
Total	3,197,251	9,934	421,712	152,295	269,417	862,959	947,856	674,423	243,253	37,114
Drinker	88,411	82	6,542	2,050	4,492	19,274	27,006	24,257	9,789	1,461
Nondrinker	2,979,981	9,419	398,983	144,276	254,707	810,923	883,339	621,011	222,350	33,956
Not stated	128,859	433	16,187	5,969	10,218	32,762	37,511	29,155	11,114	1,697
White										
Total	2,514,797	3,827	276,715	91,862	184,853	649,078	781,941	569,463	203,578	30,195
Drinker	66,388	47	4,604	1,438	3,166	13,340	19,895	19,337	7,964	1,201
Nondrinker	2,348,377	3,580	261,290	86,701	174,589	611,582	731,901	526,009	186,383	27,632
Not stated	100,032	200	10,821	3,723	7,098	24,156	30,145	24,117	9,231	1,362
Black										
Total	572,715	5,844	133,280	56,200	77,080	187,836	132,886	79,139	28,985	4,745
Drinker	18,842	26	1,486	449	1,037	5,034	6,230	4,295	1,561	210
Nondrinker	530,395	5,592	126,959	53,704	73,255	175,340	120,855	71,209	26,124	4,316
Not stated	23,478	226	4,835	2,047	2,788	7,462	5,801	3,635	1,300	219
					Percent					
Drinker[1]	2.9	0.9	1.6	1.4	1.7	2.3	3.0	3.8	4.2	4.1
White	2.7	1.3	1.7	1.6	1.8	2.1	2.6	3.5	4.1	4.2
Black	3.4	0.5	1.2	0.8	1.4	2.8	4.9	5.7	5.6	4.6
All races[1]					Percent distribution					
Drinker	100.0	100.0	100.0	100.0	100.0	100.0	100.0	100.0	100.0	100.0
1 drink or less	61.8	51.1	62.8	61.3	63.5	59.5	61.5	63.7	61.5	59.6
2 drinks	15.7	*	13.5	14.7	12.9	15.5	15.8	15.6	17.2	17.7
3–4 drinks	10.3	*	11.2	10.6	11.5	11.3	10.2	9.6	10.2	9.1
5 drinks or more	12.2	*	12.5	13.3	12.1	13.7	12.6	11.2	11.1	13.5
White										
Drinker	100.0	100.0	100.0	100.0	100.0	100.0	100.0	100.0	100.0	100.0
1 drink or less	68.4	*	66.6	64.7	67.5	66.3	69.5	70.0	66.7	63.8
2 drinks	14.5	*	12.3	12.8	12.1	13.4	14.1	14.9	16.7	17.8
3–4 drinks	8.6	*	9.8	10.3	9.6	9.9	8.1	8.0	8.8	7.8
5 drinks or more	8.5	*	11.2	12.2	10.8	10.3	8.3	7.2	7.8	10.6
Black										
Drinker	100.0	100.0	100.0	100.0	100.0	100.0	100.0	100.0	100.0	100.0
1 drink or less	38.5	*	52.4	52.6	52.3	42.6	36.4	34.6	33.6	34.9
2 drinks	20.6	*	17.3	21.5	15.6	21.3	21.7	19.2	20.4	19.2
3–4 drinks	16.2	*	15.0	10.9	16.6	14.8	16.8	16.8	17.3	15.8
5 drinks or more	24.8	*	15.3	15.0	15.5	21.4	25.1	29.3	28.8	30.1

[1]Includes races other than white and black.

NOTE: Excludes data for California, New York, and South Dakota, which did not require reporting of alcohol use during pregnancy.

Source: S. J. Ventura, S. M. Taffel, and T. J. Mathews, National Center for Health Statistics, *Advance Report of Maternal and Infant Health Data from the Birth Certificate, 1991*, Monthly Vital Statistics Report, Vol. 42, No. 11 (suppl.), Washington, D.C.: U.S. Department of Health and Human Services, May 11, 1994, Table 6.

C2-14. Number and Percent of Women Aged 15 to 44 Ever Tested for Human Immunodeficiency Virus (HIV) Infection, by Marital Status and Selected Risk Factors: 1990

Characteristic	Number of women in thousands	Percent ever tested	
		Self-reported tests[1]	All tests[2]
All women[3]	58,381	25.6	34.9
Race and ethnic origin			
Hispanic	5,547	23.8	29.8
Black, not Hispanic	7,526	28.5	34.8
White, not Hispanic	42,836	25.4	35.8
Education[4]			
Less than 12 years	5,618	24.6	31.0
12 years	17,247	23.1	31.3
13 years or more.	27,033	28.6	39.9
Marital status			
Never married.	20,123	26.0	35.7
Married.	31,417	23.6	32.5
Formerly married.	6,841	33.5	43.4
Age			
15–19 years.	8,483	21.5	28.7
20–24 years.	9,154	27.0	40.8
25–29 years.	10,637	33.4	40.9
30–34 years.	11,091	27.5	37.1
35–39 years.	10,111	22.0	31.5
40–44 years.	8,905	20.3	28.5
Residence in metropolitan area[5]			
MSA, central city.	12,727	31.9	39.9
MSA, other	29,981	26.1	36.4
Non–MSA	11,979	21.4	32.4
Region [5]			
Northeast	11,226	28.2	36.9
South.	18,603	28.0	39.5
Midwest	14,453	23.8	34.0
West	10,405	25.4	33.5
Poverty-level income[6]			
0–149 percent	7,918	28.1	35.5
150 percent or more	41,980	25.9	36.0

[1]Includes only tests reported in response to the question: "Have you ever had your blood tested for infection with the AIDS virus?"
[2]Category includes all tests for HIV infection, including those done in connection with blood donation.
[3]Includes "other" races and women whose HIV testing status was unknown; not shown separately because of small sample size.
[4]Women 20–44 years of age only.
[5]This variable was collected during the 1988 survey.
[6]Ratio of total family income to poverty level. Women 20–44 years of age only.

NOTES: MSA is metropolitan statistical area. AIDS is acquired immunodeficiency syndrome. HIV is human immunodeficiency virus.

Source: Jacqueline B. Wilson, National Center for Health Statistics, *Human Immunodeficiency Virus Antibody Testing In Women 15–44 Years of Age: United States, 1990*, Advance Data, No. 238, December 22, 1993, Hyattsville, MD: National Center for Health Statistics. Table 1.

C2-15. Breast Examination and Mammograms, by Selected Characteristics of Women: 1990

Risk factor	Total	Curently married	Formerly married	Never married	Currently married	Formerly married	Never married
		Number in thousands			Percent		
All women[1]	20,363	10,209	2,967	7,187	32.5	43.4	35.7
Ever had a sexually transmitted disease[2]							
Yes	2,670	1,039	652	978	34.7	54.1	49.5
No..........................	17,693	9,169	2,315	6,209	32.3	41.1	34.2
Ever had pelvic inflammatory disease							
Yes	2,673	1,326	590	757	30.0	36.6	43.3
No..........................	17,690	8,883	2,377	6,430	32.9	45.5	35.0
Number of lifetime male sexual partners							
Never had intercourse	871	– – –	– – –	871	– – –	– – –	*17.4
1 man........................	3,919	2,953	36	929	29.7	12.2	33.7
2–5 men.......................	8,959	4,299	1,457	3,203	30.9	42.9	41.5
6 or more men	6,615	2,957	1,474	2,184	39.1	46.9	47.2
Age at first intercourse							
Never had intercourse	871	– – –	– – –	871	– – –	– – –	*17.4
Under 15 years...................	1,858	781	320	756	39.1	40.7	35.7
15–17 years.....................	8,381	3,829	1,224	3,328	33.0	39.4	42.7
18–19 years.....................	5,550	3,025	1,189	1,336	31.7	52.5	43.4
20 or more years.................	3,703	2,573	234	896	31.1	34.5	41.9

[1]Includes women with missing data on row variables.
[2]A woman is identified as having had a sexually transmitted disease if she indicated that she had ever had one or more of the following: genital warts, gonorrhea, chlamydia, or genital herpes.

Source: Jacqueline B. Wilson, National Center for Health Statistics, *Human Immunodeficiency Virus Antibody Testing In Women 15–44 Years of Age: United States, 1990,* Advance Data, No. 238, December 22, 1993, Hyattsville, MD: National Center for Health Statistics. Table 4.

C2-16. Participation in Sports of Persons Seven Years Old and Over, by Sex: 1989 and 1994

Based on the National Health Interview Survey and subject to sampling error

CHARACTERISTIC	POPULATION 18 YEARS AND OVER					POPULATION 35 YEARS AND OVER		
	Total (1,000)	Percent who—				Total (1,000)	Percent who had a mammogram	
		Had a breast exam [1]	Knew how to do BSE [2]	Did a BSE monthly [2,3]	Had a PAP smear [4]		Ever	In the past 3 years
Total [5]	95,169	53.1	88.1	43.1	50.1	59,934	57.7	50.5
Race:								
White.	81,255	53.1	88.8	42.3	49.7	52,188	58.9	51.5
Black.	11,212	55.3	86.0	50.9	54.3	6,282	51.3	44.9
Hispanic origin:								
Hispanic.	7,709	50.4	74.7	44.1	49.1	3,704	49.4	42.3
Non-Hispanic	87,151	53.4	89.2	43.1	50.1	56,029	58.2	51.0
Marital status:								
Currently married.	58,398	55.8	90.6	44.5	53.5	38,074	61.5	55.0
Formerly married	21,650	45.5	84.8	43.8	39.1	18,536	51.7	43.4
Never married	15,031	53.1	82.8	36.4	51.5	3,312	47.4	38.9
Educational attainment:								
Less than 12 years	20,326	43.0	76.9	43.9	37.9	14,714	44.9	37.4
12 years.	38,634	52.2	89.7	43.6	49.6	24,234	59.0	51.8
More than 12 years	35,964	59.7	92.8	42.2	57.2	20,798	65.5	58.5
Labor force status:								
Employed.	53,833	55.9	91.3	42.9	54.7	30,067	60.5	53.5
Unemployed	2,659	52.9	90.2	40.7	51.1	1,140	52.9	46.2
Not in the labor force . . .	38,677	49.2	83.4	43.8	43.4	28,727	55.1	47.5
Income:								
Less than $10,000	11,930	45.5	80.0	42.2	41.0	7,203	40.9	32.7
$10,000 to $19,999	16,740	47.0	85.3	43.0	44.0	10,408	50.3	42.5
$20,000 to $34,999	20,445	53.0	90.6	42.3	50.1	11,948	58.9	52.0
$35,000 to $49,999	14,149	58.3	93.3	43.1	55.2	8,545	62.9	56.6
$50,000 or more	17,405	61.4	92.5	41.5	58.9	11,710	71.4	64.5

[1] In the past year by a professional.   [2] BSE=Breast self-examination.   [3] On average over the past year.   [4] In the past year.   [5] Includes persons whose characteristics are unknown.

Source: U.S. National Center for Health Statistics, *Health Promotion and Disease Prevention, United States 1990, Vital and Health Statistics,* series 10, No. 185.

Source: U.S. Bureau of the Census, *Statistical Abstract of the United States: 1994,* (114th edition), Washington, D.C.: U.S. Government Printing Office, 1994, Table 212.

C2-17. Percentage of Persons 18 Years of Age and Over Who Exercised or Played Sports Regularly: 1990

(In millions of participants. Participation is more than once. Ranked by 1994 female participation.)

SPORT	FEMALE		MALE	
	1994	1989	1994	1989
Exercise walking	45.3	42.9	25.5	23.7
Swimming	31.3	37.3	29.0	33.2
Bicycle Riding	22.9	28.6	26.9	28.4
Exercising w/equipment	22.6	15.0	21.2	16.5
Camping	19.9	21.9	23.0	24.6
Aerobic exercising	18.8	20.9	4.4	4.2
Bowling	17.8	19.6	19.6	21.3
Fishing	16.6	16.1	29.1	36.2
Billiards/Pool	12.5	10.0	21.5	19.6
Boating (motor/power)	11.3	12.0	15.1	17.0
Hiking	11.3	10.9	14.0	12.6
Work out at club	10.5	NA	NA	NA
Step Aerobics	10.0	NA	1.5	NA
In-line roller skating	9.3	NA	10.2	NA
Volleyball	8.9	12.1	8.5	13.0
Running/jogging	8.7	10.3	11.9	14.5
Roller skating/2x2	8.6	13.1	5.4	8.3
Dart throwing	8.4	6.3	12.8	11.2
Softball	8.0	8.7	10.1	13.4
Basketball	7.7	7.1	20.5	19.1
Golf	5.9	5.7	18.7	17.4
Tennis	5.1	8.4	6.5	10.4
Calisthenics	4.9	8.3	3.6	6.8
Ice/figure skating	4.8	4.2	3.0	2.8
Skiing, Alpine	4.3	4.1	6.3	6.9
Soccer	4.3	3.7	8.2	7.5
Backpack/wilderness camping	3.9	4.1	5.9	7.3
Canoeing	3.7	3.7	4.8	5.7
Water skiing	2.9	4.2	4.5	6.6
Baseball	2.8	3.3	12.3	12.1
Snorkeling	2.7	NA	3.2	NA
Target shooting	2.6	NA	9.6	NA
Football	2.4	1.9	13.2	12.8
Hunting w/firearms	2.3	1.6	14.1	16.1
Sailing	1.9	1.9	2.2	2.8
Skiing-cross country	1.9	2.5	1.7	2.4
Racquetball	1.4	2.1	3.9	6.2
Archery	1.1	1.2	5.1	4.4
Skateboarding	1.0	1.6	3.9	5.8
Scuba (open water)	0.7	0.5	1.5	1.5
Snowboarding	0.4	0.4	1.7	1.2
Windsurfing	0.3	NA	0.4	NA
Ice Hockey	0.2	0.2	1.7	1.3

Source: National Sportings Goods Association, 1699 Wall St.
Mt. Prospect, IL 60056 Phone: 708-439-4000 (Thomas Doyle)

Source: National Sporting Goods Association, 1699 Wall St., Mt. Prospect, IL 60056 (Telephone: Thomas Doyle, 708-439-4000), unpublished.

C2-18. Percentage of Persons 18 Years of Age and Over Who Specified Exercise Needs to Be Performed Three Times a Week and Maintained 20 Minutes per Session to Strengthen the Heart and Lungs: 1990

(Data are based on household interviews of the civilian noninstitutionalized population. The survey design, general qualifications, and information on the reliability of the estimates are given in Appendix I. Definitions of Terms are given in Appendix II]

Characteristic	Both sexes 18 years and over	Male					Female				
		Total	18–29 years	30–44 years	45–64 years	65 years and over	Total	18–29 years	30–44 years	45–64 years	65 years and over
All persons[1]	40.7	44.0	56.1	44.3	35.6	36.9	37.7	44.2	40.1	34.6	29.1
Education level											
Less than 12 years	25.9	29.3	45.0	23.2	20.6	29.5	22.8	28.1	21.6	22.0	21.1
12 years	37.0	40.3	51.5	37.3	32.0	37.1	34.4	38.5	34.1	33.4	30.5
More than 12 years	52.1	54.3	66.1	53.9	46.6	47.5	49.8	56.7	49.7	45.1	42.3
13–15 years	48.5	50.3	65.2	46.5	37.5	42.2	47.0	53.9	44.8	42.5	42.2
16 years or more	55.8	57.9	67.6	59.5	52.4	51.4	53.2	61.7	54.4	47.8	42.3
Income											
Less than $10,000	32.9	40.4	61.8	28.8	22.0	26.1	28.9	38.3	27.2	21.4	24.8
$10,000–$19,999	32.3	35.3	47.9	33.3	24.3	30.6	29.9	36.5	30.0	24.8	27.5
$20,000–$34,999	40.5	42.6	56.0	40.3	30.9	41.4	38.5	43.7	39.0	34.9	33.4
$35,000–$49,999	46.1	47.2	57.6	49.6	33.3	47.4	44.8	53.2	44.4	38.8	41.3
$50,000 or more	51.7	54.1	62.7	54.8	49.5	49.6	49.1	57.1	50.7	44.5	37.5
Race											
White	41.5	44.1	55.0	45.0	36.3	37.8	39.1	46.4	42.1	35.7	29.9
Black	34.3	42.2	61.7	39.6	28.3	25.1	27.9	32.2	29.4	25.5	19.1
Hispanic origin											
Hispanic	34.9	38.4	46.7	38.5	24.4	32.1	31.9	35.1	33.4	27.8	21.2
Non-Hispanic	41.2	44.5	57.3	44.7	36.3	37.1	38.3	45.6	40.7	35.2	29.4
Geographic region											
Northeast	37.4	41.8	53.6	43.5	34.1	31.8	33.5	42.8	36.5	31.1	21.9
Midwest	41.5	43.8	55.5	45.4	36.0	33.3	39.3	46.7	40.2	37.3	30.9
South	39.0	42.8	56.7	42.3	32.1	37.6	35.7	42.6	38.4	31.3	27.7
West	45.9	48.3	58.0	46.8	41.8	45.7	43.5	45.4	46.1	41.1	38.5
Marital status											
Currently married	39.4	40.7	49.0	42.7	35.7	38.0	38.0	40.8	40.0	36.2	31.6
Formerly married	34.3	40.4	48.2	48.1	35.9	32.8	31.8	35.6	39.5	31.7	27.5
Never married	51.3	56.3	61.3	49.7	32.3	33.5	45.0	49.2	42.4	25.0	25.0
Employment status											
Currently employed	43.2	45.6	55.7	45.2	37.0	36.0	40.3	46.0	40.5	34.7	32.4
Unemployed	42.7	43.4	53.5	40.8	28.9	*34.6	42.0	46.8	40.6	34.7	*34.6
Not in labor force	35.4	38.6	59.7	30.6	30.4	37.1	33.8	39.4	39.0	34.5	28.7

[1]Includes persons with unknown sociodemographic characteristics.

NOTE: Denominator for each cell excludes unknowns.

Source: National Center for Health Statistics, *Health Promotion and Disease Prevention: United States, 1990,* Vital and Health Statistics Series 10, No. 185 (National Health Survey), Hyattsville, MD: National Center for Health Statistics, 1993, Table 16.

C2-19. Ratio of Persons 18 Years of Age or Over Reporting Favorable Health Practices: 1990 Compared with 1985

Data are based on household interviews of the civilian noninstitutionalized population. The survey design, general qualifications, and information on the reliability of the estimates are given in appendix I.

Characteristic	Both sexes 18 years and over	Male Total	Male 18–29 years	Male 30–44 years	Male 45–64 years	Male 65 years and over	Female Total	Female 18–29 years	Female 30–44 years	Female 45–64 years	Female 65 years and over
All persons[1]	5.2	4.9	4.0	6.0	5.3	3.0	5.5	5.2	7.5	5.4	2.8
Education level											
Less than 12 years	2.8	2.4	2.5	3.1	2.0	2.0	3.3	4.6	4.2	3.2	2.1
12 years	4.4	3.3	2.7	4.0	3.8	2.2	5.3	4.8	6.5	5.3	3.6
More than 12 years	7.2	7.3	6.0	8.0	8.4	5.2	7.2	5.8	9.2	7.2	3.0
13–15 years	5.9	6.1	5.0	6.4	7.9	4.9	5.7	4.8	7.2	6.3	*2.3
16 years or more	8.6	8.4	7.8	9.2	8.7	5.4	8.9	7.7	11.0	8.1	*3.8
Income											
Less than $10,000	3.2	2.5	3.0	*3.0	*2.1	*1.4	3.7	4.2	4.8	4.3	2.2
$10,000–$19,999	3.7	3.2	3.1	3.8	3.1	2.7	4.1	4.2	4.9	4.2	3.3
$20,000–$34,999	5.5	4.5	5.1	5.2	3.3	3.6	6.5	6.7	8.3	5.5	3.7
$35,000–$49,999	6.9	6.4	4.6	7.7	6.2	*4.4	7.5	7.0	8.1	7.5	*5.2
$50,000 or more	6.9	6.8	3.4	8.0	7.8	*4.6	7.1	4.5	9.4	6.2	*2.8
Race											
White	5.5	5.2	4.3	6.4	5.6	3.3	5.7	5.4	7.8	5.6	2.9
Black	3.9	3.1	2.9	3.5	4.1	*0.5	4.6	4.5	6.2	4.0	*2.0
Hispanic origin											
Hispanic	3.4	2.9	*2.2	3.5	*3.0	*3.5	3.9	3.4	4.6	4.7	*1.1
Non-Hispanic	5.4	5.0	4.2	6.2	5.5	3.0	5.7	5.4	7.7	5.5	2.9
Geographic region											
Northeast	5.2	4.7	4.5	5.3	5.8	*2.0	5.5	4.6	7.7	5.0	4.0
Midwest	6.0	5.8	4.8	7.9	5.5	3.5	6.2	6.5	8.0	5.4	3.6
South	4.5	3.8	2.6	4.8	4.7	2.3	5.1	5.2	6.9	5.4	1.4
West	5.5	5.5	4.9	6.2	5.6	4.7	5.6	4.1	7.8	5.8	2.9
Marital status											
Currently married	5.8	5.2	5.5	5.9	5.6	3.0	6.3	5.7	8.2	5.5	3.2
Formerly married	4.0	3.9	*3.5	5.0	3.9	*2.3	4.1	5.2	5.6	5.1	2.5
Never married	4.5	4.1	3.0	7.2	*5.1	*5.2	4.9	4.7	5.8	*5.8	*4.0
Employment status											
Currently employed	5.9	5.4	4.3	6.1	5.8	4.0	6.4	5.4	7.8	6.1	*2.2
Unemployed	4.3	3.6	*2.1	*4.6	*5.2	*–	5.0	*3.4	7.7	*3.5	*6.4
Not in labor force	3.9	3.1	3.1	4.4	3.3	2.8	4.3	5.1	6.7	4.5	2.9

[1]Includes persons with unknown sociodemographic characteristics.

NOTE: Denominator for each cell includes unknowns.

Source: National Center for Health Statistics, *Health Promotion and Disease Prevention: United States, 1990,* Vital and Health Statistics Series 10, No. 185 (National Health Survey), Hyattsville, MD: National Center for Health Statistics, 1993, Table 21.

C2-20. Ratio of Persons 18 Years and Over Reporting Favorable Health Practices: 1990 Compared with 1985

Characteristic	Favorable health practices				
	Currently trying to lose weight[1]	Exercised or played sports regularly	Heard of fetal alcohol syndrome[2]	Wore seatbelts all or most of the time	One or more working smoke detectors in home
	Ratio of the proportion reporting practice in 1990 to proportion reporting the practice in 1985				
All persons 18 years of age and over	0.95	1.02	1.16	1.87	1.31
Sex					
Male	0.94	1.03	1.14	1.84	1.31
Female	0.96	1.00	1.17	1.90	1.31

Source: National Center for Health Statistics, *Health Promotion and Disease Prevention: United States, 1990*, Vital and Health Statistics Series 10, No. 185 (National Health Survey), Hyattsville, MD: National Center for Health Statistics, 1993, Table G.

C3. REPRODUCTIVE HEALTH

Sexual Activity

C3-1. Percentage of Women Who Have Ever Had Intercourse and Who Had Intercourse in the Three Months before the Survey, by Marital Status and Age: 1982 and 1988 (National Survey of Family Growth)

Age-group	All women				Never married*				Formerly married*	
	Ever had intercourse		Last 3 months		Ever had intercourse		Last 3 months		Last 3 months	
	1982	1988	1982	1988	1982	1988	1982	1988	1982	1988
15–44	**86.4**	**88.5**	**77.4**	**77.6**	**59.3**	**65.5**	**44.9**	**49.0**	**67.8**	**60.8**
15–19	47.1	53.2	40.0	42.5	42.1	49.5	34.3	38.5	†	†
20–24	85.7	86.4	75.5	75.8	72.3	74.8	54.4	59.9	85.9	63.2
25–29	96.7	94.8	89.3	85.4	83.8	79.9	60.3	61.1	78.9	63.8
30–34	98.0	98.0	89.7	88.2	81.3	84.8	52.5	53.6	70.3	67.5
35–39	97.9	97.9	88.8	86.5	67.5	78.1	42.4	50.8	60.7	62.6
40–44	98.2	98.9	85.5	84.3	63.0	84.5	22.9‡	33.6	52.4	48.9

*Not cohabiting. †Fewer than 20 respondents.
‡Denotes proportion with relative standard error of 30 percent or more.

Source: Jacqueline D. Forrest and Susheela Singh, The Alan Guttmacher Institute, *The Sexual and Reproductive Behavior of American Women, 1982–1988*, Family Planning Perspectives, Vol. 22, No. 5, September/October, 1990, Table 3. Reprinted with permission.

C3-2. Percentages of Women Aged 15 to 19 Who Have Ever Had Sexual Intercourse, by Race/Hispanic Origin, Age, and Poverty Level: 1982 and 1988 (National Survey of Family Growth)

Race/ethnicity and poverty level	15–19		15–17		18–19	
	1982	1988	1982	1988	1982	1988
Total	**47.1**	**53.2**	**32.6**	**38.4**	**64.1**	**74.4**
Race/ethnicity						
Non-Hispanic white	44.5	52.4	29.8	36.2	60.8	74.3
Non-Hispanic black	59.0	60.8	44.4	50.5	79.1	78.0
Hispanic	50.6	48.5	35.6	36.1	70.1	70.0
Poverty level						
<200%	55.6	56.5	45.7	41.6	65.0	80.9
≥200%	39.7	50.1	23.0	35.0	63.0	69.0

Source: Jacqueline D. Forrest and Susheela Singh, The Alan Guttmacher Institute, *The Sexual and Reproductive Behavior of American Women, 1982–1988*, Family Planning Perspectives, Vol. 22, No. 5, September/October, 1990, Table 4 (p. 208). Reprinted with permission.

C3-3. Percentage of Girls Aged 12 to 19 Who Have Ever Had Sexual Intercourse: 1988

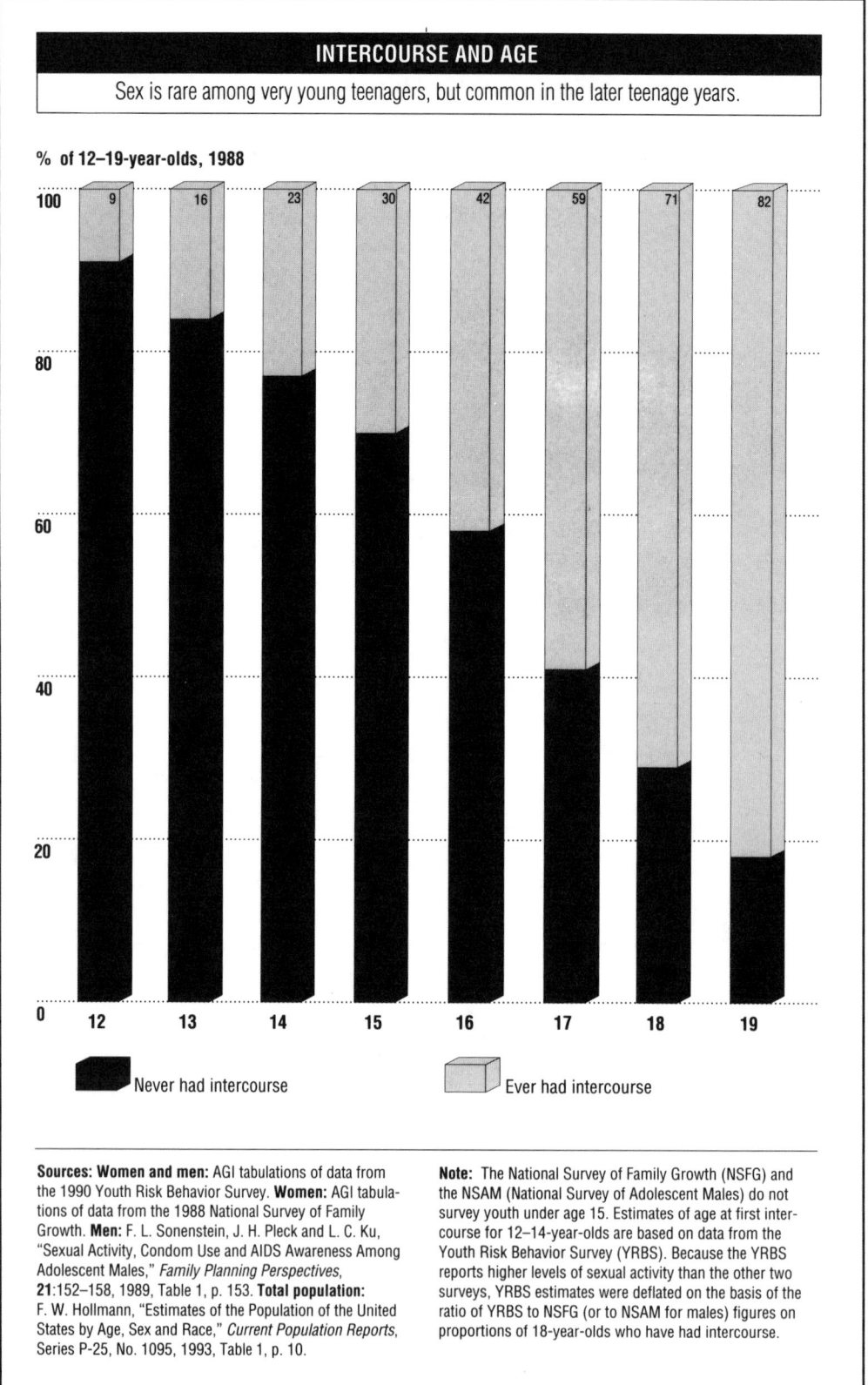

Source: The Alan Guttmacher Institute, *Sex and America's Teenagers*, New York: The Alan Guttmacher Institute, 1994, Figure 9. Reprinted with permission.

C3-4. Percentage of Women and Men Who Have Had Intercourse by Age 18: Selected Years 1956–58 to 1986–88

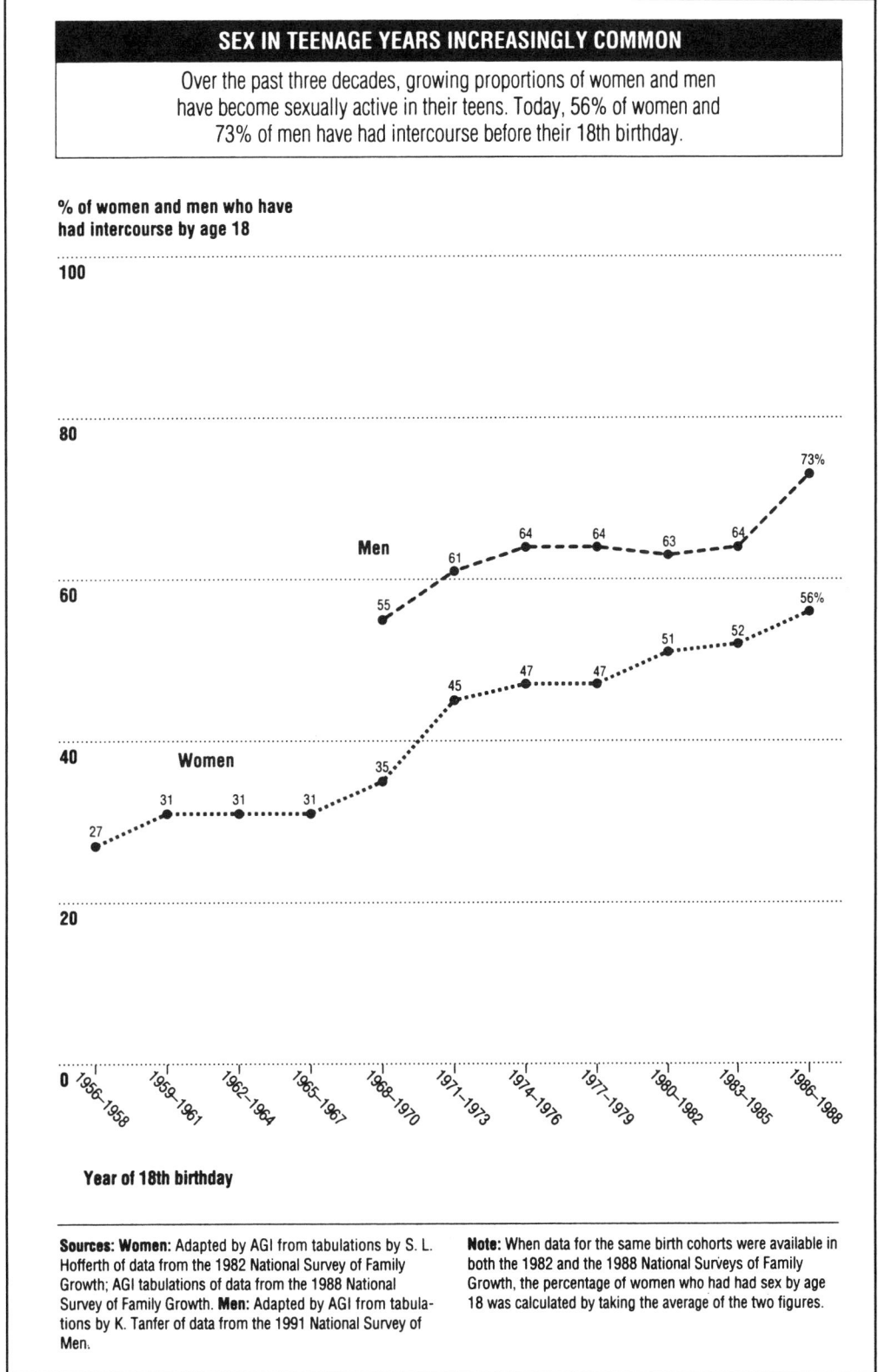

SEX IN TEENAGE YEARS INCREASINGLY COMMON

Over the past three decades, growing proportions of women and men have become sexually active in their teens. Today, 56% of women and 73% of men have had intercourse before their 18th birthday.

% of women and men who have had intercourse by age 18

Year of 18th birthday

Sources: Women: Adapted by AGI from tabulations by S. L. Hofferth of data from the 1982 National Survey of Family Growth; AGI tabulations of data from the 1988 National Survey of Family Growth. **Men:** Adapted by AGI from tabulations by K. Tanfer of data from the 1991 National Survey of Men.

Note: When data for the same birth cohorts were available in both the 1982 and the 1988 National Surveys of Family Growth, the percentage of women who had had sex by age 18 was calculated by taking the average of the two figures.

Source: The Alan Guttmacher Institute, *Sex and America's Teenagers,* New York: The Alan Guttmacher Institute, 1994, Figure 10. Reprinted with permission.

C3-5. Percentage of Women Aged 15 to 19 Who Have Ever Had Intercourse, by Selected Characteristics: 1988

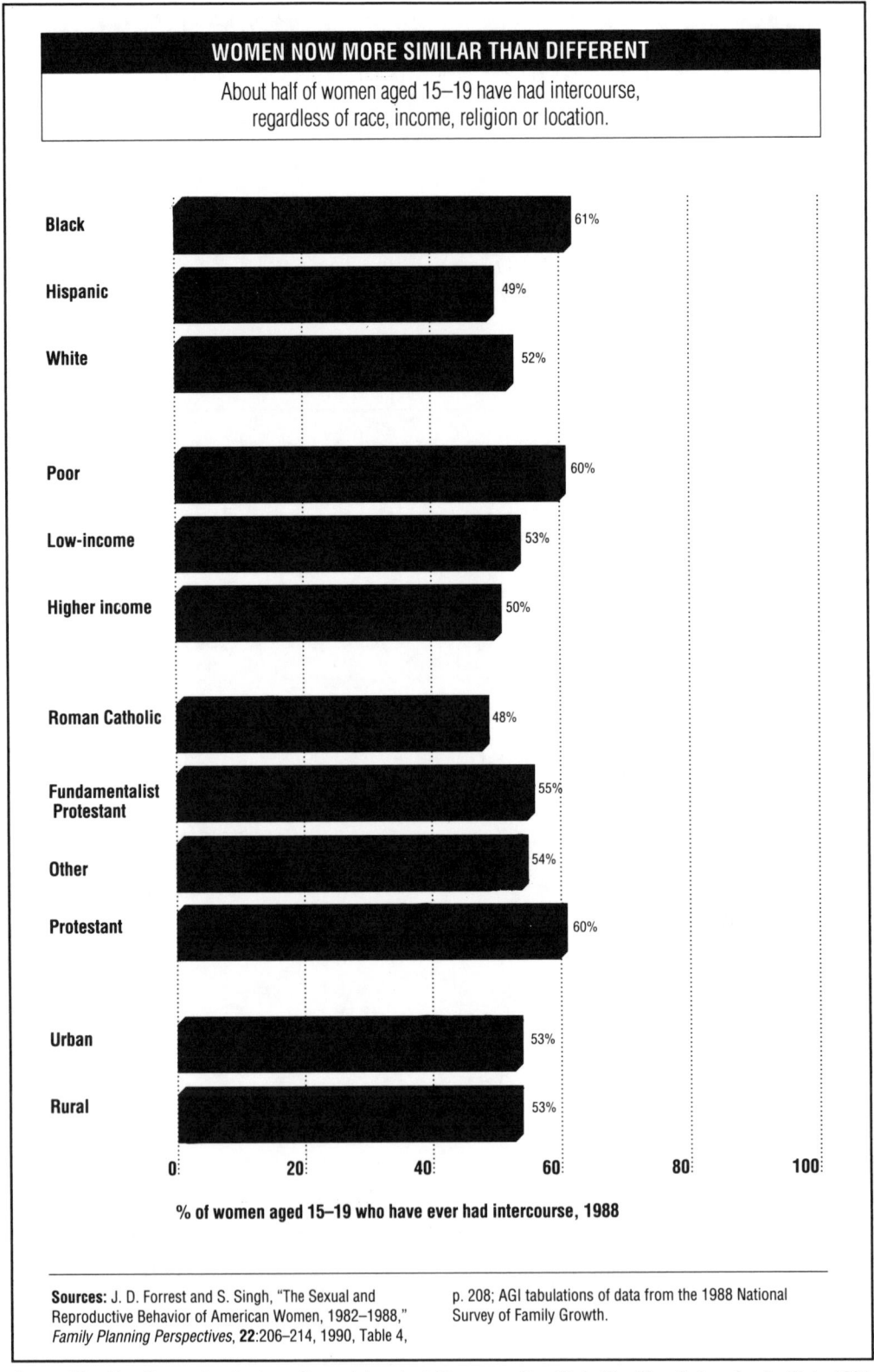

WOMEN NOW MORE SIMILAR THAN DIFFERENT

About half of women aged 15–19 have had intercourse, regardless of race, income, religion or location.

Characteristic	%
Black	61%
Hispanic	49%
White	52%
Poor	60%
Low-income	53%
Higher income	50%
Roman Catholic	48%
Fundamentalist Protestant	55%
Other	54%
Protestant	60%
Urban	53%
Rural	53%

% of women aged 15–19 who have ever had intercourse, 1988

Sources: J. D. Forrest and S. Singh, "The Sexual and Reproductive Behavior of American Women, 1982–1988," *Family Planning Perspectives,* **22**:206–214, 1990, Table 4, p. 208; AGI tabulations of data from the 1988 National Survey of Family Growth.

Source: The Alan Guttmacher Institute, *Sex and America's Teenagers,* New York: The Alan Guttmacher Institute, 1994, Figure 15. Reprinted with permission.

Use of Contraceptives

C3-6. Contraceptive Use and Method for Women 15 to 44 Years Old, by Age: 1982, 1988, and 1990

Statistics are based on samples of the female population of the United States.

Contraceptive status and method	15–24 years			25–34 years			35–44 years		
	1990[1]	1988	1982	1990	1988	1982	1990	1988	1982
	Number in thousands								
All women.	17,637	18,592	20,150	21,728	21,726	19,644	19,016	17,582	14,305
	Percent distribution								
Total	100.0	100.0	100.0	100.0	100.0	100.0	100.0	100.0	100.0
Sterile	3.8	3.1	3.3	26.4	27.0	27.9	64.6	61.3	60.0
Surgically sterile	3.1	2.4	2.6	24.8	26.0	26.4	61.1	58.6	57.2
Contraceptively sterile	2.8	2.2	2.4	22.1	23.3	21.5	48.6	46.7	39.0
Female	2.3	1.6	1.3	16.2	16.6	14.8	32.9	32.5	26.8
Male	*0.5	*0.6	*1.1	5.9	6.7	6.7	15.7	14.2	12.2
Noncontraceptively sterile	*0.3	*0.2	*0.2	2.7	2.7	4.9	12.5	11.9	18.2
Female	*0.3	*0.2	*0.2	2.7	2.7	4.6	12.5	11.9	17.4
Male	0.0	0.0	0.0	0.0	0.0	*0.3	0.0	0.0	*0.8
Nonsurgically sterile	*0.7	0.7	*0.7	1.6	1.0	1.5	3.5	2.7	2.8
Pregnant or post partum	7.0	5.0	6.3	7.9	7.6	6.5	1.2	1.1	*1.0
Seeking pregnancy	1.8	2.7	3.5	7.6	5.8	6.2	2.0	2.4	2.5
Other nonuser[1]	46.4	45.7	48.6	17.1	16.6	14.3	12.0	13.5	13.8
Never had intercourse	26.4	30.0	32.5	2.8	3.6	2.7	1.3	1.6	2.0
No intercourse in last 1 month[2] . . .	7.7	11.4	10.6	7.1	8.2	7.1	6.4	7.7	6.7
Had intercourse in last 1 month[2] . .	12.3	4.3	5.5	7.2	4.8	4.5	4.3	4.2	5.1
Nonsurgical contraceptors	41.2	43.5	38.4	41.3	43.0	45.2	20.1	21.7	22.5
Pill	23.9	29.7	23.5	22.0	21.6	17.1	4.7	3.0	2.3
IUD	*0.2	*0.1	1.4	*0.4	1.4	6.5	1.8	2.1	4.2
Diaphragm	*0.2	1.3	3.7	2.3	4.8	6.8	2.4	4.1	2.4
Condom	13.9	9.5	5.5	11.0	9.1	7.6	6.7	7.7	7.0
Periodic abstinence[3]	1.0	*0.6	1.2	2.0	1.7	2.8	1.6	1.8	2.6
Natural family planning	*0.1	*0.2	*0.1	*0.4	*0.5	*0.6	*0.2	*0.4	*0.3
Withdrawal	*0.6	1.5	1.2	*0.6	1.9	1.2	*0.5	*0.6	*0.8
Other methods	1.4	0.8	1.9	3.0	2.5	3.2	2.4	2.4	3.2

[1]For 0.9 percent of U.S. women 15–24 years of age in 1990, contraceptive status was not ascertained and imputation was not performed. This group was proportionately distributed across all categories.
[2]The 3-month classification could not be used in this analysis because the necessary questions were not asked in the 1990 survey.
[3]Includes natural family planning and other types of periodic abstinence.

Source: Linda S. Peterson, National Center for Health Statistics, *Contraceptive Use in the United States: 1982–90*, Advance Data From Vital and Health Statistics, No. 260, Hyattsville, MD: National Center for Health Statistics, February 14, 1995, Table 2.

C3-7. Contraceptives Users, by Method and Age: 1988

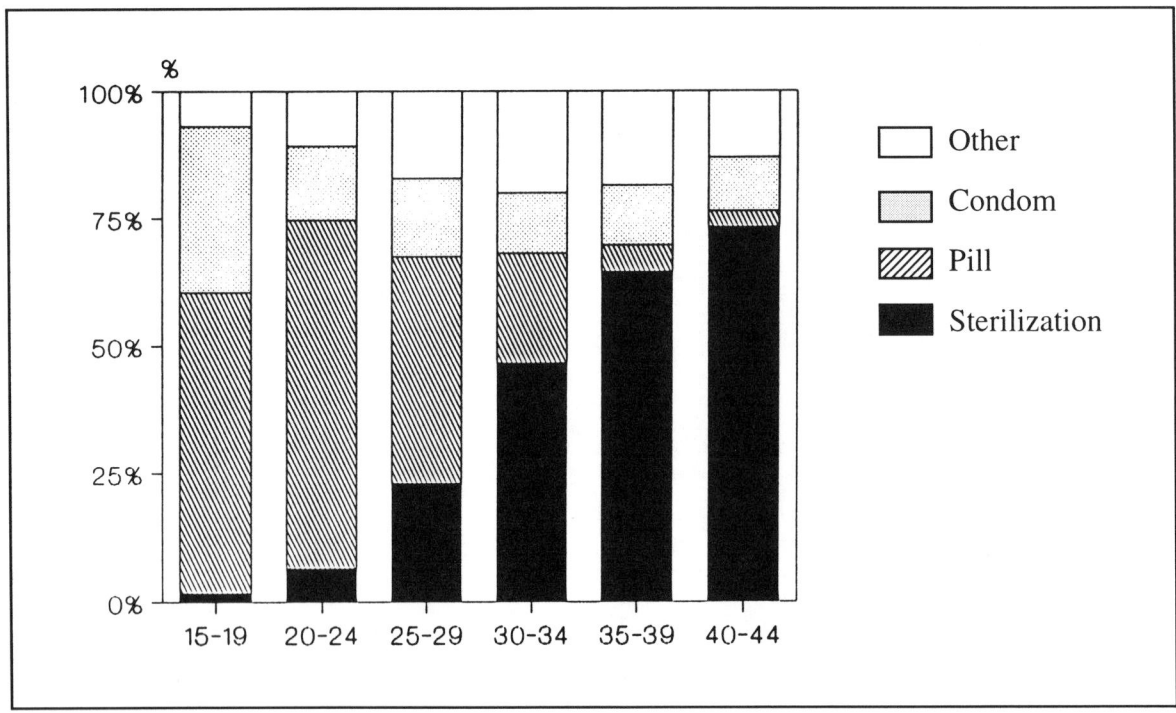

Source: Jacqueline D. Forrest, The Alan Guttmacher Institute, "Levels and Determinants of U.S. Fertility," presentation at The Population and Consumption Task Force of the President's Council on Sustainable Development, October 27, 1994, unpublished.

C3-8. Method of Contraception by Women 15 to 44 Years Old, by Selected Characteristics: 1988 and 1990

Statistics are based on a sample of the female population of the United States.

Age, race, and marital status	Number of women in thousands	Number of women using a method	Percent using any method	All methods	Female sterilization	Male sterilization	Pill	IUD	Diaphragm	Condom	Periodic abstinence[1]	Other
1990:[2]												
All women	58,381	34,516	59.3	100.0	29.5	12.6	28.5	1.4	2.8	17.7	2.7	4.8
Age												
15–19	8,483	2,623	31.5	100.0	0.0	0.0	52.0	0.0	0.0	44.0	*1.0	*3.0
15–17	4,944	1,165	24.3	100.0	0.0	0.0	41.1	0.0	0.0	51.9	*2.2	*4.7
18–19	3,539	1,458	41.2	100.0	0.0	0.0	60.7	0.0	0.0	37.6	0.0	*1.7
20–24	9,154	5,065	55.3	100.0	8.0	*1.8	55.4	*0.8	*0.6	25.3	2.8	5.3
25–29	10,637	6,385	60.0	100.0	17.4	5.0	47.3	*0.4	2.3	19.0	2.7	5.9
30–34	11,091	7,344	66.2	100.0	32.7	13.0	23.9	*0.9	4.7	15.9	3.5	5.4
35–39	10,111	7,138	70.6	100.0	44.2	19.8	10.6	3.3	3.3	10.3	3.4	5.2
40–44	8,905	5,962	66.9	100.0	52.0	26.5	*2.2	*1.8	3.8	9.2	*1.6	2.9
Race and origin												
Hispanic	5,500	2,856	52.2	100.0	33.1	6.4	31.4	*1.9	1.5	17.1	3.7	5.1
White non-Hispanic	42,968	25,928	60.5	100.0	27.3	15.5	28.5	1.3	3.0	17.0	2.7	4.7
Black non-Hispanic	7,510	4,412	58.7	100.0	41.0	*1.3	28.5	*1.4	*1.6	19.4	*1.2	5.6
Marital status												
Currently married	30,561	21,608	70.7	100.0	33.5	19.2	20.6	1.4	4.1	14.0	3.5	3.8
Divorced, separated, widowed	7,033	4,026	57.3	100.0	52.1	*2.8	22.4	*2.5	*0.9	9.7	*0.6	9.0
Never married	20,788	8,882	43.0	100.0	9.6	*1.1	50.5	*0.8	*0.6	30.1	1.8	5.5
1988:												
All women	57,900	34,912	60.3	100.0	27.5	11.7	30.7	2.0	5.7	14.6	2.3	5.4
Age												
15–19	9,179	2,950	32.1	100.0	*1.5	*0.2	58.8	0.0	*1.0	32.8	*0.8	4.8
15–17	5,404	1,076	19.9	100.0	0.0	0.0	53.3	0.0	*0.7	40.4	*0.9	*4.7
18–19	3,775	1,874	49.6	100.0	*2.4	*0.4	61.9	0.0	*1.2	28.4	*0.8	*4.9
20–24	9,413	5,550	59.0	100.0	4.6	*1.8	68.2	*0.3	3.7	14.5	*1.7	5.2
25–29	10,796	6,967	64.5	100.0	17.0	6.0	44.5	*1.3	5.5	15.6	2.4	7.6
30–34	10,930	7,437	68.0	100.0	32.5	14.0	21.5	2.9	8.9	12.0	2.7	5.5
35–39	9,583	6,726	70.2	100.0	44.9	19.7	5.2	*2.7	7.7	11.8	3.0	5.1
40–44	7,999	5,282	66.0	100.0	51.1	22.2	3.2	3.7	3.9	10.5	*2.2	3.2
Race and origin												
Hispanic	5,557	2,799	50.4	100.0	31.7	4.3	33.4	5.0	*2.4	13.6	*2.5	7.1
White non-Hispanic	42,575	26,799	62.9	100.0	25.6	14.3	29.5	1.5	6.6	15.2	2.3	5.0
Black non-Hispanic	7,408	4,208	56.8	100.0	37.8	*0.9	38.1	3.2	2.0	10.1	2.1	5.9
Marital status												
Currently married	29,147	21,657	74.3	100.0	31.4	17.3	20.4	2.0	6.2	14.3	2.8	5.6
Divorced, separated, widowed	7,695	4,429	57.6	100.0	50.7	3.6	25.3	3.6	5.3	5.9	*1.9	3.8
Never married	21,058	8,826	41.9	100.0	6.4	1.8	59.0	*1.3	4.9	19.6	*1.3	5.7

[1] Includes natural family planning and other types of periodic abstinence.
[2] Percentages for 1990 were calculated excluding cases for whom contraceptive status was not ascertained. Overall, contraceptive status was not ascertained for only 0.3 percent of U.S. women in 1990.

Source: Linda S. Peterson, National Center for Health Statistics, *Contraceptive Use in the United States: 1982–90*, Advance Data From Vital and Health Statistics, No. 260, Hyattsville, MD: National Center for Health Statistics, February 14, 1995, Table 4.

C3-9. Method of Contraception of Women 15 to 44 Years Old, by Years of School Completed, Poverty Status, and Future Birth Intentions: 1988 and 1990

Statistics are based on a sample of the female population of the United States.

Age, race, and marital status	Number of women in thousands	Number of women using a method	Percent using any method	All methods	Female sterilization	Male sterilization	Pill	IUD	Diaphragm	Condom	Periodic abstinence[1]	Other
1990:[2]												
All women.	58,381	34,516	59.3	100.0	29.5	12.6	28.5	1.4	2.8	17.7	2.7	4.8
Income (percent of poverty level)[3]												
0–149	8,350	4,959	59.4	100.0	47.2	6.2	24.8	*1.1	*0.6	14.9	*1.7	3.6
150–299.	13,191	8,734	66.2	100.0	38.5	11.8	26.6	2.5	1.9	12.9	2.3	3.5
300 and over.	26,369	16,872	64.0	100.0	25.1	16.4	27.3	1.0	4.2	16.8	3.5	5.7
Education (years)[3]												
0–11	5,525	3,351	60.6	100.0	58.0	6.8	18.4	*1.7	*0.2	11.7	*1.1	*2.2
12.	17,507	11,598	66.2	100.0	38.4	15.7	26.8	*1.1	1.7	11.0	2.0	3.3
13 and over.	26,831	16,930	63.1	100.0	22.3	13.7	28.0	1.7	4.6	19.3	3.7	6.7
Children ever born												
0	24,205	10,451	43.4	100.0	3.3	4.7	53.0	*0.8	2.1	28.2	2.7	5.2
1	10,927	6,066	55.6	100.0	13.0	9.6	34.9	*1.7	4.5	20.7	4.1	11.4
2	13,385	9,910	74.0	100.0	42.3	17.6	16.9	1.7	3.7	12.3	2.6	3.0
3 and over	9,864	8,089	82.0	100.0	60.0	19.2	6.1	*1.5	*1.5	8.3	*1.7	*1.6
Fertility intentions												
More children.	25,119	11,770	47.0	100.0	*0.7	*0.2	52.9	*0.6	3.0	30.8	3.9	7.9
No more children	29,405	20,545	69.9	100.0	49.1	21.1	12.5	1.7	2.5	8.8	1.7	2.5
1988:												
All women.	57,900	34,912	60.3	100.0	27.5	11.7	30.7	2.0	5.7	14.6	2.3	5.4
Income (percent of poverty level)[3]												
0–149	10,115	6,091	60.2	100.0	42.8	5.2	31.3	3.3	2.3	10.2	*1.8	3.2
150–299.	12,134	8,137	67.1	100.0	34.5	13.1	26.6	2.4	5.0	11.4	1.7	5.3
300 and over.	26,472	17,734	67.0	100.0	23.5	15.1	27.8	1.7	8.0	14.5	3.0	6.3
Education (years)[3]												
0–11	7,103	4,276	60.2	100.0	51.9	6.9	22.5	3.8	*1.3	6.4	*1.6	5.6
12.	17,594	11,880	67.5	100.0	34.3	15.0	29.4	1.7	2.8	10.7	1.7	4.4
13 and over.	24,024	15,806	65.8	100.0	20.7	12.6	28.7	2.2	10.0	16.4	3.2	6.3
Children ever born												
0	25,129	11,057	44.0	100.0	2.6	4.8	57.9	*0.9	6.6	20.2	1.8	5.4
1	9,906	5,982	60.4	100.0	14.8	8.2	37.6	3.0	8.8	15.9	3.6	8.1
2	13,237	10,275	77.6	100.0	40.5	16.5	15.1	2.2	5.3	12.0	2.7	5.7
3 and over	9,628	7,598	78.9	100.0	56.4	17.8	7.0	2.6	2.7	9.0	1.6	3.0
Fertility intentions												
More children.	25,374	12,460	49.1	100.0	0.0	*0.1	58.7	1.0	7.6	22.4	2.9	7.4
No more children	29,440	20,854	70.8	100.0	46.1	19.3	12.9	2.5	3.7	9.7	1.8	4.0

[1]Includes natural family planning and other types of periodic abstinence.
[2]Percentages for 1990 were calculated excluding cases for whom contraceptive status was not ascertained. Overall, contraceptive status was not ascertained for only 0.3 percent of U.S. women in 1990.
[3]Data on education and income pertain only to women 20–44 years of age (see Definition of terms).

Source: Linda S. Peterson, National Center for Health Statistics, *Contraceptive Use in the United States: 1982–90*, Advance Data From Vital and Health Statistics, No. 260, Hyattsville, MD: National Center for Health Statistics, February 14, 1995, Table 5.

C3-10. Percentage of Women Aged 15 to 19 Who Request Contraceptive Services within the First Year after Intercourse: 1988

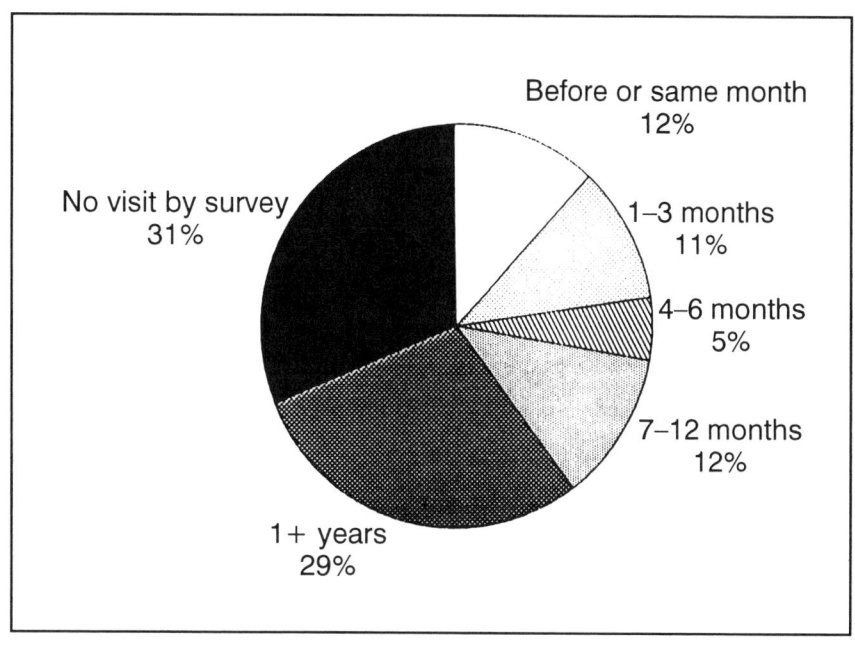

Source: Jacqueline D. Forrest, The Alan Guttmacher Institute, "Levels and Determinants of U.S. Fertility," presentation at The Population and Consumption Task Force of the President's Council on Sustainable Development, October 27, 1994, unpublished.

C3-11. Contraceptive Use among Women at Risk of Pregnancy (1988) and Women with Unintended Pregnancies (1987)

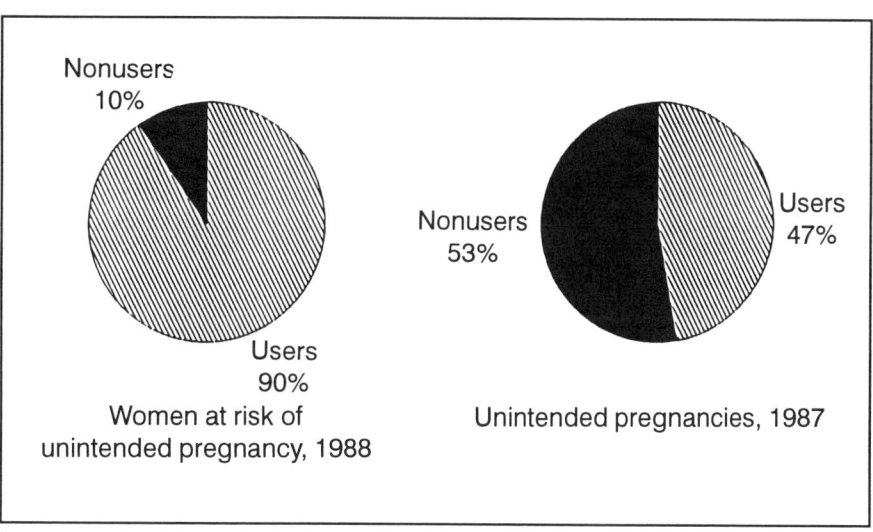

Source: Jacqueline D. Forrest, The Alan Guttmacher Institute, "Levels and Determinants of U.S. Fertility," presentation at The Population and Consumption Task Force of the President's Council on Sustainable Development, October 27, 1994, unpublished.

C3-12. Estimated Percentage of Women Becoming Pregnant in One Year of Intercouse Using No Contraceptive Method, by Age: 1988

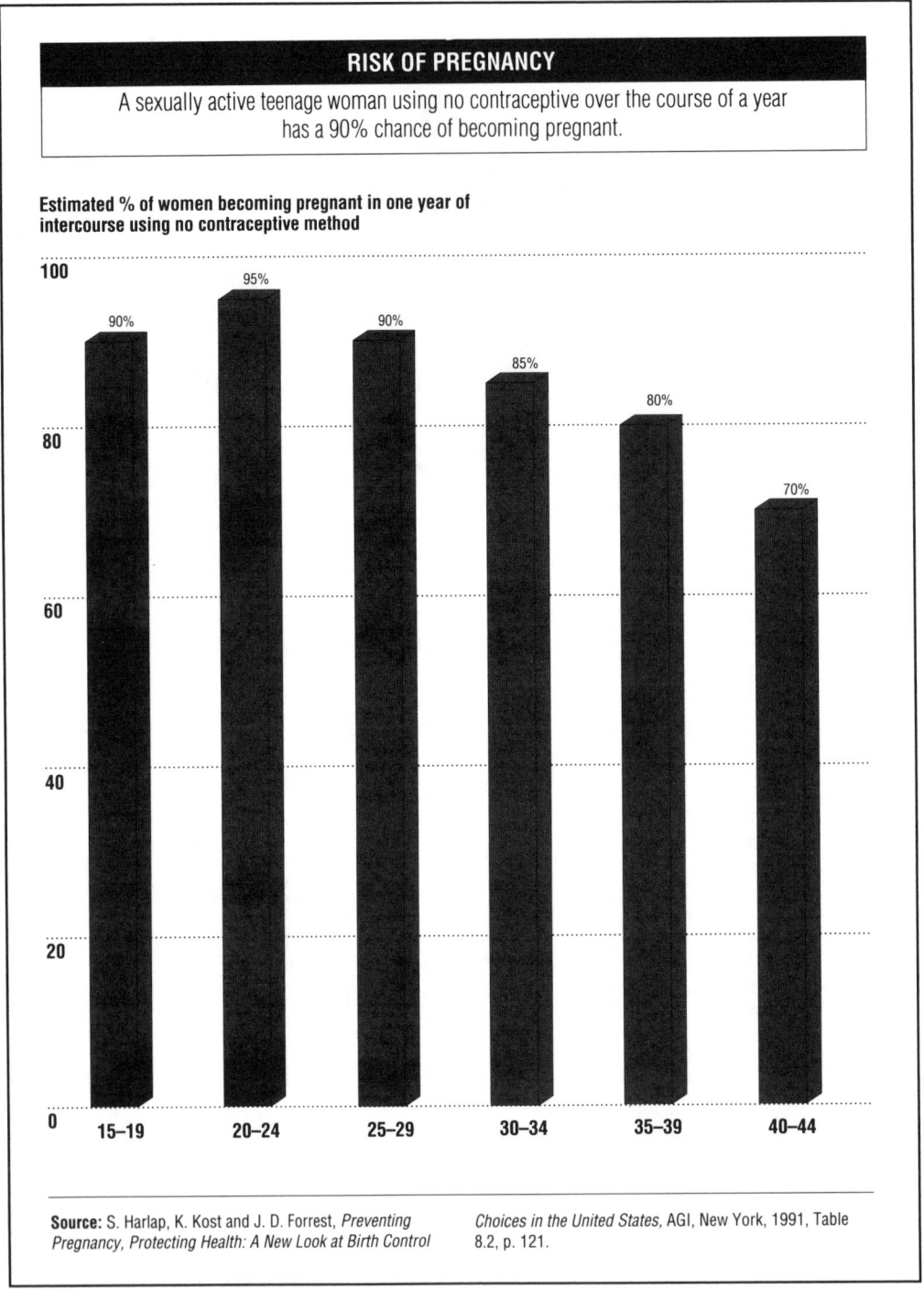

RISK OF PREGNANCY

A sexually active teenage woman using no contraceptive over the course of a year has a 90% chance of becoming pregnant.

Estimated % of women becoming pregnant in one year of intercourse using no contraceptive method

Source: S. Harlap, K. Kost and J. D. Forrest, *Preventing Pregnancy, Protecting Health: A New Look at Birth Control* *Choices in the United States*, AGI, New York, 1991, Table 8.2, p. 121.

Source: The Alan Guttmacher Institute, Sex and America's Teenagers, New York: The Alan Guttmacher Institute, 1994, Figure 19. Reprinted with permission.

Abortions

C3-13. Estimated Number, Rate, and Ratio of Abortions, by Race: 1975 to 1992

[Refers to women 15 to 44 years old at time of abortion]

	ALL RACES				WHITE				BLACK AND OTHER			
	Women 15-44 years old (1,000)	Abortions			Women 15-44 years old (1,000)	Abortions			Women 15-44 years old (1,000)	Abortions		
YEAR		Number (1,000)	Rate per 1,000 women	Ratio per 1,000 live births [1]		Number (1,000)	Rate per 1,000 women	Ratio per 1,000 live births [1]		Number (1,000)	Rate per 1,000 women	Ratio per 1,000 live births [1]
1975	47,606	1,034	21.7	331	40,857	701	17.2	276	6,749	333	49.3	565
1978	50,920	1,410	27.7	413	43,427	969	22.3	356	7,493	440	58.7	665
1979	52,016	1,498	26.8	420	44,266	1,062	24.0	373	7,750	435	56.2	625
1980	53,048	1,554	29.3	428	44,942	1,094	24.3	376	8,106	460	56.5	642
1981	53,901	1,577	29.3	430	45,494	1,108	24.3	377	8,407	470	55.9	645
1982	54,679	1,574	28.8	428	46,049	1,095	23.8	373	8,630	479	55.5	646
1983 [2]	55,340	1,575	28.5	436	46,506	1,084	23.3	376	8,834	491	55.5	670
1984	56,061	1,577	28.1	423	47,023	1,087	23.1	366	9,038	491	54.3	646
1985	56,754	1,589	28.0	422	47,512	1,076	22.6	360	9,242	513	55.5	659
1986 [2]	57,483	1,574	27.4	416	48,010	1,045	21.8	350	9,473	529	55.9	661
1987	57,964	1,559	27.1	405	48,288	1,017	21.1	338	9,676	542	56.0	648
1988	58,192	1,591	27.3	401	48,325	1,026	21.2	333	9,867	565	57.3	638
1989 [2]	58,365	1,557	26.8	380	48,104	1,006	20.9	309	10,261	561	54.7	650
1990 [2]	58,700	1,609	27.4	389	48,224	1,039	21.5	318	10,476	570	54.4	655
1991	59,076	1,557	26.3	378	(NA)	(NA)	(NA)	(NA)	(NA)	(NA)	(NA)	(NA)
1992	59,008	1,529	25.9	379	(NA)	(NA)	(NA)	(NA)	(NA)	(NA)	(NA)	(NA)

NA Not available. [1] Live births are those which occurred from July 1 of year shown through June 30 of the following year (to match time of conception with abortions). Births are classified by race of child 1972-1988, and by race of mother after 1988. [2] Total numbers of abortions in 1983 and 1986 have been estimated by interpolation; 1989 and 1990 have been estimated using trends in CDC data.

Source: U.S. Bureau of the Census, *Statistical Abstract of the United States: 1994*, (114th edition), Washington, D.C.: U.S. Government Printing Office, 1994, Table 111.

C3-14. Abortions, by Selected Characteristics of Women: 1980, 1985, and 1990

[Number of abortions from surveys conducted by source; characteristics from the U.S. Centers for Disea abortion surveillance summaries, with adjustments for changes in States reporting data to the CDC each year]

CHARACTERISTIC	NUMBER (1,000)			PERCENT DISTRIBUTION			ABORTION RATIO [1]		
	1980	1985	1990 [1]	1980	1985	1990 [1]	1980	1985	1990 [1]
Total abortions	1,554	1,589	1,609	100	100	100	300	297	290
Age of woman:									
Less than 15 years old	15	17	13	1	1	1	607	624	515
15 to 19 years old	445	399	351	29	25	22	451	462	403
20 to 24 years old	549	548	532	35	35	33	310	328	326
25 to 29 years old	304	336	360	20	21	22	213	219	224
30 to 34 years old	153	181	216	10	11	13	213	203	196
35 to 39 years old	67	87	106	4	5	7	317	280	249
40 years old and over	21	21	29	1	1	2	461	409	354
Race of woman:									
White	1,094	1,076	1,039	70	68	65	274	265	241
Black and other	460	513	570	30	32	35	392	397	396
Marital status of woman:									
Married	320	281	284	21	18	18	98	88	88
Unmarried	1,234	1,307	1,325	79	82	82	649	605	527
Number of prior live births:									
None	900	872	780	58	55	49	365	358	316
One	305	349	396	20	22	25	208	219	230
Two	216	240	280	14	15	17	283	288	292
Three	83	85	102	5	5	6	288	281	279
Four or more	51	43	50	3	3	3	251	230	223
Number of prior induced abortions:									
None	1,043	944	891	67	60	55	(NA)	(NA)	(NA)
One	373	416	443	24	26	28	(NA)	(NA)	(NA)
Two or more	138	228	275	9	14	17	(NA)	(NA)	(NA)
Weeks of gestation: [2]									
Less than 9 weeks	800	811	850	52	51	53	(NA)	(NA)	(NA)
9 to 10 weeks	417	425	418	27	27	26	(NA)	(NA)	(NA)
11 to 12 weeks	202	198	185	13	12	12	(NA)	(NA)	(NA)
13 weeks or more	136	154	155	9	10	10	(NA)	(NA)	(NA)
One	373	416	(NA)	24	26	(NA)	(NA)	(NA)	(NA)
Two or more	138	228	(NA)	9	14	(NA)	(NA)	(NA)	(NA)
Weeks of gestation: [2]									
Less than 9 weeks	800	811	(NA)	52	51	(NA)	(NA)	(NA)	(NA)
9 to 10 weeks	417	425	(NA)	27	27	(NA)	(NA)	(NA)	(NA)
11 to 12 weeks	202	198	(NA)	13	12	(NA)	(NA)	(NA)	(NA)
13 weeks or more	136	154	(NA)	9	10	(NA)	(NA)	(NA)	(NA)

NA Not available. [1] Number of abortions per 1,000 abortions and live births. Live births are those which occurred from July 1 of year shown through June 30 of the following year (to match time of conception with abortions). [2] Beginning 1985, data not exactly comparable with prior years because of a change in the method of calculation.

Source of tables 111 and 112: S.K. Henshaw and J. Van Vort, eds., *Abortion Factbook, 1992 Edition: Readings, Trends, and State and Local Data to 1988*, The Alan Guttmacher Institute, New York, NY, 1992 (copyright); S.K. Henshaw and J. Van Vort, *Abortion Services in the United States, 1991 and 1992; Family Perspectives, 26:100, 1994*; and unpublished data.

Source: U.S. Bureau of the Census, *Statistical Abstract of the United States: 1994*, (114th edition), Washington, D.C.: U.S. Government Printing Office, 1994, Table 112.

C3-15. Number and Rate of Abortions per 1,000 Women, and Abortion/Live Birth Ratio, by State of Occurrence: 1980, 1985, and 1992

[Number of abortions from surveys of hospitals, clinics, and physicians identified as providers of abortion services conducted by The Alan Guttmacher Institute. Abortion rates are computed per 1,000 women 15 to 44 years of age on July 1 of specified year; abortion ratios are computed as the number of abortions per 1,000 live births from July 1 of year shown to June 30 of following year, by State of occurrence]

DIVISION, REGION, AND STATE	NUMBER OF ABORTIONS (1,000)			RATE PER 1,000 WOMEN, 15 TO 44 YEARS OLD			RATIO: ABORTIONS PER 1,000 LIVE BIRTHS		
	1980	1985	1992	1980	1985	1992	1980	1985	1992
United States	1,554	1,589	1,529	29.3	28.0	25.9	428	422	379
Northeast	396	407	379	34.9	(NA)	32.1	604	(NA)	506
New England	84	85	78	28.9	28.6	25.2	530	504	429
Maine	5	5	4	18.6	18.6	14.7	289	306	282
New Hampshire	5	7	4	21.1	29.0	14.6	347	419	269
Vermont	4	3	3	30.4	26.2	21.2	466	448	393
Massachusetts	46	40	41	33.5	29.3	28.4	609	533	472
Rhode Island	7	8	7	30.7	35.5	30.0	529	572	461
Connecticut	19	22	20	25.6	29.3	26.2	561	550	444
Middle Atlantic	312	322	300	37.0	37.6	34.6	627	607	530
New York	188	195	195	45.8	47.4	46.2	780	746	694
New Jersey	56	69	55	32.8	39.6	31.0	591	672	460
Pennsylvania	69	57	50	26.1	21.3	18.6	423	348	302
Midwest	318	289	262	23.3	(NA)	18.9	336	(NA)	287
East North Central	243	221	205	24.9	22.1	20.7	369	356	313
Ohio	67	57	50	26.8	22.4	19.5	397	357	294
Indiana	20	16	16	15.3	12.2	12.0	227	202	185
Illinois	69	65	68	25.9	23.8	25.4	374	372	361
Michigan	65	64	56	29.7	28.7	25.2	457	486	393
Wisconsin	22	18	15	20.1	15.7	13.6	292	246	223
West North Central	75	68	57	19.2	16.7	14.3	260	252	221
Minnesota	20	17	16	20.7	16.6	15.6	288	257	251
Iowa	9	10	7	14.3	15.0	11.4	195	248	185
Missouri	22	20	14	19.4	17.3	11.6	273	261	175
North Dakota	3	3	1	21.5	18.5	10.7	235	230	149
South Dakota	1	2	1	9.0	10.6	6.8	103	140	92
Nebraska	6	7	6	17.9	18.2	15.7	227	268	246
Kansas	14	10	13	25.6	18.2	22.4	343	264	353
South	457	453	450	25.9	(NA)	22.0	369	(NA)	323
South Atlantic	255	257	269	29.4	27.1	25.9	462	429	397
Delaware	4	5	6	25.9	30.9	35.2	395	451	502
Maryland	31	30	31	29.2	26.9	26.4	571	480	454
District of Columbia	29	24	21	168.3	145.9	138.4	1,569	1,186	1,104
Virginia	32	34	35	24.2	24.0	22.7	417	412	373
West Virginia	3	5	3	6.9	10.1	7.7	104	185	134
North Carolina	32	34	36	22.8	22.6	22.4	377	379	357
South Carolina	14	11	12	18.2	13.7	14.2	274	228	229
Georgia	38	38	40	28.4	26.1	24.0	395	397	350
Florida	74	77	85	35.5	31.8	30.0	547	465	438
East South Central	66	57	54	19.2	15.8	14.9	271	258	228
Kentucky	13	10	10	15.1	11.0	11.4	215	189	191
Tennessee	26	22	19	23.6	19.1	16.2	352	315	243
Alabama	21	19	17	23.1	20.2	18.2	331	333	277
Mississippi	6	6	8	10.6	9.7	12.4	132	142	176
West South Central	137	139	127	24.5	21.8	19.6	306	290	266
Arkansas	6	5	7	12.3	10.1	13.5	173	159	213
Louisiana	18	19	14	17.6	17.4	13.4	218	240	195
Oklahoma	11	13	9	16.4	17.1	12.5	221	269	193
Texas	102	101	97	30.0	25.5	23.1	367	320	297
West	383	440	438	36.8	(NA)	34.1	486	(NA)	446
Mountain	68	75	70	25.0	23.6	21.0	302	316	280
Montana	4	4	3	20.1	19.0	18.2	265	288	298
Idaho	3	3	2	12.7	11.1	7.2	141	155	97
Wyoming	1	1	-	9.5	7.9	4.3	107	125	74
Colorado	23	24	20	31.4	28.8	23.6	447	438	362
New Mexico	8	6	6	27.0	17.4	17.7	358	219	228
Arizona	16	22	21	25.0	29.9	24.1	310	373	295
Utah	4	4	4	12.3	11.1	9.3	97	116	104
Nevada	9	10	13	46.6	40.5	44.2	697	641	591
Pacific	315	365	368	41.0	42.8	38.7	561	594	501
Washington	37	31	33	37.5	28.0	27.7	522	458	447
Oregon	18	15	16	28.3	22.3	23.9	396	374	372
California	250	304	304	43.7	47.9	42.1	598	640	519
Alaska	2	4	2	17.9	27.7	16.5	196	283	222
Hawaii	8	11	12	34.4	43.7	46.0	441	611	617

NA Not available.

Source: S.K. Henshaw and J. Van Vort, eds., *Abortion Factbook, 1992 Edition: Readings, Trends, and State and Local Data to 1988*, The Alan Guttmacher Institute, New York, NY, 1992 (copyright); S.K. Henshaw and J. Vam Vort, *Abortion Services in the United States, 1991 and 1992*, Family Planning Perspectives, 26:100, 1994; and unpublished data.

Source: U.S. Bureau of the Census, *Statistical Abstract of the United States: 1994*, (114th edition), Washington, D.C.: U.S. Government Printing Office, 1994, Table 113.

C3-16. Proportion of Unintended Pregnancies Aborted: 1988

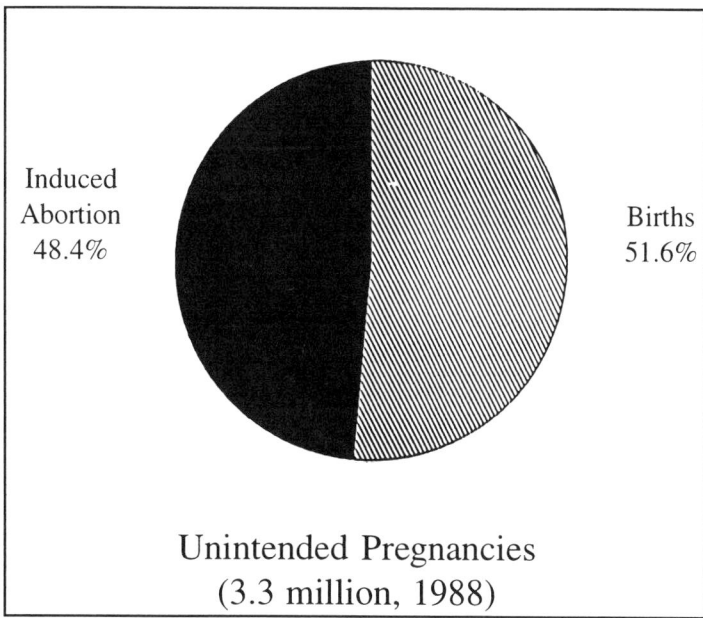

Induced
Abortion
48.4%

Births
51.6%

Unintended Pregnancies
(3.3 million, 1988)

Source: Jacqueline D. Forrest, The Alan Guttmacher Institute, "Levels and Determinants of U.S. Fertility," presentation at The Population and Consumption Task Force of the President's Council on Sustainable Development, October 27, 1994, unpublished.

Prenatal Care, Health Behavior during Pregnancy, and Deliveries

C3-17. Percent Low Birthweight Babies, by Race: 1970 to 1992

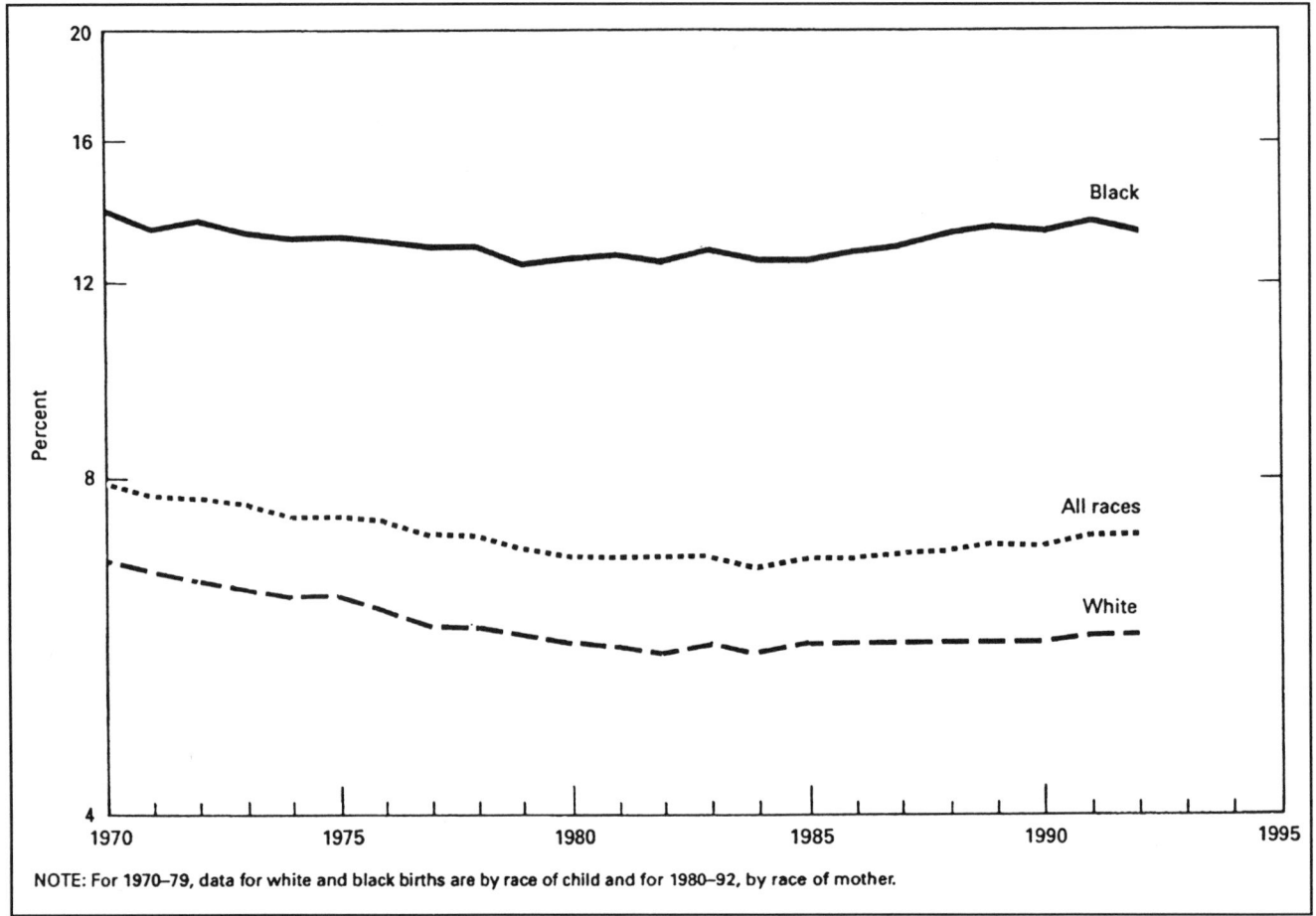

NOTE: For 1970–79, data for white and black births are by race of child and for 1980–92, by race of mother.

Source: S. J. Ventura, J. A. Martin, S. M. Taffel, et. al., National Center for Health Statistics, *Advance Report of Final Natality Statistics, 1992*, Monthly Vital Statistics Report, Vol. 43, No. 5 (suppl.), (PHS) 95-1120 4-0677, Washington, D.C.: U.S. Department of Health and Human Services, October 25, 1994, Figure 5.

C3-18. Percentage of Mothers with Early Prenatal Care and Mothers with Late or No Prenatal Care for United States and State of Residence: 1992

[By place of residence]

State	Percent beginning care in 1st trimester			Percent late [1] or no care		
	All races [2]	White	Black	All races [2]	White	Black
United States.	77.7	80.8	63.9	5.2	4.2	9.9
Alabama.	77.1	84.2	63.7	4.7	2.6	8.7
Alaska	83.1	85.8	81.7	3.0	2.2	*
Arizona	71.3	73.0	66.6	8.1	7.5	10.1
Arkansas	72.3	77.0	57.3	6.5	4.7	12.2
California	75.1	74.9	72.3	5.3	5.4	6.3
Colorado	79.0	80.1	67.6	4.9	4.5	8.8
Connecticut.	87.5	89.8	72.8	2.6	1.9	7.0
Delaware	80.5	86.7	61.3	4.7	2.6	11.2
District of Columbia	56.9	87.0	52.3	13.9	3.1	16.0
Florida	77.9	82.2	64.4	4.6	3.5	8.0
Georgia	75.8	82.6	64.2	5.4	3.5	8.6
Hawaii	73.6	76.8	65.9	5.7	3.7	4.7
Idaho.	76.6	76.8	69.6	5.2	5.1	*
Illinois	78.2	82.6	63.2	5.0	3.7	9.6
Indiana.	78.3	80.4	61.7	4.9	4.2	10.4
Iowa	86.2	86.9	72.0	2.4	2.2	5.6
Kansas	83.6	85.0	71.3	3.2	2.8	7.0
Kentucky	80.1	81.6	65.8	4.2	3.7	8.4
Louisiana	76.3	85.5	63.9	5.8	2.7	10.1
Maine	87.3	87.4	80.2	1.8	1.8	*
Maryland	85.0	90.7	72.8	3.7	1.8	7.7
Massachusetts.	87.2	89.1	74.4	2.1	1.7	5.2
Michigan.	80.8	84.9	65.6	3.7	2.5	8.4
Minnesota.	81.8	84.9	52.4	3.5	2.4	13.8
Mississippi	74.9	84.8	64.6	5.0	2.4	7.7
Missouri	80.5	84.0	64.0	4.2	2.9	10.6
Montana.	78.2	80.9	81.3	4.2	3.2	*
Nebraska	82.3	83.7	66.4	3.2	2.8	7.9
Nevada	71.5	73.5	54.7	7.8	7.0	13.8
New Hampshire	87.3	87.5	72.8	2.1	2.0	*
New Jersey.	81.5	86.1	62.7	4.6	2.8	11.8
New Mexico	61.7	64.6	53.3	9.9	8.6	12.7
New York	74.7	79.9	56.9	6.8	4.8	13.8
North Carolina	79.4	85.8	64.7	4.2	2.4	8.4
North Dakota.	82.2	84.4	73.0	2.8	2.0	*
Ohio.	82.3	85.3	66.4	3.9	2.7	10.1
Oklahoma.	74.6	77.9	58.9	6.4	5.1	12.1
Oregon	78.7	79.3	65.7	4.0	3.8	8.3
Pennsylvania.	79.6	84.3	54.8	5.2	3.1	16.9
Rhode Island	88.5	90.4	73.8	2.0	1.5	5.5
South Carolina	71.3	80.8	56.1	6.9	3.9	11.8
South Dakota.	79.0	82.3	65.8	5.0	2.8	*
Tennessee	79.6	83.6	67.2	4.0	2.7	7.6
Texas	70.3	71.2	62.8	9.2	8.9	12.1
Utah	85.0	86.0	71.1	2.5	2.1	*
Vermont	84.5	84.7	75.0	2.7	2.6	*
Virginia	81.8	86.6	68.1	3.7	2.4	7.6
Washington.	79.8	81.0	68.9	4.0	3.7	7.8
West Virginia	76.7	77.5	55.4	4.2	3.9	13.2
Wisconsin.	82.0	85.8	60.2	3.6	2.5	10.7
Wyoming	79.0	79.8	66.2	4.3	3.9	*

[1] Care beginning in 3d trimester.
[2] Includes races other than white and black.

Source: S. J. Ventura, J. A. Martin, S. M. Taffel, et. al., National Center for Health Statistics, *Advance Report of Final Natality Statistics, 1992*, Monthly Vital Statistics Report, Vol. 43, No. 5 (suppl.), (PHS) 95-1120 4-0677, Washington, D.C.: U.S. Department of Health and Human Services, October 25, 1994, Table 34.

C3-19. Percentage of White and Black Mothers with Early Prenatal Care: 1970 to 1991

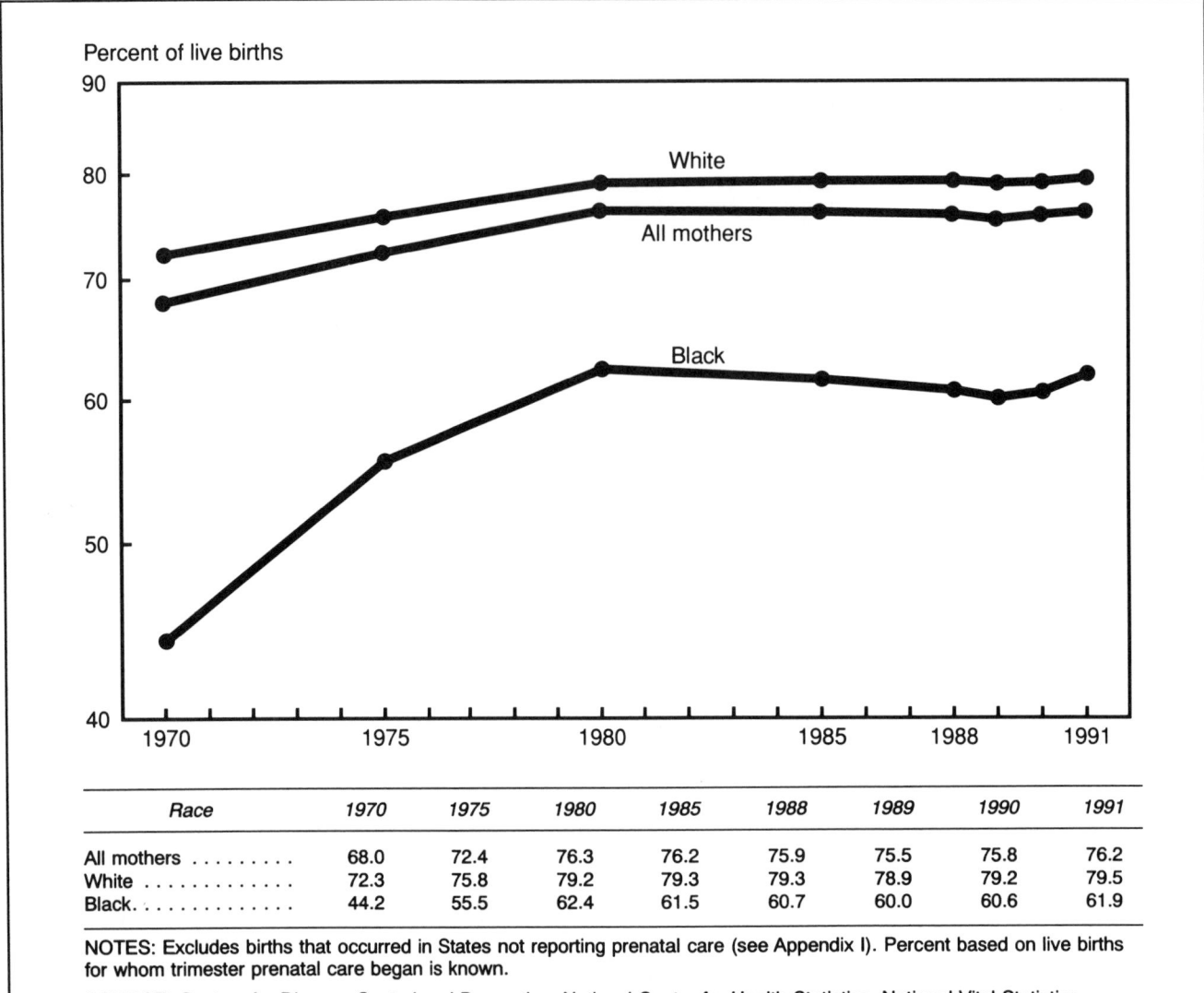

Percent of live births

Race	1970	1975	1980	1985	1988	1989	1990	1991
All mothers	68.0	72.4	76.3	76.2	75.9	75.5	75.8	76.2
White	72.3	75.8	79.2	79.3	79.3	78.9	79.2	79.5
Black.	44.2	55.5	62.4	61.5	60.7	60.0	60.6	61.9

NOTES: Excludes births that occurred in States not reporting prenatal care (see Appendix I). Percent based on live births for whom trimester prenatal care began is known.

SOURCE: Centers for Disease Control and Prevention, National Center for Health Statistics, National Vital Statistics System. See related *Health, United States, 1993*, table 9.

Source: National Center for Health Statistics, *Health, United States, 1993*, (PHS) 94-1232, Washington, D.C.: U.S. Government Printing Office, 1994, Figure 6.

C3-20. Percentage of Mothers with Early Prenatal Care, by Race and Hispanic Origin of Mother: 1991

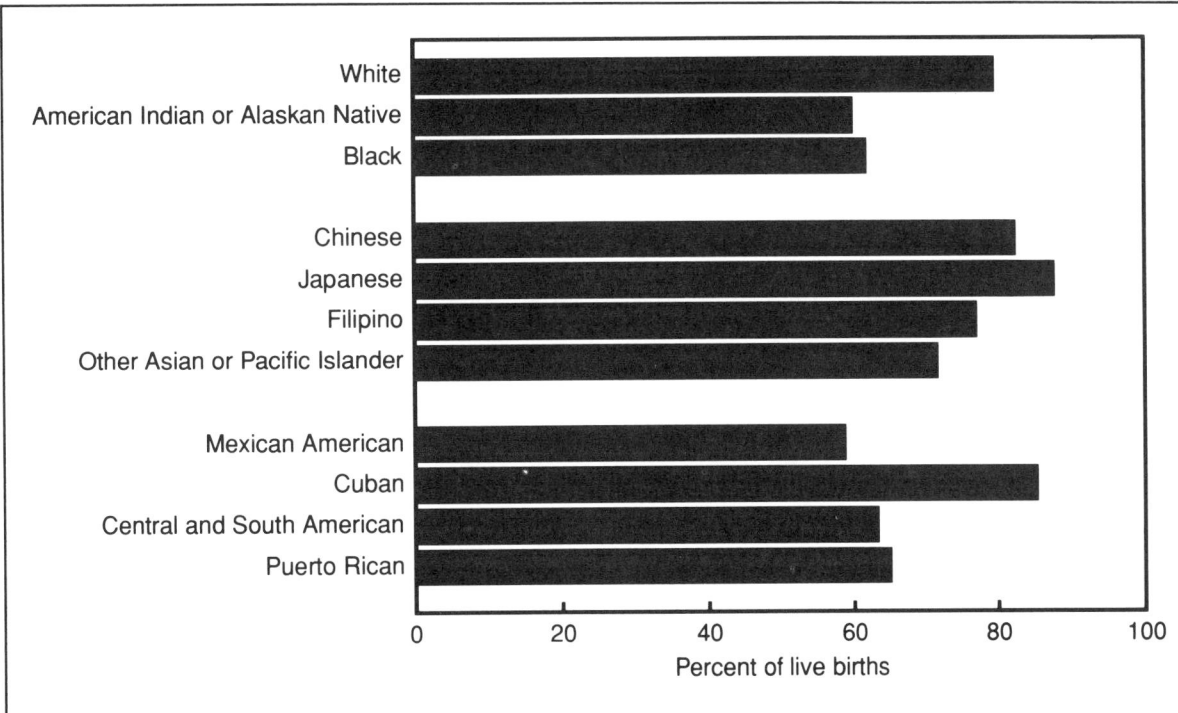

Race and Hispanic origin	Percent
White	79.5
American Indian or Alaskan Native.	59.9
Black.	61.9
Chinese.	82.3
Japanese.	87.7
Filipino	77.1
Other Asian or Pacific Islander[1]	71.7
Mexican American	58.7
Cuban	85.4
Central and South American	63.4
Puerto Rican	65.0

[1]Includes Hawaiians and part Hawaiians.

NOTES: Percent is based on live births for whom trimester prenatal care began is known. The race groups white, black, Asian or Pacific Islander subgroups, and American Indian or Alaskan Native include persons of Hispanic and non-Hispanic origin. Conversely, persons of Hispanic origin may be of any race. Data for Hispanic subgroups exclude data from New Hampshire (see Appendix I)

SOURCE: Centers for Disease Control and Prevention, National Center for Health Statistics, National Vital Statistics System. See related *Health, United States, 1993*, table 9.

Source: National Center for Health Statistics, *Health, United States, 1993*, (PHS) 94-1232, Washington, D.C.: U.S. Government Printing Office, 1994, Figure 7.

C3-21. Number of Live Births, by Mother's Smoking Status, Age, and Race: 1992 (46 Reporting States and the District of Columbia)

Smoking status, smoking measure, and race of mother	All ages	Under 15 years	Age of mother 15–19 years Total	15–17 years	18–19 years	20–24 years	25–29 years	30–34 years	35–39 years	40–49 years
All races[1]					Number					
Total	3,080,239	9,772	397,738	147,376	250,362	825,367	891,828	667,846	248,391	39,297
Smoker	506,023	652	71,812	22,401	49,411	163,134	139,729	94,014	32,295	4,387
Nonsmoker	2,486,246	8,831	315,174	120,870	194,304	639,953	726,855	553,655	208,190	33,588
Not stated	87,970	289	10,752	4,105	6,647	22,280	25,244	20,177	7,906	1,322
White										
Total	2,413,588	3,809	259,314	88,637	170,677	616,031	732,081	563,415	206,826	32,112
Smoker	420,713	531	62,506	19,379	43,127	138,063	114,596	76,046	25,480	3,491
Nonsmoker	1,925,482	3,148	189,921	66,784	123,137	461,887	597,346	470,766	174,866	27,548
Not stated	67,393	130	6,887	2,474	4,413	16,081	20,139	16,603	6,480	1,073
Black										
Total	556,629	5,704	127,181	54,642	72,539	183,265	127,147	78,324	30,055	4,953
Smoker	74,450	100	7,346	2,305	5,041	21,591	22,361	16,214	6,067	771
Nonsmoker	465,256	5,450	116,344	50,832	65,512	156,266	100,718	59,481	22,989	4,008
Not stated	16,923	154	3,491	1,505	1,986	5,408	4,068	2,629	999	174
					Percent					
Smoker[1]	16.9	6.9	18.6	15.6	20.3	20.3	16.1	14.5	13.4	11.6
White	17.9	14.4	24.8	22.5	25.9	23.0	16.1	13.9	12.7	11.2
Black	13.8	1.8	5.9	4.3	7.1	12.1	18.2	21.4	20.9	16.1
All races[1]					Percent distribution					
Smoker	100.0	100.0	100.0	100.0	100.0	100.0	100.0	100.0	100.0	100.0
1–5 cigarettes	21.4	38.7	27.2	31.2	25.4	21.7	20.2	19.6	18.6	18.4
6–10 cigarettes	40.4	40.4	43.5	44	43.3	41.3	40	38.6	36.8	34.9
11–15 cigarettes	6.5	4.8	5.2	4.4	5.6	6.4	6.9	7.1	6.5	7.0
16–20 cigarettes	26.3	14.3	21	18	22.4	26	27.4	27.9	29.3	29.8
21–30 cigarettes	3.7	*	2.2	1.8	2.3	3.2	3.9	4.7	5.6	6.0
31–40 cigarettes	1.4	*	0.8	0.6	0.9	1.2	1.4	1.9	2.8	3.3
41 cigarettes or more	0.2	*	0.1	0.1	0.1	0.2	0.2	0.2	0.4	0.5
White										
Smoker	100.0	100.0	100.0	100.0	100.0	100.0	100.0	100.0	100.0	100.0
1–5 cigarettes	18.7	34.6	24.3	28.3	22.5	18.6	17.3	17.2	16.3	16.2
6–10 cigarettes	39.9	42.3	44.2	45.0	43.8	41.2	39.1	37.4	35.2	33.9
11–15 cigarettes	7.2	5.2	5.6	4.7	6.0	7.0	7.7	7.9	7.1	7.6
16–20 cigarettes	28.3	16.3	22.6	19.3	24.1	28.2	29.7	29.9	31.3	31.2
21–30 cigarettes	4.2	*	2.4	2.0	2.5	3.6	4.5	5.3	6.4	6.9
31–40 cigarettes	1.5	*	0.8	0.6	0.9	1.2	1.6	2.0	3.2	3.7
41 cigarettes or more	0.2	*	0.1	*	0.1	0.2	0.2	0.2	0.5	*
Black										
Smoker	100.0	100.0	100.0	100.0	100.0	100.0	100.0	100.0	100.0	100.0
1–5 cigarettes	35.4	57.1	48.0	52.1	46.2	39.2	34.1	29.9	27.0	27.1
6–10 cigarettes	42.9	31.9	38.4	35.5	39.8	42.6	44.1	44.1	43.0	38.9
11–15 cigarettes	3.0	*	2.1	1.7	2.2	2.5	3.1	3.6	3.9	4.5
16–20 cigarettes	16.0	*	9.9	9.0	10.3	13.8	16.3	19.1	21.8	24.2
21–30 cigarettes	1.5	*	0.8	*	0.8	1.2	1.5	1.9	2.3	2.9
31–40 cigarettes	0.9	*	0.7	*	0.6	0.7	0.8	1.2	1.6	*
41 cigarettes or more	0.2	*	*	*	*	0.1	0.2	0.2	0.4	*

[1]Includes races other than white and black.

NOTE: Excludes data for California, Indiana, New York, and South Dakota, which did not require reporting of tobacco use during pregnancy.

Source: S. J. Ventura, J. A. Martin, S. M. Taffel, et. al., National Center for Health Statistics, *Advance Report of Final Natality Statistics, 1992*, Monthly Vital Statistics Report, Vol. 43, No. 5 (suppl.), (PHS) 95-1120 4-0677, Washington, D.C.: U.S. Department of Health and Human Services, October 25, 1994, Table 28.

C3-22. Number of Live Births by Mother's Smoking Status, Age, and Race or National Origin: 1990 (45 Reporting States and the District of Columbia)

[For a listing of reporting areas see Technical Appendix, table A]

Smoking status and race of mother	All ages	Under 15 years	15-19 years			20-24 years	25-29 years	30-34 years	35-39 years	40-49 years
			Total	15-17 years	18-19 years					
Number										
All races¹	3,103,146	9,316	404,409	142,181	262,228	824,541	954,363	651,077	225,704	33,736
Smoker	551,080	673	81,125	24,121	57,004	175,392	165,336	95,789	26,803	3,962
Non-smoker	2,437,784	8,309	309,073	112,970	196,103	619,916	754,631	530,214	187,364	28,277
Not stated	114,282	334	14,211	5,090	9,121	29,233	34,396	25,074	9,537	1,497
White	2,443,822	3,535	264,695	84,647	180,048	620,227	788,908	550,146	188,729	27,582
Smoker	455,940	540	69,911	20,743	49,168	146,105	135,591	77,487	23,123	3,183
Non-smoker	1,899,598	2,845	185,457	60,749	124,708	452,733	625,839	451,907	157,664	23,153
Not stated	88,284	150	9,327	3,155	6,172	21,389	27,478	20,752	7,942	1,246
Black	557,392	5,567	129,517	53,984	75,533	180,432	133,583	76,977	27,060	4,256
Smoker	85,002	114	9,419	2,780	6,639	26,066	27,020	16,639	5,082	662
Non-smoker	450,942	5,286	115,632	49,415	66,217	147,454	101,042	57,194	20,904	3,430
Not stated	21,448	167	4,466	1,789	2,677	6,912	5,521	3,144	1,074	164
American Indian²	29,556	120	5,487	1,959	3,528	9,537	7,921	4,421	1,730	340
Smoker	6,373	15	1,297	450	847	2,175	1,711	850	280	45
Non-smoker	22,129	98	3,953	1,416	2,537	7,032	5,939	3,430	1,390	287
Not stated	1,054	7	237	93	144	330	271	141	60	8
Chinese	7,525	3	127	46	81	677	2,596	2,765	1,185	172
Smoker	143	–	14	2	12	20	33	49	23	4
Non-smoker	6,969	3	110	43	67	633	2,429	2,539	1,097	158
Not stated	413	–	3	1	2	24	134	177	65	10
Japanese	4,735	1	177	46	131	501	1,433	1,725	763	135
Smoker	370	–	31	10	21	71	109	105	46	8
Non-smoker	4,228	1	143	36	107	421	1,287	1,563	689	124
Not stated	137	–	3	–	3	9	37	57	28	3
Hawaiian	5,477	14	1,013	349	664	1,760	1,538	794	316	42
Smoker	1,132	2	224	59	165	365	302	177	55	7
Non-smoker	4,270	12	773	285	488	1,370	1,218	605	258	34
Not stated	75	–	16	5	11	25	18	12	3	1
Filipino	9,367	11	692	243	449	2,036	2,782	2,443	1,168	235
Smoker	479	1	58	23	35	134	134	102	42	8
Non-smoker	8,495	8	613	213	400	1,835	2,539	2,215	1,071	214
Not stated	393	2	21	7	14	67	109	126	55	13
Other Asian or Pacific Islander	43,328	57	2,473	835	1,638	8,832	15,013	11,421	4,587	945
Smoker	1,558	1	158	49	109	435	413	364	144	43
Non-smoker	39,340	49	2,185	748	1,437	7,934	13,787	10,399	4,136	850
Not stated	2,430	7	130	38	92	463	813	658	307	52
Percent										
SMOKERS										
All races¹	18.4	7.5	20.8	17.6	22.5	22.1	18.0	15.3	13.3	12.3
White	19.4	16.0	27.4	25.5	28.3	24.4	17.8	14.6	12.8	12.1
Black	15.9	2.1	7.5	5.3	9.1	15.0	21.1	22.5	19.6	16.2
American Indian²	22.4	*	24.7	24.1	25.0	23.6	22.4	19.9	16.8	13.6
Chinese	2.0	*	*	*	*	3.1	1.3	1.9	2.1	*
Japanese	8.0	*	17.8	*	16.4	14.4	7.8	6.3	6.3	*
Hawaiian	21.0	*	22.5	17.2	25.3	21.0	19.9	22.6	17.6	*
Filipino	5.3	*	8.6	9.7	8.0	6.8	5.0	4.4	3.8	*
Other Asian or Pacific Islander	3.8	*	6.7	6.1	7.1	5.2	2.9	3.4	3.4	4.8

¹ Includes births of other races not shown separately.
² Includes Aleuts and Eskimos.

Source: National Center for Health Statistics, *Vital Statistics of the United States, 1990,* Vol. 1 (Natality), Washington, D.C.: U.S. Government Printing Office, 1994, Table 1-129.

C3-23. Number of Live Births by Mother's Age and Smoking Status and Hispanic Origin: 1992 (45 Reporting States and the District of Columbia)

Origin of mother	Smoking status				Age of mother									
	Total	Smoker	Nonsmoker	Not stated	All ages	Under 15 years	15–19 years			20–24 years	25–29 years	30–34 years	35–39 years	40–49 years
							Total	15–17 years	18–19 years					
	Number				Percent smokers									
All origins[1]	3,064,249	502,897	2,473,412	87,940	16.9	6.9	18.5	15.6	20.0	20.3	16.1	14.5	13.4	11.5
Hispanic	324,649	18,081	294,919	11,649	5.8	3.4	5.8	5.3	6.0	6.1	5.5	5.7	5.7	5.0
Mexican	203,564	8,317	187,051	8,196	4.3	3.4	4.1	3.8	4.2	4.2	4.1	4.7	4.6	4.6
Puerto Rican	35,960	4,390	30,215	1,355	12.7	*	11.2	9.4	12.2	13.9	13.0	12.5	11.5	9.7
Cuban	10,022	590	9,350	82	5.9	*	6.6	*	6.1	6.3	5.2	6.4	6.9	*
Central and South American	35,508	890	33,724	894	2.6	*	3.0	3.1	3.0	2.3	2.4	2.8	3.2	*
Other and unknown Hispanic	39,595	3,894	34,579	1,122	10.1	*	9.5	8.5	10.1	11.3	9.8	9.1	10.3	10.2
Non-Hispanic[2]	2,714,613	480,240	2,161,480	72,893	18.2	7.4	20.6	17.5	22.2	22.3	17.2	15.2	14.1	12.3
White	2,063,552	396,714	1,613,497	53,341	19.7	20.9	29.9	28.3	30.4	26.2	17.4	14.7	13.5	12.1
Black	546,925	73,399	457,364	16,162	13.8	1.8	5.9	4.3	7.0	12.1	18.3	21.6	21.0	16.4

[1]Includes origin not stated.
[2]Includes races other than white and black.

NOTE: Excludes data for California, Indiana, New Hampshire, New York, and South Dakota, which did not require reporting of either Hispanic origin of mother or tobacco use during pregnancy.

Source: S. J. Ventura, J. A. Martin, S. M. Taffel, et. al., National Center for Health Statistics, *Advance Report of Final Natality Statistics, 1992*, Monthly Vital Statistics Report, Vol. 43, No. 5 (suppl.), (PHS) 95-1120 4-0677, Washington, D.C.: U.S. Department of Health and Human Services, October 25, 1994, Table 29.

C3-24. Births to Mothers Who Smoked during Pregnancy, by Educational Attainment and Race of Mother: 1992 (46 Reporting States and the District of Columbia)

Smoking measure and race of mother	Total	Years of school completed by mother					
		0–8 years	9–11 years	12 years	13–15 years	16 years or more	Not stated
		Number					
All races[1]	3,080,239	144,221	515,655	1,143,580	646,489	581,145	49,149
White	2,413,588	116,035	350,357	877,591	520,880	514,397	34,328
Black	556,629	20,455	148,517	230,587	105,876	40,578	10,616
		Percent					
Smoker[1]	16.9	16.8	30.6	20.1	12.0	3.9	17.2
White	17.9	18.3	35.9	22.1	12.6	4.0	17.5
Black	13.8	11.4	19.3	13.5	10.1	4.7	20.3
All races[1]		Percent distribution					
Smoker	100.0	100.0	100.0	100.0	100.0	100.0	100.0
10 cigarettes or less	61.9	55.9	60.5	61.2	64.8	73.9	63.7
11–20 cigarettes	32.8	35.6	33.5	33.8	30.7	22.5	30.8
21 cigarettes or more	5.4	8.5	6.0	5.1	4.4	3.6	5.6
White							
Smoker	100.0	100.0	100.0	100.0	100.0	100.0	100.0
10 cigarettes or less	58.6	53.5	56.3	58.0	62.3	73.0	59.9
11–20 cigarettes	35.5	37.3	37.0	36.5	32.8	23.1	33.7
21 cigarettes or more	5.9	9.2	6.8	5.5	4.9	3.8	6.5
Black							
Smoker	100.0	100.0	100.0	100.0	100.0	100.0	100.0
10 cigarettes or less	78.3	72.3	77.6	79.2	79.1	81.0	74.1
11–20 cigarettes	19.0	23.9	19.3	18.4	18.9	17.7	23.0
21 cigarettes or more	2.6	3.9	3.1	2.3	2.0	1.2	2.9

[1]Includes races other than white and black.

NOTE: Excludes data for California, Indiana, New York, and South Dakota, which did not require reporting of tobacco use during pregnancy.

Source: S. J. Ventura, J. A. Martin, S. M. Taffel, et. al., National Center for Health Statistics, *Advance Report of Final Natality Statistics, 1992*, Monthly Vital Statistics Report, Vol. 43, No. 5 (suppl.), (PHS) 95-1120 4-0677, Washington, D.C.: U.S. Department of Health and Human Services, October 25, 1994, Table 30.

C3-25. Number of Live Births, by Mother's Drinking Status and Age and Race: 1992 (47 Reporting States and the District of Columbia)

Drinking status, drinking measure, and race of mother	All ages	Under 15 years	Age of mother							
			15–19 years			20–24 years	25–29 years	30–34 years	35–39 years	40–49 years
			Total	15–17 years	18–19 years					
All races [1]					*Number*					
Total	3,164,379	9,973	409,406	151,457	257,949	850,586	916,905	683,809	253,578	40,122
Drinker	78,651	82	5,381	1,701	3,680	16,613	22,864	22,723	9,634	1,354
Nondrinker	2,993,122	9,586	392,528	145,397	247,131	810,132	867,819	639,965	235,712	37,380
Not stated	92,606	305	11,497	4,359	7,138	23,841	26,222	21,121	8,232	1,388
White										
Total	2,487,502	3,908	268,377	91,608	176,769	637,837	754,963	578,066	211,503	32,848
Drinker	57,494	46	3,744	1,169	2,575	11,059	16,150	17,725	7,659	1,111
Nondrinker	2,359,345	3,732	257,205	87,794	169,411	609,541	718,027	543,085	197,139	30,616
Not stated	70,663	130	7,428	2,645	4,783	17,237	20,786	17,256	6,705	1,121
Black										
Total	566,055	5,806	129,734	55,737	73,997	186,549	129,060	79,409	30,472	5,025
Drinker	18,262	30	1,251	398	853	4,756	5,906	4,412	1,711	196
Nondrinker	529,591	5,608	124,786	53,752	71,034	176,008	118,767	72,117	27,666	4,639
Not stated	18,202	168	3,697	1,587	2,110	5,785	4,387	2,880	1,095	190
					Percent					
Drinker [1]	2.6	0.8	1.4	1.2	1.5	2.0	2.6	3.4	3.9	3.5
White	2.4	1.2	1.4	1.3	1.5	1.8	2.2	3.2	3.7	3.5
Black	3.3	0.5	1.0	0.7	1.2	2.6	4.7	5.8	5.8	4.1
All races [1]					*Percent distribution*					
Drinker	100.0	100.0	100.0	100.0	100.0	100.0	100.0	100.0	100.0	100.0
1 drink or less	60.7	62.7	59.6	59.3	59.7	58.3	60.1	62.6	62.3	58.1
2 drinks	16.5	*	17.0	17.3	16.8	16.2	16.2	16.5	16.8	19.0
3–4 drinks	10.5	*	11.2	11.1	11.2	11.6	10.7	9.9	9.9	9.9
5 drinks or more	12.3	*	12.3	12.3	12.3	13.9	13.0	11.0	11.0	12.9
White										
Drinker	100.0	100.0	100.0	100.0	100.0	100.0	100.0	100.0	100.0	100.0
1 drink or less	67.9	*	64.0	62.2	64.8	65.4	69.2	69.1	67.9	62.6
2 drinks	15.2	*	14.9	17.0	14.0	14.9	14.3	15.6	16.2	18.6
3–4 drinks	8.5	*	10.1	9.8	10.2	9.2	8.1	8.1	8.5	9.0
5 drinks or more	8.4	*	11.0	11.0	11.0	10.5	8.4	7.2	7.4	9.8
Black										
Drinker	100.0	100.0	100.0	100.0	100.0	100.0	100.0	100.0	100.0	100.0
1 drink or less	37.5	*	48.0	52.6	46.0	42.6	34.8	34.4	33.9	31.7
2 drinks	21.1	*	22.8	18.2	24.8	20.1	22.1	20.6	20.8	23.2
3–4 drinks	16.9	*	14.0	14.2	14.0	16.3	17.8	17.4	16.9	14.1
5 drinks or more	24.5	*	15.1	15.0	15.2	21.0	25.3	27.6	28.4	31.0

[1] Includes races other than white and black.

NOTE: Excludes data for California, New York, and South Dakota, which did not require reporting of alcohol use during pregnancy.

Source: S. J. Ventura, J. A. Martin, S. M. Taffel, et. al., National Center for Health Statistics, *Advance Report of Final Natality Statistics, 1992*, Monthly Vital Statistics Report, Vol. 43, No. 5 (suppl.), (PHS) 95-1120 4-0677, Washington, D.C.: U.S. Department of Health and Human Services, October 25, 1994, Table 32.

C3-26. Number of Live Births, by Mother's Drinking Status, Age, and Race or Asian National Origin: 1990 (46 Reporting States and the District of Columbia)

Drinking status and race of mother	All ages	Age of mother								
		Under 15 years	15-19 years			20-24 years	25-29 years	30-34 years	35-39 years	40-49 years
			Total	15-17 years	18-19 years					
Number										
All races [1]	3,189,360	9,524	416,744	146,311	270,433	849,898	981,555	666,713	230,500	34,426
Drinker	101,329	80	7,391	2,129	5,262	22,295	32,968	27,081	10,079	1,435
Non-drinker	2,959,930	9,067	393,279	138,436	254,843	794,681	910,083	611,621	209,865	31,334
Not stated	128,101	377	16,074	5,746	10,328	32,922	38,504	28,011	10,556	1,657
White	2,519,599	3,638	274,431	87,673	186,758	642,180	813,669	564,411	193,068	28,202
Drinker	78,050	45	5,346	1,554	3,792	15,729	25,234	22,048	8,434	1,214
Non-drinker	2,341,350	3,414	258,234	82,445	175,789	601,949	757,366	518,985	175,801	25,601
Not stated	100,199	179	10,851	3,674	7,177	24,502	31,069	23,378	8,833	1,387
Black	566,865	5,671	132,027	55,061	76,966	183,632	135,700	78,098	27,425	4,312
Drinker	20,321	26	1,651	444	1,207	5,731	6,893	4,439	1,403	178
Non-drinker	523,617	5,465	125,608	52,702	72,906	170,504	122,903	70,314	24,863	3,960
Not stated	22,927	180	4,768	1,915	2,853	7,397	5,904	3,345	1,159	174
American Indian [2]	29,661	120	5,507	1,963	3,544	9,572	7,954	4,437	1,730	341
Drinker	2,094	9	341	114	227	659	608	338	127	12
Non-drinker	26,391	103	4,913	1,752	3,161	8,542	7,041	3,933	1,540	319
Not stated	1,176	8	253	97	156	371	305	166	63	10
Chinese	7,610	3	127	46	81	682	2,633	2,795	1,196	174
Drinker	79	–	–	–	–	2	20	42	13	2
Non-drinker	7,100	3	124	45	79	652	2,473	2,572	1,115	161
Not stated	431	–	3	1	2	28	140	181	68	11
Japanese	4,768	1	177	46	131	502	1,442	1,739	771	136
Drinker	95	–	–	–	–	7	22	32	27	7
Non-drinker	4,522	1	174	46	128	483	1,376	1,649	713	126
Not stated	151	–	3	–	3	12	44	58	31	3
Hawaiian	5,489	14	1,015	349	666	1,764	1,541	795	318	42
Drinker	153	–	17	5	12	41	45	37	12	1
Non-drinker	5,226	14	976	337	639	1,689	1,468	739	300	40
Not stated	110	–	22	7	15	34	28	19	6	1
Filipino	9,445	11	696	244	452	2,049	2,805	2,467	1,181	236
Drinker	93	–	3	1	2	25	23	32	7	3
Non-drinker	8,935	9	667	234	433	1,955	2,666	2,305	1,113	220
Not stated	417	2	26	9	17	69	116	130	61	13
Other Asian or Pacific Islander	43,679	57	2,484	839	1,645	8,893	15,137	11,530	4,628	950
Drinker	403	–	30	10	20	94	113	101	49	16
Non-drinker	40,636	50	2,314	789	1,525	8,304	14,143	10,702	4,247	876
Not stated	2,640	7	140	40	100	495	881	727	332	58
Percent										
DRINKERS										
All races [1]	3.3	0.9	1.8	1.5	2.0	2.7	3.5	4.2	4.6	4.4
White	3.2	1.3	2.0	1.9	2.1	2.5	3.2	4.1	4.6	4.5
Black	3.7	.5	1.3	.8	1.6	3.3	5.3	5.9	5.3	4.3
American Indian [2]	7.4	·	6.5	6.1	6.7	7.2	7.9	7.9	7.6	·
Chinese	1.1	·	·	·	·	·	.8	1.6	1.2	·
Japanese	2.1	·	·	·	·	·	1.6	1.9	3.6	·
Hawaiian	2.8	·	·	·	·	2.4	3.0	4.8	·	·
Filipino	1.0	·	·	·	·	1.3	.9	1.4	·	·
Other Asian or Pacific Islander	1.0	·	1.3	·	1.3	1.1	.8	.9	1.1	·

[1] Includes births of other races not shown separately.
[2] Includes Aleuts and Eskimos.

Source: National Center for Health Statistics, *Vital Statistics of the United States, 1990*, Vol. 1 (Natality), Washington, D.C.: U.S. Government Printing Office, 1994, Table 1-135.

Adoption

C3-27. Percentage of Babies Born to Never-Married Mothers Placed for Adoption, by Race: 1965–72, 1973–81, and 1982–88

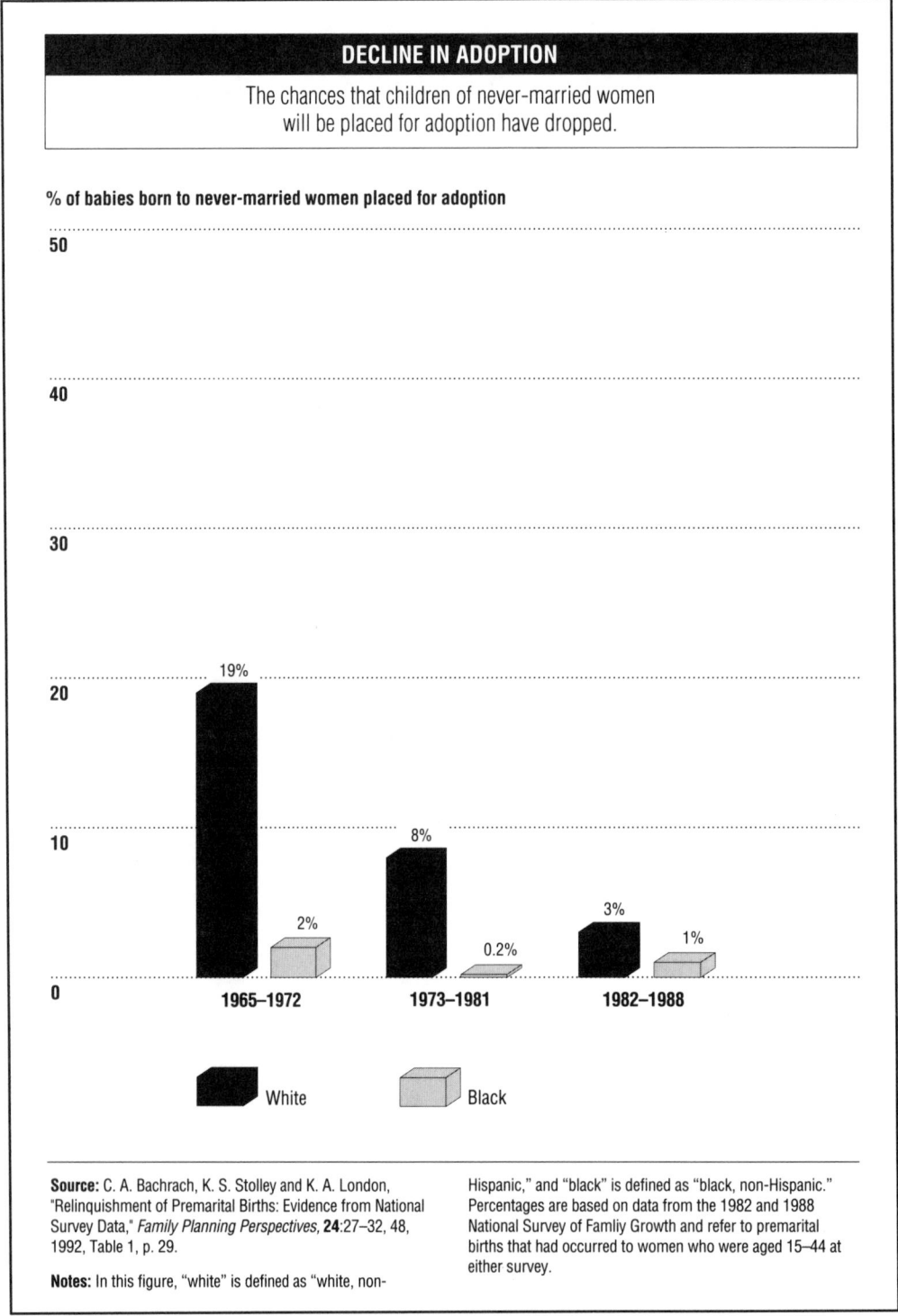

DECLINE IN ADOPTION

The chances that children of never-married women
will be placed for adoption have dropped.

% of babies born to never-married women placed for adoption

Source: C. A. Bachrach, K. S. Stolley and K. A. London, "Relinquishment of Premarital Births: Evidence from National Survey Data," *Family Planning Perspectives,* **24**:27–32, 48, 1992, Table 1, p. 29.

Notes: In this figure, "white" is defined as "white, non-Hispanic," and "black" is defined as "black, non-Hispanic." Percentages are based on data from the 1982 and 1988 National Survey of Famliy Growth and refer to premarital births that had occurred to women who were aged 15–44 at either survey.

Source: The Alan Guttmacher Institute, *Sex and America's Teenagers*, New York: The Alan Guttmacher Institute, 1994, Figure 39. Reprinted with permission.

C3-28. Children Living with Adoptive Married-Couple Parents and Living with Biological and Step-Parents, by Race and Hispanic Origin of Mother: 1980 to 1990

TYPE OF PARENT	ALL RACES [1]			WHITE			BLACK			His-panic origin,[2] 1990
	1980	1985	1990	1980	1985	1990	1980	1985	1990	
NUMBER (1,000)										
Own children under 18 years, total	47,248	45,347	45,448	42,329	39,942	39,732	3,775	3,816	3,671	4,568
Biological mother and father	39,523	37,213	37,026	35,852	33,202	32,975	2,698	2,661	2,336	3,703
Biological mother-stepfather	5,355	6,049	6,643	4,362	4,918	5,258	877	952	1,149	699
Stepmother-biological father	727	740	608	664	676	549	46	50	38	38
Adoptive mother and father.	1,350	866	974	1,209	754	815	119	76	97	101
Unknown mother or father	293	479	197	242	391	135	35	77	51	27
PERCENT DISTRIBUTION										
Own children under 18 years, total	100.0	100.0	100.0	100.0	100.0	100.0	100.0	100.0	100.0	100.0
Biological mother and father	83.7	82.1	81.5	84.7	83.1	83.0	71.5	69.7	63.6	81.1
Biological mother-stepfather	11.3	13.3	14.6	10.3	12.3	13.2	23.2	24.9	31.3	15.3
Stepmother-biological father	1.5	1.6	1.3	1.6	1.7	1.4	1.2	1.3	1.0	0.8
Adoptive mother and father.	2.9	1.9	2.1	2.9	1.9	2.1	3.1	2.0	2.6	2.2
Unknown mother or father	0.6	1.1	0.4	0.6	1.0	0.3	0.9	2.0	1.4	0.6

[1] Includes other races not shown separately.   [2] Persons of Hispanic origin may be of any race.

Source: U.S. Bureau of the Census, *Current Population Reports*, P23-180.

Source: U.S. Bureau of the Census, *Statistical Abstract of the United States: 1994*, (114th edition), Washington, D.C.: U.S. Government Printing Office, 1994, Table 79.

Sexually Transmitted Diseases

C3-29. Estimated Percentage Risk of Acquiring a Sexually Transmitted Disease (STD) in One Act of Unprotected Intercourse with an Infected Partner, by Sex: 1992

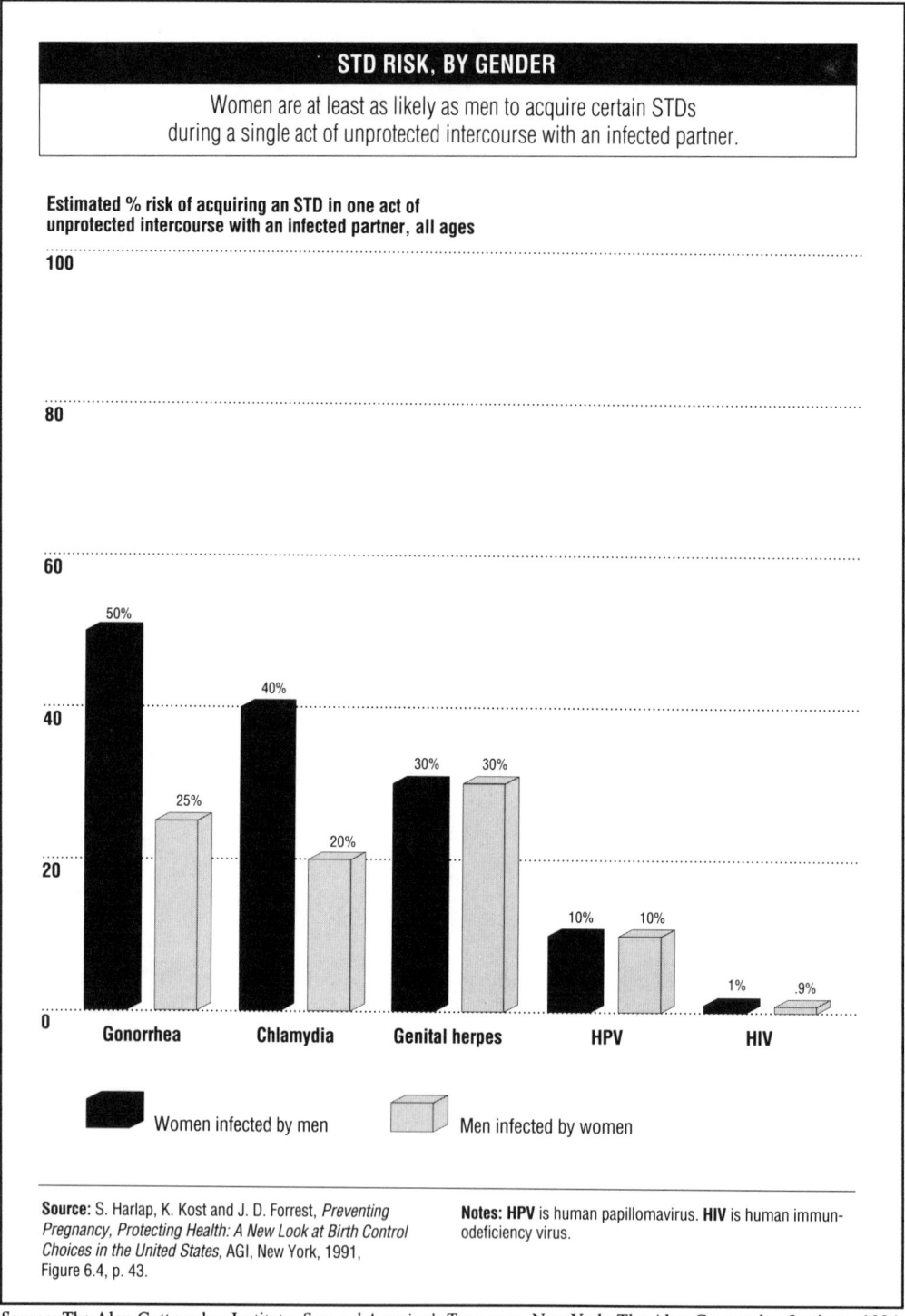

STD RISK, BY GENDER

Women are at least as likely as men to acquire certain STDs during a single act of unprotected intercourse with an infected partner.

Estimated % risk of acquiring an STD in one act of unprotected intercourse with an infected partner, all ages

■ Women infected by men   ▢ Men infected by women

Source: S. Harlap, K. Kost and J. D. Forrest, *Preventing Pregnancy, Protecting Health: A New Look at Birth Control Choices in the United States*, AGI, New York, 1991, Figure 6.4, p. 43.

Notes: HPV is human papillomavirus. **HIV** is human immunodeficiency virus.

Source: The Alan Guttmacher Institute, *Sex and America's Teenagers*, New York: The Alan Guttmacher Institute, 1994, Figure 20. Reprinted with permission.

C3-30. Reported Cases of Gonnorrhea among Women, by State and Outlying Areas: 1989 to 1993

State/Area	Cases					Rates per 100,000 Population				
	1989	1990	1991	1992	1993	1989	1990	1991	1992	1993
Alabama	9,134	10,242	9,011	7,583	6,679	435.2	486.7	423.6	353.7	311.6
Alaska	461	500	420	338	364	178.2	192.2	155.8	122.0	131.4
Arizona	2,005	2,076	2,030	1,872	1,885	109.4	111.9	106.8	96.4	97.1
Arkansas	3,386	3,696	3,185	3,880	3,550	278.6	303.5	259.5	314.1	287.4
California	27,484	20,584	17,696	16,014	12,605	188.2	138.5	116.6	103.6	81.5
Colorado	2,028	1,741	1,837	2,303	1,941	122.6	104.7	108.0	133.1	112.1
Connecticut	4,469	3,675	2,925	2,841	2,335	263.9	216.9	172.2	166.6	136.9
Delaware	1,566	1,549	1,370	827	770	461.6	451.3	391.4	232.6	216.6
Florida	19,973	17,398	14,047	11,515	10,086	306.1	260.6	204.9	164.4	144.0
Georgia	19,316	21,340	17,463	13,586	6,544	585.3	640.1	512.4	391.6	188.6
Hawaii	244	290	327	272	356	45.4	53.3	58.7	47.7	62.5
Idaho	95	88	97	67	102	19.0	17.4	18.7	12.7	19.3
Illinois	18,530	16,614	14,460	13,017	11,159	315.7	282.6	243.8	218.0	186.9
Indiana	5,263	5,327	5,219	4,392	3,993	185.0	186.5	180.9	151.2	137.5
Iowa	1,519	1,174	1,055	918	1,027	106.3	82.0	73.4	63.7	71.3
Kansas	2,570	2,431	2,145	2,122	1,897	203.8	192.5	168.7	166.0	148.4
Kentucky	2,535	2,732	2,719	2,098	2,126	133.8	143.8	142.1	109.1	110.5
Louisiana	6,216	4,921	5,123	5,329	5,122	281.9	224.8	232.4	240.4	231.1
Maine	135	127	94	53	37	21.6	20.2	14.8	8.3	5.8
Maryland	10,043	10,297	9,182	7,162	5,725	412.4	418.1	366.7	282.0	225.4
Massachusetts	3,516	3,201	2,629	1,581	1,426	112.4	102.3	84.2	50.6	45.7
Michigan	14,410	14,652	12,278	10,291	8,987	302.7	306.4	254.9	212.5	185.6
Minnesota	1,498	2,007	1,437	1,492	1,271	67.7	90.0	63.7	65.5	55.8
Mississippi	7,884	7,804	7,727	6,637	5,548	587.2	581.3	571.6	488.4	408.2
Missouri	9,755	9,346	7,788	6,814	5,859	369.2	352.3	291.4	253.4	217.8
Montana	102	120	62	53	50	25.3	29.8	15.2	13.0	12.2
Nebraska	998	908	901	803	434	123.6	112.2	110.5	98.0	53.0
Nevada	1,064	971	925	766	652	190.5	164.6	147.3	116.7	99.3
New Hampshire	84	109	128	62	43	14.9	19.3	22.6	10.9	7.6
New Jersey	6,121	6,154	4,077	2,679	2,798	153.2	154.1	101.6	66.4	69.3
New Mexico	633	588	524	475	547	82.8	76.4	66.8	59.7	68.7
New York	19,519	21,183	20,164	16,035	15,051	208.4	226.2	214.5	170.0	159.6
North Carolina	13,276	14,433	15,677	11,596	10,749	392.6	422.7	452.0	330.3	306.2
North Dakota	80	56	39	33	32	24.7	17.5	12.2	10.3	10.0
Ohio	18,389	19,901	17,731	13,859	11,051	327.7	354.1	313.2	243.6	194.2
Oklahoma	3,209	3,219	3,288	2,947	2,356	198.4	199.3	201.9	179.7	143.7
Oregon	1,304	1,137	976	807	565	91.9	78.7	65.9	53.6	37.5
Pennsylvania	14,045	15,475	11,078	9,389	8,472	227.2	250.1	178.1	150.3	135.7
Rhode Island	553	458	555	291	194	106.2	87.7	106.1	55.4	36.9
South Carolina	6,621	5,861	4,683	3,955	3,935	371.5	325.9	255.4	212.5	211.5
South Dakota	148	190	200	102	148	41.8	53.7	56.1	28.4	41.3
Tennessee	8,584	8,748	9,820	7,211	6,442	341.1	346.0	383.0	278.4	248.7
Texas	16,937	16,762	17,537	16,103	13,889	198.5	194.4	199.3	180.1	155.3
Utah	198	176	133	180	165	23.1	20.3	15.0	19.9	18.2
Vermont	34	27	24	10	13	11.9	9.4	8.3	3.4	4.5
Virginia	6,561	7,078	7,188	6,908	5,089	210.3	224.5	224.3	212.6	156.6
Washington	3,024	2,458	2,340	1,984	1,755	126.4	100.2	92.7	77.0	68.1
West Virginia	753	752	592	415	354	80.2	80.7	63.4	44.4	37.8
Wisconsin	4,809	4,235	2,471	1,336	1,682	193.8	169.5	97.8	52.5	66.0
Wyoming	53	69	45	41	51	23.2	30.5	19.7	17.8	22.1
U.S.TOTAL[1]	304,994	300,149	266,507	224,023	190,220	241.0	235.5	206.3	171.5	145.7
Guam	42	81	82	35	40	63.6	118.3	142.4	58.9	67.3
Puerto Rico	414	389	192	120	160	24.6	23.1	10.6	6.6	8.8
Virgin Islands	116	129	104	44	36	238.2	294.2	186.0	76.4	62.5
OUTLYING AREAS	572	599	378	199	236	31.8	33.3	19.6	10.3	12.2
TOTAL	305,566	300,748	266,885	224,222	190,456	238.1	232.7	203.5	169.2	143.7

[1]Includes cases reported by Washington, D.C.

SOURCE: Centers for Disease Control and Prevention

Source: Centers for Disease Control, *Special Focus Profiles From the Sexually Transmitted Disease Surveillance: 1993*, U.S. Department of Health and Human Services, Public Health Service, December 1994, Table 12.

C3-31. Age-Specific Rates of Gonorrhea among Women 15 to 44 Years of Age: 1981 to 1993

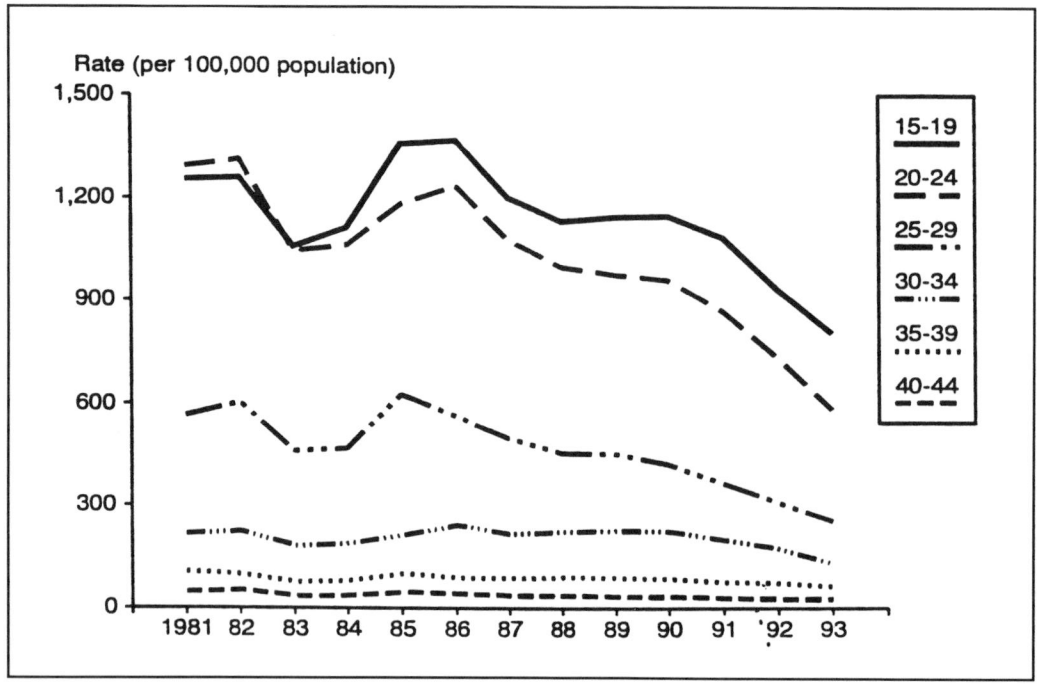

Source: Centers for Disease Control, *Special Focus Profiles From the Sexually Transmitted Disease Surveillance: 1993*, U.S. Department of Health and Human Services, Public Health Service, December 1994, Figure I.

C3-32. Reported Rates of Gonorrhea for 15- to 19-Year-Old Women, by Race and Ethnicity: 1981 to 1993

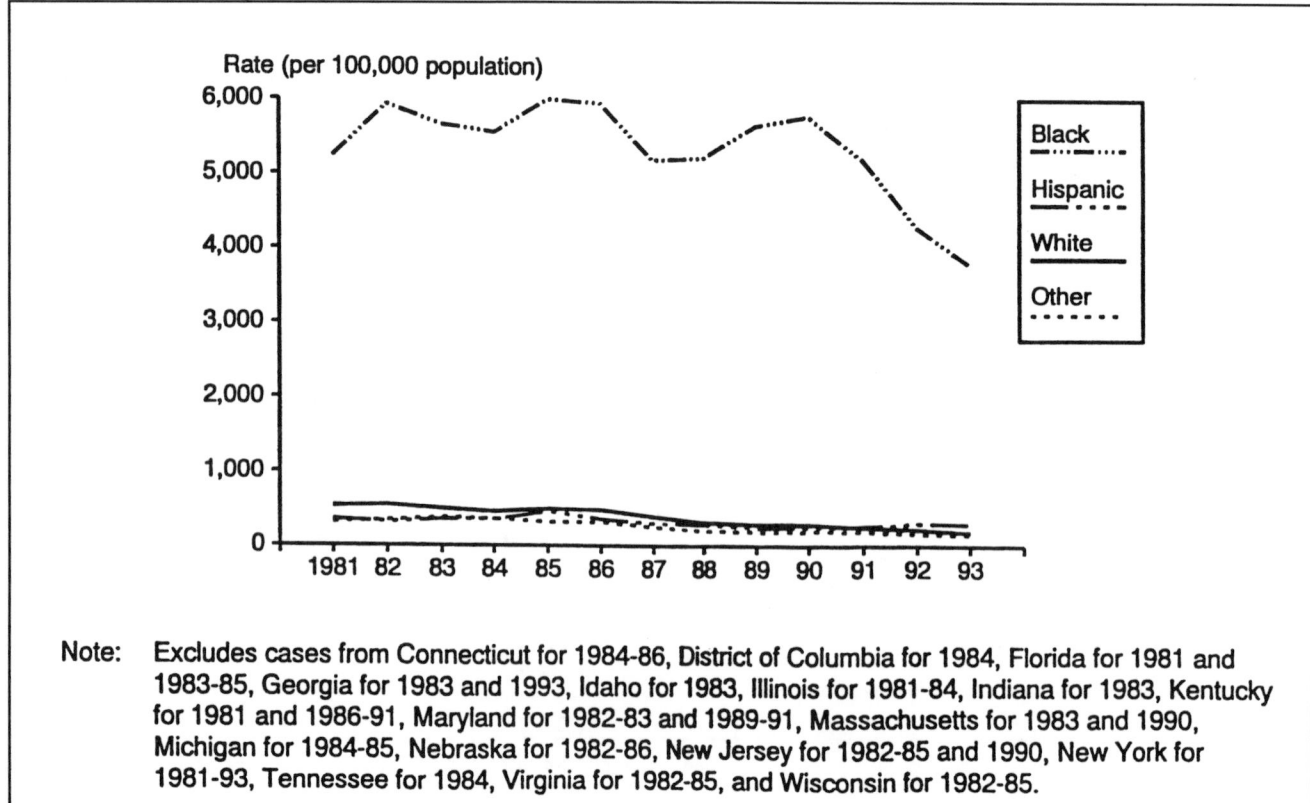

Note: Excludes cases from Connecticut for 1984-86, District of Columbia for 1984, Florida for 1981 and 1983-85, Georgia for 1983 and 1993, Idaho for 1983, Illinois for 1981-84, Indiana for 1983, Kentucky for 1981 and 1986-91, Maryland for 1982-83 and 1989-91, Massachusetts for 1983 and 1990, Michigan for 1984-85, Nebraska for 1982-86, New Jersey for 1982-85 and 1990, New York for 1981-93, Tennessee for 1984, Virginia for 1982-85, and Wisconsin for 1982-85.

Source: Centers for Disease Control, *Special Focus Profiles From the Sexually Transmitted Disease Surveillance: 1993*, U.S. Department of Health and Human Services, Public Health Service, December 1994, Figure N.

C3-33. Chlamydia Rates for Women, by State: 1993

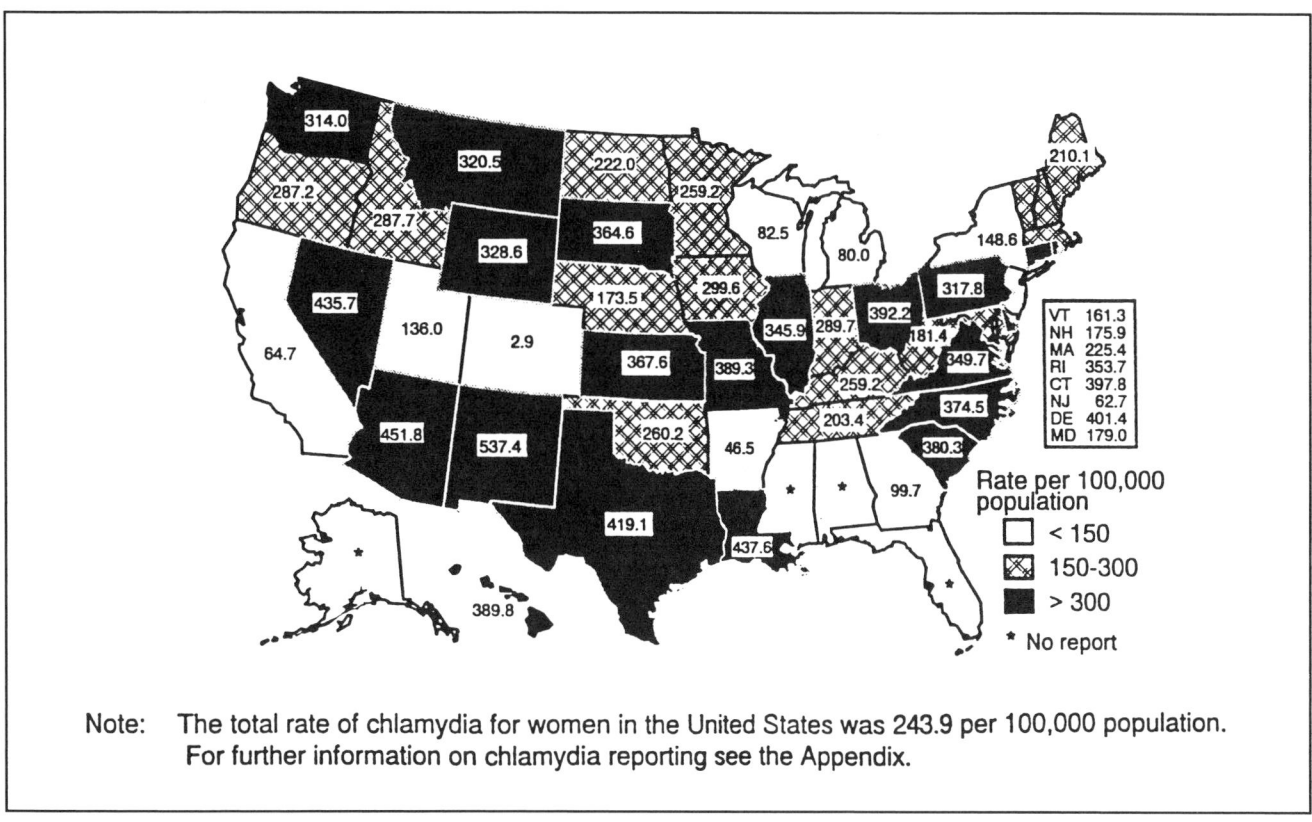

VT	161.3
NH	175.9
MA	225.4
RI	353.7
CT	397.8
NJ	62.7
DE	401.4
MD	179.0

Rate per 100,000 population

☐ < 150
▨ 150-300
■ > 300
* No report

Note: The total rate of chlamydia for women in the United States was **243.9** per 100,000 population. For further information on chlamydia reporting see the Appendix.

Source: Centers for Disease Control, *Special Focus Profiles From the Sexually Transmitted Disease Surveillance: 1993*, U.S. Department of Health and Human Services, Public Health Service, December 1994, Figure B.

C3-34. Ectopic Pregnancy Rates, by Race: 1970–74 to 1985–89

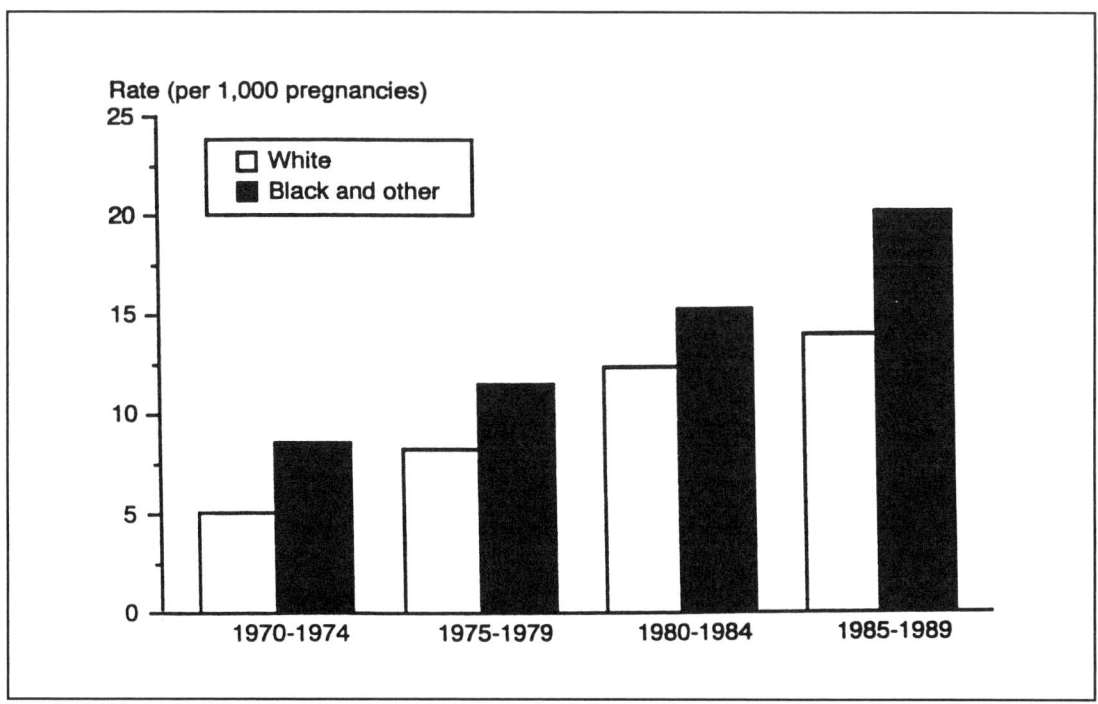

Source: Centers for Disease Control, *Special Focus Profiles From the Sexually Transmitted Disease Surveillance: 1993*, U.S. Department of Health and Human Services, Public Health Service, December 1994, Figure Q.

C3-35. Reported Cases and Rates of Primary and Secondary Syphilis among Women, by State and Outlying Areas: 1989 to 1993

State/Area	Cases					Rates Per 100,000 Population				
	1989	1990	1991	1992	1993	1989	1990	1991	1992	1993
Alabama	397	639	726	479	389	18.9	30.4	34.1	22.3	18.1
Alaska	3	5	6	3	3	1.2	1.9	2.2	1.1	1.1
Arizona	106	236	140	56	34	5.8	12.7	7.4	2.9	1.8
Arkansas	193	302	463	492	300	15.9	24.8	37.7	39.8	24.3
California	2,096	1,730	1,059	587	369	14.4	11.6	7.0	3.8	2.4
Colorado	15	11	31	22	37	0.9	0.7	1.8	1.3	2.1
Connecticut	508	395	211	117	79	30.0	23.3	12.4	6.9	4.6
Delaware	97	101	94	105	57	28.6	29.4	26.9	29.5	16.0
Florida	2,961	2,297	1,186	719	500	45.4	34.4	17.3	10.3	7.1
Georgia	1,614	1,694	1,321	818	447	48.9	50.8	38.8	23.6	12.9
Hawaii	2	5	2	2	1	0.4	0.9	0.4	0.4	0.2
Idaho	1	6	4	0	0	0.2	1.2	0.8	0.0	0.0
Illinois	349	726	1,110	1,085	702	5.9	12.4	18.7	18.2	11.8
Indiana	35	47	84	127	168	1.2	1.6	2.9	4.4	5.8
Iowa	13	40	29	25	30	0.9	2.8	2.0	1.7	2.1
Kansas	31	40	91	138	60	2.5	3.2	7.2	10.8	4.7
Kentucky	27	59	47	74	147	1.4	3.1	2.5	3.8	7.6
Louisiana	660	1,271	1,474	1,392	1,357	29.9	58.1	66.9	62.8	61.2
Maine	4	2	3	4	3	0.6	0.3	0.5	0.6	0.5
Maryland	346	505	458	267	142	14.2	20.5	18.3	10.5	5.6
Massachusetts	221	251	203	132	56	7.1	8.0	6.5	4.2	1.8
Michigan	223	432	579	428	269	4.7	9.0	12.0	8.8	5.6
Minnesota	25	35	38	48	28	1.1	1.6	1.7	2.1	1.2
Mississippi	340	549	550	731	943	25.3	40.9	40.7	53.8	69.4
Missouri	60	112	263	527	638	2.3	4.2	9.8	19.6	23.7
Montana	0	1	3	3	1	0.0	0.2	0.7	0.7	0.2
Nebraska	14	6	7	11	7	1.7	0.7	0.9	1.3	0.9
Nevada	88	51	34	16	9	15.8	8.6	5.4	2.4	1.4
New Hampshire	11	11	7	12	8	2.0	1.9	1.2	2.1	1.4
New Jersey	693	810	523	292	147	17.3	20.3	13.0	7.2	3.6
New Mexico	9	16	15	13	11	1.2	2.1	1.9	1.6	1.4
New York	2,146	2,283	1,690	1,297	580	22.9	24.4	18.0	13.8	6.1
North Carolina	517	773	901	1,207	931	15.3	22.6	26.0	34.4	26.5
North Dakota	1	1	0	0	0	0.3	0.3	0.0	0.0	0.0
Ohio	86	250	268	381	601	1.5	4.4	4.7	6.7	10.6
Oklahoma	49	115	88	159	133	3.0	7.1	5.4	9.7	8.1
Oregon	103	50	39	19	10	7.3	3.5	2.6	1.3	0.7
Pennsylvania	1,096	1,247	695	410	280	17.7	20.2	11.2	6.6	4.5
Rhode Island	18	13	22	11	6	3.5	2.5	4.2	2.1	1.1
South Carolina	408	483	709	659	472	22.9	26.9	38.7	35.4	25.4
South Dakota	0	2	1	1	0	0.0	0.6	0.3	0.3	0.0
Tennessee	610	964	760	562	525	24.2	38.1	29.6	21.7	20.3
Texas	1,728	2,286	2,261	1,595	1,188	20.3	26.5	25.7	17.8	13.3
Utah	4	3	3	1	4	0.5	0.3	0.3	0.1	0.4
Vermont	1	2	1	1	0	0.4	0.7	0.3	0.3	0.0
Virginia	265	414	390	368	319	8.5	13.1	12.2	11.3	9.8
Washington	178	141	76	34	29	7.4	5.7	3.0	1.3	1.1
West Virginia	9	9	20	10	2	1.0	1.0	2.1	1.1	0.2
Wisconsin	55	184	274	294	282	2.2	7.4	10.8	11.5	11.1
Wyoming	1	0	1	2	2	0.4	0.0	0.4	0.9	0.9
U.S. TOTAL[1]	18,774	22,088	19,311	15,936	12,429	14.8	17.3	14.9	12.2	9.5
Guam	0	0	0	0	0	0.0	0.0	0.0	0.0	0.0
Puerto Rico	254	188	231	212	216	15.1	11.2	12.7	11.7	11.9
Virgin Islands	6	0	27	9	7	12.3	0.0	48.3	15.6	12.2
OUTLYING AREAS	260	188	258	221	223	14.4	10.5	13.3	11.4	11.5
TOTAL	19,034	22,276	19,569	16,157	12,652	14.8	17.2	14.9	12.2	9.5

[1]Includes cases reported by Washington, D.C.

SOURCE: Centers for Disease Control and Prevention

Source: Centers for Disease Control, *Special Focus Profiles From the Sexually Transmitted Disease Surveillance: 1993*, U.S. Department of Health and Human Services, Public Health Service, December 1994, Table 24.

C3-36. Acquired Immunodeficiency Syndrome (AIDS) Cases, by Age at Diagnosis, Sex, Race, and Hispanic Origin: 1985 to 1993

[Data are based on reporting by State health departments]

Age at diagnosis, sex, race, and Hispanic origin	All years[1]	All years[1]	1985	1987	1988	1989	1990	1991	1992	January–September 1993	12 months ending September 30, 1993
	Percent distribution	Number, by year of report									Cases per 100,000 population[2]
All races	. . .	328,392	8,189	21,048	30,648	33,511	41,558	43,574	45,603	83,814	37.0
Male											
All males, 13 years and over . . .	100.0	285,063	7,538	19,047	27,049	29,549	36,300	37,530	38,917	70,396	80.2
White, not Hispanic	56.4	160,861	4,787	12,304	16,008	17,470	20,903	20,613	20,763	36,336	54.3
Black, not Hispanic	28.8	82,110	1,704	4,315	7,153	8,031	10,268	11,082	12,107	23,047	244.3
Hispanic	13.7	38,914	987	2,245	3,647	3,714	4,731	5,403	5,540	10,125	125.3
American Indian[3]	0.2	614	7	24	34	60	72	75	97	223	36.9
Asian or Pacific Islander[4]	0.7	1,992	48	131	163	214	255	259	283	540	20.0
13–19 years	0.3	934	31	67	84	90	102	99	94	299	. . .
20–29 years	18.2	51,945	1,468	3,784	5,449	5,692	6,814	6,459	6,350	12,052	. . .
30–39 years	46.3	131,858	3,610	8,855	12,581	13,868	16,802	17,332	17,819	32,116	. . .
40–49 years	24.8	70,729	1,657	4,283	6,105	6,809	8,908	9,628	10,337	18,935	. . .
50–59 years	7.6	21,657	605	1,474	1,990	2,240	2,651	2,896	3,079	5,289	. . .
60 years and over	2.8	7,940	167	584	840	850	1,023	1,116	1,238	1,705	. . .
Female											
All females, 13 years and over . .	100.0	38,684	522	1,682	3,034	3,370	4,540	5,375	5,942	12,789	13.4
White, not Hispanic	26.6	10,288	141	544	854	948	1,225	1,358	1,454	3,379	4.6
Black, not Hispanic	56.1	21,707	285	894	1,650	1,893	2,539	3,109	3,398	7,171	64.3
Hispanic	16.2	6,285	92	230	497	493	736	859	1,024	2,091	27.0
American Indian[3]	0.3	103	3	3	6	9	10	11	15	43	6.5
Asian or Pacific Islander[4]	0.6	228	1	11	22	17	19	25	37	86	3.1
13–19 years	1.1	418	4	11	23	29	63	55	57	157	. . .
20–29 years	24.3	9,418	173	480	768	889	1,104	1,223	1,370	2,962	. . .
30–39 years	47.1	18,224	236	750	1,503	1,615	2,091	2,538	2,715	6,131	. . .
40–49 years	17.9	6,919	44	229	411	507	788	995	1,245	2,523	. . .
50–59 years	5.6	2,148	26	92	151	172	275	342	344	681	. . .
60 years and over	4.0	1,557	39	120	178	158	219	222	211	335	. . .
Children											
All children, under 13 years	100.0	4,645	129	319	565	592	718	669	744	629	1.7
White, not Hispanic	21.1	979	27	85	149	111	159	146	128	110	0.4
Black, not Hispanic	57.7	2,680	83	160	300	339	384	403	470	380	6.9
Hispanic	20.2	937	19	71	112	135	168	113	137	128	2.6
American Indian[3]	0.3	14	–	2	–	2	3	2	3	2	0.4
Asian or Pacific Islander[4]	0.5	22	–	1	4	3	4	4	1	4	0.2
Under 1 year	39.2	1,820	54	141	190	241	284	247	302	224	. . .
1–12 years	60.8	2,825	75	178	375	351	434	422	442	405	. . .

[1]Includes cases prior to 1985.
[2]Resident population estimates for 1992 based on extrapolation from 1990 census counts from the U.S. Bureau of the Census.
[3]Includes Aleut and Eskimo.
[4]Includes Chinese, Japanese, Filipino, Hawaiian and part Hawaiian, and other Asian or Pacific Islander.

NOTES: The AIDS case reporting definitions were expanded in 1985, 1987, and 1993. See Appendix II. Excludes residents of U.S. territories. Data are updated periodically because of reporting delays. Data for all years have been updated through September 30, 1993. Data as of December 31, 1993, are available in the Centers for Disease Control and Prevention, HIV/AIDS Surveillance Report Year-End edition, February 1994.

SOURCE: Centers for Disease Control and Prevention, National Center for Infectious Diseases, Division of HIV/AIDS.

Source: Centers for Disease Control, *Special Focus Profiles From the Sexually Transmitted Disease Surveillance: 1993*, U.S. Department of Health and Human Services, Public Health Service, December 1994, Table 61.

C4. HEALTH INSURANCE

C4-1. Health Insurance Coverage, by Sex, and by Race and Hispanic Origin: 1991

Health insurance coverage	Both sexes	Male	Female	White Total	White Not of Hispanic origin	Black	Hispanic origin[1]	Not of Hispanic origin
1991								
All persons (in thousands)..................	244,658	118,795	125,862	205,468	187,679	30,342	20,756	223,901
	(100.0)	(100.0)	(100.0)	(100.0)	(100.0)	(100.0)	(100.0)	(100.0)
Percent Distribution								
Covered by private or government: health insurance:								
Less than 12 months	19.2	20.7	17.8	17.9	15.8	26.6	38.9	17.4
No months	7.0	7.8	6.2	6.5	5.5	9.3	16.8	6.1
1 to 4 months.........................	3.7	4.0	3.3	3.4	2.9	5.3	7.5	3.3
5 to 8 months.........................	4.8	5.0	4.6	4.3	3.8	8.0	9.7	4.3
9 to 11 months	3.8	3.9	3.7	3.7	3.6	4.0	4.9	3.7
12 months.............................	80.8	79.3	82.2	82.1	84.2	73.4	61.1	82.6
1 to 12 months	93.0	92.2	93.8	93.5	94.5	90.7	83.2	93.9
Covered by private health insurance:								
Less than 12 months	29.7	29.3	30.0	26.0	23.0	51.2	56.8	27.1
No months	16.4	15.7	17.1	13.6	11.3	33.0	37.3	14.5
1 to 4 months.........................	4.5	4.6	4.3	4.0	3.6	7.5	7.3	4.2
5 to 8 months.........................	5.1	5.2	5.1	4.8	4.4	7.8	8.6	4.8
9 to 11 months	3.6	3.8	3.5	3.7	3.7	2.9	3.7	3.6
12 months.............................	70.3	70.7	70.0	74.0	77.0	48.8	43.2	72.9
1 to 12 months	83.6	84.3	82.9	86.4	88.7	67.0	62.7	85.5
Covered by Medicaid:								
Less than 12 months	93.7	95.4	92.2	95.7	96.6	81.7	86.5	94.4
No months	89.2	91.4	87.1	92.0	93.4	71.7	76.4	90.4
1 to 4 months.........................	2.2	2.0	2.3	1.8	1.6	4.5	5.1	1.9
5 to 8 months.........................	1.4	1.1	1.7	1.1	1.0	3.3	3.0	1.3
9 to 11 months	0.9	0.8	1.0	0.8	0.6	2.1	2.1	0.8
12 months.............................	6.3	4.6	7.8	4.3	3.4	18.3	13.5	5.6
1 to 12 months	10.8	8.6	12.9	8.0	6.6	28.3	23.6	9.6

[1]May be of any race.

Source: Robert L. Bennefield, U.S. Bureau of the Census, *Dynamics of Economic Well-Being: Health Insurance, 1990 to 1992*, Current Population Reports, P70-37, Washington, D.C.: U.S. Government Printing Office, 1994, Table A.

C4-2. Number of Months in a Married-Couple Family with Health Insurance Coverage: 1990 to 1992

Health insurance coverage	No months	Member of married-couple family				
		1 to 30 months			31 to 32 months	
		Total	1 to 18 months	19 to 30 months	Total	32 months
All persons (in thousands)...............	58,903	23,125	11,857	11,268	153,783	153,032
	(100.0)	(100.0)	(100.0)	(100.0)	(100.0)	(100.0)
Percent Distribution						
Covered by private or government health insurance:						
Less than 32 months	31.1	43.5	43.1	43.9	20.3	20.2
No months	5.2	2.9	3.1	2.7	3.4	3.4
1 to 6 months.........................	3.4	4.0	2.9	5.1	1.8	1.8
7 to 12 months	4.1	5.1	4.7	5.6	2.3	2.3
13 to 18 months	3.1	5.7	5.9	5.5	2.1	2.1
19 to 24 months	5.7	9.6	9.6	9.7	3.6	3.6
25 to 30 months	8.4	13.6	13.9	13.2	6.2	6.1
31 months............................	1.1	2.5	2.9	2.0	0.9	0.9
32 months.............................	68.9	56.5	56.9	56.1	79.7	79.8
Covered by private health insurance:						
Less than 32 months	53.3	53.7	54.5	53.0	25.8	25.6
No months	23.5	10.6	11.8	9.4	7.2	7.2
1 to 6 months.........................	5.7	6.4	5.7	7.2	2.4	2.4
7 to 12 months	5.4	6.8	7.3	6.3	2.6	2.6
13 to 18 months	3.4	5.6	6.0	5.2	2.0	2.0
19 to 24 months	6.1	8.5	8.4	8.6	3.9	3.9
25 to 30 months	8.5	13.7	13.3	14.1	6.7	6.7
31 months............................	0.7	2.1	2.0	2.2	0.9	0.9
32 months.............................	46.7	46.3	45.5	47.0	74.2	74.4
Covered by Medicaid:						
Less than 32 months	86.7	96.1	94.5	97.8	98.5	98.5
No months	75.9	80.2	79.6	80.8	93.3	93.4
1 to 6 months.........................	2.4	5.0	3.9	6.2	2.2	2.2
7 to 12 months	2.3	3.6	2.8	4.5	1.3	1.3
13 to 18 months	1.4	2.3	2.4	2.1	0.5	0.5
19 to 24 months	2.0	2.5	2.5	2.5	0.6	0.5
25 to 30 months	2.2	2.3	2.9	1.6	0.6	0.6
31 months............................	-	-	-	-	-	-
32 months.............................	13.3	3.9	5.5	2.2	1.5	1.5

Source: Robert L. Bennefield, U.S. Bureau of the Census, *Dynamics of Economic Well-Being: Health Insurance, 1990 to 1992*, Current Population Reports, P70-37, Washington, D.C.: U.S. Government Printing Office, 1994, Table I.

C4-3. Number of Months in a Family with a Female Householder, No Husband Present, with Related Children Under 18 Years, and Health Insurance Coverage: 1990 to 1992

Health insurance coverage	No months	Member of family with female householder				
		1 to 30 months			31 to 32 months	
		Total	1 to 18 months	19 to 30 months	Total	32 months
All persons (in thousands).................	195,499	15,060	9,984	5,076	25,252	25,052
	(100.0)	(100.0)	(100.0)	(100.0)	(100.0)	(100.0)
Percent Distribution						
Covered by private or government health insurance:						
Less than 32 months	22.3	47.1	49.5	42.2	35.0	34.9
No months	3.5	3.8	4.2	3.0	5.8	5.8
1 to 6 months..........................	2.1	4.5	4.5	4.4	3.5	3.5
7 to 12 months	2.6	6.0	6.1	5.9	4.7	4.7
13 to 18 months	2.4	5.4	5.9	4.4	3.5	3.4
19 to 24 months	4.1	10.9	11.6	9.5	6.4	6.4
25 to 30 months	6.7	14.2	14.7	13.3	9.8	9.9
31 months.............................	1.0	2.2	2.5	1.7	1.3	1.3
32 months.............................	77.7	52.9	50.5	57.8	65.0	65.1
Covered by private health insurance:						
Less than 32 months	29.8	61.4	63.0	58.2	63.4	63.5
No months	8.2	16.5	15.4	18.8	34.9	35.1
1 to 6 months..........................	2.9	8.0	8.0	8.1	6.8	6.8
7 to 12 months	3.1	8.2	7.8	8.9	6.1	6.0
13 to 18 months	2.4	5.5	6.3	4.0	3.0	2.9
19 to 24 months	4.6	8.7	9.7	6.7	5.1	5.2
25 to 30 months	7.6	12.7	13.4	11.2	6.9	6.9
31 months.............................	1.0	1.7	2.3	-	0.5	0.5
32 months.............................	70.2	38.6	37.0	41.8	36.6	36.5
Covered by Medicaid:						
Less than 32 months	97.9	93.1	94.7	89.8	76.5	76.3
No months	92.6	70.5	71.2	69.0	59.6	59.5
1 to 6 months..........................	2.1	6.6	7.3	5.1	3.2	3.2
7 to 12 months	1.3	5.0	6.0	3.1	3.4	3.3
13 to 18 months	0.5	3.4	4.0	2.4	2.6	2.6
19 to 24 months	0.7	3.9	3.4	5.0	3.1	3.1
25 to 30 months	0.6	3.2	2.7	4.2	3.8	3.8
31 months.............................	-	-	-	1.0	0.7	0.7
32 months.............................	2.1	6.9	5.3	10.2	23.5	23.7

Source: Robert L. Bennefield, U.S. Bureau of the Census, *Dynamics of Economic Well-Being: Health Insurance, 1990 to 1992,* Current Population Reports, P70-37, Washington, D.C.: U.S. Government Printing Office, 1994, Table J.

C4-4. Labor Force Status of Wage and Salary Workers with 32 Months of Continuous Health Insurance Coverage, by Sex, and by Race and Hispanic Origin: 1990 to 1992

[Based on workers 18 to 64 years old. Numbers in thousands]

Health insurance coverage	Both sexes	Male	Female	White Total	White Not of Hispanic origin	Black	Hispanic origin[1]	Not of Hispanic origin
Worked Full-Period, Full-Time								
All persons	53,372	32,435	20,937	46,172	43,437	5,406	3,228	50,144
	(100.0)	(100.0)	(100.0)	(100.0)	(100.0)	(100.0)	(100.0)	(100.0)
Percent Distribution								
Covered by private or government health insurance	87.5	87.6	87.4	88.7	90.0	78.3	70.4	88.6
Covered by private health insurance	86.9	86.8	87.1	88.2	89.5	77.0	69.3	88.1
Covered by employer-provided health insurance	67.2	71.0	61.3	68.3	69.3	59.9	55.5	68.0
Worked Full-Period, Part-Time								
All persons	4,803	1,080	3,723	4,186	3,941	479	259	4,544
	(100.0)	(100.0)	(100.0)	(100.0)	(100.0)	(100.0)	(100.0)	(100.0)
Percent Distribution								
Covered by private or government health insurance	77.9	67.3	81.0	81.5	83.7	53.6	45.4	79.7
Covered by private health insurance	74.3	60.3	78.4	78.6	81.0	44.2	39.9	76.3
Covered by employer-provided health insurance	19.3	20.3	19.1	20.3	20.6	14.5	14.5	19.6
Workers With One or More Work Interruptions								
All persons	75,635	29,861	45,773	62,887	57,214	10,052	6,662	68,973
	(100.0)	(100.0)	(100.0)	(100.0)	(100.0)	(100.0)	(100.0)	(100.0)
Percent Distribution								
Covered by private or government health insurance	62.0	54.1	67.2	63.6	65.9	53.2	41.3	64.0
Covered by private health insurance	52.4	46.6	56.2	56.2	59.0	31.2	27.5	54.8
Covered by employer-provided health insurance	14.9	21.6	10.6	15.6	16.1	12.3	9.9	15.4

[1]Persons of Hispanic origin may be of any race.

Source: Robert L. Bennefield, U.S. Bureau of the Census, *Dynamics of Economic Well-Being: Health Insurance, 1990 to 1992*, Current Population Reports, P70-37, Washington, D.C.: U.S. Government Printing Office, 1994, Table K.

C4-5. Persons with Job Separations, by Method of Health Insurance Coverage before and after Job Separation, by Age and Sex: 1990 to 1992

[Numbers in thousands; data as of the first job separation in the period]

Age and sex	Before job separation				After job separation			
		Own name		Not own name or none (percent)		Own name		Not own name or none (percent)
	Total	Employer provided (percent)	Other (percent)		Total	Employer provided (percent)	Other (percent)	
MEN								
Total	20,140	36.5	9.0	54.5	20,140	24.5	10.4	65.1
16 to 19 years	3,802	5.4	3.2	91.4	3,802	1.7	4.1	94.3
20 to 24 years	3,282	22.8	10.8	66.3	3,282	11.9	10.9	77.2
25 to 34 years	4,828	39.5	8.5	52.0	4,828	23.4	9.5	67.2
35 to 54 years	5,155	50.0	7.9	42.1	5,155	34.3	10.2	55.5
55 years or more	3,073	62.3	16.6	21.2	3,073	51.3	19.5	29.2
WOMEN								
Total	22,599	23.2	7.1	69.7	22,599	14.4	8.3	77.3
16 to 19 years	3,923	4.9	2.5	92.6	3,923	1.6	3.7	94.7
20 to 24 years	3,601	22.6	4.8	72.6	3,601	10.6	6.6	82.7
25 to 34 years	6,032	26.1	3.6	70.3	6,032	14.4	5.1	80.5
35 to 54 years	6,360	26.8	6.4	66.8	6,360	17.1	7.7	75.2
55 years or more	2,684	36.1	25.8	38.1	2,684	32.1	25.8	42.1

Source: Wilfred Masumura and Paul Ryscavage, U.S. Bureau of the Census, *Dynamics of Economic Well-Being: Labor Force and Income, 1990 to 1992,* Current Population Reports, Series P70-40, Washington, D.C.: U.S. Government Printing Office, November 1994, Table R.

C4-6. Percentage of Women 50 to 64 Years Old Who Received Cancer Screening within the Past Year, by Type of Procedure, Health Insurance Coverage, and Educational Attainment: 1992

Type of procedure and health insurance coverage	Sample size	Educational attainment		
		Total	*0–12 years*	*13 years or more*
		Percent and standard error		
Mammogram				
Total.	1,171	49.6 (1.8)	44.8 (2.1)	60.6 (3.1)
Private coverage	910	55.4 (2.0)	51.0 (2.5)	63.3 (3.2)
HMO	190	62.1 (4.0)	62.8 (5.6)	61.0 (6.8)
Fee-for-service	720	53.6 (2.3)	48.1 (2.8)	64.0 (3.6)
Medicaid	90	38.3 (6.9)	38.0 (7.1)	*
Uninsured	130	19.3 (4.1)	19.2 (4.2)	*
Clinical breast examination (CBE)				
Total.	1,168	60.8 (1.8)	57.4 (2.2)	68.4 (2.6)
Private coverage	906	65.2 (2.0)	62.2 (2.6)	70.7 (2.6)
HMO	188	70.5 (3.7)	71.8 (5.7)	68.7 (5.5)
Fee-for-service	718	63.8 (2.1)	60.0 (2.7)	71.3 (2.9)
Medicaid	90	52.0 (7.5)	52.1 (7.8)	*
Uninsured	132	38.2 (5.9)	37.7 (6.4)	*
Pap test				
Total.	1,171	53.4 (1.7)	49.5 (2.1)	62.2 (2.9)
Private coverage	909	57.9 (1.9)	54.4 (2.4)	64.2 (3.0)
HMO	192	64.7 (3.5)	63.8 (5.0)	66.1 (5.8)
Fee-for-service	717	56.0 (2.2)	52.1 (2.6)	63.5 (3.3)
Medicaid	92	41.0 (7.0)	40.1 (7.2)	*
Uninsured	129	32.0 (5.9)	31.5 (6.2)	*

NOTES: Based on the one-fourth of the NHIS sample that received the Cancer Control questions. HMO includes all persons who reported HMO coverage, regardless of other coverage reported. Persons with Medicaid who did not report HMO coverage are classified as Medicaid. Uninsured persons are those who did not report private, Medicare, Medicaid, military/CHAMPUS, or public assistance coverage.

Source: Diane M. Makuc, Virginia Freid, and P. Ellen Parsons, National Center for Health Statistics, *Health Insurance and Cancer Screening Among Women*, Advance Data, No. 254, August 3, 1994, Hyattsville, MD: National Center for Health Statistics, Table 2.

Social Characteristics

D1. MARRIAGE AND DIVORCE

Marriage is still popular in the United States but so is divorce, delaying marriage, living together, and avoiding marriage altogether by staying single. In 1993, 2.3 million couples married. The number of marriages has varied over the last 50 years from the highest number in 1984 (almost 2.5 million) to the lowest in 1958 (1.5 million).

Beginning in the late 1960s, the rate of first marriages and remarriages began to fall. The marriage rate cycles partly in response to wars, economic change, and variation in the number of adults reaching marriageable ages. The marriage rate per 1,000 unmarried women aged 15 to 44, for example, reached a record high of 199 in 1946 and has drifted down to 87 in 1993, an indication that fewer eligible women are marrying than did so in the past.

Most American women are not rushing into their first marriages. Compared to 1970, brides and grooms were less likely to be under age 25 (in 1970, 11 percent of brides were 25 to 39 years old; in 1990, 41 percent were that old). Half the women who married for the first time in 1993 were 25 years old or older, much older than the median age of 20 to 22 years old that had been the situation since 1890. In 1975, 63 percent of women aged 20 to 24 had married compared to 38 percent in 1990. A result of this is that more unmarried women find themselves at risk of pregnancy and thereby of heading a one-parent family (see Section A4), with the consequent economic implications (see Section B6). Marriages among Black teenagers have become rare.

The move away from early marriage may mean the overall proportion of women ever marrying will be about 90 percent rather than the 95 percent of past cohorts of women. The proportion of women aged 35 to 39 who have never married has more than doubled, from 5 percent in 1970 to 13 percent in 1993. The difference between White and Black women in the likelihood of ever marrying is striking. Black women have historically married later than White women, but by their 40s, there was little difference. Among Black women aged 35 to 39, 30 percent had never married by 1993, compared to 10 percent of White women. In 1980, only 12 percent of Black women and 5 percent of White women that age had never married, another indication of significant change. Census Bureau projections indicate only three in four Black women will ever marry compared to nine in ten White women. Data from the National Center for Health Statistics shows that the rate of marriage in 1990 was 76 percent higher for White women than Black women and 55 percent higher for White men than Black men.

One thing that hasn't changed much is the "seven-year itch." The median duration of marriage has remained about seven years since at least 1970. In addition, from 1970 to 1990, the divorce rate rose by one-third (from 3.5 divorces per 1,000 persons to 4.7 divorces), and the marriage rate fell about 8 percent. During the 1980s, the divorce rate started to stabilize and even dropped slightly at the end of the decade. Nevertheless, a high proportion of marriages still end in divorce.

Economic distress, such as low income and unemployment, can be related to the breakup of families. Poverty does not necessarily break up a family, but poor two-parent families were almost twice as likely as nonpoor families to break up within a two-year period during the mid-1980s.

Census Bureau projections indicate 4 in 10 first marriages will end in divorce, down from previous projections that about half of marriages would end in divorce eventually. It appears the likelihood of divorce for women in their 20s is lower than among women of the Baby Boom. Even with a decline in divorce, the United States has among the highest percentages of marriages ending in divorce in the world.

When children are involved, custody is awarded entirely to the wife in about three-fourths of the cases; otherwise, custody was joint or to the husband. In 1992, 9.9 million women were the custodial parent and 1.6 million men were the custodial parent. Black women are more likely to retain sole custody of children after a divorce than are other women. Nearly 5 million custodial mothers expected child support, as did 400,000 men. Among the custodial mothers who were supposed to receive child support from the absent fathers, three-fourths received some payments but only about half received the full amount. The average child support award of custodial mothers was about $3,000 a year compared to $2,300 for custodial fathers. These payments made up about 17 percent of the custodial mothers' total income and 7 percent of the custodial fathers' income. Custodial mothers were nearly three times as likely to be in poverty as the custodial father (35 percent versus 13 percent).

The likelihood of remarriage after divorce has been declining but is still widespread. As a result, in one-fourth of married-couple families with children, the children were either adopted or stepchildren. White women are more likely than Black or Hispanic women to remarry, and the median number of years between ending a first marriage and remarriage has increased. In 1965–69, half of women had remarried within 2 years of their divorce; in 1980–84, it took 5 years before half of divorced women remarried. Between 1975 and 1990, the proportion of women aged 50 to 54 divorced from their first husbands who had remarried dropped from 74 percent to 63 percent. The Census Bureau projects that the near-term levels of remarriage after divorce may be about two-thirds.

In 1993, there were 6 unmarried couples for every 100 married couples, compared to only 1 in 100 in 1970. In about one-third of the 2.2 million households with a female householder and an unrelated adult who reported they were partners, both adults were women.

D2. LIVING ARRANGEMENTS

Most adult women are married, and so the great majority of women live in a family setting. White women, however, are less likely (79 percent) than Black (83 percent) or Hispanic (87 percent) women to be living with a family.

Those parents who wonder whether their adult children will ever leave home will be interested to know that about 6.4 million women aged 20 years or older lived in the home of their parents in 1993, and most were under age 30. Conversely, over 2.2 million young adult women (18 to 24 years old) maintained their own homes in 1993.

Nearly 12 million women lived alone in 1993, which accounted for the largest share of persons living alone (6 in 10). Living alone is especially common among elderly widows. Of adults under 25 years, only 3 percent of women lived alone. By comparison, for women 75 years and older, 52 percent lived alone. In the

1970s, an increasing proportion of young women lived alone, but there has been no increase since 1980. Hispanic women are generally about half as likely as White and Black women to live alone. Among women 75 years and older, over half (54 percent) of White women lived alone compared with 44 percent of Black women and 35 percent of Hispanic women.

More than seven in ten persons living in nursing homes are women. Almost half of the women are 85 years or older. Most people will be surprised to learn that only 28 percent of women aged 85 and older live in nursing homes, while 72 percent of these oldest old women live in the community.

Young girls under age 18 are more likely to be living with only their mother than two decades ago—the result of the increase in the numbers of divorce and of mothers who have never married. In 1993, 23 percent of all children lived with their mother only, compared to 10 percent of children in 1970; among Blacks, the percentages were 54 percent of children in 1993 and 11 percent in 1970. About 1.7 million girls under 18 lived in the homes of their grandparents.

D3. HOUSEHOLD COMPOSITION

Because of delays and decline in marriages and changes in the patterns of childbearing, divorce, and remarriage since 1970, the mix of households has changed. Most households, 7 in 10 in 1993, were family households. That's a large majority, but a smaller proportion than in 1970 when families constituted 8 in 10 households. There has also been an enormous change in the proportion of households that are married couples with children: 26 percent in 1993 compared to 40 percent in 1970. Most married couples had no children—the opposite of 1970. The increase over the last two decades in single-parent households is remarkable. The proportion increased from 12 percent of family groups with children in 1970 to 26 percent in 1993. Also, women are somewhat more likely to live alone: in 1993, 15 percent of all households constituted women living alone compared to 12 percent in 1970.

Changes in Black families have been substantial. In 1970, 64 percent of Black families with children were married couples compared to only 37 percent in 1993. Likewise, 90 percent of White families with children were married couples in 1970 as were 76 percent in 1993. Change was less dramatic among Hispanic families. In 1970, 74 percent of Hispanic families were two-parent groups, compared to 65 percent in 1993.

Nearly 3 in 5 Black families with children were headed by the mother alone in 1993 compared to 20 percent for Whites. The 24 percent of Hispanic family groups with children headed by a woman alone in 1970 increased to 30 percent in 1993.

The marital status of mothers with children running households by themselves has changed radically since 1970. In 1970, 36 percent of the women were married but their husbands were absent from the household and another 18 percent were widows; only 7 percent had never been married. In 1993, one-third of all mothers had never been married, only 4 percent were widows, and 18 percent were married with no husband in the household. In 1970, less than 3 percent of White mothers heading their households and 15 percent of Black women had never married, compared to 21 percent and 55 percent, respectively, in 1993.

There were six times as many single mothers as single fathers in 1993. There has been a very small increase in the proportion of father/child families with no wife present: from 1 percent in 1970 to 4 percent in 1993 of White family groups with children and from 3 to 5 percent of such Black families.

D4. EDUCATION

Women are now more qualified for a wider variety of occupations than ever before because they have increased their level of education and varied the fields in which they have studied. Women 25 years and older are more likely to be enrolled in college than was the case two decades ago, and their levels of enrollment in 1990 exceeded those of men. In 1990, men averaged eight years after receipt of their bachelor's degree to finish a doctorate, compared to eleven years for women. In that same year, men and women both took about five years to complete a professional degree.

In 1980, half of adult Black women had at least a high school diploma compared to seven in ten White women. By 1994, the gap had narrowed. Nearly three in four Black women had graduated from high school, compared to eight in ten White women. The gap between Black and White women with a college degree remained during that period, although both greatly increased their proportions among all women. Black women with a college degree increased from 8 percent to 13 percent, and White women with a college degree increased from 14 percent to 20 percent.

There has also been significant achievement in reducing high school dropout rates among young women. In 1970, nearly one in five women aged 14 to 34 were high school dropouts; in 1993, that proportion had been cut in half. And among women, three in four high school dropouts live in urban America, and half of these women live in central cities.

D5. EDUCATIONAL FIELDS OF STUDY

Women received more than half of the bachelor's and master's degrees in the nation in 1990. The fields in which women professionals receive degrees is a factor in their relatively low pay when compared to men. Among women receiving bachelor's degrees in 1990, their major educational fields were among the lower-paying fields for professionals, including business management, education, social sciences and history, health professions (more than half were nurses), and general psychology. The predominant fields for women receiving their master's degree were the same as above with the addition of public administration as an important field. Women received more than one-third of the doctorate degrees, medical degrees, and law degrees conferred to students in 1991–92. One-third of the doctorates awarded to women were in the education and health professions.

D6. EDUCATIONAL OUTCOMES

Personal enrichment, values, and lifelong economic status are related to educational attainment. For example, among high school seniors in 1992, there was little difference in opinion between young men and women in the importance of successful and steady work; men valued income level more than women and considered having children less important than did the young women. A greater proportion of 1992 female high school seniors than 1972 female high school seniors thought success at work and finding steady work was very important. Income level was markedly more important to 1992 female high school seniors than 1972 high school seniors (29 percent versus 10 percent, respectively); but correcting inequalities was less important (24 percent in 1992 and 31 percent in 1972).

Higher education is associated with higher participation in the labor force and higher incomes for women. Overall, 57 percent of adult women (25 years and over) participated in the labor force in 1993. Only 28 percent of women who are high school dropouts were in the labor force compared to 75 percent of women with at least a bachelor's degree. In addition, women who are high school dropouts are five times as likely to be unemployed as are college-educated women.

Among college-educated Black adults, more women than men were employed in 1993. Two-thirds of these well-educated women worked in professional jobs and executive positions; more than one in four were in technical, sales, and administrative support jobs. By contrast, about three in five college-educated Black men were in professional or executive positions. Almost three in four White, non-Hispanic women with a college education held executive or professional jobs.

Among women with earnings in 1992, high school dropouts made about one-third of the annual earnings of women with a bachelor's degree. Women with a doctorate or professional degree had median earnings about 1.5 times that of women with a bachelor's degree. The lack of a high school diploma or a bachelor's degree also meant more sporadic work during the year.

D7. VOTING AND POLITICAL INVOLVEMENT

Women have, in the last three decades, been somewhat more likely to report voting than men. Sixty-two percent of women reported voting in the 1992 presidential election. The 1992 turnout of women exceeded that of men by about 2 percentage points and was 4 percentage points higher than the 1988 turnout among women. In the 1992 presidential election, the reported turnout was highest among White women (65 percent); by comparison, 57 percent of Black women and 31 percent of Hispanic women reported voting. Women 55 and older are the most likely to vote. In 1992, over half of all women reported they identified more with the Democratic party than with the Republican party. One in five considered themselves "strong" Democrats.

More women are holding public office and at higher levels than ever before. In the 103rd U.S. Congress (1993), 47 Representatives and 7 Senators were women. By comparison, in the 97th Congress (1981), 19 Representatives and 2 Senators were women. In 1993, nearly 1,600 women were elected to a state office.

D8. VICTIMS OF CRIME

In every category of personal crimes, women had lower victimization rates than did men. For example, women were half as likely as men to experience robberies or aggravated assaults. In addition, White women are less likely than Black women to be crime victims. Specifically, Black women are 4 to 5 times as likely as White women to be murdered. Women under 25 years old are more likely than older women to be victims of crimes of violence. About 1 million women a year are the victims of violence by intimates. Women are more likely than men to be the crime victims of people they know, and three-fourths of lone-offender violence against women was perpetrated by someone they knew.

D9. CRIMINAL OFFENDERS

Women are convicted of a small but growing proportion of all offenses. Drug offenses in particular have made women an increasingly larger proportion of the prison population. In 1978, less than 10,000 women were inmates of local jails compared to 41,000 in 1992. The female state prison inmate population increased from less than 23,000 in 1986 to nearly 40,000 in 1991, a 75 percent increase in only 5 years. The 6,900 women in federal prisons were nearly 8 percent of the total federal prison population in 1993.

Most women in state prisons were Black, unemployed at the time of their arrest, had at least a high school education or equivalency (GED), and were either married or had been married before their imprisonment. More than four in ten women in state prisons reported they had been physically or sexually abused before their incarceration.

At the end of 1993, 35 women were under sentence of death in the United States. Of these, 22 were White, non-Hispanic, 10 were Black, non-Hispanic, and 3 were of Hispanic origin. Of the women in state prisons for murder, they were almost twice as likely to have killed a husband, ex-husband, or boyfriend as another relative.

D1. MARRIAGE AND DIVORCE

D1-1. Marriage and Marriage Rates: 1940 to 1993

[Data refer only to events occurring within the United States. Alaska included beginning 1959 and Hawaii beginning 1960. Beginning with 1978, data include nonlicensed marriages registered in California; see Technical notes. Rates per 1,000 population enumerated as of April 1 for 1940, 1950, 1960, 1970, and 1980 and estimated as of July 1 for all other years]

| Year | Number | Rate per 1,000 population— | | | | |
		Total population	Men 15 years of age and over[1]	Women 15 years of age and over[1]	Unmarried women 15 years of age and over	Unmarried women 15–44 years of age
Provisional:						
1993	2,334,000	9.0	- - -	- - -	52.3	86.8
1992	2,362,000	9.3	- - -	- - -	53.3	88.2
1991	2,371,000	9.4	- - -	- - -	54.2	89.0
Final:						
1990	2,443,489	9.8	26.0	24.1	54.5	91.3
1989	2,403,268	9.7	25.8	23.9	54.2	91.2
1988	2,395,926	9.8	26.0	24.0	54.6	91.0
1987	2,403,378	9.9	26.3	24.3	55.7	92.4
1986	2,407,099	10.0	26.6	24.5	56.2	93.9
1985	2,412,625	10.1	27.0	24.9	57.0	94.9
1984	2,477,192	10.5	28.0	25.8	59.5	99.0
1983	2,445,604	10.5	28.0	25.7	59.9	99.3
1982	2,456,278	10.6	28.5	26.1	61.4	101.9
1981	2,422,145	10.6	28.4	26.1	61.7	103.1
1980	2,390,252	10.6	28.5	26.1	61.4	102.6
1979	2,331,337	10.4	28.1	25.8	63.6	107.9
1978	2,282,272	10.3	28.0	25.7	64.1	109.1
1977	2,178,367	9.9	27.2	25.0	63.6	109.8
1976	2,154,807	9.9	27.4	25.2	65.2	113.4
1975	2,152,662	10.0	27.9	25.6	66.9	118.5
1974	2,229,667	10.5	29.4	27.1	72.0	128.4
1973	2,284,108	10.8	30.7	28.2	76.0	137.3
1972	2,282,154	10.9	31.3	28.8	77.9	141.3
1971	2,190,481	10.6	30.7	28.2	76.2	138.9
1970	2,158,802	10.6	31.1	28.4	76.5	140.2
1969	2,145,000	10.6	31.4	28.9	80.0	149.1
1968	2,069,000	10.4	30.8	28.3	79.1	147.2
1967	1,927,000	9.7	29.1	26.9	76.4	145.2
1966	1,857,000	9.5	28.4	26.4	75.6	145.1
1965	1,800,000	9.3	27.9	26.0	75.0	144.3
1964	1,725,000	9.0	27.1	25.3	74.6	146.2
1963	1,654,000	8.8	26.4	24.7	73.4	143.3
1962	1,577,000	8.5	25.5	23.9	71.2	138.4
1961	1,548,000	8.5	25.5	24.0	72.2	145.4
1960	1,523,000	8.5	25.4	24.0	73.5	148.0
1959	1,494,000	8.5	25.2	23.8	73.6	149.8
1958	1,451,000	8.4	24.8	23.5	72.0	146.3
1957	1,518,000	8.9	26.4	24.9	78.0	157.4
1956	1,585,000	9.5	27.8	26.4	82.4	165.6
1955	1,531,000	9.3	27.2	25.8	80.9	161.1
1954	1,490,000	9.2	26.9	25.4	79.8	154.3
1953	1,546,000	9.8	28.2	26.7	83.7	163.3
1952	1,539,318	9.9	28.3	26.8	83.2	159.9
1951	1,594,694	10.4	29.4	28.1	86.6	164.9
1950	1,667,231	11.1	30.7	29.8	90.2	166.4
1949	1,579,798	10.6	29.4	28.5	86.7	158.0
1948	1,811,155	12.4	34.0	33.0	98.5	174.7
1947	1,991,878	13.9	37.9	36.8	106.2	182.7
1946	2,291,045	16.4	44.5	42.8	118.1	199.0
1945	1,612,992	12.2	35.8	30.5	83.6	138.2
1944	1,452,394	10.9	31.2	27.8	76.5	124.5
1943	1,577,050	11.7	32.2	30.6	83.0	133.5
1942	1,772,132	13.2	35.6	34.8	93.0	147.6
1941	1,695,999	12.7	34.0	33.7	88.5	138.4
1940	1,595,879	12.1	32.3	32.3	82.8	122.4

[1]Rates for 1981–88 are revised and may differ from rates published previously.

Source: U.S. Bureau of the Census, *Population Profile of the United States: 1993*, Current Population Reports, Special Studies Series P23-185, Washington, D.C.: U.S. Government Printing Office, May 1993, Table 1.

D1-2. Percentage of Ever-Married Women Divorced after First Marriage, by Age: June 1975 and June 1990

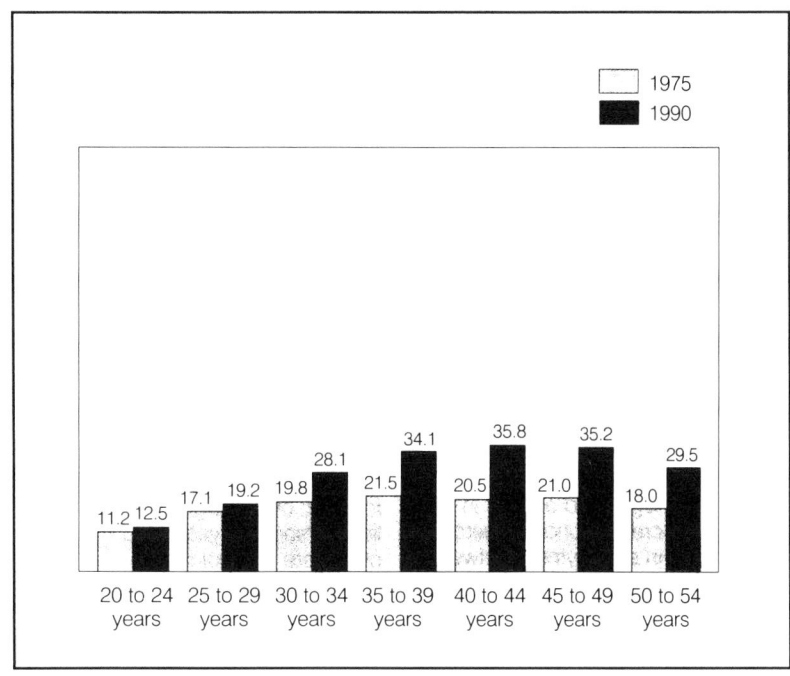

Source: U.S. Bureau of the Census, *Population Profile of the United States: 1993,* Current Population Reports, Special Studies Series P23-185, Washington, D.C.: U.S. Government Printing Office, May 1993, Figure 22.

D1-3. Marriages and Divorces: 1970 to 1988

[See also *Historical Statistics, Colonial Times to 1970*, series B 214-217]

YEAR	MARRIAGES [1]						DIVORCES AND ANNULMENTS		
	Number (1,000)	Rate per 1,000 population					Number (1,000)	Rate per 1,000 population	
		Total	Men, 15 yrs. old and over	Women, 15 yrs. old and over	Unmarried women			Total	Married women, 15 yrs. old and over
					15 yrs. old and over	15 to 44 yrs. old			
1970	2,159	10.6	31.1	28.4	76.5	140.2	708	3.5	14.9
1975	2,153	10.0	27.9	25.6	66.9	118.5	1,036	4.8	20.3
1980	2,390	10.6	28.5	26.1	61.4	102.6	1,189	5.2	22.6
1981	2,422	10.6	28.4	26.1	61.7	103.1	1,213	5.3	22.6
1982	2,456	10.6	28.4	26.1	61.4	101.9	1,170	5.0	21.7
1983	2,446	10.5	28.0	25.7	59.9	99.3	1,158	4.9	21.3
1984	2,477	10.5	28.1	25.8	59.5	99.0	1,169	5.0	21.5
1985	2,413	10.1	26.9	24.8	57.0	94.9	1,190	5.0	21.7
1986	2,407	10.0	26.5	24.5	56.2	93.9	1,178	4.9	21.2
1987	2,403	9.9	26.2	24.2	55.7	92.4	1,166	4.8	20.8
1988	2,396	9.7	25.9	23.9	54.6	91.0	1,167	4.7	20.7

[1] Beginning 1980, includes nonlicensed marriages registered in California.

Source: U.S. Bureau of the Census, *Statistical Abstract of the United States: 1993*, (113th edition), Washington, D.C.: U.S. Government Printing Office, 1993, Table 140.

D1-4. Median Duration of Marriage, Median Age at Divorce, and Children Involved: 1970 to 1988

[Data cover divorce-registration area. Based on a sample and subject to sampling variability; for details, see source. Median age computed on data by single years of age. See also *Historical Statistics, Colonial Times to 1970*, series B218]

DURATION OF MARRIAGE, AGE AT DIVORCE, AND CHILDREN INVOLVED	1970	1975	1980	1981	1982	1983	1984	1985	1986	1987	1988
Median duration of marriage (years).	6.7	6.5	6.8	7.0	7.0	7.0	6.9	6.8	6.9	7.0	7.1
Median age at divorce:											
Men (years)	32.9	32.2	32.7	33.1	33.6	34.0	34.3	34.4	34.6	34.9	35.1
Women (years)	29.8	29.5	30.3	30.6	31.1	31.5	31.7	31.9	32.1	32.5	32.6
Estimated number of children involved											
in divorce (1,000)	870	1,123	1,174	1,180	1,108	1,091	1,081	1,091	1,064	1,038	1,044
Avg. number of children per decree	1.22	1.08	0.98	0.97	0.94	0.94	0.92	0.92	0.90	0.89	0.89
Rate per 1,000 children under 18 years of age.	12.5	16.7	17.3	18.7	17.6	17.4	17.2	17.3	16.8	16.3	16.4

Source of tables 142-144: U.S. National Center for Health Statistics of the United States, *Vital Statistics of the United States*, annual, *Monthly Vital Statistics Report;* and unpublished data.

Source: U.S. Bureau of the Census, *Statistical Abstract of the United States: 1993*, (113th edition), Washington, D.C.: U.S. Government Printing Office, 1993, Table 144.

D1-5. Marital Status of Persons 15 Years and Over, by Age, Sex, and Race: March 1994

Numbers in thousands.

Race, region, and marital status	Total, 15 years and over Male	Female	15 to 24 years Male	Female	25 to 34 years Male	Female	35 to 44 years Male	Female	45 to 54 years Male	Female	55 to 64 years Male	Female	65 years and over Male	Female
BLACK														
United States														
Total	10,630	12,869	2,580	2,816	2,499	2,980	2,312	2,719	1,379	1,670	883	1,152	978	1,532
Percent	100.0	100.0	100.0	100.0	100.0	100.0	100.0	100.0	100.0	100.0	100.0	100.0	100.0	100.0
Never married	47.1	40.3	94.0	89.7	58.2	51.4	31.5	26.7	17.1	13.8	12.0	8.2	5.6	5.1
Married, spouse present	36.2	28.9	5.0	7.2	30.4	29.1	45.0	38.3	55.6	43.3	60.6	40.2	63.1	27.5
Married, spouse absent .	6.0	8.9	0.5	2.2	5.6	10.2	10.9	13.3	7.1	13.7	8.0	11.7	6.0	3.5
Widowed.............	2.8	10.3	0.1	0.2	-	0.4	0.6	2.3	2.4	7.7	7.5	23.7	18.1	54.8
Divorced	8.0	11.6	0.4	0.8	5.7	8.9	12.0	19.4	17.8	21.5	11.9	16.1	7.2	9.1
South														
Total	5,931	7,070	1,497	1,565	1,328	1,624	1,262	1,530	788	899	499	606	557	846
Percent	100.0	100.0	100.0	100.0	100.0	100.0	100.0	100.0	100.0	100.0	100.0	100.0	100.0	100.0
Never married	45.4	38.4	93.3	87.6	55.4	47.0	27.9	24.4	17.0	13.0	10.1	8.1	4.7	5.1
Married, spouse present	38.0	31.4	5.7	8.6	33.1	32.2	48.9	41.2	56.9	45.8	60.5	44.2	65.0	30.3
Married, spouse absent .	6.3	9.1	0.7	2.8	5.4	10.7	12.4	12.7	6.9	14.4	10.2	11.0	4.9	3.8
Widowed.............	2.9	10.1	-	0.2	-	0.5	0.7	2.4	2.3	7.2	8.0	26.0	18.4	52.6
Divorced	7.5	10.9	0.3	0.8	6.1	9.6	10.1	19.2	17.0	19.6	11.3	10.6	7.1	8.3
North and West														
Total	4,699	5,799	1,083	1,251	1,171	1,357	1,050	1,189	590	770	383	546	421	686
Percent	100.0	100.0	100.0	100.0	100.0	100.0	100.0	100.0	100.0	100.0	100.0	100.0	100.0	100.0
Never married	49.2	42.6	94.9	92.2	61.5	56.7	35.8	29.7	17.4	14.7	14.5	8.4	6.9	5.0
Married, spouse present	33.9	25.8	4.0	5.4	27.4	25.4	40.3	34.5	53.9	40.5	60.7	35.8	60.5	24.2
Married, spouse absent .	5.6	8.7	0.3	1.5	5.8	9.6	9.2	14.0	7.3	12.7	5.1	12.4	7.4	3.2
Widowed.............	2.7	10.5	0.3	0.2	-	0.3	0.6	2.2	2.6	8.4	7.0	21.2	17.8	57.6
Divorced	8.7	12.5	0.5	0.7	5.3	8.0	14.2	19.6	18.9	23.7	12.8	22.3	7.3	10.1
WHITE, NOT HISPANIC														
United States														
Total	73,575	78,470	12,501	12,256	14,807	14,944	15,702	15,554	11,477	11,748	8,194	8,591	10,894	15,378
Percent	100.0	100.0	100.0	100.0	100.0	100.0	100.0	100.0	100.0	100.0	100.0	100.0	100.0	100.0
Never married	27.6	20.2	89.2	79.4	35.7	22.4	14.2	8.5	7.0	4.7	4.7	3.5	4.5	4.0
Married, spouse present	60.2	56.2	9.5	16.9	55.1	63.8	70.3	73.0	78.1	72.4	80.0	70.4	76.8	42.6
Married, spouse absent .	2.0	2.6	0.6	1.9	2.5	3.8	2.9	3.3	2.1	2.7	2.3	1.9	1.6	1.4
Widowed.............	2.3	11.3	-	0.1	0.1	0.6	0.3	1.0	0.7	4.0	2.7	12.1	12.5	46.3
Divorced	7.8	9.8	0.6	1.7	6.6	9.6	12.3	14.2	12.0	16.2	10.3	12.2	4.7	5.6
South														
Total	23,920	25,654	4,070	3,968	4,851	4,829	4,933	5,072	3,804	3,824	2,650	2,896	3,612	5,065
Percent	100.0	100.0	100.0	100.0	100.0	100.0	100.0	100.0	100.0	100.0	100.0	100.0	100.0	100.0
Never married	24.9	17.5	86.1	73.8	31.0	18.4	10.7	6.3	5.7	3.9	3.3	2.5	3.3	2.7
Married, spouse present	62.8	58.2	12.0	21.6	58.5	66.3	73.2	75.2	79.9	73.7	81.1	69.2	80.1	44.2
Married, spouse absent .	2.2	2.7	0.9	2.2	2.8	3.7	3.2	3.3	1.7	3.3	2.1	2.0	1.9	1.5
Widowed.............	2.1	11.3	-	0.1	0.1	0.5	0.4	1.0	1.1	3.4	2.5	12.9	10.2	45.8
Divorced	8.0	10.2	1.0	2.3	7.6	11.1	12.4	14.1	11.7	15.8	10.9	13.4	4.6	5.8
North and West														
Total	49,655	52,816	8,431	8,288	9,956	10,114	10,769	10,482	7,673	7,924	5,544	5,694	7,282	10,313
Percent	100.0	100.0	100.0	100.0	100.0	100.0	100.0	100.0	100.0	100.0	100.0	100.0	100.0	100.0
Never married	29.0	21.5	90.6	82.0	38.0	24.3	15.8	9.5	7.7	5.0	5.3	4.0	5.0	4.7
Married, spouse present	59.0	55.2	8.4	14.7	53.5	62.5	69.0	71.9	77.3	71.8	79.5	71.0	75.2	41.9
Married, spouse absent .	2.0	2.5	0.5	1.8	2.3	3.8	2.8	3.3	2.4	2.4	2.3	1.8	1.4	1.4
Widowed.............	2.4	11.3	-	0.1	0.1	0.6	0.2	1.0	0.5	4.3	2.7	11.7	13.6	46.5
Divorced	7.7	9.5	0.4	1.5	6.1	8.8	12.3	14.2	12.1	16.5	10.1	11.6	4.7	5.6

Source: Claudette E. Bennett, U.S. Bureau of the Census, The Black Population in the United States: March 1994 and 1993, Current Population Reports, Series P20-480, Washington, D.C.: U.S. Government Printing Office, January 1995, Table 4.

D1-6. Interval from Puberty to Marriage: 1890 and 1988

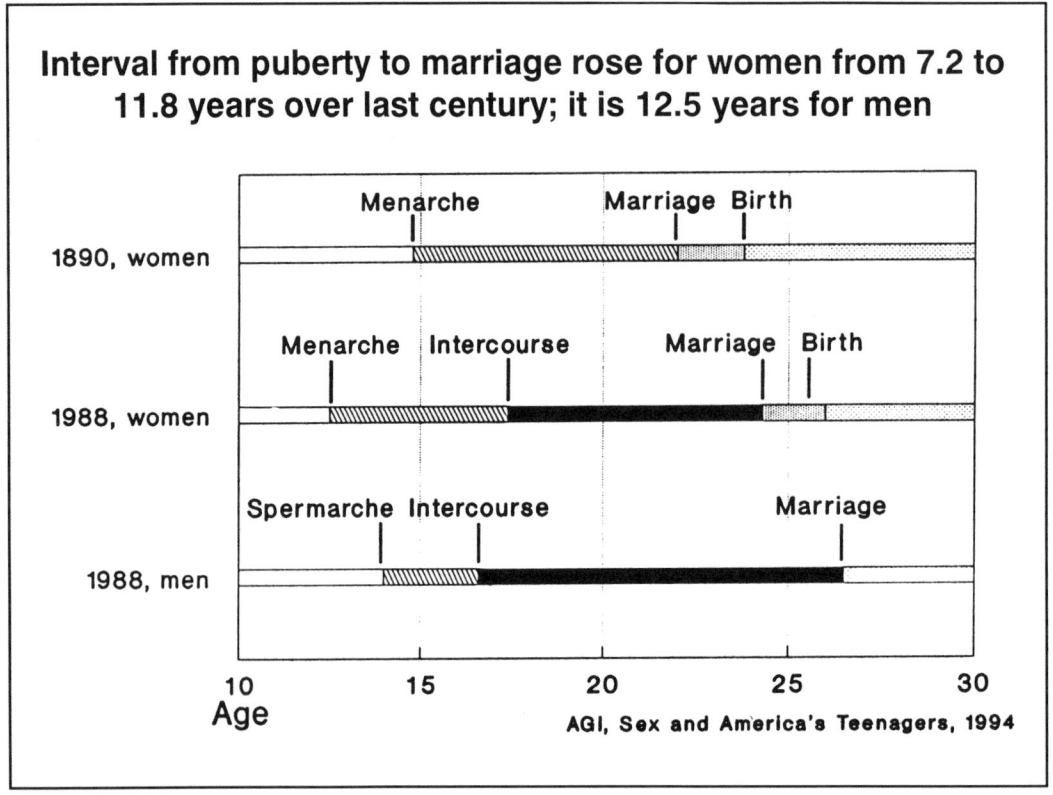

Interval from puberty to marriage rose for women from 7.2 to 11.8 years over last century; it is 12.5 years for men

Source: Jacqueline D. Forrest, The Alan Guttmacher Institute, "Levels and Determinants of U.S. Fertility," presentation at The Population and Consumption Task Force of the President's Council on Sustainable Development, October 27, 1994, unpublished.

D1-7. Median Age at First Marriage, by Sex: 1890 to 1993

Year	Men	Women	Year	Men	Women
1993.....................	26.5	24.5			
			1955.....................	22.6	20.2
1990.....................	26.1	23.9	1950.....................	22.8	20.3
1985.....................	25.5	23.3	1940.....................	24.3	21.5
1980.....................	24.7	22.0	1930.....................	24.3	21.3
1975.....................	23.5	21.1	1920.....................	24.6	21.2
1970.....................	23.2	20.8	1910.....................	25.1	21.6
1965.....................	22.8	20.6	1900.....................	25.9	21.9
1960.....................	22.8	20.3	1890.....................	26.1	22.0

Note: A standard error of 0.1 years is appropriate to measure sampling variability for any of the above median ages at first marriage, based on Current Population Survey data.

Source: Arlene F. Saluter, U.S. Bureau of the Census, *Marital Status and Living Arrangements: March 1993*, Current Population Reports, P20-478, Washington, D.C.: U.S. Government Printing Office, 1994, Table B.

D1-8. Life-Cycle Events of Women, by Year of Woman's Birth: June 1985

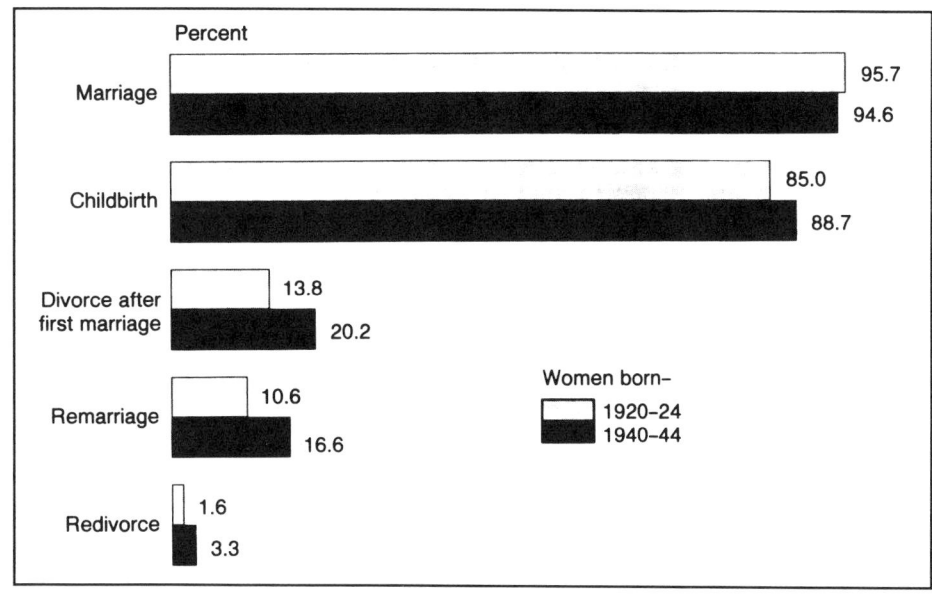

Source: Arthur J. Norton and Louisa F. Miller, U.S. Bureau of the Census, "The Family Life Cycle: 1985," *Work and Family Patterns of American Women*, Current Population Reports, Series P-23, No. 165, Washington, D.C.: U.S. Government Printing Office, 1990, Figure 1.

D1-9. Ever-Married Mothers at Stages of the Family Life Cycle, by Year of Birth: 1985

Stage	All mothers born 1920-54	Birth cohort						
		1920-24	1925-29	1930-34	1935-39	1940-44	1945-49	1950-54
Total (in thousands)	40581	4819	5181	4930	5199	6212	7118	7122
Median age at—								
First marriage.	20.4	21.0	20.7	20.2	19.9	20.3	20.5	20.3
Birth of first child	22.3	23.3	22.7	22.0	21.5	21.9	22.4	22.4
Birth of last child	28.8	31.5	31.1	30.1	28.7	28.0	27.9	27.3
Years between age at—								
First marriage and first birth.	1.9	2.3	2.0	1.8	1.6	1.6	1.9	2.1
First birth and last birth	6.5	8.2	8.4	8.1	7.2	6.1	5.5	4.9
Average number of children								
per woman.	2.89	3.18	3.38	3.45	3.27	2.82	2.44	2.20

Source: Arthur J. Norton and Louisa F. Miller, U.S. Bureau of the Census, "The Family Life Cycle: 1985," *Work and Family Patterns of American Women*, Current Population Reports, Series P-23, No. 165, Washington, D.C.: U.S. Government Printing Office, 1990, Table A.

D1-10. Ever-Married Childless Women at Stages of Marital Life, by Year of Birth: 1985

Stage	All childless women born 1920-54	Birth cohort						
		1920-24	1925-29	1930-34	1935-39	1940-44	1945-49	1950-54
Women ever married (thous.)..	5000	636	590	456	394	526	913	1485
Median age at first marriage..	23.3	24.0	22.5	22.5	24.8	22.7	23.3	23.5
Women married once, currently married (thous.).......	2775	311	333	227	207	276	536	887
Median age at first marriage.	24.7	25.3	23.9	23.2	25.7	23.1	24.4	25.7
Women married once, currently divorced (thous.)......	733	43	43	68	70	82	165	263
Median age at:								
First marriage	22.9	(B)	(B)	(B)	(B)	22.6	23.0	21.8
First separation	30.4	(B)	(B)	(B)	(B)	31.4	30.9	27.0
First divorce	31.5	(B)	(B)	(B)	(B)	33.3	31.8	28.3
Women married twice (currently married), divorced after first marriage (thous.)	608	58	55	59	49	81	117	189
Median age at:								
First marriage	20.6	(B)	(B)	(B)	(B)	22.3	21.3	20.1
First separation	26.8	(B)	(B)	(B)	(B)	30.1	26.7	24.6
First divorce	27.6	(B)	(B)	(B)	(B)	30.3	27.9	25.6
Second marriage.........	31.9	(B)	(B)	(B)	(B)	34.2	32.4	29.6

B Base less than 75,000.

Source: Arthur J. Norton and Louisa F. Miller, U.S. Bureau of the Census, "The Family Life Cycle: 1985," *Work and Family Patterns of American Women*, Current Population Reports, Series P-23, No. 165, Washington, D.C.: U.S. Government Printing Office, 1990, Table I.

D1-11. Divorces and Annulments and Rates: 1940 to 1990

[Data refer only to events occurring within the United States. Alaska included beginning with 1959, and Hawaii, beginning with 1960. Rates per 1,000 population enumerated as of April 1 for 1940, 1950, 1960, 1970, and 1980 and estimated as of July 1 for all other years]

Year	Divorces and annulments	Rate per 1,000 — Total population [1]	Rate per 1,000 — Married women 15 years and over
1990	1,182,000	4.7	20.9
1989	1,157,000	4.7	20.4
1988	1,167,000	4.8	20.7
1987	1,166,000	4.8	20.8
1986	1,178,000	4.9	21.2
1985	1,190,000	5.0	21.7
1984	1,169,000	5.0	21.5
1983	1,158,000	5.0	21.3
1982	1,170,000	5.1	21.7
1981	1,213,000	5.3	22.6
1980	1,189,000	5.2	22.6
1979	1,181,000	5.3	22.8
1978	1,130,000	5.1	21.9
1977	1,091,000	5.0	21.1
1976	1,083,000	5.0	21.1
1975	1,036,000	4.8	20.3
1974	977,000	4.6	19.3
1973	915,000	4.3	18.2
1972	845,000	4.0	17.0
1971	773,000	3.7	15.8
1970	708,000	3.5	14.9
1969	639,000	3.2	13.4
1968	584,000	2.9	12.5
1967	523,000	2.6	11.2
1966	499,000	2.5	10.9
1965	479,000	2.5	10.6
1964	450,000	2.4	10.0
1963	428,000	2.3	9.6
1962	413,000	2.2	9.4
1961	414,000	2.3	9.6
1960	393,000	2.2	9.2
1959	395,000	2.2	9.3
1958	368,000	2.1	8.9
1957	381,000	2.2	9.2
1956	382,000	2.3	9.4
1955	377,000	2.3	9.3
1954	379,000	2.4	9.5
1953	390,000	2.5	9.9
1952	392,000	2.5	10.1
1951	381,000	2.5	9.9
1950	385,000	2.6	10.3
1949	397,000	2.7	10.6
1948	408,000	2.8	11.2
1947	483,000	3.4	13.6
1946	610,000	4.3	17.9
1945	485,000	3.5	14.4
1944	400,000	2.9	12.0
1943	359,000	2.6	11.0
1942	321,000	2.4	10.1
1941	293,000	2.2	9.4
1940	264,000	2.0	8.8

[1] Rates for 1981–88 are revised and may differ from rates published previously.

Source: Sally C. Clarke, National Center for Health Statistics, *Advance Report of Final Divorce Statistics, 1989 and 1990*, Monthly Vital Statistics Report, Vol. 43, No. 9 (suppl.), Washington, D.C.: U.S. Department of Health and Human Services, March 22, 1995, Table 1.

D1-12. Median and Mean Age of Husband and Wife at Time of Divorce Decree, by Number of This Marriage, in Divorce-Registration Area: 1970 to 1990

[Based on sample data. Means and medians computed on data by single years of age]

Year	Number of marriage of husband						Number of marriage of wife					
			Remarriage						Remarriage			
	Total	First marriage	Total¹	Second marriage	Third marriage or more	Number of marriage not stated	Total	First marriage	Total¹	Second marriage	Third marriage or more	Number of marriage not stated
	Median age in years											
1990	35.6	33.2	41.5	40.4	44.9	35.1	33.2	31.1	38.2	37.3	40.6	32.8
1989	35.4	32.9	41.2	40.2	44.3	35.6	32.9	30.9	37.7	36.8	40.2	33.1
1988	35.1	32.7	40.8	39.7	44.1	35.3	32.6	30.6	37.5	36.6	40.1	32.7
1987	34.9	32.6	40.4	39.5	43.7	35.1	32.5	30.5	37.3	36.4	39.8	32.6
1986	34.6	32.4	40.0	39.2	43.5	34.9	32.1	30.2	37.0	36.1	39.4	32.2
1985	34.4	32.2	39.8	38.8	43.0	34.5	31.9	30.0	36.8	36.0	39.1	31.8
1984	34.3	32.2	39.6	38.5	42.7	34.4	31.7	30.0	36.4	35.7	38.5	31.5
1983	34.0	32.1	39.3	38.3	42.6	34.1	31.5	29.8	36.3	35.5	38.9	31.3
1982	33.6	31.7	39.1	38.0	42.4	33.7	31.1	29.5	35.8	35.0	38.8	30.9
1981	33.1	31.4	38.5	37.4	42.4	33.4	30.6	29.1	35.3	34.5	38.5	30.6
1980	32.7	31.0	38.3	37.3	41.9	32.8	30.3	28.8	35.2	34.3	38.3	30.1
1979	32.5	30.8	38.4	37.3	42.4	32.5	30.1	28.6	35.3	34.4	38.5	29.9
1978	32.0	30.5	38.2	36.9	41.1	32.5	29.7	28.3	35.1	33.9	38.7	29.7
1977	32.4	30.5	39.3	38.0	43.8	32.5	29.9	28.2	35.7	34.6	40.1	29.9
1976	32.3	30.2	39.6	38.2	44.3	31.9	29.7	28.1	36.2	34.9	40.8	29.2
1975	32.2	30.1	39.9	38.3	44.9	32.8	29.5	27.9	36.4	35.1	40.8	29.7
1974	32.2	30.2	40.3	38.7	45.0	32.0	29.5	27.7	36.7	35.4	41.3	29.2
1973	32.4	30.4	40.8	39.3	45.8	31.7	29.7	27.8	37.3	36.0	42.0	28.7
1972	32.6	30.4	40.9	39.4	45.6	32.4	29.8	27.9	37.7	36.2	42.6	29.6
1971	32.9	30.5	41.5	40.0	46.3	32.6	29.8	27.7	37.9	36.5	42.2	29.6
1970	32.9	30.5	41.5	39.9	46.5	33.1	29.8	27.7	38.2	36.5	42.8	29.3
	Mean age in years											
1990	37.3	35.0	43.1	41.9	46.5	37.2	34.8	32.9	39.5	38.6	41.9	34.7
1989	37.2	34.8	42.9	41.8	46.1	37.4	34.6	32.7	39.2	38.3	41.6	34.7
1988	36.9	34.7	42.5	41.5	45.8	37.0	34.4	32.5	39.0	38.2	41.5	34.3
1987	36.8	34.6	42.3	41.3	45.5	37.2	34.2	32.4	38.8	38.0	41.4	34.4
1986	36.5	34.4	42.1	41.0	45.2	36.6	33.9	32.2	38.6	37.8	41.1	33.8
1985	36.4	34.3	41.9	41.0	44.9	36.4	33.7	32.0	38.5	37.7	41.2	33.6
1984	36.2	34.2	41.6	40.7	44.6	36.4	33.6	31.9	38.2	37.5	40.5	33.6
1983	36.1	34.1	41.4	40.5	44.6	36.1	33.5	31.8	38.1	37.2	41.0	33.1
1982	35.7	33.7	41.3	40.3	44.6	35.8	33.1	31.4	37.9	37.0	40.7	32.9
1981	35.4	33.4	40.9	39.8	44.5	35.8	32.7	31.1	37.6	36.7	40.5	32.7
1980	35.1	33.2	40.6	39.6	43.7	35.3	32.4	30.8	37.4	36.5	40.4	32.3
1979	35.0	33.1	40.7	39.7	44.2	35.4	32.3	30.7	37.4	36.6	40.5	32.5
1978	34.8	32.9	40.5	39.5	43.8	35.0	32.1	30.5	37.2	36.2	40.5	32.1
1977	35.1	33.0	41.4	40.4	45.3	35.1	32.4	30.5	38.1	37.2	41.6	32.2
1976	35.1	32.9	41.7	40.4	45.6	34.6	32.3	30.4	38.3	37.1	42.2	31.8
1975	35.0	32.8	41.7	40.4	45.8	35.6	32.3	30.3	38.5	37.4	42.1	32.5
1974	35.1	32.9	42.1	40.9	46.1	35.1	32.3	30.3	38.8	37.6	42.6	32.1
1973	35.3	33.1	42.4	41.1	46.4	34.9	32.5	30.4	39.1	38.0	42.7	31.6
1972	35.4	33.2	42.4	41.1	46.4	35.3	32.6	30.5	39.3	38.0	43.4	32.4
1971	35.6	33.2	42.7	41.4	46.8	35.2	32.7	30.4	39.4	38.2	43.0	32.3
1970	35.6	33.2	42.8	41.4	47.1	35.4	32.7	30.4	39.3	38.1	43.4	32.2

¹Includes remarried, number not stated.

Source: Sally C. Clarke, National Center for Health Statistics, *Advance Report of Final Divorce Statistics, 1989 and 1990,* Monthly Vital Statistics Report, Vol. 43, No. 9 (suppl.), Washington, D.C.: U.S. Department of Health and Human Services, March 22, 1995, Table 7.

D1-13. Percentages of Two-Parent Families that Ended within Two Years, by Poverty Status: Mid-1980s

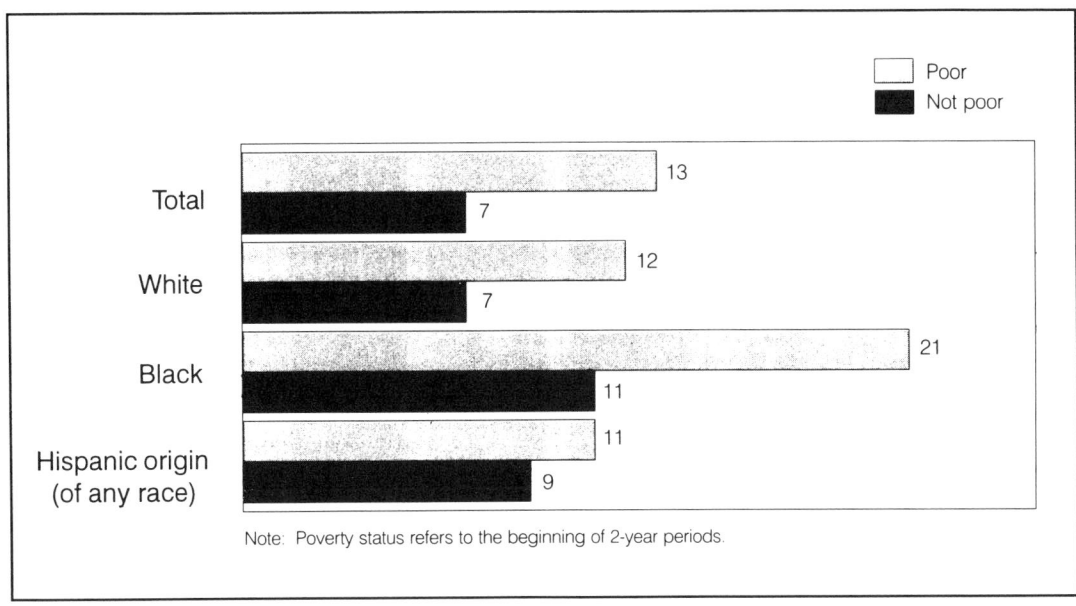

Note: Poverty status refers to the beginning of 2-year periods.

Source: Arlene F. Saluter, U.S. Bureau of the Census, *Marital Status and Living Arrangements: March 1993*, Current Population Reports, P20-478, Washington, D.C.: U.S. Government Printing Office, 1994, Figure 17.

D1-14. First Marriage Dissolution and Years until Remarriage for Women, by Race and Hispanic Origin: 1988

[For women 15 to 44 years old. Based on 1988 National Survey of Family Growth. Marriage dissolution includes death of spouse, separation because of marital discord, and divorce.]

ITEM	Number (1,000)	YEARS UNTIL REMARRIAGE (cummulative percent)					
		All	1	2	3	4	5
ALL RACES [1]							
Year of dissolution of first marriage:							
All years	11,577	56.8	20.6	32.8	40.7	46.2	49.7
1980-84	3,504	47.5	16.3	28.1	36.4	[2]41.1	[2]45.4
1975-79	3,235	65.3	21.9	36.0	44.7	52.7	55.4
1970-74	1,887	83.2	24.9	38.6	47.9	56.4	61.2
1965-69	1,013	89.9	32.6	48.7	60.2	65.0	72.8
WHITE							
Year of dissolution of first marriage:							
All years	10,103	59.9	21.9	35.2	43.5	49.4	53.0
1980-84	3,030	51.4	18.2	31.1	40.3	[2]45.2	[2]49.8
1975-79	2,839	69.5	23.2	38.5	46.9	55.6	58.4
1970-74	1,622	87.5	24.9	39.8	49.8	59.3	64.3
1965-69	893	91.0	34.7	52.3	64.9	69.3	76.9
BLACK							
Year of dissolution of first marriage:							
All years	1,166	34.0	10.9	16.5	19.6	22.7	25.0
1980-84	380	19.7	[3]4.7	[3]10.6	[3]12.9	[2]14.8	[2]14.8
1975-79	301	32.3	[3]11.4	[3]15.6	18.5	22.2	24.9
1970-74	227	59.0	22.3	29.4	35.3	38.7	42.3
1965-69	98	81.2	[3]20.9	[3]27.3	[3]31.3	40.8	52.1
Hispanic, [4] all years	942	44.7	12.5	16.6	22.7	27.8	29.9

[1] Includes other races.   [2] The percent having remarried is biased downward because the women had not completed the indicated number of years since dissolution of first marriage at the time of the survey.   [3] Figure does not meet standard of reliability or precision.   [4] Hispanic persons may be of any race.

Source: National Center for Health Statistics, *Advance Data from Vital and Health Statistics*, No. 194.

Source: U.S. Bureau of the Census, *Statistical Abstract of the United States: 1993*, (113th edition), Washington, D.C.: U.S. Government Printing Office, 1993, Table 145.

D1-15. Rates of First Marriage, Divorce, and Remarriage: 1921 to 1989

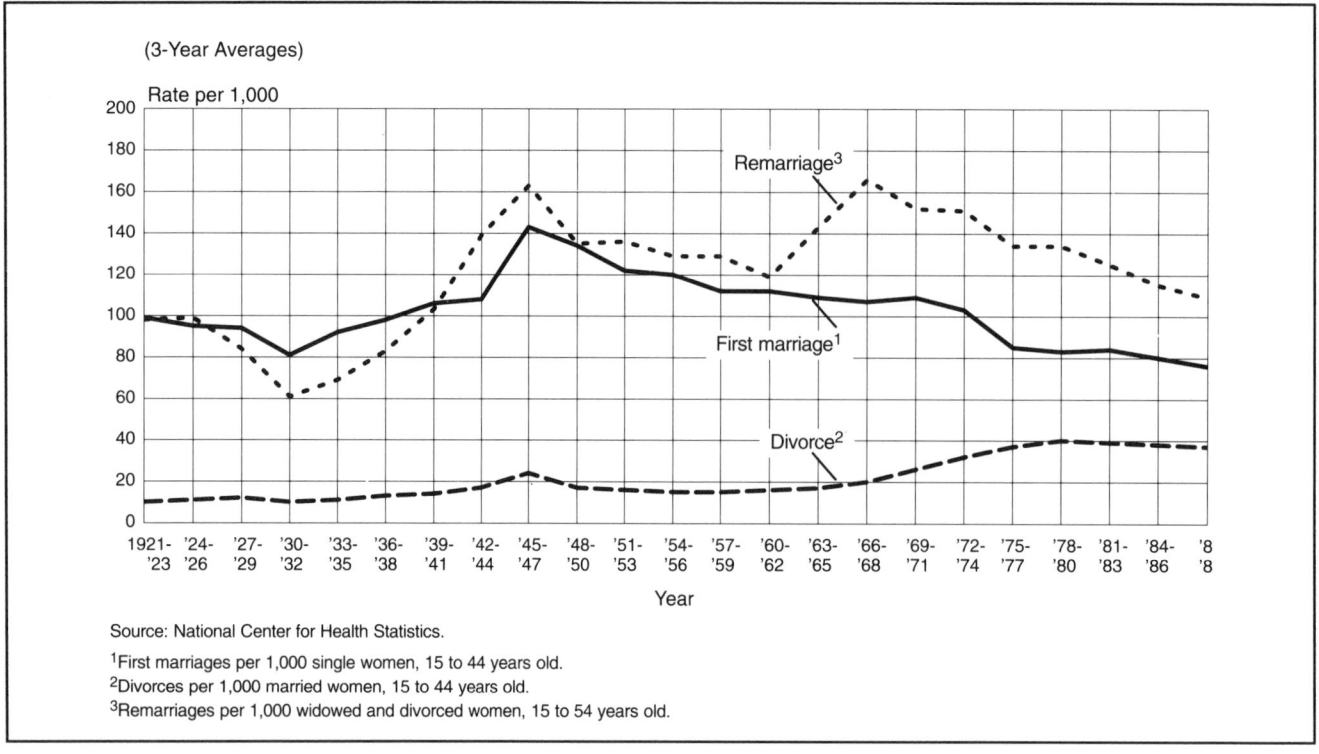

Source: National Center for Health Statistics.

[1]First marriages per 1,000 single women, 15 to 44 years old.
[2]Divorces per 1,000 married women, 15 to 44 years old.
[3]Remarriages per 1,000 widowed and divorced women, 15 to 54 years old.

Source: Arthur J. Norton and Louisa F. Miller, U.S. Bureau of the Census, *Marriage, Divorce, and Remarriage in the 1990's,* Current Population Reports, Special Studies Series P23-180, October 1992, Washington, D.C.: Government Printing Office, Figure 1.

D1-16. Numbers and Rates of First Marriage, Divorce, and Remarriage: 3-Year Averages, 1921 to 1989

Period	First marriage		Divorce		Remarriage	
	Thousands	Rate[1]	Thousands	Rate[2]	Thousands	Rate[3]
1921 to 1923	990	99	158	10	186	98
1924 to 1926	992	95	177	11	200	99
1927 to 1929	1,025	94	201	12	181	84
1930 to 1932	919	81	183	10	138	61
1933 to 1935	1,081	92	196	11	162	69
1936 to 1938	1,183	98	243	13	201	83
1939 to 1941	1,312	106	269	14	254	103
1942 to 1944	1,247	108	360	17	354	139
1945 to 1947	1,540	143	526	24	425	163
1948 to 1950	1,326	134	397	17	360	135
1951 to 1953	1,190	122	388	16	370	136
1954 to 1956	1,182	120	379	15	353	129
1957 to 1959	1,128	112	381	15	359	129
1960 to 1962	1,205	112	407	16	345	119
1963 to 1965	1,311	109	452	17	415	143
1966 to 1968	1,440	107	535	20	511	166
1969 to 1971	1,649	109	702	26	515	152
1972 to 1974	1,662	103	907	32	601	151
1975 to 1977	1,508	85	1,070	37	646	134
1978 to 1980	1,580	83	1,167	40	754	134
1981 to 1983	1,632	84	1,191	39	822	125
1984 to 1986	1,595	80	1,179	38	838	115
1987 to 1989[4]	1,564	76	1,165	37	837	109

Source: National Center for Health Statistics.

[1]First marriages per 1,000 single women, 15 to 44 years old.
[2]Divorces per 1,000 married women, 15 to 44 years old.
[3]Remarriages per 1,000 widowed and divorced women, 15 to 54 years old.
[4]Data on first marriages and remarriages are not available for 1989. The proportions for 1988 were applied to 1989 marriages (12 months handing in December).

Source: Arthur J. Norton and Louisa F. Miller, U.S. Bureau of the Census, *Marriage, Divorce, and Remarriage in the 1990's,* Current Population Reports, Special Studies Series P23-180, October 1992, Washington, D.C.: Government Printing Office, Table A.

D1-17. Percentage of Women Whose First Marriage Ended in Divorce or May Eventually End in Divorce: June 1990

(Universe is ever-married women 20 to 54)

Age	Ended in divorce by June 1990	May end in divorce if their future experience is similar to older cohorts during:[1]	
		1975 to 1980	1985 to 1990
20 to 24.............................	12.5	49.2	37.6
25 to 29.............................	19.2	46.4	39.0
30 to 34.............................	28.1	46.2	40.8
35 to 39.............................	34.1	44.8	42.0
40 to 44.............................	35.8	41.9	39.9
45 to 49.............................	35.2	38.7	36.2
50 to 54.............................	29.5	32.0	30.2

[1]Increments through age 65.

Source: Arthur J. Norton and Louisa F. Miller, U.S. Bureau of the Census, *Marriage, Divorce, and Remarriage in the 1990's*, Current Population Reports, Special Studies Series P23-180, October 1992, Washington, D.C.: Government Printing Office, Table C.

D1-18. Marriage Experience for Women, by Age, Race, and Hispanic Origin: 1975, 1980, 1985, and 1990

(Universe is women 20 to 54 years)

Category	All races				White				Black				Hispanic origin[1]		
	1975	1980	1985	1990	1975	1980	1985	1990	1975	1980	1985	1990	1980	1985	1990
Percent ever married															
20 to 24	62.5	49.5	43.3	38.5	64.9	52.2	46.6	41.3	47.5	33.3	23.9	23.5	55.4	56.7	45.8
25 to 29	87.2	78.6	74.0	69.0	88.8	81.0	77.4	73.2	76.5	62.3	53.4	45.0	80.2	78.4	69.6
30 to 34	93.1	89.9	85.8	82.2	93.9	91.6	88.1	85.6	87.1	77.9	70.9	61.1	88.3	88.0	83.0
35 to 39	95.5	94.3	91.6	89.4	96.2	95.3	93.1	91.4	90.1	87.4	80.7	74.9	91.2	91.6	88.9
40 to 44	95.8	95.1	94.6	92.0	95.9	95.8	95.6	93.4	95.1	89.7	86.1	82.1	94.2	90.3	92.8
45 to 49	95.9	95.9	94.4	94.4	95.9	96.4	95.1	95.1	95.4	92.5	88.4	89.7	94.4	91.1	91.7
50 to 54	95.8	95.3	95.2	95.5	96.0	95.8	95.4	96.1	94.6	92.1	93.4	91.9	95.0	92.5	91.8
Percent divorced after first marriage															
20 to 24	11.2	14.2	13.9	12.5	11.3	14.7	14.4	12.8	10.6	10.5	11.0	9.6	9.4	11.0	6.8
25 to 29	17.1	20.7	21.0	19.2	17.7	21.0	21.5	19.8	20.5	20.2	18.2	17.8	13.9	14.8	13.5
30 to 34	19.8	26.2	29.3	28.1	20.0	25.8	29.0	28.6	20.5	31.4	34.4	26.6	21.1	19.2	19.9
35 to 39	21.5	27.2	32.0	34.1	21.2	26.7	32.0	34.6	22.7	32.9	34.6	35.8	21.9	26.3	29.7
40 to 44	20.5	26.1	32.1	35.8	19.7	25.5	32.0	35.2	27.4	33.7	36.9	45.1	19.7	22.8	26.6
45 to 49	21.0	23.1	29.0	35.2	20.3	22.7	28.4	35.5	26.9	29.0	36.0	39.8	23.9	24.3	24.6
50 to 54	18.0	21.8	25.7	29.5	16.8	21.0	24.6	28.5	29.7	29.0	33.7	39.2	22.5	21.8	22.9
Percent remarried after divorce															
20 to 24	47.9	45.5	44.3	38.1	50.1	47.0	46.0	39.3	(B)	(B)	(B)	(B)	(B)	(B)	(B)
25 to 29	60.2	53.4	55.3	51.8	62.0	56.4	58.3	52.8	43.1	27.9	25.4	44.4	(B)	50.5	49.5
30 to 34	64.4	60.9	61.4	59.6	67.5	63.3	64.3	61.4	41.8	42.0	41.1	42.0	58.3	44.9	45.9
35 to 39	69.5	64.9	63.0	65.0	70.9	66.9	64.9	66.5	62.6	50.6	44.8	54.0	45.2	57.1	51.2
40 to 44	69.7	67.4	64.7	67.1	71.9	68.6	67.5	69.5	57.1	58.4	45.4	50.3	(B)	50.6	53.9
45 to 49	69.6	69.2	67.9	65.9	70.7	70.4	69.6	67.2	61.7	62.7	54.6	55.0	(B)	78.9	51.0
50 to 54	73.5	72.0	68.2	63.0	73.4	72.6	68.4	65.4	73.7	72.7	64.3	50.2	(B)	(B)	62.2
Percent redivorced after remarriage															
20 to 24	(NA)	8.5	8.7	13.1	(NA)	(NA)	(NA)	(NA)	(NA)	(NA)	(NA)	(NA)	(NA)	(NA)	(NA)
25 to 29	(NA)	15.6	18.2	17.8	(NA)	(NA)	(NA)	(NA)	(NA)	(NA)	(NA)	(NA)	(NA)	(NA)	(NA)
30 to 34	(NA)	19.1	20.0	22.7	(NA)	(NA)	(NA)	(NA)	(NA)	(NA)	(NA)	(NA)	(NA)	(NA)	(NA)
35 to 39	(NA)	24.7	26.9	28.5	(NA)	(NA)	(NA)	(NA)	(NA)	(NA)	(NA)	(NA)	(NA)	(NA)	(NA)
40 to 44	(NA)	28.4	33.0	30.6	(NA)	(NA)	(NA)	(NA)	(NA)	(NA)	(NA)	(NA)	(NA)	(NA)	(NA)
45 to 49	(NA)	25.1	33.8	36.4	(NA)	(NA)	(NA)	(NA)	(NA)	(NA)	(NA)	(NA)	(NA)	(NA)	(NA)
50 to 54	(NA)	29.0	27.3	34.5	(NA)	(NA)	(NA)	(NA)	(NA)	(NA)	(NA)	(NA)	(NA)	(NA)	(NA)

B Base is less than 75,000.
NA Not available.

[1]Persons of Hispanic origin may be of any race. No Hispanic data are available for 1975.

Source: Arthur J. Norton and Louisa F. Miller, U.S. Bureau of the Census, *Marriage, Divorce, and Remarriage in the 1990's*, Current Population Reports, Special Studies Series P23-180, October 1992, Washington, D.C.: Government Printing Office, Table B.

D1-19. Presence and Marital Status of Parent for Children under 18 Years Living with Only One Parent, by Age, Sex, and Race: March 1993

[Numbers in thousands. For meaning of symbols, see text]

Characteristic	All races				Black				White				White, not Hispanic			
	Total	Under 3	Under 6	6 to 17	Total	Under 3	Under 6	6 to 17	Total	Under 3	Under 6	6 to 17	Total	Under 3	Under 6	6 to 17
NUMBER																
Total	17,872	3,254	6,492	11,379	6,080	1,294	2,405	3,674	11,110	1,838	3,853	7,257	8,818	1,384	2,925	5,893
Living with mother only. .	15,586	2,822	5,627	9,959	5,757	1,221	2,264	3,493	9,256	1,507	3,168	6,088	7,237	1,120	2,381	4,855
Never married.	5,511	1,813	3,067	2,443	3,317	978	1,693	1,625	2,015	779	1,271	744	1,208	532	834	374
Husband absent	3,739	536	1,220	2,519	1,272	139	364	908	2,322	375	816	1,506	1,738	293	611	1,127
Widowed.	649	45	111	539	137	14	25	111	478	30	78	400	382	22	64	318
Divorced	5,687	428	1,230	4,457	1,032	90	182	850	4,441	324	1,004	3,437	3,910	273	872	3,038
Mother householder . . .	12,696	1,870	4,075	8,620	4,770	839	1,698	3,072	7,460	971	2,240	5,221	5,912	736	1,700	4,212
Never married.	4,012	1,103	2,047	1,973	2,548	636	1,202	1,347	1,344	428	775	569	774	298	504	270
Husband absent	3,208	381	946	2,263	1,147	109	313	834	1,942	264	609	1,333	1,446	208	454	992
Widowed.	585	40	97	488	135	14	24	111	418	25	67	351	342	18	53	290
Divorced	4,881	347	985	3,896	940	80	159	781	3,756	255	789	2,967	3,350	212	689	2,661
Living with father only . .	2,286	432	865	1,420	322	74	142	181	1,854	332	684	1,170	1,581	265	544	1,038
Never married.	747	314	515	233	173	56	96	77	533	237	389	145	409	187	292	117
Wife absent.	475	44	116	359	62	10	23	40	387	33	90	297	315	24	70	246
Widowed.	114	1	7	106	14	-	3	11	94	-	3	91	76	-	-	76
Divorced	950	74	228	722	73	9	20	53	840	63	202	638	781	55	182	599
Father householder	1,957	373	722	1,235	256	59	111	145	1,610	294	583	1,026	1,378	236	468	911
Never married.	611	266	434	177	121	41	71	51	462	211	346	117	357	170	264	93
Wife absent.	412	38	93	320	54	10	20	34	332	26	70	262	273	17	54	219
Widowed.	106	1	7	99	14	-	3	11	90	-	3	88	73	-	-	72
Divorced	828	68	187	641	66	9	17	49	725	57	164	560	675	49	149	525
PERCENT																
Total	100.0	100.0	100.0	100.0	100.0	100.0	100.0	100.0	100.0	100.0	100.0	100.0	100.0	100.0	100.0	100.0
Living with mother only. .	87.2	86.7	86.7	87.5	94.7	94.4	94.1	95.1	83.3	82.0	82.2	83.9	82.1	80.9	81.4	82.4
Never married.	35.4	64.2	54.5	24.5	57.6	80.1	74.8	46.5	21.8	51.7	40.1	12.2	16.7	47.5	35.0	7.7
Husband absent	24.0	19.0	21.7	25.3	22.1	11.4	16.1	26.0	25.1	24.9	25.8	24.7	24.0	26.2	25.7	23.2
Widowed.	4.2	1.6	2.0	5.4	2.4	1.1	1.1	3.2	5.2	2.0	2.5	6.6	5.3	2.0	2.7	6.5
Divorced	36.5	15.2	21.9	44.8	17.9	7.4	8.0	24.3	48.0	21.5	31.7	56.5	54.0	24.4	36.6	62.6
Mother householder. . . .	71.0	57.5	62.8	75.8	78.5	64.8	70.6	83.6	67.1	52.8	58.1	71.9	67.0	53.2	58.1	71.5
Never married.	31.6	59.0	50.2	22.9	53.4	75.8	70.8	43.8	18.0	44.1	34.6	10.9	13.1	40.5	29.6	6.4
Husband absent	25.3	20.4	23.2	26.3	24.0	13.0	18.4	27.1	26.0	27.2	27.2	25.5	24.5	28.3	26.7	23.6
Widowed.	4.6	2.1	2.4	5.7	2.8	1.7	1.4	3.6	5.6	2.6	3.0	6.7	5.8	2.4	3.1	6.9
Divorced	38.4	18.6	24.2	45.2	19.7	9.5	9.4	25.4	50.3	26.3	35.2	56.8	56.7	28.8	40.5	63.2
Living with father only . .	12.8	13.3	13.3	12.5	5.3	5.7	5.9	4.9	16.7	18.1	17.8	16.1	17.9	19.1	18.6	17.6
Never married.	32.7	72.7	59.5	16.4	53.7	75.7	67.6	42.5	28.7	71.4	56.9	12.4	25.9	70.6	53.7	11.3
Wife absent.	20.8	10.2	13.4	25.3	19.3	13.5	16.2	22.1	20.9	9.9	13.2	25.4	19.9	9.1	12.9	23.7
Widowed.	5.0	0.2	0.8	7.5	4.3	-	2.1	6.1	5.1	-	0.4	7.8	4.8	-	-	7.3
Divorced	41.6	17.1	26.4	50.8	22.7	12.2	14.1	29.3	45.3	19.0	29.5	54.5	49.4	20.8	33.5	57.7
Father householder	11.0	11.5	11.1	10.9	4.2	4.6	4.6	3.9	14.5	16.0	15.1	14.1	15.6	17.1	16.0	15.5
Never married.	31.2	71.3	60.1	14.3	47.3	69.5	64.0	35.2	28.7	71.8	59.3	11.4	25.9	72.0	56.4	10.2
Wife absent.	21.1	10.2	12.9	25.9	21.1	16.9	18.0	23.4	20.6	8.8	12.0	25.5	19.8	7.2	11.5	24.0
Widowed.	5.4	0.3	1.0	8.0	5.5	-	2.7	7.6	5.6	-	0.5	8.6	5.3	-	-	7.9
Divorced	42.3	18.2	25.9	51.9	25.8	15.3	15.3	33.8	45.0	19.4	28.1	54.6	49.0	20.8	31.8	57.6

Source: Claudette E. Bennett, U.S. Bureau of the Census, *The Black Population in the United States: March 1994 and 1993*, Current Population Reports, Series P20-480, Washington, D.C.: U.S. Government Printing Office, January 1995, Table H.

D1-20. Living Arrangements of Children under 18 Years, by Marital Status and Selected Characteristics of Parent: March 1993

Numbers in thousands. Characteristics are shown for householder or reference person in married-couple situations.

Subject	Total, living with one or both parents	Living with both parents	Living with mother only					Living with father only				
				Marital status of mother					Marital status of father			
			Total	Divorced	Married, spouse absent	Widowed	Never married	Total	Divorced	Married, spouse absent	Widowed	Never married
ALL RACES												
Children under 18 years -------	65 052	47 181	15 586	5 687	3 739	649	5 511	2 286	950	475	114	747
Number of siblings in household:												
None ------------------	12 732	7 616	4 247	1 489	701	169	1 888	868	384	116	39	329
One -------------------	26 529	20 053	5 570	2 412	1 326	246	1 586	905	403	204	47	252
Two -------------------	15 955	12 366	3 239	1 183	906	152	998	350	127	112	15	96
Three -----------------	6 203	4 579	1 507	383	505	41	578	117	36	22	5	54
Four ------------------	2 222	1 564	622	121	163	27	311	36	–	17	2	17
Five or more ----------	1 411	1 002	401	100	138	14	149	9	–	4	5	–
Mean number of siblings ----	1.43	1.48	1.35	1.21	1.60	1.31	1.33	.94	.81	1.22	1.10	.90
Age of parent:												
15 to 19 years --------	529	57	447	4	33	–	410	26	–	2	–	24
20 to 24 years --------	3 278	1 243	1 854	166	320	7	1 362	181	6	14	–	161
25 to 29 years --------	8 338	4 878	3 081	873	743	36	1 429	378	74	35	7	263
30 to 34 years --------	14 497	10 402	3 645	1 458	879	86	1 222	450	193	103	1	154
35 to 39 years --------	15 875	12 181	3 227	1 525	860	168	675	467	222	135	22	87
40 to 44 years --------	12 625	10 146	2 098	1 041	623	137	296	381	259	69	23	30
45 to 49 years --------	6 323	5 259	845	452	205	108	81	218	135	46	25	12
50 to 54 years --------	2 290	1 907	257	127	52	59	19	127	44	49	20	14
55 to 59 years --------	776	659	82	31	20	23	8	35	7	18	10	–
60 to 64 years --------	321	286	18	4	–	10	4	18	11	3	2	2
65 years and over -----	199	162	33	5	5	18	5	4	–	2	3	–
Education of parent:												
Less than 9th grade ----	3 893	2 691	1 052	173	384	94	401	150	26	51	14	59
9th to 12 grade, no diploma --	7 799	3 890	3 479	800	840	102	1 737	430	140	74	18	199
High school graduate (including equivalency) --	22 519	15 638	5 964	2 225	1 340	221	2 178	916	385	179	32	320
Some college, no degree or associate degree ----	16 307	12 021	3 815	1 776	888	143	1 008	471	239	106	17	109
Bachelor's degree ------	9 332	8 188	939	475	235	65	164	205	93	48	15	49
Graduate or professional degree ---	5 202	4 752	337	237	53	24	23	113	67	17	18	11
Percent high school graduates--	82.0	86.1	70.9	82.9	67.3	69.7	61.2	74.6	82.6	73.8	71.8	65.5
Employment status of parent:												
In the labor force ------	54 345	42 812	9 531	4 310	2 152	363	2 706	2 002	828	404	103	667
Employed -----------	50 603	40 579	8 295	3 989	1 831	332	2 143	1 730	728	363	97	542
Both parents employed ----	25 885	25 885	(X)	(X)	(X)	(X)	(X)	(X)	(X)	(X)	(X)	(X)
Full time -------	46 019	38 025	6 435	3 304	1 396	195	1 540	1 559	685	328	77	470
Part time -------	4 584	2 554	1 860	685	435	137	603	171	44	35	20	72
Unemployed -------------	3 742	2 233	1 236	321	321	31	563	273	100	42	6	125
Not in the labor force --------	9 751	3 417	6 055	1 377	1 587	286	2 804	279	119	69	11	81
Presence of adults other than parent:												
Other relatives present only --	11 074	6 819	3 757	1 088	846	239	1 583	497	198	86	45	169
Nonrelatives present only ----	3 319	429	2 069	939	303	69	758	821	281	72	13	455
Other relatives and nonrelatives present -------	565	171	312	111	66	17	117	82	17	14	2	49
No adults other than parent -------	50 095	39 761	9 449	3 549	2 523	323	3 053	886	454	303	54	75
Family income:												
Under $2,500 ---------	1 564	341	1 121	223	363	40	495	102	32	14	–	56
$2,500 to $4,999 ---------	2 330	308	1 942	548	469	22	903	80	27	16	4	34
$5,000 to $7,499 ---------	2 687	572	1 980	509	538	56	877	134	33	42	1	58
$7,500 to $9,999 ---------	2 490	742	1 608	533	375	30	670	139	53	31	1	54
$10,000 to $12,499 ---------	2 808	1 272	1 377	432	413	42	490	159	51	25	3	80
$12,500 to $14,999 ---------	2 059	1 051	935	333	270	25	306	74	18	32	–	23
$15,000 to $19,999 ---------	4 706	2 886	1 585	632	377	109	466	236	108	36	12	80
$20,000 to $24,999 ---------	4 640	3 069	1 284	589	251	100	344	286	115	45	22	103
$25,000 to $29,999 ---------	4 604	3 373	1 017	512	205	57	244	213	103	44	11	56
$30,000 to $39,999 ---------	8 832	7 270	1 247	657	182	77	331	315	151	79	8	78
$40,000 to $49,999 ---------	8 213	7 257	703	377	156	36	134	253	122	43	18	71
$50,000 and over ---------	20 119	19 039	786	341	141	55	250	294	138	68	34	54
Mean income ---------------	41 558	49 971	17 859	21 471	15 378	23 782	15 115	29 494	31 034	30 397	59 467	22 410
Median income ---------------	35 166	43 578	12 073	17 014	10 752	20 059	9 292	23 305	26 649	24 437	36 970	18 406
Percent below poverty level ---	21.2	10.6	52.9	38.4	58.9	32.3	66.3	23.7	18.1	26.7	8.8	31.1
Percent below 125 percent of poverty level ----	26.6	15.2	60.3	45.8	67.8	39.2	72.7	32.2	24.9	33.9	12.3	43.4
Area of residence:												
Inside metropolitan areas ---------	50 069	35 743	12 611	4 341	3 083	484	4 702	1 716	668	378	98	573
1,000,000 or more ---------	27 351	19 218	7 249	2 216	1 838	277	2 918	885	309	229	34	313
Inside central cities ---------	10 624	6 110	4 110	961	1 005	130	2 013	405	87	131	18	168
Outside central cities ---------	16 727	13 107	3 139	1 255	832	147	905	480	221	99	16	145
Under 1,000,000 ---------	22 718	16 525	5 362	2 125	1 246	207	1 784	831	359	149	64	260
Inside central cities ---------	8 378	5 234	2 778	998	612	89	1 079	366	149	80	15	122
Outside central cities ---------	14 340	11 291	2 584	1 126	634	118	705	465	210	68	49	138
Outside metropolitan areas ---------	14 983	11 438	2 976	1 346	656	165	808	570	282	97	16	175
Tenure[1]:												
Owned ---------------	40 876	34 682	5 010	2 354	1 103	377	1 176	1 184	588	255	84	258
Rented ---------------	24 176	12 499	10 576	3 334	2 636	272	4 334	1 101	362	220	29	490
Public housing ---------------	4 158	837	3 198	771	778	25	1 624	123	34	29	6	53
Private housing ---------------	20 018	11 662	7 379	2 562	1 859	247	2 711	978	328	190	23	437

[1]Refers to tenure of householder (who may or may not be the child's parent.)

Source: Arlene F. Saluter, U.S. Bureau of the Census, *Marital Status and Living Arrangements: March 1993,* Current Population Reports, P20-478, Washington, D.C.: U.S. Government Printing Office, 1994, Table 6.

D1-21. Married Couples of Same or Mixed Races and Origins: 1970 to 1993

In thousands. As of March, except as noted. Persons 15 years old and over. Persons of Hispanic origin may be of any race. Except as noted, based on Current Population Survey.

RACE AND ORIGIN OF SPOUSES	1970 [1]	1980	1990	1993
Married couples, total.	44,598	49,714	53,256	54,199
RACE				
Same race couples	43,922	48,264	50,889	51,437
White/White	40,578	44,910	47,202	47,782
Black/Black.	3,344	3,354	3,687	3,655
Interracial couples	310	651	964	1,195
Black/White.	65	167	211	242
Black husband/White wife.	41	122	150	182
White husband/Black wife.	24	45	61	60
White/other race [2]	233	450	720	920
Black/other race [2]	12	34	33	33
All other couples [2]	366	799	1,401	1,567
HISPANIC ORIGIN				
Hispanic/Hispanic	1,368	1,906	3,085	3,419
Hispanic/other origin (not Hispanic)	584	891	1,193	1,206
All other couples (not of Hispanic origin)	42,645	46,917	48,979	49,573

[1] As of April and based on Census of Population. [2] Excluding White and Black.

Source of tables 60–62: U.S. Bureau of the Census, *Current Population Reports,* P20–450; and earlier reports; and unpublished data.

Source: U.S. Bureau of the Census, *Statistical Abstract of the United States: 1993,* (113th edition), Washington, D.C.: U.S. Government Printing Office, 1993, Table 62.

D1-22. Mean Duration of Marriage at Time of Divorce Decree, by Race of Husband and Wife: 1989 and 1990 (27 Reporting States and the District of Columbia)

[Based on sample data. Mean duration in years]

Race of husband	Race of wife									
	1990					1989				
	All races	White	Black	Other races	Not stated	All races	White	Black	Other races	Not stated
All races	9.3	9.2	10.2	8.4	9.0	9.2	9.1	9.9	8.6	8.8
White	9.2	9.2	6.4	7.6	8.8	9.2	9.2	7.0	7.9	8.1
Black	10.1	7.1	10.3	5.8	13.4	9.8	6.1	10.0	6.8	*
Other races	8.2	6.6	5.3	9.1	*	8.0	6.4	5.2	9.1	*
Not stated	8.9	7.6	*	*	8.9	8.7	6.9	*	*	8.8

NOTE: The 27 reporting States were Alabama, Alaska, Connecticut, Delaware, Georgia, Hawaii, Idaho, Illinois, Iowa, Kansas, Kentucky, Maryland, Missouri, Montana, Nebraska, New York, Oregon, Pennsylvania, Rhode Island, South Carolina, South Dakota, Tennessee, Utah, Vermont, Virginia, Wisconsin, and Wyoming.

Source: Sally C. Clarke, National Center for Health Statistics, *Advance Report of Final Divorce Statistics, 1989 and 1990,* Monthly Vital Statistics Report, Vol. 43, No. 9 (suppl.), Washington, D.C.: U.S. Department of Health and Human Services, March 22, 1995, Table 15.

D1-23. Percent Never Married, by Sex and Age: 1970 and 1992

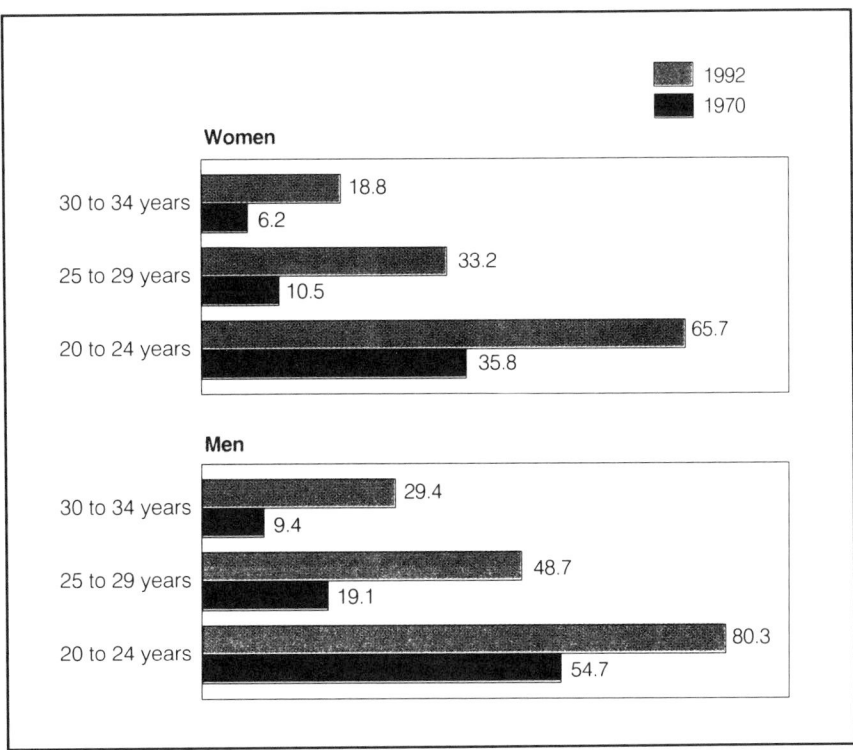

Source: U.S. Bureau of the Census, *Population Profile of the United States: 1993*, Current Population Reports, Special Studies Series P23-185, Washington, D.C.: U.S. Government Printing Office, May 1993, Figure 19.

D1-24. Percent Never Married, by Age, Sex, Race, and Hispanic Origin: 1993, 1980, and 1970

Age	Women			Men		
	1993	1980	1970	1993	1980	1970
ALL RACES						
20 to 24 years	66.8	50.2	35.8	81.0	68.8	54.7
25 to 29 years	33.1	20.9	10.5	48.4	33.1	19.1
30 to 34 years	19.3	9.5	6.2	30.1	15.9	9.4
35 to 39 years	12.5	6.2	5.4	19.7	7.8	7.2
40 to 44 years	9.0	4.8	4.9	10.8	7.1	6.3
45 to 54 years	5.4	4.7	4.9	6.9	6.1	7.5
55 to 64 years	4.3	4.5	6.8	6.6	5.3	7.8
65 years and over	4.4	5.9	7.7	4.4	4.9	7.5
WHITE						
20 to 24 years	63.8	47.2	34.6	79.0	67.0	54.4
25 to 29 years	28.7	18.3	9.2	46.2	31.4	17.8
30 to 34 years	15.5	8.1	5.5	27.3	14.2	9.2
35 to 39 years	9.9	5.2	4.6	17.1	6.6	6.1
40 to 44 years	7.3	4.3	4.8	9.8	6.7	5.7
45 to 54 years	4.6	4.4	4.9	6.1	5.6	7.1
55 to 64 years	3.7	4.4	7.0	5.9	5.2	7.6
65 years and over	4.4	6.1	8.0	4.4	4.8	7.4
BLACK						
20 to 24 years	81.2	68.5	43.5	89.6	79.3	56.1
25 to 29 years	57.3	37.2	18.8	61.1	44.2	28.4
30 to 34 years	43.3	19.0	10.8	48.3	30.0	9.2
35 to 39 years	29.7	12.2	12.1	38.7	18.5	15.8
40 to 44 years	21.8	9.0	6.9	20.4	10.8	11.2
45 to 54 years	11.9	7.7	4.4	14.4	11.7	10.4
55 to 64 years	8.9	5.7	4.7	14.6	5.9	9.1
65 years and over	4.3	4.5	4.2	5.8	5.5	5.7
HISPANIC ORIGIN*						
20 to 24 years	55.2	42.8	33.4	71.3	61.8	49.9
25 to 29 years	30.9	22.5	13.7	46.2	28.9	19.4
30 to 34 years	17.9	11.2	8.4	28.9	12.1	11.0
35 to 39 years	12.8	6.6	6.9	21.5	5.8	7.6
40 to 44 years	9.3	7.9	6.3	12.4	6.5	7.1
45 to 54 years	7.8	7.1	6.1	10.9	6.4	6.2
55 to 64 years	6.5	7.8	6.7	5.9	4.3	6.0
65 years and over	8.3	5.4	7.7	3.9	9.7	8.8

*Persons of Hispanic origin may be of any race.

Source of Hispanic data for 1970: 1970 Census of Population, *U.S. Summary*, table 203.

Source: Arlene F. Saluter, U.S. Bureau of the Census, *Marital Status and Living Arrangements: March 1993*, Current Population Reports, P20-478, Washington, D.C.: U.S. Government Printing Office, 1994, Table C.

D1-25. Unmarried-Couple Households, by Presence of Children: 1970 to 1993

[Numbers in thousands]

Year	Total married couples	Unmarried couples			Ratio of unmarried couples per 100 married couples
		Total	Without children under 15 years	With children under 15 years	
1993	54,199	3,510	2,274	1,236	6
1990	56,112	2,856	1,966	891	5
1985	51,114	1,983	1,380	603	4
1980	49,714	1,589	1,159	431	3
1970 Census	44,593	523	327	196	1

Source of 1970 data: 1970 Census of Population, PC(2)-4B, *Persons by Family Characteristics*, table 11.

Source: Arlene F. Saluter, U.S. Bureau of the Census, *Marital Status and Living Arrangements: March 1993*, Current Population Reports, P20-478, Washington, D.C.: U.S. Government Printing Office, 1994, Table B, Figure 17, Table D.

D1-26. Households with Two Unrelated Adults, by Marital Status, Age, and Female Householders: March 1993

Numbers in thousands.

Subject	Households with two unrelated adults	Age of householder					Marital status of householder				
		Under 25 years	25 to 34 years	35 to 44 years	45 to 64 years	65 years and over	Never married	Married, spouse absent		Widowed	Divorced
								Separated	Other		
FEMALE HOUSEHOLDERS											
Total	2 168	520	832	358	304	153	1 243	83	13	203	627
Partner of opposite sex	1 455	323	579	260	196	95	751	57	3	138	506
No children under 15 years in household	938	198	286	177	181	95	497	12	2	120	307
Age of partner:											
Under 25 years	167	122	30	4	7	3	148	1	–	5	13
25 to 34 years	303	69	182	41	8	3	221	5	1	4	72
35 to 44 years	193	7	57	86	39	4	89	3	–	5	97
45 to 64 years	197	–	14	45	108	29	33	2	1	42	118
65 years and over	78	–	2	1	20	55	6	1	–	64	8
Marital status of partner:											
Never married	539	178	208	77	49	27	400	5	1	35	99
Married, spouse absent	60	4	12	14	19	10	17	6	–	7	29
Separated	51	4	12	14	12	9	16	6	–	7	22
Widowed	46	–	–	1	11	34	–	–	–	39	8
Divorced	293	16	66	85	102	24	80	2	1	39	171
With children under 15 years in household	516	125	294	83	15	–	254	44	2	18	198
Age of partner:											
Under 25 years	117	74	41	1	–	–	81	6	–	2	29
25 to 34 years	248	48	164	33	4	–	124	18	–	6	101
35 to 44 years	110	3	67	37	3	–	36	8	2	8	57
45 to 64 years	39	–	22	12	5	–	14	11	–	3	12
65 years and over	3	–	–	–	3	–	–	3	–	–	–
Marital status of partner:											
Never married	326	107	170	41	8	–	199	23	2	8	95
Married, spouse absent	38	6	23	9	–	–	10	14	–	2	12
Separated	34	5	23	6	–	–	9	14	–	2	9
Widowed	1	–	–	–	1	–	–	1	–	–	–
Divorced	151	12	100	33	5	–	45	5	–	9	91
Partner of same sex	713	197	253	98	107	58	492	26	10	65	121
No children under 15 years in household	595	181	183	79	94	58	442	9	8	61	75
Age of partner:											
Under 25 years	198	144	44	4	5	–	184	4	4	2	4
25 to 34 years	190	31	115	22	15	7	152	3	4	8	24
35 to 44 years	95	4	23	41	24	2	60	1	–	3	31
45 to 64 years	66	2	–	12	35	18	34	–	1	19	12
65 years and over	46	–	–	–	15	31	12	1	–	28	5
Marital status of partner:											
Never married	471	176	160	57	56	21	396	5	8	13	48
Married, spouse absent	19	4	4	1	5	6	11	–	–	6	2
Separated	7	1	2	–	2	2	5	–	–	2	–
Widowed	31	–	–	2	10	19	4	1	–	23	3
Divorced	74	1	19	18	22	13	31	3	–	18	21
With children under 15 years in household	119	16	70	19	13	–	50	17	2	4	46
Age of partner:											
Under 25 years	34	8	22	1	3	–	9	6	–	2	17
25 to 34 years	55	4	43	3	5	–	27	8	–	1	20
35 to 44 years	21	1	5	13	1	–	11	2	–	1	8
45 to 64 years	7	3	–	–	3	–	4	1	–	–	1
65 years and over	2	–	–	2	–	–	–	–	2	–	–
Marital status of partner:											
Never married	64	9	41	9	4	–	26	9	–	2	26
Married, spouse absent	17	1	12	–	5	–	4	5	–	2	6
Separated	16	1	10	–	5	–	2	5	–	2	6
Widowed	7	1	–	4	1	–	3	1	2	–	1
Divorced	31	5	17	6	3	–	18	1	–	–	12

Source: Arlene F. Saluter, U.S. Bureau of the Census, *Marital Status and Living Arrangements: March 1993*, Current Population Reports, P20-478, Washington, D.C.: U.S. Government Printing Office, 1994, Table 8.

D1-27. Ratio of Unmarried Men per 100 Unmarried Women, by Metropolitan Areas: 1990

```
(Unmarried includes never-married, widowed, and divorced persons 15 years
old and over.  Metropolitan areas as defined June 30,1990)

RANK
ORDER   METROPOLITAN AREAS                                          RATIO
-----------------------------------------------------------------------

220 ABILENE, TX MSA                                                 79.40
239 AKRON, OH PMSA                                                  78.67
294 ALBANY, GA MSA                                                  75.64
179 ALBANY-SCHENECTADY-TROY, NY MSA                                 81.58
118 ALBUQUERQUE, NM MSA                                             85.44
284 ALEXANDRIA, LA MSA                                              76.65
223 ALLENTOWN-BETHLEHEM-EASTON, PA-NJ MSA                           79.20
353 ALTOONA, PA MSA                                                 69.42
261 AMARILLO, TX MSA                                                77.55
 27 ANAHEIM-SANTA ANA, CA PMSA                                      99.23
  8 ANCHORAGE, AK MSA                                              112.45
142 ANDERSON, IN MSA                                                83.40
305 ANDERSON, SC MSA                                                75.01
 58 ANN ARBOR, MI PMSA                                              92.50
244 ANNISTON, AL MSA                                                78.44
103 APPLETON-OSHKOSH-NEENAH, WI MSA                                 87.02
344 ASHEVILLE, NC MSA                                               71.14
150 ATHENS, GA MSA                                                  82.93
140 ATLANTA, GA MSA                                                 83.69
206 ATLANTIC CITY, NJ MSA                                           80.10
158 AUGUSTA, GA-SC MSA                                              82.47
 68 AURORA-ELGIN, IL PMSA                                           90.70
 39 AUSTIN, TX MSA                                                  96.02
 45 BAKERSFIELD, CA MSA                                             95.49
170 BALTIMORE, MD MSA                                               81.97
144 BANGOR, ME MSA                                                  83.22
199 BATON ROUGE, LA MSA                                             80.63
221 BATTLE CREEK, MI MSA                                            79.32
256 BEAUMONT-PORT ARTHUR, TX MSA                                    77.95
324 BEAVER COUNTY, PA PMSA                                          73.63
 93 BELLINGHAM, WA MSA                                              88.32
279 BENTON HARBOR, MI MSA                                           76.79
238 BERGEN-PASSAIC, NJ PMSA                                         78.70
234 BILLINGS, MT MSA                                                78.88
 50 BILOXI-GULFPORT, MS MSA                                         93.51
204 BINGHAMTON, NY MSA                                              80.24
342 BIRMINGHAM, AL MSA                                              71.63
187 BISMARCK, ND MSA                                                81.15
122 BLOOMINGTON, IN MSA                                             85.14
```

D1-27. Ratio of Unmarried Men per 100 Unmarried Women, by Metropolitan Areas: 1990 *(continued)*

262	BLOOMINGTON-NORMAL, IL MSA	77.50
106	BOISE CITY, ID MSA	86.46
183	BOSTON, PMSA	81.40
169	BOSTON-LAWRENCE-SALEM, MA-NH CMSA	82.03
31	BOULDER-LONGMONT, CO PMSA	98.56
354	BRADENTON, FL MSA	68.41
4	BRAZORIA, TX PMSA	116.71
11	BREMERTON, WA MSA	108.30
217	BRIDGEPORT-MILFORD, CT PMSA	79.49
128	BRISTOL, CT PMSA	84.63
112	BROCKTON, MA PMSA	85.74
276	BROWNSVILLE-HARLINGEN, TX MSA	76.95
10	BRYAN-COLLEGE STATION, TX MSA	111.40
289	BUFFALO, NY PMSA	76.37
287	BUFFALO-NIAGARA FALLS, NY CMSA	76.52
322	BURLINGTON, NC MSA	73.73
133	BURLINGTON, VT MSA	84.35
306	CANTON, OH MSA	74.99
116	CASPER, WY MSA	85.56
196	CEDAR RAPIDS, IA MSA	80.74
23	CHAMPAIGN-URBANA-RANTOUL, IL MSA	101.33
46	CHARLESTON, SC MSA	95.42
348	CHARLESTON, WV MSA	70.65
219	CHARLOTTE-GASTONIA-ROCK HILL, NC-SC MSA	79.42
146	CHARLOTTESVILLE, VA MSA	83.06
329	CHATTANOOGA, TN-GA MSA	73.04
52	CHEYENNE, WY MSA	93.22
172	CHICAGO, IL PMSA	81.89
143	CHICAGO-GARY-LAKE COUNTY, IL-IN-WI CMSA	83.39
100	CHICO, CA MSA	87.41
282	CINCINNATI, OH-KY-IN PMSA	76.72
274	CINCINNATI-HAMILTON, OH-KY-IN CMSA	77.03
7	CLARKSVILLE-HOPKINSVILLE, TN-KY MSA	112.71
314	CLEVELAND, OH PMSA	74.48
290	CLEVELAND-AKRON-LORAIN, OH CMSA	76.01
25	COLORADO SPRINGS, CO MSA	99.42
117	COLUMBIA, MO MSA	85.46
134	COLUMBIA, SC MSA	84.29
60	COLUMBUS, GA-AL MSA	92.10
131	COLUMBUS, OH MSA	84.59
119	CORPUS CHRISTI, TX MSA	85.43
332	CUMBERLAND, MD-WV MSA	72.73
95	DALLAS, TX PMSA	88.02
89	DALLAS-FORT WORTH, TX CMSA	88.47
84	DANBURY, CT PMSA	88.74
341	DANVILLE, VA MSA	71.72
241	DAVENPORT-ROCK ISLAND-MOLINE, IA-IL MSA	78.60
252	DAYTON-SPRINGFIELD, OH MSA	78.08
189	DAYTONA BEACH, FL MSA	81.14
202	DECATUR, AL MSA	80.31
327	DECATUR, IL MSA	73.40
98	DENVER, CO PMSA	87.46
83	DENVER-BOULDER, CO CMSA	88.88

D1-27. Ratio of Unmarried Men per 100 Unmarried Women, by Metropolitan Areas: 1990 *(continued)*

```
317 DES MOINES, IA MSA                                      74.28
201 DETROIT, MI PMSA                                        80.34
188 DETROIT-ANN ARBOR, MI CMSA                              81.15
209 DOTHAN, AL MSA                                          79.86
240 DUBUQUE, IA MSA                                         78.64
161 DULUTH, MN-WI MSA                                       82.37
190 EAU CLAIRE, WI MSA                                      81.13
175 EL PASO, TX MSA                                         81.72
181 ELKHART-GOSHEN, IN MSA                                  81.54
185 ELMIRA, NY MSA                                          81.27
299 ENID, OK MSA                                            75.35
214 ERIE, PA MSA                                            79.52
127 EUGENE-SPRINGFIELD, OR MSA                              84.71
325 EVANSVILLE, IN-KY MSA                                   73.49
328 FALL RIVER, MA-RI PMSA                                  73.18
 77 FARGO-MOORHEAD, ND-MN MSA                               89.29
  3 FAYETTEVILLE, NC MSA                                   117.66
 65 FAYETTEVILLE-SPRINGDALE, AR MSA                         90.99
205 FITCHBURG-LEOMINSTER, MA MSA                            80.15
243 FLINT, MI MSA                                           78.45
336 FLORENCE, AL MSA                                        72.20
334 FLORENCE, SC MSA                                        72.32
 66 FORT COLLINS-LOVELAND, CO MSA                           90.85
257 FORT LAUDERDALE-HOLLYWOOD-POMPANO BEACH, FL PMSA        77.87
270 FORT MYERS-CAPE CORAL, FL MSA                           77.27
152 FORT PIERCE, FL MSA                                     82.85
263 FORT SMITH, AR-OK MSA                                   77.46
 20 FORT WALTON BEACH, FL MSA                              101.70
193 FORT WAYNE, IN MSA                                      80.93
 76 FORT WORTH-ARLINGTON, TX PMSA                           89.40
 78 FRESNO, CA MSA                                          89.21
350 GADSDEN, AL MSA                                         69.86
 42 GAINESVILLE, FL MSA                                     95.70
 97 GALVESTON-TEXAS CITY, TX PMSA                           87.71
225 GARY-HAMMOND, IN PMSA                                   79.17
 82 GLENS FALLS, NY MSA                                     88.93
 16 GRAND FORKS, ND MSA                                    104.19
178 GRAND RAPIDS, MI MSA                                    81.59
 96 GREAT FALLS, MT MSA                                     88.02
 90 GREELEY, CO MSA                                         88.39
141 GREEN BAY, WI MSA                                       83.60
297 GREENSBORO-WINSTON-SALEM-HIGH POINT, NC MSA             75.45
200 GREENVILLE-SPARTANBURG, SC MSA                          80.61
 30 HAGERSTOWN, MD MSA                                      98.56
237 HAMILTON-MIDDLETOWN, OH PMSA                            78.73
236 HARRISBURG-LEBANON-CARLISLE, PA MSA                     78.74
159 HARTFORD, CT PMSA                                       82.43
147 HARTFORD-NEW BRITAIN-MIDDLETOWN, CT CMSA                83.02
139 HICKORY-MORGANTON, NC MSA                               83.71
 13 HONOLULU, HI MSA                                       105.22
126 HOUMA-THIBODAUX, LA MSA                                 84.91
 57 HOUSTON, TX PMSA                                        92.67
 51 HOUSTON-GALVESTON-BRAZORIA, TX CMSA                     93.31
```

D1-27. Ratio of Unmarried Men per 100 Unmarried Women, by Metropolitan Areas: 1990 *(continued)*

333	HUNTINGTON-ASHLAND, WV-KY-OH MSA	72.67
94	HUNTSVILLE, AL MSA	88.30
268	INDIANAPOLIS, IN MSA	77.28
49	IOWA CITY, IA MSA	94.23
24	JACKSON, MI MSA	101.24
320	JACKSON, MS MSA	74.01
351	JACKSON, TN MSA	69.72
113	JACKSONVILLE, FL MSA	85.65
1	JACKSONVILLE, NC MSA	223.64
232	JAMESTOWN-DUNKIRK, NY MSA	78.94
163	JANESVILLE-BELOIT, WI MSA	82.30
110	JERSEY CITY, NJ PMSA	85.85
286	JOHNSON CITY-KINGSPORT-BRISTOL, TN-VA MSA	76.56
300	JOHNSTOWN, PA MSA	75.30
55	JOLIET, IL PMSA	93.07
319	JOPLIN, MO MSA	74.12
198	KALAMAZOO, MI MSA	80.66
227	KANKAKEE, IL MSA	79.08
246	KANSAS CITY, MO-KS MSA	78.39
115	KENOSHA, WI PMSA	85.58
2	KILLEEN-TEMPLE, TX MSA	122.75
277	KNOXVILLE, TN MSA	76.86
323	KOKOMO, IN MSA	73.72
260	LA CROSSE, WI MSA	77.63
176	LAFAYETTE, LA MSA	81.64
19	LAFAYETTE-WEST LAFAYETTE, IN MSA	102.01
194	LAKE CHARLES, LA MSA	80.88
22	LAKE COUNTY, IL PMSA	101.56
235	LAKELAND-WINTER HAVEN, FL MSA	78.85
216	LANCASTER, PA MSA	79.50
145	LANSING-EAST LANSING, MI MSA	83.12
316	LAREDO, TX MSA	74.34
53	LAS CRUCES, NM MSA	93.16
14	LAS VEGAS, NV MSA	104.65
44	LAWRENCE, KS MSA	95.50
174	LAWRENCE-HAVERHILL, MA-NH PMSA	81.75
5	LAWTON, OK MSA	115.63
226	LEWISTON-AUBURN, ME MSA	79.08
251	LEXINGTON-FAYETTE, KY MSA	78.19
129	LIMA, OH MSA	84.62
108	LINCOLN, NE MSA	86.23
291	LITTLE ROCK-NORTH LITTLE ROCK, AR MSA	75.96
304	LONGVIEW-MARSHALL, TX MSA	75.14
191	LORAIN-ELYRIA, OH PMSA	81.11
37	LOS ANGELES-ANAHEIM-RIVERSIDE, CA CMSA	96.43
41	LOS ANGELES-LONG BEACH, CA PMSA	95.76
309	LOUISVILLE, KY-IN MSA	74.80
61	LOWELL, MA-NH PMSA	91.95
81	LUBBOCK, TX MSA	88.96
346	LYNCHBURG, VA MSA	71.04
307	MACON-WARNER ROBBINS, GA MSA	74.96
74	MADISON, WI MSA	89.67
182	MANCHESTER, NH MSA	81.52

D1-27. Ratio of Unmarried Men per 100 Unmarried Women, by Metropolitan Areas: 1990 (continued)

135	MANSFIELD, OH MSA	84.21
230	MCALLEN-EDINBURG-MISSION, TX MSA	78.99
137	MEDFORD, OR MSA	84.04
69	MELBOURNE-TITUSVILLE-PALM BAY, FL MSA	90.69
269	MEMPHIS, TN-AR-MS MSA	77.28
32	MERCED, CA MSA	98.56
249	MIAMI-FORT LAUDERDALE, FL CMSA	78.24
242	MIAMI-HIALEAH, FL PMSA	78.48
91	MIDDLESEX-SOMERSET-HUNTERDON, NJ PMSA	88.39
102	MIDDLETOWN, CT PMSA	87.23
254	MIDLAND, TX MSA	78.03
210	MILWAUKEE, WI PMSA	79.78
208	MILWAUKEE-RACINE, WI CMSA	79.96
120	MINNEAPOLIS-ST PAUL, MN-WI MSA	85.42
312	MOBILE, AL MSA	74.59
111	MODESTO, CA MSA	85.83
303	MONMOUTH-OCEAN, NJ PMSA	75.24
339	MONROE, LA MSA	72.06
302	MONTGOMERY, AL MSA	75.26
283	MUNCIE, IN MSA	76.70
138	MUSKEGON, MI MSA	83.87
85	NAPLES, FL MSA	88.74
71	NASHUA, NH PMSA	90.49
224	NASHVILLE, TN MSA	79.19
149	NASSAU-SUFFOLK, NY PMSA	82.93
308	NEW BEDFORD, MA MSA	74.82
153	NEW BRITAIN, CT PMSA	82.77
212	NEW HAVEN-MERIDEN, CT MSA	79.67
29	NEW LONDON-NORWICH, CT-RI MSA	98.73
281	NEW ORLEANS, LA MSA	76.72
285	NEW YORK, NY PMSA	76.62
229	NEW YORK-NORTHERN NEW JERSEY-LONG ISLAND, NY-NJ-CT CMSA	79.05
213	NEWARK, NJ PMSA	79.54
271	NIAGARA FALLS, NY PMSA	77.24
33	NORFOLK-VIRGINIA BEACH-NEWPORT NEWS, VA MSA	98.43
207	NORWALK, CT PMSA	80.10
86	OAKLAND, CA PMSA	88.71
298	OCALA, FL MSA	75.36
160	ODESSA, TX MSA	82.42
166	OKLAHOMA CITY, OK MSA	82.17
180	OLYMPIA, WA MSA	81.58
186	OMAHA, NE-IA MSA	81.25
34	ORANGE COUNTY, NY PMSA	97.16
70	ORLANDO, FL MSA	90.60
338	OWENSBORO, KY MSA	72.14
26	OXNARD-VENTURA, CA PMSA	99.32
105	PANAMA CITY, FL MSA	86.54
330	PARKERSBURG-MARIETTA, WV-OH MSA	72.92
99	PASCAGOULA, MS MSA	87.43
265	PAWTUCKET-WOONSOCKET-ATTLEBORO, RI-MA PMSA	77.36
130	PENSACOLA, FL MSA	84.60
273	PEORIA, IL MSA	77.11
250	PHILADELPHIA, PA-NJ PMSA	78.24

D1-27. Ratio of Unmarried Men per 100 Unmarried Women, by Metropolitan Areas: 1990 (continued)

```
233 PHILADELPHIA-WILMINGTON-TRENTON, PA-NJ-DE-MD CMSA        78.93
 80 PHOENIX, AZ MSA                                          89.04
203 PINE BLUFF, AR MSA                                       80.30
340 PITTSBURGH, PA PMSA                                      72.04
337 PITTSBURGH-BEAVER VALLEY, PA CMSA                        72.16
266 PITTSFIELD, MA MSA                                       77.31
272 PORTLAND, ME MSA                                         77.14
123 PORTLAND, OR PMSA                                        85.13
114 PORTLAND-VANCOUVER, OR-WA CMSA                           85.59
136 PORTSMOUTH-DOVER-ROCHESTER, NH-ME MSA                    84.13
 36 POUGHKEEPSIE, NY MSA                                     96.59
245 PROVIDENCE RI PMSA                                       78.42
264 PROVIDENCE-PAWTUCKET-FALL RIVER, RI-MA CMSA             77.44
107 PROVO-OREM, UT MSA                                       86.45
192 PUEBLO, CO MSA                                           81.06
177 RACINE, WI PMSA                                          81.59
168 RALEIGH-DURHAM, NC MSA                                   82.05
 62 RAPID CITY, SD MSA                                       91.66
231 READING, PA MSA                                          78.97
151 REDDING, CA MSA                                          82.89
 18 RENO, NV MSA                                            103.52
 54 RICHLAND-KENNEWICK-PASCO, WA MSA                         93.12
296 RICHMOND-PETERSBURG, VA MSA                              75.45
 43 RIVERSIDE-SAN BERNARDINO, CA PMSA                        95.60
345 ROANOKE, VA MSA                                          71.09
255 ROCHESTER, MN MSA                                        78.00
184 ROCHESTER, NY MSA                                        81.36
173 ROCKFORD, IL MSA                                         81.88
 88 SACRAMENTO, CA MSA                                       88.59
247 SAGINAW-BAY CITY-MIDLAND, MI MSA                         78.32
101 SALEM, OR MSA                                            87.35
318 SALEM-GLOUCESTER, MA PMSA                                74.27
  9 SALINAS-SEASIDE-MONTEREY, CA MSA                        112.01
 72 SALT LAKE CITY-OGDEN, UT MSA                             90.42
215 SAN ANGELO, TX MSA                                       79.51
167 SAN ANTONIO, TX MSA                                      82.13
 12 SAN DIEGO, CA MSA                                       105.33
 48 SAN FRANCISCO, CA PMSA                                   94.30
 47 SAN FRANCISCO-OAKLAND-SAN JOSE, CA CMSA                  94.34
 17 SAN JOSE, CA PMSA                                       103.63
 38 SANTA BARBARA-SANTA MARIA-LOMPOC, CA MSA                 96.30
 56 SANTA CRUZ, CA PMSA                                      92.76
 75 SANTA FE, NM MSA                                         89.47
125 SANTA ROSA-PETALUMA, CA PMSA                             85.03
355 SARASOTA, FL MSA                                         65.57
248 SAVANNAH, GA MSA                                         78.28
326 SCRANTON-WILKES-BARRE, PA MSA                            73.43
 64 SEATTLE, WA PMSA                                         91.53
 59 SEATTLE-TACOMA, WA CMSA                                  92.40
228 SHARON, PA MSA                                           79.07
 79 SHEBOYGAN, WI MSA                                        89.18
335 SHERMAN-DENISON, TX MSA                                  72.27
343 SHREVEPORT, LA MSA                                       71.54
```

D1-27. Ratio of Unmarried Men per 100 Unmarried Women, by Metropolitan Areas: 1990 (continued)

267	SIOUX CITY, IA-NE MSA	77.29
275	SIOUX FALLS, SD MSA	76.98
218	SOUTH BEND-MISHAWAKA, IN MSA	79.43
155	SPOKANE, WA MSA	82.68
352	SPRINGFIELD, IL MSA	69.63
315	SPRINGFIELD, MA MSA	74.46
288	SPRINGFIELD, MO MSA	76.47
35	ST CLOUD, MN MSA	97.00
347	ST JOSEPH, MO MSA	70.93
293	ST LOUIS, MO-IL MSA	75.85
301	STAMFORD, CT PMSA	75.28
6	STATE COLLEGE, PA MSA	112.98
331	STEUBENVILLE-WEIRTON, OH-WV MSA	72.87
28	STOCKTON, CA MSA	98.79
195	SYRACUSE, NY MSA	80.82
40	TACOMA, WA PMSA	95.76
197	TALLAHASSEE, FL MSA	80.69
311	TAMPA-ST PETERSBURG-CLEARWATER, FL MSA	74.65
157	TERRE HAUTE, IN MSA	82.54
310	TEXARKANA, TX-TEXARKANA, AR MSA	74.79
258	TOLEDO, OH MSA	77.69
280	TOPEKA, KS MSA	76.73
162	TRENTON, NJ PMSA	82.32
104	TUCSON, AZ MSA	86.60
222	TULSA, OK MSA	79.29
171	TUSCALOOSA, AL MSA	81.95
295	TYLER, TX MSA	75.47
109	UTICA-ROME, NY MSA	85.96
21	VALLEJO-FAIRFIELD-NAPA, CA PMSA	101.68
92	VANCOUVER, WA PMSA	88.38
211	VICTORIA, TX MSA	79.71
156	VINELAND-MILLVILLE-BRIDGETON, NJ PMSA	82.60
67	VISALIA-TULARE-PORTERVILLE, CA MSA	90.84
164	WACO, TX MSA	82.22
124	WASHINGTON, DC-MD-VA MSA	85.08
253	WATERBURY, CT MSA	78.04
313	WATERLOO-CEDAR FALLS, IA MSA	74.50
87	WAUSAU, WI MSA	88.65
292	WEST PALM BEACH-BOCA RATON-DELRAY BEACH, FL MSA	75.92
349	WHEELING, WV-OH MSA	70.48
121	WICHITA FALLS, TX MSA	85.18
132	WICHITA, KS MSA	84.52
259	WILLIAMSPORT, PA MSA	77.65
165	WILMINGTON, DE-NJ-MD PMSA	82.20
278	WILMINGTON, NC MSA	76.81
154	WORCESTER, MA MSA	82.76
73	YAKIMA, WA MSA	90.24
148	YORK, PA MSA	82.98
321	YOUNGSTOWN-WARREN, OH MSA	73.74
63	YUBA CITY, CA MSA	91.53
15	YUMA, AZ MSA	104.64

Note: The presence of a military base, college or university, correctional facility, nursing home, etc., in a metropolitan area may have a significant impact on the size of the ratio. For more information contact Marriage and Family Statistics Branch, Population Division, U.S. Bureau of the Census, Washington, D.C. 20233 (301) 763-7987.

Source: Marriage and Family Statistics Branch, Population Division, Bureau of the Census, *1990 Ratio of Unmarried Men Per 100 Unmarried Women by Metropolitan Areas in the United States,* 1990 Census Population, CPH-L-152.

D1-28. Child Custody Awards, by Race of Parents: 1989 (13 Reporting States) and 1990 (17 Reporting States)

[Based on sample data]

	Custody awarded to:									
	1990					1989				
Race of husband and wife	Total[1]	Husband	Wife	Joint	Other person	Total[1]	Husband	Wife	Joint	Other person
Husband	*Number*									
All races	184,036	18,684	132,692	29,754	2,906	168,923	16,167	120,458	30,354	1,944
White	157,449	16,466	111,155	27,247	2,581	145,990	14,434	101,892	28,078	1,586
Black	15,895	970	13,791	879	255	13,997	939	11,974	817	267
Other	1,758	318	1,181	231	28	1,665	166	1,247	219	33
Race not stated.	8,934	930	6,565	1,397	42	7,271	628	5,345	1,240	58
Wife										
All races	184,036	18,684	132,692	29,754	2,906	168,923	16,167	120,458	30,354	1,944
White	157,392	16,185	111,445	27,190	2,572	146,254	14,245	102,396	28,070	1,543
Black	15,102	894	13,209	767	232	13,359	810	11,513	772	264
Other	2,193	556	1,306	298	33	1,905	375	1,257	234	39
Race not stated.	9,349	1,049	6,732	1,499	69	7,405	737	5,292	1,278	98
Husband	*Percent distribution*									
All races	100.0	10.2	72.1	16.2	1.6	100.0	9.6	71.3	18.0	1.2
White	100.0	10.5	70.6	17.3	1.6	100.0	9.9	69.8	19.2	1.1
Black	100.0	6.1	86.8	5.5	1.6	100.0	6.7	85.5	5.8	1.9
Other	100.0	18.1	67.2	13.1	*	100.0	10.0	74.9	13.2	*
Race not stated.	100.0	10.4	73.5	15.6	*	100.0	8.6	73.5	17.1	*
Wife										
All races	100.0	10.2	72.1	16.2	1.6	100.0	9.6	71.3	18.0	1.2
White	100.0	10.3	70.8	17.3	1.6	100.0	9.7	70.0	19.2	1.1
Black	100.0	5.9	87.5	5.1	1.5	100.0	6.1	86.2	5.8	2.0
Other	100.0	25.4	59.6	13.6	*	100.0	19.7	66.0	12.3	*
Race not stated.	100.0	11.2	72.0	16.0	*	100.0	10.0	71.5	17.3	*

[1]Total of children for whom custody was reported does not necessarily equal the reported number of children under 18 years of age.

NOTES: Of the 31 States in the divorce-registration area, 13 reported custody and race of husband and wife in 1989—Alabama, Connecticut, Idaho, Illinois, Kansas, Missouri, Montana, Oregon, Pennsylvania, Tennessee, Utah, Wisconsin, and Wyoming. In 1990 an additional five States reported—Alaska, Nebraska, Rhode Island, Vermont, and Virginia. Wisconsin ceased to report.

Source: Sally C. Clarke, National Center for Health Statistics, *Advance Report of Final Divorce Statistics, 1989 and 1990*, Monthly Vital Statistics Report, Vol. 43, No. 9 (suppl.), Washington, D.C.: U.S. Department of Health and Human Services, March 22, 1995, Table 20.

D1-29. Child Support—Award and Recipiency Status of Women: 1981 to 1989

[Women with own children under 21 years of age present from absent fathers. For 1989, women 15 years old and over as of April 1990; for previous years, women 18 years old and over as of April of following year. Covers civilian noninstitutional population. Based on Current Population Survey.]

AWARD AND RECIPIENCY STATUS	ALL WOMEN						WOMEN BELOW THE POVERTY LEVEL					
	Number (1,000)			Percent distribution			Number (1,000)			Percent distribution		
	1981	1985	1989	1981	1985	1989	1981	1985	1989	1981	1985	1989
Total	8,387	8,808	9,955	100	100	100	2,566	2,797	3,206	100	100	100
Payments awarded	4,969	5,396	5,748	59	61	58	1,018	1,130	1,387	40	40	43
Supposed to receive payments .	4,043	4,381	4,953	48	50	50	806	905	1,190	31	32	37
Not supposed to receive payments	926	1,015	795	11	12	8	212	225	197	8	8	6
Payments not awarded	3,417	3,411	4,207	41	39	42	1,547	1,668	1,819	60	60	57
Supposed to receive payments .	4,043	4,381	4,953	100	100	100	806	905	1,190	100	100	100
Actually received payments	2,902	3,243	3,725	72	74	75	495	595	813	61	66	68
Received full amount	1,888	2,112	2,546	47	48	51	(NA)	(NA)	(NA)	(NA)	(NA)	(NA)
Received partial amount	1,014	1,131	1,179	25	26	24	(NA)	(NA)	(NA)	(NA)	(NA)	(NA)
Did not receive payments	1,140	1,138	1,228	28	26	25	311	310	377	39	34	32

NA Not available.

Source: U.S. Bureau of the Census, *Current Population Reports*, P60-173.

Source: U.S. Bureau of the Census, *Statistical Abstract of the United States: 1994*, (114th edition), Washington, D.C.: U.S. Government Printing Office, 1994, Table 604.

D1-30. Child Support and Alimony—Selected Characteristics of Women: 1989

[Alimony data are for ever-divorced and currently separated women.]

RECIPIENCY STATUS OF WOMEN	Unit	Total [1]	AGE			RACE		His-panic [2]	CURRENT MARITAL STATUS			
			18 to 29 years	30 to 39 years	40 years and over	White	Black		Divor-ced	Mar-ried [3]	Never mar-ried	Sepa-rated
CHILD SUPPORT												
All women, total	1,000 . .	9,955	3,066	4,175	2,566	6,905	2,770	1,112	3,056	2,531	2,950	1,352
Payments awarded	1,000 . .	5,748	1,408	2,685	1,632	4,661	955	452	2,347	1,999	704	648
Percent of total	Percent .	58	46	64	64	68	35	41	77	79	24	48
Supposed to receive child support in 1989	1,000 . .	4,953	1,208	2,413	1,309	4,048	791	364	2,123	1,685	583	527
Percent received payment .	Percent .	75	76	74	76	77	70	70	77	72	73	80
Mean child support	Dollars .	2,995	1,981	3,032	3,903	3,132	2,263	2,965	3,322	2,931	1,888	3,060
Percent of total income .	Percent .	19	20	18	19	19	16	20	17	20	20	21
Women with incomes below the poverty level in 1989	1,000 . .	3,206	1,531	1,189	434	1,763	1,314	536	820	176	1,590	612
Payments awarded	1,000 . .	1,387	608	568	195	962	384	177	577	127	389	288
Percent of total	Percent .	43	40	48	45	55	29	33	70	72	25	47
Supposed to receive child support in 1989	1,000 . .	1,190	507	500	168	827	325	148	525	106	334	221
Percent received payment .	Percent .	68	68	67	72	68	70	64	66	67	69	74
Mean child support	Dollars .	1,889	1,515	2,167	2,316	1,972	1,674	1,824	2,112	2,275	1,553	1,717
Percent of total income .	Percent .	37	33	36	56	39	32	37	38	52	34	35
ALIMONY												
All women, total	1,000 . .	20,610	2,464	6,093	12,051	17,245	2,863	1,499	8,888	7,738	(X)	2,790
Number awarded payments . . .	1,000 . .	3,189	184	610	2,394	2,801	305	171	1,472	1,170	(X)	316
Percent of total	Percent .	16	8	10	20	16	11	11	17	15	(X)	11
Supposed to receive pay-ments	1,000 . .	922	85	267	569	787	98	63	567	170	(X)	164
Women with incomes below the poverty level in 1989	1,000 . .	3,692	726	1,206	1,758	2,640	931	477	1,860	420	(X)	1,147
Number awarded payments . . .	1,000 . .	429	60	96	273	340	76	31	223	55	(X)	110
Percent of total	Percent .	12	8	8	16	13	8	6	12	13	(X)	10
Supposed to receive pay-ments	1,000 . .	178	43	56	79	149	26	21	112	11	(X)	54

X Not applicable. [1] Includes other items, not shown separately. [2] Hispanic women may be of any race. [3] Remarried women whose previous marriage ended in divorce.

Source: U.S. Bureau of the Census, *Current Population Reports*, P60-173.

Source: U.S. Bureau of the Census, *Statistical Abstract of the United States: 1994*, (114th edition), Washington, D.C.: U.S. Government Printing Office, 1994, Table 605.

D1-31. Child Support Award Status, Receipt and Income of Custodial Parents: Spring 1992

(Numbers in thousands. Custodial parents 15 years and older with own children under 21 years of age present from absent parents as of spring 1992.)

Characteristics	Custodial parents		Custodial mothers		Custodial fathers	
	Number	Percent	Number	Percent	Number	Percent
ALL CUSTODIAL PARENTS						
Total	11,502	(X)	9,918	(X)	1,584	(X)
With child support agreement or award	6,190	(X)	5,542	(X)	648	(X)
Supposed to receive payments in 1991	5,326	100.0	4,883	100.0	443	100.0
Actually received payments in 1991	4,006	75.2	3,728	76.3	278	62.8
Received the full amount due	2,742	51.5	2,552	52.3	189	42.7
Received partial payments	1,265	23.8	1,176	24.1	89	20.1
Received no payments in 1991	1,320	24.8	1,156	23.7	164	37.0
Mean Income and Child Support:						
Received child support payments in 1991:						
Mean total money income	$19,217	(X)	$18,144	(X)	$33,579	(X)
Mean child support received	$2,961	(X)	$3,011	(X)	$2,292	(X)
Received the full amount due:						
Mean total money income	$20,050	(X)	$19,310	(X)	$30,012	(X)
Mean child support received	$3,543	(X)	$3,618	(X)	$2,536	(X)
Received partial payments:						
Mean total money income	$17,411	(X)	$15,611	(X)	$41,163	(X)
Mean child support received	$1,699	(X)	$1,694	(X)	$1,773	(X)
Received no payments in 1991:						
Mean total money income	$15,919	(X)	$14,602	(X)	$25,184	(X)
Without child support agreement or award	5,312	(X)	4,376	(X)	936	(X)
Mean total money income	$13,283	(X)	$10,226	(X)	$27,578	(X)

Source: U.S. Bureau of the Census, Press Release CB95-95, May 13, 1995

D2. LIVING ARRANGEMENTS

D2-1. Marital Status of Persons 15 Years and Over, by Family Status, Age, Sex, Race, and Hispanic Origin: March 1993

[Numbers in thousands.]

Subject	Total, 15 years and over	15 to 17 years	18 and 19 years	20 to 24 years	25 to 29 years	30 to 34 years	35 to 39 years	40 to 44 years	45 to 54 years	55 to 64 years	65 to 74 years	75 to 84 years	85 years and over
WHITE, NOT HISPANIC													
Female													
Total	78 452	3 417	2 224	6 348	7 071	8 246	8 071	7 371	11 493	8 826	8 595	5 206	1 584
Householder	23 508	13	133	1 258	1 875	2 123	2 014	1 981	3 178	2 735	3 837	3 228	1 134
Family householder	10 229	10	65	560	1 051	1 360	1 394	1 340	1 771	1 102	959	465	154
Nonfamily householder	13 279	3	69	698	824	763	619	640	1 407	1 633	2 879	2 763	980
Living alone	11 816	3	42	332	545	593	505	517	1 259	1 531	2 808	2 727	955
Living with nonrelatives	1 463	–	27	366	280	170	114	124	149	102	70	36	25
One nonrelative	1 256	–	23	293	235	146	103	112	130	91	69	32	22
Male, 15 years or older	726	–	11	147	150	73	69	74	82	51	47	14	6
Female, 15 years or older	530	–	12	145	85	73	34	38	48	40	22	18	16
Two or more nonrelatives	207	–	4	73	44	24	11	12	18	11	1	4	3
Not householder	54 944	3 404	2 091	5 090	5 196	6 123	6 057	5 390	8 315	6 091	4 758	1 978	450
In families	51 750	3 336	1 905	4 275	4 516	5 645	5 781	5 179	8 100	5 965	4 704	1 931	414
Child of householder	9 224	3 180	1 638	2 451	769	404	314	189	195	67	18	1	–
With children under 18 years	693	30	53	201	162	105	92	34	15	1	–	–	–
Not in families	3 194	69	186	815	681	478	276	211	215	126	54	47	36
Married, spouse present	44 455	33	211	1 900	4 099	5 780	6 003	5 357	8 383	6 189	4 710	1 626	164
Householder	3 526	2	11	163	394	557	536	405	583	420	334	98	21
Not householder	40 929	31	200	1 736	3 706	5 223	5 467	4 951	7 800	5 769	4 376	1 527	143
Married, spouse absent	1 861	3	19	149	267	256	283	259	282	158	98	79	8
Householder	1 453	–	8	81	174	207	240	222	237	129	80	69	6
Family householder	961	–	8	64	130	162	201	191	135	44	22	4	–
Nonfamily householder	492	–	–	17	43	45	39	31	103	84	58	65	6
Living alone	466	–	–	13	39	37	38	25	102	84	58	65	6
Living with nonrelatives	25	–	–	4	4	8	2	6	1	–	–	–	–
One nonrelative	24	–	–	4	4	8	1	6	1	–	–	–	–
Male, 15 years or older	7	–	–	–	–	2	1	3	–	–	–	–	–
Female, 15 years or older	17	–	–	4	4	6	–	2	1	–	–	–	–
Two or more nonrelatives	1	–	–	–	–	–	1	–	–	–	–	–	–
Not householder	408	3	11	67	94	49	43	37	45	30	18	10	2
In families	267	3	11	55	60	20	20	19	34	18	18	10	–
Child of householder	177	3	6	47	57	14	20	9	16	4	1	–	–
With children under 18 years	109	3	2	36	46	8	12	4	–	–	–	–	–
Not in families	141	–	–	13	33	29	23	18	11	12	–	–	2
Widowed	9 018	1	–	2	19	44	82	109	439	1 115	2 926	3 021	1 258
Householder	7 988	–	–	–	14	36	67	89	412	1 025	2 688	2 669	987
Family householder	1 613	–	–	–	10	26	59	67	216	332	484	311	108
Nonfamily householder	6 375	–	–	–	4	9	9	22	197	693	2 204	2 358	879
Living alone	6 224	–	–	–	3	7	7	21	184	655	2 155	2 334	858
Living with nonrelatives	151	–	–	–	2	2	2	1	12	38	49	24	21
One nonrelative	147	–	–	–	2	2	2	1	12	35	49	23	21
Male, 15 years or older	87	–	–	–	2	–	2	1	6	23	35	12	6
Female, 15 years or older	60	–	–	–	–	2	–	–	6	12	14	11	14
Two or more nonrelatives	4	–	–	–	–	–	–	–	–	3	–	1	1
Not householder	1 030	1	–	2	5	8	15	20	26	90	238	352	271
In families	878	1	–	1	–	3	8	6	20	62	210	322	245
Child of householder	34	–	–	1	–	3	8	5	6	7	5	–	–
With children under 18 years	13	–	–	1	–	3	7	3	–	–	–	–	–
Not in families	152	–	–	1	5	6	7	14	6	28	28	30	27
Divorced	7 608	2	10	167	674	909	934	1 119	1 891	1 056	569	224	53
Householder	6 104	–	3	85	425	626	717	941	1 610	941	514	198	44
Family householder	3 147	–	2	69	328	461	534	615	764	266	86	16	7
Nonfamily householder	2 957	–	1	16	97	166	182	326	846	676	428	183	37
Living alone	2 587	–	1	9	60	120	143	248	743	635	415	177	37
Living with nonrelatives	370	–	–	8	37	45	39	78	103	41	14	5	–
One nonrelative	320	–	–	7	35	38	32	71	84	35	12	4	–
Male, 15 years or older	250	–	–	4	32	28	28	57	65	23	10	1	–
Female, 15 years or older	70	–	–	2	3	10	5	14	19	12	2	3	–
Two or more nonrelatives	50	–	–	1	2	7	7	7	18	6	1	1	–
Not householder	1 504	2	7	82	249	283	217	178	281	114	55	26	9
In families	658	–	3	44	96	101	77	68	135	60	44	21	9
Child of householder	422	–	2	37	78	87	69	53	67	25	3	–	–
With children under 18 years	177	–	2	21	41	47	33	19	13	–	–	–	–
Not in families	846	2	4	38	153	182	140	110	146	54	11	5	–
Never married	15 510	3 379	1 984	4 130	2 011	1 257	768	527	498	307	292	255	101
Householder	4 437	11	111	928	868	697	454	324	335	220	221	193	75
Family householder	982	8	43	263	188	154	65	62	73	40	32	36	17
Nonfamily householder	3 456	3	68	665	680	543	389	262	262	180	189	157	58
Living alone	2 539	3	41	311	443	429	318	223	230	157	181	150	54
Living with nonrelatives	917	–	27	353	237	115	71	39	33	23	7	7	4
One nonrelative	765	–	23	282	194	97	68	34	33	20	7	5	2
Male, 15 years or older	382	–	11	143	117	43	38	12	10	5	2	1	–
Female, 15 years or older	383	–	12	139	77	55	30	22	22	16	5	4	2
Two or more nonrelatives	151	–	4	72	43	17	3	5	–	3	–	2	2
Not householder	11 073	3 367	1 873	3 202	1 143	560	315	204	163	87	71	62	26
In families	9 052	3 300	1 692	2 451	657	313	211	134	113	55	57	50	18
Child of householder	8 392	3 176	1 620	2 317	586	277	187	106	86	30	7	1	–
With children under 18 years	283	26	47	109	51	32	18	–	–	–	–	–	–
Not in families	2 021	67	181	751	486	247	103	69	50	32	14	12	8

¹May be of any race.

D2-1. Marital Status of Persons 15 Years and Over, by Family Status, Age, Sex, Race, and Hispanic Origin: March 1993 *(continued)*

[Numbers in thousands.]

Subject	Total, 15 years and over	15 to 17 years	18 and 19 years	20 to 24 years	25 to 29 years	30 to 34 years	35 to 39 years	40 to 44 years	45 to 54 years	55 to 64 years	65 to 74 years	75 to 84 years	85 years and over
BLACK													
Female													
Total	12 495	800	520	1 342	1 409	1 502	1 382	1 139	1 620	1 201	960	482	137
Householder	6 085	1	72	449	690	821	774	620	899	721	592	355	92
Family householder	4 267	1	59	342	562	694	658	531	632	396	236	109	47
Nonfamily householder	1 818	–	13	107	128	127	117	89	267	325	355	246	45
Living alone	1 648	–	4	84	95	114	106	80	228	316	346	231	43
Living with nonrelatives	170	–	10	22	33	13	11	8	40	9	9	15	2
One nonrelative	151	–	10	20	33	10	6	8	36	6	9	13	2
Male, 15 years or older	125	–	6	13	25	10	5	7	33	3	9	11	2
Female, 15 years or older	21	–	3	6	7	–	–	1	1	–	–	1	–
Two or more nonrelatives	20	–	–	3	–	2	5	–	4	3	–	2	–
Not householder	6 410	799	448	893	719	682	607	519	721	481	369	126	45
In families	6 053	784	433	819	643	627	571	484	687	469	365	125	45
Child of householder	2 261	680	360	572	239	185	97	44	46	22	9	5	–
With children under 18 years	508	32	56	157	103	91	39	20	9	–	–	–	–
Not in families	357	15	15	74	77	55	36	35	34	11	3	1	–
Married, spouse present	3 720	2	5	182	394	522	519	471	736	471	332	77	8
Householder	587	–	–	39	57	106	72	75	128	57	40	14	–
Not householder	3 133	2	5	143	337	416	446	396	609	414	292	63	8
Married, spouse absent	1 100	6	7	56	150	161	166	155	189	136	50	18	5
Householder	918	–	5	35	115	130	151	136	161	125	41	14	5
Family householder	730	–	5	25	113	118	146	123	109	70	12	4	5
Nonfamily householder	187	–	–	9	1	12	5	13	52	55	30	11	–
Living alone	183	–	–	9	1	11	5	13	49	55	29	11	–
Living with nonrelatives	5	–	–	–	–	–	–	–	3	–	1	–	–
One nonrelative	3	–	–	–	–	–	–	–	1	–	1	–	–
Male, 15 years or older	3	–	–	–	–	–	–	–	1	–	1	–	–
Female, 15 years or older	–	–	–	–	–	–	–	–	–	–	–	–	–
Two or more nonrelatives	2	–	–	–	–	–	–	–	2	–	–	–	–
Not householder	182	6	2	21	35	31	15	19	29	11	9	4	–
In families	146	6	2	19	28	26	12	13	19	8	9	4	–
Child of householder	78	4	–	6	22	23	9	2	9	3	–	–	–
With children under 18 years	37	–	–	4	9	15	5	2	2	–	–	–	–
Not in families	36	–	–	2	7	6	3	6	10	3	–	–	–
Widowed	1 401	–	–	3	3	6	25	43	142	303	426	338	113
Householder	1 222	–	–	–	3	6	22	39	122	278	385	288	78
Family householder	562	–	–	–	3	6	22	33	84	148	152	82	34
Nonfamily householder	659	–	–	–	–	–	–	7	38	131	233	206	44
Living alone	625	–	–	–	–	–	–	7	30	126	226	195	42
Living with nonrelatives	34	–	–	–	–	–	–	–	9	5	7	12	2
One nonrelative	27	–	–	–	–	–	–	–	6	–	7	10	2
Male, 15 years or older	24	–	–	–	–	–	–	–	6	3	6	10	2
Female, 15 years or older	–	–	–	–	–	–	–	–	–	–	6	10	2
Two or more nonrelatives	7	–	–	–	–	–	–	–	2	2	–	2	–
Not householder	180	–	–	3	–	–	3	3	19	24	41	50	35
In families	171	–	–	2	–	–	3	3	17	23	38	49	35
Child of householder	38	–	–	2	–	–	2	2	8	12	6	5	–
With children under 18 years	2	–	–	2	–	–	–	–	–	–	–	–	–
Not in families	8	–	–	–	–	–	–	–	2	2	3	1	–
Divorced	1 408	2	4	12	54	163	261	221	361	185	109	35	–
Householder	1 215	–	–	9	35	140	223	183	330	171	96	30	–
Family householder	813	–	–	3	27	119	188	151	215	85	19	5	–
Nonfamily householder	403	–	–	6	8	20	35	32	114	86	76	25	–
Living alone	360	–	–	6	4	20	29	28	92	83	76	22	–
Living with nonrelatives	42	–	–	–	4	–	6	4	22	3	–	3	–
One nonrelative	39	–	–	–	4	–	3	4	22	3	–	3	–
Male, 15 years or older	35	–	–	–	4	–	3	3	21	3	–	2	–
Female, 15 years or older	4	–	–	–	–	–	–	1	1	–	–	1	–
Two or more nonrelatives	3	–	–	–	–	–	3	–	–	–	–	–	–
Not householder	193	2	4	4	19	23	38	38	32	15	13	5	–
In families	116	2	4	1	8	16	17	25	15	11	13	5	–
Child of householder	62	2	4	–	4	12	14	10	12	3	–	–	–
With children under 18 years	35	–	–	–	2	10	13	7	2	–	–	–	–
Not in families	77	–	–	2	12	7	21	13	17	4	–	–	–
Never married	4 867	790	504	1 089	808	650	411	248	192	106	44	14	11
Householder	2 144	1	68	366	480	439	306	186	159	90	30	10	9
Family householder	1 575	1	54	275	362	345	230	149	97	37	13	5	8
Nonfamily householder	569	–	13	92	119	94	77	37	63	53	16	4	1
Living alone	480	–	4	69	90	83	72	33	57	52	15	4	1
Living with nonrelatives	90	–	10	22	29	12	5	4	6	1	1	–	–
One nonrelative	81	–	10	20	29	9	3	4	6	–	1	–	–
Male, 15 years or older	64	–	6	13	22	9	2	4	6	–	1	–	–
Female, 15 years or older	18	–	3	6	7	–	–	–	–	–	–	–	–
Two or more nonrelatives	8	–	–	3	–	2	2	–	–	1	–	–	–
Not householder	2 723	789	436	723	328	211	104	63	33	16	14	4	2
In families	2 493	774	422	653	274	172	92	47	27	13	14	4	2
Child of householder	2 063	675	356	563	205	142	72	29	15	2	3	–	–
With children under 18 years	421	32	56	151	87	58	22	11	5	–	–	–	–
Not in families	230	15	15	70	54	40	12	16	6	3	–	–	–

See footnotes at end of table.

D2-1. Marital Status of Persons 15 Years and Over, by Family Status, Age, Sex, Race, and Hispanic Origin: March 1993 *(continued)*

[Numbers in thousands.]

Subject	Total, 15 years and over	15 to 17 years	18 and 19 years	20 to 24 years	25 to 29 years	30 to 34 years	35 to 39 years	40 to 44 years	45 to 54 years	55 to 64 years	65 to 74 years	75 to 84 years	85 years and over
HISPANIC[1] -													
Female													
Total	8 047	554	395	1 001	1 004	1 036	934	714	1 002	693	462	193	61
Householder	2 255	9	39	197	279	306	281	232	342	262	189	88	30
Family householder	1 638	6	27	157	217	249	245	192	267	162	84	20	11
Nonfamily householder	617	2	12	39	61	57	36	40	75	100	105	69	20
Living alone	524	1	2	26	38	45	31	31	69	94	102	66	20
Living with nonrelatives	93	2	10	13	24	13	5	9	7	6	3	3	-
One nonrelative	80	2	10	10	20	10	5	9	5	5	3	3	-
Male, 15 years or older	57	2	9	5	13	6	4	6	4	4	3	1	-
Female, 15 years or older	22	-	1	5	7	4	1	2	-	1	-	2	-
Two or more nonrelatives	12	-	-	3	4	3	-	-	2	1	-	-	-
Not householder	5 792	545	356	804	725	730	653	482	659	431	272	104	30
In families	5 359	514	321	689	641	669	609	464	640	418	266	100	28
Child of householder	1 234	447	228	296	109	66	33	21	22	7	5	-	-
With children under 18 years	186	22	24	51	31	28	20	5	5	-	-	-	-
Not in families	434	31	35	116	84	61	44	18	19	13	7	4	2
Married, spouse present	4 080	16	59	377	577	668	610	470	655	382	213	44	8
Householder	400	-	5	39	72	68	54	45	71	28	19	1	-
Not householder	3 679	16	55	339	505	600	556	425	584	354	195	43	8
Married, spouse absent	517	1	4	56	72	78	75	68	83	56	21	5	-
Householder	377	-	1	24	49	67	59	56	69	38	12	2	-
Family householder	327	-	1	21	47	60	56	52	59	24	5	1	-
Nonfamily householder	50	-	-	3	2	7	3	4	10	14	7	1	-
Living alone	46	-	-	2	2	5	3	4	10	13	7	-	-
Living with nonrelatives	4	-	-	1	-	1	-	1	-	1	-	1	-
One nonrelative	4	-	-	1	-	1	-	1	-	1	-	1	-
Male, 15 years or older	4	-	-	1	-	1	-	1	-	1	-	1	-
Female, 15 years or older	-	-	-	-	-	-	-	-	-	-	-	-	-
Two or more nonrelatives	-	-	-	-	-	-	-	-	-	-	-	-	-
Not householder	140	1	3	32	23	11	16	11	13	18	8	3	-
In families	119	1	3	27	21	8	11	7	11	18	8	3	-
Child of householder	48	1	2	19	9	5	6	1	3	-	1	-	-
With children under 18 years	29	-	2	12	8	3	3	-	2	-	-	-	-
Not in families	21	-	-	4	2	3	5	4	3	-	-	-	-
Widowed	525	-	-	2	2	8	12	22	39	125	164	113	38
Householder	371	-	-	2	1	6	10	18	31	103	112	68	21
Family householder	176	-	-	2	1	5	8	14	20	62	42	15	7
Nonfamily householder	195	-	-	-	-	1	2	3	11	41	70	53	14
Living alone	187	-	-	-	-	1	1	3	10	39	67	52	14
Living with nonrelatives	8	-	-	-	-	-	1	-	1	2	3	1	-
One nonrelative	7	-	-	-	-	-	1	-	1	1	3	1	-
Male, 15 years or older	5	-	-	-	-	-	1	-	-	1	3	-	-
Female, 15 years or older	1	-	-	-	-	-	-	-	1	1	-	1	-
Two or more nonrelatives	1	-	-	-	-	-	-	-	-	1	-	-	-
Not householder	154	-	-	-	2	2	3	5	8	21	52	44	17
In families	144	-	-	-	2	2	3	5	7	20	49	41	15
Child of householder	4	-	-	-	-	-	1	2	1	-	-	-	-
With children under 18 years	4	-	-	-	-	-	1	2	1	-	-	-	-
Not in families	10	-	-	-	-	-	-	-	1	2	3	3	2
Divorced	641	-	-	13	43	98	117	88	147	85	39	6	4
Householder	481	-	-	8	27	62	83	67	122	70	35	4	4
Family householder	349	-	-	8	24	52	75	53	84	36	15	-	1
Nonfamily householder	132	-	-	-	3	10	8	13	38	33	20	4	3
Living alone	118	-	-	-	3	7	8	10	33	31	20	3	3
Living with nonrelatives	14	-	-	-	-	2	-	4	5	2	-	1	-
One nonrelative	12	-	-	-	-	1	-	4	4	2	-	1	-
Male, 15 years or older	10	-	-	-	-	1	-	4	4	2	-	-	-
Female, 15 years or older	2	-	-	-	-	1	-	-	1	-	-	1	-
Two or more nonrelatives	2	-	-	-	-	1	-	-	1	-	-	-	-
Not householder	160	-	-	6	16	36	35	21	25	15	4	3	-
In families	81	-	-	1	5	13	13	14	18	11	4	3	-
Child of householder	38	-	-	1	5	8	8	7	6	3	-	-	-
With children under 18 years	20	-	-	1	3	8	7	-	-	-	-	-	-
Not in families	79	-	-	5	11	23	22	8	7	4	-	-	-
Never married	2 285	536	332	553	310	186	119	66	78	45	25	25	10
Householder	626	9	34	125	131	104	75	46	49	24	12	14	5
Family householder	386	6	22	88	75	64	51	27	33	12	3	3	2
Nonfamily householder	240	2	12	37	56	40	24	19	16	11	8	11	3
Living alone	173	1	2	25	33	31	20	15	16	10	8	11	3
Living with nonrelatives	66	2	10	12	24	9	4	4	1	1	-	-	-
One nonrelative	57	2	10	9	20	7	4	4	-	1	-	-	-
Male, 15 years or older	38	2	9	4	13	5	3	2	-	-	-	-	-
Female, 15 years or older	19	-	1	5	7	3	1	2	-	1	-	-	-
Two or more nonrelatives	9	-	-	3	4	2	-	-	1	-	-	-	-
Not householder	1 659	528	298	428	179	82	44	20	29	22	13	11	5
In families	1 371	499	267	338	112	52	27	13	22	15	9	11	5
Child of householder	1 095	445	224	262	88	39	12	10	7	4	3	-	-
With children under 18 years	97	21	20	28	15	7	3	3	3	-	-	-	-
Not in families	288	28	31	90	68	30	17	7	7	7	4	-	-

[1]May be of any race.

Source: Arlene F. Saluter, U.S. Bureau of the Census, *Marital Status and Living Arrangements: March 1993,* Current Population Reports, P20-478, Washington, D.C.: U.S. Government Printing Office, 1994, Table 7.

D2-2. Persons Living Alone, by Age and Sex: 1993, 1980, and 1970

(Numbers in thousands)

Age	1993			1980			1970		
	Total persons	Living alone		Total persons	Living alone		Total persons	Living alone	
		Number	Percent		Number	Percent		Number	Percent of total
Both sexes	197,254	23,642	12.0	171,862	18,296	10.6	148,325	10,851	7.3
15 to 24 years	34,429	1,186	3.4	41,452	1,726	4.2	38,536	556	1.4
25 to 34 years	41,864	3,735	8.9	36,615	3,259	8.9	24,861	893	3.6
35 to 44 years	40,342	3,286	8.1	25,426	1,470	5.8	23,156	711	3.1
45 to 54 years	28,503	3,048	10.7	22,698	1,705	7.5	23,253	1,303	5.6
55 to 64 years	21,247	3,033	14.3	21,476	2,809	13.1	18,642	2,319	12.4
65 to 74 years	18,362	4,330	23.6	15,293	3,851	25.2	12,357	2,815	22.8
75 years and over	12,508	5,025	40.2	8,901	3,477	39.1	7,518	2,256	30.0
Men	94,854	9,436	9.9	81,947	6,966	8.5	70,559	3,532	5.0
15 to 24 years	17,210	665	3.9	20,558	947	4.6	18,695	274	1.5
25 to 34 years	20,856	2,282	10.9	18,051	1,975	10.9	12,191	535	4.4
35 to 44 years	19,904	1,972	9.9	12,435	945	7.6	11,277	398	3.5
45 to 54 years	13,847	1,465	10.6	10,938	804	7.4	11,224	513	4.6
55 to 64 years	10,205	1,057	10.4	10,014	809	8.1	8,835	639	7.2
65 to 74 years	8,114	1,046	12.9	6,657	775	11.6	5,393	611	11.3
75 years and over	4,717	948	20.1	3,296	711	21.6	2,943	563	19.1
Women	102,400	14,206	13.9	89,914	11,330	12.6	77,766	7,319	9.4
15 to 24 years	17,218	521	3.0	20,895	779	3.7	19,841	282	1.4
25 to 34 years	21,007	1,451	6.9	18,565	1,284	6.9	12,670	358	2.8
35 to 44 years	20,438	1,313	6.4	12,991	525	4.0	11,879	313	2.6
45 to 54 years	14,655	1,583	10.8	11,760	901	7.7	12,029	790	6.6
55 to 64 years	11,042	1,976	17.9	11,462	2,000	17.4	9,807	1,680	17.1
65 to 74 years	10,249	3,284	32.0	8,637	3,076	35.6	6,964	2,204	31.6
75 years and over	7,790	4,078	52.3	5,605	2,766	49.3	4,575	1,693	37.0

*1970 is shown for the population 14 years and older.

Source: Arlene F. Saluter, U.S. Bureau of the Census, *Marital Status and Living Arrangements: March 1993,* Current Population Reports, P20-478, Washington, D.C.: U.S. Government Printing Office, 1994, Table E.

D2-3. Percent Living Alone, by Age and Sex: 1970, 1980, and 1993

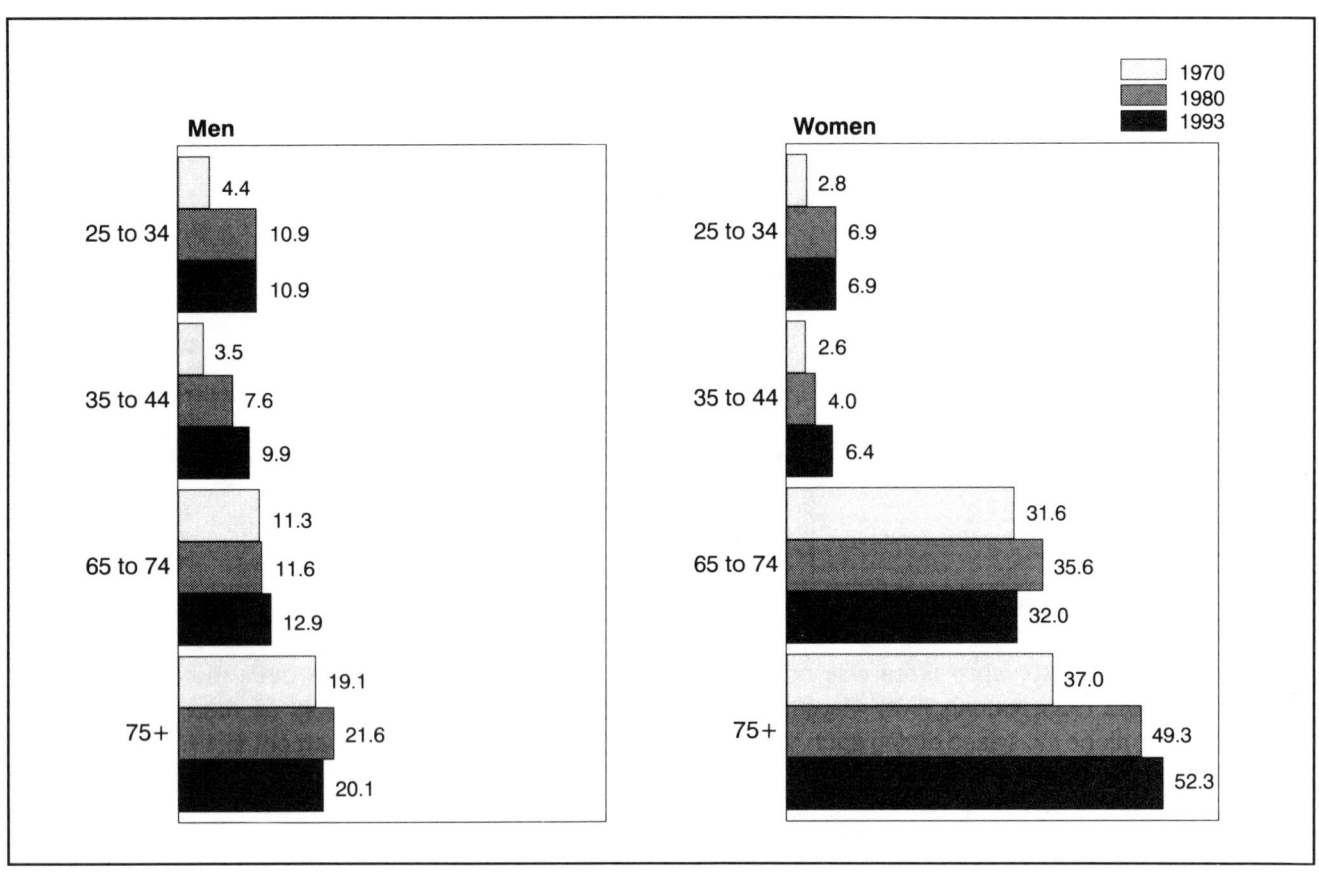

Source: Arlene F. Saluter, U.S. Bureau of the Census, *Marital Status and Living Arrangements: March 1993*, Current Population Reports, P20-478, Washington, D.C.: U.S. Government Printing Office, 1994, Figure 3.

D2-4. Persons Living in Nursing Homes, by Age and Sex: 1980 and 1990

Age	1980 Number	1980 Percent	1990 Number	1990 Percent	Percent change, 1980 to 1990	1990 Male	1990 Female
Total	1,426,371	100.0	1,772,032	100.0	24.2	493,609	1,278,423
Under 35 years	29,418	2.1	19,362	1.1	-34.2	11,880	7,482
35 to 44 years	20,764	1.5	27,303	1.5	31.5	16,178	11,125
45 to 54 years	42,857	3.0	40,903	2.3	-4.6	21,662	19,241
55 to 64 years	100,374	7.0	93,701	5.3	-6.6	46,844	46,857
65 to 74 years	238,962	16.8	244,676	13.8	2.4	97,873	146,803
75 to 79 years	219,571	15.4	245,972	13.9	12.0	75,542	170,430
80 to 84 years	286,679	20.1	361,330	20.4	26.0	88,362	272,968
85 to 89 years	276,251	19.4	378,612	21.4	37.1	135,268	603,517
90 to 94 years	158,807	11.1	247,648	14.0	55.9	(NA)	(NA)
95 years and over	52,688	3.7	112,525	6.4	113.6	(NA)	(NA)
Under 25 years	12,902	0.9	4,231	0.2	-67.2	2,399	1,832
Under 55 years	93,039	6.5	87,568	4.9	-5.9	49,720	37,848
Under 65 years	193,413	13.6	181,269	10.2	-6.3	96,564	84,705
65 years and over	1,232,958	86.4	1,590,763	89.8	29.0	397,045	1,193,718
85 years and over	487,746	34.2	738,785	41.7	51.5	135,268	603,517
Percentage of age groups							
Under 65 years	--	0.1	--	0.1	--	0.1	0.1
65 to 74 years	--	1.5	--	1.4	--	1.2	1.4
75 to 84 years	--	6.6	--	6.1	--	4.4	7.1
85 to 89 years	--	17.6	--	18.6	--	16.1	27.7
90 to 94 years	--	29.1	--	33.1	--	(NA)	(NA)
95 years and over	--	41.0	--	47.1	--	(NA)	(NA)
65 years and over	--	4.8	--	5.1	--	3.2	6.4
85 years and over	--	21.8	--	24.5	--	16.1	27.7
90 years and over	--	31.4	--	36.5	--	(NA)	(NA)

(NA) - Not available, included in previous age groups.
—Not applicable.
Note: In the 1990 decennial census, "Nursing homes" include skilled-nursing facilities, intermediate-care facilities, long-term care rooms in wards or buildings on the grounds of hospitals, or long-term care rooms/nursing wings in congregate housing facilities. Also included are nursing, convalescent, and rest rooms, such as soldiers', sailors', veterans', and fraternal or religious homes for the aged, with or without nursing care.
Source: U.S. Bureau of the Census, Decennial Censuses. 1990 Census of Population, prepared from the Census Analysis System; 1980 Census of Population,

Source: Cynthia M. Taeuber, U.S. Bureau of the Census, *Nursing Home Population: 1990 Census of Population and Housing (CPH-L-137),* Press Release CB93-117, June 28, 1993, Table 2.

D2-5. Living Arrangements of Children under 18 Years of Age and Presence of Parents, by Race and Hispanic Origin: 1993, 1980, and 1970

(Numbers in thousands. Excludes persons under 18 years old who were maintaining households or family groups and spouses)

Living arrangements	1933	1980	1970	Percent distribution		
				1993	1980	1970
ALL RACES						
Children under 18 years.................	66,893	63,427	69,162	100.0	100.0	100.0
Living with:						
Two parents	47,181	48,624	58,939	70.5	76.7	85.2
One parent	17,872	12,466	8,199	26.7	19.7	11.9
Mother only............................	15,586	11,406	7,452	23.3	18.0	10.8
Father only	2,286	1,060	748	3.4	1.7	1.1
Other relatives	1,443	1,949	1,547	2.2	3.1	2.2
Nonrelatives only.......................	398	388	477	0.6	0.6	0.7
WHITE						
Children under 18 years.................	53,075	52,242	58,790	100.0	100.0	100.0
Living with:						
Two parents	40,996	43,200	52,624	77.2	82.7	89.5
One parent	11,110	7,901	5,109	20.9	15.1	8.7
Mother only............................	9,256	7,059	4,581	17.4	13.5	7.8
Father only	1,854	842	528	3.5	1.6	0.9
Other relatives	726	887	696	1.4	1.7	1.2
Nonrelatives only.......................	243	254	362	0.5	0.5	0.6
BLACK						
Children under 18 years.................	10,660	9,375	9,422	100.0	100.0	100.0
Living with:						
Two parents	3,796	3,956	5,508	35.6	42.2	58.5
One parent	6,079	4,297	2,996	57.0	45.8	31.8
Mother only............................	5,757	4,117	2,783	54.0	43.9	29.5
Father only	322	180	213	3.0	1.9	2.3
Other relatives	657	999	820	6.2	10.7	8.7
Nonrelatives only.......................	127	123	97	1.2	1.3	1.0
HISPANIC ORIGIN*						
Children under 18 years.................	7,776	5,459	4,006	100.0	100.0	100.0
Living with:						
Two parents	5,017	4,116	3,111	64.5	75.4	77.7
One parent	2,472	1,152	(NA)	31.8	21.1	(NA)
Mother only............................	2,176	1,069	(NA)	28.0	19.6	(NA)
Father only	296	83	(NA)	3.8	1.5	(NA)
Other relatives	228	183	(NA)	2.9	3.4	(NA)
Nonrelatives only.......................	58	8	(NA)	0.7	0.1	(NA)

NA Not available.

* Persons of Hispanic origin may be of any race.

Source of Hispanic data for 1970: 1970 Census of Population, PC(2)-1C, *Persons of Spanish Origin*.

Source: Arlene F. Saluter, U.S. Bureau of the Census, *Marital Status and Living Arrangements: March 1993*, Current Population Reports, P20-478, Washington, D.C.: U.S. Government Printing Office, 1994, Table F.

D2-6. Household Relationship and Presence of Parents for Children under 18 Years of Age, by Age, Sex, Race, and Hispanic Origin of Child: March 1993

[Numbers in thousands.

Subject	Total, under 18 years¹	Under 1 year	1 and 2 years	3 to 5 years	6 to 9 years	10 to 14 years	15 to 17 years	Total, under 6 years	Total, 6 to 11 years	Total, 12 to 17 years
ALL RACES										
Both sexes	66 893	4 031	7 929	11 676	14 924	18 427	9 906	23 636	22 512	20 745
In households	66 849	4 022	7 913	11 672	14 920	18 423	9 899	23 607	22 504	20 738
Child of householder	61 099	3 527	6 930	10 562	13 659	17 258	9 163	21 019	20 737	19 343
Grandchild of householder	3 368	334	603	689	769	617	355	1 627	1 023	718
Other relative of householder	1 100	103	198	183	188	232	196	484	283	333
Nonrelative of householder	1 282	58	182	238	304	315	185	478	460	344
Living with both parents	47 181	2 891	5 584	8 180	10 687	13 077	6 762	16 655	16 094	14 431
Child of householder	46 446	2 788	5 425	8 009	10 540	12 977	6 707	16 222	15 905	14 319
Grandchild of householder	475	61	91	115	114	66	29	266	136	72
Other relative of householder	206	32	46	45	29	28	26	123	45	38
Nonrelative of householder	54	11	22	11	4	6	–	44	8	2
Living with mother only	15 586	939	1 883	2 805	3 391	4 257	2 311	5 627	5 131	4 828
Child of householder	12 696	597	1 273	2 205	2 755	3 737	2 128	4 075	4 252	4 368
Grandchild of householder	1 647	249	371	350	346	229	101	970	455	221
Other relative of householder	447	64	122	87	75	72	26	274	101	72
Nonrelative of householder	797	29	116	163	214	219	56	308	323	166
Living with father only	2 286	158	274	433	448	610	363	865	698	722
Child of householder	1 957	141	232	349	363	544	328	722	580	655
Grandchild of householder	229	11	29	68	65	37	20	108	81	40
Other relative of householder	22	4	2	3	3	6	5	8	6	8
Nonrelative of householder	77	2	12	13	17	22	10	27	30	19
Living with neither parent	1 797	33	172	255	394	479	464	460	581	756
Grandchild of householder	1 017	14	113	156	244	285	206	282	350	384
Other relative of householder	426	3	28	48	81	126	139	79	132	215
Nonrelative of householder	354	17	31	51	69	67	119	99	98	157
Foster child	206	14	26	38	48	44	36	77	67	61
In group quarters	44	9	16	4	4	4	7	29	8	8
Male	34 303	2 069	4 066	5 962	7 661	9 406	5 140	12 097	11 565	10 642
In households	34 282	2 061	4 061	5 961	7 659	9 404	5 136	12 083	11 561	10 638
Child of householder	31 363	1 795	3 577	5 423	6 999	8 795	4 773	10 795	10 625	9 942
Grandchild of householder	1 703	170	292	346	402	322	171	807	539	356
Other relative of householder	585	60	106	91	96	121	110	258	150	177
Nonrelative of householder	632	36	86	101	161	166	83	223	247	163
Living with both parents	24 330	1 493	2 910	4 240	5 510	6 674	3 503	8 643	8 268	7 418
Child of householder	23 925	1 424	2 835	4 157	5 436	6 603	3 470	8 416	8 159	7 350
Grandchild of householder	246	40	34	49	55	48	20	123	75	48
Other relative of householder	126	21	29	30	17	16	14	79	28	19
Nonrelative of householder	33	9	12	4	2	6	–	25	6	2
Living with mother only	7 847	469	959	1 377	1 704	2 128	1 210	2 805	2 609	2 433
Child of householder	6 381	303	646	1 090	1 368	1 859	1 115	2 039	2 144	2 198
Grandchild of householder	856	117	198	183	178	124	56	498	240	119
Other relative of householder	224	36	65	41	39	33	10	141	49	34
Nonrelative of householder	385	12	51	64	119	111	28	127	176	82
Living with father only	1 212	76	116	220	232	363	205	412	370	429
Child of householder	1 056	68	96	176	196	333	188	340	322	394
Grandchild of householder	105	5	10	36	32	13	9	51	35	19
Other relative of householder	13	4	–	–	1	6	3	4	4	5
Nonrelative of householder	37	–	9	8	3	12	5	17	9	11
Living with neither parent	894	22	76	124	213	240	218	223	314	357
Grandchild of householder	496	8	50	78	137	137	86	136	190	170
Other relative of householder	221	–	13	21	39	66	83	34	69	119
Nonrelative of householder	176	14	14	25	37	37	49	53	55	68
Foster child	109	11	14	21	24	29	10	46	41	22
In group quarters	21	8	5	–	2	2	3	13	4	4
Female	32 589	1 962	3 862	5 714	7 263	9 020	4 766	11 539	10 947	10 103
In households	32 567	1 961	3 852	5 711	7 261	9 019	4 763	11 524	10 943	10 100
Child of householder	29 736	1 732	3 352	5 139	6 659	8 463	4 391	10 223	10 112	9 401
Grandchild of householder	1 665	165	312	343	367	295	184	819	484	362
Other relative of householder	515	43	92	91	92	111	86	226	133	156
Nonrelative of householder	650	22	96	137	143	149	102	255	214	181
Living with both parents	22 851	1 398	2 674	3 940	5 177	6 404	3 258	8 012	7 826	7 013
Child of householder	22 521	1 364	2 589	3 852	5 104	6 374	3 237	7 805	7 746	6 970
Grandchild of householder	229	21	56	66	59	18	9	144	61	24
Other relative of householder	80	11	17	15	12	12	12	44	17	19
Nonrelative of householder	21	2	10	6	2	–	–	19	2	–
Living with mother only	7 739	470	924	1 428	1 687	2 129	1 101	2 822	2 522	2 395
Child of householder	6 314	294	628	1 115	1 387	1 878	1 013	2 036	2 108	2 170
Grandchild of householder	791	132	174	167	168	105	45	472	216	103
Other relative of householder	223	28	57	47	36	39	15	132	51	39
Nonrelative of householder	412	16	65	100	95	108	28	181	147	84
Living with father only	1 074	81	159	213	215	247	158	453	328	293
Child of householder	901	74	135	172	167	212	140	382	258	261
Grandchild of householder	124	6	18	32	32	24	11	57	46	21
Other relative of householder	9	–	2	3	2	–	2	4	2	2
Nonrelative of householder	40	1	3	6	14	11	5	10	21	8
Living with neither parent	903	11	96	130	182	239	245	237	267	399
Grandchild of householder	521	6	63	78	108	148	119	146	161	214
Other relative of householder	204	3	15	27	42	61	56	45	63	96
Nonrelative of householder	178	3	17	26	32	30	70	46	43	89
Foster child	96	3	12	17	24	15	27	31	26	39
In group quarters	23	1	11	3	3	2	3	15	4	4

¹Excludes householders, subfamily reference persons, and their spouses.
²May be of any race.

Source: Arlene F. Saluter, U.S. Bureau of the Census, *Marital Status and Living Arrangements: March 1993,* Current Population Reports, P20-478, Washington, D.C.: U.S. Government Printing Office, 1994, Table 4.

D3. HOUSEHOLD COMPOSITION

D3-1. Household Composition, by Presence of Own Children under 18: 1993, 1990, 1980, and 1970

(Numbers in thousands)

Type of household	1993 Number	1993 Percent	1990 Number	1990 Percent	1980 Number	1980 Percent	1970 Number	1970 Percent	Average annual percent change 1990-93	Average annual percent change 1980-90	Average annual percent change 1970-80
All households.............	96,391	100.0	93,347	100.0	80,776	100.0	63,401	100.0	1.1	1.4	2.4
Family households..............	68,144	70.7	66,090	70.8	59,550	73.7	51,456	81.2	1.0	1.0	1.5
No own children under 18	34,887	36.2	33,801	36.2	28,528	35.3	22,725	35.8	1.1	1.7	2.3
With own children under 18. ...	33,257	34.5	32,289	34.6	31,022	38.4	28,732	45.3	1.0	0.4	0.8
Married-couple family..........	53,171	55.2	52,317	56.0	49,112	60.8	44,728	70.5	0.5	0.6	0.9
No own children under 18 ...	28,464	29.5	27,780	29.8	24,151	29.9	19,196	30.3	0.8	1.4	2.3
With own children under 18. .	24,707	25.6	24,537	26.3	24,961	30.9	25,532	40.3	0.2	-0.2	-0.2
Other family, male householder.	3,026	3.1	2,884	3.1	1,733	2.1	1,228	1.9	1.6	5.1	3.4
No own children under 18 ...	1,702	1.8	1,731	1.9	1,117	1.4	887	1.4	-0.6	4.4	2.3
With own children under 18. .	1,324	1.4	1,153	1.2	616	0.8	341	0.5	4.6	6.3	5.9
Other family, female householder...............	11,947	12.4	10,890	11.7	8,705	10.8	5,500	8.7	3.1	2.2	4.6
No own children under 18 ...	4,721	4.9	4,290	4.6	3,261	4.0	2,642	4.2	3.2	2.7	2.1
With own children under 18. .	7,226	7.5	6,599	7.1	5,445	6.7	2,858	4.5	3.0	1.9	6.4
Nonfamily households..........	28,247	29.3	27,257	29.2	21,226	26.3	11,945	18.8	1.2	2.5	5.7
Living alone...............	23,642	24.5	22,999	24.6	18,296	22.7	10,851	17.1	0.9	2.3	5.2
Male householder.............	12,254	12.7	11,606	12.4	8,807	10.9	4,063	6.4	1.8	2.8	7.7
Living alone...............	9,436	9.8	9,049	9.7	6,966	8.6	3,532	5.6	1.4	2.6	6.8
Female householder	15,993	16.6	15,651	16.8	12,419	15.4	7,882	12.4	0.7	2.3	4.5
Living alone...............	14,206	14.7	13,950	14.9	11,330	14.0	7,319	11.5	0.6	2.1	4.4

Source: Steve W. Rawlings, U.S. Bureau of the Census, *Household and Family Characteristics: March 1993,* Current Population Reports, P20–477. Washington, D.C.: U.S. Government Printing Office, 1994, Table A.

D3-2. Household Composition: 1970, 1980, 1990, and 1993

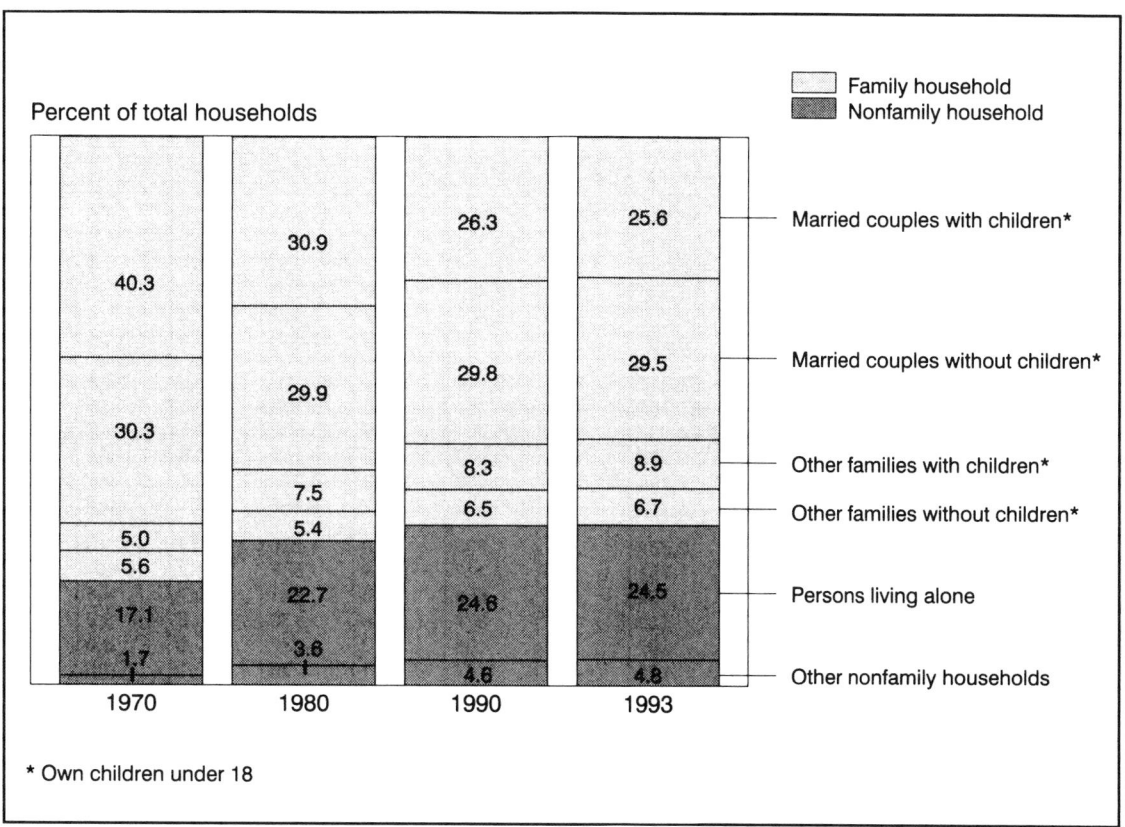

Source: Steve W. Rawlings, U.S. Bureau of the Census, *Household and Family Characteristics: March 1993,* Current Population Reports, P20–477. Washington, D.C.: U.S. Government Printing Office, 1994, Figure 1.

D3-3. Type of Family as Percentage of All Families, by Race: 1970 to 1993

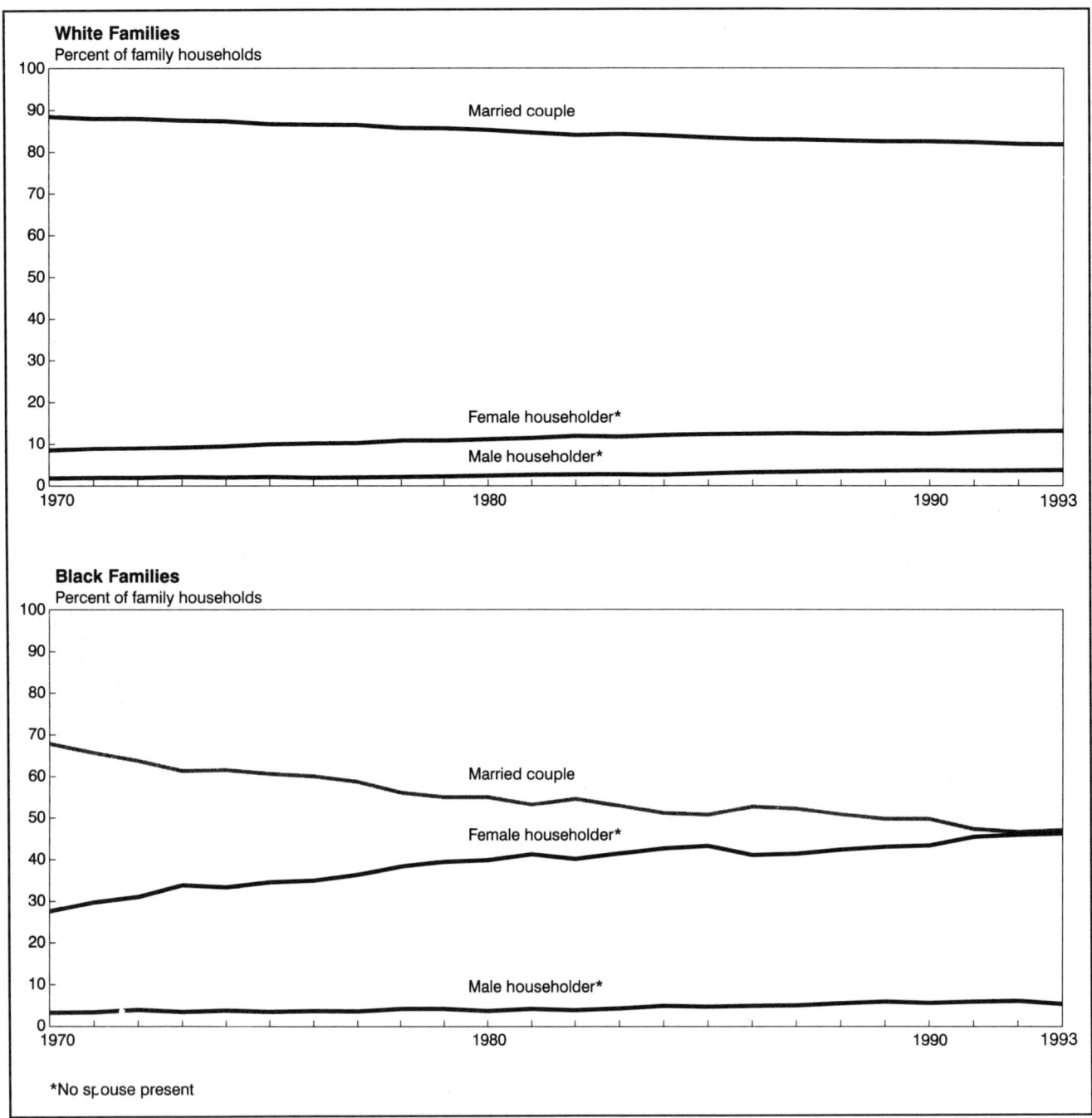

Source: Steve W. Rawlings, U.S. Bureau of the Census, *Household and Family Characteristics: March 1993*, Current Population Reports, P20-477, Washington, D.C.: U.S. Government Printing Office, 1994, Figure 4.

D3-4. Family Households, by Type, Race, and Hispanic Origin of Householder: 1993, 1990, 1980, and 1970

(Numbers in thousands)

Type of family	1993		1990		1980		1970		Average annual percent change		
	Number	Percent	Number	Percent	Number	Percent	Number	Percent	1990-93	1980-90	1970-80
ALL RACES											
Family households	68,144	100.0	66,090	100.0	59,550	100.0	51,456	100.0	1.0	1.0	1.5
Married-couple families	53,171	78.0	52,317	79.2	49,112	82.5	44,728	86.9	0.5	0.6	0.9
Male householder, no wife present	3,026	4.4	2,884	4.4	1,733	2.9	1,228	2.4	1.6	5.1	3.4
Female householder, no husband present	11,947	17.5	10,890	16.5	8,705	14.6	5,500	10.7	3.1	2.2	4.6
WHITE											
Family households	57,858	100.0	56,590	100.0	52,243	100.0	46,166	100.0	0.7	0.8	1.2
Married-couple families	47,601	82.3	46,981	83.0	44,751	85.7	41,029	88.9	0.4	0.5	0.9
Male householder, no wife present	2,409	4.2	2,303	4.1	1,441	2.8	1,038	2.2	1.5	4.7	3.3
Female householder, no husband present	7,848	13.6	7,306	12.9	6,052	11.6	4,099	8.9	2.4	1.9	3.9
BLACK											
Family households	7,888	100.0	7,470	100.0	6,184	100.0	4,856	100.0	1.8	1.9	2.4
Married-couple families	3,748	47.5	3,750	50.2	3,433	55.5	3,317	68.3	–	0.9	0.3
Male householder, no wife present	460	5.8	446	6.0	256	4.1	181	3.7	1.0	5.6	3.5
Female householder, no husband present	3,680	46.7	3,275	43.8	2,495	40.3	1,358	28.0	3.9	2.7	6.1
ASIAN OR PACIFIC ISLANDER+											
Family households	1,662	100.0	1,531	100.0	818	100.0	NA	NA	2.7	6.3	NA
Married-couple families	1,335	80.3	1,256	82.0	691	84.5	NA	NA	2.0	6.0	NA
Male householder, no wife present	95	5.7	86	5.6	39	4.8	NA	NA	3.3	7.9	NA
Female householder, no husband present	232	14.0	188	12.3	88	10.8	NA	NA	7.0	7.6	NA
HISPANIC*											
Family households	5,318	100.0	4,840	100.0	3,029	100.0	2,004	100.0	3.1	4.7	4.1
Married-couple families	3,674	69.1	3,395	70.1	2,282	75.3	1,615	80.6	2.6	4.0	3.5
Male householder, no wife present	407	7.7	329	6.8	138	4.6	82	4.1	7.1	8.7	5.2
Female householder, no husband present	1,238	23.3	1,116	23.1	610	20.1	307	15.3	3.5	6.0	6.9

- Zero or rounds to zero.
NA Not available.
+ 1980 Data for Asian or Pacific Islander from 1980 Census of Population, Vol. 1, Table 141.
* Persons of Hispanic origin may be of any race. 1970 Hispanic data from 1970 Census of Population, Vol. II, 4A, Table 6.

Source: Steve W. Rawlings, U.S. Bureau of the Census, *Household and Family Characteristics: March 1993,* Current Population Reports, P20-477, Washington, D.C.: U.S. Government Printing Office, 1994, Table E.

D3-5. Composition of Family Groups with Children, by Race and Hispanic Origin: 1970, 1980, 1990, and 1993

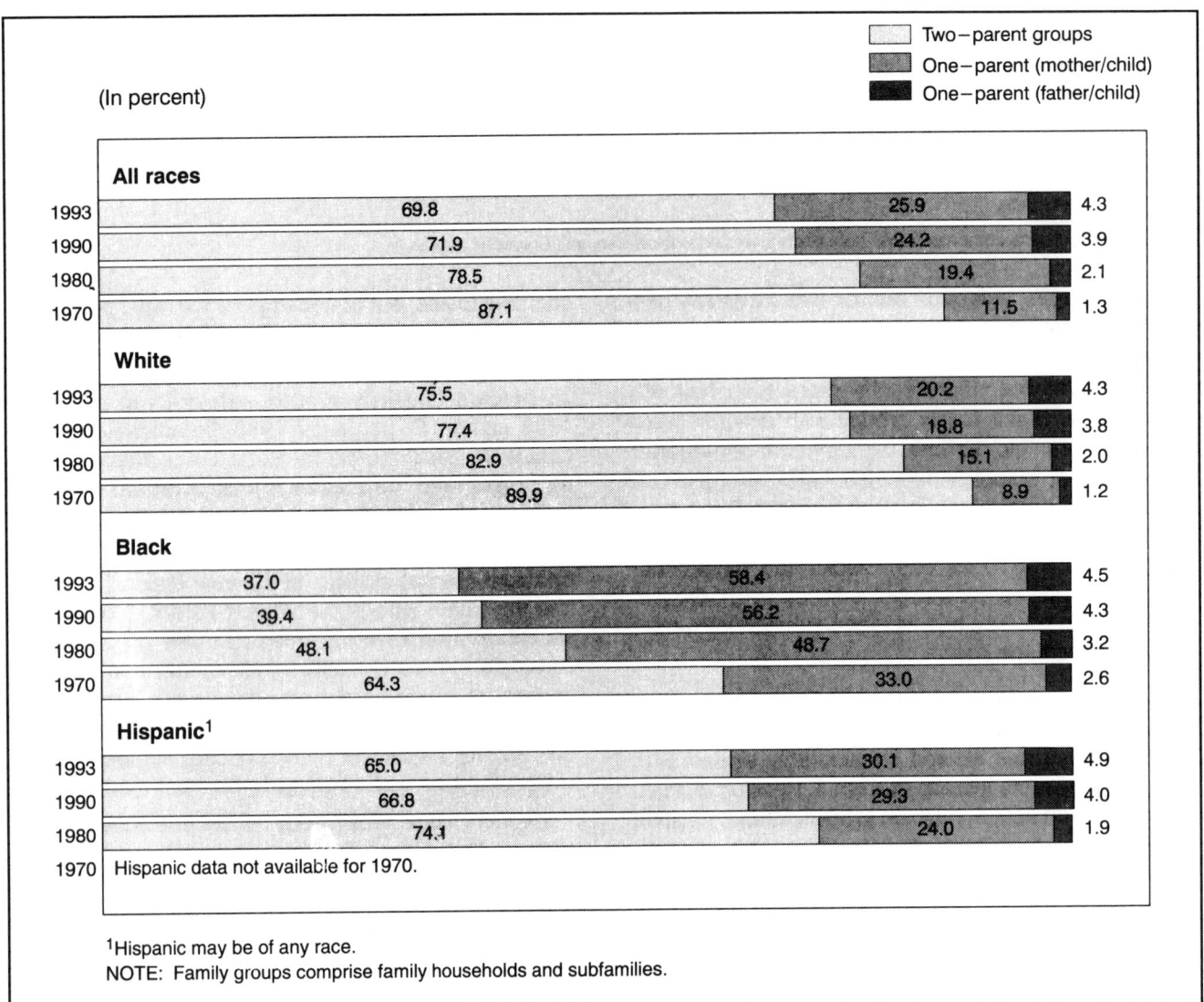

¹Hispanic may be of any race.
NOTE: Family groups comprise family households and subfamilies.

Source: Steve W. Rawlings, U.S. Bureau of the Census, *Household and Family Characteristics: March 1993*, Current Population Reports, P20-477, Washington, D.C.: U.S. Government Printing Office, 1994, Figure 5.

D3-6. One-Parent Family Groups, by Race, Hispanic Origin, and Marital Status of Householder or Reference Persons in Survey: 1993, 1990, 1980, and 1970

(Numbers in thousands)

Subject	1993 Number	1993 Percent	1990 Number	1990 Percent	1980 Number	1980 Percent	1970 Number	1970 Percent	Average annual percent change 1990-93	Average annual percent change 1980-90	Average annual percent change 1970-80
ALL RACES											
One-parent family groups	10,901	100.0	9,749	100.0	6,920	100.0	3,808	100.0	3.7	3.4	6.0
Maintained by mother.........	9,339	85.7	8,398	86.1	6,230	90.0	3,415	89.7	3.5	3.0	6.0
Never married	3,448	31.6	2,775	28.5	1,063	15.4	248	6.5	7.2	9.6	14.6
Married, spouse absent	1,974	18.1	1,836	18.8	1,743	25.2	1,377	36.2	2.4	0.5	2.4
Separated	1,670	15.3	1,557	16.0	1,483	21.4	962	25.3	2.3	0.5	4.3
Divorced	3,497	32.1	3,194	32.8	2,721	39.3	1,109	29.1	3.0	1.6	9.0
Widowed	420	3.9	593	6.1	703	10.2	682	17.9	-11.5	-1.7	0.3
Maintained by father	1,562	14.3	1,351	13.9	690	10.0	393	10.3	4.8	6.7	5.6
Never married	510	4.7	345	3.5	63	0.9	22	0.6	13.0	(B)	(B)
Married, spouse absent	288	2.6	217	2.2	181	2.6	247	6.5	9.4	1.8	-3.1
Divorced	683	6.3	700	7.2	340	4.9	(NA)	(NA)	-0.8	7.2	(NA)
Widowed	80	0.7	89	0.9	107	1.5	124	3.3	-3.6	-1.8	-1.5
WHITE											
One-parent family groups	7,167	100.0	6,389	100.0	4,664	100.0	2,638	100.0	3.8	3.1	5.7
Maintained by mother	5,901	82.3	5,310	83.1	4,122	88.4	2,330	88.3	3.5	2.5	5.7
Never married	1,478	20.6	1,139	17.8	379	8.1	73	2.8	8.7	11.0	16.5
Spouse absent...........	1,288	18.0	1,206	18.9	1,033	22.1	796	30.2	2.2	1.5	2.6
Separated	1,091	15.2	1,015	15.9	840	18.0	477	18.1	2.4	1.9	5.7
Divorced	2,825	39.4	2,553	40.0	2,201	47.2	930	35.3	3.4	1.5	8.6
Widowed	311	4.3	411	6.4	511	11.0	531	20.1	-9.3	-2.2	-0.4
Maintained by father	1,265	17.7	1,079	16.9	542	11.6	307	11.6	5.3	6.9	5.7
Never married	356	5.0	253	4.0	32	0.7	18	0.7	11.4	(B)	(B)
Spouse absent*...........	239	3.3	169	2.6	141	3.0	196	7.4	11.6	1.8	-3.3
Divorced	606	8.5	591	9.3	288	6.2	(NA)	(NA)	0.8	7.2	(NA)
Widowed	64	0.9	65	1.0	82	1.8	93	3.5	(B)	-2.3	-1.3
BLACK											
One-parent family groups	3,377	100.0	3,081	100.0	2,114	100.0	1,148	100.0	3.1	3.8	6.1
Maintained by mother	3,135	92.8	2,860	92.8	1,984	93.9	1,063	92.6	3.1	3.7	6.2
Never married	1,871	55.4	1,572	51.0	665	31.5	173	15.1	5.8	8.6	13.5
Spouse absent...........	611	18.1	570	18.5	667	31.6	570	49.7	2.3	-1.6	1.6
Separated	532	15.8	502	16.3	616	29.1	479	41.7	1.9	-2.0	2.5
Divorced	562	16.6	574	18.6	477	22.6	172	15.0	-0.7	1.9	10.2
Widowed	91	2.7	144	4.7	174	8.2	148	12.9	-15.3	-1.9	1.6
Maintained by father.........	242	7.2	221	7.2	129	6.1	85	7.4	3.0	5.4	4.2
Never married	130	3.8	74	2.4	30	1.4	4	0.3	(B)	(B)	(B)
Spouse absent*...........	38	1.1	38	1.2	37	1.8	50	4.4	(B)	(B)	(B)
Divorced	61	1.8	93	3.0	43	2.0	(NA)	(NA)	-14.1	(B)	(B)
Widowed	13	0.4	18	0.6	19	0.9	30	2.6	(B)	(B)	(B)
HISPANIC+											
One-parent family groups	1,344	100.0	1,140	100.0	568	100.0	(NA)	(NA)	5.5	7.0	(NA)
Maintained by mother	1,157	86.1	1,003	88.0	526	92.6	(NA)	(NA)	4.8	6.5	(NA)
Never married	476	35.4	361	31.7	120	21.1	(NA)	(NA)	9.2	11.0	(NA)
Spouse absent...........	318	23.7	314	27.5	199	35.0	(NA)	(NA)	0.4	4.6	(NA)
Separated	252	18.8	249	21.8	170	29.9	(NA)	(NA)	0.4	3.8	(NA)
Divorced	304	22.6	266	23.3	162	28.5	(NA)	(NA)	4.5	5.0	(NA)
Widowed	58	4.3	62	5.4	46	8.1	(NA)	(NA)	(B)	(B)	(NA)
Maintained by father.........	187	13.9	138	12.1	42	7.4	(NA)	(NA)	10.1	(B)	(NA)
Never married	88	6.5	62	5.4	7	1.2	(NA)	(NA)	(B)	(B)	(NA)
Spouse absent*...........	40	3.0	26	2.3	13	2.3	(NA)	(NA)	(B)	(B)	(NA)
Divorced	46	3.4	40	3.5	13	2.3	(NA)	(NA)	(B)	(B)	(NA)
Widowed	14	1.0	9	0.8	8	1.4	(NA)	(NA)	(B)	(B)	(NA)

* Data for 1970 include divorced fathers.
B Base less than 75,000
NA Not available.
+ May be of any race.

Note: Family groups comprise family households, related subfamilies and unrelated subfamilies.

Source: Steve W. Rawlings, U.S. Bureau of the Census, *Household and Family Characteristics: March 1993,* Current Population Reports, P20-477, Washington, D.C.: U.S. Government Printing Office, 1994, Table H.

D4. EDUCATION

D4-1. School Enrollment, by Sex and Educational Level: 1960 to 1992

(In millions. As of Oct. For the civilian, noninstitutional population. For 1960, persons 5 to 34 years old; 1970–1979 3 to 34 years old; beginning 1980, 3 years old and over. Elementary includes kindergarten and grades 1–8; high school, grades 9–12; and college, 2-year and 4-year colleges, universities, and graduate and professional schools. Data for college represent degree-credit enrollment)

YEAR	ALL LEVELS [1]			ELEMENTARY			HIGH SCHOOL			COLLEGE		
	Total	Male	Female	Total	Male	Female	Total	Male	Female	Total	Male	Female
1960	46.3	24.2	22.0	32.4	16.7	15.7	10.2	5.2	5.1	3.6	2.3	1.2
1970	60.4	31.4	28.9	37.1	19.0	18.1	14.7	7.4	7.3	7.4	4.4	3.0
1975	61.0	31.6	29.4	33.8	17.3	16.5	15.7	8.0	7.7	9.7	5.3	4.4
1976	60.5	31.2	29.3	33.3	17.0	16.2	15.7	8.1	7.7	10.0	5.3	4.7
1977	60.0	30.8	29.2	32.4	16.6	15.8	15.8	8.0	7.7	10.2	5.4	4.8
1978	58.6	30.1	28.6	31.5	16.1	15.3	15.5	7.8	7.6	9.8	5.1	4.7
1979	57.9	29.5	28.3	30.9	15.9	15.0	15.1	7.7	7.4	10.0	5.0	5.0
1980	58.6	29.6	29.1	30.6	15.8	14.9	14.6	7.3	7.3	11.4	5.4	6.0
1981 [2]	58.4	29.5	28.9	30.1	15.5	14.7	14.4	7.3	7.1	11.8	5.6	6.2
1981 [3]	59.9	30.3	29.6	31.0	15.9	15.0	14.7	7.5	7.3	12.1	5.8	6.3
1982	59.4	30.0	29.4	30.7	15.8	14.9	14.2	7.2	7.0	12.3	5.9	6.4
1983	59.3	30.1	29.2	30.6	15.7	14.8	14.1	7.1	7.0	12.4	6.0	6.3
1984	58.9	29.9	29.0	30.3	15.6	14.7	13.9	7.1	6.8	12.3	6.0	6.3
1985	59.8	30.0	29.7	30.7	15.7	15.0	14.1	7.2	6.9	12.5	5.9	6.6
1986	60.1	30.4	29.7	31.1	7.1	15.0	14.0	7.1	6.9	12.4	5.8	6.6
1986 [4]	60.5	30.6	30.0	31.1	16.1	15.0	14.2	7.2	7.0	12.7	6.0	6.7
1987	60.6	30.7	29.9	31.6	16.3	15.3	13.8	7.0	6.8	12.7	6.0	6.7
1988	61.1	30.7	30.5	32.2	16.6	15.6	13.2	6.7	6.4	13.1	5.9	7.2
1989	61.5	30.8	30.7	32.5	16.7	15.8	12.9	6.6	6.3	13.2	6.0	7.2
1990	63.0	31.5	31.5	33.2	17.1	16.0	12.8	6.5	6.4	13.6	6.2	7.4
1991	63.9	32.1	31.8	33.8	17.3	16.4	13.1	6.8	6.4	14.1	6.4	7.6
1992	64.6	32.2	32.3	34.3	17.7	16.6	13.3	6.8	6.5	14.0	6.2	7.8

[1] Beginning 1970, includes nursery schools, not shown separately. [2] Based on 1970 population controls. [3] Based on 1980 population controls. [4] Revised. Data beginning 1986, based on a revised edit and tabulation package.

Source: U.S. Bureau of the Census, *Current Population Reports*, P20-474; and earlier reports.

Source: U.S. Bureau of the Census, *Statistical Abstract of the United States: 1994*, (114th edition), Washington, D.C.: U.S. Government Printing Office, 1994, Table 231.

D4-2. Percentage of Population 3 to 34 Years Old Enrolled in School[1], by Race/Ethnicity, Sex, and Age: October 1975 and October 1993

Year and age	Total				Male				Female			
	All races	White, non-Hispanic	Black, non-Hispanic	Hispanic origin	All races	White, non-Hispanic	Black, non-Hispanic	Hispanic origin	All races	White, non-Hispanic	Black, non-Hispanic	Hispanic origin
1	2	3	4	5	6	7	8	9	10	11	12	13
1975												
Total, 3 to 34 years	53.7	53.0	57.7	54.8	56.1	55.2	60.4	58.1	51.5	50.8	55.3	51.7
3 and 4 years	31.5	31.0	34.4	27.3	30.9	31.1	31.4	26.7	32.1	30.9	37.5	27.9
5 and 6 years	94.7	95.1	94.4	92.1	94.4	94.8	94.8	89.7	95.1	95.4	94.0	94.4
7 to 9 years	99.3	99.4	99.3	99.6	99.2	99.2	99.4	99.6	99.5	99.6	99.2	99.5
10 to 13 years	99.3	99.3	99.1	99.2	98.9	99.0	98.9	98.8	99.6	99.6	99.3	99.7
14 and 15 years	98.2	98.5	97.4	95.6	98.4	98.6	97.6	97.4	98.0	98.4	97.2	93.8
16 and 17 years	89.0	89.5	86.8	86.2	90.7	91.2	88.1	88.3	87.2	87.8	85.5	84.0
18 and 19 years	46.9	46.8	46.9	44.0	49.9	49.4	49.6	51.9	44.2	44.2	44.6	37.1
20 and 21 years	31.2	32.1	26.7	27.5	35.3	36.7	28.4	31.3	27.4	27.8	25.3	24.3
22 to 24 years	16.2	16.4	13.9	14.1	20.0	20.8	14.5	15.9	12.6	12.2	13.4	12.5
25 to 29 years	10.1	10.1	9.4	8.3	13.1	13.2	11.6	11.9	7.2	7.2	7.6	5.3
30 to 34 years	6.6	6.6	7.1	5.5	7.7	7.5	8.7	7.2	5.6	5.8	5.9	4.1
1993												
Total, 3 to 34 years	51.8	51.4	53.5	48.9	52.6	52.2	55.7	47.4	51.0	50.6	51.5	50.6
3 and 4 years	40.4	43.1	40.1	26.8	41.5	44.1	42.4	27.0	39.3	42.0	37.6	26.7
5 and 6 years	95.4	95.7	94.5	93.8	95.5	95.4	96.8	93.6	95.2	96.0	91.9	93.9
7 to 9 years	99.4	99.5	99.0	99.6	99.5	99.5	99.3	99.8	99.4	99.5	98.7	99.4
10 to 13 years	99.5	99.5	99.8	99.2	99.6	99.6	100.0	98.8	99.5	99.5	99.7	99.6
14 and 15 years	98.9	99.1	98.5	97.6	99.0	99.3	99.0	96.9	98.7	98.9	97.9	98.2
16 and 17 years	94.0	95.0	94.9	88.3	95.0	96.2	96.0	89.1	92.9	93.7	93.7	87.4
18 and 19 years	61.6	63.6	57.4	50.0	61.6	62.5	63.2	47.7	61.7	64.8	51.8	51.9
20 and 21 years	42.7	46.1	29.9	31.8	42.5	47.0	24.0	31.6	42.9	45.2	34.9	32.0
22 to 24 years	23.6	24.9	18.0	13.7	25.5	26.7	19.5	12.8	21.8	23.1	16.6	14.5
25 to 29 years	10.2	10.2	10.0	7.7	9.6	9.9	9.4	5.5	10.8	10.5	10.4	10.2
30 to 34 years	5.9	6.0	5.3	5.1	5.2	5.2	2.8	5.4	6.6	6.7	7.3	4.8

[1] Includes enrollment in any type of graded public, parochial, or other private schools. Includes nursery schools, kindergartens, elementary schools, high schools, colleges, universities, and professional schools. Attendance may be on either a full-time or part-time basis and during the day or night. Enrollments in "special" schools, such as trade schools, business colleges, or correspondence schools, are not included.

NOTE.—Data are based upon sample surveys of the civilian noninstitutional population.

SOURCE: U.S. Department of Commerce, Bureau of the Census, Current Population Survey, unpublished data. (This table was prepared March 1994.)

Source: National Center for Education Statistics, *Digest of Education Statistics, 1994*, NCES 94-115, Washington, D.C.: U.S. Government Printing Office, 1994, Table 7.

D4-3. College Enrollment, by Selected Characteristics: 1980 to 1990

[In thousands. As of fall. Totals may differ from other tables because of adjustments to underreported and nonreported racial/ethnic data. Nonresident alien students are not distributed among racial/ethnic groups]

CHARACTERISTIC	1980	1984	1988	1990
Total	12,086.8	12,233.0	13,043.1	13,710.2
Male	5,868.1	5,858.3	5,998.2	6,238.5
Female	6,218.7	6,374.7	7,044.9	7,471.6
Public	9,456.4	9,456.4	10,156.4	10,740.6
Private	2,630.4	2,776.6	2,886.7	2,969.7
2-year	4,521.4	4,526.9	4,868.1	5,181.0
4-year	7,565.4	7,706.1	8,175.0	8,529.1
Undergraduate	10,469.1	10,610.8	11,304.2	11,862.9
Graduate	1,340.9	1,343.7	1,471.9	1,573.6
Professional	276.8	278.5	267.1	273.6
White [1]	9,833.0	9,814.7	10,283.2	10,674.8
Male	4,772.9	4,689.9	4,711.6	4,840.8
Female	5,060.1	5,124.7	5,571.6	5,834.0
Public	7,656.1	7,542.4	7,963.8	8,339.5
Private	2,176.9	2,272.3	2,319.4	2,335.2
2-year	3,558.5	3,514.3	3,701.5	3,917.9
4-year	6,274.5	6,300.4	6,581.6	6,756.8
Undergraduate	8,480.7	8,484.0	8,906.7	9,231.3
Graduate	1,104.7	1,087.3	1,153.2	1,221.1
Professional	247.7	243.4	223.2	222.4
Black [1]	1,106.8	1,075.8	1,129.6	1,223.3
Male	463.7	436.8	442.7	476.3
Female	643.0	639.0	686.9	747.0
Public	876.1	844.0	881.1	952.3
Private	230.7	231.8	248.5	270.9
2-year	472.5	458.7	473.3	508.7
4-year	634.3	617.0	656.3	714.6
Undergraduate	1,018.8	994.9	1,038.8	1,123.8
Graduate	75.1	67.4	76.5	83.6
Professional	12.8	13.4	14.3	15.8
Hispanic	471.7	534.9	680.0	758.1
Male	231.6	253.8	310.3	344.1
Female	240.1	281.2	369.6	413.9
Public	406.2	456.1	586.9	648.3
Private	65.5	78.9	93.1	109.8

CHARACTERISTIC	1980	1984	1988	1990
2-year	255.1	288.8	383.9	413.6
4-year	216.6	246.1	296.0	344.5
Undergraduate	433.1	495.2	631.2	701.8
Graduate	32.1	31.7	39.5	45.8
Professional	6.5	8.0	9.3	10.5
American Indian [1]	83.9	83.6	92.5	102.6
Male	37.8	37.4	39.1	43.0
Female	46.1	46.1	53.4	59.7
Public	74.2	72.1	81.1	90.3
Private	9.7	11.4	11.5	12.4
2-year	47.0	45.5	50.4	54.4
4-year	36.9	38.1	42.1	48.2
Undergraduate	77.9	77.8	85.9	95.1
Graduate	5.2	4.8	5.6	6.4
Professional	0.8	1.0	1.1	1.1
Asian [1]	286.4	389.5	496.7	554.8
Male	151.3	210.0	259.2	286.6
Female	135.2	179.5	237.5	268.2
Public	239.7	322.7	405.7	445.3
Private	46.7	66.8	91.0	109.5
2-year	124.3	167.1	199.3	211.8
4-year	162.1	222.4	297.4	343.0
Undergraduate	248.7	343.0	436.6	484.8
Graduate	31.6	37.1	45.7	51.7
Professional	6.1	9.3	14.4	18.4
Nonresident alien	305.0	334.6	361.2	396.6
Male	210.8	230.4	235.3	247.6
Female	94.2	104.1	125.9	149.0
Public	204.1	219.0	237.8	264.8
Private	100.8	115.5	123.3	131.8
2-year	64.1	52.5	59.6	74.5
4-year	240.9	282.1	301.5	322.1
Undergraduate	209.9	215.8	205.0	226.1
Graduate	92.2	115.3	151.4	165.2
Professional	2.9	3.4	4.7	5.4

[1] Non-Hispanic.
Source: U.S. National Center for Education Statistics, *Digest of Education Statistics*, 1992.

Source: U.S. Bureau of the Census, *Statistical Abstract of the United States: 1993*, (113th edition), Washington, D.C.: U.S. Government Printing Office, 1993, Table 273.

D4-4. Enrollment in Institutions of Higher Education, by Sex: Fall 1979 to Fall 2004 (Middle Alternative Projections)

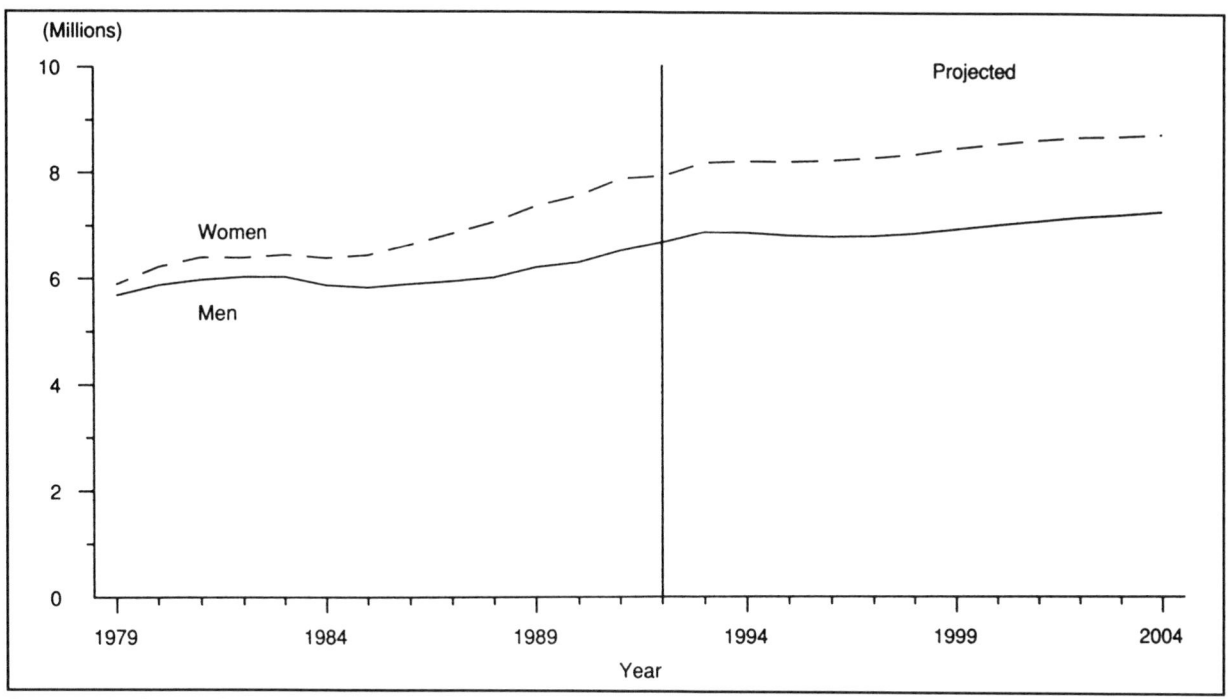

Source: National Center for Education Statistics, *Projections of Education Statistics to 2004*, NCES 93-256, Washington, D.C.: U.S. Government Printing Office, 1993, Figure 12.

D4-5. Years of School Completed by Persons Age 25 and Over, by Sex and Race: 1940 to 1993

Age, year, and sex	All races				White [1]				Black and other races [1]			
	Percent, by years of school completed			Median years of school completed	Percent, by years of school completed			Median years of school completed	Percent, by years of school completed			Median years of school completed
	Less than 5 years of elementary school	4 years of high school or more	4 or more years of college		Less than 5 years of elementary school	4 years of high school or more	4 or more years of college		Less than 5 years of elementary school	4 years of high school or more	4 or more years of college	
1	2	3	4	5	6	7	8	9	10	11	12	13
Males												
25 and over												
April 1940	15.1	22.7	5.5	8.6	12.0	24.2	5.9	8.7	46.2	6.9	1.4	5.4
April 1950	12.2	32.6	7.3	9.0	9.8	34.6	7.9	9.3	36.9	12.6	2.1	6.4
April 1960	9.4	39.5	9.7	10.3	7.4	41.6	10.3	10.6	27.7	20.0	3.5	7.9
March 1970	5.9	55.0	14.1	12.2	4.5	57.2	15.0	12.2	17.9	35.4	6.8	9.9
March 1980	3.6	69.2	20.9	12.6	2.7	71.0	22.1	12.6	10.3	55.3	11.9	12.2
March 1990	2.7	77.7	24.4	12.8	2.2	79.1	25.3	12.8	5.9	69.1	18.3	12.6
March 1991	2.7	78.5	24.3	12.8	2.2	79.8	25.4	12.8	6.0	70.1	17.8	12.6
March 1992	2.3	81.0	24.3	12.9	1.9	82.3	25.2	12.9	4.5	73.0	18.8	12.6
March 1993	2.2	81.8	24.8	12.9	1.8	83.0	25.7	13.0	4.7	74.9	19.0	12.7
Females												
25 and over												
April 1940	12.4	26.3	3.8	8.7	9.8	28.1	4.0	8.8	37.5	8.4	1.2	6.1
April 1950	10.0	36.0	5.2	9.6	8.1	38.2	5.4	10.0	28.6	14.7	2.4	7.2
April 1960	7.4	42.5	5.8	10.7	6.0	44.7	6.0	11.0	19.7	23.1	3.6	8.5
March 1970	4.7	55.4	8.2	12.1	3.9	57.7	8.6	12.2	11.9	36.6	5.6	10.3
March 1980	3.2	68.1	13.6	12.4	2.5	70.1	14.0	12.5	7.6	54.1	10.4	12.1
March 1990	2.2	77.5	18.4	12.7	1.8	79.0	19.0	12.7	5.0	68.4	15.1	12.5
March 1991	2.1	78.3	18.8	12.7	1.8	79.9	19.3	12.7	4.1	69.1	15.8	12.5
March 1992	2.0	80.6	18.6	12.8	1.7	82.0	19.1	12.8	3.8	72.9	15.9	12.6
March 1993	2.0	81.3	19.2	12.8	1.7	82.5	19.7	12.8	3.5	74.5	16.5	12.7

[1]Persons of Hispanic origin are included, as appropriate, in the "white" or in the "black and other races" category.

NOTE: —Data for 1975 and subsequent years are for the noninstitutional population.

SOURCE: U.S. Department of Commerce, Bureau of the Census, U.S. Census of Population, 1960, Vol. 1, part 1; current Population Reports, Series P-20; Series P-19, No. 4; 1960 Census Monograph, "Education of the American Population," by John K. Folger and Charles B. Nam; and unpublished data from the Current Population Survey; and U.S. Department of Labor, Bureau of Labor Statistics, Office of Employment and Unemployment Statistics, "Educational Attainment of Workers, March 1991." (This table was prepared May 1994.)

Source: National Center for Education Statistics, *Digest of Education Statistics, 1994*, NCES 94-115, Washington, D.C.: U.S. Government Printing Office, 1994, Table 8.

D4-6. Educational Attainment of Persons 25 Years Old and Over, by Sex, Race, and Ethnicity: 1960 to 1993

(In percent. For persons 25 years old and over. 1960, 1970 and 1980 as of April 1 and based on sample data from the censuses of population. Other years as of March and based on the Current Population survey.)

YEAR	ALL RACES [1]		WHITE		BLACK		ASIAN AND PACIFIC ISLANDER		HISPANIC [2]	
	Male	Female	Male	Female	Male	Female	Male	Female	Male	Female
COMPLETED 4 YEARS OF HIGH SCHOOL OR MORE										
1960	39.5	42.5	41.6	44.7	18.2	21.8	(NA)	(NA)	(NA)	(NA)
1965	48.0	49.9	50.2	52.2	25.8	28.4	(NA)	(NA)	(NA)	(NA)
1970	51.9	52.8	54.0	55.0	30.1	32.5	(NA)	(NA)	37.9	34.2
1975	63.1	62.1	65.0	64.1	41.6	43.3	(NA)	(NA)	39.5	36.7
1980	67.3	65.8	69.6	68.1	50.8	51.5	(NA)	(NA)	67.3	65.8
1985	74.4	73.5	76.0	75.1	58.4	60.8	(NA)	(NA)	48.5	47.4
1990	77.7	77.5	79.1	79.0	65.8	66.5	84.0	77.2	50.3	51.3
1991	78.5	78.3	79.8	79.9	66.7	66.7	83.8	80.0	51.4	51.2
1992 [3]	79.7	79.2	81.1	80.7	67.0	68.2	(NA)	(NA)	53.7	51.5
1993 [3]	80.5	80.0	81.8	81.3	69.6	71.1	(NA)	(NA)	52.9	53.2
COMPLETED 4 YEARS OF COLLEGE OR MORE										
1960	9.7	5.8	10.3	6.0	2.8	3.3	(NA)	(NA)	(NA)	(NA)
1965	12.0	7.1	12.7	7.3	4.9	4.5	(NA)	(NA)	(NA)	(NA)
1970	13.5	8.1	14.4	8.4	4.2	4.6	(NA)	(NA)	7.8	4.3
1975	17.6	10.6	18.4	11.0	6.7	6.2	(NA)	(NA)	8.3	4.6
1980	20.1	12.8	21.3	13.3	8.4	8.3	(NA)	(NA)	9.4	6.0
1985	23.1	16.0	24.0	16.3	11.2	11.0	(NA)	(NA)	9.7	7.3
1990	24.4	18.4	25.3	19.0	11.9	10.8	44.9	35.4	9.8	8.7
1991	24.3	18.8	25.4	19.3	11.4	11.6	43.2	35.5	10.0	9.4
1992 [3]	24.3	18.6	25.2	19.1	11.9	12.0	(NA)	(NA)	10.2	8.5
1993 [3]	24.8	19.2	25.7	19.7	11.9	12.4	(NA)	(NA)	9.5	8.5

NA Not available.   [1] Includes other races, not shown separately.   [2] Persons of Hispanic origin may be of any race.
[3] Beginning 1992, persons high school graduates and those with a BA degree or higher.

Source: U.S. Bureau of the Census, *U.S. Census of Population, 1960, 1970, and 1980, vol.1;* and *Current Population Reports* P20-459, P20-462, P20-475; and unpublished data.

Source: U.S. Bureau of the Census, *Statistical Abstract of the United States: 1994*, (114th edition), Washington, D.C.: U.S. Government Printing Office, 1994, Table 233.

D4-7. Educational Attainment of Persons 25 Years Old and Over, by Race and Sex: 1980, 1990, and 1994

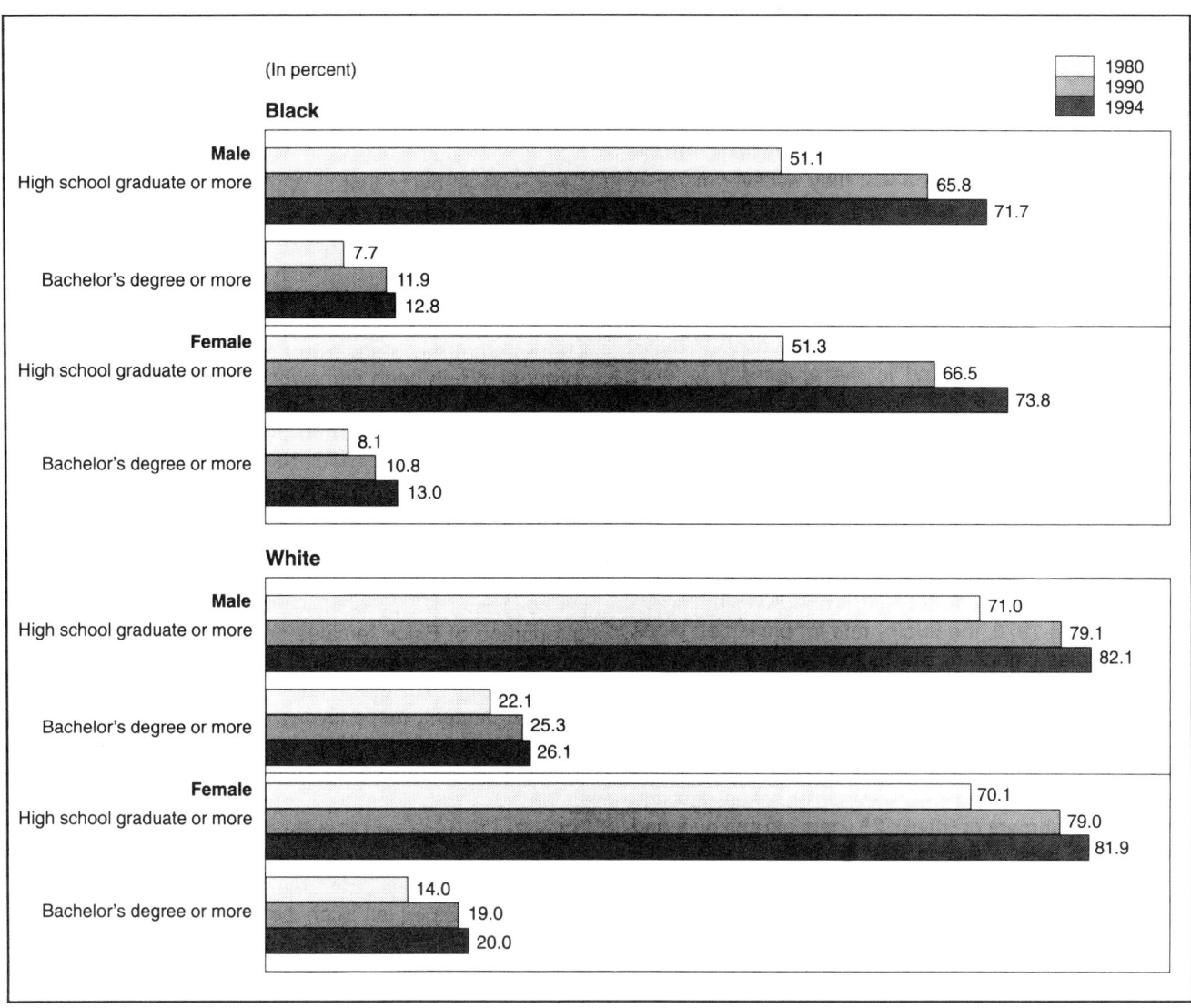

(In percent)

Legend: 1980, 1990, 1994

Black

Male
High school graduate or more
- 51.1
- 65.8
- 71.7

Bachelor's degree or more
- 7.7
- 11.9
- 12.8

Female
High school graduate or more
- 51.3
- 66.5
- 73.8

Bachelor's degree or more
- 8.1
- 10.8
- 13.0

White

Male
High school graduate or more
- 71.0
- 79.1
- 82.1

Bachelor's degree or more
- 22.1
- 25.3
- 26.1

Female
High school graduate or more
- 70.1
- 79.0
- 81.9

Bachelor's degree or more
- 14.0
- 19.0
- 20.0

Source: Claudette E. Bennett, U.S. Bureau of the Census, *The Black Population in the United States: March 1994 and 1993*, Current Population Reports, Series P20-480, Washington, D.C.: U.S. Government Printing Office, January 1995, Figure 2.

D4-8. Highest Level of Education Attained by Persons Age 18 and Over, by Age and Sex: 1993

[In thousands]

Age, sex, and race	Total population [1]	Elementary level		High school			College					
		Less than 7 years	7 or 8 years	1 to 3 years	4 years	Grad-uate	Some college	Associ-ate	Bach-elor's	Master's	First-profes-sional	Doctor-ate
1	2	3	4	5	6	7	8	9	10	11	12	13
Total												
18 and over	187,135	7,199	8,610	18,553	3,063	65,140	35,626	11,471	25,388	8,411	2,247	1,427
18 and 19 years old	6,508	64	95	1,855	654	1,827	1,987	26	—	—	—	—
20 to 24 years old	17,802	271	252	1,744	296	5,724	6,544	1,089	1,769	101	11	2
25 years old and over	162,826	6,864	8,263	14,953	2,113	57,589	27,095	10,356	23,619	8,310	2,236	1,425
25 to 29 years old	19,603	398	327	1,588	290	6,994	3,897	1,471	3,828	580	185	45
30 to 34 years old	22,261	502	378	1,683	331	8,042	4,151	1,843	3,969	942	292	127
35 to 39 years old	21,467	519	342	1,448	191	7,524	4,138	1,856	3,745	1,199	321	185
40 to 49 years old	34,662	900	777	2,194	360	11,592	6,590	2,644	5,748	2,787	656	414
50 to 59 years old	23,434	1,037	1,040	2,362	292	8,847	3,588	1,235	2,837	1,502	380	314
60 to 64 years old	10,529	659	798	1,347	164	4,024	1,284	410	1,095	495	121	132
65 years old and over	30,870	2,849	4,602	4,331	486	10,567	3,446	897	2,396	806	280	209
Men												
18 and over	89,694	3,615	4,062	8,808	1,561	29,523	17,004	5,076	12,922	4,409	1,656	1,060
18 and 19 years old	3,263	38	41	1,071	382	851	857	11	—	—	—	—
20 to 24 years old	8,786	141	144	928	167	2,905	3,227	463	767	40	4	—
25 years old and over	77,644	3,436	3,866	6,809	1,011	25,766	12,920	4,601	12,154	4,368	1,652	1,060
25 to 29 years old	9,767	257	171	786	149	3,565	1,894	657	1,851	294	116	27
30 to 34 years old	11,089	292	197	863	188	4,003	1,945	813	1,971	498	196	88
35 to 39 years old	10,606	249	194	736	111	3,717	1,950	867	1,840	579	243	119
40 to 49 years old	16,987	457	396	1,034	181	5,191	3,235	1,212	3,057	1,448	481	294
50 to 59 years old	11,280	542	590	1,034	135	3,773	1,738	522	1,566	853	283	244
60 to 64 years old	5,084	315	430	631	65	1,663	644	210	636	273	108	109
65 years old and over	12,832	1,324	1,887	1,725	182	3,817	1,515	320	1,234	424	226	177
Women												
18 and over	97,442	3,584	4,548	9,745	1,503	35,618	18,622	6,396	12,466	4,002	591	368
18 and 19 years old	3,244	25	43	784	271	976	1,130	15	—	—	—	—
20 to 24 years old	9,016	130	108	816	129	2,819	3,317	626	1,001	60	7	2
25 years old and over	85,181	3,428	4,398	8,144	1,102	31,823	14,175	5,755	11,465	3,942	584	366
25 to 29 years old	9,836	140	155	802	141	3,429	2,003	814	1,977	287	69	18
30 to 34 years old	11,171	210	181	820	143	4,003	2,207	1,029	1,998	444	96	39
35 to 39 years old	10,861	270	148	712	80	3,807	2,188	989	1,905	620	78	65
40 to 49 years old	17,675	443	381	1,160	179	6,401	3,355	1,432	2,691	1,339	175	120
50 to 59 years old	12,154	495	451	1,328	156	5,073	1,851	713	1,271	649	98	70
60 to 64 years old	5,445	344	368	716	99	2,361	640	199	460	222	14	22
65 years old and over	18,038	1,526	2,714	2,606	303	6,750	1,931	577	1,163	382	54	32

[1] Civilian noninstitutional population.

—Data non applicable or not available.

NOTE: Data are based on a sample survey of the noninstitutional population. Although cells with fewer than 75,000 people are subject to relatively wide sampling variation, they are included in the table to permit various types of aggregations. Because of rounding, details may not add to totals.

SOURCE: U.S. Department of Commerce, Bureau of the Census, Current Population Survey, unpublished data. (This table was prepared May 1994.)

Source: Claudette E. Bennett, U.S. Bureau of the Census, *The Black Population in the United States: March 1994 and 1993*, Current Population Reports, Series P20-480, Washington, D.C.: U.S. Government Printing Office, January 1995, Table 9.

D4-9. Percent of High School Dropouts among Persons 14 to 34 Years Old[1], by Age, Race/Ethnicity, and Sex: October 1970 and October 1993

Year, race/ethnicity, and sex	Total, 14 to 34 years	14 and 15 years	16 and 17 years	18 and 19 years	20 and 21 years	22 to 24 years	25 to 29 years	30 to 34 years
1	2	3	4	5	6	7	8	9
October 1970								
All races	17.0	1.8	8.0	16.2	16.6	18.7	22.5	26.5
Male	16.2	1.7	7.1	16.0	16.1	17.9	21.4	26.2
Female	17.7	1.9	8.9	16.3	16.9	19.4	23.6	26.8
White[2]	15.2	1.7	7.3	14.1	14.6	16.3	19.9	24.6
Male	14.4	1.7	6.3	13.3	14.1	15.3	19.0	24.2
Female	16.0	1.8	8.4	14.8	15.1	17.2	20.7	24.9
Black[2]	30.0	2.4	12.8	31.2	29.6	37.8	44.4	43.5
Male	30.4	2.0	13.3	36.4	29.6	39.5	43.1	45.9
Female	29.5	2.8	12.4	26.6	29.6	36.4	45.6	41.5
October 1993[3]								
All races	10.6	1.1	4.8	11.8	13.4	12.9	12.1	11.8
Male	11.1	1.0	4.0	12.1	13.9	13.5	13.2	12.7
Female	10.1	1.2	5.7	11.5	12.9	12.3	11.1	10.8
White, non-Hispanic	7.3	0.9	3.9	9.5	9.8	8.4	8.2	7.5
Male	7.8	0.7	3.1	10.1	9.7	9.4	8.7	8.5
Female	6.8	1.1	4.7	8.7	9.9	7.4	7.6	6.6
Black, non-Hispanic	12.5	1.2	4.5	12.8	19.0	17.0	13.3	14.8
Male	12.1	1.0	3.5	10.5	22.8	14.7	15.0	13.7
Female	12.9	1.4	5.5	15.2	15.8	19.1	11.9	15.7
Hispanic origin	30.7	2.4	9.9	28.3	29.0	37.8	38.5	38.9
Male	32.0	3.1	8.4	32.2	28.9	39.8	40.8	39.3
Female	29.3	1.8	11.8	25.0	29.0	35.8	35.8	38.5

[1] "Status" dropouts.

[2] Includes persons of Hispanic origin.

[3] Because of changes in data collection procedures, data may not be comparable with figures for earlier years.

NOTE.—"Status" dropouts are persons who are not enrolled in school and who are not high school graduates. People who have received GED credentials are counted as graduates. Data are based upon sample surveys of the civilian noninstitutional population.

SOURCE: U.S. Department of Commerce, Bureau of the Census, Current Population Survey, and unpublished data. (This table was prepared May 1994.)

Source: National Center for Education Statistics, *Digest of Education Statistics, 1994*, NCES 94-115, Washington, D.C.: U.S. Government Printing Office, 1994, Table 103.

D4-10. Educational Attainment in Urban and Rural Areas, by Sex: 1990

Data based on sample and subject to sampling variability.

United States Urban and Rural and Size of Place	United States	Urban Total	Inside urbanized area Total	Inside urbanized area Central place	Inside urbanized area Urban fringe	Outside urbanized area Place of 10,000 or more	Outside urbanized area Place of 2,500 to 9,999	Rural Total	Rural Place of 1,000 to 2,499	Rural Place of less than 1,000	Rural farm
EDUCATIONAL ATTAINMENT											
Persons 18 to 24 years	26 234 893	20 954 809	17 571 449	9 695 915	7 875 534	1 865 573	1 517 787	5 280 084	611 644	305 481	274 045
High school graduate (includes equivalency)	8 126 562	6 109 449	5 068 121	2 649 480	2 418 641	517 973	523 355	2 017 113	229 403	124 889	97 977
Some college or associate degree	9 941 932	8 373 415	6 934 074	3 849 581	3 084 493	889 811	549 530	1 568 517	190 230	83 580	92 246
Bachelor's degree or higher	1 991 840	1 784 910	1 607 497	853 109	754 388	109 225	68 188	206 930	24 647	10 276	12 922
Persons 25 years and over	158 868 436	119 363 595	101 451 903	49 688 973	51 762 930	8 423 834	9 487 858	39 504 841	4 556 715	2 456 759	2 625 244
Less than 5th grade	4 271 677	3 265 734	2 712 701	1 822 085	890 616	254 167	298 866	1 005 943	129 959	64 162	47 412
5th to 8th grade	12 230 534	8 183 431	6 451 767	3 824 924	2 626 843	756 395	975 269	4 047 103	512 725	319 031	306 877
9th to 12th grade, no diploma	22 841 507	16 519 925	13 759 857	7 731 145	6 028 712	1 262 147	1 497 921	6 321 582	723 002	412 385	336 954
High school graduate (includes equivalency)	47 642 763	33 535 142	27 804 320	13 096 880	14 707 440	2 577 409	3 153 413	14 107 621	1 610 472	934 727	1 025 554
Some college, no degree	29 779 777	23 358 570	20 133 324	9 458 681	10 674 643	1 580 729	1 644 517	6 421 207	736 764	360 787	415 523
Associate degree, occupational program	5 233 002	3 872 448	3 279 108	1 494 940	1 784 168	281 883	311 457	1 360 554	152 564	82 271	97 319
Associate degree, academic program	4 558 923	3 673 128	3 227 151	1 394 130	1 833 021	221 935	224 042	885 795	96 361	39 603	50 327
Bachelor's degree	20 832 567	17 299 746	15 437 802	6 854 942	8 582 860	956 019	905 925	3 532 821	394 282	165 689	242 404
Master's degree	7 520 469	6 270 053	5 596 862	2 530 595	3 066 267	350 246	322 945	1 250 416	138 992	56 195	71 938
Professional school degree	2 751 791	2 348 208	2 121 866	1 017 679	1 104 187	113 469	112 873	403 583	46 519	17 145	22 543
Doctorate degree	1 205 426	1 037 210	927 145	462 972	464 173	69 435	40 630	168 216	15 075	4 764	8 393
Females 25 years and over	83 654 171	63 517 937	53 816 395	26 559 578	27 256 817	4 547 388	5 154 154	20 136 234	2 464 142	1 314 016	1 284 435
Less than 5th grade	2 161 459	1 737 940	1 459 452	979 528	479 924	128 643	149 845	423 519	62 914	29 231	17 604
5th to 8th grade	6 546 831	4 597 279	3 616 801	2 148 326	1 468 475	428 016	552 462	1 949 552	282 319	166 886	124 974
9th to 12th grade, no diploma	12 360 377	9 118 618	7 556 672	4 268 968	3 287 704	715 759	846 187	3 241 759	402 077	224 366	164 142
High school graduate (includes equivalency)	26 850 606	19 341 708	16 087 048	7 478 461	8 608 587	1 467 617	1 787 043	7 508 898	899 486	507 793	509 283
Some college, no degree	15 520 115	12 250 265	10 543 654	4 986 943	5 556 711	837 658	868 953	3 269 850	392 641	194 366	215 423
Associate degree, occupational program	2 920 672	2 173 205	1 835 633	838 678	996 955	161 050	176 522	747 467	86 441	46 111	53 692
Associate degree, academic program	2 538 505	2 038 632	1 788 237	771 109	1 017 128	123 427	126 968	499 873	56 063	23 840	30 357
Bachelor's degree	10 015 766	8 303 050	7 388 520	3 373 280	4 015 240	467 173	447 357	1 712 716	197 223	87 948	120 915
Master's degree	3 581 055	2 979 413	2 654 556	1 263 356	1 391 200	170 251	154 606	601 642	65 269	25 680	37 620
Professional school degree	857 999	713 784	644 827	320 252	324 575	33 339	35 618	144 215	16 407	6 684	8 562
Doctorate degree	300 786	264 043	245 995	130 677	110 318	14 455	8 593	36 743	3 302	1 111	1 863
Persons 25 years and over	158 868 436	119 363 595	101 451 903	49 688 973	51 762 930	8 423 834	9 487 858	39 504 841	4 556 715	2 456 759	2 625 244
Percent:											
Less than 5th grade	2.7	2.7	2.7	3.7	1.7	3.0	3.1	2.5	2.9	2.6	1.8
High school graduate or higher	75.2	76.6	77.4	73.1	81.6	73.0	70.8	71.2	70.0	67.6	73.7
Male	75.7	77.6	78.4	74.1	82.4	74.2	71.8	70.3	70.4	67.2	71.3
Female	74.8	75.7	76.5	72.2	80.8	72.0	70.0	72.1	69.7	68.0	76.1
Some college or higher	45.2	48.5	50.0	46.7	53.1	42.4	37.5	35.5	34.7	29.6	34.6
Bachelor's degree or higher	20.3	22.6	23.7	21.9	25.5	17.7	14.6	13.6	13.1	9.9	13.2
Male	23.3	26.3	27.6	25.0	30.1	20.7	17.0	14.8	14.9	10.7	13.2
Female	17.6	19.3	20.3	19.2	21.4	15.1	12.5	12.4	11.5	9.2	13.2
Males 25 to 34 years	21 709 473	16 921 715	14 656 657	7 514 640	7 142 017	1 119 287	1 145 771	4 787 758	514 655	274 716	226 888
Percent:											
High school graduate or higher	82.7	83.6	84.0	80.7	87.5	82.0	80.5	79.5	80.9	80.6	85.1
Bachelor's degree or higher	22.9	25.9	27.3	25.7	29.0	18.9	14.8	12.2	12.9	9.7	11.8
Females 25 to 34 years	21 757 561	16 993 292	14 701 583	7 487 177	7 214 406	1 113 125	1 178 584	4 764 269	537 535	280 456	208 953
Percent:											
High school graduate or higher	85.5	85.8	86.1	82.6	89.7	84.3	83.2	84.4	84.0	83.8	87.5
Bachelor's degree or higher	22.6	25.0	26.3	25.1	27.6	17.9	14.6	14.1	13.4	10.8	15.9

Source: U.S. Bureau of the Census, *Social and Economic Characteristics of the United States: 1990 Census of Population,* CP-2-1, Washington, D.C.: U.S. Government Printing Office, 1993, Table 17.

D4-11. Average Time Spent Earning Advanced Degrees, by Sex: Spring 1990

(Numbers in thousands)

| | Years from end of Bachelor's to: | | | | | | | | |
| | Doctorate | | | Professional | | | Master's | | |
	Total	Mean	Standard error	Total	Mean	Standard error	Total	Mean	Standard error
Both sexes	1056	8.97	0.49	2054	5.07	0.32	7599	6.47	0.19
Male	833	8.36	0.54	1547	5.23	0.36	3996	5.78	0.23
Female.........................	223	11.24	1.09	506	4.61	0.67	3603	7.24	0.30

Source: Robert Kominski and Rebecca Sutterlin, *What's It Worth? Educational Background and Economic Status: Spring 1990,* Current Population Reports, P70-32, Washington, D.C.: U.S. Government Printing Office, December 1992, Table C.

D4-12. Bachelor's Degrees, by Sex of Recipient: 1978–79 to 2003–2004 (Middle Alternative Projections)

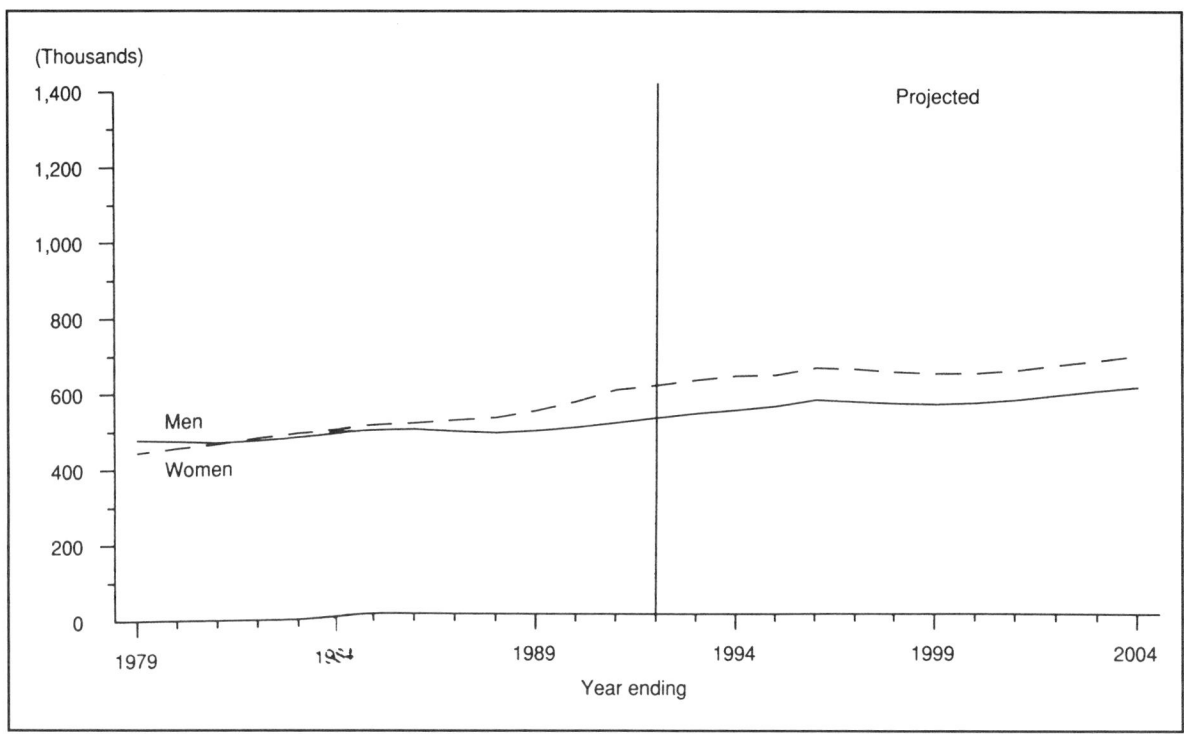

Source: National Center for Education Statistics, *Projections of Education Statistics to 2004,* NCES 93-256 Washington, D.C.: U.S. Government Printing Office, 1993, Figure 36.

D4-13. Doctor's Degrees, by Sex of Recipient: 1978–79 to 2003–04 (Middle Alternative Projections)

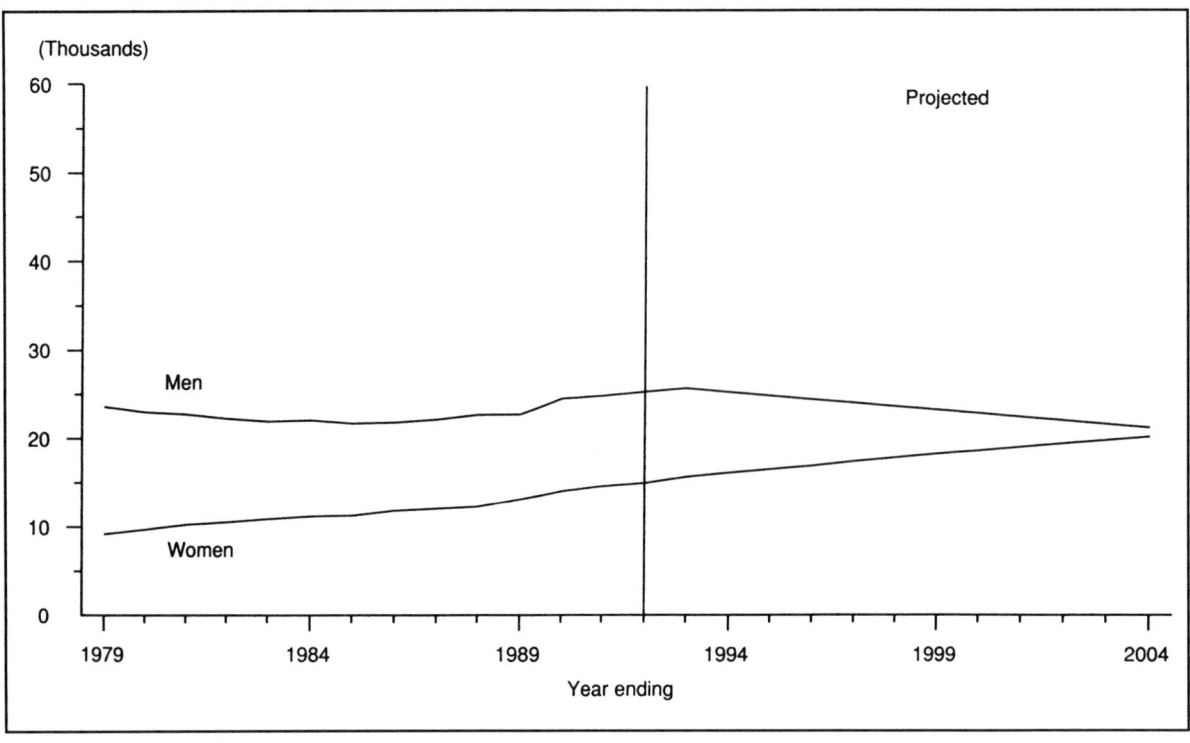

Source: National Center for Education Statistics, *Projections of Education Statistics to 2004*, NCES 93-256, Washington, D.C.: U.S. Government Printing Office, 1993, Figure 40.

D4-14. Earned Degrees Conferred by Institutions of Higher Education, by Level of Degree and Sex of Student: 1869–70 to 2004–05

Year	Associate degrees			Bachelor's degrees			Master's degrees			First-professional degrees			Doctor's degrees		
	Total	Men	Women	Total	Men	Women	Total	Men	Women	Total	Men	Women	Total	Men	Women
1869–70	—	—	—	[1]9,371	[1]7,993	[1]1,378	0	0	0	(2)	(2)	(2)	1	1	0
1879–80	—	—	—	[1]12,896	[1]10,411	[1]2,485	879	868	11	(2)	(2)	(2)	54	51	3
1889–90	—	—	—	[1]15,539	[1]12,857	[1]2,682	1,015	821	194	(2)	(2)	(2)	149	147	2
1899–1900	- -	—	—	[1]27,410	[1]22,173	[1]5,237	1,583	1,280	303	(2)	(2)	(2)	382	359	23
1909–10	—	—	—	[1]37,199	[1]28,762	[1]8,437	2,113	1,555	558	(2)	(2)	(2)	443	399	44
1919–20	—	—	—	[1]48,622	[1]31,980	[1]16,642	4,279	2,985	1,294	(2)	(2)	(2)	615	522	93
1929–30	—	—	—	[1]122,484	[1]73,615	[1]48,869	14,969	8,925	6,044	(2)	(2)	(2)	2,299	1,946	353
1939–40	—	—	—	[1]186,500	[1]109,546	[1]76,954	26,731	16,508	10,223	(2)	(2)	(2)	3,290	2,861	429
1949–50	—	—	—	[1]432,058	[1]328,841	[1]103,217	58,183	41,220	16,963	(2)	(2)	(2)	6,420	5,804	616
1959–60	—	—	—	[1]392,440	[1]254,063	[1]138,377	74,435	50,898	23,537	(2)	(2)	(2)	9,829	8,801	1,028
1960–61	—	—	—	365,174	224,538	140,636	84,609	57,830	26,779	25,253	24,577	676	10,575	9,463	1,112
1961–62	—	—	—	383,961	230,456	153,505	91,418	62,603	28,815	25,607	24,836	771	11,622	10,377	1,245
1962–63	—	—	—	411,420	241,309	170,111	98,684	67,302	31,382	26,590	25,753	837	12,822	11,448	1,374
1963–64	—	—	—	461,266	265,349	195,917	109,183	73,850	35,333	27,209	26,357	852	14,490	12,955	1,535
1964–65	—	—	—	493,757	282,173	211,584	121,167	81,319	39,848	28,290	27,283	1,007	16,467	14,692	1,775
1965–66	111,607	63,779	47,828	520,115	299,287	220,828	140,602	93,081	47,521	30,124	28,982	1,142	18,237	16,121	2,116
1966–67	139,183	78,356	60,827	558,534	322,711	235,823	157,726	103,109	54,617	31,695	30,401	1,294	20,617	18,163	2,454
1967–68	159,441	90,317	69,124	632,289	357,682	274,607	176,749	113,552	63,197	33,939	32,402	1,537	23,089	20,183	2,906
1968–69	183,279	105,661	77,618	728,845	410,595	318,250	193,756	121,531	72,225	35,114	33,595	1,519	26,158	22,722	3,436
1969–70	206,023	117,432	88,591	792,317	451,097	341,220	208,291	125,624	82,667	34,578	32,794	1,784	29,912	25,890	4,022
1970–71	252,610	144,395	108,215	839,730	475,594	364,136	230,509	138,146	92,363	37,946	35,544	2,402	32,107	27,530	4,577
1971–72	292,119	166,317	125,802	887,273	500,590	386,683	251,633	149,550	102,083	43,411	40,723	2,688	33,363	28,090	5,273
1972–73	316,174	175,413	140,761	922,362	518,191	404,171	263,371	154,468	108,903	50,018	46,489	3,529	34,777	28,571	6,206
1973–74	343,924	188,591	155,333	945,776	527,313	418,463	277,033	157,842	119,191	53,816	48,530	5,286	33,816	27,365	6,451
1974–75	360,171	191,017	169,154	922,933	504,841	418,092	292,450	161,570	130,880	55,916	48,956	6,960	34,083	26,817	7,266
1975–76	391,454	209,996	181,458	925,746	504,925	420,821	311,771	167,248	144,523	62,649	52,892	9,757	34,064	26,267	7,797
1976–77	406,377	210,842	195,535	919,549	495,545	424,004	317,164	167,783	149,381	64,359	52,374	11,985	33,232	25,142	8,090
1977–78	412,246	204,718	207,528	921,204	487,347	433,857	311,620	161,212	150,408	66,581	52,270	14,311	32,131	23,658	8,473
1978–79	402,702	192,091	210,611	921,390	477,344	444,046	301,079	153,370	147,709	68,848	52,652	16,196	32,730	23,541	9,189
1979–80	400,910	183,737	217,173	929,417	473,611	455,806	298,081	150,749	147,332	70,131	52,716	17,415	32,615	22,943	9,672
1980–81	416,377	188,638	227,739	935,140	469,883	465,257	295,739	147,043	148,696	71,956	52,792	19,164	32,958	22,711	10,247
1981–82	434,515	196,939	237,576	952,998	473,364	479,634	295,546	145,532	150,014	72,032	52,223	19,809	32,707	22,224	10,483
1982–83	456,441	207,141	249,300	969,510	479,140	490,370	289,921	144,697	145,224	73,136	51,310	21,826	32,775	21,902	10,873
1983–84	452,416	202,762	249,654	974,309	482,319	491,990	284,263	143,595	140,668	74,407	51,334	23,073	33,209	22,064	11,145
1984–85	454,712	202,932	251,780	979,477	482,528	496,949	286,251	143,390	142,861	75,063	50,455	24,608	32,943	21,700	11,243
1985–86	446,047	196,166	249,881	987,823	485,923	501,900	288,567	143,508	145,059	73,910	49,261	24,649	33,653	21,819	11,834
1986–87[3]	436,308	190,842	245,466	991,264	480,782	510,482	289,349	141,269	148,080	71,617	46,523	25,094	34,041	22,061	11,980
1987–88	435,085	190,047	245,038	994,829	477,203	517,626	299,317	145,163	154,154	70,735	45,484	25,251	34,870	22,615	12,255
1988–89	436,764	186,316	250,448	1,018,755	483,346	535,409	310,621	149,354	161,267	70,856	45,046	25,810	35,720	22,648	13,072
1989–90	455,102	191,195	263,907	1,051,344	491,696	559,648	324,301	153,653	170,648	70,988	43,961	27,027	38,371	24,401	13,970
1990–91	481,720	198,634	283,086	1,094,538	504,045	590,493	337,168	156,482	180,686	71,948	43,846	28,102	39,294	24,756	14,538
1991–92	504,231	207,481	296,750	1,136,553	520,811	615,742	352,838	161,842	190,996	74,146	45,071	29,075	40,659	25,557	15,102
1992–93[4]	497,000	207,000	290,000	1,145,000	529,000	616,000	364,000	170,000	194,000	73,900	43,900	30,000	41,200	25,600	15,600
1993–94[4]	504,000	210,000	294,000	1,165,000	537,000	628,000	370,000	176,000	194,000	74,700	44,000	30,700	41,300	25,200	16,100
1994–95[4]	518,000	216,000	302,000	1,178,000	548,000	630,000	377,000	182,000	195,000	75,100	44,100	31,000	41,300	24,800	16,500
1995–96[4]	518,000	215,000	303,000	1,214,000	565,000	649,000	383,000	188,000	195,000	75,300	44,200	31,100	41,300	24,400	16,900
1996–97[4]	516,000	214,000	302,000	1,206,000	560,000	646,000	389,000	194,000	195,000	74,700	44,100	30,600	41,400	24,000	17,400
1997–98[4]	517,000	214,000	303,000	1,194,000	556,000	638,000	383,000	188,000	195,000	74,300	44,000	30,300	41,400	23,600	17,800
1998–99[4]	522,000	216,000	306,000	1,187,000	553,000	634,000	378,000	182,000	196,000	74,000	43,900	30,100	41,400	23,200	18,200
1999–2000[4]	528,000	219,000	309,000	1,190,000	556,000	634,000	371,000	176,000	195,000	73,900	43,800	30,100	41,400	22,800	18,600
2000–01[4]	538,000	223,000	315,000	1,203,000	563,000	640,000	364,000	170,000	194,000	73,800	43,700	30,100	41,400	22,400	19,000
2001–02[4]	547,000	227,000	320,000	1,229,000	575,000	654,000	364,000	170,000	194,000	73,700	43,600	30,100	41,400	22,000	19,400
2002–03[4]	554,000	230,000	324,000	1,254,000	587,000	667,000	363,000	170,000	193,000	73,800	43,500	30,300	41,400	21,600	19,800
2003–04[4]	554,000	230,000	324,000	1,254,000	587,000	667,000	363,000	170,000	193,000	73,800	43,500	30,300	41,400	21,600	19,800
2004–05[4]	554,000	230,000	324,000	1,254,000	587,000	667,000	363,000	170,000	193,000	73,800	43,500	30,300	41,400	21,600	19,800

[1] Includes first-professional degrees.

[2] First-professional degrees are included with bachelor's degrees.

[3] Revised from previously published data.

[4] Projected.

—Data not available.

NOTE.—Some data have been revised from previously published figures. Because of rounding, details may not add to totals.

SOURCE: U.S. Department of Education, National Center for Education Statistics, *Earned Degrees Conferred; Projections of Education Statistics to 2004*; and Integrated Postsecondary Education Data System (IPEDS), "Completions" surveys. (This table was prepared August 1994.)

Source: National Center for Education Statistics, *Projections of Education Statistics to 2004*, NCES 93-256, Washington, D.C.: U.S. Government Printing Office, 1993, Table 234.

D4-15. Educational Attainment of Husband, by Educational Attainment of Wife for Married Couples, by Age of Husband, Race, and Hispanic Origin: March 1993

[In thousands. Noninstitutional population]

Education of husband, age, race, and Hispanic origin	All wives	Not high school graduate — Total	Elementary — None-4th grade	Elementary — 5th-8th grade	High School — 9th-11th grade	High school graduate or more — Total	High school graduate only	Some college no degree	Associate degree	Bachelor's degree	Advanced degree
ALL RACES											
18 Years and Over											
All husbands	54 198	8 476	666	2 766	5 044	45 722	21 525	9 310	3 960	7 816	3 111
Not high school graduate	9 852	5 548	597	2 179	2 772	4 304	3 270	638	229	135	33
Elementary: None to 4th grade	881	756	359	275	123	125	99	10	10	5	–
5th to 8th grade	3 828	2 479	171	1 471	837	1 350	1 045	194	61	38	12
High school: 9th to 11th grade	5 142	2 312	67	434	1 812	2 830	2 126	433	158	92	21
High school graduate	44 346	2 928	69	587	2 272	41 418	18 255	8 672	3 731	7 681	3 079
High School Graduate Only	18 054	2 056	39	437	1 580	15 998	11 311	2 512	1 016	938	221
College: Some, no degree	9 127	508	10	83	416	8 619	3 400	3 249	675	1 007	288
Associate degree	3 271	179	3	33	144	3 092	1 159	634	733	420	146
Bachelor's degree	8 491	147	14	26	107	8 344	1 711	1 548	812	3 432	840
Advanced degree	5 403	38	3	8	26	5 365	675	729	494	1 884	1 583
18 to 24 Years											
All husbands	1 567	316	8	62	246	1 251	684	341	110	108	7
Not high school graduate	361	211	8	48	155	150	124	18	8	–	–
Elementary: None to 4th grade	12	11	5	5	1	1	1	–	–	–	–
5th to 8th grade	63	46	–	22	24	17	15	3	–	–	–
High school: 9th to 11th grade	286	154	3	21	130	132	108	16	8	–	–
High school graduate	1 206	105	–	14	91	1 102	560	323	102	108	7
High School Graduate Only	672	79	–	11	68	593	416	115	39	21	2
College: Some, no degree	345	24	–	3	21	321	96	164	32	29	1
Associate degree	86	–	–	–	–	86	36	17	24	9	–
Bachelor's degree	100	2	–	–	2	98	12	28	8	49	1
Advanced degree	4	–	–	–	–	4	–	–	–	1	3
25 to 34 Years											
All husbands	10 861	1 238	68	298	872	9 623	3 940	2 157	956	2 065	505
Not high school graduate	1 326	678	59	230	389	648	458	127	36	22	6
Elementary: None to 4th grade	85	75	37	24	14	10	8	1	1	–	–
5th to 8th grade	306	213	11	143	60	93	61	20	5	4	3
High school: 9th to 11th grade	935	389	12	63	315	545	388	105	30	18	3
High school graduate	9 535	560	8	68	483	8 975	3 482	2 030	921	2 043	499
High School Graduate Only	4 007	407	7	49	350	3 601	2 317	694	281	282	27
College: Some, no degree	2 041	83	–	9	73	1 958	625	767	199	287	80
Associate degree	799	55	2	8	45	744	231	151	211	126	24
Bachelor's degree	1 970	13	–	2	11	1 958	258	322	175	1 052	151
Advanced degree	718	3	–	–	3	714	52	95	54	295	218
35 to 44 Years											
All husbands	13 649	1 278	102	342	834	12 371	4 917	2 724	1 298	2 459	972
Not high school graduate	1 351	719	89	256	374	631	435	120	54	17	5
Elementary: None to 4th grade	109	100	53	37	10	9	7	2	–	–	–
5th to 8th grade	388	252	22	151	79	136	97	25	11	2	1
High school: 9th to 11th grade	855	368	14	68	285	487	331	94	43	15	4
High school graduate	12 298	558	13	85	460	11 740	4 482	2 604	1 244	2 442	967
High School Graduate Only	4 309	377	2	57	319	3 932	2 669	684	280	243	56
College: Some, no degree	2 595	107	2	16	89	2 488	852	1 032	234	287	83
Associate degree	1 118	41	–	7	34	1 077	333	238	273	171	61
Bachelor's degree	2 709	30	9	4	16	2 679	506	480	313	1 115	266
Advanced degree	1 567	3	–	1	2	1 564	122	171	144	627	501
45 to 54 Years											
All husbands	10 670	1 315	132	374	809	9 354	4 248	1 831	777	1 620	879
Not high school graduate	1 430	773	116	256	401	657	503	97	24	28	4
Elementary: None to 4th grade	139	118	75	24	20	20	15	–	4	2	–
5th to 8th grade	494	311	34	168	109	183	134	30	5	11	2
High school: 9th to 11th grade	798	344	8	64	273	454	354	67	15	15	2
High school graduate	9 240	542	16	117	409	8 698	3 744	1 734	753	1 591	875
High School Graduate Only	3 456	361	11	79	272	3 094	2 197	461	175	197	64
College: Some, no degree	1 865	104	3	19	82	1 760	745	623	106	226	61
Associate degree	683	34	–	11	23	649	276	138	115	72	48
Bachelor's degree	1 668	36	–	9	28	1 631	335	291	184	598	223
Advanced degree	1 569	6	2	–	4	1 562	190	221	173	499	479
55 to 64 Years											
All husbands	7 884	1 455	137	407	911	6 429	3 618	1 153	427	789	443
Not high school graduate	1 852	961	125	308	528	891	707	105	56	20	3
Elementary: None to 4th grade	171	146	76	42	29	24	16	3	3	2	–
5th to 8th grade	768	462	44	228	190	306	250	34	15	5	1
High school: 9th to 11th grade	913	352	5	38	309	561	441	68	37	12	2
High school graduate	6 033	495	12	99	383	5 538	2 911	1 048	371	769	439
High School Graduate Only	2 662	366	6	82	278	2 296	1 791	290	114	65	36
College: Some, no degree	1 084	74	3	10	61	1 010	506	323	57	91	33
Associate degree	334	25	1	3	21	309	176	42	61	19	11
Bachelor's degree	1 069	20	2	2	16	1 049	285	256	71	322	115
Advanced degree	883	10	–	2	8	874	153	137	69	270	245

See footnote at end of table.

D4-15. Educational Attainment of Husband, by Educational Attainment of Wife for Married Couples, by Age of Husband, Race, and Hispanic Origin: March 1993 (continued)

[In thousands. Noninstitutional population]

Education of husband, age, race, and Hispanic origin	All wives	Education of wife									
		Not high school graduate				High school graduate or more					
		Total	Elementary		High School	Total	High school graduate only	College			
			None–4th grade	5th–8th grade	9th–11th grade			Some college no degree	Associate degree	Bachelor's degree	Advanced degree
ALL RACES—Con.											
65 Years and Over											
All husbands	9 568	2 874	219	1 284	1 371	6 694	4 118	1 104	392	775	305
Not high school graduate	3 533	2 206	199	1 081	925	1 327	1 042	171	52	48	14
Elementary: None to 4th grade	366	306	114	142	50	60	52	5	2	1	–
5th to 8th grade	1 810	1 195	61	759	375	615	487	82	24	16	5
High school: 9th to 11th grade	1 357	705	24	180	501	652	503	83	25	31	9
High school graduate	6 035	668	20	203	446	5 366	3 076	933	340	727	291
High School Graduate Only	2 948	466	14	159	294	2 482	1 921	268	128	129	36
College: Some, no degree	1 198	116	2	26	89	1 082	576	340	48	87	30
Associate degree	251	24	–	3	21	227	105	49	48	22	2
Bachelor's degree	976	47	3	10	34	929	316	172	61	296	84
Advanced degree	661	15	1	5	9	646	158	105	55	192	138
WHITE											
18 Years and Over											
All husbands	48 385	7 303	526	2 408	4 369	41 082	19 504	8 261	3 555	6 981	2 782
Not high school graduate	8 442	4 707	472	1 876	2 358	3 736	2 880	514	201	111	30
Elementary: None to 4th grade	664	577	291	216	70	87	67	10	8	3	–
5th to 8th grade	3 348	2 148	135	1 284	730	1 200	935	168	57	28	12
High school: 9th to 11th grade	4 430	1 982	46	377	1 559	2 448	1 878	336	136	80	18
High school graduate	39 942	2 596	54	532	2 011	37 346	16 623	7 747	3 354	6 870	2 752
High School Graduate Only	16 183	1 824	36	394	1 394	14 359	10 223	2 221	908	813	194
College: Some, no degree	8 237	457	8	78	370	7 781	3 147	2 856	606	907	265
Associate degree	2 934	162	3	29	130	2 772	1 055	563	650	373	131
Bachelor's degree	7 695	121	6	23	92	7 574	1 569	1 431	755	3 035	784
Advanced degree	4 894	33	1	8	24	4 861	631	675	436	1 742	1 377
BLACK											
18 Years and Over											
All husbands	3 865	794	41	232	520	3 071	1 455	805	261	390	159
Not high school graduate	1 065	581	40	214	327	484	334	104	22	20	3
Elementary: None to 4th grade	151	120	20	53	47	32	29	1	–	2	–
5th to 8th grade	348	224	11	128	86	124	92	21	2	9	–
High school: 9th to 11th grade	565	237	10	33	195	328	213	83	20	9	3
High school graduate	2 800	213	1	18	193	2 587	1 121	701	239	370	157
High School Graduate Only	1 415	167	–	16	152	1 247	798	246	86	97	20
College: Some, no degree	661	34	–	3	31	627	183	307	47	70	20
Associate degree	215	5	–	–	5	210	73	51	47	27	12
Bachelor's degree	336	4	–	–	4	332	61	71	30	139	31
Advanced degree	174	3	1	–	2	171	6	26	29	36	73
HISPANIC ORIGIN[1]											
18 Years and Over											
All husbands	3 965	1 801	368	787	646	2 163	1 211	489	165	214	84
Not high school graduate	1 856	1 436	347	649	440	420	310	77	16	13	4
Elementary: None to 4th grade	419	382	234	113	34	38	29	4	2	2	–
5th to 8th grade	764	619	85	418	116	145	96	36	6	5	3
High school: 9th to 11th grade	673	435	28	117	290	237	184	37	8	7	1
High school graduate	2 109	365	21	138	206	1 743	901	412	148	201	80
High School Graduate Only	1 040	240	15	86	139	800	586	131	33	43	7
College: Some, no degree	534	79	3	29	47	455	171	188	44	39	12
Associate degree	159	24	1	11	11	136	57	29	36	11	2
Bachelor's degree	247	18	1	12	6	229	70	43	18	74	26
Advanced degree	128	5	1	1	3	123	17	21	18	33	34

[1]Persons of Hispanic origin may be of any race.

Source: Robert Kominski and Andrea Adams, U.S. Bureau of the Census, *Educational Attainment in the United States: March 1993 and 1992.* Current Population Reports, P20-476, Washington, D.C.: U.S. Government Printing Office, 1994, Table 5.

D5. EDUCATIONAL FIELDS OF STUDY

D5-1. Earned Degrees Conferred, by Field of Study and Level of Degree: 1971 to 1990

LEVEL AND FIELD OF STUDY	1971	1980	1985	1988	1989	1990	PERCENT FEMALE 1971	PERCENT FEMALE 1990
Bachelor's, total	839,730	929,417	979,477	994,829	1,018,755	1,049,657	43.4	53.2
Agriculture and natural resources	12,672	22,802	18,107	14,222	13,492	13,070	4.2	31.5
Architecture and environmental design	5,570	9,132	9,325	8,603	9,150	9,261	11.9	39.1
Area and ethnic studies	2,582	2,840	2,867	3,453	3,945	4,399	52.4	60.0
Business and management	114,865	185,361	233,351	243,725	247,175	249,081	9.1	46.7
Communications [1]	10,802	28,616	42,083	46,726	48,645	51,283	35.3	60.6
Computer and information sciences	2,388	11,154	38,878	34,523	30,454	27,434	13.6	30.1
Education	176,614	118,169	88,161	91,287	97,082	104,715	74.5	78.1
Engineering [1]	50,046	68,893	96,105	88,706	85,225	82,110	0.8	13.8
Foreign languages	19,945	11,133	9,954	10,045	10,780	11,326	74.6	73.4
Health sciences	25,190	63,607	64,513	60,754	59,138	58,816	77.1	84.3
Home economics	11,167	18,411	15,555	14,855	14,715	14,987	97.3	90.1
Law	545	683	1,157	1,303	1,976	1,582	5.0	67.8
Letters	64,933	33,497	34,091	39,551	43,387	48,075	65.5	67.0
Liberal/general studies	5,461	20,069	19,191	21,790	23,498	24,956	29.0	58.3
Library and archival sciences	1,013	398	202	123	122	84	92.0	81.0
Life sciences	35,743	46,370	38,445	36,755	36,059	37,170	29.1	50.7
Mathematics	24,801	11,378	15,146	15,904	15,218	14,597	38.0	46.5
Military sciences	357	251	299	350	419	417	0.3	7.9
Multi/interdisciplinary studies	8,306	14,404	15,727	17,353	18,215	19,188	28.4	54.4
Parks and recreation	1,621	5,753	4,593	4,078	4,183	4,404	34.7	55.9
Philosophy, religion, and theology	11,890	13,276	12,439	11,526	11,742	12,010	25.5	30.9
Physical sciences	21,412	23,410	23,732	17,806	17,186	16,131	13.8	31.2
Psychology	37,880	41,962	39,811	45,003	48,737	53,586	44.5	71.5
Protective services	2,045	15,015	12,510	13,367	14,698	15,387	9.2	37.8
Public affairs	6,252	18,422	13,838	14,294	15,270	16,241	60.2	67.3
Social sciences [2]	155,236	103,519	91,461	100,288	107,914	116,925	36.8	44.2
Visual and performing arts	30,394	40,892	37,936	36,638	37,925	39,695	59.7	61.4
Unclassified	-	-	-	1,801	2,405	2,727		49.1
Master's, total	230,509	298,081	286,251	299,317	310,621	323,844	40.1	52.6
Agriculture and natural resources	2,457	3,976	3,928	3,479	3,245	3,373	5.9	33.4
Architecture and environmental design	1,705	3,139	3,275	3,159	3,383	3,492	13.8	36.4
Area and ethnic studies	1,032	852	879	903	1,004	1,198	38.3	45.2
Business and management	26,481	55,006	67,527	69,655	73,521	77,203	3.9	34.0
Communications [1]	1,856	3,082	3,669	3,925	4,257	4,369	34.6	60.8
Computer and information sciences	1,588	3,647	7,101	9,197	9,414	9,643	10.3	27.7
Education	88,952	103,951	76,137	77,867	82,533	86,057	56.2	75.8
Engineering [1]	16,443	16,243	21,557	23,388	24,572	24,848	1.1	13.8
Foreign languages	4,755	2,236	1,724	1,844	1,898	1,995	65.5	68.6
Health sciences	5,445	15,068	17,383	18,665	19,293	20,354	55.9	77.7
Home economics	1,452	2,690	2,383	2,053	2,166	2,153	93.9	85.6
Law	955	1,817	1,796	1,880	2,013	1,869	4.8	29.9
Letters	11,148	6,807	5,934	6,194	6,676	7,223	60.2	66.0
Liberal/general studies	549	1,373	1,180	1,354	1,450	1,594	44.3	65.2
Library and archival sciences	7,001	5,374	3,893	3,713	3,953	4,349	81.3	77.9
Life sciences	5,728	6,510	5,059	4,784	4,961	4,861	33.6	51.1
Mathematics	5,191	2,860	2,882	3,442	3,447	3,677	29.2	40.0
Military sciences	2	46	119	49	-	-		
Multi/interdisciplinary studies	1,157	3,579	3,184	3,098	3,236	3,505	30.9	42.3
Parks and recreation	218	647	544	461	452	430	29.8	58.4
Philosophy, religion, and theology	4,036	5,126	5,519	5,913	5,924	6,012	27.1	36.2
Physical sciences	6,367	5,219	5,796	5,733	5,723	5,447	13.3	26.4
Psychology	4,431	7,806	8,408	7,872	8,552	9,231	37.2	67.6
Protective services	194	1,805	1,235	1,024	1,047	1,151	10.3	30.8
Public affairs	8,215	18,413	16,045	17,290	17,918	17,993	49.2	65.6
Social sciences [2]	16,476	12,101	10,380	10,294	10,867	11,419	28.5	40.8
Visual and performing arts	6,675	8,708	8,714	7,937	8,265	8,546	47.4	56.1
Unclassified	-	-	-	4,144	851	1,852		60.3
Doctorate's, total	32,107	32,615	32,943	34,870	35,720	38,238	14.3	36.3
Agriculture and natural resources	1,086	991	1,213	1,142	1,183	1,272	2.9	19.1
Architecture and environmental design	36	79	89	98	86	97	8.3	28.9
Area and ethnic studies	144	151	137	140	113	128	16.7	46.9
Business and management	807	792	866	1,109	1,149	1,142	2.9	24.4
Communications [1]	145	193	234	234	253	269	13.1	46.5
Computer and information sciences	128	240	248	428	551	623	2.3	14.4
Education	6,403	7,941	7,151	6,553	6,800	6,922	21.2	57.7
Engineering [1]	3,638	2,507	3,230	4,191	4,523	4,965	0.6	8.7
Foreign languages	781	549	437	411	420	512	38.0	59.0
Health sciences	459	771	1,199	1,261	1,436	1,543	16.3	54.8
Home economics	123	192	276	309	265	303	61.0	70.6
Law	20	40	105	89	76	113	0.0	20.4
Letters	1,857	1,500	1,239	1,172	1,234	1,266	28.0	55.3
Life sciences	3,645	3,636	3,432	3,629	3,520	3,844	16.3	37.7
Mathematics	1,199	724	699	750	866	915	7.8	18.5
Multi/interdisciplinary studies	80	295	285	261	257	311	13.8	34.7
Philosophy, religion, and theology	866	1,693	1,608	1,604	1,627	1,730	5.8	15.0
Physical sciences	4,390	3,089	3,403	3,809	3,858	4,168	5.6	19.3
Psychology	1,782	2,768	2,908	2,987	3,222	3,353	24.0	57.8
Public affairs	185	372	431	470	429	495	23.8	53.7
Social sciences [2]	3,659	3,219	2,851	2,781	2,885	3,023	13.9	32.6
Visual and performing arts	621	655	693	725	752	842	22.2	43.9
Other and unclassified	53	218	209	717	215	402	28.3	45.3

- Represents zero.   [1] Includes technologies.   [2] Includes history.

Source: U.S. Department of Education, National Center for Education Statistics, *Digest of Education Statistics*, annual.

Source: U.S. Bureau of the Census, *Statistical Abstract of the United States: 1993*, (113th edition), Washington, D.C.: U.S. Government Printing Office, 1993, Table 293.

D5-2. Doctor's Degrees Conferred, by Racial/Ethnic Group, Major Field of Study, and Sex of Student: 1991–92

Major field of study	Total							Men							Women						
	Total	White, non-His-panic	Black, non-His-panic	His-panic	Asian/ Pacific Islander	Amer-ican Indian/ Alas-kan Native	Non-resi-dent alien	Total	White, non-His-panic	Black, non-His-panic	His-panic	Asian/ Pacific Islander	Amer-ican Indian/ Alas-kan Native	Non-resi-dent alien	Total	White, non-His-panic	Black, non-His-panic	His-panic	Asian/ Pacific Islander	Amer-ican Indian/ Alas-kan Native	Non-resi-dent alien
1	2	3	4	5	6	7	8	9	10	11	12	13	14	15	16	17	18	19	20	21	22
All fields, total[1]	40,090	25,813	1,223	811	1,559	118	10,566	25,168	14,674	576	458	1,062	65	8,333	14,922	11,139	647	353	497	53	2,233
Agriculture and natural resources	1,214	590	10	14	35	1	564	963	443	9	13	26	1	471	251	147	1	1	9	0	93
Architecture and related programs	132	68	3	5	3	0	53	93	43	2	1	3	0	44	39	25	1	4	0	0	9
Area, ethnic, and cultural studies	155	105	18	0	4	0	28	90	60	9	0	3	0	18	65	45	9	0	1	0	10
Biological sciences/life sciences	4,243	2,785	57	89	214	11	1,087	2,620	1,683	34	53	123	8	719	1,623	1,102	23	36	91	3	368
Business management and administrative services	1,242	700	27	11	63	2	439	953	484	17	9	54	1	388	289	216	10	2	9	1	51
Communications	252	177	18	6	9	1	41	131	84	10	4	7	0	26	121	93	8	2	2	1	15
Communications technologies	3	3	0	0	0	0	0	1	1	0	0	0	0	0	2	2	0	0	0	0	0
Computer and information sciences	772	366	5	6	45	1	349	669	301	3	6	40	1	318	103	65	2	0	5	0	31
Education	6,864	5,404	513	187	100	36	624	2,783	2,149	175	86	32	16	325	4,081	3,255	338	101	68	20	299
Engineering	5,488	2,102	44	58	414	11	2,859	4,961	1,840	38	49	364	6	2,664	527	262	6	9	50	5	195
Engineering-related technologies	11	5	1	0	0	0	5	11	5	1	0	0	0	5	0	0	0	0	0	0	0
English language and literature/ letters	1,273	1,034	32	12	28	4	163	537	425	13	7	13	2	77	736	609	19	5	15	2	86
Foreign languages and literatures	850	514	13	66	18	1	238	378	218	4	27	8	1	120	472	296	9	39	10	0	118
Health professions and related sciences	1,661	1,161	45	26	68	3	358	698	396	15	15	34	0	238	963	765	30	11	34	3	120
Home economics and vocational home economics	293	209	12	5	6	0	61	71	45	5	1	0	0	20	222	164	7	4	6	0	41
Law and legal studies	68	15	0	5	2	0	46	50	11	0	4	1	0	34	18	4	0	1	1	0	12
Liberal arts and sciences, general studies, and humanities	67	55	4	1	0	0	7	30	23	0	1	0	0	6	37	32	4	0	0	0	1
Library science	50	36	2	2	2	0	8	16	11	1	1	2	0	1	34	25	1	1	0	0	7
Mathematics	1,082	460	2	11	55	2	552	851	350	2	8	40	0	451	231	110	0	3	15	2	101
Multi/interdisciplinary studies	231	153	3	5	8	1	61	144	89	0	4	7	1	43	87	64	3	1	1	0	18
Parks, recreation, leisure and fitness studies	61	34	5	0	3	0	19	41	23	3	0	1	0	14	20	11	2	0	2	0	5
Philosophy and religion	475	376	10	6	14	2	67	365	287	9	3	11	1	54	110	89	1	3	3	1	13
Physical sciences and science technologies	4,391	2,470	31	75	224	6	1,585	3,429	1,923	23	51	158	5	1,269	962	547	8	24	66	1	316
Precision production trades	0	0	0	0	0	0	0	0	0	0	0	0	0	0	0	0	0	0	0	0	0
Protective services	24	18	0	1	0	0	5	13	10	0	0	0	0	3	11	8	0	0	1	0	2
Psychology	3,373	2,931	118	102	58	12	152	1,359	1,177	36	39	21	3	83	2,014	1,754	82	63	37	9	69
Public administration and services	432	306	36	9	14	2	65	204	131	16	1	4	2	50	228	175	20	8	10	0	15
Military technologies	0	0	0	0	0	0	0	0	0	0	0	0	0	0	0	0	0	0	0	0	0
Social sciences and history	3,218	2,052	107	63	112	13	871	2,126	1,242	63	41	71	9	700	1,092	810	44	22	41	4	171
Theological studies/religious vocations	1,259	958	88	25	39	5	144	1,077	815	74	21	31	5	131	182	143	14	4	8	0	13
Transportation and material moving	0	0	0	0	0	0	0	0	0	0	0	0	0	0	0	0	0	0	0	0	0
Visual and performing arts	906	726	19	22	19	4	116	504	405	14	13	7	3	62	402	321	5	9	12	1	54

[1] Reported racial/ethnic distributions of students by level of degree, field of degree, and sex were used to estimate race/ethnicity for students whose race/ethnicity was not reported. Excludes 389 men and 180 women whose racial/ethnic group and field of study were not available.

NOTE.—To facilitate trend comparisons, certain aggregations have been made of the degree fields as reported in the IPEDS "Completions" survey: "Agriculture and natural resources" includes Agribusiness and agriculture production; Agricultural sciences, and Conservation and renewable natural resources; and "Business management and administrative services" includes Business and management, Business and office, Marketing and distribution, and Consumer and personal services.

SOURCE: U.S. Department of Education, National Center for Education Statistics, Integrated Postsecondary Education Data System (IPEDS), "Completions" survey. (This table was prepared April 1994.)

Source: National Center for Education Statistics, *Digest of Education Statistics, 1994*, NCES 94-115, Washington, D.C.: U.S. Government Printing Office, 1994, Table 261.

D5-3. First-Professional Degrees in Dentistry, Medicine, and Law, by Sex: 1949–50 to 1991–92

Year	Dentistry (D.D.S. or D.M.D.)				Medicine (M.D.)				Law (LL.B. or J.D.)			
	Number of institutions conferring degrees	Degrees conferred			Number of institutions conferring degrees	Degrees conferred			Number of institutions conferring degrees	Degrees conferred		
		Total	Men	Women		Total	Men	Women		Total	Men	Women
1	2	3	4	5	6	7	8	9	10	11	12	13
1949–50	40	2,579	2,561	18	72	5,612	5,028	584	(¹)	(¹)	(¹)	(¹)
1951–52	41	2,918	2,895	23	72	6,201	5,871	330	(¹)	(¹)	(¹)	(¹)
1953–54	42	3,102	3,063	39	73	6,712	6,377	335	(¹)	(¹)	(¹)	(¹)
1955–56	42	3,009	2,975	34	73	6,810	6,464	346	131	8,262	7,974	288
1957–58	43	3,065	3,031	34	75	6,816	6,469	347	131	9,394	9,122	272
1959–60	45	3,247	3,221	26	79	7,032	6,645	387	134	9,240	9,010	230
1961–62	46	3,183	3,166	17	81	7,138	6,749	389	134	9,364	9,091	273
1963–64	46	3,180	3,168	12	82	7,303	6,878	425	133	10,679	10,372	307
1965–66	47	3,178	3,146	32	84	7,673	7,170	503	136	13,246	12,776	470
1967–68	48	3,422	3,375	47	85	7,944	7,318	626	138	16,454	15,805	649
1969–70	48	3,718	3,684	34	86	8,314	7,615	699	145	14,916	14,115	801
1970–71	48	3,745	3,703	42	89	8,919	8,110	809	147	17,421	16,181	1,240
1971–72	48	3,862	3,819	43	92	9,253	8,423	830	147	21,764	20,266	1,498
1972–73	51	4,047	3,992	55	97	10,307	9,388	919	152	27,205	25,037	2,168
1973–74	52	4,440	4,355	85	99	11,356	10,093	1,263	151	29,326	25,986	3,340
1974–75	52	4,773	4,627	146	104	12,447	10,818	1,629	154	29,296	24,881	4,415
1975–76	56	5,425	5,187	238	107	13,426	11,252	2,174	166	32,293	26,085	6,208
1976–77	57	5,138	4,764	374	109	13,461	10,891	2,570	169	34,104	26,447	7,657
1977–78	57	5,189	4,623	566	109	14,279	11,210	3,069	169	34,402	25,457	8,945
1978–79	58	5,434	4,794	640	109	14,786	11,381	3,405	175	35,206	25,180	10,026
1979–80	58	5,258	4,558	700	112	14,902	11,416	3,486	179	35,647	24,893	10,754
1980–81	58	5,460	4,672	788	116	15,505	11,672	3,833	176	36,331	24,563	11,768
1981–82	59	5,282	4,467	815	119	15,814	11,867	3,947	180	35,991	23,965	12,026
1982–83	59	5,585	4,631	954	118	15,484	11,350	4,134	177	36,853	23,550	13,303
1983–84	60	5,353	4,302	1,051	119	15,813	11,359	4,454	179	37,012	23,382	13,630
1984–85	59	5,339	4,233	1,106	120	16,041	11,167	4,874	181	37,491	23,070	14,421
1985–86 ²	59	5,046	3,907	1,139	120	15,938	11,022	4,916	181	35,844	21,874	13,970
1986–87 ²	58	4,741	3,603	1,138	121	15,428	10,431	4,997	179	36,056	21,561	14,495
1987–88	57	4,477	3,300	1,177	122	15,358	10,278	5,080	180	35,397	21,067	14,330
1988–89	58	4,265	3,124	1,141	124	15,460	10,310	5,150	182	35,634	21,069	14,565
1989–90	57	4,100	2,834	1,266	124	15,075	9,923	5,152	182	36,485	21,079	15,406
1990–91	55	3,699	2,510	1,189	121	15,043	9,629	5,414	179	37,945	21,643	16,302
1991–92	52	3,593	2,431	1,162	120	15,243	9,796	5,447	177	38,848	22,260	16,588

¹ Data prior to 1955–56 are not shown because they lack comparability with the figures for subsequent years.

² Revised from previously published data.

SOURCE: U.S. Department of Education, National Center for Education Statistics, "Degrees and Other Formal Awards Conferred" surveys, and Integrated Postsecondary Education Data System (IPEDS), "Completions" surveys. (This table was prepared March 1994.)

Source: National Center for Education Statistics, *Digest of Education Statistics, 1994*, NCES 94-115, Washington, D.C.: U.S. Government Printing Office, 1994, Tables 249.

D6. EDUCATIONAL OUTCOMES

D6-1. Life Values of High School Seniors, by Sex: 1972, 1982, and 1992

| Value | Percent of 1972 seniors | | | | | | Percent of 1982 seniors | | | | | | Percent of 1992 seniors | |
| | 1972 | | 1974 (2 years after high school) | | 1976 (4 years after high school) | | 1982 | | 1984 (2 years after high school) | | 1986 (4 years after high school) | | | |
	Male	Female	Male	Female	Male	Female	Male	Female	Male	Female	Male	Female	Male	Female
1	2	3	4	5	6	7	8	9	10	11	12	13	14	15
Being successful in work	86.5	83.0	81.2	74.9	80.3	69.7	88.2	85.5	88.7	84.2	84.0	77.2	89.0	89.6
Finding steady work	82.3	73.7	74.7	59.9	79.3	62.1	88.0	84.4	87.4	83.3	84.2	76.3	87.1	88.6
Having lots of money	26.0	9.8	17.8	9.1	17.7	9.4	41.3	24.1	35.8	20.9	27.8	16.9	45.3	29.4
Being a leader in the community	14.9	8.0	8.5	4.4	9.2	4.2	11.3	5.9	13.7	6.4	9.5	4.5	—	—
Correcting inequalities	22.5	31.1	16.6	18.2	16.2	17.1	11.8	11.7	13.3	13.9	10.7	10.9	17.0	23.6
Having children	—	—	—	—	—	—	37.0	47.0	42.7	56.3	41.4	56.2	39.0	49.2
Having a happy family life	78.6	85.7	83.1	86.7	84.2	86.4	81.6	86.3	86.1	90.2	86.8	87.8	—	—
Providing better opportunities for my children	66.6	66.2	59.5	61.6	59.8	58.8	71.0	68.7	72.1	69.9	68.4	67.4	74.5	76.5
Living closer to parents or relatives	6.8	8.2	8.3	12.4	7.7	11.9	15.0	15.7	15.6	20.1	12.9	19.8	15.2	18.7
Moving from area	14.3	14.6	8.3	7.4	6.7	6.4	14.4	12.8	10.5	9.1	9.0	7.4	20.7	20.1
Having strong friendships	81.2	78.7	76.5	74.7	76.1	72.1	80.4	79.1	80.1	79.7	76.5	75.0	79.8	80.0
Having leisure time	—	—	60.9	55.1	65.4	60.1	70.2	68.8	74.5	72.0	70.1	68.9	65.3	62.0

—Question not asked.

NOTE.—Percentages are based on the total sample members who responded to the individual survey items in each survey period.

SOURCE: U.S. Department of Education, National Center for Education Statistics, "National Longitudinal Study," "High School and Beyond" surveys, and "National Education Longitudinal Study, Second Followup." (This table was prepared April 1994.)

Source: National Center for Education Statistics, *Digest of Education Statistics, 1994*, NCES 94-115, Washington, D.C.: U.S. Government Printing Office, 1994, Table 364.

D6-2. Four-Month Average Income, Earnings, Work Activity, and Educational Attainment, by Sex and Age: Spring 1990

Educational attainment	Monthly income		Monthly earnings		Months with work activity	
	Mean	Standard error	Mean	Standard error	Mean	Standard error
TOTAL, 18 YEARS AND OVER						
Both sexes	$1,599	$16	$1,284	$15	2.60	0.01
Doctorate	4,545	340	3,855	304	3.45	0.11
Professional	5,554	457	4,961	455	3.37	0.09
Master's....................................	3,211	203	2,822	202	3.34	0.05
Bachelor's.................................	2,489	52	2,116	41	3.17	0.02
Associate	1,879	54	1,672	51	3.26	0.05
Vocational.................................	1,568	58	1,237	50	2.83	0.06
Some college, no degree..................	1,545	33	1,280	31	2.88	0.02
High school graduate only................	1,357	19	1,077	16	2.64	0.02
Not a high school graduate................	856	12	492	12	1.58	0.02
Male....................................	2,148	26	1,792	24	3.00	0.01
Doctorate	4,915	407	4,168	363	3.43	0.12
Professional	6,367	573	5,647	575	3.40	0.10
Master's....................................	3,748	144	3,285	136	3.53	0.05
Bachelor's.................................	3,235	91	2,763	66	3.48	0.04
Associate	2,380	95	2,185	95	3.54	0.06
Vocational.................................	2,085	128	1,737	98	3.22	0.10
Some college, no degree..................	2,002	58	1,729	59	3.14	0.04
High school graduate only................	1,853	36	1,542	30	3.09	0.02
Not a high school graduate................	1,166	22	776	22	2.10	0.04
Female	1,096	18	819	17	2.24	0.01
Doctorate	3,162	501	2,683	450	3.52	0.21
Professional	3,070	471	2,866	455	3.29	0.19
Master's....................................	2,614	388	2,309	388	3.14	0.07
Bachelor's.................................	1,698	36	1,428	41	2.85	0.05
Associate	1,425	53	1,207	43	3.01	0.07
Vocational.................................	1,290	54	968	52	2.62	0.09
Some college, no degree..................	1,115	32	857	20	2.63	0.04
High school graduate only................	943	17	689	14	2.26	0.02
Not a high school graduate................	579	11	239	8	1.11	0.02

Source: Robert Kominski and Rebecca Sutterlin, *What's It Worth? Educational Background and Economic Status: Spring 1990*, Current Population Reports, P70-32, Washington, D.C.: U.S. Government Printing Office, December 1992, Table 2.

D6-3. Educational Attainment of Persons 16 Years Old and Over, by Labor Force Status, Age, Sex, Race, and Hispanic Origin: March 1993

[Numbers in thousands. Civilian noninstitutional population]

Age, sex, labor force, race, and Hispanic origin	Total	Elementary None-4th grade	Elementary 5th-8th grade	High School 9th-11th grade	High School High school graduate	College Some college no degree	College Associate degree	College Bachelor's degree	College Advanced degree	Percent: High school graduate or more	Percent: Bachelor's degree or more
ALL RACES											
Male											
Civilian labor force	68 835	751	2 699	7 785	22 978	13 094	4 357	11 046	6 124	83.7	24.9
16 and 17 years	1 276	2	57	1 190	22	4	–	–	–	2.1	–
18 to 24 years	9 066	44	261	1 725	3 238	2 731	392	652	23	77.6	7.5
25 years and over	58 493	705	2 380	4 870	19 718	10 359	3 965	10 394	6 101	86.4	28.2
25 to 29 years	8 890	68	297	831	3 291	1 675	627	1 700	401	86.5	23.6
30 to 34 years	10 140	106	286	910	3 681	1 780	761	1 864	753	87.2	25.8
35 to 44 years	18 306	173	490	1 248	5 981	3 506	1 451	3 503	1 955	89.6	29.8
45 to 54 years	12 368	161	528	921	3 978	2 198	765	1 983	1 833	87.0	30.9
55 to 64 years	6 840	153	551	766	2 231	937	291	1 028	882	78.5	27.9
65 years and over	1 949	44	228	194	557	264	71	316	277	76.1	30.4
Employed	62 981	624	2 358	6 373	20 787	12 180	4 113	10 575	5 972	85.1	26.3
16 and 17 years	940	2	41	874	20	2	–	–	–	2.4	–
18 to 24 years	7 786	38	222	1 308	2 731	2 485	381	599	22	79.9	8.0
25 years and over	54 255	584	2 094	4 190	18 036	9 693	3 732	9 976	5 951	87.3	29.4
25 to 29 years	8 041	56	264	652	2 898	1 550	598	1 636	387	87.9	25.2
30 to 34 years	9 339	90	241	756	3 343	1 656	705	1 809	739	88.4	27.3
35 to 44 years	16 998	149	428	1 066	5 447	3 272	1 368	3 358	1 911	90.3	31.0
45 to 54 years	11 579	128	449	824	3 702	2 079	719	1 886	1 792	87.9	31.8
55 to 64 years	6 433	130	495	704	2 104	881	280	983	856	79.3	28.6
65 years and over	1 863	31	218	188	542	255	62	302	266	76.5	30.5
Unemployed	5 854	127	341	1 412	2 192	914	244	471	152	67.9	10.6
16 and 17 years	336	–	16	316	2	2	–	–	–	1.3	–
18 to 24 years	1 280	5	39	417	507	246	11	53	1	64.0	4.3
25 years and over	4 238	122	286	680	1 682	666	233	418	151	74.3	13.4
25 to 29 years	849	12	33	179	393	124	29	64	14	73.6	9.2
30 to 34 years	800	16	45	153	337	125	56	54	14	73.2	8.5
35 to 44 years	1 307	24	62	182	534	234	83	145	44	79.5	14.4
45 to 54 years	789	33	80	98	275	119	45	97	41	73.2	17.5
55 to 64 years	406	23	57	62	128	55	11	45	26	65.1	17.4
65 years and over	85	13	10	6	15	8	9	14	11	67.3	29.5
Not in labor force	23 466	1 029	3 427	5 684	6 318	3 684	649	1 748	926	56.8	11.4
16 and 17 years	2 114	4	165	1 916	26	2	–	–	–	1.4	–
18 to 24 years	2 845	21	49	820	443	1 306	78	108	20	68.7	4.5
25 years and over	18 506	1 003	3 213	2 947	5 849	2 376	571	1 640	906	61.3	13.8
25 to 29 years	698	21	43	101	206	165	21	113	29	76.5	20.3
30 to 34 years	761	43	54	141	289	110	32	71	21	68.7	12.2
35 to 44 years	1 369	56	119	228	497	244	72	110	43	70.5	11.2
45 to 54 years	1 431	88	180	262	466	215	66	91	62	62.9	10.7
55 to 64 years	3 364	158	514	502	1 130	392	132	336	201	65.1	16.0
65 years and over	10 883	637	2 303	1 713	3 261	1 252	249	918	550	57.2	13.5
Female											
Civilian labor force	57 558	318	1 265	5 235	20 515	12 257	4 740	9 232	3 995	88.2	23.0
16 and 17 years	1 091	–	29	1 049	12	1	–	–	–	1.1	–
18 to 24 years	8 091	21	77	896	2 666	2 963	533	882	54	87.7	11.6
25 years and over	48 376	297	1 160	3 289	17 838	9 293	4 207	8 351	3 941	90.2	25.4
25 to 29 years	7 156	17	80	457	2 369	1 497	679	1 720	337	92.3	28.7
30 to 34 years	8 235	40	117	528	2 955	1 656	834	1 600	506	91.7	25.6
35 to 44 years	15 598	102	284	831	5 413	3 236	1 488	2 762	1 482	92.2	27.2
45 to 54 years	10 780	74	240	798	4 194	1 921	829	1 571	1 153	89.7	25.3
55 to 64 years	5 191	51	268	501	2 302	799	307	576	387	84.2	18.5
65 years and over	1 415	14	170	175	605	184	69	122	76	74.7	14.0
Employed	53 997	276	1 117	4 413	19 192	11 609	4 549	8 958	3 884	89.2	23.8
16 and 17 years	836	–	8	815	11	1	–	–	–	1.4	–
18 to 24 years	7 264	13	54	674	2 358	2 770	500	843	52	89.8	12.3
25 years and over	45 897	263	1 055	2 923	16 823	8 838	4 049	8 115	3 832	90.8	26.0
25 to 29 years	6 628	15	66	356	2 150	1 403	646	1 668	324	93.4	30.1
30 to 34 years	7 724	36	102	449	2 747	1 554	806	1 550	479	92.4	26.3
35 to 44 years	14 839	86	241	736	5 105	3 086	1 456	2 678	1 451	92.8	27.8
45 to 54 years	10 329	69	226	737	4 001	1 859	777	1 536	1 123	90.0	25.7
55 to 64 years	4 997	47	258	474	2 230	755	295	561	378	84.4	18.8
65 years and over	1 380	11	161	170	590	181	69	122	76	75.2	14.3
Unemployed	3 561	43	148	822	1 323	648	191	274	111	71.6	10.8
16 and 17 years	255	–	20	234	1	–	–	–	–	.3	–
18 to 24 years	827	8	23	221	308	193	34	38	2	69.5	4.9
25 years and over	2 479	35	105	366	1 015	455	158	236	109	79.6	13.9
25 to 29 years	527	3	15	101	219	94	33	51	12	77.6	12.1
30 to 34 years	511	4	15	79	208	102	28	49	27	80.9	15.0
35 to 44 years	760	17	43	94	308	150	33	84	31	79.8	15.2
45 to 54 years	451	5	14	60	193	62	52	35	30	82.4	14.4
55 to 64 years	194	4	10	27	71	44	13	16	9	78.7	12.4
65 years and over	35	2	9	5	16	3	–	1	–	(B)	(B)
Not in labor force	43 096	1 426	5 282	9 058	15 127	6 370	1 648	3 228	958	63.4	9.7
16 and 17 years	2 177	7	124	1 997	36	12	–	–	–	2.2	–
18 to 24 years	4 158	44	164	1 105	1 119	1 483	107	120	15	68.4	3.2
25 years and over	36 762	1 375	4 994	5 955	13 972	4 874	1 540	3 109	943	66.5	11.0
25 to 29 years	2 660	31	167	486	1 051	498	131	257	38	74.3	11.1
30 to 34 years	2 932	56	179	436	1 044	551	195	399	72	77.1	16.1
35 to 44 years	4 827	168	279	630	1 766	837	308	667	171	77.7	17.4
45 to 54 years	3 870	118	366	617	1 571	543	191	360	103	71.6	12.0
55 to 64 years	5 851	273	675	1 052	2 395	698	206	385	166	65.8	9.4
65 years and over	16 623	728	3 328	2 735	6 144	1 747	508	1 040	392	59.1	8.6

¹Persons of Hispanic origin may be of any race.

Source: Robert Kominski and Andrea Adams, U.S. Bureau of the Census, *Educational Attainment in the United States: March 1993 and 1992*, Current Population Reports, P20-476, Washington, D.C.: U.S. Government Printing Office, 1994, Table 6.

D6-4. Occupation of Longest Job in 1993, by Educational Attainment of Year-Round, Full-Time Workers 25 Years Old and Over, Sex, and Race

(Numbers in thousands. Persons as of March 1994.)

Occupation of longest job	Total		Not a high school graduate		High school graduate		Some college or associate degree		Bachelor's degree or more	
	Male	Female	Male	Female	Male	Female	Male	Female	Male	Female
BLACK										
Number										
Total[1]	3,960	3,999	623	391	1,543	1,390	1,042	1,404	753	814
Executive, administrative, and managerial workers	364	429	10	8	55	56	91	178	209	187
Professional specialty workers	331	543	5	7	22	53	70	124	233	359
Technical and related support workers	131	229	-	1	27	50	82	137	22	40
Sales workers	251	210	12	7	74	85	84	71	81	47
Administrative support workers, including clerical	316	1,143	31	44	117	406	121	558	47	134
Private household workers	-	24	-	7	-	15	-	2	-	-
Protective service workers	212	73	24	3	47	22	97	30	44	18
Service workers, except private household	401	733	77	183	213	356	80	179	31	16
Farming, fishing, and forestry workers	67	6	36	4	22	1	6	-	4	-
Precision production, craft, and repair workers	646	136	93	19	358	71	151	36	44	9
Machine operators, assemblers, and inspectors	450	360	112	83	248	211	85	62	4	4
Transportation and material moving workers	500	42	137	9	239	22	103	11	21	-
Handlers, equipment cleaners, helpers, and laborers	290	72	85	15	121	43	71	14	12	-
Percent										
Total[1]	100.0	100.0	100.0	100.0	100.0	100.0	100.0	100.0	100.0	100.0
Executive, administrative, and managerial workers	9.2	10.7	1.6	2.1	3.5	4.0	8.7	12.7	27.7	22.9
Professional specialty workers	8.4	13.6	0.8	1.8	1.4	3.8	6.7	8.8	31.0	44.1
Technical and related support workers	3.3	5.7	-	0.4	1.8	3.6	7.9	9.8	2.9	4.9
Sales workers	6.3	5.2	1.9	1.8	4.8	6.1	8.1	5.0	10.8	5.8
Administrative support workers, including clerical	8.0	28.6	5.0	11.2	7.6	29.2	11.6	39.8	6.2	16.5
Private household workers	-	0.6	-	1.7	-	1.1	-	0.1	-	-
Protective service workers	5.4	1.8	3.8	0.8	3.1	1.6	9.3	2.2	5.9	2.2
Service workers, except private household	10.1	18.3	12.4	46.7	13.8	25.6	7.7	12.8	4.1	1.9
Farming, fishing, and forestry workers	1.7	0.1	5.8	1.1	1.4	0.1	0.5	-	0.6	-
Precision production, craft, and repair workers	16.3	3.4	15.0	4.9	23.2	5.1	14.5	2.6	5.8	1.1
Machine operators, assemblers, and inspectors	11.4	9.0	18.0	21.3	16.1	15.2	8.2	4.4	0.6	0.5
Transportation and material moving workers	12.6	1.0	22.0	2.3	15.5	1.6	9.9	0.8	2.8	-
Handlers, equipment cleaners, helpers, and laborers	7.3	1.8	13.7	3.9	7.9	3.1	6.8	1.0	1.6	-

See footnote at end of table.

D6-4. Occupation of Longest Job in 1993, by Educational Attainment of Year-Round, Full-Time Workers 25 Years Old and Over, Sex, and Race *(continued)*

(Numbers in thousands. Persons as of March 1994.)

Occupation of longest job	Total		Not a high school graduate		High school graduate		Some college or associate degree		Bachelor's degree or more	
	Male	Female	Male	Female	Male	Female	Male	Female	Male	Female
WHITE, NOT HISPANIC										
Number										
Total[1]	36,009	23,351	2,725	1,292	11,457	8,160	9,620	7,083	12,207	6,817
Executive, administrative, and managerial workers	6,645	4,409	156	88	1,160	1,126	1,677	1,536	3,652	1,658
Professional specialty workers	5,605	4,307	23	19	289	219	778	749	4,516	3,321
Technical and related support workers	1,121	1,078	19	15	215	263	503	552	384	248
Sales workers	4,671	2,528	151	161	1,212	1,037	1,453	745	1,856	585
Administrative support workers, including clerical	1,967	6,545	81	155	680	3,197	668	2,473	537	720
Private household workers	5	64	-	17	3	24	2	17	-	7
Protective service workers	1,074	129	36	3	360	40	463	46	214	40
Service workers, except private household	1,228	2,030	202	392	549	1,001	350	504	127	133
Farming, fishing, and forestry workers	1,197	199	246	32	511	90	292	57	149	20
Precision production, craft, and repair workers	6,899	615	840	83	3,365	327	2,212	162	482	42
Machine operators, assemblers, and inspectors	2,184	1,090	361	236	1,217	647	517	173	90	34
Transportation and material moving workers	2,301	145	413	30	1,304	69	458	37	126	8
Handlers, equipment cleaners, helpers, and laborers	1,111	213	197	61	592	120	247	31	74	1
Percent										
Total[1]	100.0	100.0	100.0	100.0	100.0	100.0	100.0	100.0	100.0	100.0
Executive, administrative, and managerial workers	18.5	18.9	5.7	6.8	10.1	13.8	17.4	21.7	29.9	24.3
Professional specialty workers	15.6	18.4	0.8	1.5	2.5	2.7	8.1	10.6	37.0	48.7
Technical and related support workers	3.1	4.6	0.7	1.1	1.9	3.2	5.2	7.8	3.1	3.6
Sales workers	13.0	10.8	5.5	12.5	10.6	12.7	15.1	10.5	15.2	8.6
Administrative support workers, including clerical	5.5	28.0	3.0	12.0	5.9	39.2	6.9	34.9	4.4	10.6
Private household workers	-	0.3	-	1.3	-	0.3	-	0.2	-	0.1
Protective service workers	3.0	0.6	1.3	0.2	3.1	0.5	4.8	0.7	1.8	0.6
Service workers, except private household	3.4	8.7	7.4	30.3	4.8	12.3	3.6	7.1	1.0	2.0
Farming, fishing, and forestry workers	3.3	0.9	9.0	2.5	4.5	1.1	3.0	0.8	1.2	0.3
Precision production, craft, and repair workers	19.2	2.6	30.8	6.4	29.4	4.0	23.0	2.3	3.9	0.6
Machine operators, assemblers, and inspectors	6.1	4.7	13.2	18.2	10.6	7.9	5.4	2.4	0.7	0.5
Transportation and material moving workers	6.4	0.6	15.2	2.3	11.4	0.8	4.8	0.5	1.0	0.1
Handlers, equipment cleaners, helpers, and laborers	3.1	0.9	7.2	4.7	5.2	1.5	2.6	0.4	0.6	-

[1]Armed forces not included.

Source: Claudette E. Bennett, U.S. Bureau of the Census, *The Black Population in the United States: March 1994 and 1993*, Current Population Reports, Series P20-480, Washington, D.C.: U.S. Government Printing Office, January 1995, Table 14.

D6-5. Total Annual Money Earnings of Persons 25 Years Old and Over[1], by Educational Attainment, Sex, and Age: 1992

Sex, earnings, and age	Total	Less than 9th grade	Some high school (no diploma)	High school graduate (includes equiva-lency)	College						
					Some college, no degree	Associate degree	Bachelor's degree or more				
							Total	Bachelor's degree	Master's degree	Professional degree	Doctor's degree
1	2	3	4	5	6	7	8	9	10	11	12
Men					Number, in thousands						
Total	77,644	7,302	7,820	25,766	12,920	4,601	19,234	12,154	4,368	1,652	1,060
With earnings	60,356	3,230	4,983	20,268	10,831	4,072	16,975	10,667	3,887	1,505	916
				Percentage distribution of men with earnings							
Total	100.0	100.0	100.0	100.0	100.0	100.0	100.0	100.0	100.0	100.0	100.0
$1 to $2,499 or loss	4.6	11.8	7.5	4.4	4.4	3.4	2.8	3.0	2.8	1.5	2.6
$2,500 to $7,499	7.6	19.1	14.3	8.3	7.2	5.1	3.5	4.0	3.4	0.5	2.1
$7,500 to $12,499	9.4	20.5	18.5	10.7	7.9	6.5	4.8	5.4	4.1	2.7	4.6
$12,500 to $14,999	3.9	8.0	6.8	4.8	3.2	2.9	2.0	2.4	1.7	1.0	0.4
$15,000 to $17,499	6.1	8.9	7.9	7.7	6.9	5.5	2.9	3.6	1.8	0.9	1.9
$17,500 to $19,999	4.4	5.1	5.5	5.6	4.6	4.7	2.3	2.7	1.9	0.7	2.0
$20,000 to $22,499	6.5	7.1	9.1	8.1	6.6	6.7	3.6	4.2	2.8	1.9	2.2
$22,500 to $24,999	3.9	3.6	4.5	4.8	3.9	4.2	2.4	3.0	1.8	0.9	1.6
$25,000 to $29,999	9.7	5.5	8.1	12.1	10.7	10.7	7.1	8.3	5.8	4.0	3.7
$30,000 to $34,999	9.1	3.3	5.8	10.2	10.5	11.6	8.3	9.3	7.6	5.6	4.4
$35,000 to $39,999	7.9	2.4	3.8	8.0	9.0	9.9	8.7	9.4	8.2	5.6	8.2
$40,000 to $44,999	6.4	1.6	2.6	5.1	8.2	7.9	8.5	8.8	9.8	4.9	5.9
$45,000 to $49,999	4.2	1.0	2.1	3.3	4.1	6.0	6.2	6.4	7.3	2.7	4.1
$50,000 to $64,999	8.3	1.1	2.6	4.5	8.2	9.3	15.6	14.4	18.8	12.8	21.6
$65,000 to $74,999	2.4	0.4	0.3	1.1	1.4	2.2	5.8	4.4	7.7	8.3	9.6
$75,000 to $99,999	2.8	0.2	0.1	0.8	1.6	2.1	7.5	5.8	7.9	16.1	11.8
$100,000 and over	2.7	0.3	0.3	0.5	1.5	1.2	7.9	4.8	6.4	29.8	13.4
				Median earnings							
All ages, 25 and over	$26,472	$12,206	$15,928	$22,765	$26,873	$30,052	$40,590	$36,691	$43,371	$70,728	$52,285
25 to 34 years	21,692	10,235	13,449	20,016	21,537	25,489	31,973	31,119	35,555	39,342	36,485
35 to 44 years	30,306	14,366	16,606	25,587	30,536	31,270	44,211	40,903	45,831	85,870	54,527
45 to 54 years	32,817	15,317	20,674	28,084	34,243	36,542	48,783	41,898	51,104	78,822	59,155
55 to 64 years	26,703	15,971	20,352	23,934	29,633	30,462	42,344	40,467	37,429	80,185	55,179
65 years and over	9,093	4,817	6,941	8,307	9,257	11,247	19,554	16,333	12,406	48,318	37,440
Women					Number, in thousands						
Total	85,181	7,826	9,246	31,823	14,175	5,755	16,356	11,465	3,942	584	366
With earnings	51,246	1,649	3,507	18,882	9,918	4,391	12,898	8,824	3,247	498	329
				Percentage distribution of women with earnings							
Total	100.0	100.0	100.0	100.0	100.0	100.0	100.0	100.0	100.0	100.0	100.0
$1 to $2,499 or loss	10.0	19.8	16.5	11.0	9.6	7.9	6.7	7.7	5.2	2.6	2.7
$2,500 to $7,499	14.2	27.5	23.3	17.0	13.9	9.8	7.6	8.3	6.1	5.2	7.6
$7,500 to $12,499	16.1	28.2	27.4	19.8	15.2	13.9	7.7	8.7	5.5	5.6	3.3
$12,500 to $14,999	5.9	7.3	7.5	7.2	6.0	5.5	3.3	3.8	2.3	2.6	1.2
$15,000 to $17,499	7.7	5.9	8.8	9.6	8.3	7.3	4.7	5.6	3.0	0.6	1.8
$17,500 to $19,999	5.6	3.0	3.5	6.6	6.7	6.5	4.0	4.7	2.9	0.6	1.2
$20,000 to $22,499	7.4	3.0	3.9	7.7	8.9	9.3	6.7	7.6	4.6	5.8	3.9
$22,500 to $24,999	4.4	1.6	2.0	4.3	4.9	5.4	5.1	5.6	4.1	2.2	4.5
$25,000 to $29,999	9.3	2.1	3.8	7.4	10.6	12.0	12.6	12.9	12.8	8.9	6.1
$30,000 to $34,999	6.6	0.5	1.2	4.5	6.7	8.0	11.3	10.6	14.2	7.8	7.0
$35,000 to $39,999	4.3	0.6	0.7	2.2	3.5	6.1	8.9	7.7	11.2	13.5	10.3
$40,000 to $44,999	3.0	0.4	0.5	1.3	2.5	3.1	6.9	5.6	10.2	6.0	12.1
$45,000 to $49,999	1.7	0.0	0.5	0.4	1.2	2.7	4.2	3.6	5.2	5.8	6.7
$50,000 to $64,999	1.3	0.0	0.3	0.2	0.9	1.0	3.6	2.9	4.6	5.6	8.5
$65,000 to $74,999	1.6	0.0	0.1	0.6	0.7	1.3	4.4	3.1	6.0	9.9	15.8
$75,000 to $99,999	0.5	0.1	0.1	0.2	0.2	0.3	1.4	1.1	1.3	6.8	4.2
$100,000 and over	0.3	0.0	0.1	0.0	0.2	0.1	1.0	0.5	0.9	10.3	3.0
				Median earnings							
All ages, 25 and over	$16,227	$7,942	$9,784	$13,266	$16,611	$19,642	$26,417	$24,126	$30,934	$37,249	$39,901
25 to 34 years	16,022	7,503	9,205	12,261	15,588	18,427	24,748	23,604	27,088	35,667	—
35 to 44 years	17,286	8,392	9,558	14,145	17,174	20,415	27,551	25,245	30,850	40,000	40,218
45 to 54 years	17,977	9,845	11,395	15,240	19,324	21,112	30,454	25,818	34,669	44,824	41,490
55 to 64 years	14,017	7,906	10,064	12,805	16,825	20,227	27,240	21,757	33,037	—	—
65 years and over	6,292	4,665	4,993	6,768	6,010	6,894	7,807	6,593	9,078	—	—

[1] Includes full-time and part-time workers.
—Data not available.

NOTE.—Because of rounding, details may not add to totals.

SOURCE: U.S. Department of Commerce, Bureau of the Census, *Current Population Reports*, Series P–60, *Money Income of Households, Families, and Persons in the United States: 1992*. (This table was prepared August 1994.)

Source: National Center for Education Statistics, *Digest of Education Statistics, 1994*, NCES 94-115, Washington, D.C.: U.S. Government Printing Office, 1994, Table 370.

D7. VOTING AND POLITICAL INVOLVEMENT

D7-1. Reported Voting and Registration, by Race, Hispanic Origin, Sex, and Age: November 1992

November 1992. Numbers in thousands.

Region, race, Hispanic origin, sex, and age	All persons	Reported registered		Reported voted		Reported that they did not vote[1]				
						Total	Registered	Not registered		
		Number	Percent	Number	Percent			Total[2]	Not a U.S. citizen	Do not know and not reported on registration[3]
UNITED STATES										
All Races										
Both Sexes										
Total, 18 years and over............	185,684	126,578	68.2	113,866	61.3	71,818	12,712	59,106	11,900	10,638
18 to 20 years.........................	9,727	4,696	48.3	3,749	38.5	5,979	947	5,032	857	821
21 to 24 years.........................	14,644	8,091	55.3	6,693	45.7	7,951	1,398	6,553	1,288	1,075
25 to 34 years.........................	41,603	25,223	60.6	22,120	53.2	19,483	3,103	16,380	3,675	2,223
35 to 44 years.........................	39,716	27,503	69.2	25,269	63.6	14,447	2,234	12,213	2,800	2,144
45 to 54 years.........................	28,058	20,785	74.1	19,292	68.8	8,766	1,493	7,273	1,435	1,466
55 to 64 years.........................	21,089	16,231	77.0	15,107	71.6	5,982	1,124	4,858	955	1,107
65 to 74 years.........................	18,445	14,685	79.6	13,607	73.8	4,839	1,078	3,760	538	952
75 years and over	12,401	9,364	75.5	8,030	64.8	4,371	1,334	3,037	352	850
Male										
Total, 18 years and over............	88,557	59,254	66.9	53,312	60.2	35,245	5,942	29,303	6,065	5,327
18 to 20 years.........................	4,876	2,274	46.6	1,786	36.6	3,090	488	2,602	444	405
21 to 24 years.........................	7,158	3,797	53.0	3,086	43.1	4,072	711	3,361	722	597
25 to 34 years.........................	20,465	11,869	58.0	10,324	50.4	10,141	1,545	8,597	2,031	1,251
35 to 44 years.........................	19,509	13,153	67.4	11,995	61.5	7,514	1,158	6,357	1,444	1,059
45 to 54 years.........................	13,608	9,956	73.2	9,287	68.2	4,321	668	3,652	697	799
55 to 64 years.........................	10,012	7,725	77.2	7,203	71.9	2,809	522	2,287	398	527
65 to 74 years.........................	8,289	6,745	81.4	6,318	76.2	1,971	427	1,544	218	410
75 years and over	4,640	3,736	80.5	3,313	71.4	1,327	424	904	113	279
Female										
Total, 18 years and over............	97,126	67,324	69.3	60,554	62.3	36,573	6,770	29,803	5,834	5,311
18 to 20 years.........................	4,851	2,421	49.9	1,962	40.5	2,889	459	2,430	413	416
21 to 24 years.........................	7,486	4,294	57.4	3,607	48.2	3,879	687	3,192	566	478
25 to 34 years.........................	21,138	13,354	63.2	11,795	55.8	9,342	1,558	7,784	1,645	972
35 to 44 years.........................	20,207	14,350	71.0	13,274	65.7	6,933	1,076	5,856	1,356	1,085
45 to 54 years.........................	14,450	10,829	74.9	10,005	69.2	4,445	825	3,620	738	667
55 to 64 years.........................	11,077	8,506	76.8	7,904	71.4	3,173	602	2,571	558	580
65 to 74 years.........................	10,157	7,940	78.2	7,289	71.8	2,868	652	2,216	320	541
75 years and over	7,761	5,628	72.5	4,717	60.8	3,044	911	2,133	240	571
White										
Both Sexes										
Total, 18 years and over............	157,837	110,684	70.1	100,405	63.6	57,432	10,279	47,153	8,284	8,289
18 to 20 years.........................	7,743	3,938	50.9	3,187	41.2	4,555	750	3,805	566	585
21 to 24 years.........................	11,939	6,808	57.0	5,745	48.1	6,194	1,064	5,130	912	787
25 to 34 years.........................	34,640	21,631	62.4	19,193	55.4	15,447	2,437	13,010	2,596	1,633
35 to 44 years.........................	33,644	23,964	71.2	22,186	65.9	11,459	1,778	9,680	1,901	1,643
45 to 54 years.........................	24,071	18,243	75.8	17,013	70.7	7,058	1,230	5,829	963	1,156
55 to 64 years.........................	18,208	14,270	78.4	13,357	73.4	4,851	913	3,938	706	887
65 to 74 years.........................	16,400	13,281	81.0	12,365	75.4	4,035	916	3,119	382	836
75 years and over	11,192	8,550	76.4	7,360	65.8	3,832	1,190	2,642	257	762
Male										
Total, 18 years and over............	75,915	52,383	69.0	47,552	62.6	28,364	4,831	23,533	4,298	4,116
18 to 20 years.........................	3,876	1,897	48.9	1,510	39.0	2,366	387	1,979	302	279
21 to 24 years.........................	5,874	3,238	55.1	2,710	46.1	3,164	528	2,637	527	435
25 to 34 years.........................	17,286	10,360	59.9	9,130	52.8	8,156	1,230	6,927	1,460	933
35 to 44 years.........................	16,752	11,617	69.3	10,677	63.7	6,075	940	5,135	1,006	809
45 to 54 years.........................	11,826	8,886	75.1	8,315	70.3	3,511	571	2,940	470	633
55 to 64 years.........................	8,706	6,859	78.8	6,428	73.8	2,278	432	1,846	292	406
65 to 74 years.........................	7,385	6,115	82.8	5,754	77.9	1,631	360	1,271	156	364
75 years and over	4,210	3,411	81.0	3,028	71.9	1,181	383	798	85	258
Female										
Total, 18 years and over............	81,922	58,301	71.2	52,853	64.5	29,068	5,448	23,621	3,986	4,173
18 to 20 years.........................	3,867	2,041	52.8	1,677	43.4	2,190	364	1,826	264	305
21 to 24 years.........................	6,064	3,571	58.9	3,035	50.0	3,029	536	2,494	385	352
25 to 34 years.........................	17,354	11,271	64.9	10,063	58.0	7,291	1,208	6,083	1,136	701
35 to 44 years.........................	16,892	12,347	73.1	11,509	68.1	5,383	838	4,545	896	834
45 to 54 years.........................	12,245	9,356	76.4	8,698	71.0	3,548	658	2,889	493	523
55 to 64 years.........................	9,502	7,411	78.0	6,929	72.9	2,573	481	2,091	414	482
65 to 74 years.........................	9,015	7,166	79.5	6,610	73.3	2,404	556	1,848	226	472
75 years and over	6,982	5,139	73.6	4,331	62.0	2,651	807	1,844	173	504

See footnotes at end of table.

D7-1. Reported Voting and Registration, by Race, Hispanic Origin, Sex, and Age: November 1992 *(continued)*

(November 1992. Numbers in thousands. For meaning of symbols, see text)

Region, race, Hispanic origin, sex, and age	All persons	Reported registered		Reported voted		Reported that they did not vote[1]				
								Not registered		
		Number	Percent	Number	Percent	Total	Registered	Total[2]	Not a U.S. citizen	Do not know and not reported on registration[3]
UNITED STATES—CONTINUED										
Black										
Both Sexes										
Total, 18 years and over	21,039	13,442	63.9	11,371	54.0	9,668	2,070	7,598	1,044	1,870
18 to 20 years	1,501	638	42.5	474	31.6	1,027	164	863	103	176
21 to 24 years	2,042	1,106	54.2	821	40.2	1,221	284	936	116	230
25 to 34 years	5,295	3,107	58.7	2,518	47.6	2,777	589	2,188	348	479
35 to 44 years	4,515	2,976	65.9	2,589	57.3	1,926	387	1,538	274	419
45 to 54 years	2,861	2,040	71.3	1,821	63.7	1,040	219	821	118	235
55 to 64 years	2,181	1,611	73.9	1,452	66.6	729	159	570	52	170
65 to 74 years	1,634	1,219	74.6	1,083	66.3	551	137	415	17	94
75 years and over	1,010	744	73.7	613	60.7	397	131	266	16	68
Male										
Total, 18 years and over	9,425	5,727	60.8	4,786	50.8	4,639	941	3,698	548	965
18 to 20 years	745	307	41.2	218	29.2	527	89	438	47	96
21 to 24 years	940	471	50.1	319	33.9	621	152	469	60	134
25 to 34 years	2,388	1,283	53.7	1,009	42.2	1,379	274	1,105	216	260
35 to 44 years	2,027	1,295	63.9	1,113	54.9	914	181	732	138	207
45 to 54 years	1,267	838	66.2	757	59.7	510	82	428	59	125
55 to 64 years	984	710	72.1	640	65.0	344	70	274	18	94
65 to 74 years	724	533	73.7	475	65.6	249	58	190	8	37
75 years and over	350	290	82.7	256	73.0	95	34	61	2	12
Female										
Total, 18 years and over	11,614	7,715	66.4	6,585	56.7	5,029	1,129	3,899	496	905
18 to 20 years	756	331	43.8	256	33.9	500	75	425	56	79
21 to 24 years	1,102	635	57.6	503	45.6	599	132	467	56	96
25 to 34 years	2,907	1,824	62.7	1,509	51.9	1,398	315	1,083	133	219
35 to 44 years	2,488	1,682	67.6	1,476	59.3	1,012	206	806	136	212
45 to 54 years	1,595	1,202	75.4	1,065	66.8	530	137	393	59	110
55 to 64 years	1,197	901	75.3	812	67.8	385	89	296	34	75
65 to 74 years	910	686	75.3	608	66.8	303	78	225	9	57
75 years and over	659	454	68.9	357	54.2	302	97	205	14	56
Hispanic origin[4]										
Both Sexes										
Total, 18 years and over	14,688	5,137	35.0	4,238	28.9	10,450	899	9,551	5,910	995
18 to 20 years	1,159	267	23.1	183	15.8	976	85	891	483	93
21 to 24 years	1,636	429	26.2	310	18.9	1,327	119	1,207	722	120
25 to 34 years	4,177	1,239	29.7	1,000	23.9	3,177	239	2,938	1,930	237
35 to 44 years	3,322	1,160	34.9	979	29.5	2,343	181	2,162	1,353	251
45 to 54 years	1,954	851	43.5	731	37.4	1,223	120	1,103	678	143
55 to 64 years	1,257	624	49.6	566	45.0	691	58	633	401	72
65 to 74 years	767	385	50.3	319	41.6	447	66	381	199	54
75 years and over	417	182	43.6	151	36.1	267	31	235	145	26
Male										
Total, 18 years and over	7,273	2,337	32.1	1,946	26.8	5,327	391	4,936	3,132	519
18 to 20 years	563	110	19.5	72	12.8	491	38	454	259	46
21 to 24 years	855	178	20.8	124	14.5	731	54	677	413	82
25 to 34 years	2,182	562	25.8	464	21.3	1,717	98	1,619	1,100	121
35 to 44 years	1,669	540	32.4	447	26.8	1,222	93	1,129	722	127
45 to 54 years	983	416	42.4	363	36.9	620	53	566	354	78
55 to 64 years	535	276	51.6	252	47.1	283	24	259	164	37
65 to 74 years	340	186	54.8	159	46.7	181	27	154	71	18
75 years and over	147	69	46.8	66	44.9	81	3	78	49	10
Female										
Total, 18 years and over	7,415	2,800	37.8	2,291	30.9	5,124	508	4,615	2,778	476
18 to 20 years	595	158	26.5	111	18.6	485	47	438	224	47
21 to 24 years	781	250	32.1	186	23.8	596	65	531	309	38
25 to 34 years	1,995	676	33.9	535	26.8	1,460	141	1,319	830	116
35 to 44 years	1,654	620	37.5	533	32.2	1,121	87	1,033	631	123
45 to 54 years	971	435	44.7	368	37.9	603	67	537	324	65
55 to 64 years	722	348	48.2	314	43.5	408	34	374	237	35
65 to 74 years	427	199	46.7	161	37.6	266	39	227	128	35
75 years and over	270	113	41.8	85	31.3	186	29	157	96	16

[1]Includes persons reported as "did not know," and "not reported" on voting.
[2]In addition to those reported as "not registered," total includes those "not a U.S. citizen," and "not reported" on registration.
[3]Includes "do not know" and "not reported" on citizenship.
[4]Persons of Hispanic origin may be of any race.

Source: Jerry T. Jennings, U.S. Bureau of the Census, *Voting and Registration in the Election of November 1992,* Current Population Reports, P20-466, Washington, D.C.: U.S. Government Printing Office, April 1993, Table 2.

D7-2. Percent Reported Voted in Presidential Election Years, by Sex: November 1964 to 1992

(Numbers in thousands. Civilian noninstitutional population)

	Presidential elections of—							
	1992	1988	1984	1980	1976	1972	1968	1964
UNITED STATES								
Total, voting age	185,684	178,098	169,963	157,085	146,548	136,203	116,535	110,604
Percent voted.................	61.3	57.4	59.9	59.2	59.2	63.0	67.8	69.3
Male..............................	60.2	56.4	59.0	59.1	59.6	64.1	69.8	71.9
Female...........................	62.3	58.3	60.8	59.4	58.8	62.0	66.0	67.0

Source: Current Population Reports, Series P-20, Nos. 174, 228, 293, 344, 383, 414, 440, and table 2 of this report.

Source: Jerry T. Jennings, U.S. Bureau of the Census, *Voting and Registration in the Election of November 1992*, Current Population Reports, P20-466, Washington, D.C.: U.S. Government Printing Office, April 1993, Table A.

D7-3. Political Party Identification of the Adult Population, by Degree of Attachment, 1970 to 1992

[In percent. Covers citizens of voting-age living in private housing units in the contiguous United States. Data are from the National Election Studies and are based on a sample and subject to sampling variability; for details, see source]

YEAR AND SELECTED CHARACTERISTIC	Total	Strong Demo-crat	Weak Demo-crat	Inde-pendent Demo-crat	Inde-pendent	Inde-pendent Repub-lican	Weak Repub-lican	Strong Repub-lican	Apolitical
1970.............................	100	20	24	10	13	8	15	9	1
1972.............................	100	15	26	11	13	11	13	10	1
1976.............................	100	15	25	12	15	10	14	9	1
1980.............................	100	18	23	11	13	10	14	9	2
1984.............................	100	17	20	11	11	12	15	12	2
1986.............................	100	18	22	10	12	11	15	11	2
1988.............................	100	18	18	12	11	13	14	14	2
1990.............................	100	20	19	12	11	12	15	10	2
1992, total [1]	100	18	18	14	12	12	14	11	1
Year of birth:									
1959 or later (Under 34 years old) .	100	10	19	17	15	14	15	9	2
1943 to 1958 (34 to 49 years old)..	100	17	18	14	11	13	15	11	1
1927 to 1942 (50 to 65 years old)..	100	22	17	13	11	12	13	13	1
1911 to 1926 (66 to 81 years old)..	100	30	15	11	8	9	13	13	(Z)
1895 to 1910 (82 to 97 years old)..	100	30	14	9	10	7	11	19	(Z)
Sex:									
Male	100	16	15	13	12	14	15	13	1
Female	100	20	19	15	11	11	14	9	1
Race:									
White......................	100	15	17	15	12	13	16	13	1
Black......................	100	41	23	13	13	3	3	2	3
Education:									
Grade school	100	35	16	14	11	4	9	9	3
High school	100	20	19	15	13	12	12	9	2
College	100	14	17	14	11	14	17	14	(Z)

Z Less than 0.5 percent. [1] Includes other characteristics, not shown separately.

Source: Center for Political Studies, University of Michigan, Ann Arbor, MI, unpublished data. Data prior to 1988 published in Warren E. Miller and Santa A. Traugott, *American National Election Studies Data Sourcebook, 1952-1986*, Harvard University Press, Cambridge, MA, 1989, (copyright).

Source: Bureau of the Census, *Statistical Abstract of the United States: 1994*, (114th ed.) Washington, D.C.: U.S. Government Printing Office, 1994, Table 446.

D7-4. Members of Congress: 1981 to 1993

[As of beginning of first session of each Congress, (January 3). Figures for Representatives exclude vacancies]

MEMBERS OF CONGRESS AND YEAR	Male	Female	Black[1]	Hispanic[2]	AGE[3] (in years)						SENIORITY[4]				
					Under 40	40 to 49	50 to 59	60 to 69	70 to 79	80 and over	Less than 2 years	2 to 9 years	10 to 19 years	20 to 29 years	30 years or more
REPRESENTATIVES															
97th Cong., 1981	416	19	17	6	94	142	132	54	12	1	77	231	96	23	8
98th Cong., 1983	413	21	21	8	86	145	132	57	13	1	83	224	88	28	11
99th Cong., 1985	412	22	20	10	71	154	131	59	17	2	49	237	104	34	10
100th Cong., 1987	412	23	23	11	63	153	137	56	24	2	51	221	114	37	12
101st Cong., 1989	408	25	24	10	41	163	133	74	20	2	39	207	139	35	13
102d Cong., 1991	407	28	25	11	39	152	134	86	20	4	55	178	147	44	11
103d Cong., 1993[5]	388	47	38	17	47	151	128	89	12	3	118	141	132	32	12
SENATORS															
97th Cong., 1981	98	2	-	-	9	35	36	14	6	-	19	51	17	11	2
98th Cong., 1983	98	2	-	-	7	28	39	20	3	3	5	61	21	10	3
99th Cong., 1985	98	2	-	-	4	27	38	25	4	2	8	56	27	7	2
100th Cong., 1987	98	2	-	-	5	30	36	22	5	2	14	41	36	7	2
101st Cong., 1989	98	2	-	-	-	30	40	22	6	2	23	22	43	10	2
102d Cong., 1991	98	2	-	-	-	23	46	24	5	2	5	34	47	10	4
103d Cong., 1993[5]	93	7	1	-	1	16	48	22	11	1	15	30	39	11	5

- Represents zero.   [1] Source: Joint Center for Political and Economic Studies, Washington, DC, *Black Elected Officials: A National Roster*, annual (copyright).   [2] Source: National Association of Latino Elected and Appointed Officials, Washington, DC, *National Roster of Hispanic Elected Officials*, annual.   [3] Some members do not provide date of birth.   [4] Represents consecutive years of service.   [5] Includes members elected to fill vacant seats through June 14, 1993.

Source: Except as noted, compiled by U.S. Bureau of the Census from data published in *Congressional Directory*, biennial.

Source: Bureau of the Census, *Statistical Abstract of the United States: 1994,* (114th ed.) Washington, D.C.: U.S. Government Printing Office, 1994, Table 437.

D7-5. Women Holding State and Local Public Offices: 1985 to 1993

STATE	State-wide elective executive office[1][2] 1993	State legislature[1] 1993	County governing boards 1988	Mayors and municipal council members 1985	STATE	State-wide elective executive office[1][2] 1993	State legislature[1] 1993	County governing boards 1988	Mayors and municipal council members 1985
United States	72	1,524	1,653	14,672	Missouri	2	37	17	-
Alabama	1	8	7	281	Montana	1	30	18	110
Alaska	-	13	17	233	Nebraska	[3]2	10	27	241
Arizona	2	30	8	87	Nevada	3	17	10	15
Arkansas	2	14	71	365	New Hampshire	-	142	8	113
California	2	27	56	465	New Jersey	-	15	15	451
Colorado	3	35	18	315	New Mexico	1	22	17	86
Connecticut	2	47	(X)	240	New York	-	35	131	797
Delaware	3	9	2	57	North Carolina	-	31	45	337
Dist. of Columbia	(X)	(X)	(X)	7	North Dakota	4	24	11	174
Florida	1	28	51	311	Ohio	1	28	25	1,129
Georgia	-	41	28	251	Oklahoma	[3]3	13	5	312
Hawaii	-	18	8	3	Oregon	3	25	20	344
Idaho	1	32	14	141	Pennsylvania	2	25	35	-
Illinois	1	41	152	-	Rhode Island	2	37	(X)	30
Indiana	4	29	10	-	South Carolina	1	22	36	184
Iowa	3	22	35	732	South Dakota	2	21	16	149
Kansas	2	48	24	445	Tennessee	-	16	117	144
Kentucky	1	7	17	-	Texas	[3]2	29	30	786
Louisiana	2	11	32	183	Utah	2	14	2	137
Maine	-	59	3	243	Vermont	1	61	(X)	87
Maryland	-	46	21	133	Virginia	-	17	49	211
Massachusetts	-	46	5	217	Washington	4	58	15	341
Michigan	1	30	123	2,779	West Virginia	-	22	11	202
Minnesota	2	55	37	542	Wisconsin	1	36	241	-
Mississippi	-	19	8	176	Wyoming	2	22	5	86

- Represents zero.   X Not applicable.   [1] As of January.   [2] Excludes women elected to the judiciary, women appointed to State cabinet-level positions, women elected to executive posts by the legislature, and elected members of university Board of Trustees or board of education.   [3] Includes one official who was appointed to an elective position.

Source: Center for the American Woman and Politics, Eagleton Institute of Politics, Rutgers University, New Brunswick, NJ, information releases, (copyright).

Source: Bureau of the Census, *Statistical Abstract of the United States: 1994,* (114th ed.) Washington, D.C.: U.S. Government Printing Office, 1994, Table 445.

D8. VICTIMS OF CRIME

D8-1. Victimization Rates for Persons 12 Years and Over, by Type of Crime and Sex and Race of Victims: 1992

Type of crime	Rate per 1,000 persons age 12 and over			
	Male		Female	
	White	Black	White	Black
All personal crimes	**97.5**	**134.8**	**80.4**	**91.0**
Crimes of violence	36.2	63.0	24.1	40.0
Completed	12.4	26.9	8.5	16.9
Attempted	23.7	36.0	15.5	23.1
Rape	0.5	1.6 *	0.8	1.0 *
Robbery	6.5	21.8	2.9	10.5
Completed	3.7	17.6	2.2	6.4
With injury	1.1	6.7	1.2	3.4
Without injury	2.6	10.9	1.0	2.9 *
Attempted	2.8	4.2	0.7	4.1
With injury	0.6	1.9 *	0.2 *	0.7 *
Without injury	2.2	2.2 *	0.5	3.4
Assault	29.1	39.7	20.4	28.5
Aggravated	10.6	24.4	5.2	13.3
Completed with injury	4.0	8.4	1.6	5.3
Attempted with weapon	6.6	15.9	3.7	8.0
Simple	18.6	15.3	15.2	15.1
Completed with injury	4.5	0.9 *	4.5	4.7
Attempted without weapon	14.0	14.4	10.6	10.4
Crimes of theft	**61.4**	**71.8**	**56.3**	**51.1**
Completed	57.5	65.8	53.0	49.9
Attempted	3.8	6.0	3.3	1.2 *
Personal larceny with contact	1.6	6.3	2.5	3.2
Personal larceny without contact	59.8	65.6	53.9	47.9
Completed	56.0	59.5	51.0	46.7
Attempted	3.8	6.0	2.9	1.2 *
Population age 12 and over	85,056,100	10,796,420	90,557,960	13,075,870

Note: Detail may not add to total shown because of rounding.
* Estimate is based on about 10 or fewer sample cases.

Source: Bureau of Justice Statistics, U.S. Department of Justice, *Criminal Victimization in the United States, 1992,* A National Crime Victimization Survey Report, NCJ-145125, March 1994, Table 7.

D8-2. Victimization Rates for Persons 12 Years and Over, by Race, Sex, and Age of Victims and Type of Crime: 1992

Race, sex, and age	Total population	Rate per 1,000 persons in each age group	
		Crimes of violence	Crimes of theft
White			
Male			
12–15	5,782,290	91.3	114.6
16–19	5,534,440	88.6	96.4
20–24	7,623,060	83.8	124.6
25–34	17,401,400	38.7	73.5
35–49	23,339,990	22.0	49.8
50–64	13,931,220	11.4	33.1
65 and over	11,443,680	6.4	14.9
Female			
12–15	5,522,070	57.9	79.7
16–19	5,362,500	51.9	104.9
20–24	7,508,090	51.0	97.5
25–34	17,414,450	32.6	70.1
35–49	23,673,130	20.0	58.1
50–64	14,916,270	7.6	31.9
65 and over	16,161,410	2.7	18.2
Black			
Male			
12–15	1,115,770	73.9	90.5
16–19	987,030	158.1	75.9
20–24	1,132,150	131.2	111.4
25–34	2,387,690	55.7	101.9
35–49	2,773,950	41.3	57.2
50–64	1,436,810	23.2 *	40.8
65 and over	962,990	12.4 *	13.1 *
Female			
12–15	1,103,220	92.7	64.4
16–19	1,052,120	94.8	67.7
20–24	1,314,120	77.7	70.0
25–34	2,872,230	48.1	68.7
35–49	3,370,440	12.9	46.1
50–64	1,821,880	12.1 *	36.7
65 and over	1,541,840	9.6 *	9.1 *

* Estimate is based on about 10 or fewer sample cases.

Source: Bureau of Justice Statistics, U.S. Department of Justice, *Criminal Victimization in the United States, 1992*, A National Crime Victimization Survey Report, NCJ-145125, March 1994, Table 11.

D8-3. Percentage of Victimizations Involving Strangers, by Sex and Age of Victims and Type of Crime: 1992

Sex and age	Crimes of violence	Completed violent crimes	Attempted violent crimes	Rape	Robbery Total	Robbery With injury	Robbery Without injury	Assault Total	Assault Aggravated	Simple
Both sexes	60.1 %	59.1 %	60.7 %	48.3 %	80.9 %	81.7 %	80.4 %	55.6 %	66.7 %	49.5 %
12–15	49.5	45.7	51.7	57.5 *	76.7	100.0 *	67.5	45.3	43.3	46.2
16–19	62.0	64.5	60.6	38.8 *	72.1	74.3	71.1	60.0	73.7	49.6
20–24	66.7	59.8	70.6	63.3 *	80.7	72.7	84.6	64.0	68.7	61.8
25–34	57.7	58.7	57.1	38.8 *	79.6	79.2	79.9	52.3	73.6	42.4
35–49	61.2	61.8	60.9	34.1 *	84.9	87.8	83.6	56.6	71.4	46.7
50–64	66.3	65.0	66.9	100.0 *	92.5	83.7 *	100.0	55.2	57.9	53.9
65 and over	68.1	86.8	58.1	0.0 *	100.0	100.0 *	100.0 *	57.2	58.7 *	56.0 *
Male	70.3	73.3	68.5	68.6 *	89.3	94.0	87.3	65.2	74.0	59.3
12–15	51.0	48.2	52.7	100.0 *	76.8	100.0 *	67.2	45.4	39.0	48.4
16–19	71.7	80.0	67.0	0.0 *	79.5	92.6	72.9	70.1	83.9	56.8
20–24	77.0	72.1	79.4	100.0 *	92.9	92.1 *	93.3	72.5	76.2	70.6
25–34	76.2	84.3	71.8	70.2 *	96.1	93.1	97.3	70.2	86.8	59.5
35–49	71.7	77.3	68.4	45.3 *	91.5	100.0 *	88.9	67.0	75.9	58.6
50–64	73.3	83.4	68.6	100.0 *	93.8	85.5 *	100.0 *	61.5	71.6 *	57.6
65 and over	65.8	80.2 *	56.8 *	0.0 *	100.0 *	100.0 *	100.0 *	57.2 *	48.8 *	64.3 *
Female	46.0	40.1	49.4	34.3 *	64.8	66.0	63.7	42.9	53.2	38.7
12–15	47.3	41.3	50.3	49.6 *	76.2 *	100.0 *	68.5 *	45.2	49.5	43.4
16–19	45.6	38.1	49.8	45.3 *	59.3	40.6 *	67.9 *	42.1	46.6	40.0
20–24	50.2	43.7	54.7	28.2 *	55.4 *	39.7 *	64.7 *	50.7	54.0	49.4
25–34	36.6	35.1	37.8	24.7 *	55.0	69.1	32.5 *	32.9	49.5	27.9
35–49	48.4	40.2	52.4	23.9 *	72.9	76.9 *	69.1 *	45.0	63.7	36.7
50–64	56.6	38.0 *	64.6	0.0 *	89.4 *	80.3 *	100.0 *	48.2	46.5 *	49.2 *
65 and over	71.6	100.0 *	59.8 *	0.0 *	100.0 *	100.0 *	100.0 *	57.1 *	75.7 *	45.8 *

* Estimate is based on about 10 or fewer sample cases.

Source: Bureau of Justice Statistics, U.S. Department of Justice, *Criminal Victimization in the United States, 1992*, A National Crime Victimization Survey Report, NCJ-145125, March 1994, Table 38.

D8-4. Percentage of Victimizations Involving Strangers, by Sex and Race of Victims and Type of Crime: 1992

Sex and race	Crimes of violence	Completed violent crimes	Attempted violent crimes	Rape	Robbery Total	Robbery With injury	Robbery Without injury	Assault Total	Assault Aggravated	Simple
Both sexes										
White	60.4 %	57.3 %	62.0 %	50.7 %	79.9 %	77.9 %	80.9 %	56.9 %	69.2 %	51.2 %
Black	60.0	65.6	55.9	39.6 *	82.3	86.3	79.6	50.4	57.9	41.4
Male										
White	70.6	70.6	70.7	74.8 *	88.6	90.1	88.1	66.5	75.0	61.7
Black	71.5	82.0	63.6	53.4 *	90.5	100.0	84.2	61.8	70.8	47.3
Female										
White	45.9	39.1	49.6	36.6 *	61.5	63.3	59.9	44.0	58.2	39.2
Black	45.1	44.1	45.9	21.9 *	68.2	63.0 *	71.7	37.4	38.4	36.5

* Estimate is based on about 10 or fewer sample cases.

Source: Bureau of Justice Statistics, U.S. Department of Justice, *Criminal Victimization in the United States, 1992*, A National Crime Victimization Survey Report, NCJ-145125, March 1994, Table 39.

D8-5. Victim/Offender Relationship and Sex of Victim, by Type of Violent Victimization Committed by Lone Offenders: 1992–93

Victim/offender relationship	Average annual percent of victimizations				
	Total	Rape/Sex - ual assault	Robbery	Aggravated assault	Simple assault
Female victims					
Intimate	29%	26%	28%	28%	29%
Spouse	9	5	6	5	11
Ex-spouse	4	5	5	5	4
Boy/girlfriend (or ex-)	16	16	18	17	15
Other relative	9	3	5	7	11
Acquaintance	40	53	19	36	41
Stranger	23	18	48	30	19
Male victims					
Intimate	4%	*	3%	5%	3%
Spouse	1	*	*	1	1
Ex-spouse	1	*	*	*	1
Boy/girlfriend (or ex-)	2	*	2	3	1
Other relative	3	*	2	4	3
Acquaintance	44	54	26	40	49
Stranger	49	46	69	51	45

Note: Intimate includes spouse or ex-spouse, boyfriend or girlfriend, and ex-boyfriend or ex-girlfriend. Detail may not add to total because of rounding.
*Ten or fewer sample cases.

Source: Bureau of Justice Statistics, "Violence Against Women: Estimates from the Redesigned Survey," Special Report NCJ-154348, National Crime Victimization Survey, August 1995, Table 4.

D8-6. Average Annual Rate of Violent Victimization, by Sex of Victim, Victim/Offender Relationship, and Type of Crime Committed by Lone Offenders: 1992–93

Type of crime	Average annual rates per 1,000 persons age 12 or older			
	Intimate	Other relative	Acquaintance/ friend	Stranger
Female victims				
Crimes of violence	9.3	2.8	12.9	7.4
Rape/Sexual assault	1.0	.1	2.0	.7
Robbery	.7	.1	.5	1.2
Aggravated assault	1.5	.4	2.0	1.6
Simple assault	6.1	2.2	8.5	3.9
Annual average number of violent crimes	1,008,000	304,500	1,402,500	802,300
Male victims				
Crimes of violence	1.4	1.2	17.2	19.0
Rape/Sexual assault	*	*	.2	.2
Robbery	.1	.1	.9	2.4
Aggravated assault	.5	.4	3.8	4.8
Simple assault	.8	.7	12.4	11.6
Annual average number of violent crimes	143,400	122,000	1,754,000	1,933,100

Note: Intimate includes spouse or ex-spouse, boyfriend or girlfriend, and ex-boyfriend or ex-girlfriend. Average annual numbers have been rounded to the nearest 100.
*Ten or fewer sample cases.

Source: Bureau of Justice Statistics, "Violence Against Women: Estimates from the Redesigned Survey," Special Report NCJ-154348, National Crime Victimization Survey, August 1995, Table 5.

D8-7. Average Annual Rate of Violent Victimizations of Women by a Lone Offender, by Victim Characteristics and Victim/Offender Relationship: 1992–93

Victim characteristic	Average annual rate of violent victimization per 1,000 females age 12 or older				
	Total	Intimate	Other relative	Acquaint-ance/friend	Stranger
Crimes of violence	36.1	9.3	2.8	12.9	7.4
Race					
White	35.2	9.1	2.6	12.5	7.1
Black	44.6	10.9	3.5	17.2	9.5
Other	27.8	6.5	4.5	8.4	5.7
Ethnicity					
Hispanic	33.9	7.3	3.2	10.0	9.0
Non-Hispanic	36.3	9.4	2.8	13.2	7.2
Age					
12–18	74.6	9.6	6.1	39.1	11.9
19–29	63.7	21.3	4.7	18.2	13.9
30–45	37.5	10.8	2.8	12.4	7.4
46–64	12.5	2.2	1.2	4.1	3.7
65 or over	4.8	1.2	0.3	1.1	1.2
Education					
Some high school or less	47.7	9.9	4.7	20.5	7.5
High school graduate	27.9	9.2	2.2	8.8	4.9
Some college or more	35.9	8.7	2.1	11.6	9.6
Annual family income					
Less than $9,999	57.1	19.9	6.1	18.5	7.8
$10,000–$14,999	46.8	13.3	4.0	14.1	9.1
$15,000–$19,999	42.2	10.9	3.1	17.3	7.0
$20,000–$29,999	38.0	9.5	2.7	14.8	7.9
$30,000–$49,999	30.6	5.4	1.8	11.5	8.4
$50,000 or more	24.8	4.5	1.8	9.7	6.3
Marital status					
Married	16.9	2.7	1.6	5.7	4.9
Widowed	10.4	1.9	0.6	3.6	2.5
Divorced	61.8	23.1	4.2	19.5	10.2
Separated	123.5	82.2	10.0	19.9	7.4
Never married	63.9	12.0	4.6	27.2	12.9
Location of residence					
Urban	45.4	10.7	3.0	15.9	10.8
Suburban	33.6	9.2	2.7	11.5	7.1
Rural	29.5	7.7	2.7	12.2	3.7

Note: Rates of violence for this table include rapes, sexual assaults, robberies, and aggravated and simple assaults from the NCVS. Rates exclude homicide victimizations. Relationship specific rates do not add to the total because some victims did not identify their relationship to the offender.

Source: Bureau of Justice Statistics, "Violence Against Women: Estimates from the Redesigned Survey," Special Report NCJ-154348, National Crime Victimization Survey, August 1995, Table 6.

D8-8. Murder Victims, by Age, Sex, and Race: 1992

AGE	Total	Sex			Race			
		Male	Female	Unknown	White	Black	Other	Unknown
Total	**22,540**	**17,576**	**4,936**	**28**	**10,647**	**11,175**	**548**	**170**
Percent distribution	100.0	78.0	21.9	0.1	47.2	49.6	2.4	0.8
Under 18 yrs. old	2,428	1,748	679	1	1,103	1,240	72	13
18 yrs. old and over	19,803	15,608	4,193	2	9,409	9,820	469	105
Infant (under 1 yr. old)	254	137	116	1	147	99	3	5
1 to 4 yrs. old	408	237	171	-	204	192	12	-
5 to 9 yrs. old	126	64	62	-	60	56	10	-
10 to 14 yrs. old	351	230	121	-	163	171	14	3
15 to 19 yrs. old	2,851	2,444	407	-	1,114	1,664	60	13
20 to 24 yrs. old	4,181	3,551	630	-	1,614	2,451	97	19
25 to 29 yrs. old	3,455	2,749	706	-	1,479	1,891	69	16
30 to 34 yrs. old	3,045	2,382	662	1	1,420	1,530	76	19
35 to 39 yrs. old	2,231	1,706	525	-	1,145	1,027	51	8
40 to 44 yrs. old	1,650	1,262	388	-	858	731	47	14
45 to 49 yrs. old	1,072	819	253	-	634	396	35	7
50 to 54 yrs. old	695	519	175	1	406	265	21	3
55 to 59 yrs. old	449	356	93	-	281	146	18	4
60 to 64 yrs. old	412	307	105	-	283	120	6	3
65 to 69 yrs. old	315	205	110	-	187	120	7	1
70 to 74 yrs. old	262	159	103	-	177	80	4	1
75 yrs. old and over	474	229	245	-	340	121	11	2
Age unknown	309	220	64	25	135	115	7	52

- Represents zero.

Source: U.S. Federal Bureau of Investigation, *Crime in the United States*, annual.

Source: U.S. Bureau of the Census, *Statistical Abstract of the United States: 1994*, (114th edition), Washington, D.C.: U.S. Government Printing Office, 1994, Table 306.

D8-9. Homicide Victims, by Race and Sex: 1970 to 1991

[**Rates per 100,000 resident population in specified group.** Excludes deaths to nonresidents of United States. Beginning 1980, deaths classified according to the ninth revision of the *International Classification of Diseases;* for earlier years, classified according to revision in use at the time; see text, section 2. See also *Historical Statistics, Colonial Times to 1970*, series H 971-978]

YEAR	HOMICIDE VICTIMS					HOMICIDE RATE [2]				
	Total [1]	White		Black		Total [1]	White		Black	
		Male	Female	Male	Female		Male	Female	Male	Female
1970	16,848	5,865	1,938	7,265	1,569	8.3	6.8	2.1	67.6	13.3
1975	21,310	8,222	2,751	8,092	1,929	9.9	9.0	2.9	69.0	14.9
1980	24,278	10,381	3,177	8,385	1,898	10.7	10.9	3.2	66.6	13.5
1981	23,646	9,941	3,125	8,312	1,825	10.3	10.4	3.1	64.8	12.7
1982	22,358	9,260	3,179	7,730	1,743	9.6	9.6	3.1	59.1	12.0
1983	20,191	8,355	2,880	6,822	1,672	8.6	8.6	2.8	51.4	11.3
1984	19,796	8,171	2,956	6,563	1,677	8.4	8.3	2.9	48.7	11.2
1985	19,893	8,122	3,041	6,616	1,666	8.3	8.2	2.9	48.4	11.0
1986	21,731	8,567	3,123	7,634	1,861	9.0	8.6	3.0	55.0	12.1
1987	21,103	7,979	3,149	7,518	1,969	8.7	7.9	3.0	53.3	12.6
1988	22,032	7,994	3,072	8,314	2,089	9.0	7.9	2.9	58.0	13.2
1989	22,909	8,337	2,971	8,888	2,074	9.2	8.2	2.8	61.1	12.9
1990	24,932	9,147	3,006	9,981	2,163	10.0	9.0	2.8	69.2	13.5
1991	26,513	9,581	3,201	10,628	2,330	10.5	9.3	3.0	72.0	14.2

[1] Includes races not shown separately.   [2] Rate based on enumerated population figures as of April 1 for 1970, 1980, and 1990; July 1 estimates for other years.

Source: U.S. National Center for Health Statistics, *Vital Statistics of the United States*, annual, and unpublished data.

Source: U.S. Bureau of the Census, *Statistical Abstract of the United States: 1994*, (114th edition), Washington, D.C.: U.S. Government Printing Office, 1994, Table 307.

D9. CRIMINAL OFFENDERS

D9-1. Jail Inmates, by Sex, Race, and Hispanic Origin: 1978 to 1992

[Excludes Federal and State prisons or other correctional institutions; institutions exclusively for juveniles; State-operated jails in Alaska, Connecticut, Delaware, Hawaii, Rhode Island, and Vermont; and other facilities which retain persons for less than 48 hours. As of June 30. For 1978, 1983, and 1988, data based on National Jail Census; for other years, based on sample survey and subject to sampling variability]

CHARACTERISTIC	1978	1983	1985	1987	1988	1989	1990	1991	1992
Total Inmates [1]	158,394	223,552	256,615	295,873	343,569	395,553	405,320	426,479	444,584
Percent of rated capacity	65	85	94	98	101	108	104	101	99
Male	148,839	207,783	235,909	270,172	313,158	356,050	368,002	386,865	403,768
Female	9,555	15,769	19,077	23,920	30,411	37,253	37,318	39,614	40,816
White	89,418	130,118	151,403	168,647	166,302	201,732	186,989	190,333	191,362
Black	65,104	87,508	102,646	124,267	141,979	185,910	174,335	187,618	195,156
Other races	3,872	5,926	2,566	2,959	3,932	7,911	5,321	5,391	5,831
Hispanic [2]	16,349	31,297	35,926	41,422	51,455	55,377	57,449	60,129	62,961
Non-Hispanic	142,045	192,254	220,689	254,451	292,114	340,176	347,871	366,350	381,623
Adult [3]	156,783	221,815	254,986	294,092	341,893	393,303	403,019	424,129	441,781
Awaiting arraignment or trial	77,453	113,984	127,059	150,101	175,669	204,291	207,358	217,671	223,840
Convicted	75,438	107,660	123,409	139,394	166,224	189,012	195,661	206,458	217,940
Juvenile [4]	1,611	1,736	1,629	1,781	1,676	2,250	2,301	2,350	2,804

[1] For 1985, 1987, 1989-1992, includes juveniles not shown separately by sex, and for 1988 and 1990-1992 includes 31,356, 38,675, 43,138, and 52,235 persons, respectively, of unknown race not shown separately.   [2] Hispanic persons may be of any race.   [3] Includes inmates not classified by conviction status.   [4] Juveniles are persons whose age makes them initially subject to juvenile court authority although they are sometimes tried as adults in criminal court.

Source: U.S. Bureau of Justice Statistics, *Profile of Jail Inmates, 1978 and 1989; Jail Inmates*, annual; and *1988 Census of Local Jails.*

Source: U.S. Bureau of the Census, *Statistical Abstract of the United States: 1994*, (114th edition), Washington, D.C.: U.S. Government Printing Office, 1994, Table 338.

D9-2. Female Prisoners in State and Federal Institutions, by Security Classification, Type of Offense, and Jurisdiction: 1993

By security classification, type of offense, and jurisdiction, 1993

| Jurisdiction | Security classification | | | | Type of offense | | | | | |
	Maximum	Medium	Minimum	Other	Violent offenses	Property offenses	Victimless offenses	Drug/alcohol offenses	Domestic violence offenses	Other
Alabama[a]	128	580	257	--	502	424	--	156	--	33
Alaska	2	36	26	86	46	35	--	32	--	37
Arizona	24	444	413	144	214	347	--	413	--	21
Arkansas	87	388	75	--	193	259	--	91	--	7
California	--	--	--	--	1,716	2,486	324	2,716	--	281
Connecticut	179	236	424	23	--	164	--	231	--	467
Delaware	12	47	155	45	132	30	1	5	60	50
District of Columbia	0	599	142	--	137	4	--	439	--	161
Florida	6	752	1,596	136	1,039	581	77	938	--	3
Georgia	204	530	666	340	601	649	57	406	--	27
Hawaii	0	123	35	21	32	56	52	39	0	--
Idaho	0	19	41	55	14	60	14	52	--	1
Illinois	136	439	973	117	616	525	0	459	0	65
Indiana	355	322	99	--	122	318	132	204	0	--
Iowa	27	105	86	48	75	101	--	63	--	--
Kansas	43	83	165	26	97	86	NA	107	NA	27
Kentucky	2	221	121	58	159	142	0	82	0	19
Louisiana	51	311	162	0	166	170	5	147	0	0
Maryland	117	360	268	132	181	0	436	182	7	49
Massachusetts	0	380	55	241	229	155	405	236	0	14
Michigan[a]	110	43	885	687	656	12	514	372	0	10
Minnesota	3	100	42	71	53	66	0	51	28	18
Mississippi	39	267	161	1	191	234	--	181	--	--
Missouri	87	190	420	217	280	413	0	202	0	19
Montana	0	11	18	12	27	32	0	7	0	0
Nebraska	49	43	44	42	46	64	1	53	NA	12
Nevada	26	136	215	39	99	140	18	179	--	--
New Hampshire	25	70	55	15	9 [a]	35 [a]	--	131 [a]	--	--
New Jersey	358	0	481	0	159	183	34	429	25	--
New Mexico	3	105	88	18	50 [a]	44 [a]	63 [a]	68 [a]	--	--
New York	712	1,873	883	0	930	287	--	2,251	--	--
North Carolina	1	453	553	88	364	355	NA	312	NA	64
North Dakota	2	5	7	0	5	9	0	0	0	0
Ohio	62	795	1,422	252	836	1,138	109	577	50	5
Oklahoma	116	118	610	238	371	370	NA	553	NA	327
Oregon	10	92	194	59	159	95	10	91	NA	--
Pennsylvania	459	252	415	0	421	0	0	320	0	--
Rhode Island	0	91	46	28	12	0	19	--	--	15
South Carolina	35	366	520	69	277	401	40	251	2	19
South Dakota	14	48	22	0	34	3	9	22	13	3
Tennessee	4	212	136	20	200	109	--	56	--	31
Virginia	0	665	0	0	214	312	0	139	0	--
Washington	49	113	464	0	183	109	0	354	0	--
West Virginia	4	50	50	0	30	20	45	5	4	0
Wisconsin	78	69	176	50	135	130	17	89	--	--
Wyoming	1	35	19	5	18	3	27	10	2	--
Federal Bureau of Prisons	95	151	1,972	3,312	243	455	225	3,649	--	805

Note: This information was collected through a survey mailed to the departments of correction in the 50 States, the District of Columbia, and the Federal Bureau of Prisons in December 1993. Colorado, Maine, and Utah did not respond to the survey. Information was unavailable for Texas and Vermont. The Source presents the information as submitted by the responding agencies. No attempt is made by the Source to verify the information received.

[a]The data are estimates.

Source: Contact Publishing, *Corrections Compendium* (Lincoln, NE: Contact Publishing, January 1994), pp. 8, 9. Table adapted by SOURCEBOOK staff. Reprinted by permission.

Source: Kathleen Maguire and Ann L. Pastore (eds.), Bureau of Justice Statistics, U.S. Department of Justice, *Sourcebook of Criminal Justice Statistics, 1993*, Washington, D.C.: U.S. Government Printing Office, 1994, Table 6-36.

D9-3. State Prison Inmates, by Sex: 1986 and 1991

	State prison inmates		Percent change
	1986	1991	
Female	22,777	39,917	75.2%
Male	464,603	728,246	52.9%

Note: Data are based on custody counts from the National Prisoner Statistics program.

Source: Tracy Snell, Bureau of Justice Statistics, U.S. Department of Justice, *Women in Prison—Survey of State Prison Inmates, 1991*, March 1994, pg. 2.

D9-4. Characteristics of State Prison Inmates, by Sex: 1986 and 1991

Characteristic	Percent of female inmates		Percent of male inmates	
	1991	1986	1991	1986
Race/Hispanic origin				
White non-Hispanic	36.2%	39.7%	35.4%	39.5%
Black non-Hispanic	46.0	46.0	45.5	45.2
Hispanic	14.2	11.7	16.8	12.7
Other[a]	3.6	2.5	2.3	2.5
Age				
17 or younger	.1%	.2%	.7%	.5%
18-24	16.3	22.3	21.6	26.9
25-34	50.4	50.5	45.5	45.5
35-44	25.5	19.6	22.6	19.4
45-54	6.1	5.5	6.6	5.2
55 or older	1.7	1.8	3.2	2.5
Median age	31 years	29 years	30 years	29 years
Marital status				
Married	17.3%	20.1%	18.1%	20.4%
Widowed	5.9	6.7	1.6	1.6
Divorced	19.1	20.5	18.4	18.0
Separated	12.5	11.0	5.9	5.8
Never married	45.1	41.7	55.9	54.3
Education[b]				
8th grade or less	16.0%	16.5%	19.6%	20.9%
Some high school	45.8	49.7	46.2	50.6
High school graduate	22.7	19.1	21.9	17.7
Some college or more	15.5	14.8	12.3	10.8
Pre-arrest employment				
Employed	46.7%	47.1%	68.5%	70.1%
Full time	35.7	37.1	56.5	58.4
Part time	11.0	10.0	12.0	11.7
Unemployed	53.3%	52.9%	31.5%	30.0%
Looking	19.2	22.0	16.2	17.8
Not looking	34.1	30.9	15.3	12.2
Number of inmates	38,796	19,812	672,847	430,604

Note: In 1991, data were missing on marital status for 1.1% of cases, on education for 0.8%, and on prearrest employment for 0.7%. In 1986, data were missing for race and Hispanic origin for 0.4% of cases, on marital status for 0.1%, on education for 0.4%, and on prearrest employment for 0.5%.
[a] Includes Asians, Pacific Islanders, American Indians, Alaska Natives, and other racial groups.
[b] Based on highest grade completed.

Source: Tracy Snell, Bureau of Justice Statistics, U.S. Department of Justice, *Women in Prison—Survey of State Prison Inmates, 1991*, March 1994, Table 1.

D9-5. Most Serious Offense of State Prison Inmates, by Sex: 1986 and 1991

	Percent of prison inmates			
	1991		1986	
Most serious offense	Female	Male	Female	Male
All offenses	100.0 %	100.0 %	100.0 %	100.0 %
Violent offenses	32.2 %	47.4 %	40.7 %	55.2 %
Murder[a]	11.7	10.5	13.0	11.2
Negligent manslaughter	3.4	1.7	6.8	3.0
Kidnaping	.4	1.2	.9	1.7
Rape	.4	3.7	.2	4.5
Other sexual assault	1.3	6.2	.9	4.7
Robbery	7.8	15.2	10.6	21.3
Assault	6.2	8.3	7.1	8.1
Other violent[b]	1.1	.5	1.2	.8
Property offenses	28.7 %	24.6 %	41.2 %	30.5 %
Burglary	4.5	12.9	5.9	17.0
Larceny/theft	11.1	4.5	14.7	5.6
Motor vehicle theft	.7	2.3	.5	1.4
Arson	1.0	.7	1.2	.7
Fraud	10.2	2.4	17.0	3.2
Stolen property	1.0	1.4	1.6	2.0
Other property[c]	.1	.5	.4	.5
Drug offenses	32.8 %	20.7 %	12.0 %	8.4 %
Possession	11.8	7.3	4.0	2.9
Trafficking	19.8	13.0	7.3	5.3
Other/unspecified	1.3	.4	.7	.2
Public-order offenses	5.7 %	7.0 %	5.1 %	5.2 %
Weapons	.5	1.9	.9	1.5
Other public-order[d]	5.1	5.1	4.3	3.7
Other offenses	.6 %	.4 %	.9 %	.7 %
Number of inmates	38,462	665,719	19,761	430,151

Note: Excludes an estimated 7,462 inmates in 1991 and 505 inmates in 1986 for whom offense was unknown. Detail may not add to total because of rounding.
[a]Includes nonnegligent manslaughter.
[b]Includes blackmail, extortion, hit-and-run driving with bodily injury, child abuse, and criminal endangerment.
[c]Includes destruction of property, vandalism, hit-and-run driving without bodily injury, trespassing, and possession of burglary tools.
[d]Includes escape from custody, driving while intoxicated, offenses against morals and decency, and commercialized vice.

Source: Tracy Snell, Bureau of Justice Statistics, U.S. Department of Justice, *Women in Prison—Survey of State Prison Inmates, 1991*, March 1994, Table 2.

D9-6. Percentage of Women Serving a Sentence in State Prison for Murder, by Relationship of Victim: 1991

Relationship of victim to offender	Percent of females serving a sentence for homicide*
Intimate	31.9%
Relative	17.0
Well known	14.3
Acquaintance	12.8
Known by sight only	2.7
Stranger	21.3

*Homicide includes murder, negligent manslaughter, and nonnegligent manslaughter.

Source: Tracy Snell, Bureau of Justice Statistics, U.S. Department of Justice, *Women in Prison—Survey of State Prison Inmates, 1991*, March 1994, pg. 3.

D9-7. Prior Physical or Sexual Abuse of State Prison Inmates, by Sex: 1991

	Percent of State prison inmates		
	Total	Female	Male
Ever physically or sexually abused before current incarceration			
No	86.1%	56.8%	87.8%
Yes	13.9	43.2	12.2
Before age 18	11.9%	31.7%	10.7%
After age 18	4.2	24.5	3.0
Physically abused	11.3	33.5	10.0
Sexually abused	6.8	33.9	5.3
Number of inmates	700,475	38,109	662,367
Relationship of abuser to inmate*			
Intimate	11.2%	49.8%	3.0%
Spouse/ex-spouse	6.1	30.5	1.0
Boyfriend/girlfriend	6.6	27.6	2.2
Relative	68.1	56.1	70.6
Parent/guardian	53.7	37.7	57.1
Other relative	22.6	26.5	21.7
Friend/acquaintance	22.8	20.1	23.4
Someone else	21.2	19.6	21.6
Refusal to answer	1.1	1.3	1.1

Note: Sexual abuse includes fondling, incest, molestation, sodomy, rape, and other types of sexual assault. Detail adds to more than total because some inmates were abused both before and after age 18 or were both sexually and physically abused; inmates may also have reported more than one abuser.
*Based on those inmates who were abused and knew their abuser.

Source: Tracy Snell, Bureau of Justice Statistics, U.S. Department of Justice, *Women in Prison—Survey of State Prison Inmates, 1991*, March 1994, Table 8.

D9-8. Women under Sentence of Death in State Prisons, by Race and State: December 31, 1993

State	Women under sentence of death 12/31/93		
	Total	White	Black
Total	35	24	11
Alabama	4	2	2
California	4	3	1
Florida	4	3	1
Illinois	4	2	2
Oklahoma	4	3	1
Pennsylvania	3	1	2
Texas	3	2	1
Missouri	2	2	0
North Carolina	2	2	0
Arizona	1	1	0
Idaho	1	1	0
Mississippi	1	1	0
Nevada	1	0	1
Tennessee	1	1	0

Source: James Stephan and Pter Brien, Bureau of Justice Statistics, U.S. Department of Justice, Capital Punishment, 1993, NCJ-150042, December 1994, pg. 8.

D9-9. Race and Hispanic Origin of State Prisoners under Sentence of Death, by Sex: December 31, 1993

	White	Black	Other
Male	1,542	1,098	41
Hispanic	187	11	5
Female	24	11	0
Hispanic	2	1	0

Source: James Stephan and Pter Brien, Bureau of Justice Statistics, U.S. Department of Justice, *Capital Punishment, 1993,* NCJ-150042, December 1994, pg. 8.

D9-10. Federal Prisoners, by Sex: 1993

United States, 1990-93

	1990		1991		1992		1993	
	Number	Percent	Number	Percent	Number	Percent	Number	Percent
Total	65,347	100.0 %	71,608	100.0 %	79,859	100.0 %	89,129	100.0 %
Sex								
Male	60,346	92.3	65,954	92.1	73,460	92.0	82,251	92.3
Female	5,001	7.7	5,654	7.9	6,399	8.0	6,878	7.7

Note: These data include Federal Bureau of Prisons designated population only, which refers to prisoners who have been assigned to a facility. Data for age is missing for 26 prisoners in 1990, 8 in 1991, 27 in 1992, and 5 in 1993.

Source: Kathleen Maguire and Ann L. Pastore (eds.), Bureau of Justice Statistics, U.S. Department of Justice, *Sourcebook of Criminal Justice Statistics, 1993*, Washington, D.C.: U.S. Government Printing Office, 1994, Table 6-64.

D9-11. Federal Prisoners, by Sex and Type of Facilities: 1993

United States, 1993[a]

| | Total | | Prisoners confined in: | | | |
| | | | Bureau of Prisons facilities | | Contract facilities[b] | |
	Number	Percent	Number	Percent	Number	Percent
Total	89,129	100.0 %	80,358	100.0 %	8,771	100.0 %
Sex						
Male	82,251	92.3	74,548	92.8	7,703	87.8
Female	6,878	7.7	5,810	7.2	1,068	12.2

[a]Percents may not sum to total because of rounding.
[b]Facilities operated by an entity other than the Federal Bureau of Prisons that house Bureau prisoners under contract, e.g., community corrections centers.

Source: Kathleen Maguire and Ann L. Pastore (eds.), Bureau of Justice Statistics, U.S. Department of Justice, *Sourcebook of Criminal Justice Statistics, 1993*, Washington, D.C.: U.S. Government Printing Office, 1994, Table 6-65.

Guide to Information Sources

The United States has a decentralized statistical system. This means that many federal agencies produce statistics. Such a wide variety of sources is often confusing to those trying to find data on a particular question or issue. Statistical handbooks such as this one, therefore, can be used as a guide to appropriate data sources.

Most federal agencies have a central number to help data users find the right persons within the agency for particular statistics. Much of the data on women comes from the Bureau of the Census, the Bureau of Labor Statistics, the National Center for Health Statistics, the National Center for Education Statistics, and the Bureau of Justice Statistics. Agencies often have unpublished data available to the public, so it's worth a telephone call if you do not find what you want. More agencies are making their data available on Internet, on diskettes, and on CD-ROM as well. Check libraries for the publications, especially those with a government documents section. Most publications are available for purchase from the information offices of the issuing agency or from the Superintendent of Documents, U.S. Government Printing Office, Washington, DC 20402, 202-783-3238.

Call the U.S. Bureau of the Census for decennial census data (including for states and local areas), population estimates and projections, demographic characteristics (e.g., age, sex, race and ethnicity, marital status, living arrangements, family types), social characteristics (e.g., education, child care arrangements, voting), and economic characteristics (e.g., occupation, income, poverty, public assistance, assets, pensions). The general telephone number for help is 301-457-4100. The Census Bureau also has a home page on the Internet that includes data files. If your local system has Mosaic or Netscape client software, use this address: (http://www.census.gov/). Otherwise, telephone 301-457-4100 or send an e-mail to (webmaster@census.gov) for additional options and direct e-mail addresses.

Call the Bureau of Labor Statistics for current statistics on labor force status, employment and unemployment, consumer expenditures, prices, productivity, technological trends in industries, compensation, working conditions, and the glass ceiling. The general telephone number for help is 202-606-5886. The Internet address is: (http://www.cdc.gov/nchswww/nchshome.htm) and the e-mail address is: (nchsquery@nch10a.em.cdc.gov).

Call the National Center for Health Statistics for statistics on births, deaths, causes of death, life expectancy, marriage and divorce, and health status. The general number for help is 301-436-8500. The Internet address is: (http://www.cdc.gov/nchswww/nchshome.htm). The e-mail address is: (nchsquery@nch10a.em.edc.gov).

Call the National Center for Education Statistics for information about fields of study, degrees conferred, and educational institutions. The general number for help is 1-800-424-1616.

Call the Bureau of Justice Statistics (BJS) for statistics. on crime victimization, law enforcement, state felony courts, corrections, drugs and crime, justice expenditure and employment, criminal history information systems, census of jails, and state and federal justice statistics. The BJS e-mail address is: (askncjrs@aspensys.com), or the Clearinghouse toll-free number is 1-800-732-3277 (staffed 8:30 a.m. to 7 p.m. Eastern Standard Time or leave a message anytime). Their "Fax-on-Demand" service is 301-251-5550.

Glossary

Most definitions given here are standard. Others vary according to the particular data set. Some have been changed over time. Data users should always review concept definitions for the particular data set they are using, especially when they wish to make historical comparisons.

Abortion Data are for legal abortions only. Definition varies among states in terms of when and conditions under which one may be performed.

Age Usually based on the age of the person at the person's last birthday.

Age-Adjusted Death Rate (AADR) Eliminates the effect of age structure on the death rate. The AADR is computed as a weighted average of age-specific death rates for specific age categories, where each category is weighted by the proportion of the total resident population enumerated in a particular census (1940 commonly used now) in that category. This can roughly be interpreted as the crude death rate that would be observed in Year X as a result of Year X age-specific mortality rates if the age structure had remained unchanged since 1940 (or whichever census is used as the standard). The AADR is affected by changes or differences in age distribution with the age-specific categories which are usually 11 ten-year age groups.

Assets Includes interest-earning assets, stocks and mutual fund shares, real estate (own home, rental property, vacation homes, and land holdings), own business or profession, mortgages held by sellers, and motor vehicles.

Average A single number or value that is used to represent the "typical value" of a group of numbers. Averages include means, medians, and per person quantities. It is a measure of "location" or "central tendency" of a group of numbers.

Average Annual Percent Change Computed by a compound interest formula unless stated otherwise. The formula assumes that the rate of change is constant throughout a specified compounding period (one year for annual rates of change). An exponential formula is usually preferred to measure population change. The exponential formula applies the amount of change continuously to the base whereas the compound interest formula applies the amount of change at the end of each compounding period.

Birth Expectations The number of children women aged 18 to 39 (regardless of marital status) said they expect to have in the future.

Birth, Live The complete expulsion or extraction from its mother of a product of conception, irrespective of the duration of pregnancy, which, after such separation, breathes or shows other evidence of life, such as heartbeat, pulsation of the umbilical cord, or definite movement of voluntary muscles, whether the umbilical cord has been cut or the placenta is attached; each product of such a birth is considered liveborn.

Births, Out-of-Wedlock (Illegitimate) Births to women occurring in the 12 months preceding the survey date, and who were currently divorced, widowed, or never married at the time of the survey.

Birth-Registration Area Established in 1915 with 10 states and the District of Columbia. By 1933, every state participated. In 1990, an estimated 99.3 percent of all live births were registered. For White births, registration was 99.4 percent complete and for all other births, 98.5 percent complete.

Cause of Death The underlying condition listed on the death certificate and classified by a system of internationally agreed-upon rules.

Census Individual count of each person within a defined geographic area as of a given day.

Children Ever Born Number of babies women aged 18 to 44 said they had ever had. Does not include stillbirths. Women were told to include children born in previous marriages, children no longer living, children away from home, and children still living at home. Data are probably less complete for children born out of wedlock than for children born in wedlock.

Constant Dollars Estimates representing an effort to remove the effects of price changes from statistical series reported in dollar terms. Usually derived by dividing current dollar estimates by a price index (such as the Consumer Price Index) for the specified period. The result is a series as it would exist if prices were the same as they were in the base year, that is, as if the dollar had constant purchasing power across time. Changes in the constant dollar series would reflect only changes in real volume of output, income, or expenditures.

Crude Birth Rate (CBR) Number of births per 1,000 population. Influenced by the age-sex distribution of the population, the CBR does not accurately reflect trends in fertility. Generally, the greater the proportion of childbearing-age females in the population, the greater the potential for a high CBR.

Crude Death Rate (CDR) Number of deaths per 1,000 population. This does not accurately reflect trends in mortality conditions because it is heavily dependent on the age structure of the population.

Current Dollars Reflects actual prices or costs prevailing during the specified year(s).

Disability Any temporary or long-term reduction of a person's activity as a result of an acute or chronic condition. It is often measured in terms of the days a person's activity has been reduced.

Divorce Rate Indicates the number of divorces (not the number of people being divorced) per 1,000 population in a given year. Also called the crude divorce rate.

Earnings Wages or salaries received by employees for pay; net nonfarm self-employment income received by persons operating their own nonfarm business, partnership, or professional practice; and net farm self-employment income received by persons operating farms. This amount may be a loss since losses can be reported from self-employment income.

Elderly Conventionally refers to the group aged 65 or older although there is no official definition.

Employed Comprised of (1) all civilians who, during the specified week, did any work at all as paid employees or in their own business or profession, or on their own farm, or who worked 15 hours or more as unpaid workers on a farm or in a business operated by a member of the family, and (2) all those who were not working but who had jobs or businesses from which they were temporary absent because of illness, bad weather, vacation, or labor-management dispute, or because they were taking time off for personal reasons, whether or not they were paid by their employers for time off, and whether or not they were seeking other jobs. Excluded from the employed group are persons whose only activity consisted of work around their own house or volunteer work.

Family A group of two or more persons, including the person maintaining the household, who live in the same household and who are related by birth, marriage, or adoption. A married-couple family is maintained by a husband and wife. More than one family may live in a household.

Food Stamps Food coupons which can be used to purchase food. The program is a federally funded program to permit low income households to have a more nutritious diet. Food stamps are a "noncash benefit."

General Fertility Rate (GFR) Ratio of live births to women aged 15 to 44 years. GFR is a measure of the fertility of women in this broad age group and can be influenced by shifts in the age distribution in this 30-year span. For example, an increased proportion of childbearing women over 35 decreases the GFR.

Hispanic Origin In censuses and surveys of the Census Bureau, Hispanic origin is determined by a question (separate from the race question) that asks for self-identification of a person's origin or descent. Persons designated as of Hispanic origin are those who said their origin was Mexican, Puerto Rican, Cuban, Central or South American, or some other Hispanic group. In these surveys, persons of Hispanic origin may be of any race. Vital statistics assign ethnicity on the basis of a person's parents, if of the same ethnicity; if different, origin is determined by that of the father. Regardless of the designation of the child, beginning with the 1989 data year, birth data are tabulated primarily by the origin of the mother. In a few surveys and administrative record data sets, Hispanic origin is considered as a race rather than as an ethnicity.

Household All the persons who occupy a housing unit. This includes related family members and any unrelated persons such as lodgers, foster children, or employees who share the housing unit. A person living alone in a housing unit or a group of unrelated persons sharing the unit as partners or roommates is counted as a household.

Householder The person (or one of the persons) in whose name the housing unit is owned or rented (maintained). The householder is also called the "reference person" and is the one to whom the relationship of all other household members, if any, are recorded. Use of the term "householder" began in 1980 and replaced the term "head of household." A "family householder" lives with at least one other person related by birth, marriage, or adoption. A person who lives alone or with one or more unrelated persons only is a "nonfamily householder." A "female householder" is a woman reported as the person maintaining a household in which no one is listed as her husband. She may be of any marital status and she may live alone, with relatives, and/or with nonrelatives.

Housing Unit House, apartment, or other group of rooms, or single room occupied or intended for occupancy as separate living quarters (occupants do not live or eat with other persons in the structure and have either direct access to their unit or have a kitchen or cooking equipment for exclusive use of the occupant).

In Labor Force Persons 15 years and over are classified as in the labor force if they were employed as civilians, unemployed, or in the armed forces during the survey week. The "civilian labor force" includes all civilians classified as employed or unemployed.

Income Total money received regularly from all sources in specified period. The following sources are usually included: (1) money wages or salary; (2) net income from nonfarm self employment; (3) net income from farm self employment; (4) Social Security or Railroad Retirement; (5) Supplemental Security Income; (6) public assistance or welfare payments; (7) interest; (8) dividends, income from estates or trusts, or net rental income; (9) veteran's payments or unemployment and worker's compensation; (10) private pensions or government employee pensions; (11) alimony or child support, regular contributions from persons not living in the household, and other periodic income. Household (family) income includes amounts only of those who were members of the household (family) at the time of the survey. Amounts shown are "gross" income before payments such as personal income taxes, Social Security, union dues, Medicare deductions. It does not include noncash benefits, proceeds from property sale, savings withdrawals, refunds, rebates, loans, gifts, or one-time lump-sum amounts such as insurance settlements or inheritances.

Income Deficit The difference between total income of families and unrelated individuals below the poverty level and their respective poverty thresholds. This provides an estimate of the amount that would be required to raise the incomes of all poor families and unrelated individuals to these poverty thresholds. The income deficit is a measure of the degree of impoverishment of a family or unrelated individual. Apparent differences in the average income deficits by the race and sex of the householder, to some extent, may be a function of differences in family size and composition.

Income, Mean The amount obtained by dividing the total income of a group by the number of units in that group. The means for households, families, and unrelated individuals are based on all households, families, and unrelated individuals. The means for persons are based only on persons with income.

Income, Median The amount that divides the distribution into two equal groups, one having incomes above the median, and the other having incomes below the median. Medians for households, families, and unrelated individuals are based on all households, families, and unrelated individuals. Medians for persons are based only on persons with income.

Layoff Release from a job because of slack work, material shortages, inventory taking, plant remodeling, installation of machinery, or like reasons. Released workers expect recall even if the date is not specified exactly.

Liabilities Includes debts secured by any asset, credit card or store bills, bank loans, and other unsecured debts.

Life Expectancy Hypothetical estimate of the average additional years a person can expect to live based on age-specific death rates for a given year. Changes in morality trends over time modify actual life expectancies.

Living Arrangements Living alone or with other persons and the relationship of persons to the reference person.

Mean (Arithmetic) Derived by summing the individual item values of a particular group and dividing the total by the number of items. The arithmetic mean is often referred to as the "average."

Median Point at which a group is divided exactly in half when each item in a group is ranked by size.

Need for Personal Assistance Includes only persons whose limitation is because of a health condition that lasted or was expected to a last a specified time period (usually 3 or 6 months, depending on the survey).

Net Worth Sum of the market value of assets minus liabilities (secured or unsecured).

Noncash Benefits Benefits received in a form other than money which improve the economic well-being of the recipient. Two major categories include public transfers and employer- or union-provided benefits to employees. Public transfers include food stamps, the school lunch program, public and other subsidized housing, Medicare and Medicaid health insurance, and military health benefits. Employee benefits include pension plans and group health insurance plans.

Not in Labor Force Civilians not classified as employed or unemployed. This includes persons engaged only in own home housework, attending school, or those unable to work because of long-term physical or mental illness, persons who are retired or too old to work, seasonal workers for whom the survey week fell in an off season, persons doing unpaid family work for less than 15 hours during the survey week, and the voluntarily idle.

Occupation Related to the job held during the survey week. Persons employed at two or more jobs were reported in the job at which they worked the most hours during the survey week.

Oldest Old Generally refers to persons 80 or 85 years or older although there is no official definition of the term.

Organized Child Care Includes day care and group care centers, nursery schools and preschool facilities.

Own Children and Related Children "Own" children in a family are sons and daughters, including stepchildren and adopted children of the householder. "Related" children in a family include own children and all other children in the household who are related to the householder by blood, marriage, or adoption.

Percentage A proportion multiplied by 100.

Personal Care Activities Includes eating, dressing, and taking care of personal hygiene.

Population Pyramid Graphic display of the age and sex distribution of a population. The number or proportion of males and females in each age group sums to 100 percent of the population. The shape of the pyramid describes a population's demographic past and future.

Poverty Statistical measure of income level based on the Department of Agriculture's 1961 Economy Food Plan. It reflects different consumption requirements of families in relation to their size, composition, and age of the family householder. Income measured is limited to money only and does not include noncash benefits such as food stamps or subsidized housing. In 1993, the average poverty threshold for a family of four persons was about $14,763. The index is determined by the Office of Management and Budget.

Proportion A ratio in which the relative size of a part is compared with the size of the whole such as when a population subgroup is expressed in terms of the total population.

Public Assistance (Welfare) Cash public assistance includes payments under the Aid to Families with Dependent Children (AFDC), Supplemental Security Income (SSI), General Assistance payments, emergency assistance payments, and assistance for heating and cooling expenses.

Public (or Other) Subsidized Housing Several programs designed to provide housing to low-income families. The value of these subsidies is included in the computation of noncash benefits (see above).

Race Varies among surveys and changes over time within the same survey or among decennial censuses. In modern censuses and surveys conducted by the Bureau of the Census, for example, a person's race is self-determined and is not a biological concept. Vital statistics assign race on the basis of a person's parents. When the parents are not the same race, the child is assigned the race of the nonWhite parent. If neither parent is White, the father's race is assigned to the newborn. Beginning with the 1989 data year, birth data are tabulated primarily by the race of the mother rather than the designation for the newborn. In 1988 and prior years, the race or national origin shown in tabulations from vital statistics records was that of the newborn child. Race is usually indicated as "White," "Black," and "Other races." Other races include Asians, Pacific Islanders, American Indians, Eskimos, Aleuts, and any other races besides White or Black.

Rate A ratio of one event to another in a specified time period. Conventionally, it is the frequency of demographic events in a population in a year.

Ratio The relation of one population subgroup to another population subgroup. A ratio is obtained by dividing the number which serves as the basis of comparison into the number which is being compared to it.

Registered Death Officially recorded death in a civil register.

Remarriage Rate Number of second or higher order marriages per 1,000 population of currently divorced and widowed persons of a specified age.

Support Payment Regular cash payments made to or by someone living outside the provider's household. These include regular cash payments for the support of children and ex-spouses, whether voluntary or court ordered. This does not include cash gifts and cash transfers for educational expenses to own children living away from home. It also does not include noncash assistance such as food, clothing, and personal services.

Survival Ratio The proportion of an age group which lives from one age to the next older age group.

Total Fertility Rate (TFR) Number of births that 1,000 women would have in their lifetime if, at each year of age, they experienced the birth rates occurring to women of that age in the specified calendar year.

The sum of the age-specific fertility rates for each female age group between the ages of 10 and 50, therefore, independent of the effects of age structure. It should be stressed that the total fertility rate is an annual (or period) measure of fertility, even though it is expressed as a hypothetical lifetime (or cohort) measure. The total fertility rate is affected by the timing as well as the level of childbearing. The following example illustrates this point. The total fertility rate peaked in 1957 at 3,760. However, it now appears that the highest cohort fertility rate among women who were then in the childbearing ages will be about 3,200 for women born in the early 1930s.

Unemployed Civilians who, during the survey week, had no employment but were available for work and (1) engaged in any specific jobseeking activity within the past 4 weeks; or (2) were waiting to be called back to a job from which they had been laid off; or (3) were waiting to report to a new wage or salary job within 30 days.

Unrelated Individuals Persons not living with any relatives.

Work Experience Civilian work for pay or profit or work on a family-operated farm or business.

Year-Round, Full-Time Worker Person who worked primarily at a job for 35 or more hours per week for 50 or more weeks during the year before the survey.

Years of School Completed The highest grade of school attended by the person whether or not the grade was finished. This applies only to progress in schools which may advance a person toward an elementary school certificate or high school diploma, or a college, university, or professional school degree.

Young Old Usually refers to persons aged 60 or 65 to 74 years, although there is no official definition.

Sources Consulted

Bachu, Amara, U.S. Bureau of the Census, "Fertility of American Women: June 1992," *Current Population Reports*, P20-470, Washington, D.C.: U.S. Government Printing Office, 1993, Appendix B.

Bureau of the Census, *Statistical Abstract of the United States: 1994*, (114th ed.), Washington, D.C.: U.S. Government Printing Office, 1994.

Bureau of the Census, "Supplemental Courses for Case Studies in Surveys and Censuses," *Demography Lectures*, ISP Supplemental Course Series No. 2, Washington D.C.: U.S. Government Printing Office, 1969.

Deardorff, K., F. Hollmann, and P. Montgomery, U.S. Bureau of the Census, "United States Population Estimates, by Age, Sex, Race, and Hispanic Origin: 1990 to 1994," *Current Population Reports,* Series PPL-21, Population Division, Bureau of the Census, March 1995.

Haupt, Arthur and Thomas T. Kane, *Population Handbook*, Washington, D.C.: Population Reference Bureau, 1980.

National Center for Health Statistics, *Vital Statistics of the United States, 1989,* Vol. II, Mortality, Part A, DHHS Pub No. (PHS) 93-1101, Washington, D.C.: Government Printing Office, 1993, Section 7.

National Center for Health Statistics, *Vital Statistics of the United States: 1990,* Vol. I, Natality, Washington, D.C.: U.S. Government Printing Office, 1994.

Petersen, William and Renee Petersen, *Dictionary of Demography: Terms, Concepts, and Institutions,* New York: Greenwood Press, 1986.

Saluter, Arlene F., U.S. Bureau of the Census, "Marital Status and Living Arrangements: March 1993," *Current Population Reports*, P20-478, Washington, D.C.: U.S. Government Printing Office, 1994, Appendix A.

Shryock, Henry and Jacob S. Siegel, U.S. Bureau of the Census, *The Methods and Materials of Demography,* Vol. 2, 3d printing (rev.), Washington, D.C.: U.S. Government Printing Office, 1975, pp. 372–381.

Index

by Virgil Diodato